CHILTON'S
REPAIR MANUAL

CHEVY S-10 BLAZER
GMC S-15 JIMMY
OLDS BRAVADA
1982-91

All U.S and Canadian models of Chevrolet S-10 Blazer, GMC S-15 Jimmy and Oldsmobile Bravada Pick-Ups • gasoline and diesel engines • 2 and 4 wheel drive

President, Chilton Enterprises	David S. Loewith
Senior Vice President	Ronald A. Hoxter
Publisher and Editor-In-Chief	Kerry A. Freeman, S.A.E.
Managing Editors	Peter M. Conti, Jr. □ W. Calvin Settle, Jr., S.A.E.
Assistant Managing Editor	Nick D'Andrea
Senior Editors	Debra Gaffney □ Ken Grabowski, A.S.E., S.A.E.
	Michael L. Grady □ Richard J. Rivele, S.A.E.
	Richard T. Smith □ Jim Taylor
	Ron Webb
Director of Manufacturing	Mike D'Imperio

CHILTON BOOK COMPANY

ONE OF THE DIVERSIFIED PUBLISHING COMPANIES, A PART OF CAPITAL CITIES/ABC, INC.

CONTENTS

GENERAL INFORMATION and MAINTENANCE

ENGINE PERFORMANCE and TUNE-UP

ENGINE and ENGINE OVERHAUL

EMISSION CONTROLS

FUEL SYSTEM

CHASSIS ELECTRICAL

SAFETY NOTICE

Proper service and repair procedures are vital to the safe, reliable operation of all motor vehicles, as well as the safety of those performing repairs. This book outlines procedures for servicing and repairing vehicles using safe effective methods. The procedures contain many NOTES, CAUTIONS and WARNINGS which should be followed along with standard safety procedures to eliminate the possibility of personal injury or improper service which could damage the vehicle or compromise its safety.

It is important to note that repair procedures and techniques, tools and parts for servicing motor vehicles, as well as the skill and experience of the individual performing the work vary widely. It is not possible to anticipate all of the conceivable ways or conditions under which vehicles may be serviced, or to provide cautions as to all of the possible hazards that may result. Standard and accepted safety precautions and equipment should be used during cutting, grinding, chiseling, prying, or any other process that can cause material removal or projectiles.

Some procedures require the use of tools specially designed for a specific purpose. Before substituting another tool or procedure, you must be completely satisfied that neither your personal safety, nor the performance of the vehicle will be endangered.

Although the information in this guide is based on industry sources and is as complete as possible at the time of publication, the possibility exists that the manufacturer made later changes which could not be included here. While striving for total accuracy, Chilton Book Company cannot assume responsibilty for any errors, changes, or omissions that may occur in the compilation of this data.

PART NUMBERS

Part numbers listed in the reference are not recommendations by Chilton for any product by brand name. They are references that can be used with interchange manuals and aftermarket supplier catalogs to locate each brand supplier's discrete part number.

SPECIAL TOOLS

Special tools are recommended by the vehicle manufacturer to perform their specific job. Use has been kept to a minimum, but where absolutely necessary, they are referred to in the text by the part number of the tool manufacturer. These tools can be purchased, under the appropiate part number, from the Service Tool Division, Kent-Moore Corporation, 29784 Little Mac, Roseville MI. or an equivalent tool can be purchased locally from a tool supplier or parts outlet. Before substituting any tool for the one recommended, read the SAFETY NOTICE at the top of this page.

ACKNOWLEDGEMENTS

Chilton Book Company expresses appreciation to Chevrolet Motor Division, General Motors Corporation, Detroit, Michigan 48202; and GMC Truck and Coach Division, General Motors Corporation, Pontiac, Michigan 48053 for their generous assistance

Manufactured in the United States of America
  34567890   0987654

Chilton's Repair Manual: Chevrolet S10 Blazer, GMC S15 Jimmy and Oldsmobile Bravada 1982–91
ISBN 0–8019–8140–9 pbk.
Library of Congress Catalog Card No. 90–056130

General Information and Maintenance

HOW TO USE THIS BOOK

Chilton's Repair Manual the S-10 Blazer, S-15 Jimmy and Bravada is intended to help you learn more about the inner working of your vehicle and save you money in it's upkeep.

The first 2 Chapters will be the most used, since they contain maintenance and tune-up information and procedures. Studies have shown that a properly tuned and maintained vehicle can get at least 10 percent better gas mileage (which translates into lower operating costs) and periodic maintenance will catch minor problems before they turn into major repair bills. The other Chapters deal with the more complex systems of your vehicle. Operating systems from engine through brakes are covered. It will give you detailed instructions to help you change your own brake pads and shoes, tune-up the engine, replace sparkplugs and filters and do many more jobs that will save you money, give you personal satisfaction and help you avoid expensive problems.

A secondary purpose of this book is a reference for owners who want to understand their vehicle and/or their mechanics better. In this case, no tools at all are required. Knowing just what a particular repair job requires in parts and labor time will allow you to evaluate whether or not you're getting a fair price quote and help decipher itemized bills from a repair shop.

Before attempting any repairs or service on your vehicle, read through the entire procedure outlined in the appropriate Chapter. This will give you the overall view of what tools and supplies will be required. There is nothing more frustrating than having to walk to the bus stop on Monday morning because you were short one bolt on Sunday afternoon. So read ahead and plan ahead. Each operation should be approached logically and all procedures thoroughly understood before attempting any work. Some special tools that may be required can often be rented from local automotive jobbers or places specializing in renting tools and equipment. Check the yellow pages of your phone book.

All Chapters contain adjustments, maintenance, removal and installation procedures and overhaul procedures. When overhaul is not considered practical, we tell you how to remove the part and then how to install the new or rebuilt replacement. In this way, you at least save the labor costs. Backyard repair of such components (such as the alternator or water pump) is just not practical but the removal and installation procedure is often simple and well within the capabilities of the averge vehicle owner.

Two basic mechanic's rules should be mentioned: First, whenever the LEFT side of the vehicle or engine is referred to, it is meant to specify the DRIVER'S side of the vehicle. Conversely, the RIGHT side of the vehicle means the PASSENGER'S side. Second, all screws and bolts are removed by turning them counterclockwise and tightened by turning them clockwise.

Safety is always the most important rule. Constantly be aware of the dangers involved in working on a vehicle and take the proper precautions to avoid the risk of personal injury or damage to the vehicle. See the entry in this Chapter, Servicing Your Vehicle Safely and the SAFETY NOTICE on the acknowledgment page before attempting any service procedures and pay attention to the instructions provided. There are 3 common mistakes in mechanical work:

1. Incorrect order of assembly, disassembly or adjustment. When taking something apart or putting it together, doing things in the wrong order usually costs extra time, however, it CAN break something. Read the entire proce-

dure before beginning the disassembly. Do everything in the order in which the instructions say you should do it, even if you can't immediately see a reason for it. When you're taking something apart that is very intricate (for example, a carburetor), you might want to draw a picture of how it looks when assembled at one point, in order to make sure you get everything back in its proper position. We will supply exploded views whenever possible but sometimes the job requires more attention to detail than an illustration provides. When making adjustments, especially tune-up adjustments, do them in order. One adjustment often affects another and you cannot expect satisfactory results unless each adjustment is made only when it cannot be changed by any other.

2. Overtorquing (or undertorquing). While it is more common for overtorquing to cause damage, undertorquing can cause a fastener to vibrate loose causing serious damage, especially, when dealing with aluminum parts. Pay attention to torque specifications and utilize a torque wrench in assembly. If a torque figure is not available, remember that if you are using the right tool to do the job, you will probably not have to strain yourself to get a fastener tight enough. The pitch of most threads is so slight that the tension you put on the wrench will be multiplied many times in actual force on what you are tightening. A good example of how critical torque is can be seen in the case of spark plug installation, especially where you are putting the plug into an aluminum cylinder head. Too little torque can fail to crush the gasket, causing leakage of combustion gases and consequent overheating of the plug and engine parts. Too much torque can damage the threads or distort the plug, which changes the spark gap at the electrode. Since more and more manufacturers are using aluminum in their engine and chassis parts to save weight, a torque wrench should be in any serious do-it-yourselfer's tool box.

There are many commercial products available for ensuring that fasteners won't come loose, even if they are not torqued just right (a very common brand is Loctite®). If you're worried about getting something together tight enough to hold but loose enough to avoid mechanical damage during assembly, one of these products might offer substantial insurance. Read the label on the package and make sure the product is compatible with the materials, fluids and etc. involved before choosing one.

3. Crossthreading. This occurs when a part such as a bolt is screwed into a nut or casting at the wrong angle and forced, causing the threads to become damaged. Crossthreading is more likely to occur if access is difficult. It helps to clean and lubricate the fasteners, then start threading with the part to be installed going straight in, using your fingers. If you encounter resistance, unscrew the part and start over again at a different angle until it can be inserted and turned several turns without much effort. Keep in mind that many parts, especially spark plugs, use tapered threads, so gentle turning will automatically bring the part you're threading to the proper angle if you don't force it or resist a change in angle. Don't put a wrench on the part until it's been turned a couple of turns by hand. If you suddenly encounter resistance and the part has not seated fully, don't force it. Pull it back out and make sure it's clean and threading properly.

Always take your time and be patient, once you have some experience working on your vehicle, it will become an enjoyable hobby.

TOOLS AND EQUIPMENT

Naturally, without the proper tools and equipment, it is impossible to properly service your vehicle. It would be impossible to catalog each tool that you would need to perform each or any operation in this book. It would also be unwise for the amateur to rush out and buy an expensive set of tools on the theory that he may need one or more of them at sometime.

The best approach is to proceed slowly, gathering a good quality set of tools that are used most frequently. Don't be misled by the low cost of bargain tools. It is far better to spend a little more for better quality. Forged wrenches, 6- or 12-point sockets and fine tooth ratchets are by far preferable to their less expensive counterparts. As any good mechanic can tell you, there are few worse experiences than trying to work on a vehicle with bad tools. Your monetary savings will be far outweighed by frustration and mangled knuckles.

Begin accumulating tools that are used most frequently; those associated with routine maintenance and tune-up.

In addition to the normal assortment of screwdrivers and pliers, you should have the following tools for routine maintenance jobs:

1. SAE (or Metric) or SAE/Metric wrenches—sockets and combination open end/box end wrenches in sizes from $^1/_8$–$^3/_4$ in. (6–19mm) and a spark plug socket ($^{13}/_{16}$ in. or $^5/_8$ in. depending on plug type).

NOTE: *If possible, buy various length socket drive extensions. One break in this department is that the metric sockets available in the U.S. will all fit the ratchet handles and*

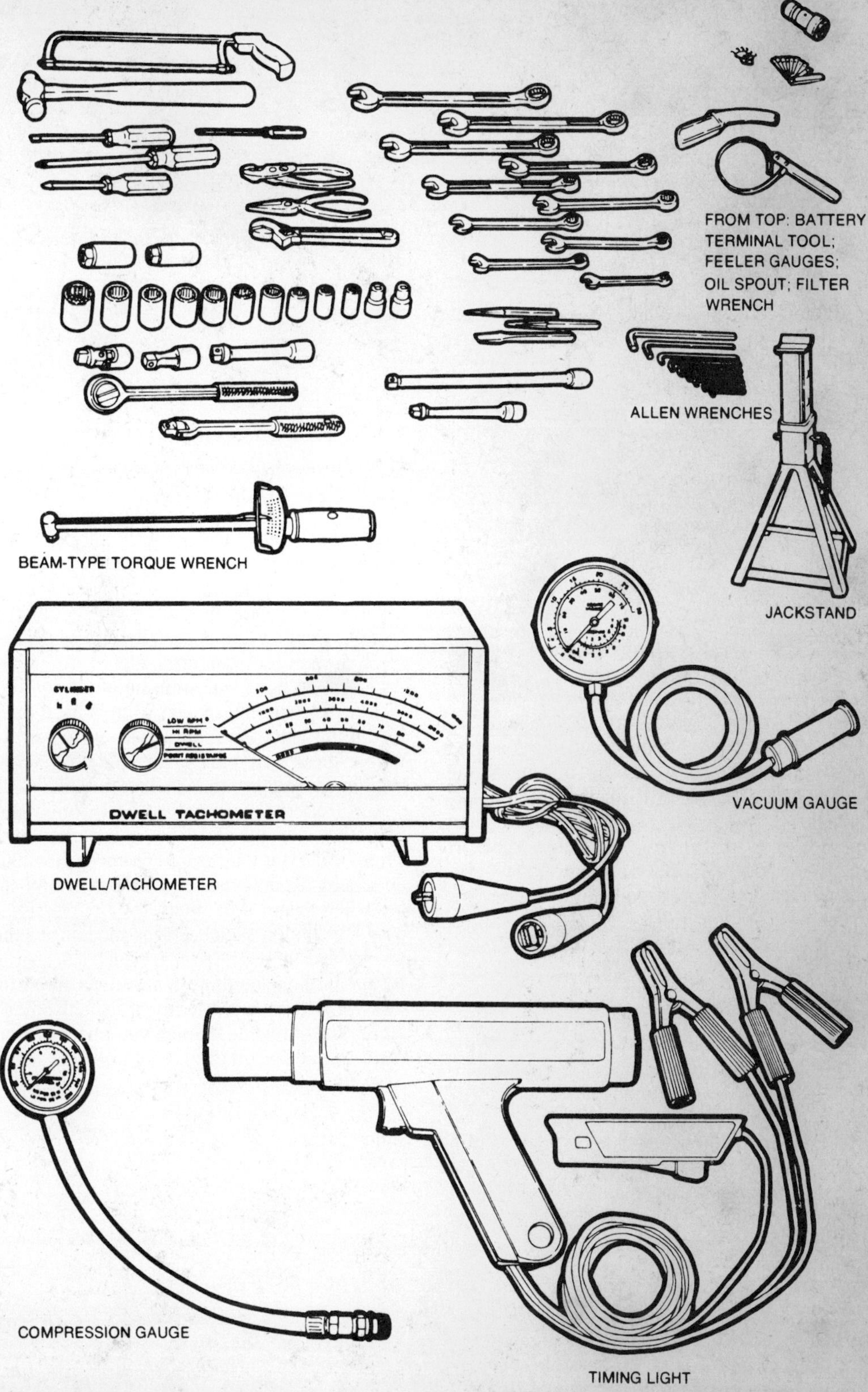

This basic collection of tools and test instruments is all you need for most maintenance on your truck.

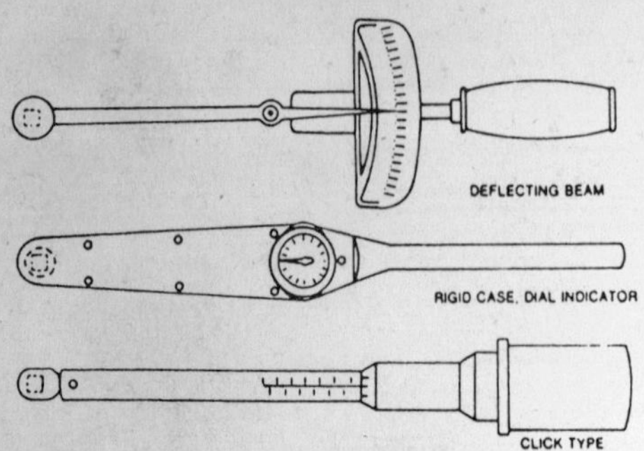

Views of the three types of torque wrenches

extensions you may already have ($^1/_4$ in., $^3/_8$ in. and $^1/_2$ in. drive).

2. Jackstands, for support
3. Oil filter wrench
4. Oil filler spout, for pouring oil
5. Grease gun, for chassis lubrication
6. Hydrometer, for checking the battery
7. A container for draining oil
8. Many rags for wiping up the inevitable mess.

In addition to the above items there are several others that are not absolutely necessary but handy to have around. These include absorbent gravel, a transmission funnel and an usual supply of lubricants, antifreeze and fluids, although these can be purchased as needed. This is a basic list for routine maintenance but only your personal needs and desires can accurately determine your list of tools. If you are serious about maintaining your own vehicle, then a floor jack is as necessary as a spark plug socket. The greatly increased utility, strength and safety of a hydraulic floor jack makes it pay for itself many times over throughout the years.

The second list of tools is for tune-ups. While the tools involved here are slightly more sophisticated, they need not be outrageously expensive. There are several inexpensive tach/dwell meters on the market that are every bit as good for the average mechanic as an expensive professional model. Just be sure it goes to at least 1,200–1,500 rpm on the tach scale and that it works on 4- or 6-cylinder engines. A basic list of tune-up equipment could include:

1. Tach/dwell meter.
2. Spark plug wrench.
3. Timing light (a DC light that works from the vehicle's battery is best, although an AC light that plugs into 110V house current will suffice at some sacrifice in brightness).
4. Wire spark plug gauge/adjusting tools.
5. Set of feeler blades.

In addition to these basic tools, there are sev-

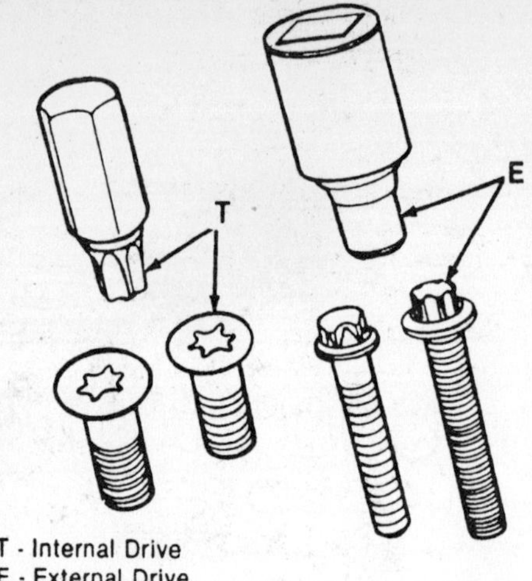

T - Internal Drive
E - External Drive

View of the 6 lobed socket head fasteners and sockets

eral other tools and gauges you may find useful. These include:

1. A compression gauge. The screw-in type is slower to use but eliminates the possibility of a faulty reading due to escaping pressure.
2. A manifold vacuum gauge.
3. A test light, volt/ohmmeter.
4. An induction meter. This is used for determining whether or not there is current in a wire. These are handy for use if a wire is broken somewhere in a wiring harness.

As a final note, you will find a torque wrench necessary for all but the most basic work. There are 3 types of torque wrenches available; deflecting beam type, dial indicator and click type. The beam type models are perfectly adequate, although the click type models are more precise and allow the user to reach the required torque without having tto assume a sometimes awkward position in reading a scale. No matter what type of torque wrench you purchase, have it calibrated periodically to ensure accuracy.

NOTE: *Special tools are occasionally necessary to perform a specific job or are recommended to make a job easier. Their use has been kept to a minimum. When a special tool is indicated, it will be referred to by manufacturer's part number, and, where possible, an illustration of the tool will be provided so an equivalent tool may be used. A list of tool manufacturers and their addresses follows:*

In the United States, contact:
Service Tool Division
Kent-Moore Corporation
29784 Little Mack
Roseville, MI 48066-2298
In Canada, contact:
Kent-Moore of Canada, Ltd.

2395 Cawthra Mississauga
Ontario, Canada L5A 3P2.

Special Tools

Normally, the use of special factory toos is avoided for repair procedures, since these are not readily available for the do-it-yourselfer mechanic. When it is possible to perform the hob with more commonly available tools, it will be pointed out but occasionally, a special tool was desigend to perform a specific function and should be used. Before substituting another tool, you should be convinced that neither your

When using an open end wrench, make sure it is the correct size

safety not the performance of the vehicle will be compromised. Special tools are available at your local General Motors dealer, at your local parts store or jobber market.

SERVICING YOUR VEHICLE SAFELY

It is virtually impossible to anticipate all of the hazards involved with automotive maintenance and service but care and common sense will prevent most accidents.

The rules of safety for mechanics range from "don't smoke around gasoline," to "use the proper tool for the job." The trick to avoiding injuries is to develop safe work habits and take every possible precaution.

Do's

• Do keep a fire extinguisher and first aid kit within easy reach.

• Do wear safety glasses or goggles when cutting, drilling, grinding or prying. If you wear glasses for the sake of vision, then they should be made of hardened glass that can serve also

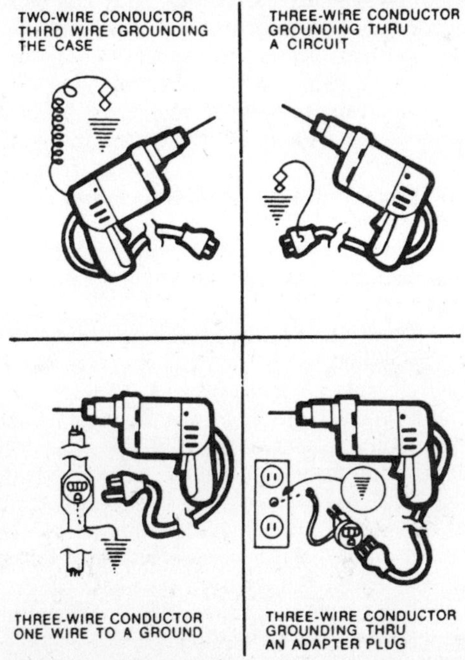

When using electric tools, make sure they are properly grounded.

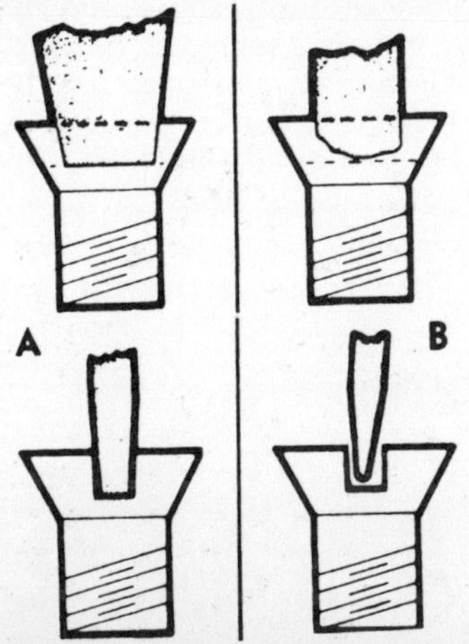

Keep screwdrivers in good shape. They should fit the slot as shown 'A'. If they look like those in 'B', they need grinding or replacing.

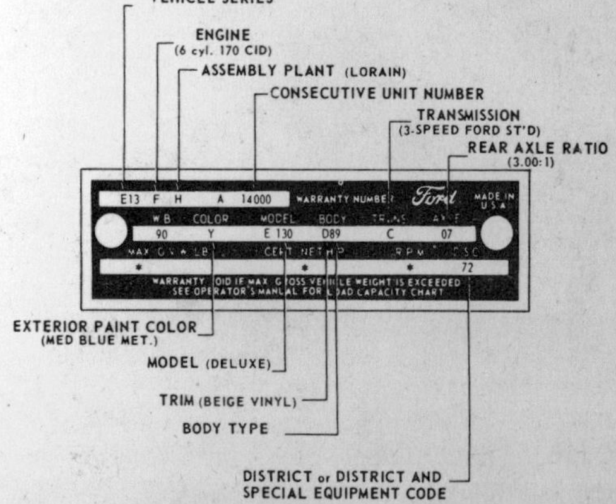

Vehicle Identification Plate

as safety glasses or wear safety goggles over your regular glasses.

• Do shield your eyes whenever you work around the battery. Batteries contain sulphuric acid. In case of contact with the eyes or skin, flush the area with water or a mixture of water and baking soda, then get medical attention immediately.

• Do use safety stands for any under-vehicle service. Jacks are for raising the vehicle; safety stands are for making sure the vehicle stays raised until you want it to come down. Whenever the vehicle is raised, block the wheels remaining on the ground and set the parking brake.

• Do use adequate ventilation when working with any chemicals. Asbestos dust resulting from brake lining wear causes cancer.

• Do disconnect the negative battery cable when working on the electrical system.

• Do follow the manufacturer's directions whenever working with potentially hazardous materials. Both brake fluid and antifreeze are poisonous if taken internally.

• Do properly maintain your tools. Loose hammer heads, mushroomed punches and chisels, frayed or poorly grounded electrical cords, excessively worn screwdrivers, spread wrenches (open end), cracked sockets, slipping ratchets or faulty droplight sockets cause accidents.

• Do use the proper size and type of tool for the job being done.

• Do when possible, pull on a wrench handle rather than push on it and adjust your stance to prevent a fall.

• Do be sure adjustable wrenches are tightly adjusted on the nut or bolt and pulled so the face is on the side of the fixed jaw.

• Do select a wrench or socket that fits the nut or bolt. The wrench or socket should sit straight, not cocked.

• Do strike squarely with a hammer—avoid glancing blows.

• Do set the parking brake and block the drive wheels if the work requires that the engine be running.

Dont's

• Don't run an engine in a garage or anywhere else without proper ventilation—EVER! Carbon monoxide is poisonous. It is absorbed by the body 400 times faster than oxygen. Carbon monoxide is odorless and colorless. Your senses cannot detect its presence. Early symptoms of monoxide poisoning include headache, irritability, improper vision (blurred or hard to focus) and/or drowsiness. When you notice any of these symptons in yourself or your helpers, stop working immediately and get to fresh, outside air. Ventilate the work area thoroughly before returning to the vehicle. It takes a long time to leave the body and can build up a deadly supply of it in your system by simply breathing in a little every day. You may not realize you are slowly poisoning yourself. Always use power vents, windows, fans or open the garage doors.

• Don't work around moving parts while wearing a necktie or other loose clothing. Short sleeves are much safer than long, loose sleeves. Hard-toed shoes with neoprene soles protect your toes and give a better grip on slippery surfaces. Jewelry such as watches, fancy belt buckles, beads or body adornment or any kind is not safe working around a vehicle. Long hair should be hidden under a hat or cap.

• Don't use pockets for tool boxes. A fall or bump can drive a screwdriver deep into your body. Even a wiping cloth hanging from the back pocket can wrap around a spinning shaft, pulley or fan.

• Don't smoke when working around gasoline, cleaning solvent or other flammable material.

• Don't smoke when working around the battery. When the battery is being charged, it gives off explosive hydrogen gas.

• Don't use gasoline to wash your hands. There are excellent soaps available. Gasoline may contain lead, and lead can enter the body through a cut, accumulating in the body until you are very ill. Gasoline also removes all the natural oils from the skin so bone dry hands will suck up oil and grease.

• Don't service the air conditioning system unless you are equipped with the necessary tools and training. The refrigerant, R-12, is extremely cold and when exposed to the air, will instantly freeze any surface it comes in contact with, including your eyes. Although the refrigerant is normally non-toxic, R-12 becomes a deadly poisonous gas in the presence of an open flame. One good whiff of the vapors from burning refrigerant can be fatal.

HISTORY

In 1983, the S-10 Chevy Blazer and the S-15 GMC Jimmy were introduced into the S-10 Pick-Up line. During 1983–85, the S-15 GMC Jimmy, 2 Wheel Drive (2WD), was available with the 2.2L Diesel engine made by Isuzu.

In 1991, the Oldsmobile Bravada was introduced but only as an All Wheel Drive (AWD) vehicle.

ENGINE IDENTIFICATION

Year	Model	Engine Displacement cu. in. (liter)	Engine Series Identification (VIN)	No. of Cylinders	Engine Type
1983	S10/15 Blazer/Jimmy 2WD	119 (1.9)	A	4	OHC
	S10/15 Blazer/Jimmy 2WD	121 (2.0)	Y	4	OHV
	S10/15 Blazer/Jimmy 2WD	173 (2.8)	B	6	OHV
	S10/15 Blazer/Jimmy 4WD	119 (1.9)	A	4	OHC
	S10/15 Blazer/Jimmy 4WD	121 (2.0)	Y	4	OHV
	S10/15 Blazer/Jimmy 4WD	173 (2.8)	B	6	OHV
	S/15 Jimmy 2WD	136 (2.2)	S	4	OHV
1984	S10/15 Blazer/Jimmy 2WD	119 (1.9)	A	4	OHC
	S10/15 Blazer/Jimmy 2WD	121 (2.0)	Y	4	OHV
	S10/15 Blazer/Jimmy 2WD	173 (2.8)	B	6	OHV
	S10/15 Blazer/Jimmy 4WD	119 (1.9)	A	4	OHC
	S10/15 Blazer/Jimmy 4WD	121 (2.0)	Y	4	OHV
	S10/15 Blazer/Jimmy 4WD	173 (2.8)	B	6	OHV
	S/15 Jimmy 2WD	136 (2.2)	S	4	OHV
1985	S10/15 Blazer/Jimmy 2WD	119 (1.9)	A	4	OHC
	S10/15 Blazer/Jimmy 2WD	151 (2.5)	E	4	OHV
	S10/15 Blazer/Jimmy 2WD	173 (2.8)	B	6	OHV
	S10/15 Blazer/Jimmy 4WD	119 (1.9)	A	4	OHC
	S10/15 Blazer/Jimmy 4WD	151 (2.5)	E	4	OHV
	S10/15 Blazer/Jimmy 4WD	173 (2.8)	B	6	OHV
	S/15 Jimmy 2WD	136 (2.2)	S	4	OHV
1986	S10/15 Blazer/Jimmy 2WD	151 (2.5)	E	4	OHV
	S10/15 Blazer/Jimmy 2WD	173 (2.8)	R	6	OHV
	S10/15 Blazer/Jimmy 4WD	151 (2.5)	E	4	OHV
	S10/15 Blazer/Jimmy 4WD	173 (2.8)	R	6	OHV
1987	S10/15 Blazer/Jimmy 2WD	151 (2.5)	E	4	OHV
	S10/15 Blazer/Jimmy 2WD	173 (2.8)	R	6	OHV
	S10/15 Blazer/Jimmy 4WD	151 (2.5)	E	4	OHV
	S10/15 Blazer/Jimmy 4WD	173 (2.8)	R	6	OHV
1988	S10/15 Blazer/Jimmy 2WD	151 (2.5)	E	4	OHV
	S10/15 Blazer/Jimmy 2WD	173 (2.8)	R	6	OHV
	S10/15 Blazer/Jimmy 4WD	173 (2.8)	R	6	OHV
	S10/15 Blazer/Jimmy 4WD	262 (4.3)	Z	6	OHV
1989	S10/15 Blazer/Jimmy 2WD	151 (2.5)	E	4	OHV
	S10/15 Blazer/Jimmy 2WD	173 (2.8)	R	6	OHV
	S10/15 Blazer/Jimmy 2WD	262 (4.3)	Z	6	OHV
	S10/15 Blazer/Jimmy 4WD	173 (2.8)	R	6	OHV
	S10/15 Blazer/Jimmy 4WD	262 (4.3)	Z	6	OHV
1990	S10/15 Blazer/Jimmy 2WD	262 (4.3)	Z	6	OHV
	S10/15 Blazer/Jimmy 4WD	262 (4.3)	Z	6	OHV
1991	S10/15 Blazer/Jimmy 2WD	262 (4.3)	Z	6	OHV
	S10/15 Blazer/Jimmy 4WD	262 (4.3)	Z	6	OHV
	Bravada	262 (4.3)	Z	6	OHV

OHV—Over Head Valves
OHC—Over Head Cam

IDENTIFICATION

Model

The S-10 Chevy Blazer and the S-15 GMC Jimmy models are available in 2-Wheel Drive (2WD) and 4-Wheel Drive (4WD). Any model with an "S" indication is known as a 2-wheel drive; any model with a "T" indication is known as a 4-wheel drive.

The Bravada, being a hybrid of the Blazer and the Jimmy, is available in All Wheel Drive (AWD).

The Gross Vehicle Weight (GVW) or maximum safe total weight of the vehicle, cargo, extra equipment and occupants. The GVW must not exceed the Gross Vehicle Weight Rating (GVWR) of your vehicle.

Vehicle

The Vehicle Identification Number (VIN) is on a plate attached to the left hand top of the

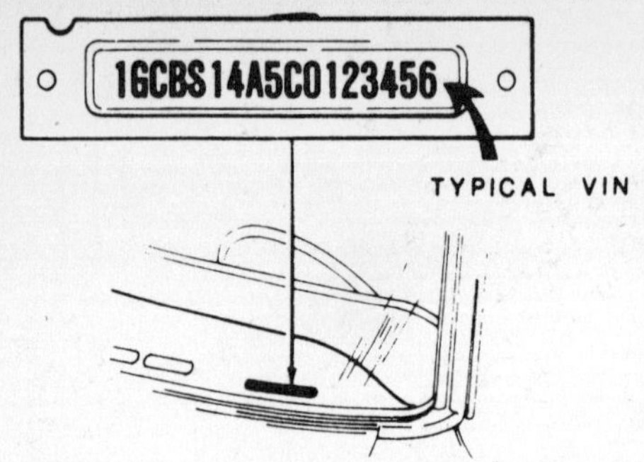

Location of the Vehicle Identification Number (VIN)

instrument panel, visible through the windshield. The Gross Vehicle Weight (GVW) or maximum safe total weight of the vehicle, cargo and passengers, is also given on the plate.

Engine

1.9L Engine

The engine identification number is on a machined flat surface, on the lower left side of the block, near the flywheel.

2.0L Engine

The engine identification number is stamped on a flat, machined surface, facing forward, on the front of the engine block, just below the head.

2.2L Diesel Engine

The engine identification number is stamped on a flat, machined surface, facing forward, on the left-front of the engine block, just below the water pump.

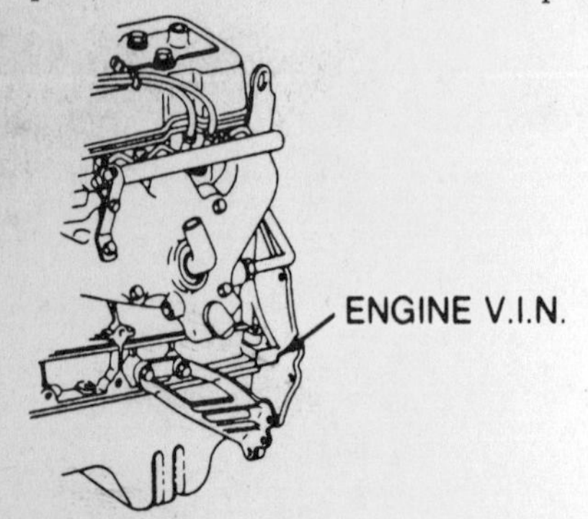

Engine identification number location—1.9L engine

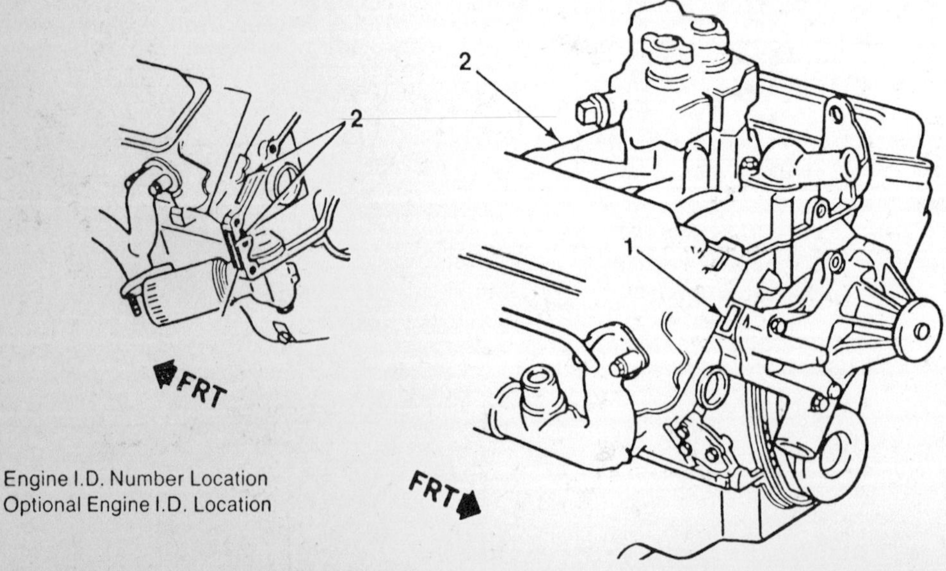

1. Engine I.D. Number Location
2. Optional Engine I.D. Location

VIN location—2.8L engine

1GCBS14A5D0123456

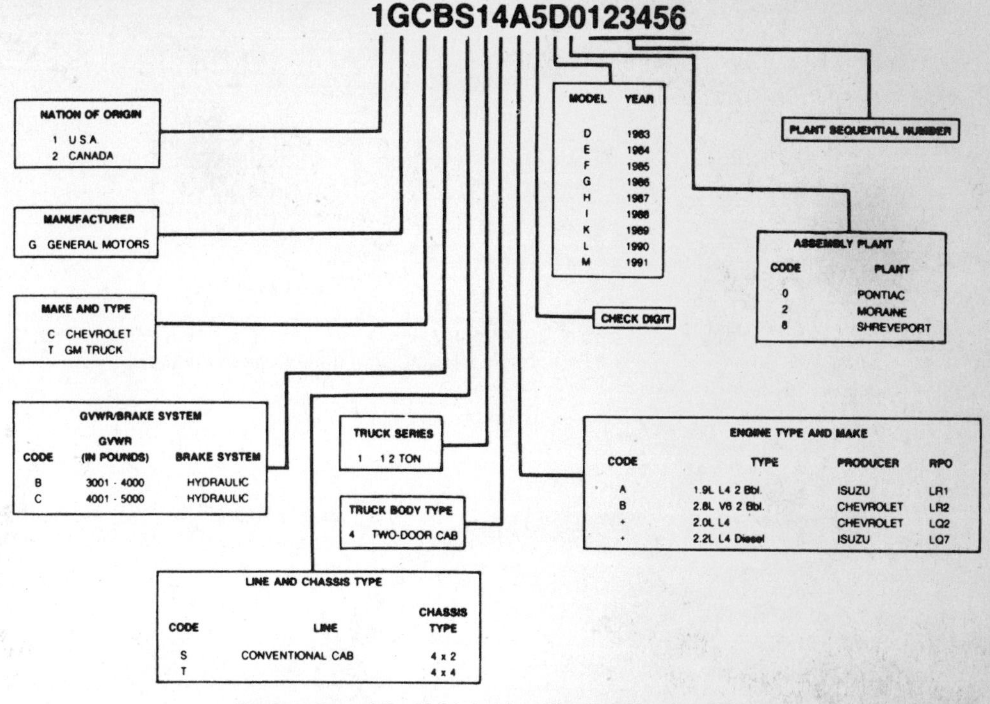

Explanation of the Vehicle Identification Number (VIN)

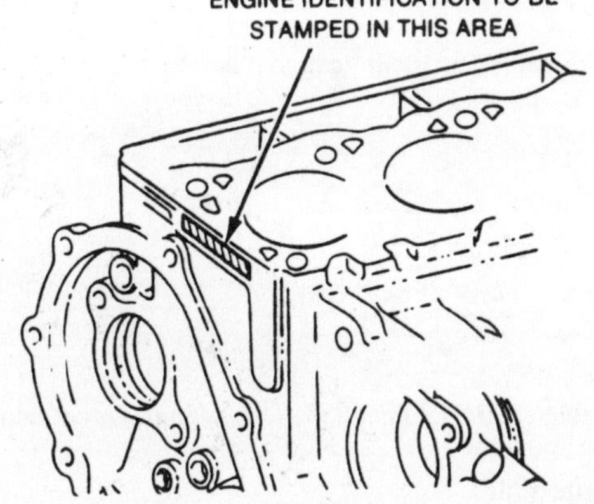

Engine identification number location—2.0L engine

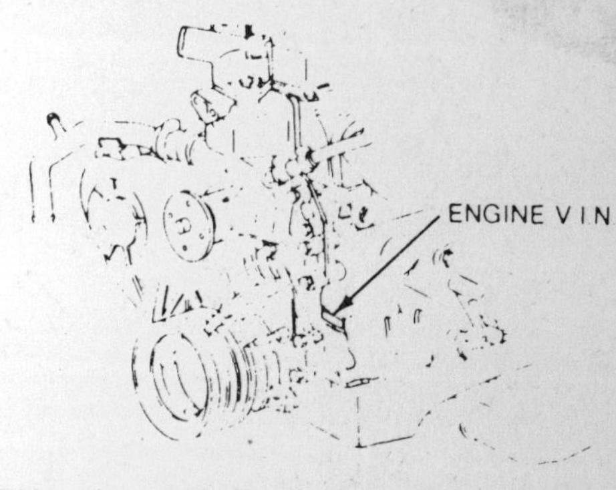

VIN location—2.2L diesel engine

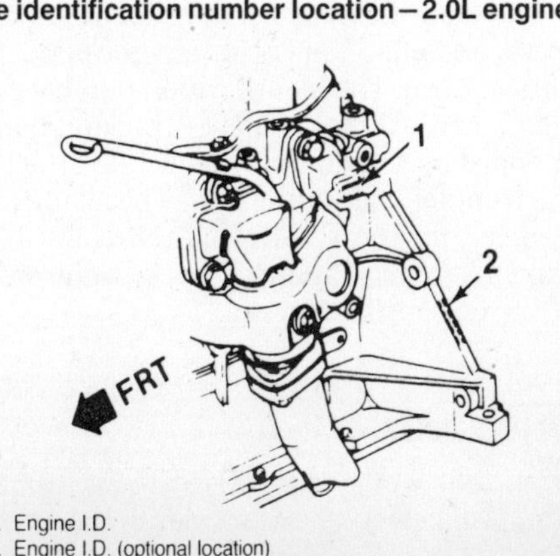

1. Engine I.D.
2. Engine I.D. (optional location)

Engine identification number location—2.5L engine

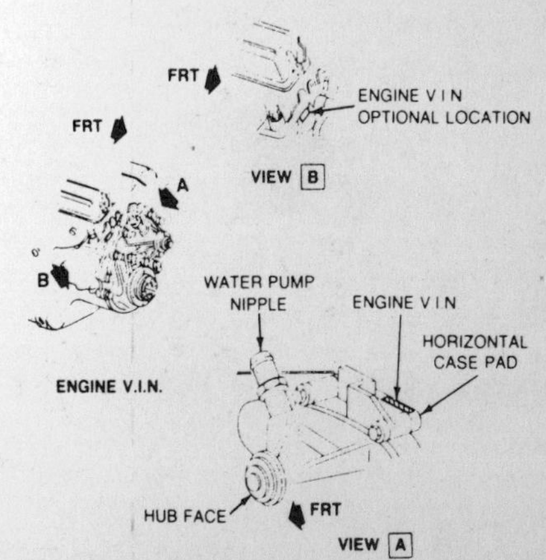

Engine identification number location—2.8L engine

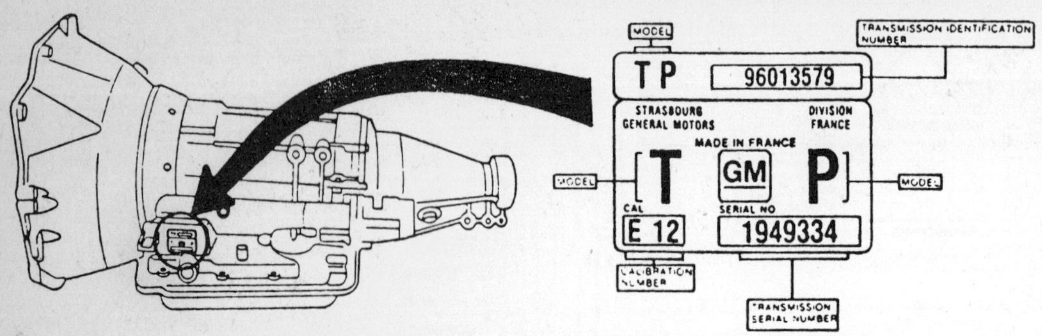

Location of the 180C and 3L30 automatic transmission identification numbers

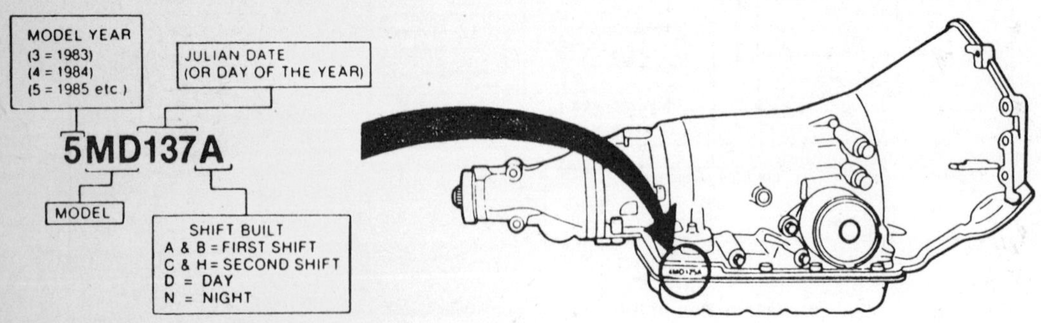

Location of the 700-R4 and 4L60 automatic transmission identification numbers

2.5L Engine

The engine identification number is stamped on a flat, machined surface, on the left rear side of the engine block, near the flywheel.

2.8L Engine

The engine identification code is stamped in 2 places. One on an upward facing, machined surface on the left front of the block, just below the head and above the water pump. The other on the right front of the engine, directly under the exhaust manifold.

4.3L Engine

The engine identification code is stamped in 2 places. One on an upward facing, machined surface on the right front of the block, just below the valve cover and above the water pump. The other, on the left rear of the engine, near the exhaust manifold.

Transmission

Manual

The transmission identification number is stamped on a metal plate which is attached to the extension housing case bolt, on the left side.

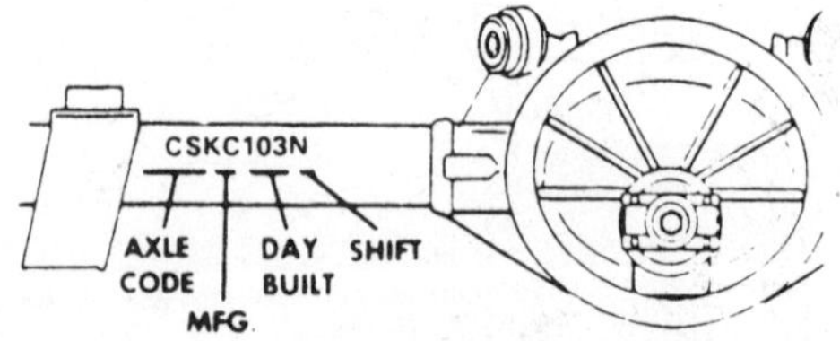

Location and explanation of the rear axle identification number

Automatic

The identification number, for the 200C, 3-speed, is stamped on either rear side of the transmission case. The identification number for the 180C and 3L30, 3-speed transmissions, is stamped on a metal plate which is attached to the front left side of the case. The identification number, for the 700-R4 and the 4L60, 4-speed transmissions, is stamped on the right rear side of the case at the pan rail.

Drive Axle

On rear axles, the identification number is stamped on the front right side of the axle tube, next to the differential. On front axles, the ID number is tamped on a tag, under one of the differential cover bolts.

MANUAL TRANSMISSION APPLICATION CHART

Transmission Type	Years	Models
Isuzu 77.5 mm 4-speed	1983–87	Blazer and Jimmy
Borg Warner 77 mm 4-speed	1983–87	Blazer and Jimmy
Borg Warner 77 mm 5-speed	1983–91	Blazer and Jimmy

TRANSFER CASE APPLICATION CHART

Transmission Case Type	Years	Models
New Process 207	1983–88	Blazer and Jimmy
New Process 231	1989–91	Blazer and Jimmy
Borg Warner 4472	1991	Bravada

Transfer Case

Blazer and Jimmy

The model 207 and 231 transfer cases are equipped with a identification tag which is attached to the rear half of the case; the tag gives the model number, the low range reduction ratio and the assembly number. If, for some reason it becomes dislodged or removed, reattach it with an adhesive sealant.

Bravada

The Borg Warner Model 4472 transfer case is equipped with an aluminum identification tag which is attached to 1 of the self tapping case bolts. The tag provides the Borg Warner part number, the General Motors part number, the serial number and the build date. If the tag becomes dislodged or removed, reattach it to the unit.

ROUTINE MAINTENANCE

Air Cleaner

The air cleaner element is a paper cartridge type, it should be replaced every year or 30,000 miles; if the vehicle is operated in heavy traffic

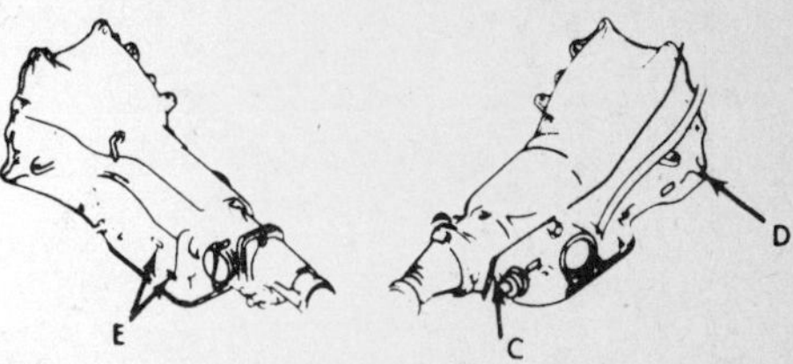

Location of the 220C automatic transmission identification numbers

or under dusty conditions, replace the element at more frequent intervals.

REMOVAL AND INSTALLATION

1. Remove the top of the air cleaner.
2. Remove and discard the paper element.
3. Using a new element, reverse the removal procedures.

Gasoline Fuel Filter

The fuel filter should be serviced every 15,000 miles; if operated under severe conditions, change it more often. Three types of fuel filters are used, a pleated-paper element type (with a internal check valve), an inline type and an in-tank type.

NOTE: *If an in-line fuel filter is used on an engine which has a filter installed in the car-*

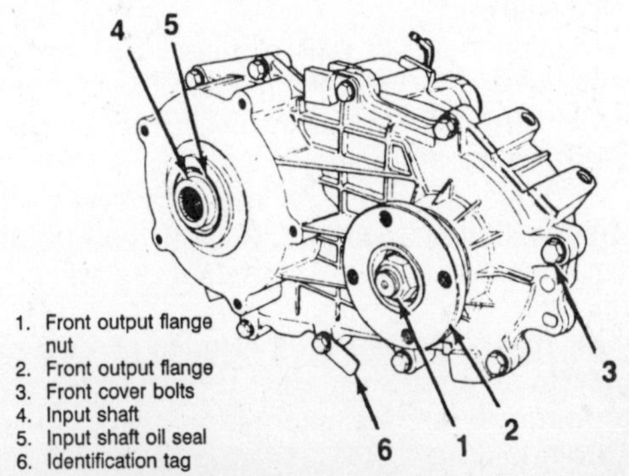

Location of the transfer case (Model 207) identification tag – Bravada

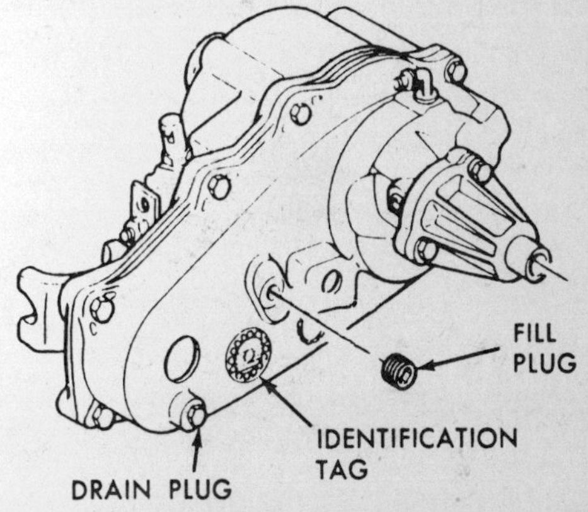

Location of the transfer case (Model 207) identification tag - Blazer and Jimmy

AUTOMATIC TRANSMISSION APPLICATION CHART

Transmission Type	Years	Models
Turbo Hydra-Matic 200C 3-speed	1983–85	Blazer and Jimmy
Turbo Hydra-Matic 700-R4 4-speed	1983–90	Blazer and Jimmy
Turbo Hydra-Matic 180C 3-speed	1987–90	Blazer and Jimmy
Turbo Hydra-Matic 3L30 3-speed	1990–91	Blazer and Jimmy
Turbo Hydra-Matic 4L60 4-speed	1990–91	Blazer, Jimmy and Bravada

In 1990, the 180C became the 3L30 and the 700-R4 became the 4L60

buretor body, be sure to change both at the same time.
CAUTION: *Filter replacement should not be attempted when the engine is HOT. Additionally, it is a good idea to place some absorbent rags under the fuel fittings to catch the gasoline which will spill out when the lines are loosened.*

REMOVAL AND INSTALLATION

There are three types of fuel filters: Internal (in the carburetor fitting), inline (in the fuel line) and in-tank (the sock on the fuel pickup tube).

Internal Filter

1. Disconnect the fuel line connection at the fuel inlet filter nut on the carburetor.
2. Remove the fuel inlet filter nut from the carburetor.
3. Remove the filter and the spring.
NOTE: *If a check valve is not present with the filter, one must be installed when the filter is replaced.*
4. Install the spring, filter and check valve (must face the fuel line), then reverse the removal procedures. Torque the filter nut-to-carburetor to 25 ft. lbs. and the fuel line-to-connector to 18 ft. lbs.; do not overtighten.
5. Start the engine and check for leaks.

Inline Filter

CAUTION: *Before disconnecting any component of the fuel system, release the fuel pressure.*
1. Remove the fuel filler cap to relieve the pressure in the fuel tank.
2. Disconnect the fuel lines from the filter.
3. Remove the fuel filter from the retainer or mounting bolt.
4. To install, reverse the removal procedures. Start the engine and check for leaks.
NOTE: *The filter has an arrow (fuel flow direction) on the side of the case, be sure to in-*

stall it correctly in the system, with the arrow facing away from the fuel tank.

In-Tank Filter

To service the in-tank fuel filter, refer to the "Electric Fuel Pump Removal and Installation" procedures in Chapter 5.

Diesel Fuel Filter

REMOVAL AND INSTALLATION

Filter Element

1. Disconnect the negative battery terminal.
2. Disconnect the water sensor wire connector from the filter assembly.
3. Disconnect the water sensor-to-main body hose.
4. Using a filter band wrench, remove the fuel filter element by turning the cartridge counterclockwise, while being careful not to spill diesel fuel from the element.
5. Drain the fuel from the element into a container and discard it. Take precautions to avoid the risk of fire during replacement procedures.
6. Remove the water and heater sensor from the bottom of the used filter element.
To install:
7. Apply a thin coat of diesel fuel to the water sensor O-ring, then install the water and heater sensor on the bottom of the replacement filter element and tighten.
8. Wipe all filter sealing surfaces clean before installing the new filter and apply a thin coat of diesel fuel to the gasket on the new fuel filter element.
9. Install the new filter element by turning it clockwise until the gasket contacts the sealing surfaces on the main filter body. Hand tighten another $2/3$ of a turn after the gasket contacts the sealing surface; do not overtighten.
10. Reconnect the water sensor wiring con-

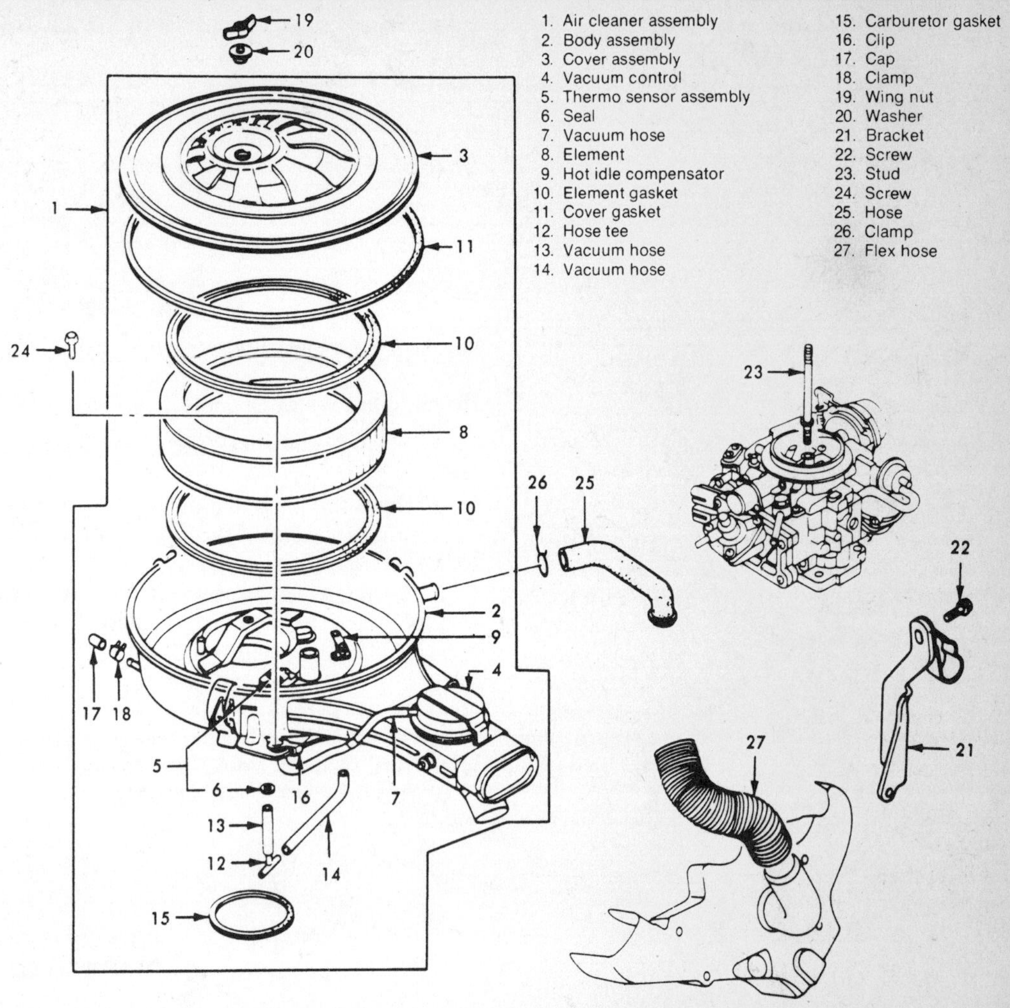

19
20
3
1
11
24
10
8
10
2
9
4
17 18
5
6
16
7
13
12
14
15
23
26 25
22
27
21
1. Air cleaner assembly
2. Body assembly
3. Cover assembly
4. Vacuum control
5. Thermo sensor assembly
6. Seal
7. Vacuum hose
8. Element
9. Hot idle compensator
10. Element gasket
11. Cover gasket
12. Hose tee
13. Vacuum hose
14. Vacuum hose
15. Carburetor gasket
16. Clip
17. Cap
18. Clamp
19. Wing nut
20. Washer
21. Bracket
22. Screw
23. Stud
24. Screw
25. Hose
26. Clamp
27. Flex hose

1.9L Thermostatic Air Cleaner (TAC) assembly—others similar

nector, then disconnect the fuel outlet hose from the injection pump and place the end in a clean container.

11. Operate the priming pump handle on the injection pump several times to fill the new filter with fuel, until fuel flows from the outlet hose. Reconnect the outlet hose to the injection pump when priming is complete.

12. Start the engine and check for leaks.

NOTE: *It is very important to prime the new filter element before starting the engine, as the shock of the diesel engine's high operating fuel pressure hitting a dry element can tear small pieces of debris away and allow them to pass into the injection pump and injectors, possibly causing injection pump or injector damage.*

A. Front
1. Upper fuel line fitting
2. Lower fuel line fitting
3. Bracket
5. Bolt
1
3
2
5
A

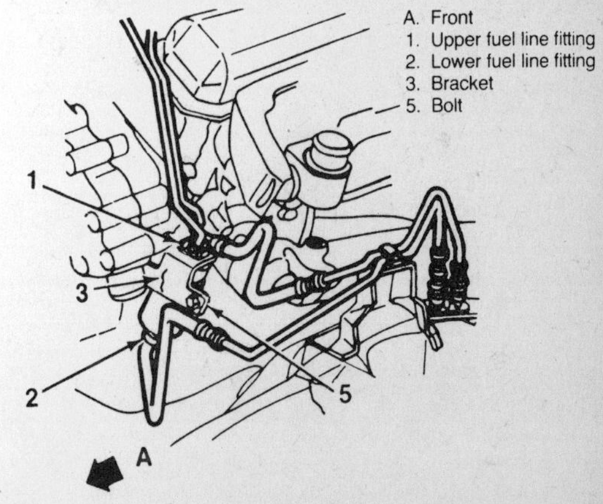

2.8L TBI in-line fuel filter

2.5L TBI in-line fuel filter

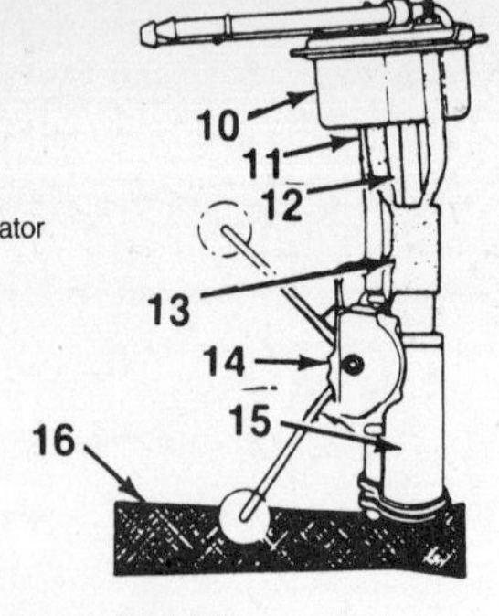

Fuel injected engine in-tank fuel filter

Filter Assembly

1. Disconnect the negative battery terminal.

2. Disconnect the water sensor electrical connector.

3. Disconnect the fuel hoses from the filter assembly.

4. Remove the filter assembly-to-bracket screws and the filter main body, element and sensors as an assembly.

5. To install, reverse the removal procedures. Refer to the ''Draining the Water Separator'' procedures in this Chapter and prime the fuel system.

Draining the Water Separator

1. Turn the engine **OFF** and allow it to cool.

2. Open the hood and place a 2 quart container under the end of the drain hose attached to the separator.

3. Turn the wing nut about 4 turns **counterclockwise** to open the drain plug, then operate the priming pump lever until all of the water is drained and only clean diesel fuel flows from the water separator.

4. Tighten the drain plug wing nut **clockwise** until securely closed; do not overtighten.

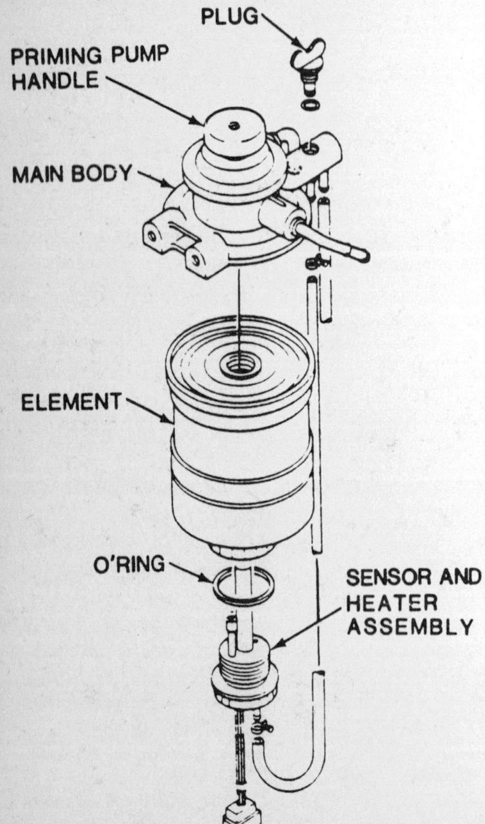

Exploded view of the diesel fuel filter assembly

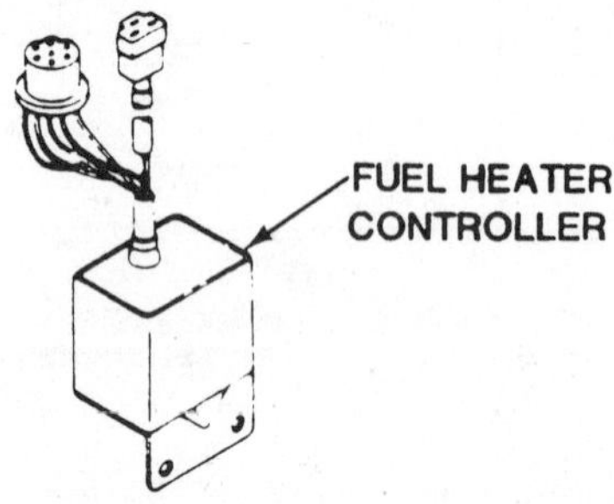

2.2L diesel fuel heater controller

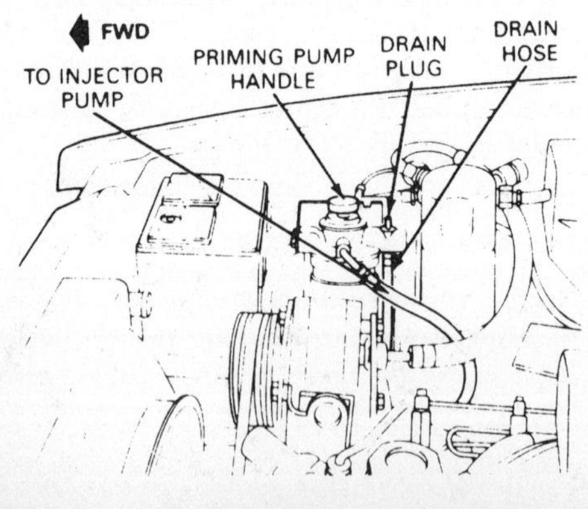

Diesel fuel filter installation

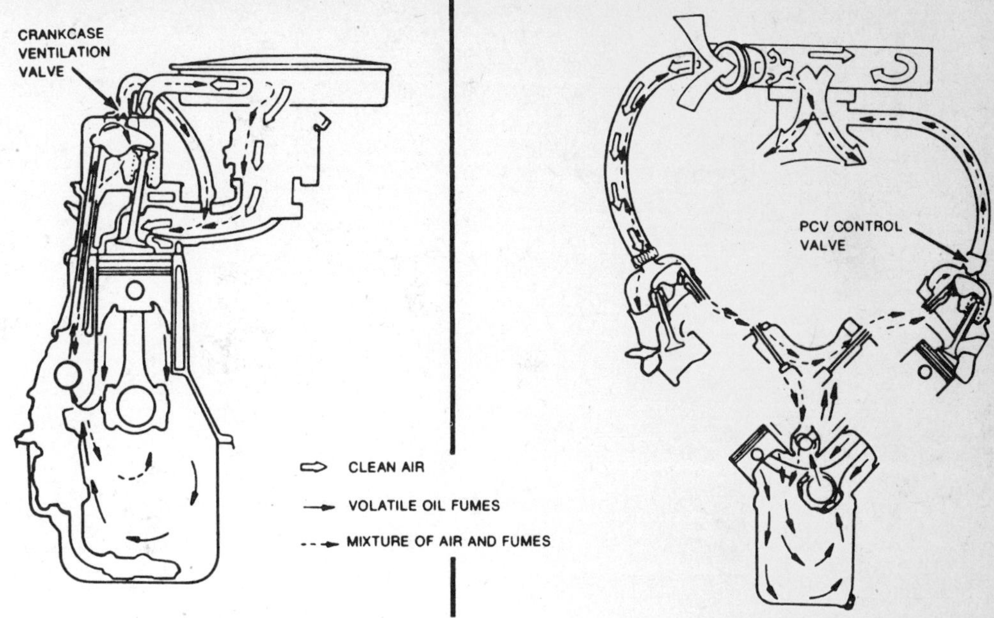

PCV flow through the engine

Again operate the priming pump handle until resistance is felt, indicating that the fuel filter is properly primed.

5. Start the engine and check for fuel leaks from the separator and fuel lines. Make sure the "Water In Fuel" light is OFF; if the light remains ON, the fuel tank must be purged of water with a siphon hose and hand pump fed into the tank through the fuel filter.

CAUTION: *Do not attempt to siphon any fuel tank contents by using mouth suction to start the siphon effect. Diesel fuel is poisonous and is by far the worst tasting stuff you can imagine. Use a hand siphon pump or power drill attachment to pull the water from the fuel tank.*

Positive Crankcase Ventilation (PCV)

The PCV valve is attached to the valve cover by a rubber grommet and connected to the intake manifold through a ventilation hose. Replace the PCV valve and the PCV filter (located in the air cleaner) every 30,000 miles under severe usage or 60,000 miles under light usage.

REMOVAL AND INSTALLATION

1. Pull the PCV from the valve cover grommet and disconnect it from the ventilation hose(s).

2. Inspect the valve for operation: (1) Shake it to see if the valve is free; (2) Blow through it (air should pass in one direction only).

NOTE: *When replacing the PCV valve, it is recommended to use a new one.*

3. To install, reverse the removal procedures.

Evaporative Canister

To limit gasoline vapor discharge into the air, this system is designed to trap fuel vapors, which normally escape from the fuel tank and the intake manifold. Vapor arrest is accomplished through the use of the charcoal canister. This canister absorbs fuel vapors and stores them until they can be removed to be burned in the engine. Removal of the vapors from the canister to the engine is accomplished by a canister mounted purge valve, the throttle valve position, a Thermostatic Vacuum Switch (TVS) or a computer controlled canister purge solenoid.

In addition to the modifications and the canister, the fuel tank requires a non-vented gas cap. The domed fuel tank positions a vent high enough above the fuel to keep the vent pipe in the vapor at all times. The single vent pipe is routed directly to the canister. From the canister, the vapors are routed to the intake system, where they will be burned during normal combustion.

SERVICING

Every 30,000 miles or 24 months, check all fuel, vapor lines and hoses for proper hookup, routing and condition. If equipped, check that the bowl vent and purge valves work properly.

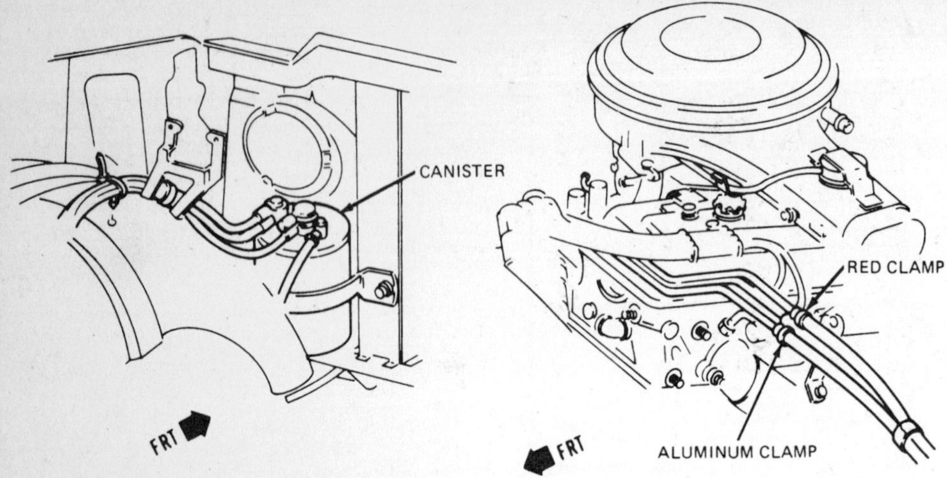

4-cylinder evaporative canister and hoses

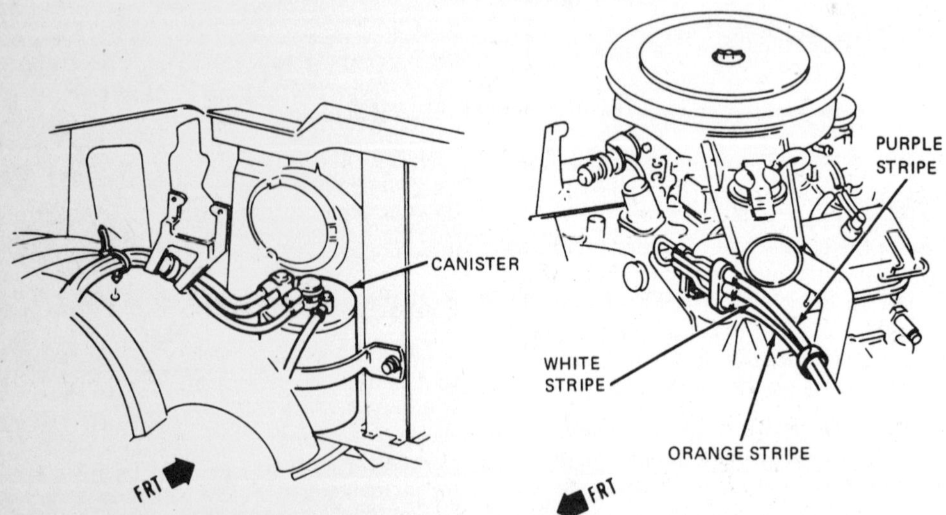

6-cylinder engine evaporative canister and hoses

Remove the canister and check for cracks or damage, then replace, if necessary.

REMOVAL AND INSTALLATION

1. Disconnect and mark the charcoal canister vent hoses.
2. Remove the canister-to-bracket bolt.
3. Lift the canister from the bracket.
4. To install, reverse the removal procedures.

CHARCOAL CANISTER SOLENOID REPLACEMENT

1. Disconnect the negative battery cable.
2. Remove the solenoid retaining bolt, the cover and the solenoid.
3. Disconnect the electrical connector and the hoses from the solenoid.

4. To install, reverse the removal procedures.

Battery

All vehicles have a Maintenance Free battery as standard equipment, eliminating the need for fluid level checks and the possibility of specific gravity tests. Nevertheless, the battery does require some attention.

Once a year, the battery terminals and the cable clamps should be cleaned. Remove the side terminal bolts and the cables, negative cable first. Clean the cable clamps and the battery terminals with a wire brush until all corrosion, grease, etc. is removed and the metal is shiny. It is especially important to clean the inside of the clamp thoroughly, since a small deposit of foreign material or oxidation there will prevent a sound electrical connection and in-

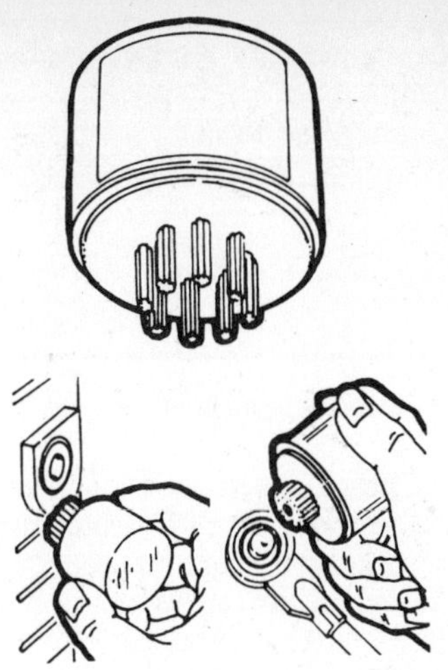

Special tools are also available for cleaning the posts and clamps on side terminal batteries

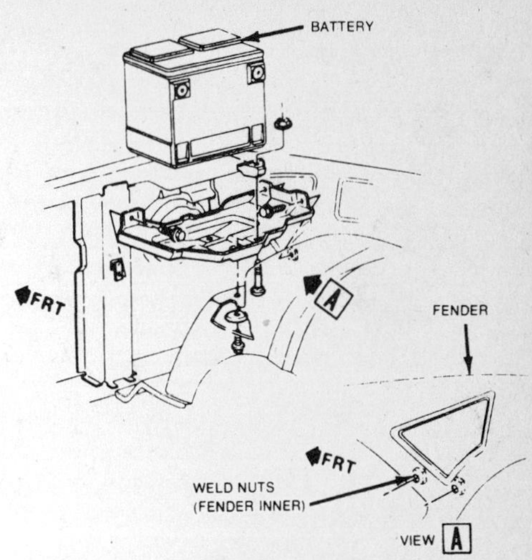

Battery tray installation

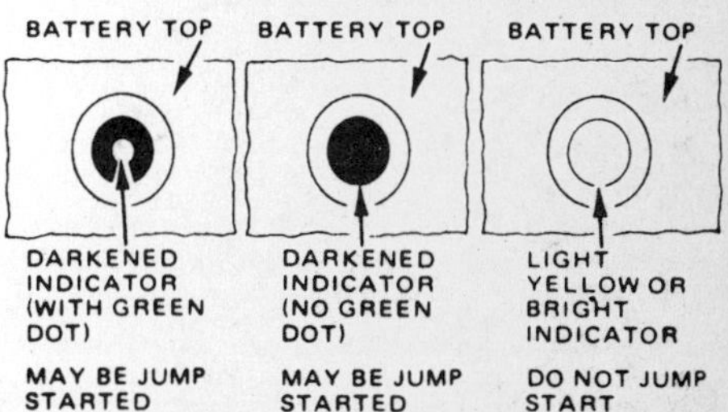

Maintenance-free batteries contain their own built in hydrometer

hibit either starting or charging. Special tools are available for cleaning the side terminal clamps and terminals.

Before installing the cables, loosen the battery hold-down clamp, remove the battery and check the battery tray. Clear it of any debris and check it for soundness. Rust should be wire brushed away and the metal given a coat of anti-rust paint. Replace the battery and tighten the hold-down clamp securely but be careful not to overtighten, which will crack the battery case.

NOTE: *Batteries can be cleaned using a solution of baking soda and water. Surface coatings on battery cases can actually conduct electricity which will cause a slight voltage drain, so make sure the battery case is clean.*

After the clamps and terminals are clean, reinstall the cables, negative cable last. Give the clamps and terminals a thin external coat of nonmetallic grease after installation, to retard corrosion.

Check the cables at the same time that the terminals are cleaned. If the cable insulation is cracked, broken or the ends are frayed, the cable should be replaced with a new one of the same length and gauge.

CAUTION: *Keep flames or sparks away from the battery. It gives off explosive hydrogen gas. The battery electrolyte contains sulphuric acid. If you should get any on your skin or in your eyes, flush the affected areas with plenty of clear water. If it lands in your eyes, seek medical help immediately.*

Testing the Maintenance Free Battery

Maintenance free batteries, do not require normal attention as far as fluid level checks are concerned. However, the terminals require pe-

riodic cleaning, which should be performed at least once a year.

The sealed top battery cannot be checked for charge in the normal manner, since there is no provision for access to the electrolyte. To check the condition of the battery:

1. If the indicator eye on top of the battery is dark, the battery has enough fluid. If the eye is lit, the electrolyte fluid is too low and the battery must be replaced.

2. If a green dot appears in the middle of the eye, the battery is sufficiently charged. Proceed to Step 4. If no green dot is visible, charge the battery as in Step 3.

3. Charge the battery at this rate:

NOTE: *Do not charge the battery for more than 50 amp-hours. If the green dot appears or if the electrolyte squirts out of the vent hole, stop the charge and proceed to Step 4.*

It may be necessary to tip the battery from side-to-side to get the green dot to appear after charging.

CAUTION: *When charging the battery, the electrical system and control unit can be quickly damaged by improper connections, high output battery chargers or incorrect service procedures.*

4. Connect a battery load tester and a voltmeter across the battery terminals (the battery cables should be disconnected from the battery). Apply a 300 amp load to the battery for 15 seconds to remove the surface charge. Remove the load.

5. Wait 15 seconds to allow the battery to recover. Apply the appropriate test load, as specified in the following chart:

Apply the load for 15 seconds while reading the voltage. Disconnect the load.

6. Check the results against the following chart. If the battery voltage is at or above the specified voltage for the temperature listed, the battery is good. It the voltage falls below what's listed, the battery should be replaced.

Early Fuel Evaporation (EFE) Heater

The EFE heating system is used on all carbureted engines. The purpose of the heating unit is to further vaporize the fuel droplets as they enter the intake manifold; vaporization of the air/fuel mixture ensures complete combustion which provides the maximum power output of the fuel used.

REMOVAL AND INSTALLATION

Heater Unit

The EFE heater unit is located directly under the carburetor and is electrically operated.

1. Disconnect the negative battery terminal. Remove the air cleaner.

2. From the carburetor, disconnect the

Battery	Test Load (Amps)
83–50	150
83-60	180
85A-60	170
87A-60	230
89A-60	270
1981103	200
1981104	250
1981105	270
1981577	260

Battery test load specifications chart

Charging Rate Amps	Time
75	40 min
50	1 hr
25	2 hr
10	5 hr

Battery charging rates chart

Temperature (°F)	Minimum Voltage
70 or above	9.6
60	9.5
50	9.4
40	9.3
30	9.1
20	8.9
10	8.7
0	8.5

Battery minimum voltage chart

vacuum hoses, electrical connectors and fuel hoses. Disconnect the EFE Heater electrical connector from the wiring harness.

3. Remove the carburetor-to-intake manifold nuts and the carburetor from the manifold. Lift the EFE Heater from the intake manifold.

4. Using a putty knife, clean the gasket mounting surfaces.

5. To install, use new gaskets and reverse the removal procedures. Torque the carburetor-to-intake manifold nuts to 13 ft. lbs.

Heater Switch

The heater switch is located near the thermostat housing on 2.8L carbureted engine, the bottom rear side of the intake manifold on 2.0L carbureted engine or the top right side of the engine on 1.9L carbureted engine.

1. Using a drain pan, position it under the radiator, then open the drain cock and drain the coolant to a level below the heater switch.

CAUTION: *When draining the coolant, keep in mind that cats and dogs are attracted by the ethylene glycol antifreeze, and are quite likely to drink any that is left in an uncovered container or in puddles on the ground. This will prove fatal in sufficient quantity. Always drain the coolant into a sealable container. Coolant should be reused unless it is contaminated or several years old.*

2. Disconnect the wiring harness connector from the EFE heater switch.

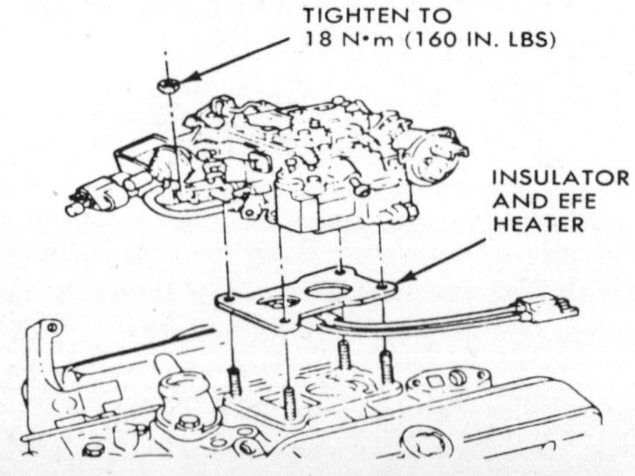

Carbureted 2.8L EFE heater assembly

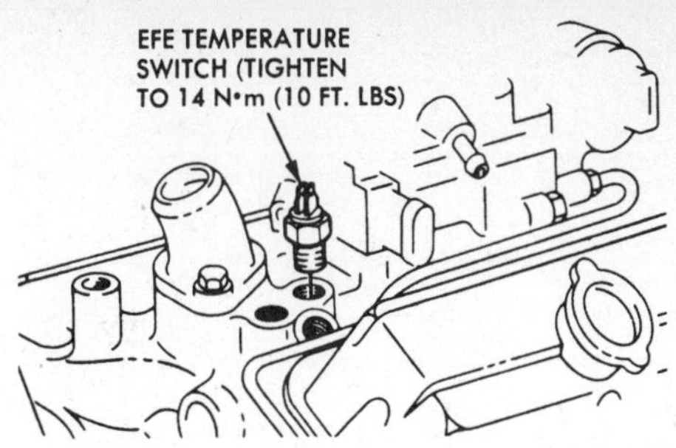

2.8L EFE heater switch

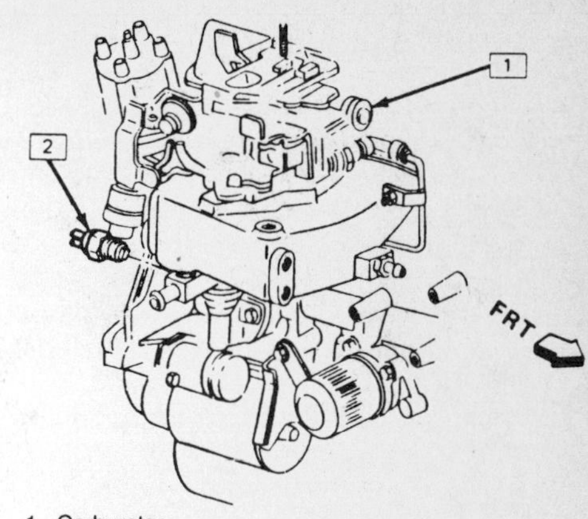

1. Carburetor
2. EFE heater switch

EFE heater switch relay on the 2.0L engine

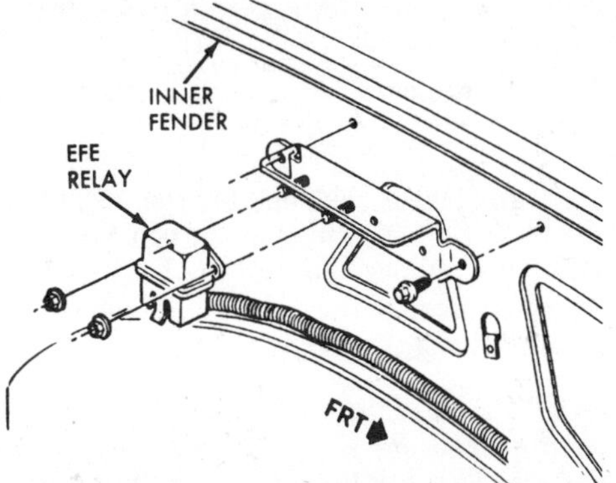

Exploded view of the EFE heater switch relay - 1982-83, others similar

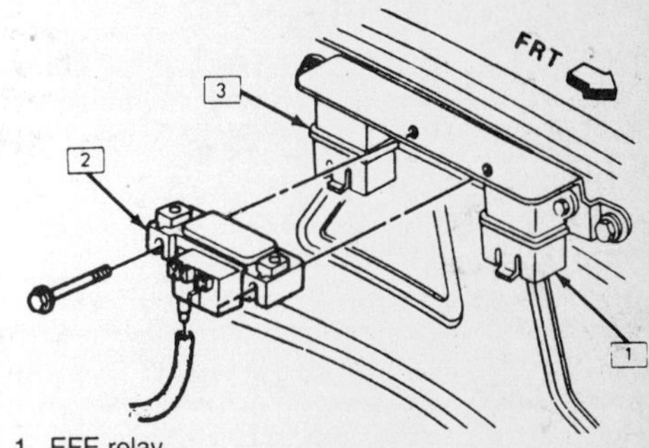

1. EFE relay
2. Manifold differential pressure sensor
3. W.O.T. relay

1984–85 EFE heater switch relay

1. Disconnect the negative battery terminal.

2. Disconnect the wiring harness connector(s) from the heater switch relay.

3. Remove the heater switch relay-to-bracket screw and the relay from the vehicle.

4. To install, use a new relay and reverse the removal procedures.

TESTING

1. Disconnect the wiring harness connector from the EFE heater switch, located near the thermostat housing on 2.8L carbureted engine, on the bottom rear side of the intake manifold on 2.0L carbureted engine or on the top right side of the engine on 1.9L carbureted engine.

NOTE: *To perform the following inspection, the engine temperature must be below 140°F (60°C).*

2. Using a 12 volt test lamp, connect it across the EFE wiring harness connector terminals. Turn the ignition switch **ON** with the engine is OFF, the lamp should glow; if the lamp glows, the EFE heater is good.

3. If the lamp does not glow, reconnect the

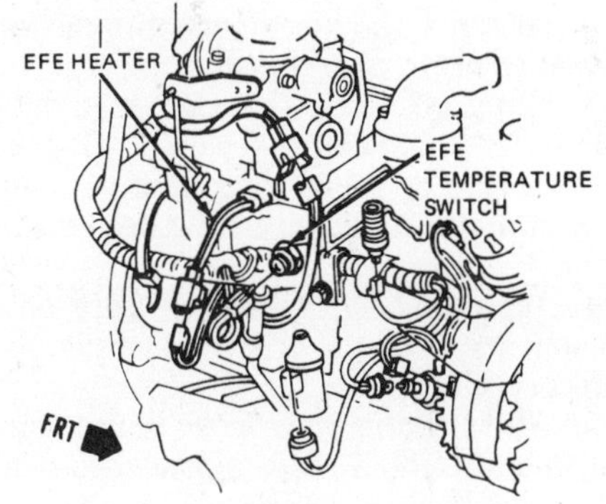

1.9L EFE heater and heater switch

3. Remove the EFE heater switch, turn it counterclockwise, from the intake manifold.

4. To install the new EFE heater switch, coat the threads with a soft setting sealant and torque it to 10 ft. lbs. Reconnect the wiring harness connector to the EFE heater switch. Refill the cooling system.

NOTE: *When applying sealant to the EFE heater, be careful not to coat the sensor and/ or the switch.*

Heater Switch Relay

The heater switch relay is located on the left-fender.

wiring harness connector to the EFE heater switch.

4. Using a DC voltmeter, place it on the 0–15 volt scale, insert the test probes into the rear of the wiring harness connector body (the black wire is to be grounded) and measure the voltage; it should read 11–13 volts.

5. If the voltage is not 11–13 volts, insure that the black wire is grounded; if the voltage is not 0 volt, the black (grounded) wire is an open circuit, repair it.

6. If the voltage is 0 volts, check for voltage-to-ground at each heater switch terminal—the voltage at each switch terminal should be 11–13 volts.

7. If 1 terminal measures 11–13 volts and the other is low or 0 volts, check the connector for deformed terminals and repair, as necessary.

8. If the electrical connector is making proper contact, replace the EFE heater switch.

9. If the voltage is not 11–13 volts at each switch terminal, check the wiring harness circuit between the heater switch and the ignition switch, then repair, as necessary.

10. Start the engine, allow it to warm to 170°F (76.7°C), then check the voltage across the EFE heater terminals; it should be 0 volts. If the voltage is not 0 volts, replace the EFE heater switch.

Drive Belts

INSPECTION

On 1983–86 vehicles, check the drive belt(s) every 15,000 miles/12 months (heavy usage) or 30,000 miles/24 months (light usage) for evidence of wear such as cracking, fraying and incorrect tension. On 1987–91 vehicles, check the drive belts every 12,000 miles (heavy usage) or 60,000 miles (light usage).

On the 1983–86 vehicles, determine the belt tension at a point halfway between the pulleys by pressing on the belt with moderate thumb pressure. The belt should deflect about 1/4 in. (6mm) over a 7–10 in. (178–254mm) span, or 1/2 in. (12.7mm) over a 13–16 in. (330–406mm) span, at this point. If the deflection is found to be too much or too little, perform the tension adjustments.

ADJUSTING TENSION

Except 4.3L Engine

NOTE: *The following procedures require the use of GM Belt Tension Gauge No. BT-33-95-ACBN (regular V-belts), BT-33-97M (poly V-belts) or equivalent.*

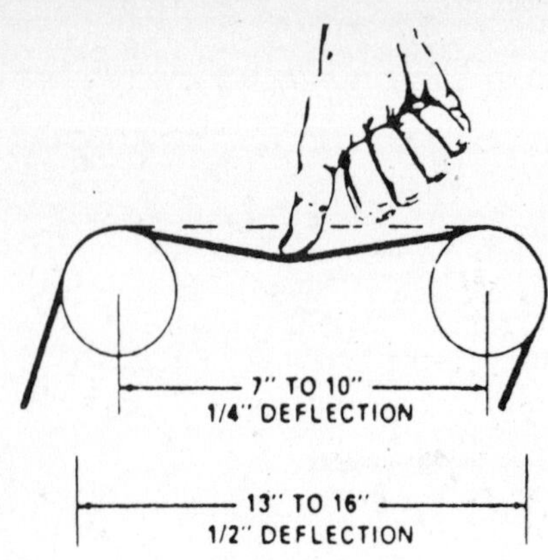

A gauge is recommended but you can check the belt tension with thumb pressure

1. If the belt is cold, operate the engine (at idle speed) for 15 minutes; the belt will seat itself in the pulleys allowing the belt fibers to relax or stretch. If the belt is hot, allow it to cool, until it is warm to the touch.

NOTE: *A used belt is one that has been rotated at least one complete revolution on the pulleys. This begins the belt seating process and it must never be tensioned to the new belt specifications.*

2. Loosen the component-to-mounting bracket bolts.

3. Using a GM Belt Tension Gauge No. BT-33-95-ACBN (standard V-belts), BT-33-97M (poly V-belts) or equivalent, place the tension gauge at the center of the belt between the longest span.

4. Applying belt tension pressure on the component, adjust the drive belt tension to the correct specifications.

5. While holding the correct tension on the component, tighten the component-to-mounting bracket bolt.

6. When the belt tension is correct, remove the tension gauge.

NOTE: *It is better to have belts too loose than too tight, because overtight belts will lead to bearing failure, particularly in the water pump and alternator. However, loose belts place an extremely high impact load on the driven components due to the whipping action of the belt.*

4.3 L Engine

The belt tensioner is spring loaded and the dirve belt will return to the tensioner position, provided the grooves in the belt match the grooves in the pulley.

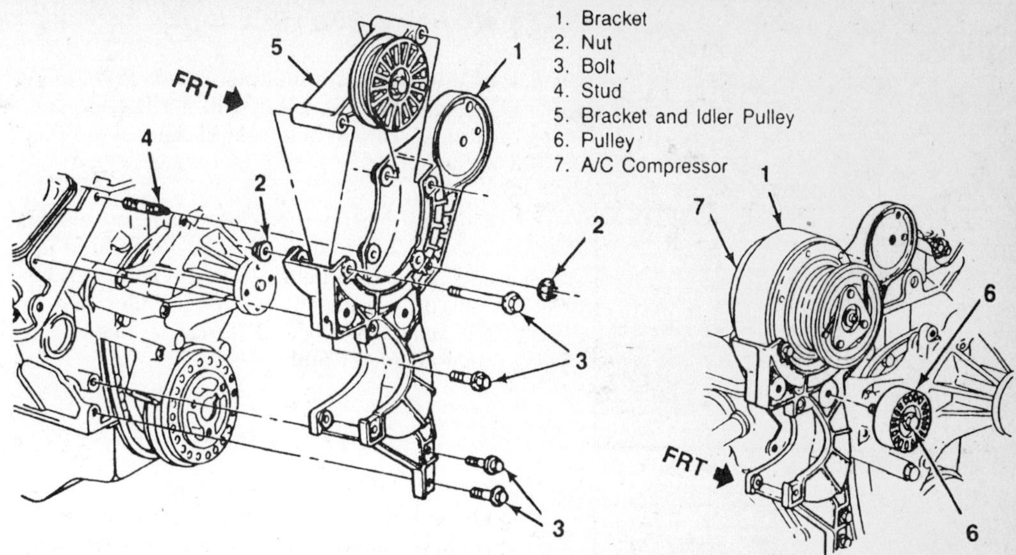

Exploded view of the idler pulley and bracket—4.3L engine

REMOVAL AND INSTALLATION

Except 4.3L Engine

1. Loosen the component-to-mounting bracket bolts.

2. Rotate the component to relieve the tension on the drive belt.

3. Slip the drive belt from the component pulley and remove it from the engine.

NOTE: *If the engine uses more than one belt, it may be necessary to remove other belts that are in front of the one being removed.*

4. To install, reverse the removal procedures. Adjust the component drive belt tension to specifications.

4.3L Engine

1. Place a tool over the tensioner pulley axis bolt.

2. Rotate the tool counterclockwise

3. Remove the drive belt.

4. Remove the tool.

To install:

5. Route the belt over the pulleys, except the drive belt tensionser pulley.

6. Place a tool over the tensioner pulley axis bolt.

7. Rotate the tool counterclockwise.

8. Install the drive belt over the belt tensioner pulley.

9. Remove the tool and check the belt for correct tracking.

Hoses

The upper/lower radiator hoses and all heater hoses should be checked for deteriora-

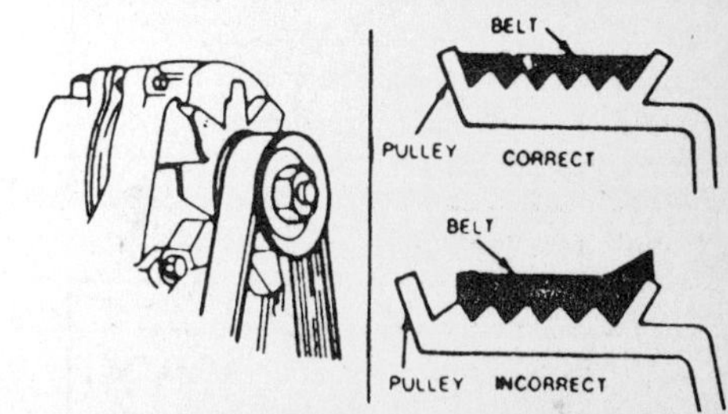

Serpentine drive belt alignment—4.3L engine

tion, leaks and loose hose clamps every 15,000 miles or 12 months.

REMOVAL AND INSTALLATION

1. Drain the cooling system.

CAUTION: *When draining the coolant, keep in mind that cats and dogs are attracted by the ethylene glycol antifreeze, and are quite likely to drink any that is left in an uncovered container or in puddles on the ground. This will prove fatal in sufficient quantity. Always drain the coolant into a sealable container. Coolant should be reused unless it is contaminated or several years old.*

2. Loosen the hose clamps at each end of the hose.

3. Working the hose back and forth, slide it off it's connection and then install a new hose, if necessary.

NOTE: *When replacing the heater hoses, maintain a 1½ in. (38mm) clearance between the hose clip-to-upper control arm and between the rear overhead heater core lines-to-exhaust pipe.*

4. To install, reverse the removal procedures. Refill the cooling system.

HOW TO SPOT WORN V-BELTS

V-Belts are vital to efficient engine operation—they drive the fan, water pump and other accessories. They require little maintenance (occasional tightening) but they will not last forever. Slipping or failure of the V-belt will lead to overheating. If your V-belt looks like any of these, it should be replaced.

Cracking or weathering

This belt has deep cracks, which cause it to flex. Too much flexing leads to heat build-up and premature failure. These cracks can be caused by using the belt on a pulley that is too small. Notched belts are available for small diameter pulleys.

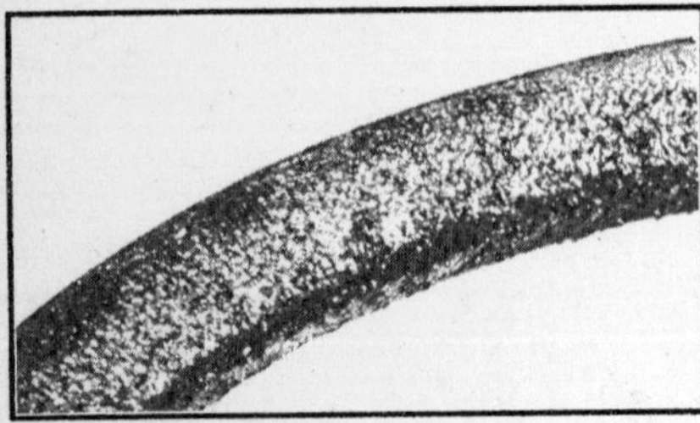

Softening (grease and oil)

Oil and grease on a belt can cause the belt's rubber compounds to soften and separate from the reinforcing cords that hold the belt together. The belt will first slip, then finally fail altogether.

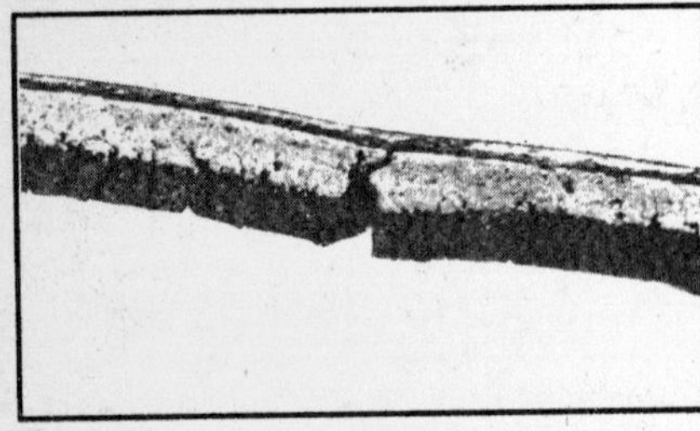

Glazing

Glazing is caused by a belt that is slipping. A slipping belt can cause a run-down battery, erratic power steering, overheating or poor accessory performance. The more the belt slips, the more glazing will be built up on the surface of the belt. The more the belt is glazed, the more it will slip. If the glazing is light, tighten the belt.

Worn cover

The cover of this belt is worn off and is peeling away. The reinforcing cords will begin to wear and the belt will shortly break. When the belt cover wears in spots or has a rough jagged appearance, check the pulley grooves for roughness.

Separation

This belt is on the verge of breaking and leaving you stranded. The layers of the belt are separating and the reinforcing cords are exposed. It's just a matter of time before it breaks completely.

HOW TO SPOT BAD HOSES

Both the upper and lower radiator hoses are called upon to perform difficult jobs in an inhospitable enviorment. They are subject to nearly 18 psi at under hood temperature often over 280F., and must circulate an hour-3 good reasons to have good hoses.

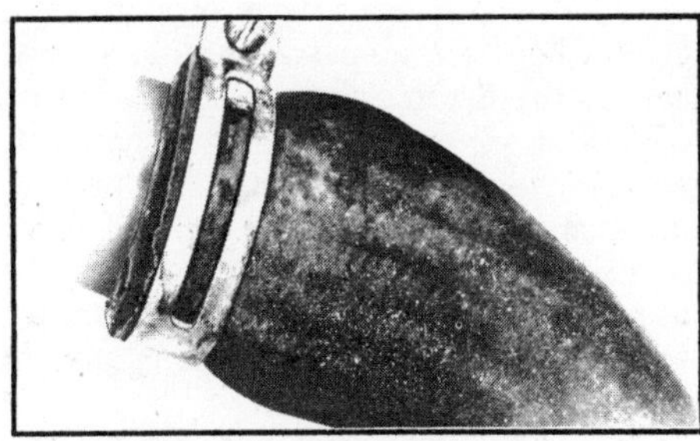

Swollen hose

A good test for any hose is to feel it for soft or spongy spots. Frequently these will appear as swollen areas of the hose. The most likely cause is oil soaking. This hose could burst at any time, when hot or under pressure.

Cracked hose

Cracked hoses can usually be seen but feel the hoses to be sure they have not hardened; a prime cause of cracking. This hose has cracked down to the reinforcing cords and could split at any of the cracks.

Frayed hose end (due to weak clamp)

Weakened clamps frequently are the cause of hose and cooling system failure. The connection between the pipe and hose has deteriorated enough to allow coolant to escape when the engine is hot.

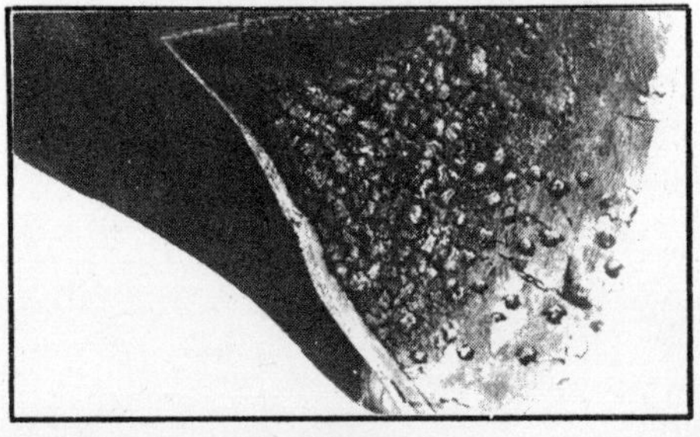

Debris in cooling system

Debris, rust and scale in the cooling system can cause the inside of a hose to weaken. This can usually be felt on the outside of the hose as soft or thinner areas.

NOTE: *Draw the hoses tight to prevent sagging or rubbing against other components; route the hoses through the clamps as installed originally. Always make sure the hose clamps are beyond the component bead and placed in the center of the clamping surface before tightening them.*

Air Conditioning

SAFETY WARNINGS

Because of the importance of the necessary safety precautions that must be exercised when working with air conditioning systems and R-12 refrigerant, a recap of the safety precautions are outlined.

• Avoid contact with a charged refrigeration system, even when working on another part of the air conditioning system or vehicle. If a heavy tool comes into contact with a section of copper tubing or a heat exchanger, it can easily cause the relatively soft material to rupture.

• When it is necessary to apply force to a fitting which contains refrigerant, as when checking that all system couplings are securely tightened, use a wrench on both parts of the fitting involved, if possible. This will avoid putting torque on the refrigerant tubing. It is advisable, when possible, to use tube or line wrenches when tightening these flare nut fittings.

• Avoid applying heat to any refrigerant line or storage vessel. Charging may be aided by using water heated to less than 125°F (52°C) to warm the refrigerant container. Never allow a refrigerant storage container to sit out in the sun or near any other heat source, such as a radiator.

• Always wear goggles when working on a system to protect the eyes. If refrigerant contacts the eyes, it is advisable in all cases to see a physician as soon as possible.

• Frostbite from liquid refrigerant should be treated by first gradually warming the area with cool water and then gently applying petroleum jelly. A physician should be consulted.

• Always keep the refrigerant can fittings capped when not in use. Avoid any sudden shock to the drum, which might occur from dropping it or from banging a heavy tool against it. Never carry a drum in the passenger compartment of a vehicle.

• Always have the system completely discharged before painting the vehicle (if the paint is to be baked on), or before welding anywhere near the refrigerant lines.

NOTE: *Any repair work to an air conditioning system should be left to a professional. Do not, under any circumstances, attempt to loosen or tighten any fittings or perform any work other than that outlined here.*

SYSTEM INSPECTION

NOTE: *The Cycling Clutch Orfice (CCOT) tube air conditioning system does not use a sight glass.*

Checking For Oil Leaks

Refrigerant leaks show up as oily areas on the various components because the compressor oil is transported around the entire system

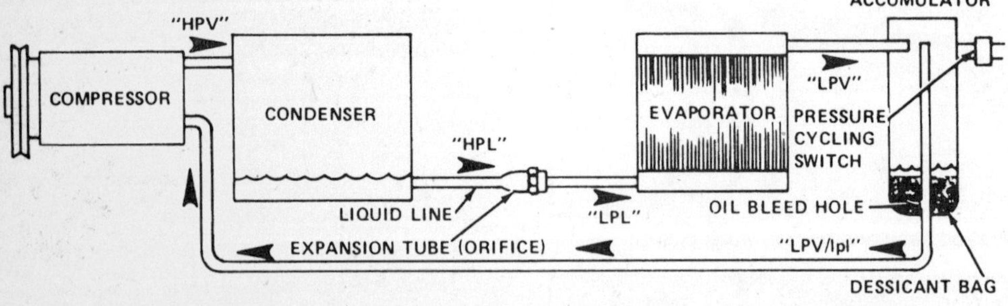

Air conditioning system schematic

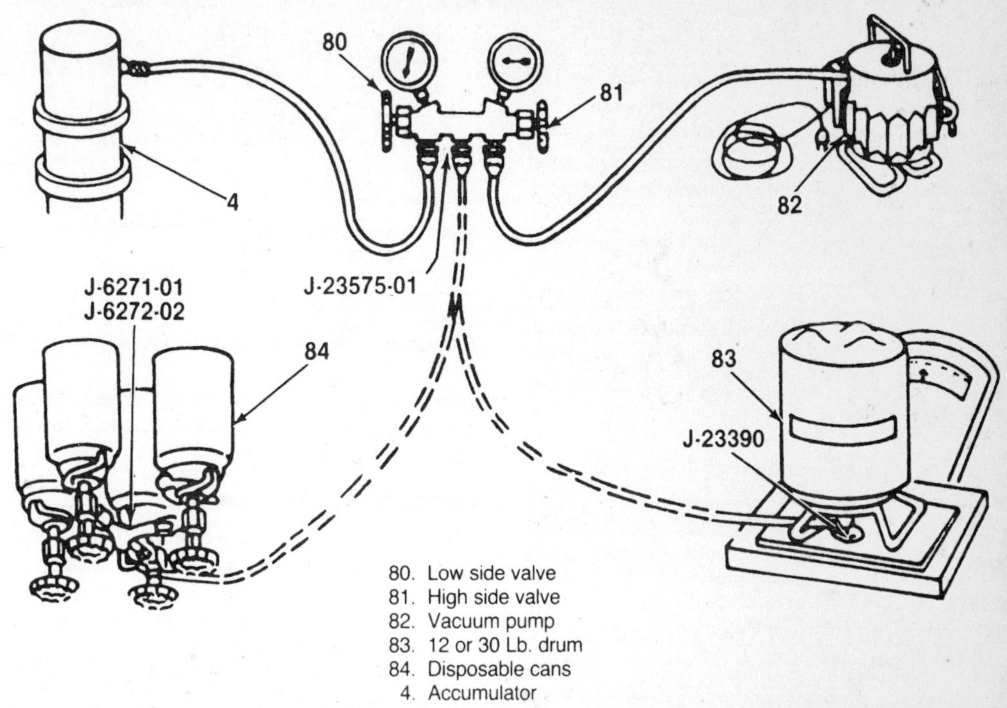

Air conditioning charging system with gauges

along with the refrigerant. Look for oily spots on all the hoses and lines, especially on the hose and tubing connections. If there are oily deposits, the system may have a leak, have it checked by a qualified repairman.

NOTE: *A small area of oil on the front of the compressor is normal and no cause for alarm.*

Checking The Compressor Belt

Refer to the Drive Belts section in this Chapter.

Keep The Condenser Clear

Periodically inspect the front of the condenser for bent fins or foreign material (dirt, buts, leaves, etc.). If any cooling fins are bent, straighten them carefully with needle-nose pliers. You can remove any debris with a stiff bristle brush or hose.

Operate The A/C System Periodically

A lot of air conditioning problems can be avoided by simply running the air conditioner at least once a week regardless of the season. Simply let the system run for at least 5 minutes a week (even in the winter) and you'll keep the internal parts lubricated as well as preventing the hoses from hardening.

Leak Testing the System

There are several methods of detecting leaks in an air conditioning system; among them, the 2 most popular are (1) halide leak detection or the open flame method and (2) electronic leak detector.

The Halide Leak Detection tool J-6084 or equivalent, is a torch like device which produces a yellow-green color when refrigerant is introduced into the flame at the burner. A purple or violet color indicates the presence of large amounts of refrigerant at the burner.

An Autobalance Refrigerant Leak Detector tool J-29547 or equivalent, is a small portable electronic device with an extended probe. With the unit activated, the probe is passed along those components of the system which contain refrigerant. If a leak is detected, the unit will sound an alarm signal or activate a display signal depending on the manufacturer's design. It is advisable to follow the manufacturer's instructions as the design and function of the detection may vary significantly.

CAUTION: *Care should be taken to operate either type of detector in well ventilated areas, so as to reduce the chance of personal injury, which may result from coming in contact with poisonous gases produced when R-12 is exposed to flame or electric spark.*

GAUGE SETS (USE)

Most of the service work performed in air conditioning requires the use of a set of 2 gauges, one for the high (head) pressure side of the system, the other for the low (suction) side.

The low side gauge records both pressure and vacuum. Vacuum readings are calibrated from 0–30 in. Hg vacuum, and the pressure graduations read from 0–60 psi.

The high side gauge measures pressure from 0–600 psi.

Both gauges are threaded into a manifold that contains 2 hand shut-off valves. Proper manipulation of these valves and the use of the attached test hoses allow the user to perform the following services:

1. Test high and low side pressures.
2. Charge the system with refrigerant.

The manifold valves are designed so they have no direct effect on the gauge readings but serve only to provide for or cut off the flow of refrigerant through the manifold. During all testing and hook-up operations, the valves are kept in a closed position to avoid disturbing the refrigeration system. The valves are Opened ONLY to purge the system of refrigerant or to charge it.

Service Valves

For the user to diagnose an air conditioning system he or she must gain entrance to the system in order to observe the pressures; the type of terminal for this purpose is the familiar Schrader valve.

The Schrader valve is similar to a tire valve stem and the process of connecting the test hoses is the same as threading a hand pump outlet hose to a bicycle tire. As the test hose is threaded to the service port the valve core is depressed, allowing the refrigerant to enter the test hose outlet. Removal of the test hose automatically closes the system.

Extreme caution must be observed when removing test hoses from the Schrader valves as

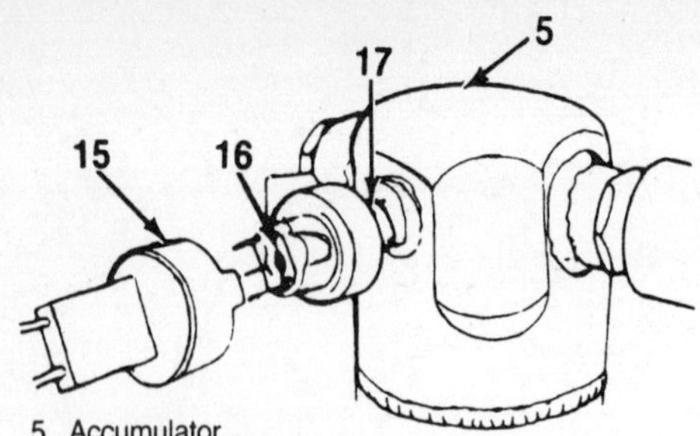

5. Accumulator
15. Electrical connector
16. Pressure cycling switch adjusting screw
17. "Schrader" type valve

A/C accumulator with Schrader valve

some refrigerant will normally escape, usually under high pressure; observe safety precautions.

Using The Manifold Gauges

The following are step-by-step procedures to guide the user to the correct gauge usage.

CAUTION: *Wear goggles or face shield during all testing operations. Backseat hand shut-off type service valves.*

1. Remove the caps from the high and low side service ports. Make sure both gauge valves are closed.

2. Connect the low side test hose to the service valve that leads to the evaporator (located between the evaporator outlet and the compressor).

3. Attach the high side test hose to the service valve that leads to the condenser.

4. Mid-position the hand shutoff type service valves.

5. Start the engine and allow it to warm-up. All testing and charging of the system should be done after the engine and system has reached normal operating temperatures, except when using certain the charging stations.

6. Adjust the air conditioner controls to Max. cold.

7. Observe the gauge readings.

When the gauges are not being used it is a good idea to:

a. Keep both hand valves in the closed position.

b. Attach both ends of the high and low service hoses to the manifold, if extra outlets are present on the manifold or plug them, if not.

c. Keep the center charging hose attached to an empty refrigerant can. This extra precaution will reduce the possibility of moisture entering the gauges. If the air and moisture have gotten into the gauges, purge the hoses by supplying refrigerant under pressure to the center hose with both gauge valves open and all openings unplugged.

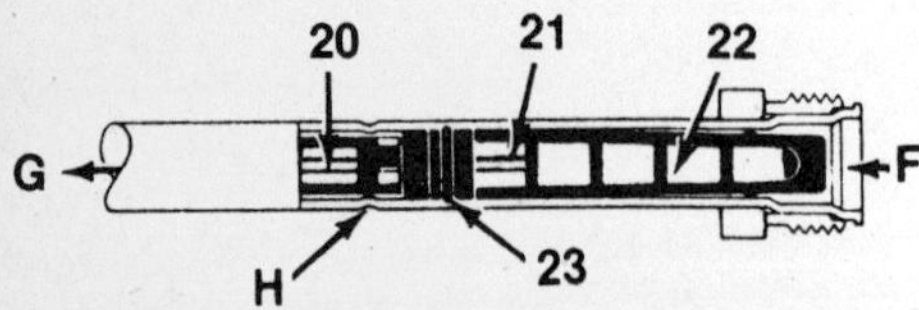

F. Inlet
G. Outlet (to evaporator)
H. Dent on tube (retains the expansion tube)
20. Outlet Screen
21. Expansion tube
22. Inlet screen
23. Seal

Sectional view of the air conditioning system orifice tube

CHARGING SYSTEM

CAUTION: *Never attempt to charge the system by opening the high pressure gauge control while the compressor is operating. The compressor accumulating pressure can burst the refrigerant container, causing sever personal injuries.*

1. Start the engine, operate it with the choke Open and normal idle speed, then position the air conditioning control lever on the Off.

2. Using 14 oz. cans of refrigerant, in the inverted position, allow about 1 lb. of refrigerant to enter the system through the low side service fitting on the accumulator.

3. After 1 lb. of refrigerant enters the system, position the control lever on Norm (the compressor will engage) and the blower motor on Hi speed; this operation will draw the remainder of the refrigerant into the system.

NOTE: *To speed up the operation, position a fan in front of the condenser; the lowering of the condenser temperature will allow refrigerant to enter the system faster.*

4. When the system is charged, turn Off the refrigerant source and allow the engine to run for 30 seconds to clear the lines and gauges.

5. With the engine running, remove the hose adapter from the accumulator service fitting (unscrew the hose quickly to prevent refrigerant from escaping).

CAUTION: *Never remove the gauge line from the adapter when the line is connected to the system; always remove the line adapter from the service fitting first.*

6. Replace the accumulator protective caps and turn the engine Off.

7. Using a leak detector, inspect the air conditioning system for leaks. If a leak is present, repair it.

Windshield Wipers

For maximum effectiveness and longest element life, the windshield and wiper blades should be kept clean. Dirt, tree sap, road tar and so on will cause streaking, smearing and blade deterioration if left on the glass. It is advisable to wash the windshield carefully with a commercial glass cleaner at least once a month. Wipe off the rubber blades with the wet rag, afterwards.

If the blades are found to be cracked, broken or torn, they should be replaced immediately. Replacement intervals will vary with usage, although ozone deterioration usually limits blade life to about one year. If the wiper pattern is smeared, streaked or if the blade chatters across the glass, the elements should be replaced. It is easiest and most sensible to replace the elements in pairs.

BLADE REPLACEMENT

1. Lift the wiper arm assembly from the windshield.

2. Depress the wiper arm-to-blade assembly pin to disconnect the blade assembly from the wiper arm.

3. To install, use new blade assemblies and reverse the removal procedures.

Tires and Wheels

TIRE ROTATION

TIRE DESIGN

Tire Types

For maximum satisfaction, tires should be used in sets of five. Mixing of different types (radial, bias-belted, fiberglass belted) should be avoided. Conventional bias tires are con-

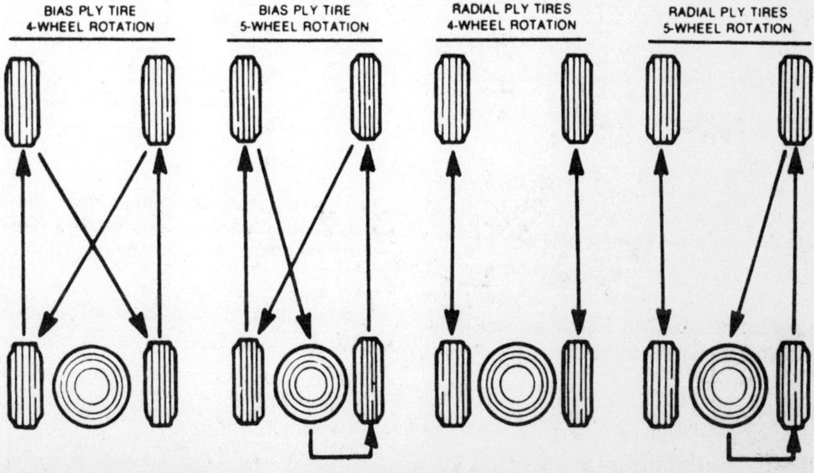

Tire rotation patterns

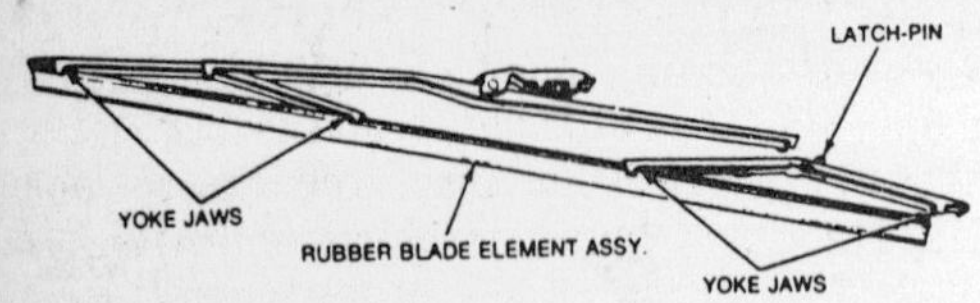

Typical windshield wiper assembly

structed so the cords run bead-to-bead at an angle. This type of construction gives rigidity to both tread and sidewall. Bias-belted tires are similar in construction to conventional bias ply tires. Belts run at an angle and also at a 90 degree angle to the bead, as in the radial tire. Tread life is improved considerably over the conventional bias tire. The radial tire differs in construction, but instead of the carcass plies running are an angle of 90 degree to each other, they run at an angle of 90 degree to the bead. This gives the tread a great deal of rigidity and the sidewall a great deal of flexibility and accounts for the characteristic bulge associated with radial tires.

The vehicles are capable of using radial tires and they are recommended. If they are used, tire sizes and wheel diameters should be selected to maintain ground clearance and tire load capacity equivalent to the minimum specified tire. Radial tires should always be used in sets of five, but in an emergency, radial tires can be used with caution on the rear axle only. If this is done, both tires on the rear should be of radial design.

NOTE: *Radial tires should never be used on only the front axle.*

Snow tires should not be operated at sustained speeds over 70 mph.

On 4-wheel drive vehicles, all tires must be of the same size, type, and tread pattern, to provide even traction on loose surfaces, to prevent driveline bind when conventional four wheel drive is used, and to prevent excessive wear on the center differential with full time four wheel drive.

Tread Depth

All tires have built-in tread wear indicator bars that show up as $1/2$ in. (12.7mm) wide smooth bands across the tire when $1/16$ in. (1.5mm) of tread remains. The appearance of tread wear indicators means that the tires should be replaced. In fact, many states have laws prohibiting the use of tires with less than $1/16$ in. (1.5mm) tread.

You can check your own tread depth with an inexpensive gauge or by using a Lincoln head penny. Slip the Lincoln penny into several into several tread grooves. If you can see the top of

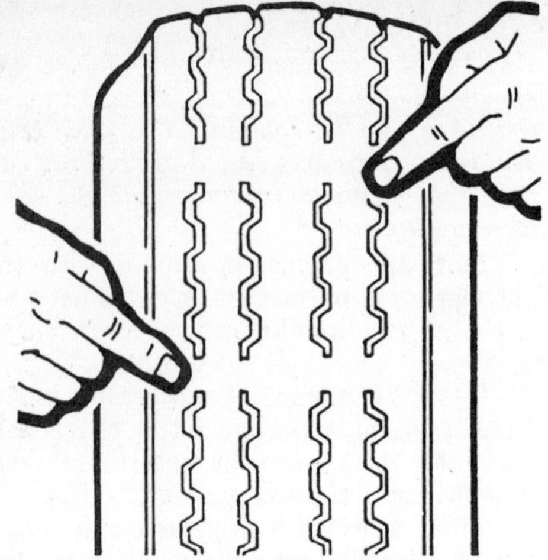

Tread wear indicators appear when the tire needs replacement

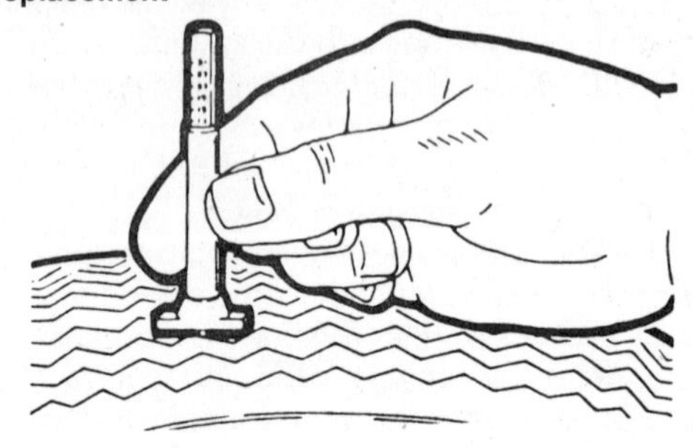

Tread wear can be accurately measured with a tread depth gauge

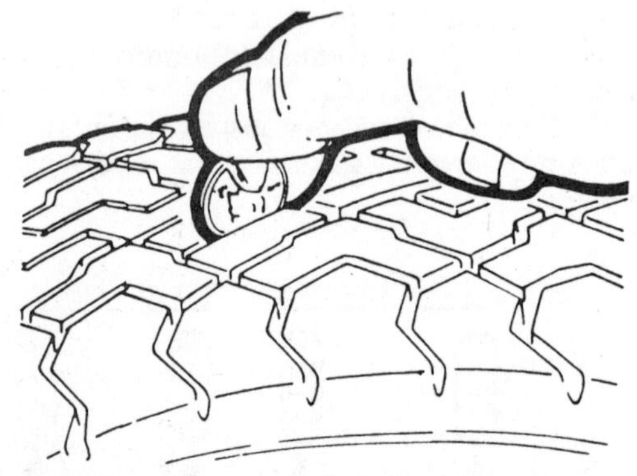

An quicker way to check tread depth is with a penny. If all of Lincoln's head is visible in two or more adjacent grooves, the tire should be replaced

Lincoln's head in 2 adjacent grooves, the tires have less than $1/16$ in. (1.5mm) tread left and should be replaced. You can measure snow tires in the same manner by using the tails side of the Lincoln penny. If you can see the top of the Lincoln memorial, it's time to replace the snow tires.

TIRE STORAGE

Store the tires at proper inflation pressures if they are mounted on wheels. All tires should be kept in a cool, dry place. If they are stored in the garage or basement, do not let them stand on a concrete floor, set them on strips of wood.

Aluminum Wheels

NOTE: *If your vehicle has aluminum wheels, be very careful when using any type of cleaner on either the wheels or the tires. Read the label on the package of the cleaner to make sure it will not damage aluminum.*

TIRE INFLATION

The inflation is the most ignored item of auto maintenance. Gasoline mileage can drop as much as 0.8 percent for every 1 pound/square inch (psi) of under inflation.

Two items should be a permanent fixture in every glove compartment: a tire pressure gauge and a tread depth gauge. Check the tire air pressure (including the spare) regularly with a pocket type gauge. Kicking the tires won't tell you a thing and the gauge on the service station air hose is notoriously inaccurate.

The tire pressures recommended for your vehicle are usually found on the glove box door or in the owner's manual. Ideally, inflation pressure should be checked when the tires are cool. When the air becomes heated it expands and the pressure increases. Every 10°F rise (or drop) in temperature means a difference of 1 psi, which also explains why the tire appears to lose air on a very cold night. When it is impossible to check the tires cold, allow for pressure build-up due to heat. If the hot pressure exceeds the cold pressure by more than 15 psi, reduce your speed, load or both. Otherwise internal heat is created in the tire. When the heat approaches the temperature at which the tire was cured, during manufacture, the tread can separate from the body.

CAUTION: *Never counteract excessive pressure build-up by bleeding off air pressure (letting some air out). This will only further raise the tire operating temperature.*

Before starting a long trip with lots of luggage, you can add about 2–4 psi to the tires to make them run cooler but never exceed the maximum inflation pressure on the side of the tire.

Factory installed wheels and tires are designed to handle loads up to and including their rated load capacity when inflated to the recommended inflation pressures. Correct tire pressures and driving techniques have an important influence on tire life. Heavy cornering, ex-cessively rapid acceleration and unnecessary braking increase tire wear. Underinflated tires can cause handling problems, poor fuel economy, shortened tire life and tire overloading.

Maximum axle load must never exceed the value shown on the side of the tire. The inflation pressure should never exceed 35 psi (standard tires) or 60 psi (compact tire).

FLUIDS AND LUBRICANTS

Fuel and Engine Oil Recommendations

ENGINE OIL

Use ONLY SG/CC or SG/CD rated oils of the recommended viscosity. Under the classification system developed by the American Petroleum Institute, the SG rating designates the highest quality oil for use in passenger vehicles. In addition, Chevrolet recommends the use of an SG/Energy Conserving oil. Oils labeled Energy Conserving (or Saving), Fuel (Gas or Gasoline) Saving, etc. are recommended due to their superior lubricating qualities (less friction—easier engine operation) and fuel saving characteristics. Pick your oil viscosity with regard to the anticipated temperatures during the period before your next oil change. Using the accompanying chart, choose the oil viscosity for the lowest expected temperature. You will be assured of easy cold starting and sufficient engine protection.

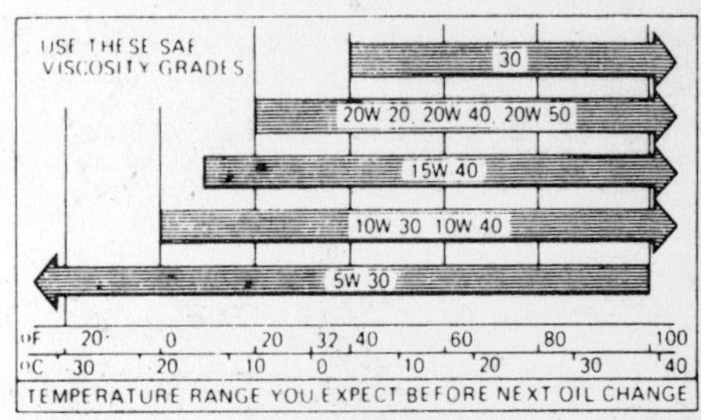

Gasoline engine oil viscosity reccommedations

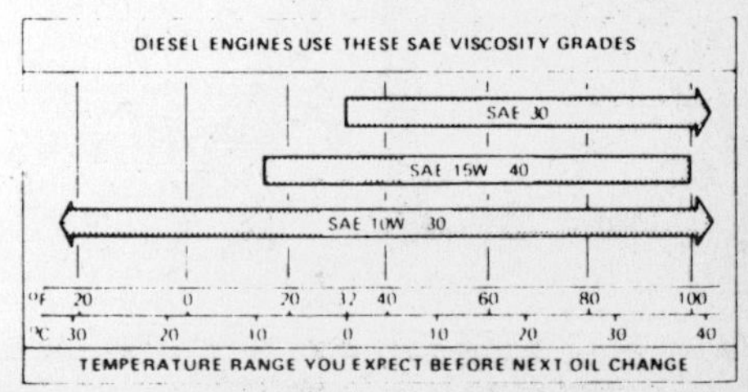

Diesel engine oil viscosity recommendation

FUEL

Gasoline

NOTE: *Some fuel additives contain chemicals that can damage the catalytic converter and/or oxygen sensor. Read all of the labels carefully before using any additive in the engine or fuel system.*

Fuel should be selected for the brand and octane which performs best with your engine. Judge a gasoline by its ability to prevent pinging, it's engine starting capabilities (cold and hot) and general all weather performance. As far as the octane rating is concerned, refer to the General Engine Specifications chart in Chapter 3 to find your engine and its compression ratio.

If the compression ratio is 9.0:1 or lower, in most cases a regular unleaded grade of gasoline can be used. If the compression ratio is 9.0:1–9.3:1, use a premium grade of unleaded fuel.

NOTE: *Your vehicle's engine fuel requirement can change with time, due to carbon buildup, which changes the compression ratio. If your vehicle's engine knocks, pings or runs on, switch to a higher grade of fuel, if possible, and check the ignition timing. Sometimes changing brands of gasoline will cure the problem. If it is necessary to retard the timing from specifications, don't change it more than a few degrees. Retarded timing will reduce the power output and the fuel mileage, plus it will increase the engine temperature.*

Diesel

A diesel-engined vehicle requires the use of diesel fuel. Two grades are manufactured, No. 1 and No. 2, although No. 2 grade is generally the only grade available. Better fuel economy results from the use of No. 2 grade fuel. In some northern parts of the USA, and in most parts of Canada, No. 1 grade fuel is available in winter, or a winterized blend of No. 2 grade is supplied in winter months. If No. 1 grade is available, it should be used whenever temperatures fall below 20°F (–7°C). Winterized No. 2 grade may also be used at these temperatures. However, unwinterized No. 2 grade should not be used below 20°F (–7°C). Cold temperatures cause unwinterized No. 2 grade to thicken (it actually gels), blocking the fuel lines and preventing the engine from running.

Do not use home heating oil or gasoline in the diesel vehicle. Do not attempt to "thin" unwinterized No. 2 diesel fuel with gasoline. Gasoline or home heating oil will damage the engine and void the manufacturer's warranty.

CAUTION: *A mixture of gasoline and diesel fuel produces an extremely potent explosive that is more volatile than gasoline alone.*

Engine

OIL CHECK LEVEL

The engine oil should be checked on a regular basis, ideally at each fuel stop. If the vehicle is used for trailer towing or for heavy-duty use, it would be safer to check more often.

When checking the oil level it is best that the oil be at operating temperature, although checking the level immediately after stopping will give a false reading because all of the oil will not have drained back into the crankcase. Be sure the vehicle is resting on a level surface, allowing time for the oil to drain back into the crankcase.

1. Open the hood and locate the dipstick. Remove it from the tube. The oil dipstick is located on the driver's side.

2. Wipe the dipstick with a clean rag.

3. Insert the dipstick fully into the tube and remove it again. Hold the dipstick horizontally and read the oil level. The level should be between the FULL and ADD marks. If the oil level is at or below the ADD mark, oil should be added as necessary. Oil is added through the capped opening on the valve cover(s) on gasoline engines. Diesel engines have a capped oil full tube at the front of the engine. Refer to the

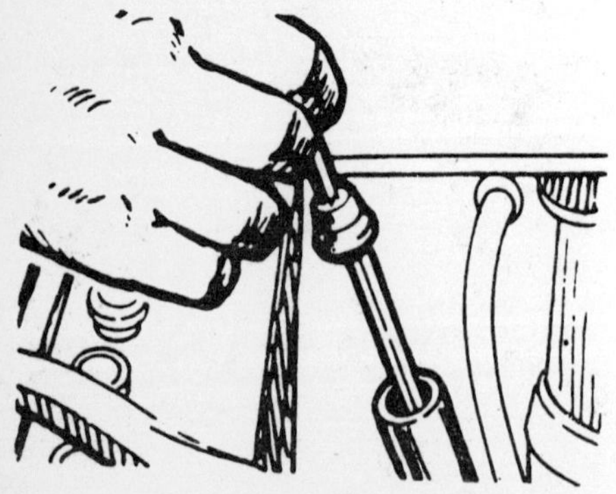

The oil level is checked with the dipstick. When checking engine oil level, note the color and smell of the oil. Oil that is black or has a gas smell indicates a need for engine service

The full level should be between the "add" and "full" marks on the dipstick

"Engine Oil and Fuel Recommendations" in this Chapter for the proper viscosity oil to use.

4. Replace the dipstick and check the level after adding oil. Be careful not to overfill the crankcase. Approximately 1 quart of oil will raise the level from ADD to FULL.

OIL AND FILTER CHANGE

Engine oil should be changed every 6000 miles for 1983–87 or 7500 miles for 1988–91 on gasoline engines and every 3000 miles on diesel engines. The oil change and filter replacement interval should be cut in half under conditions such as:

- Driving in dusty conditions.
- Continuous trailer pulling or RV use.
- Extensive or prolonged idling.
- Extensive short trip operation in freezing temperatures (when the engine is not thoroughly warmed-up).
- Frequent long runs at high speed and high ambient temperatures.
- Stop-and-go service such as delivery vehicles.

Operation of the engine in severe conditions such as a dust storm may require an immediate oil and filter change.

Chevrolet and GMC recommend changing both the oil and filter during the first oil change and the filter every other oil change thereafter. For the small price of an oil filter, it's cheap insurance to replace the filter at every oil change. One of the larger filter manufacturers points out in its advertisements that not changing the filter leaves one quart of dirty oil in the engine. This claim is true and should be kept in mind when changing your oil.

NOTE: *The oil filter on the diesel engine must be changed every oil change.*

To change the oil, the vehicle should be on a level surface and the engine should be at operating temperature. This is to ensure that the foreign matter will be drained away along with the oil and not left in the engine to form sludge. You should have available a container that will hold a minimum of 8 quarts of liquid, a wrench to fit the old drain plug, a spout for pouring in new oil and a rag or 2, which you will always need. If the filter is being replaced, you will also need a band wrench or filter wrench to fit the end of the filter.

NOTE: *If the engine is equipped with an oil cooler, this will also have to be drained, using the drain plug. Be sure to add enough oil to fill the cooler in addition to the engine.*

1. Position the vehicle on a level surface and set the parking brake or block the wheels. Slide a drain pan under the oil drain plug.

2. From under the vehicle, loosen, but do not remove the oil drain plug. Cover your hand with a rag or glove and slowly unscrew the drain plug.

CAUTION: *The engine oil will be HOT. Keep your arms, face and hands clear of the oil as it drains out.*

3. Remove the plug and let the oil drain into the pan. Do not drop the plug into the drain pan.

4. When all of the oil has drained, clean off the drain plug and reinstall it into pan. Torque the drain plug to 20 ft. lbs. for gasoline or 30 ft. lbs. for diesel engines.

5. Using an oil filter wrench, loosen the oil filter. On most Chevrolet engines, especially the V6s, the oil filter is next to the exhaust pipes. Stay clear of these, since even a passing contact will result in a painful burn.

NOTE: *If equipped with catalytic converters stay clear of the converter. The outside temperature of a hot catalytic converter can approach 1200°F (650°C).*

6. Cover your hand with a rag and spin the filter off by hand; turn it slowly.

7. Coat the rubber gasket on a new filter with a light film of clean engine oil. Screw the filter onto the mounting stud and tighten it according to the directions on the filter, usually hand-tight one turn past the point where the gasket contacts the mounting base; do not overtighten the filter.

8. Refill the engine with the specified amount of clean engine oil.

9. Run the engine for several minutes, checking for leaks. Check the level of the oil and add oil, if necessary.

When you have finished this job, you will notice that you now possess 4–5 quarts of dirty oil. The best thing to do with it is to pour it into plastic jugs, such as milk or antifreeze containers. Then, locate a service station where you can pour it into their used oil tank for recycling.

NOTE: *Pouring used motor oil into a storm drain not only pollutes the environment, it violates Federal law. Dispose of waste oil properly.*

Manual Transmission

FLUID RECOMMENDATIONS

All manual transmissions in these vehicles use Dexron® II automatic transmission fluid.

LEVEL CHECK

Remove the filler plug from the passenger's side of the transmission; the upper plug, if the transmission has 2 plugs. The oil should be level with the bottom edge of the filler hole. This should be checked at least once every 6000

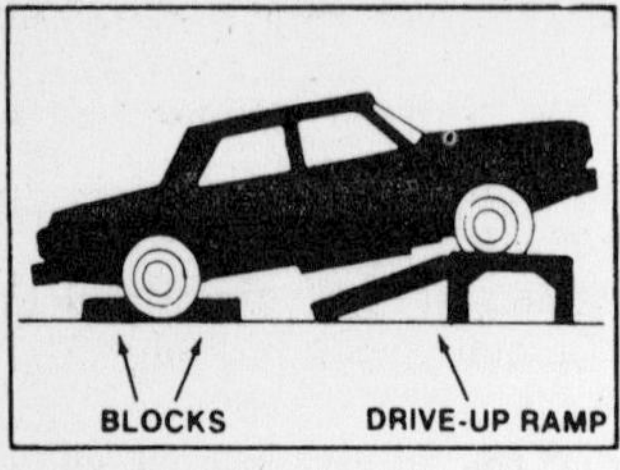

1. *Warm the car up before changing your oil. Raise the front end of the car and support it on drive-on ramps or jackstands.*

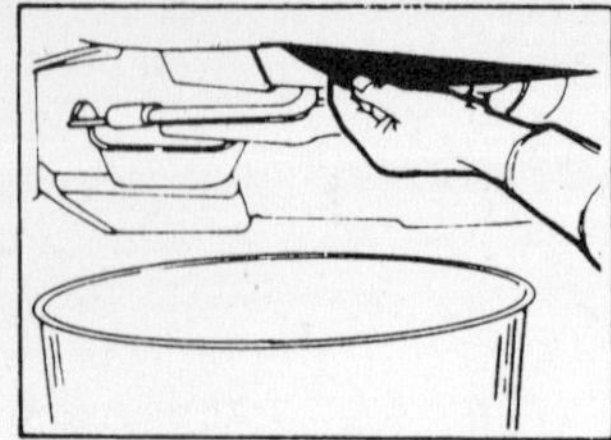

2. *Locate the drain plug on the bottom of the oil pan and slide a low flat pan of sufficient capacity under the engine to catch the oil. Loosen the plug with a wrench and turn it out the last few turns by hand. Keep a steady inward pressure on the plug to avoid hot oil from running down your arm.*

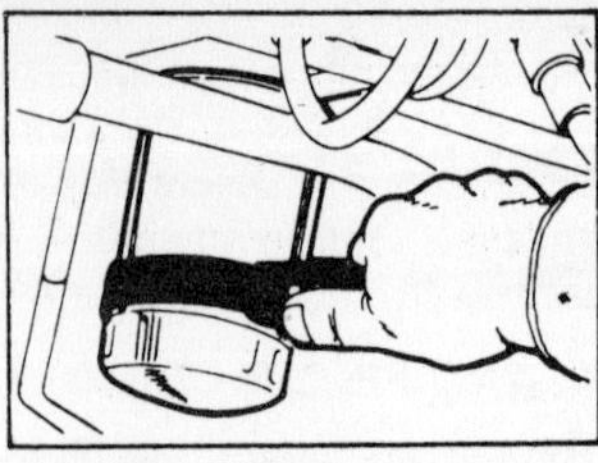

3. *Remove the oil filter with a filter wrench. The filter can hold more than a quart of oil, which will be hot. Be sure the gasket comes off with the filter and clean the mounting base on the engine.*

4. *Lubricate the gasket on the new filter with clean engine oil. A dry gasket may not make a good seal and will allow the filter to leak.*

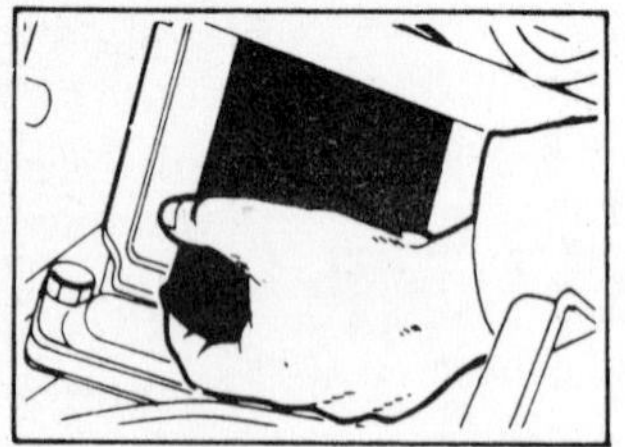

5. *Position a new filter on the mounting base and spin it on by hand. Do not use a wrench. When the gasket contacts the engine, tighten it another ½–1 turn by hand.*

6. *Using a rag, clean the drain plug and the area around the drain hole in the oil pan.*

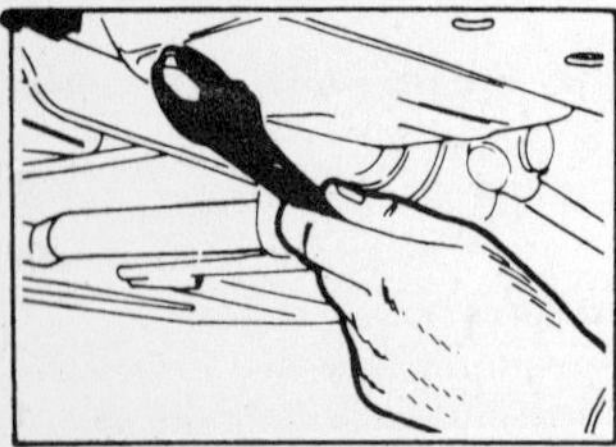

7. *Install the drain plug and tighten it finger-tight. If you feel resistance, stop and be sure you are not cross-threading the plug. Finally, tighten the plug with a wrench.*

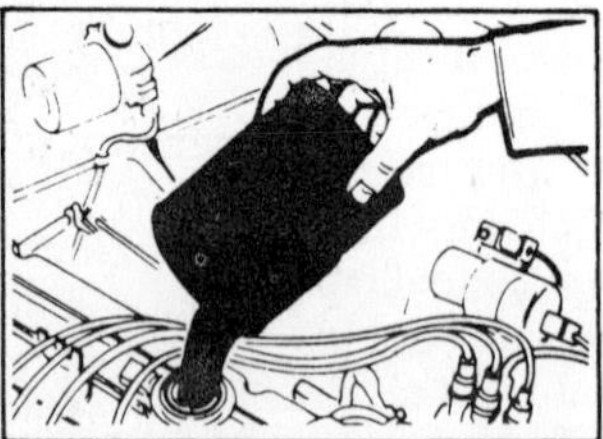

8. *Locate the oil cap on the valve cover. An oil spout is the easiest way to add oil, but a funnel will do just as well.*

9. *Start the engine and check for leaks. The oil pressure warning light will remain on for a few seconds; when it goes out, stop the engine and check the level on the dipstick.*

Changing the oil and the filter

miles or more often if any leakage or seepage is observed.

DRAIN AND REFILL

Under normal conditions, the transmission fluid should not be changed. However, if the vehicle is driven in deep water, replace the fluid.

1. Raise and safely support the vehicle.
2. Place a fluid catch pan under the transmission.
3. Remove the bottom plug and drain the fluid.
4. Install the bottom plug and refill the transmission housing.

Automatic Transmission

FLUID RECOMMENDATIONS

When adding fluid or refilling the transmission, use Dexron®II automatic transmission fluid.

LEVEL CHECK

Before checking the fluid level of the transmission, drive the vehicle for at least 15 miles to warm the fluid.

1. Place the vehicle on a level surface, apply the parking brake and block the front wheels.
2. Start the engine and move the selector through each range, then place it in **P**.

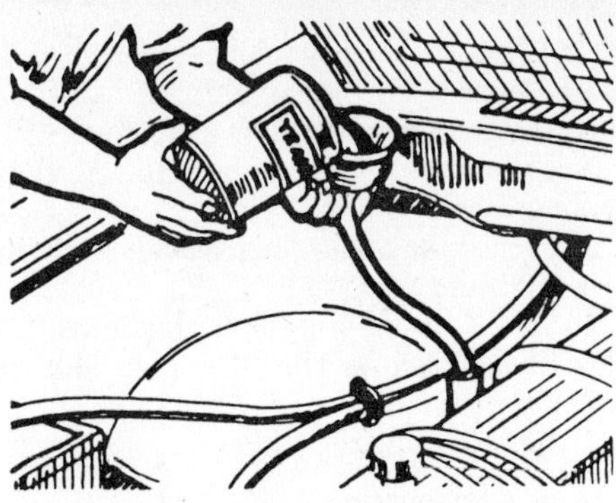

Adding automatic transmission fluid

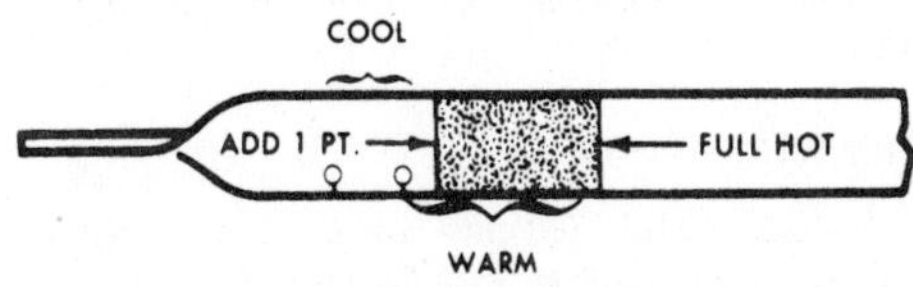

Automatic transmission fluid dipstick. When checking transmission oil, note the color and smell of the oil. Oil that is brown or has a burnt smell indicates a need for transmission service

NOTE: *When moving the selector through each range, do not race the engine.*

3. With the engine running at a low idle, remove the transmission's dipstick to check the fluid level.

4. The level should be at the Full Hot mark of the dipstick. If not, add fluid.

NOTE: *Do not overfill the transmission, damage to the seals could occur. Use Dexron®II automatic transmission fluid. One pint raises the level from ADD to FULL.*

DRAIN AND REFILL

The fluid should be changed at 15,000 mile intervals for severe usage or 30,000 mile intervals for light usage.

The vehicle should be driven 15 miles to warm the transmission fluid before the pan is removed.

NOTE: *The fluid should be drained while the transmission is warm.*

1. Raise and safely support the vehicle.

2. Place a drain pan under the transmission pan.

3. Remove the pan bolts from the front and the sides, then loosen the rear bolts 4 turns.

4. Using a small prybar, pry the pan from the transmission. This will allow the pan to partially drain. Remove the remaining pan bolts and lower the pan from the transmission.

NOTE: *If the transmission fluid is dark or has a burnt smell, transmission damage is indicated. Have the transmission checked professionally.*

5. Empty the pan, remove the gasket material and clean with a solvent.

6. Using a putty knife, clean gasket mounting surfaces.

To install:

7. To install the oil pan, use a new gasket and sealant, then reverse the removal procedures. Torque the pan bolts to 8 ft. lbs. in a criss-cross pattern.

8. Using Dexron® II automatic transmission fluid, add it through the filler tube. See the Capacities Chart to determine the proper amount of fluid to be added.

NOTE: *Do not overfill the transmission. Foaming of the fluid and subsequent transmission damage due to slippage will result.*

9. With the gearshift lever in **P**, start the engine and let it idle. Do not race the engine.

10. Apply the parking brake and move the gearshift lever through each position. Return the lever to **P**k and check the fluid level with the engine idling. The level should be between the 2 dimples on the dipstick, about 1/4 in. (6mm) below the ADD mark. Add fluid, if necessary.

11. Check the fluid level after the vehicle has been driven enough to thoroughly warm the transmission.

PAN AND FILTER SERVICE

1. Refer to the Drain and Refill procedures in this Chapter and remove the oil pan.

2. Remove the screen and the filter from the valve body.

3. Install a new filter using a new gasket or O-ring.

NOTE: *If the transmission uses a filter having a fully exposed screen, it may be cleaned and reused.*

4. To install the oil pan, use a new gasket and sealant, then reverse the removal procedures. Torque the pan bolts to 8 ft. lbs. in a criss-cross pattern. Refill the transmission.

Transfer Case

FLUID RECOMMENDATIONS

When adding fluid or refilling the transfer case, use Dexron®II automatic transmission fluid.

LEVEL CHECK

The transfer case should be checked every 12 months, at 15,000 mile intervals for severe usage or 30,000 mile intervals for light usage, whichever occurs first.

1. Raise and safely support the vehicle (level).

2. At the rear side of the transfer case, remove the filler plug.

3. Using your finger, check the fluid level, it should be level with the bottom of the filler hole.

4. If the fluid level is low, use Dexron®II automatic transmission fluid to bring the fluid up to the proper level.

5. On all except Bravada, install the filler plug and torque it to 30–40 ft. lbs. On Bravada, apply Loctite® to the filler plug and torque it to 80 inch lbs. (9 Nm).

DRAIN AND REFILL

1. Raise and safely support the vehicle.
2. Position drain pan under transfer case.
3. Remove drain and filler plugs, then drain the lubricant into the drain pan.
4. Install drain plug. Except for Bravada, torque the plug to 30–40 ft. lbs. On Bravada, apply Loctite® to the drain plug and torque it to 80 inch lbs. (9 Nm).
5. Remove the drain pan and dump the fluid into a used oil storage tank, for recycling purposes.
6. Using Dexron® II automatic transmission fluid, fill transfer case to edge of filler plug opening.
7. Except for Bravada, install filler plug and torque it to 30–40 ft. lbs. On Bravada, apply Loctite® to the filler plug and torque it to 80 inch lbs. (9 Nm).
8. Lower vehicle and check the operation of the transfer case.

Drive Axle

At least once every 2 years or 30,000 miles, the drive axle(s) should be inspected and refilled with fluid.

No draining of the axle fluid is recommended; be sure to maintain a Full fluid level of 3/8 in. below the filler plug hole.

FLUID RECOMMENDATIONS

Standard Axle

Always use SAE-80W or SAE 80W-90 GL5. Drain and refill the differential at first oil fill, then at every other oil fill.

Locking Axle

NOTE: *Never use standard differential lubricant in a positraction differential.*

Always use GM part 1052271 gear lubricant. Before refilling the rear axle, add 4 ounces of GM Fluid 1052358. Drain and refill the differential at first oil fill, then at every other oil fill.

LEVEL CHECK

The lubricant level should be checked at each chassis lubrication and maintained at 3/8 in. below the bottom of the filler plug hole.

1. Raise and safely support the vehicle; be sure the vehicle is level.
2. Remove the filler plug, located at the side of the differential carrier.
3. Check the fluid level, it should be 3/8 in. below the bottom of the filler plug hole, add fluid, if necessary.
4. Replace the filler plug.

DRAIN AND REFILL

Refer to Fluid Recommendations in this Chapter for information on when to change the fluid.

Rear Axle

1. Run the vehicle until the lubricant reaches operating temperature.
2. Raise and safely support the vehicle; be sure the vehicle is level.
3. Using a floor jack, support the drive axle. Position a drain pan under the rear axle.
4. Remove the cover from the rear of the drive axle and drain the lubricant.
5. Using a putty knife, clean the gasket mounting surfaces.
6. To install, use a new gasket, sealant and reverse the removal procedures.
7. Torque the cover-to-rear axle bolts in a criss-cross pattern to 20 ft. lbs. Using a suction gun or a squeeze bulb, install the fluid through the filler plug hole. Install the filler plug.

Front Axle

1. Run the vehicle until the lubricant reaches operating temperature.
2. Raise and safely support the vehicle; be sure the vehicle is level.
3. Using a floor jack, support the front axle. Position a drain pan under the front axle.
4. Remove the drain plug from the right side of the front axle and drain the lubricant.
5. Remove the filler plug.
6. To install the drain plug, use a sealant and torque the plug to 24 ft. lbs. (33 Nm).
7. Using a suction gun or a squeeze bulb, install the fluid through the filler plug hole.
8. Using sealant, coat the filler plug threads and torque the plug to 24 ft. lbs. (33 Nm).

Cooling System

At least once every 2 years or 30,000 miles, the engine cooling system should be inspected, flushed and refilled with fresh coolant. If the coolant is left in the system too long, it loses its ability to prevent rust and corrosion. If the coolant has too much water, it won't protect against freezing.

FLUID RECOMMENDATIONS

Using a good quality of ethylene glycol anti-freeze (one that will not effect aluminum), mix it with water until a 50–50 antifreeze solution is attained.

LEVEL CHECK

NOTE: *When checking the coolant level, the radiator need not be removed, simply check the coolant tank.*

Check the coolant recovery bottle (see through plastic bottle). With the engine Cold, the coolant should be at the ADD mark (recovery tank ¼ full). With the engine warm, the coolant should be at the FULL mark (recovery tank ½ full). If necessary, add fluid to the recovery bottle.

DRAIN AND REFILL

CAUTION: *To avoid injuries from scalding fluid and steam, do not remove the radiator cap while the engine and radiator are still HOT.*

1. *When the engine is cool, remove the radiator cap using the following procedures.*

   a. Slowly rotate the cap counterclockwise to the detent.

   b. If any residual pressure is present, WAIT until the hissing noise stops.

   c. After the hissing noise has ceased, press down on the cap and continue rotating it counterclockwise to remove it.

2. Place a fluid catch pan under the radiator, open the radiator drain valve and the engine drain plugs, then drain the coolant.

CAUTION: *When draining the coolant, keep in mind that cats and dogs are attracted by the ethylene glycol antifreeze, and are quite likely to drink any that is left in an uncovered container or in puddles on the ground. This will prove fatal in sufficient quantity. Always drain the coolant into a sealable container. Coolant should be reused unless it is contaminated or several years old.*

3. Close the drain valve and install the engine drain plugs.

4. Empty the coolant reservoir and flush it.

5. Using the correct mixture of antifreeze, fill the radiator to the bottom of the filler neck and the coolant tank to the FULL mark.

6. Install the radiator cap; make sure the arrows align with the overflow tube.

7. Run the engine until it reaches the operating temperatures, allow it to cool, then check the fluid level and add fluid, if necessary.

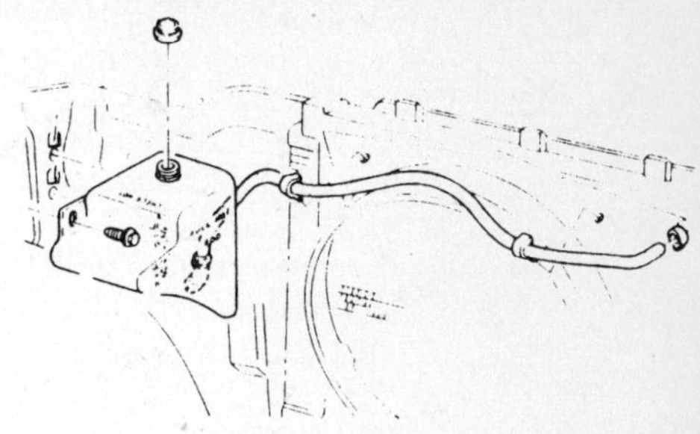

Coolant recovery system see-through bottle

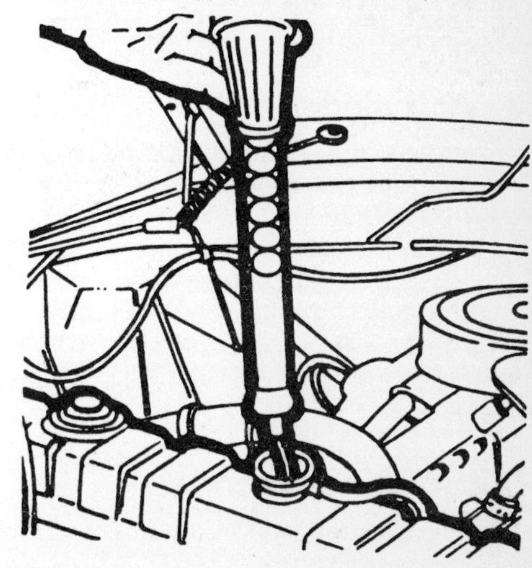

Coolant protection can be checked with a simple float-type tester

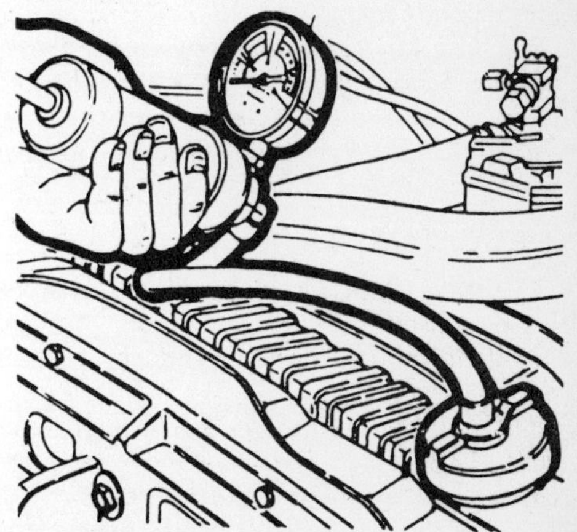

The coolant system should be pressure checked at least once a year

FLUSHING AND CLEANING THE SYSTEM

1. Refer to the Drain and Refill procedures in this Chapter, then drain the cooling system.

NOTE: *Always drain the coolant into a sealable container. Coolant should be reused unless it is contaminated or several years old.*

2. Close the drain valve and install the engine drain plugs, then add sufficient water to the cooling system.

3. Run the engine, then drain and refill the system. Perform this procedure several times, until the fluid (drained from the system) is clear.

4. Empty the coolant reservoir and flush it.

5. Using the correct mixture of antifreeze, fill the radiator to the bottom of the filler neck and the coolant tank to the FULL mark.

6. Install the radiator cap; make sure the arrows align with the overflow tube.

Master Cylinder

The vehicles are equipped with a dual braking system, allowing a vehicle to be brought to a safe stop in the event of failure in either the front or rear brakes. The dual master cylinder has 2 entirely separate reservoirs, one connected to the front brakes and the other connected to the rear brakes. In the event of failure in either portion, the remaining part is not affected.

FLUID RECOMMENDATIONS

Use only heavy-duty Delco Supreme 11 or DOT-3 brake fluid.

NOTE: *Brake fluid damages paint. It also absorbs moisture from the air; never leave a container or the master cylinder uncovered any longer than necessary. All parts in contact with the brake fluid (master cylinder, hoses, plunger assemblies and etc.) must be kept clean, since any contamination of the brake fluid will adversely affect braking performance.*

LEVEL CHECK

The brake fluid level should be inspected every 6 months.

1. Remove the master cylinder reservoir cap.

NOTE: *If equipped with a see through reservoir, it is not necessary to remove the reservoir cap unless you are adding fluid.*

2. The fluid should be $^1/_4$ in. (6mm) from top of the reservoir, if necessary, add fluid.

3. Replace the reservoir caps.

Hydraulic Clutch

NOTE: *The clutch master cylinder is mounted on the firewall next to the brake master cylinder.*

FLUID RECOMMENDATIONS

Use heavy duty Delco Supreme 11 or any brand-name DOT-3 brake fluid.

LEVEL CHECK

The hydraulic clutch reservoir should be checked at least every 6 months. Fill to the line on the reservoir.

Power Steering Pump

The power steering pump reservoir is located at the front left-side of the engine.

FLUID RECOMMENDATIONS

Use GM Power Steering Fluid No. 1050017 or equivalent.

NOTE: *Avoid using automatic transmission fluid in the power steering unit, except in an emergency.*

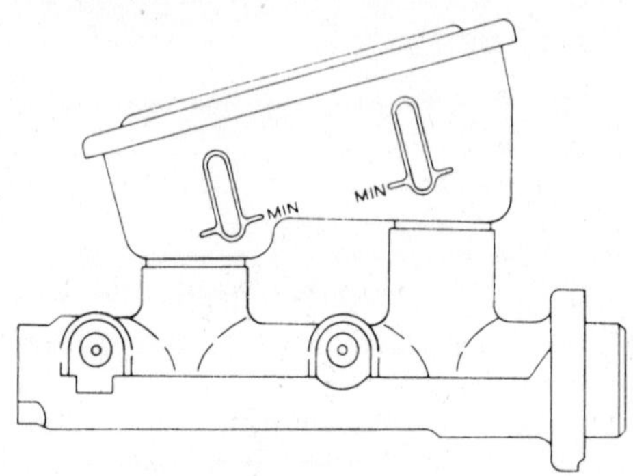

Master cylinder reservoir showing the minimum fluid level line

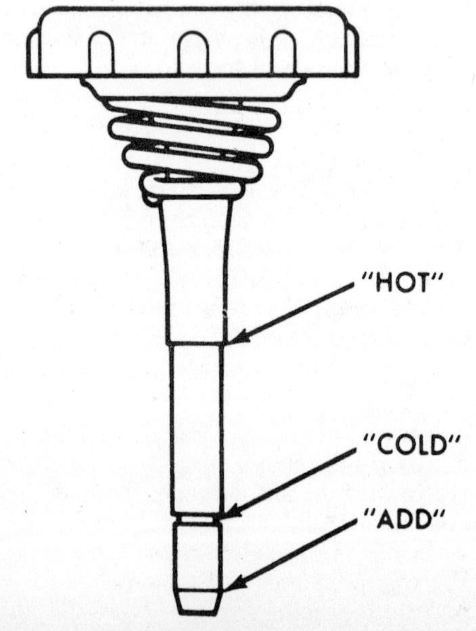

Power steering fluid dipstick

LEVEL CHECK

The power steering fluid should be checked at least every 6 months. There is a COLD and a HOT mark on the dipstick. The fluid should be checked when the engine is warm and turned OFF. If necessary, add fluid to the power steering pump reservoir.

NOTE: *On models equipped with a remote reservoir, the fluid level should be 1/2–1 in. (25.4mm) from the top when the wheels are turned to the extreme left position.*

Manual Steering Gear

The steering gear is factory-filled with a lubricant which does not require seasonal change. The housing should not be drained; no lubrication is required for the life of the gear.

FLUID RECOMMENDATIONS

Use GM steering gear lubricant No. 1052182 or equivalent.

LEVEL CHECK

The steering lubricant should be checked every 6 months or 7500 miles.

The gear should be inspected for seal leakage when specified in the "Maintenance" chart. Look for solid grease, not an oily film. If a seal is replaced or the gear overhauled, it should be refilled with lubricant.

Chassis Greasing

Chassis greasing should be performed every 6 months or 7500 miles, it can be performed with a commercial pressurized grease gun or at home by using a hand operated grease gun. Wipe the grease fittings clean before greasing in order to prevent the possibility of forcing any dirt into the component.

The 4-wheel drive front driveshaft requires special attention for lubrication. The large constant velocity joint at the front of the transfer case has a special grease fitting in the centering ball; a special needle nose adapter for a flush type fitting is required, as well as a special lubricant, GM part No. 1050679. You can only get at this fitting when it is facing up toward the floorboard, so you need a flexible hose, too.

Water resistant EP chassis lubricant (grease) conforming to GM specification 6031-M should be used for all chassis grease points.

Body Lubrication and Maintenance

HOOD LATCH AND HINGES

Clean the latch surfaces and apply clean engine oil to the latch pilot bolts and the spring anchor. Use the engine oil to lubricate the hood hinges as well. Use a chassis grease to lubricate all the pivot points in the latch release mechanism.

DOOR HINGES

The gas tank filler door, the front doors and rear door hinges should be wiped clean and lubricated with clean engine oil. Silicone spray also works well on these parts but must be applied more often. The door lock cylinders can be lubricated easily with a shot of GM silicone spray No. 1052276 or one of the many dry penetrating lubricants commercially available.

PARKING BRAKE LINKAGE

Use chassis grease on the parking brake cable where it contacts the guides, links, levers and pulleys. The grease should be a water resistant one for durability under the vehicle.

ACCELERATOR LINKAGE

Lubricate the throttle body lever, the cable and the accelerator pedal lever (at the support inside the vehicle) with clean engine oil.

TRANSMISSION SHIFT LINKAGE

Lubricate the shift linkage with water resistant chassis grease which meets GM specification No. 6031M or equivalent.

Front Wheel Bearings—2WD Only

Once every 30,000 miles, clean and repack wheel bearings with a GM Wheel Bearing Grease No. 1051344 or equivalent. Use only enough grease to completely coat the rollers. Remove any excess grease from the exposed surface of the hub and seal.

REMOVAL, PACKING AND INSTALLATION

NOTE: *The following procedures require the use of GM tools No. J-29117, J-8092, J-8850, J-8457, J-9746-02 or equivalent.*

1. Raise and support the vehicle on jackstands.

2. Remove the tire/wheel assembly.

3. Remove the caliper-to-steering knuckle bolts and the caliper from the steering knuckle. Using a wire, support the caliper from the vehicle; do not disconnect the brake line.

4. From the hub/disc assembly, remove the dust cap, the cotter pin, the spindle nut, the thrust washer and the outer bearing.

5. Grasping the hub/disc assembly firmly, pull the assembly from the axle spindle.

6. Using a small prybar, pry the grease seal from the rear of the hub/disc assembly, then remove the inner bearing.

NOTE: *Do not remove the bearing races from the hub, unless they show signs of damage.*

7. If it is necessary to remove the wheel bearing races, use the GM front bearing race removal tool J-29117 or equivalent, to drive the races from the hub/disc assembly.

8. Using solvent, clean the grease from all of the parts, then blow them dry with compressed air.

9. Inspect all of the parts for scoring, pitting or cracking, replace the parts, if necessary.

To install:

10. If the bearing races were removed, perform the following procedures to the install the them:

a. Using grease, lightly lubricate the inside of the hub/disc assembly.

b. Using the GM seal installation tools J-8092 and J-8850 or equivalent, drive the inner bearing race into the hub/disc assembly until it seats.

NOTE: *When installing the bearing races, be sure to support the hub/disc assembly with*

GM *tool J-9746-02 or equivalent.*

c. Using the GM seal installation tools J-8092 and J-8457 or equivalent, drive the outer race into the hub/disc assembly until it seats.

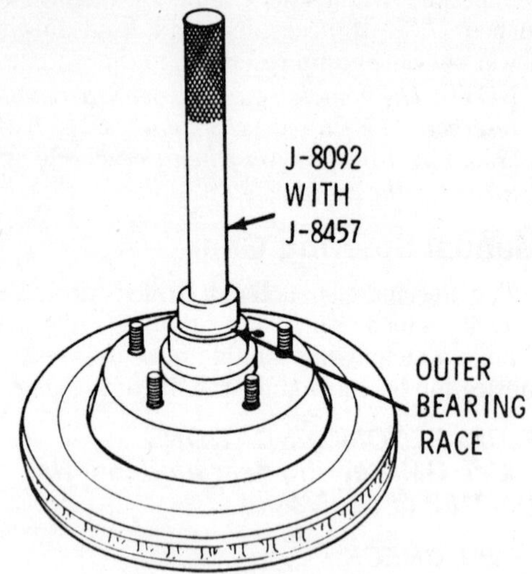

Installing the outer bearing race—2WD

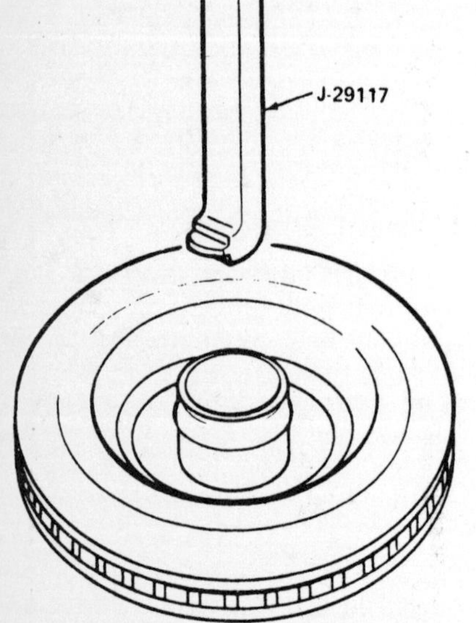

Removing the bearing race—2WD

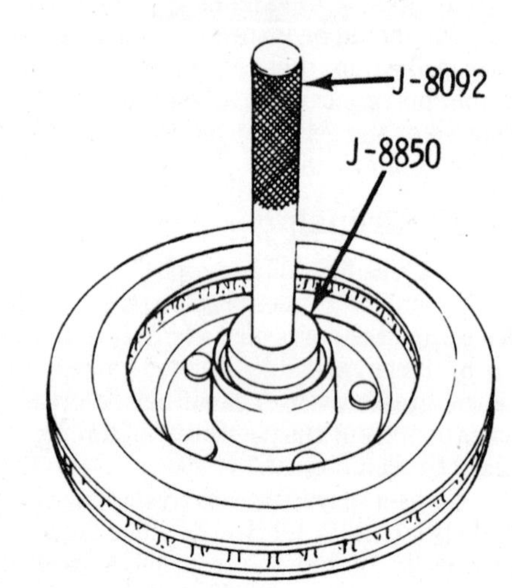

Installing the inner bearing race—2WD

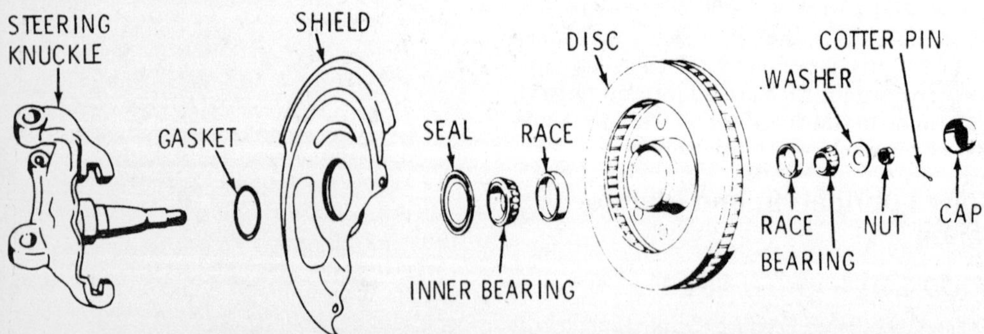

Exploded view of the front wheel bearing assembly—2WD

11. Using wheel bearing grease, lubricate the bearings, the races and the spindle; be sure to place a gob of grease (inside the hub/disc assembly) between the races to provide an ample supply of lubricant.

NOTE: *To lubricate each bearing, place a gob of grease in the palm of the hand, then roll the bearing through the grease until it is well lubricated.*

12. Place the inner wheel bearing into the hub/disc assembly. Using a flat plate, drive the new grease seal into the rear of the hub/disc assembly until it is flush with the outer surface.

13. Onto the spindle, install the hub/disc assembly, the thrust washer and the hub nut. While turning the wheel, torque the hub nut to 16 ft. lbs. until the bearings seat. Loosen the nut, retighten it and back it off until the nearest nut slot aligns with a spindle hole (not more than a $1/2$ turn).

14. Install a new cotter pin through the nut and the spindle, then bend the ends and cut off the excess pin. Install the grease cap.

15. If necessary, use a dial indicator to the check the rotor endplay. The endplay should be 0.001–0.005 in. (0.025–0.127mm); if not, readjust the hub/disc assembly.

16. Install the caliper onto the steering knuckle and torque the bolts to 37 ft. lbs. Road test the vehicle.

TRAILER TOWING

These vehicles are popular as trailer towing vehicles. Their strong construction and variety of power train combinations make them ideal for towing campers, boat trailers and utility trailers.

Factory trailer towing packages are available on most vehicles. However, if you are installing a trailer hitch and wiring on your vehicle, there are a few things you ought to know.

General Recommendations

Wiring

Wiring the vehicle for towing is fairly easy. There are a number of good wiring kits available and these should be used, rather than trying to design your own. All trailers will need brake lights, turn signals, tail lights and side marker lights. Most states require extra marker lights for overwide trailers. Also, most states have recently required back-up lights for trailers and most trailer manufacturers have been building trailers with back-up lights for several years.

Additionally, some Class I, most Class II and just about all Class III trailers will have electric brakes.

Add to this number an accessories wire, to operate the trailer internal equipment or to charge the trailer's battery and you can have as many as seven wires in the harness.

Determine the equipment on your trailer and buy the wiring kit necessary. The kit will contain all the wires needed, plus a plug adapter set which included the female plug, mounted on the bumper or hitch and the male plug, wired into or plugged into the trailer harness.

When installing the kit, follow the manufacturer's instructions. The color coding of the wires is standard throughout the industry.

One point to note: some domestic vehicles and most imported vehicles, have separate turn signals. On most domestic vehicles, the brake lights and rear turn signals operate with the same bulb. For those vehicles with separate turn signals, you can purchase an isolation unit so the brake lights won't blink whenever the turn signals are operated or you can go to your local electronics supply house and buy 4 diodes to wire in series with the brake and turn signal bulbs. Diodes will isolate the brake and turn signals. The choice is yours. The isolation units are simple and quick to install but far more expensive than the diodes. The diodes, however, require more work to install properly, since they require the cutting of each bulb's wire and soldering in place of the diode.

One, final point, the best kits are those with a spring loaded cover on the vehicle mounted socket. This cover prevents dirt and moisture from corroding the terminals. Never let the vehicle socket hang loosely; always mount it securely to the bumper or hitch.

Cooling

ENGINE

One of the most common, if not the most common, problems associated with trailer towing is engine overheating.

With factory installed trailer towing packages, a heavy duty cooling system is usually included. Heavy duty cooling systems are available as optional equipment on most vehicles, with or without a trailer package. If you have one of these extra capacity systems, you shouldn't have overheating problems.

If you have a standard cooling system, without an expansion tank, you'll definitely need to get an aftermarket expansion tank kit, preferably one with at least a 2 quart capacity. These kits are easily installed on the radiator's overflow hose and come with a pressure cap designed for expansion tanks.

Another helpful accessory is a Flex Fan.

These fan are large diameter units are designed to provide more air flow at low speeds, with blades that have deeply cupped surfaces. The blades then flex or flatten out, at high speed, when less cooling air is needed. These fans are far lighter in weight than stock fans, requiring less horsepower to drive them. Also, they are far quieter than stock fans.

If you do decide to replace your stock fan with a flex fan, note that if your vehicle has a fan clutch, a spacer between the flex fan and water pump hub will be needed.

Aftermarket engine oil coolers are helpful for prolonging engine oil life and reducing overall engine temperatures. Both of these factors increase engine life.

While not absolutely necessary in towing Class I and some Class II trailers, they are recommended for heavier Class II and all Class III towing.

Engine oil cooler systems consist of an adapter, screwed on in place of the oil filter, a remote filter mounting and a multi-tube, a finned heat exchanger, which is mounted in front of the radiator or air conditioning condenser.

TRANSMISSION

An automatic transmission is usually recommended for trailer towing. Modern automatics have proven reliable and, of course, easy to operate, in trailer towing.

The increased load of a trailer, however, causes an increase in the temperature of the automatic transmission fluid. Heat is the worst enemy of an automatic transmission. As the temperature of the fluid increases, the life of the fluid decreases.

It is essential, therefore, that you install an automatic transmission cooler.

The cooler, which consists of a multi-tube, finned heat exchanger, is usually installed in front of the radiator or air conditioning compressor and hooked inline with the transmission cooler tank inlet line. Follow the cooler manufacturer's installation instructions.

Select a cooler of at least adequate capacity, based upon the combined gross weights of the vehicle and trailer.

Cooler manufacturers recommend that you use an aftermarket cooler in addition to and not instead of, the present cooling tank in your vehicles radiator. If you do want to use it in place of the radiator cooling tank, get a cooler at least 2 sizes larger than normally necessary.

One note: transmission cooler can, sometimes, cause slow or harsh shifting in the transmission during cold weather, until the fluid has a chance to come up to normal operating temperature. Some coolers can be purchased with or retrofitted with a temperature bypass valve which will allow fluid flow through the cooler only when the fluid has reached operating temperature or above.

Trailer and Tongue Weight Limits

Trailer Weight

Trailer weight is the first, and most important, factor in determining whether or not your vehicle is suitable for towing the trailer you have in mind. The horsepower-to-weight ratio should be calculated. The basic standard is a ratio of 35:1. That is, 35 lbs. of GVW for every horsepower.

To calculate this ratio, multiply you engine's rated horsepower by 35, then subtract the weight of the vehicle, including passengers and luggage. The resulting figure is the ideal maximum trailer weight that you can tow. One point to consider: a numerically higher axle ratio can offset what appears to be a low trailer weight. If the weight of the trailer that you have in mind is somewhat higher than the weight you just calculated, you might consider changing your rear axle ratio to compensate.

Hitch Weight

There are 3 kinds of hitches: bumper mounted, frame mounted and load equalizing.

Bumper mounted hitches are those which attach solely to the vehicle's bumper. Many states prohibit towing with this type of hitch, when it attaches to the vehicle's stock bumper, since it subjects the bumper to stresses for which it was not designed. After market rear step bumpers, designed for trailer towing, are acceptable for use with bumper mounted hitches.

Frame mounted hitches can be of the type which bolts to 2 or more points on the frame, plus the bumper or just to several points on the frame. Frame mounted hitches can also be of the tongue type, for Class I towing or of the receiver type, for classes II and III.

Load equalizing hitches are usually used for large trailers. Most equalizing hitches are welded in place, they use equalizing bars and chains to level the vehicle after the trailer is connected.

The bolt-on hitches are the most common, since they are relatively easy to install.

Check the gross weight rating of your trailer. Tongue weight is usually figured as 10 percent of gross trailer weight. Therefore, a trailer with a maximum gross weight of 2000 lbs. will have a maximum tongue weight of 200 lbs. Class I trailers fall into this category. Class II trailers are those with a gross weight rating of 2000–

3500 lbs., while Class III trailers fall into the 3500–6000 lbs. category. Class IV trailers are those over 6000 lbs. and are for use with 5th wheel vehicles, only.

When you've determined the hitch that you'll need, follow the manufacturer's installation instructions, exactly, especially when it comes to fastener torques. The hitch will be subjected to a lot of stress and good hitches come with hardened bolts. Never substitute an inferior bolt for a hardened bolt.

PUSHING AND TOWING

CAUTION: *Pushing or tow your vehicle to start it may result in unusually high catalytic converter and exhaust system temperatures, which under extreme conditions may ignite the interior floor covering material above the converter.*

Pushing

Vehicles with manual transmissions can be push started.

To push start, make sure both bumpers are in reasonable alignment. Turn the ignition switch ON and engage High gear. Depress the clutch pedal. When a speed of about 10 mph is reached, slightly depress the gas pedal and slowly release the clutch. The engine should start.

NOTE: *Automatic transmission equipped vehicles cannot be started by pushing.*

Towing

The vehicles can be towed on all 4 wheels (flat towed) at speeds of less than 35 mph for distances less than 50 miles, providing that the axle, driveline and engine/transmission are operable. The transmission should be in Neutral, the engine should be OFF, the steering column unlocked, and the parking brake released.

Do not attach chains to the bumpers or bracketing. All attachments must be made to the structural members. Safety chains should be used. it should also be remembered that power steering and brake assists will not be working with the engine off.

The rear wheels must be raised off the ground or the driveshaft disconnected when the transmission is not operating properly or when speeds or over 35 mph will be used or when towing more than 50 miles.

CAUTION: *If a vehicle is towed on its front wheels only, the steering wheel must be secured with the wheels in a straight ahead position.*

JUMP STARTING

The following procedure is recommended by the manufacturer. Be sure the booster battery is 12 volt with negative ground. Follow this procedure exactly to avoid possible damage to the electrical system, especially on models equipped with computerized engine controls.

CAUTION: *Do not attempt this procedure on a frozen battery; it will probably explode. Do not attempt it on a sealed Delco Freedom battery showing a light color in the charge indicator. Be certain to observe correct polarity connections. Failure to do so will result in almost immediate computer, alternator and regulator destruction. Never allow the jumper cable ends to touch each other.*

1. Position the vehicles so they are not touching. Set the parking brake and place automatic transmission in **P** and manual transmission in Neutral. Turn OFF the lights, heater and other electrical loads. Turn both ignition switches OFF.

2. Remove the vent caps from both the booster and discharged battery. Lay a cloth over the open vent cells of each battery. This isn't necessary on batteries equipped with sponge type flame arrestor caps and it isn't possible on sealed batteries.

3. Attach one cable to the positive terminal of the booster battery and the other end to the positive terminal of the discharged battery.

NOTE: *If you are attempting to start a vehicle with the diesel engine, it is suggested that this connection be made to the battery on the driver's side of the vehicle, because this battery is closer to the starter and thus the resistance of the electrical cables is lower. From this point on, ignore the other battery in the vehicle.*

CAUTION: *Do not attempt to jump start the vehicle with a 24 volt power source.*

4. Attach one end of the remaining cable to the negative terminal of the booster battery and the other end to a good ground. Do not attach to the negative terminal of discharged batteries. Do not lean over the battery when making this last connection.

5. Start the engine of the vehicle with the booster battery. Start the engine of the vehicle with the discharged battery. If the engine will not start, disconnect the batteries as soon as possible. If this is not done, the 2 batteries will soon reach a state of equilibrium, with both too weak to start an engine. This will not be a problem of the engine of the booster vehicle is kept running fast enough. Lengthy cranking can also overheat and damage the starter.

6. Reverse the above steps to disconnect the

JUMP STARTING A DEAD BATTERY

The chemical reaction in a battery produces explosive hydrogen gas. This is the safe way to jump start a dead battery, reducing the chances of an accidental spark that could cause an explosion.

Jump Starting Precautions

1. Be sure both batteries are of the same voltage.
2. Be sure both batteries are of the same polarity (have the same grounded terminal).
3. Be sure the vehicles are not touching.
4. Be sure the vent cap holes are not obstructed.
5. Do not smoke or allow sparks around the battery.
6. In cold weather, check for frozen electrolyte in the battery. Do not jump start a frozen battery.
7. Do not allow electrolyte on your skin or clothing.
8. Be sure the electrolyte is not frozen.

CAUTION: *Make certain that the ignition key, in the vehicle with the dead battery, is in the OFF position. Connecting cables to vehicles with on-board computers will result in computer destruction if the key is not in the OFF position.*

Jump Starting Procedure

1. Determine voltages of the two batteries; they must be the same.
2. Bring the starting vehicle close (they must not touch) so that the batteries can be reached easily.
3. Turn off all accessories and both engines. Put both cars in Neutral or Park and set the handbrake.
4. Cover the cell caps with a rag—do not cover terminals.
5. If the terminals on the run-down battery are heavily corroded, clean them.
6. Identify the positive and negative posts on both batteries and connect the cables in the order shown.
7. Start the engine of the starting vehicle and run it at fast idle. Try to start the car with the dead battery. Crank it for no more than 10 seconds at a time and let it cool off for 20 seconds in between tries.
8. If it doesn't start in 3 tries, there is something else wrong.
9. Disconnect the cables in the reverse order.
10. Replace the cell covers and dispose of the rags.

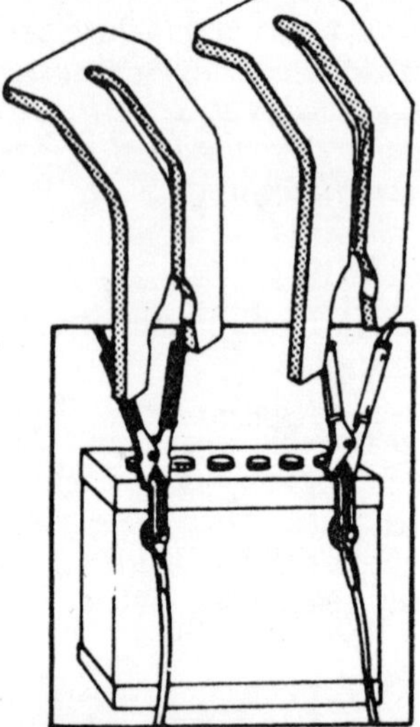

Side terminal batteries occasionally pose a problem when connecting jumper cables. There frequently isn't enough room to clamp the cables without touching sheet metal .Side terminal adaptors are available to alleviate this problem and should be removed after use.

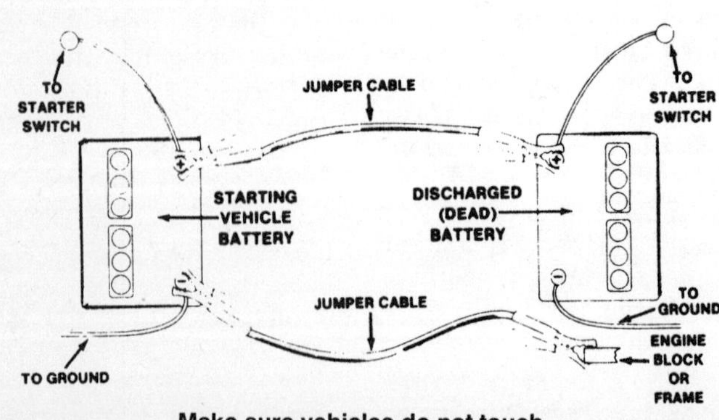

Make sure vehicles do not touch

This hook–up for negative ground cars only

booster and discharge batteries. Be certain to remove negative connections first.

7. Reinstall the vent caps. Dispose of the cloths; they may have battery acid on them.

CAUTION: *The use of any "hot shot" type of jumper system in excess of 12 volts can damage the electronic control units or cause the discharged battery to explode.*

JACKING

The jack supplied with the vehicle is meant for changing tires. It was not meant to support the vehicle while you crawl under it and work. Whenever it is necessary to get under a vehicle to perform service operations, always be sure it is adequately supported, by jackstands at the proper points. Always block the wheels when changing tires.

If your vehicle is equipped with a Positraction rear axle, do not run the engine for any reason with one rear wheel off the ground. Power will be transmitted through the rear wheel remaining on the ground, possibly causing the vehicle to drive itself off the jack.

Some of the service operations in this book require that one or both ends of the vehicle be raised and supported safely. The best arrangement for this, of course, is a grease pit or a vehicle lift but these items are seldom found in the home garage. However, small hydraulic, screw, or scissors jacks are satisfactory for raising the vehicle.

Heavy wooden blocks or adjustable jackstands should be used to support the vehicle while it is being worked on. Drive-on trestles or ramps are also a handy and a safe way to raise the vehicle, assuming their capacity is adequate. These can be bought or constructed from suitable heavy timbers or steel.

In any case, it is always best to spend a little extra time to make sure your vehicle is lifted and supported safely.

CAUTION: *Concrete blocks are not recommended. They may crumble if the load is not evenly distributed. Boxes and milk crates of any description must not be used. Shake the vehicle a few times to make sure the jackstands are securely supporting the weight before crawling under.*

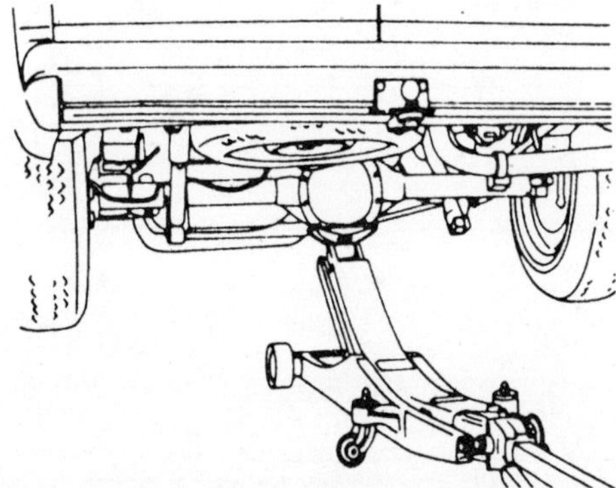

Using the rear axle to lift the rear of the vehicle

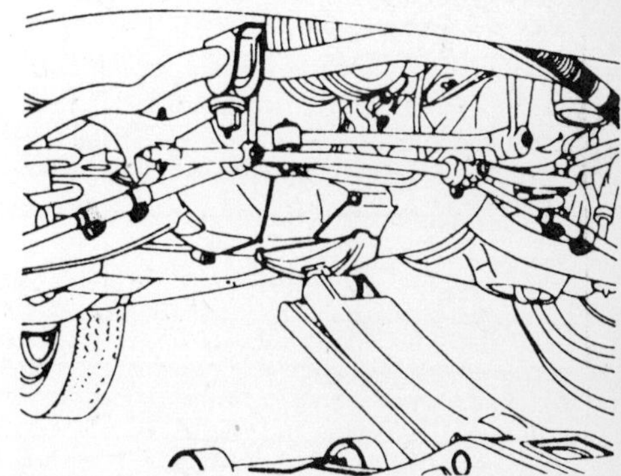

Using the crossmember to lift the front of the vehicle

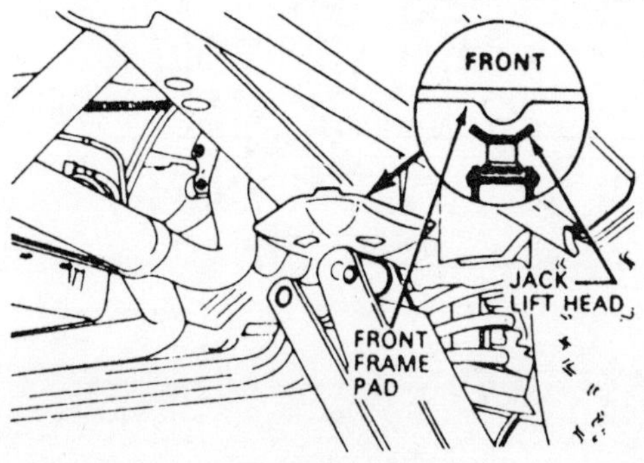

Using the front frame pad to lift the side of the vehicle

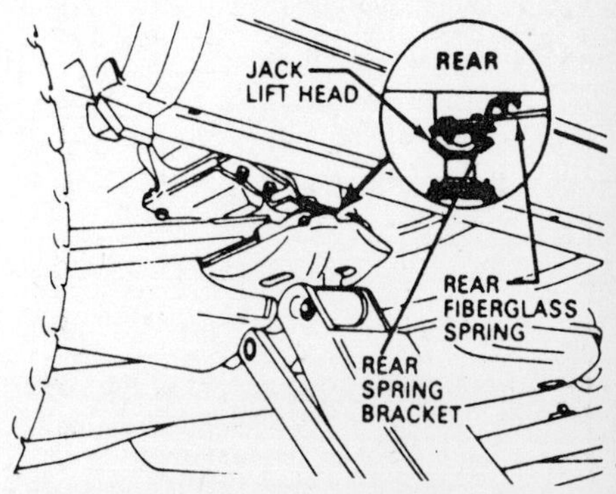

Using the rear spring bracket to lift the side of the vehicle

SCHEDULE II ②

Item No.	To Be Serviced	When to Perform Miles or Months, Whichever Occurs First Miles (000)	7.5	15	22.5	30	37.5	45	52.5	60
			The services shown in this schedule up to 60,000 miles are to be performed after 60,000 miles at the same intervals							
1	Engine Oil Change	Every 7,500 Miles or 12 Months	•	•	•	•	•	•	•	•
	Oil Filter Change	At First and Every Other Oil Change or 12 Months	•		•		•		•	
2	Chassis Lubrication	Every oil change	•	•	•	•	•	•	•	•
3	Carburetor Choke and Hoses Inspection	At 6 Months or 7,500 Miles and at 60,000 Miles	•			•				•
4	Carburetor or T.B.I. Mounting Bolt Torque Check	At 6 Months or 7,500 Miles and at 60,000 Miles	•							•
5	Engine Idle Speed Adjustment	At 6 Months or 7,500 Miles and at 60,000 Miles	•							•
6	Engine Accessory Drive Belts Inspection	Every 24 Months or 30,000 Miles				•				•
7	Cooling System Service	Every 24 Months or 30,000 Miles				•				•
8	Front Wheel Bearing Repack	Every 30,000 Miles				•				•
9	Transmission Service	30,000 Miles				•				•
10	Vacuum Advance System Inspection	Check at 6 Months or 7,500 Miles, then at 30,000 Miles, and then at 15,000 Mile intervals.	•			•		•		•
11	Spark Plugs and Wire Service	Every 30,000 Miles				•				•
12	PCV System Inspection	Every 30,000 Miles				•				•
13	ERG System Check	Every 30,000 Miles				•				•
14	Air Cleaner and PCV Filter Replacement	Every 30,000 Miles				•				•
15	Engine Timing Check	Every 30,000 Miles				•				•
16	Fuel Tank, Cap and Lines Inspection	Every 24 Months or 30,000 Miles				•				•
17	Early Fuel Evaporation System Inspection	At 7,500 Miles and at 30,000 Miles then at 30,000 Mile intervals.	•			•				•
18	Evaporative Control System Inspection	Every 30,000 Miles				•				•
19	Fuel Filter Replacement	Every 30,000 Miles				•				•
20	Valve Lash Adjustment	Every 15,000 Miles		•		•		•		•
21	Thermostatically Controlled Air Cleaner Inspection	Every 30,000 Miles				•				•

① Severe service
② Normal service

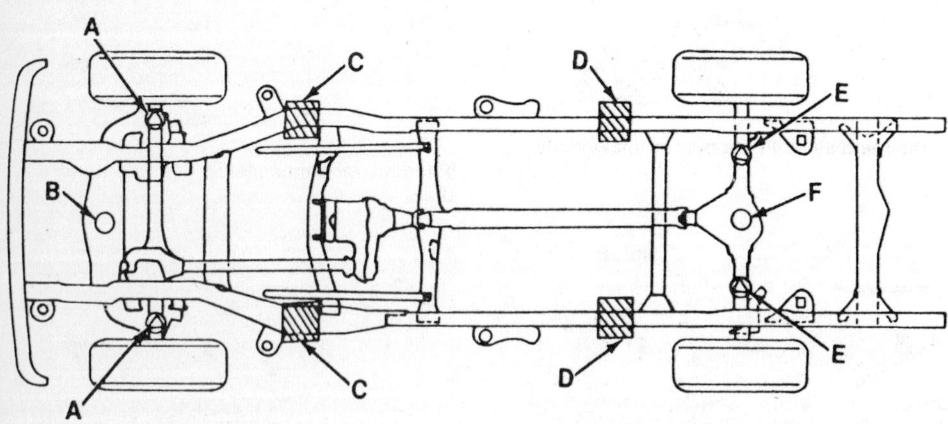

A. Lower Control Arm; Inboard of the Lower Ball Joint
B. Front Suspension Crossmember; Center
C. Frame; at Second Crossmember
D. Rear Spring; at Forward Spring Hanger
E. Axle; Inboard of Shock Absorber Hanger
F. Differential; at Center

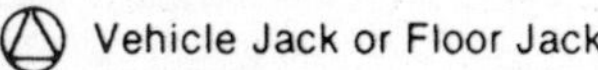
Vehicle Jack or Floor Jack

Floor Jack

Hoist

View of the 4WD lifting points — Blazer, Bravada and Jimmy

A. Lower Control Arm; Inboard of the Lower
   Ball Joint
B. Front Suspension Crossmember; Center
C. Frame; at Second Crossmember
D. Rear Spring; at Forward Spring Hanger
E. Axle; Inboard of Shock Absorber Hanger
F. Differential; at Center

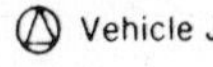

△ Vehicle Jack or Floor Jack

○ Floor Jack

▨ Hoist

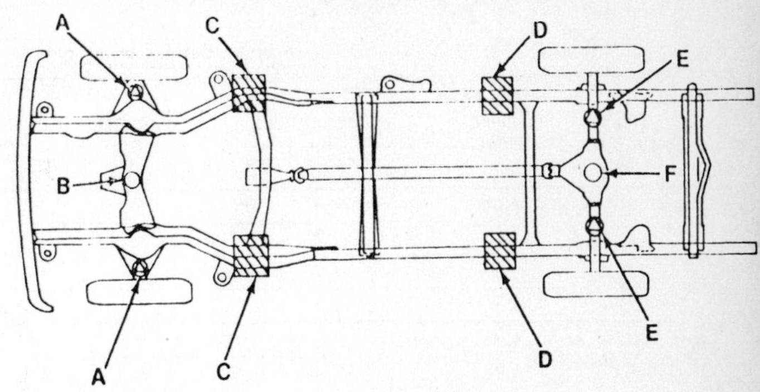

View of the 2WD lifting points—Blazer and Jimmy

MAINTENANCE INTERVALS SCHEDULE I ①

The services shown in this schedule up to 48,000 miles are to be performed after 48,000 miles at the same intervals.

Item No.	To Be Serviced	When to Perform — Miles or Months, Whichever Occurs First — Miles (000)	3	6	9	12	15	18	21	24	27	30	33	36	39	42	45	48
1	Every Oil and Oil Filter Change	Every 3,000 Miles or 3 Months	•	•	•	•	•	•	•	•	•	•	•	•	•	•	•	•
2	Chassis Lubrication	Every oil change	•	•	•	•	•	•	•	•	•	•	•	•	•	•	•	•
3	Carburetor Choke and Hose Inspection	At 6,000 Miles, then at 30,000 Miles		•								•					•	
4	Carburetor or T.B.I. Mounting Bolt Torque Check			•								•						
5	Engine Idle Speed Adjustment			•								•						
6	Engine Accessory Drive Belts Inspection	Every 12 Months or 15,000 Miles					•					•					•	
7	Cooling System Service	Every 24 Months or 30,000 Miles										•						
8	Front Wheel Bearing Repack	Every 15,000 Miles					•					•					•	
9	Transmission Service	15,000 Miles					•					•						
10	Vacuum Advance System Inspection	Check at 6,000 Miles at 30,000 Miles, and at 45,000 Miles		•								•					•	
11	Spark Plugs and Wire Service	Every 30,000 Miles										•						
12	PCV System Inspection	Every 30,000 Miles										•						
13	EGR System Check	Every 30,000 Miles										•						
14	Air Cleaner and PCV Filter Replacement	Every 30,000 Miles										•						
15	Engine Timing Check	Every 30,000 Miles										•						
16	Fuel Tank, Cap and Lines Inspection	Every 12 Months or 15,000 Miles					•					•					•	
17	Early Fuel Evaporation System Inspection	At 6,000 Miles then at 30,000 Miles		•								•						
18	Evaporative Control System Inspection	At 30,000 Miles										•						
19	Fuel Filter Replacement	Every 15,000 Miles					•					•					•	
20	Valve Lash Adjustment	Every 15,000 Miles					•					•					•	
21	Thermostatically Controlled Air Cleaner Inspection	Every 30,000 Miles										•						

CAPACITIES CHART

| Year | Engine No. Cyl. Liters | Crankcase Includes Filter (qt) | Transmission (pts) | | | Transfer Case (pts) | Drive Axle (pts) | | Fuel Tank (gal) | Cooling System (qt) | |
			4-sp	5-sp	Auto		Front	Rear		w/AC	wo/AC
1983	4-1.9L	4.0	2.5	2.2	10.0[1]	5.2	3.0	3.5	13.5[2]	9.5	9.4
	4-2.0L	4.0	2.5	2.2	10.0[1]	5.2	3.0	3.5	13.5[2]	9.7	9.6
	4-2.2L	5.0	2.5	2.2	10.0[1]	—	—	3.5	13.5[2]	10.0	10.0
	6-2.8L	4.0	2.5	2.2	10.0[1]	5.2	3.0	3.5	13.5[2]	12.0	12.0
1984	4-1.9L	4.0	2.5	2.2	10.0[1]	5.2	3.0	3.5	13.5[2]	9.5	9.4
	4-2.0L	4.0	2.5	2.2	10.0[1]	5.2	3.0	3.5	13.5[2]	9.7	9.6
	4-2.2L	5.0	2.5	2.2	10.0[1]	—	—	3.5	13.5[2]	10.0	10.0
	6-2.8L	4.0	2.5	2.2	10.0[1]	5.2	3.0	3.5	13.5[2]	12.0	12.0
1985	4-1.9L	4.0	2.5	2.2	10.0[1]	4.6	2.6	3.8	13.5[2]	9.5	9.5
	4-2.2L	5.5	2.5	2.2	10.0[1]	—	—	3.8	13.5[2]	11.5	11.5
	4-2.5L	3.0	2.5	2.2	10.0[1]	4.6	2.6	3.8	13.5[2]	12.0	12.0
	6-2.8L	4.0	2.5	2.2	10.0[1]	4.6	2.6	3.8	13.5[2]	12.0	12.0
1986	4-2.5L	3.0	2.5	2.2	10.0	4.6	2.6	3.8	13.5[2]	10.5	10.5
	6-2.8L	4.0	2.5	2.2	10.0	4.6	2.6	3.8	13.5[2]	11.6	11.6
1987	4-2.5L	3.0	2.5	2.2	10.0[3]	4.6	2.6	3.9	13.5[2]	10.5	10.5
	6-2.8L	4.0	2.5	2.2	10.0[3]	4.6	2.6	3.9	13.5[2]	11.5	11.5
1988	4-2.5L	3.0	—	2.2	10.0[3]	4.6[4]	2.6	3.9	13.0[2]	11.5	11.5
	6-2.8L	4.0	—	2.2	10.0[3]	4.6[4]	2.6	3.9	13.0[2]	10.5	10.5
	6-4.3L	4.0	—	2.2	10.0[3]	4.6[4]	2.6	3.9	13.0[2]	13.5	13.5
1989	4-2.5L	3.0	—	2.2	10.0[3]	4.4	2.6	3.9	13.0[2]	11.5	11.5
	6-2.8L	4.0	—	2.2	10.0[3]	4.4	2.6	3.9	13.0[2]	10.5	10.5
	6-4.3L	4.0	—	2.2	10.0[3]	4.4	2.6	3.9	13.0[2]	13.5	13.5
1990	6-4.3L	4.0	—	2.2	[5]	4.4	2.6	3.9	13.0[2]	13.5	13.5
1991	6-4.3L	4.0	—	2.2	[5] [9]	4.4[8]	2.6	3.9	20.0[7]	12.1[6]	12.1[6]

[1] If equipped with a 200C: 7.0 pts.
[2] Optional: 20.0 gal.
[3] If equipped with a 180C, 3-speed: 3 pts.
[4] If equipped with a 231: 2.2 pts.
[5] 180C and 3L30: 3.0 pts.
700-R4 and 4L60: 10.0 pts.
[6] Bravada without rear heater: 13.5 qts.
Bravada with rear heater: 16.5 qts.
[7] Bravada: 27 gals.
[8] Bravada: 3.0 pts.
[9] Bravada is only equipped with a 4L60: 10 pts.

TUNE-UP PROCEDURES

In order to extract the full measure of performance and economy from your engine, it is essential that it is properly tuned at regular intervals. A regular tune-up will keep your vehicle's engine running smoothly and will prevent the annoying breakdowns and poor performance associated with an untuned engine.

A complete tune-up should be performed every 30,000 miles. This interval should be halved if the vehicle is operated under severe conditions such as trailer towing, prolonged idling, start-and-stop driving, or if starting or running problems are noticed. It is assumed that the routine maintenance described in Chapter 1 has been kept up, as this will have a decided effect on the results of a tune-up. All of the applicable steps of a tune-up should be followed in order, as the result is a cumulative one.

> NOTE: *Diesel engines do not require tune-ups, as there is not an ignition system.*

If the specifications on the underhood tune-up sticker in the engine compartment disagree with the Tune-Up Specifications chart in this Chapter, the figures on the sticker must be used. The sticker often reflects changes made during the production run.

Spark Plugs

Normally, a set of spark plugs requires replacement about every 20,000–30,000 miles on vehicles equipped with an High Energy Ignition (HEI) system. Any vehicle which is subjected to severe conditions will need more frequent plug replacement.

Under normal operation, the plug gap increases about 0.001 in. (0.0254mm) for every 1000–2000 miles. As the gap increases, the plug's voltage requirement also increases. It requires a greater voltage to jump the wider gap and about 2–3 times as much voltage to fire a plug at high speeds than at idle.

When you are removing the spark plugs, work on 1 at a time. Don't start by removing the plug wires all at once, for unless you number them, they may become mixed up. Take a minute before you begin and number the wires with tape. The best location for numbering the wires is near the distributor cap.

REMOVAL

When removing the spark plugs, work on 1 at a time. Don't start by removing the plug wire

DIESEL ENGINE TUNE-UP SPECIFICATIONS

Year	VIN	Eng. No. Cyl. Displ. cc (Cu. In.)	Injection Timing (deg.)	Intake Valve Opens (deg.)	Low Idle (rpm)	Compression Pressure (psi)	Valve Clearance (in.) Intake	Exhaust	Firing Order
1983	S	4-2238 (136.6)	15B	16B	750	441①	0.016C	0.16C	1-3-4-2
1984	S	4-2238 (136.6)	15B	16B	750	441①	0.016C	0.16C	1-3-4-2
1985	S	4-2238 (136.6)	15B	16B	750	441①	0.016C	0.16C	1-3-4-2

NOTE: The underhood specifications sticker often reflects tune-up specification changes made in production. Sticker figures must be used if they disagree with those in this chart.
① @ 200 rpm

GASOLINE ENGINE TUNE-UP SPECIFICATIONS

Years	VIN	Engine No. Cyl. cc (cu. in.)	Spark Plugs Type	Gap (in.)	Ignition Time (deg.) Man. Trans.	Auto. Trans.	Idle Speed Man. Trans.	Auto Trans.	Valve Clearance In.	Exh.
1983	A	4-1950 (119)	R42XLS	0.040	6B	6B	800	900	0.006	0.010
	B	6-2800 (173)	R42TS	0.040	6B	10B	1000	750	Hyd.	Hyd.
	Y	4-2000 (121)	R42CTS	0.035	12B	12B	750	700	Hyd.	Hyd.
1984	A	4-1950 (119)	R42XLS	0.040	6B	6B	800	900	0.006	0.010
	B	6-2800 (173)	R42TS	0.040	6B	10B	1000	750	Hyd.	Hyd.
	Y	4-2000 (121)	R42CTS	0.035	12B	12B	750	700	Hyd.	Hyd.
1985	A	4-1950 (119)	R42XLS	0.040	6B	6B	800	900	0.006	0.010
	B	6-2800 (173)	R42TS	0.040	6B	10B	1000	750	Hyd.	Hyd.
	E	4-2500 (151)	R43CTS6	①	①	①	②	②	Hyd.	Hyd.
1986	E	4-2500 (151)	R43CTS6	①	①	①	②	②	Hyd.	Hyd.
	R	6-2800 (173)	R42CTS	①	①	①	②	②	Hyd.	Hyd.
1987	E	4-2500 (151)	R43CTS6	①	①	①	②	②	Hyd.	Hyd.
	R	6-2800 (173)	R43CTS	①	①	①	②	②	Hyd.	Hyd.
1988	E	4-2500 (151)	R43CTS6	①	①	①	②	②	Hyd.	Hyd.
	R	6-2800 (173)	R43CTS	①	①	①	②	②	Hyd.	Hyd.
	Z	6-4300 (262)	R43CTS	0.040	①	①	②	②	Hyd.	Hyd.
1989	E	4-2500 (151)	R43CTS6	①	①	①	②	②	Hyd.	Hyd.
	R	6-2800 (173)	R43CTS	①	①	①	②	②	Hyd.	Hyd.
	Z	6-4300 (262)	CR43TS	0.045	①	①	②	②	Hyd.	Hyd.
1990	Z	6-4300 (262)	CR43TS	0.045	①	①	②	②	Hyd.	Hyd.
1991	Z	6-4300 (262)	CR43TS	0.045	①	①	②	②	Hyd.	Hyd.

① See underhood sticker
② This function is controlled by the ECU;
No adjustment is necessary.

all at once because unless you number them, they're going to get mixed up. On some models though, it will be more convenient for you to remove all of the wires before you start to work on the plugs. If this is necessary, take a minute before you begin and number the wires with tape before you take them off. The time you spend here will pay off later on.

1. Twist the spark plug boot ½ turn and remove the boot from the plug. You may also use a plug wire removal tool designed especially for this purpose. Do not pull on the wire itself. When the wire has been removed, take a wire brush and clean the area around the plug. Make sure all the grime is removed so none will enter the cylinder after the plug has been removed.

2. Remove the plug using the proper size socket, extensions and universals as necessary.

3. If removing the plug is difficult, drip some penetrating oil (Liquid Wrench®, WD-40® or etc.) on the plug threads, allow it to work,

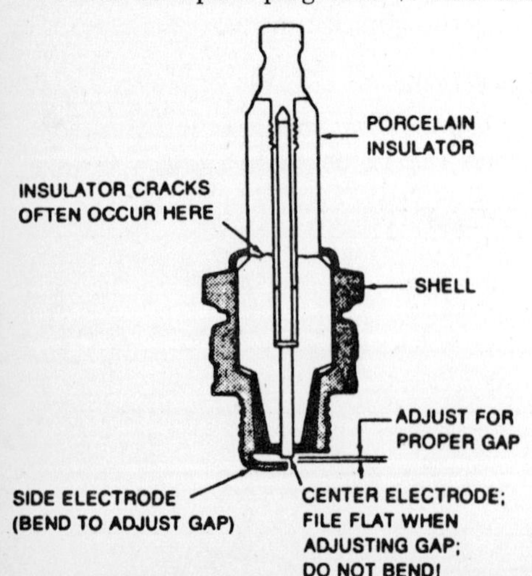

Cross-section of a spark plug

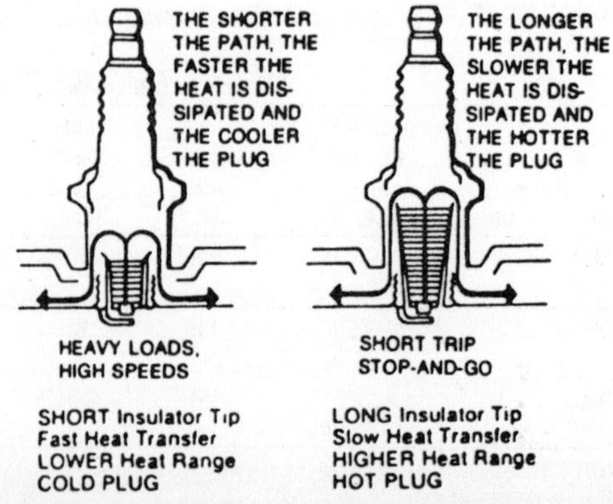

Spark plug heat range

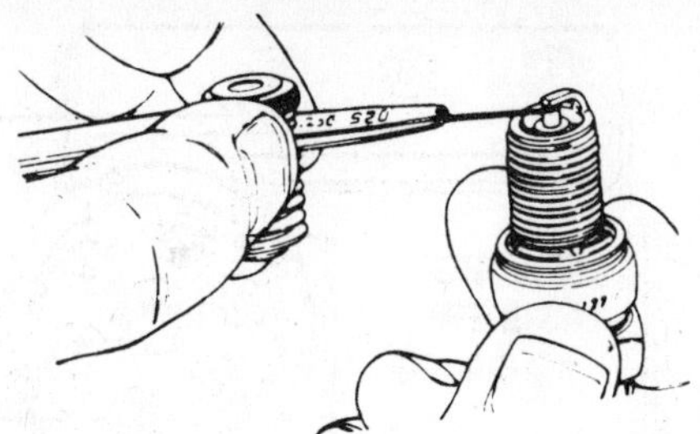

View of the distributor and coil locations—2.8L engines

then remove the plug. Also, be sure the socket is straight on the plug, especially on those hard to reach plugs.

INSPECTION

Check the plugs for deposits and wear. If they are not going to be replaced, clean the plugs thoroughly. Remember, any kind of deposit will decrease the efficiency of the plug. Plugs can be cleaned on a spark plug cleaning machine, which can sometimes be found in service stations or you can do an acceptable job of cleaning with a stiff brush. If the plugs are cleaned, the electrodes must be filed flat. Use an ignition points file, not an emery board or the like, which will leave deposits. The electrodes must be filed perfectly flat with sharp edges; rounded edges reduce the spark plug voltage by as much as 50 percent.

Check the spark plug gap before installation. The ground electrode (the L-shaped 1 connected to the body of the plug) must be parallel to the center electrode and the specified size wire gauge (see Tune-Up Specifications) should pass through the gap with a slight drag. Always check the gap on the new plugs, they are not always set correctly at the factory. Do not use a flat feeler gauge when measuring the gap, because the reading will be inaccurate.

Heat range is a term used to describe the cooling characteristics of spark plugs. Plugs with longer nosed insulators take a longer time to dissipate heat than plugs with shorter nosed insulators. These are termed "hot" or "cold" plugs, respectively. It is generally advisable to use the factory recommended plugs. However, in conditions of extremely hard use (cross-country driving in summer) going to the next cooler heat range may be advisable. If most driving is done in the city or over short distances, go to the next hotter heat range plug to eliminate fouling. If in doubt concerning the substitution of spark plugs, consult your Chevrolet, GMC or Oldsmobile dealer.

Wire gapping tools usually have a bending tool attached; use that to adjust the side electrode until the proper distance is obtained.

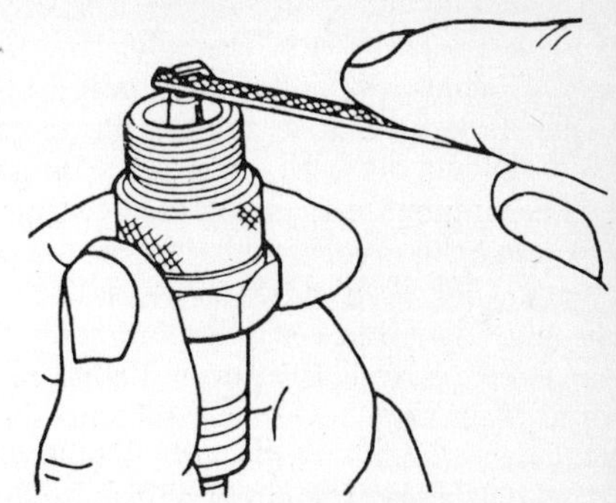

Filing an electrode square with an ignition points file

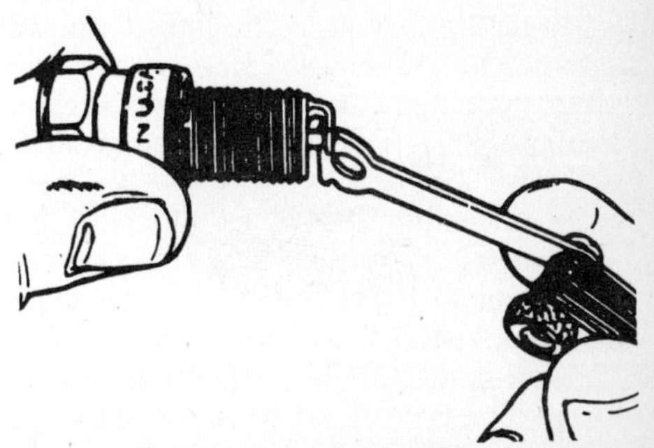

Bending the side electride to adjust the spark plug gap

Absolutely, never bend the center electrode.

Also, be careful not to bend the side electrode too far or too often; it may weaken and break off within the engine, requiring removal of the cylinder head to retrieve it.

INSTALLATION

1. Lubricate the threads of the spark plugs with a drop of oil. Install the plugs and tighten them hand tight. Take care not to cross-thread them.

2. Tighten the spark plugs with the socket. Do not apply the same amount of force you would use for a bolt; just snug them in. If a torque wrench is available, tighten to 11–15 ft. lbs.

3. Install the wire on their respective plugs. Make sure the wires are firmly connected, you will be able to feel them click into place.

Spark Plug Wires

Every 15,000 miles, visually inspect the spark plug cables for burns, cuts or breaks in the insulation. Check the spark plug boots and the nipples on the distributor cap and coil. Replace any damaged wiring.

Every 30,000 miles or so, the resistance of the wires should be checked with an ohmmeter. Wires with excessive resistance will cause misfiring and may make the engine difficult to start in damp weather. Generally, the useful life of the cables is 30,000–45,000 miles.

To check the resistance, remove the distributor cap, leaving the wires in place. Connect 1 lead of an ohmmeter to an electrode within the cap; connect the other lead to the corresponding spark plug terminal (remove it from the spark plug for this test). Replace any wire which shows a resistance over 30,000 ohms. Generally speaking, however, resistance should not be over 25,000 ohms and 30,000 ohms must be considered the outer limit of acceptability.

It should be remembered that resistance is also a function of length; the longer the wire the greater the resistance. Thus, if the wires on your van are longer than the factory originals, resistance will be higher, quite possibly outside these limits.

When installing a new set of spark plug wires, replace the wires 1 at a time, so there will be no mixup. Start by replacing the longest cable first. Install the boot firmly over the spark plug. Route the wire exactly the same as the original. Insert the distributor end of the wire firmly into the distributor cap tower, then seat the boot over the tower. Repeat the process for each wire.

HEI Plug Wire Resistance Chart

Wire Length	Minimum	Maximum
0–15 inches	3000 ohms	10,000 ohms
15–25 inches	4000 ohms	15,000 ohms
25–35 inches	6000 ohms	20,000 ohms
Over 35 inches	6000 ohms	25,000 ohms

FIRING ORDERS

NOTE: *To avoid confusion, remove and tag the wires 1 at a time, for replacement.*

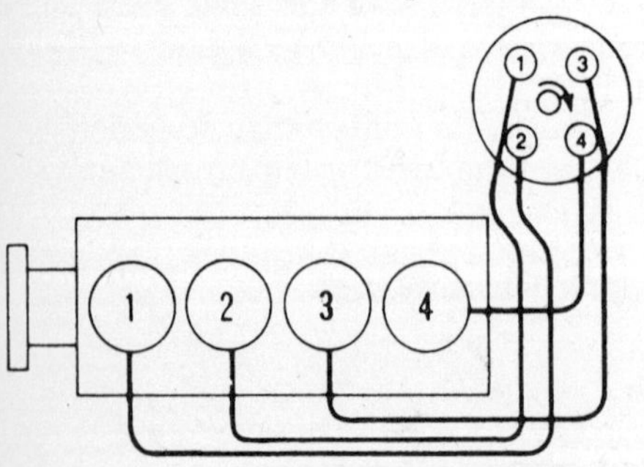

2.0L Engine
Engine Firing order: 1-3-4-2
Distributor Rotation: Clockwise

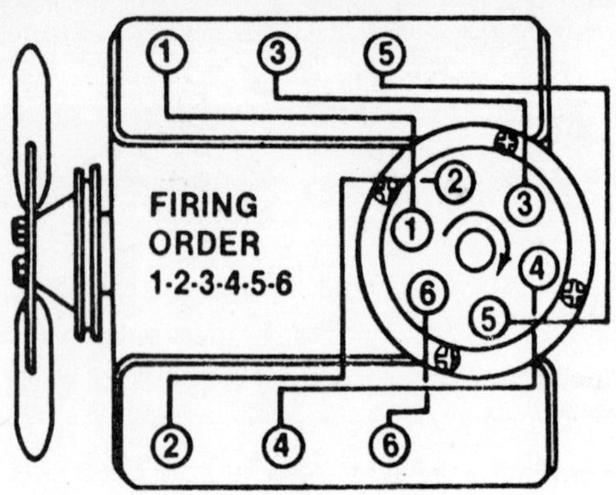

2.8L Engine
Engine Firing Order: 1-2-3-4-5-6
Distributor Rotation: Clockwise

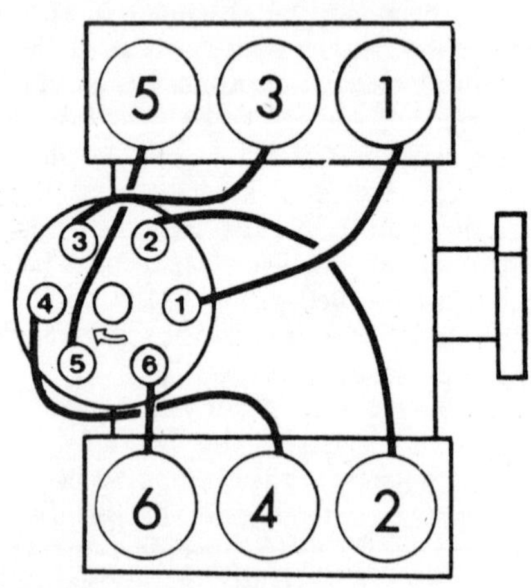

4.3L Engine
Engine Firing Order: 1-6-5-4-3-2
Distributor Rotation: Clockwise

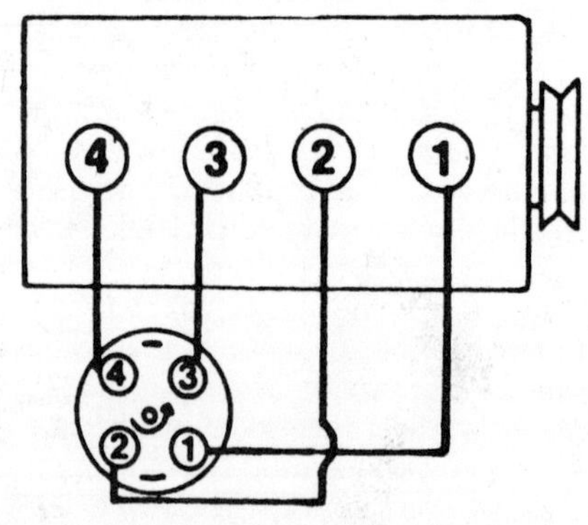

1.9L Engine
Engine Firing Order: 1-3-4-2
Distributor Rotation: Counterclockwise

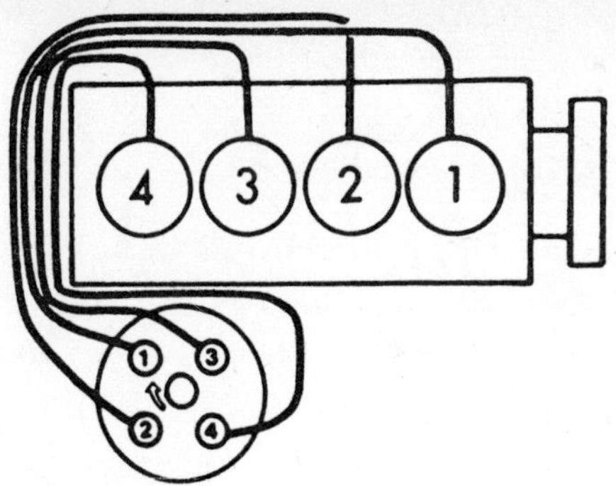

2.5L Engine
Engine Firing Order: 1-3-4-2
Distributor Rotation: Clockwise

ELECTRONIC IGNITION

GENERAL INFORMATION

The High Energy Ignition (HEI) distributor is used on all gasoline engines. The ignition coil is either mounted to the top of the distributor cap or is externally mounted on the engine, using a secondary circuit high tension wire to connect the coil to the distributor cap. Interconnecting primary wiring is routed through the engine harness.

The HEI distributor is equipped to aid in spark timing changes, necessary for emissions, economy and performance. This system is called the Electronic Spark Timing Control (EST). HEI(EST) distributors use a magnetic pick-up assembly, located inside the distributor containing a permanent magnet, a pole piece with internal teeth and a pick-up coil. When the teeth of the rotating timer core and pole piece align, an induced voltage in the pick-up coil signals the electronic module to open the coil primary circuit. As the primary current de-creases, a high voltage is induced in the secondary windings of the ignition coil, directing a spark through the rotor and high voltage leads to fire the spark plugs. The dwell period is automatically controlled by the electronic module and is increased with increasing engine rpm. The HEI system features a longer spark duration which is instrumental in firing lean and EGR (Exhaust Gas Recirculation) diluted fuel/air mixtures. The condenser (capacitor) located within the HEI distributor is provided for noise (static) suppression purposes only and is not a regularly replaced ignition system component.

All spark timing changes in the HEI(EST) distributors are performed electronically by the Electronic Control Module (ECM), which monitors information from the various engine sensors, computes the desired spark timing and signals the distributor to change the timing accordingly. Vacuum advance and centrifugal advance is used only on distributors without EST.

The distributor on the 1.9L engine uses vacuum and centrifugal advance and does not use EST.

The distributor on the 2.5L engine contains a Hall Effect Switch. It is mounted above the pick-up coil in the distributor and takes the place of the reference (R) terminal on the distributor module. The Hall Effect Switch provides a voltage signal to the ECM to tell it which cylinder will fire next.

The 2.8L and 4.3L engines are equipped with Electronic Spark Control (ESC). A knock sensor is mounted in the engine block. It is connected to the ESC module which is mounted on the cowl in the engine compartment. In response to engine knock, the sensor sends a signal to the ESC module. The module will then signal the ECM which will retard the spark timing in the distributor.

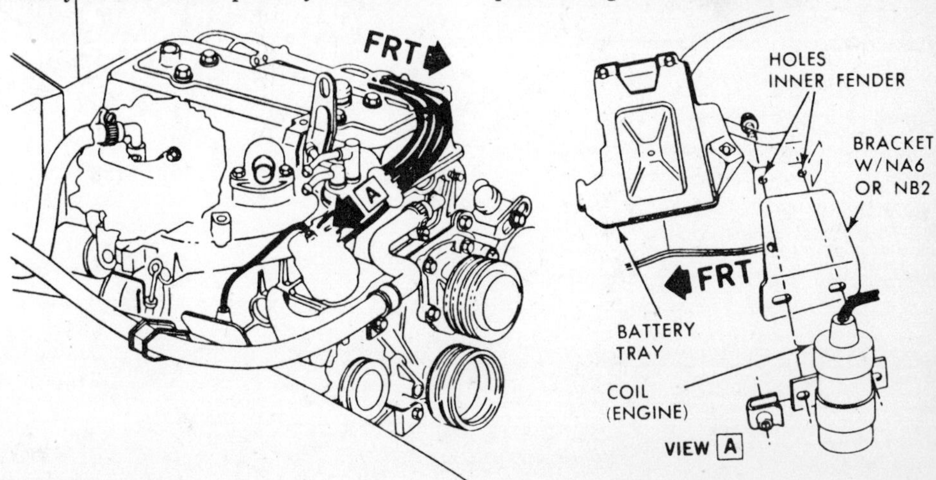

Distributor and coil locations — 1.9L and 2.0L engines

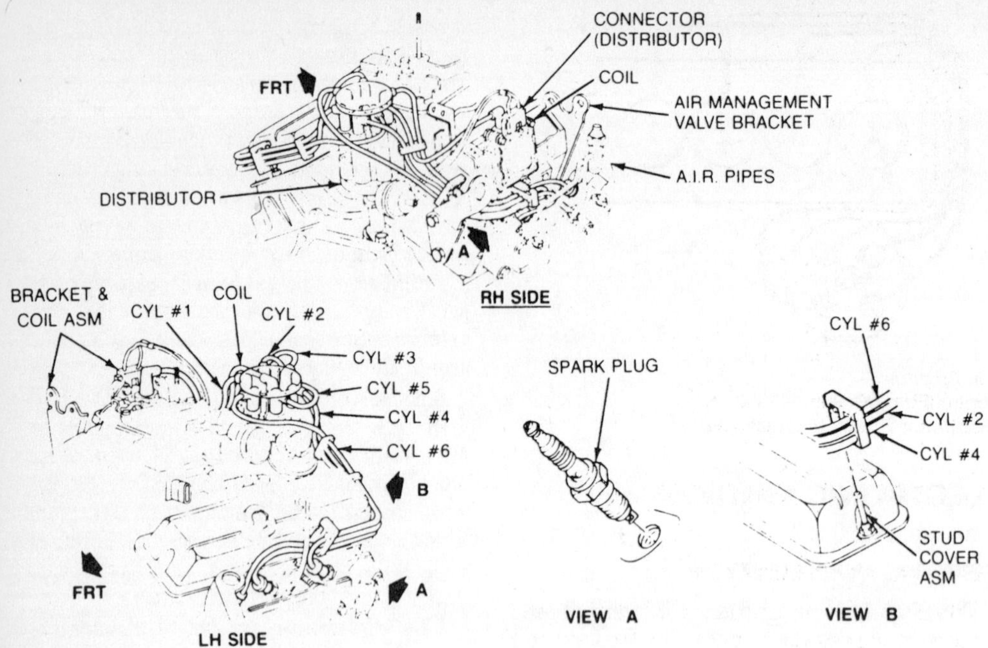

Distributor and coil locations — 2.8L engines

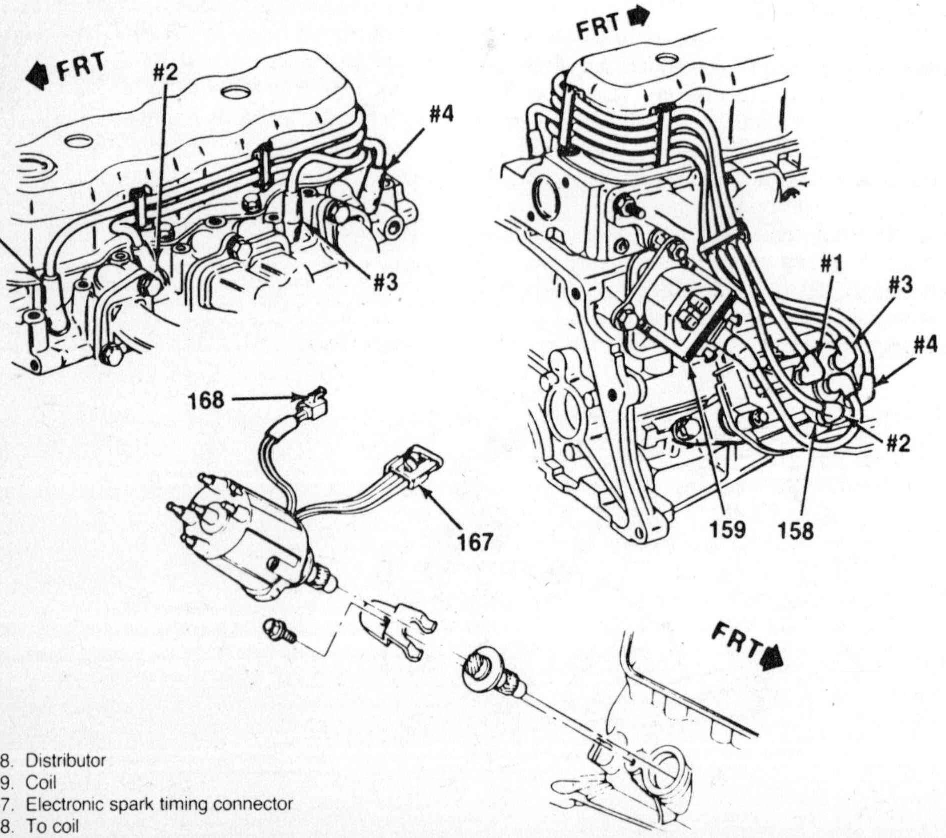

158. Distributor
159. Coil
167. Electronic spark timing connector
168. To coil

Distributor and coil locations — 2.5L engines

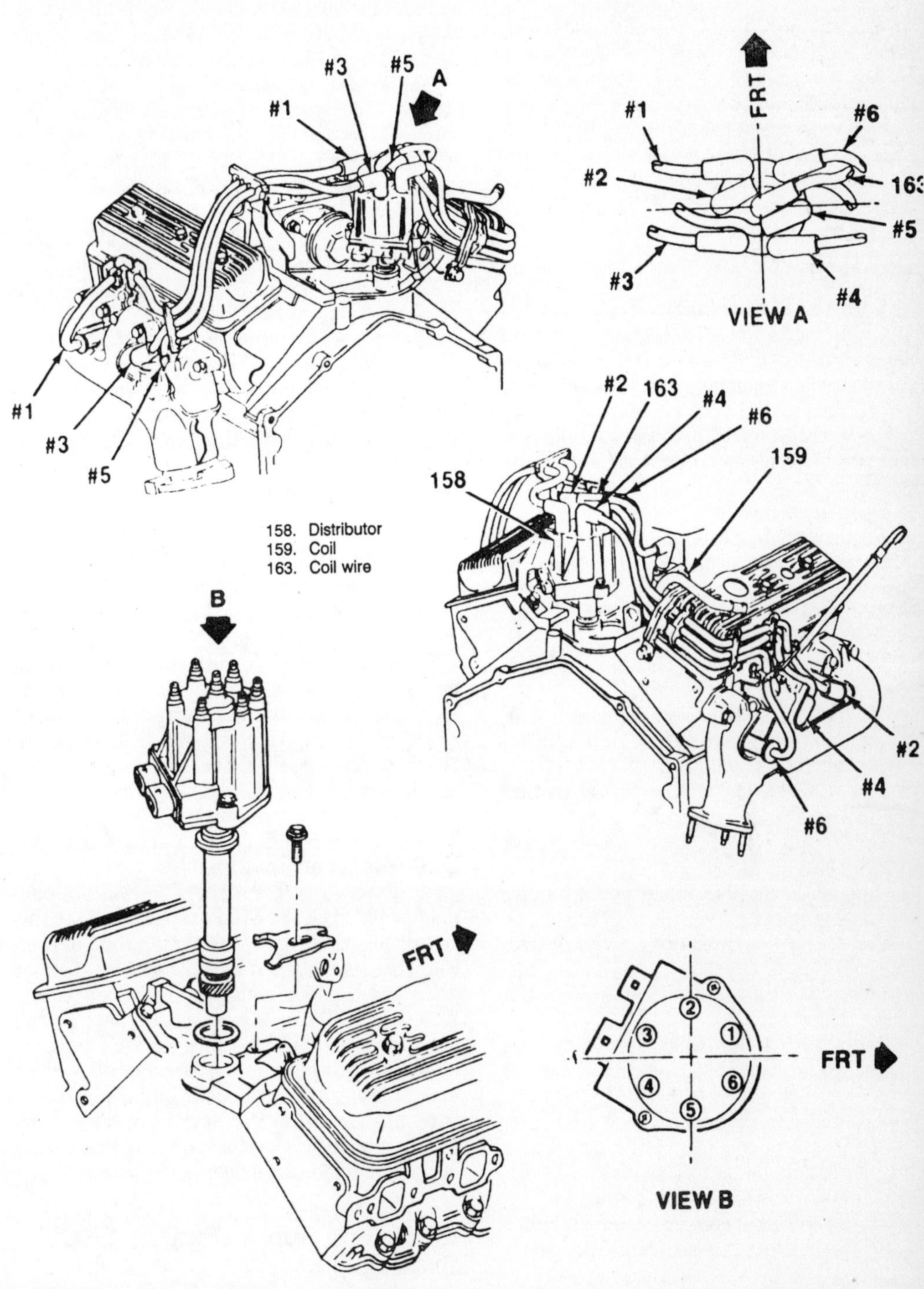

View of the distributor and coil locations—4.3L engine

Electronic Spark Timing (EST) System

The High Energy Ignition (HEI) system controls fuel combustion by providing the spark to ignite the compressed air/fuel mixture in the combustion chamber at the correct time. To provide improved engine performance, fuel economy and control of the exhaust emissions, the ECM controls distributor spark advance (timing) using the Electronic Spark Timing (EST) system.

OPERATION

The HEI (EST) distributor uses a modified module. The module has 7 terminals instead of the 4 used without EST. Two terminal arrangements are used, depending upon engine application.

To properly control ignition/combustion timing, the ECM needs to know the following information:

- Crankshaft position
- Engine speed (rpm)
- Engine load (manifold pressure or vacuum)
- Atmospheric (barometric) pressure
- Engine temperature
- Transmission gear position (certain models)

The ECM uses information from the MAP and coolant sensors in addition to rpm to calculate spark advance as follows:

- Low MAP output voltage would require MORE spark advance.
- Cold engine would require MORE spark advance.
- High MAP output voltage would require LESS spark advance.
- Hot engine would require LESS spark advance.

Incorrect operation of the EST system can cause the following:

- Detonation – low MAP output or high resistance in the coolant sensor circuit.
- Poor performance – high MAP output or low resistance in the coolant sensor circuit.

The EST system consists of the distributor module, ECM and its connecting wires. The distributor has 4 wires from the HEI module connected to a 4 terminal connector, which mates with a 4 wire connector from the ECM.

Except 2.5L Engine

The distributor 4-terminal connector is labeled A, B, C, D. Circuit functions for these terminals, except the 2.5L Hall Effect Switch model, are as follows:

1. Reference ground – Terminal A – This wire is grounded in the distributor and makes sure the ground circuit has no voltage drop, which could affect performance. If this circuit is open, it could cause poor performance.
2. Bypass – Terminal B – At approximately 400 rpm, the ECM applies 5 volts to this circuit to switch the spark timing control from the HEI module to the ECM. An open or grounded bypass circuit will set a Code 42 and the engine will run at base timing, plus a small amount of advance built into the HEI module.
3. Distributor reference – Terminal C – This provides the ECM with rpm and crankshaft position information.
4. EST – Terminal D – This triggers the HEI module. The ECM does not know what the actual timing is, but it does know when it gets its reference signal. It then advances or retards the spark timing from that point. Therefore, if the base timing is set incorrectly, the entire spark curve will be incorrect.

2.5L Engine With Hall Effect Switch

Circuit functions for the 2.5L Hall Effect Switch distributor are as follows:

1. EST – Terminal A – This triggers the HEI module. The ECM does not know what the actual timing is but it does know when it gets its reference signal. It then advances or retards the spark timing from that point. Therefore, if the base timing is set incorrectly, the entire spark curve will be incorrect.
2. Distributor reference – Terminal B – This provides the ECM with rpm and crankshaft position information.
3. Bypass – Terminal C – At approximately 400 rpm, the ECM applies 5 volts to this circuit to switch the spark timing control from the HEI module to the ECM. An open or grounded bypass circuit will set a Code 42 and the engine will run at base timing, plus a small amount of advance built into the HEI module.
4. Reference ground – Terminal D – This wire is grounded in the distributor and makes sure the ground circuit has no voltage drop, which could affect performance. If this circuit is open, it could cause poor performance.

Electronic Spark Control (ESC) System

The Electronic Spark Control (ESC) system is designed to retard spark timing up to 20 degrees to reduce detonation in the engine. This allows the engine to use maximum spark advance to improve driveability and fuel economy. Varying octane levels in gasoline can cause detonation (spark knock) in any engine.

OPERATION

The ESC system has 3 components:
- ESC Module
- ESC Knock Sensor
- ECM

The knock sensor detects abnormal vibration in the engine. The sensor is mounted in the engine block near the cylinders. The ESC module receives the knock sensor information and sends a signal to the ECM. The ECM then adjusts the Electronic Spark Timing (EST) to reduce spark knocking.

The ESC module sends a voltage signal to the ECM when no spark knocking is detected by the ESC knock sensor, and the ECM provides normal spark advance. When the knock sensor detects spark knock, the module turns off the circuit to the ECM. The ECM then retards EST to reduce spark knock.

IGNITION TIMING ADJUSTMENT

The following procedure requires the use of a distributor wrench and a timing light. When using a timing light, be sure to consult the manufacturer's recommendations for installation and usage.

Gasoline Engine

On 2.5L engine, ground the ‹cf3›A‹cf1› and ‹cf3›B‹cf1› terminals on the ALDL connector under the dash before adjusting the timing.

On all except 2.5L engine with an EST distributor, disconnect the timing connector wire, located below the heater case in the engine compartment or coming out of the wiring harness near the distributor, before adjusting the timing.

1. Timing specifications are listed on the Vehicle Emissions Control Information label, located on the radiator support. Use the timing specifications specific to your vehicle.

2. Using a timing light, connect it to the engine by performing the following procedures:

a. If using a non-inductive type, connect an adapter between the No. 1 spark plug and the spark plug wire; do not puncture the spark plug wire, for this will cause a voltage leak.

b. If using an inductive type, clamp it around the No. 1 spark plug wire.

c. If using a magnetic type, place the probe in the connector located near the damper pulley; this type must be used with special electronic timing equipment.

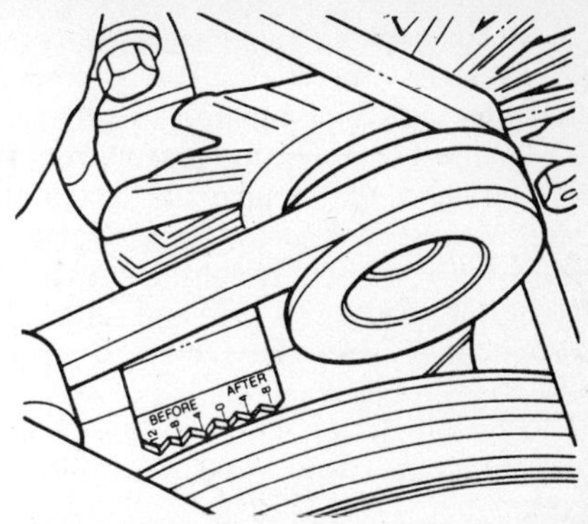

Timing marks

3. If equipped with Electric Spark Timing (EST), disconnect the timing connector wire; this allows the engine to operate in the bypass timing mode.

4. Start the engine aim the timing light at the timing mark on the damper pulley; a line on the damper pulley will align the timing mark. If necessary to adjust the timing, loosen the distributor hold-down clamp and slowly turn the distributor slightly to align the marks. When the alignment is correct, tighten the hold-down bolt.

5. Turn the engine **OFF**. Remove the timing light and reconnect the timing connector wire, if disconnected.

DIESEL ENGINE INJECTION TIMING

NOTE: *This procedure requires the use of a static timing gauge tool J-29763 or equivalent; do not attempt any injection timing adjustments without this tool.*

1. Check that notched line on the injection pump flange is in alignment with notched line on the injection pump front bracket.

2. Bring the piston in No. 1 cylinder to top dear center on compression stroke by turning the crankshaft as necessary.

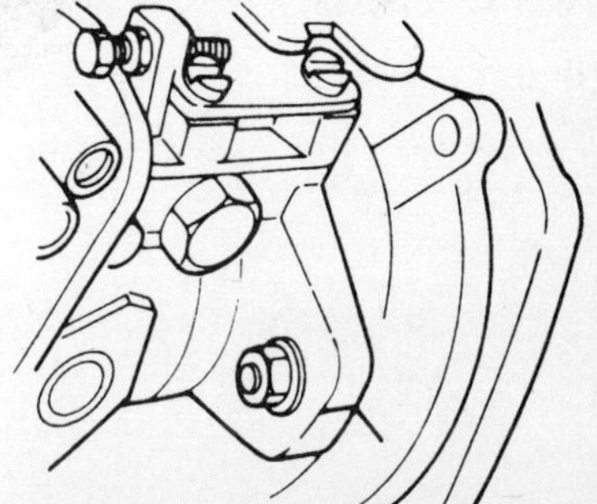

Injection pump and flange alignment

3. With the timing pulley housing cover removed, check that the timing belt is properly tensioned and that timing marks are aligned.

4. Disconnect the injection pipe(s) from the injection pump, then remove the distributor head screw and washer. Using the static timing gauge tool J-29763 or equivalent, install it into the distributor head screw hole and set the lift to approximately 0.04 in. (1mm) from the plunger.

5. Use a wrench to hold the delivery holder when loosening the sleeve nuts on the injection pump side.

6. Bring the piston in No. 1 cylinder to a point 45–60 degrees before top dead center (BTDC) by turning the crankshaft, then calibrate the dial indicator to zero.

7. Turn the crankshaft pulley slightly in both directions and check that gauge indication is stable.

8. Turn the crankshaft in the normal direction of rotation, then record the reading of the dial indicator when the timing mark (15 degrees) on the crankshaft pulley is in alignment with the pointer; the reading should be 0.020 in. (0.5mm).

9. If the reading of dial indicator deviates from the specified range, hold the crankshaft in position 15 degrees BTDC and loosen 2 nuts on injection pump flange.

10. Move the injection pump to a point where dial indicator gives reading of 0.020 in. (0.5mm), then tighten pump flange nuts.

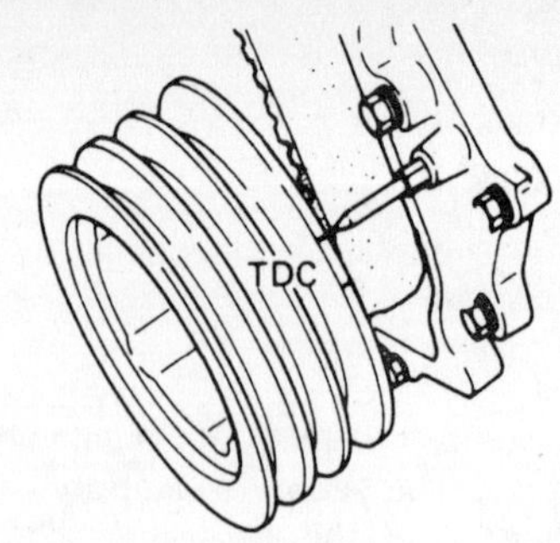

Number 1 piston at TDC

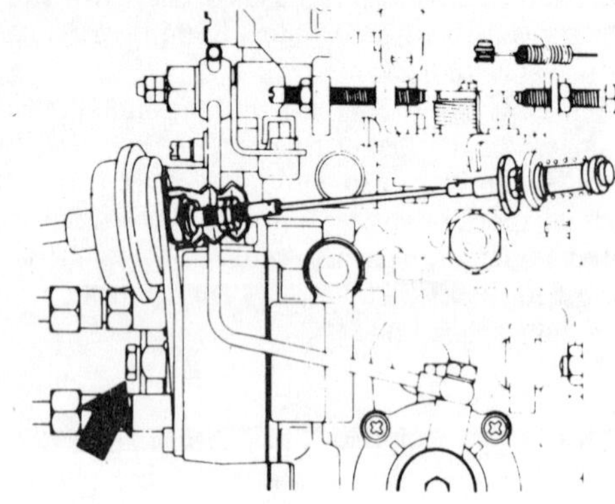

Removing the distributor screw — diesel engine

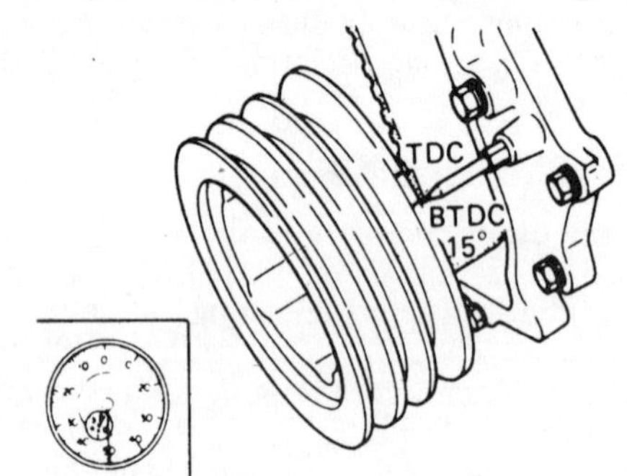

No. 1 piston 15° BTDC

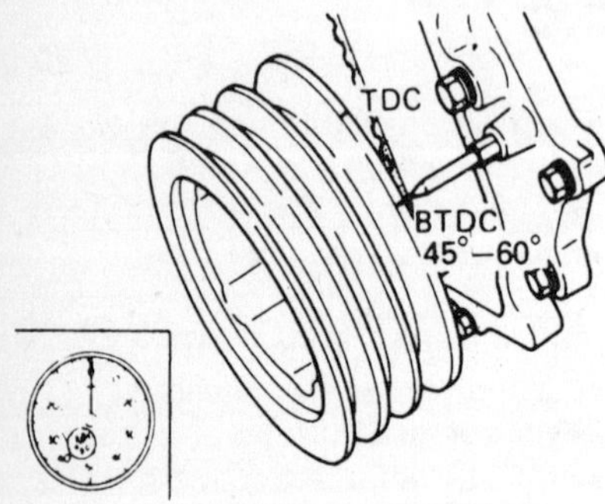

No. 1 piston 45–60° BTDC

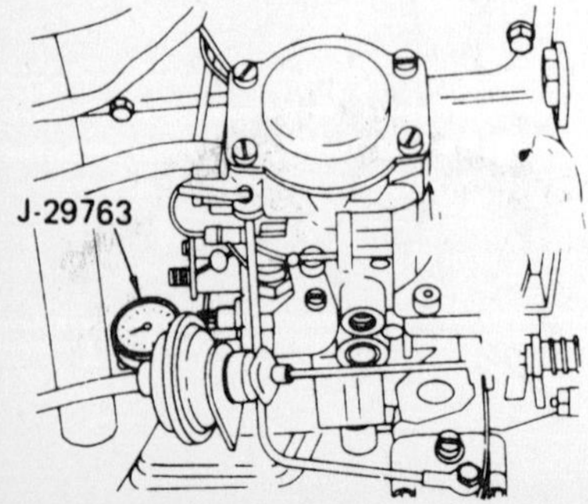

Static timing gauge installed

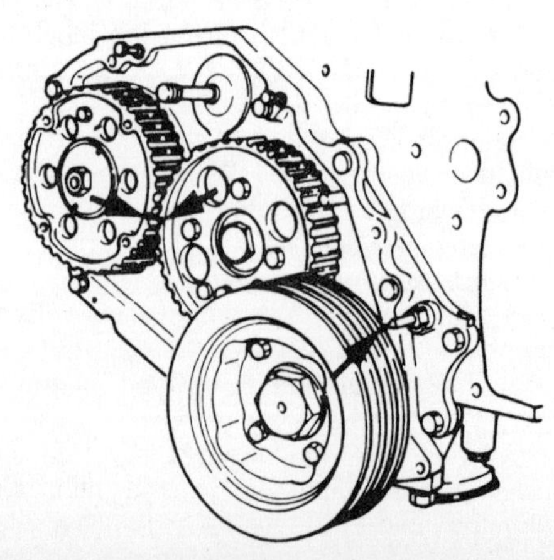

Aligning the timing marks — diesel engine

VALVE LASH

Valve adjustment determines how far the valves enter the cylinder and how long they stay open and/or closed.

NOTE: *While all valve adjustments must be made as accurately as possible, it is better to have the valve adjustment slightly loose than slightly tight, as a burned valve may result from overly tight adjustments.*

ADJUSTMENT

1.9L and 2.2L Diesel

NOTE: *The valves are adjusted with the engine Cold.*

1. Remove the rocker arm cover.

2. Make sure the rocker arm shaft nuts/bolts are torqued to 16 ft. lbs.

3. Using a wrench on the damper pulley bolt or a remote starter button, turn the engine's crankshaft until the No. 1 piston is at TDC of the compression stroke.

NOTE: *You can tell when the piston is coming up on the compression stroke by removing the spark plug and placing your thumb over the hole, you will feel the air being forced out of the spark plug hole. Stop turning the crankshaft when the TDC timing mark on the crankshaft pulley is directly aligned with the timing mark pointer.*

4. With the No. 1 cylinder on the TDC of the compression stroke, perform the following valve setting procedures:

    a. If working on the 1.9L engine, use a 0.006 in. (0.152mm) feeler gauge, to set intake valves of cylinders No. 1 and 2. Using a 0.010 in. (0.254mm) feeler gauge, set the exhaust valves of cylinders No. 1 and 3.

    b. If working on the 2.2L engine, use a 0.016 in. (0.40mm) feeler gauge, to set the intake valves of cylinders No. 1, 2 and 3, then set the exhaust valve of cylinder No. 1.

5. Rotate the engine 1 complete revolution, so cylinder No. 4 is on the TDC of its compression stroke and the timing marks are aligned.

6. With cylinder No. 4 on the TDC of the compression stroke, perform the following valve setting procedures:

    a. If working on the 1.9L engine, use a 0.006 in. (0.152mm) feeler gauge, to set intake valves of cylinders No. 3 and 4. Using a 0.010 in. (0.254mm) feeler gauge, set the exhaust valves of cylinders No. 2 and 4.

    b. If working on the 2.2L engine, use a 0.016 in. (0.40mm) feeler gauge, to set the intake valve of cylinder No. 4, then the exhaust valves of cylinders No. 2, 3 and 4.

NOTE: *When adjusting the valve clearance, loosen the locknut with an open-end wrench, then turn the adjuster screw with a screwdriver and retighten the locknut. The proper thickness feeler gauge should pass between the camshaft and the rocker with a slight drag when the clearance is correct.*

2.0L and 2.8L Engines

1. Remove the air cleaner and the rocker arm cover(s).

2. Rotate the crankshaft until the mark on the crankshaft pulley aligns with the **0** mark on the timing plate. Make sure the No. 1 cylinder is positioned on the compression stroke.

NOTE: *To determine the compression stroke, place your fingers on the No. 1 rocker arms, as the mark on the crankshaft pulley comes near the **0** mark on the timing plate. If the valves move, the engine is on the No. 4 firing position; rotate the crankshaft 1 complete revolution and realign the pulley mark with the timing plate **0** mark.*

3. With the engine in the No. 1 firing position, perform the following adjustments:

    a. If working on the 2.0L engine, adjust the intake valves of cylinders No. 1 and 2 and the exhaust valves of cylinders No. 1 and 3.

    b. If working on the 2.8L engine, adjust the intake valves of cylinders No. 1, 5 and 6

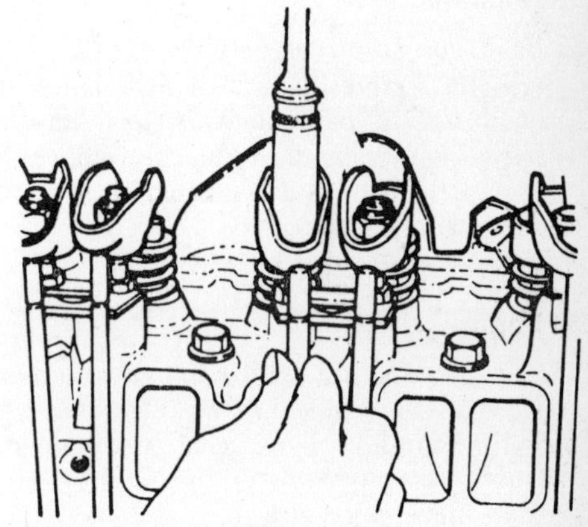

Valve adjustment

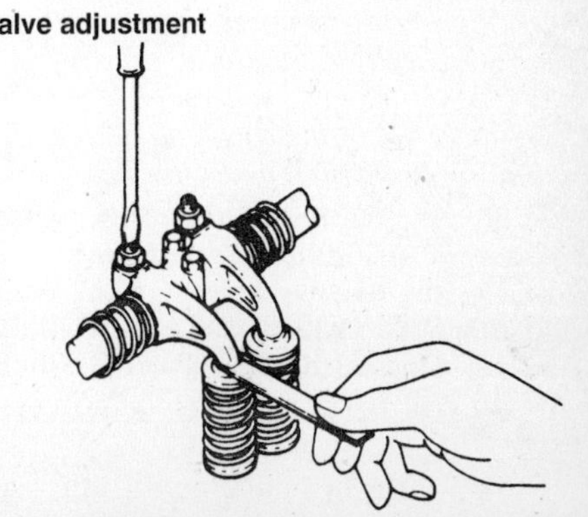

Valve clearance adjustment – 1.9L and 2.2L engines

and the exhaust valves of cylinders No. 1, 2 and 3.

4. To adjust the valves, back-out the adjusting nut until lash can be felt at the pushrod, then turn the nut until all of the lash is removed.

NOTE: *To determine is all of the lash is removed, turn the pushrod with your fingers until the movement is removed.*

5. When all of the lash has been removed, turn the adjusting an additional 1¹/₂ turns; this will center the lifter plunger.

6. Rotate the crankshaft 1 complete revolution and realign the timing marks; the engine is now positioned on the No. 4 firing position.

7. With the engine in the No. 4 firing position, perform the following procedures:

a. If working on the 2.0L engine, adjust the intake valves of cylinders No. 3 and 4 and the exhaust valves of cylinders No. 2 and 4.

b. If working on the 2.8L engine, adjust the intake valves of cylinders No. 2, 3 and 4 and the exhaust valves of cylinders No. 4, 5 and 6.

8. To compete the installation, reverse the removal procedures.

2.5L Engine

Valve lash is not adjustable on the 2.5L engine. Check that the rocker arm bolts are tightened to 22 ft. lbs. When valve lash falls out of specification (valve tap is heard), replace the rocker arm, pushrod and hydraulic lifter on the offending cylinder.

4.3L Engine

1. To prepare the engine for valve adjustment, rotate the crankshaft until the mark on the damper pulley aligns with the 0 degree mark on the timing plate and the No. 1 cylinder is on the compression stroke.

NOTE: *You can tell when the piston is coming up on the compression stroke by removing the spark plug and placing your thumb over the hole, you will feel the air being forced out of the spark plug hole. Stop turning the crankshaft when the TDC timing mark on the crankshaft pulley is directly aligned with the timing mark pointer.*

2. With the engine on the compression stroke, adjust the exhaust valves of cylinders No. 1, 5 and 6 and the intake valves of cylinders No. 1, 2 and 3 by performing the following procedures:

a. Back out the adjusting nut until lash can be felt at the pushrod.

b. While rotating the pushrod, turn the adjusting nut inward until all of the lash is removed.

c. When the play has disappeared, turn the adjusting nut inward 1 additional turn.

3. Rotate the crankshaft 1 complete revolution and align the mark on the damper pulley with the **0** degree mark on the timing plate; this is TDC of the compression stroke for the No. 4 cylinder. With the engine on the compression stroke, adjust the exhaust valves of cylinders No. 2, 3 and 4 and the intake valves of cylinders No. 4, 5 and 6, by performing the following procedures:

a. Back out the adjusting nut until lash can be felt at the pushrod.

b. While rotating the pushrod, turn the adjusting nut inward until all of the lash is removed.

c. When the play has disappeared, turn the adjusting nut inward 1 additional turn.

4. To complete the installation, reverse the removal procedures. Start the engine, the check for oil leaks and engine operation.

VALVE ARRANGEMENT

1.9L
  E–I–I–E–E–I–I–E (front-to-rear)
2.0L
  E–I–I–E–E–I–I–E (front-to-rear)
2.2L
  E–I–I–E–E–I–I–E (front-to-rear)
2.5L
  I–E–I–E–E–I–E–I (front-to-rear)
2.8L
  E–I–I–E–I–E (left bank – front-to-rear)
  E–I–E–I–I–E (right bank – front-to-rear)
4.3L
  E–I–E–I–I–E (left bank – front-to-rear)
  E–I–I–E–I–E (right bank – front-to-rear)

IDLE SPEED AND MIXTURE ADJUSTMENTS

Carbureted Engines

1.9L Engine

In order to adjust the idle mixture, first remove the plug that covers the mixture screw.

1. Set the parking brake, block the drive wheels and place the transmission in Neutral.

2. Remove the carburetor from the engine, place it on a work bench and turn it upside down.

3. Using a punch and a hammer, carefully drive the idle mixture screw metal plug from the base of the carburetor.

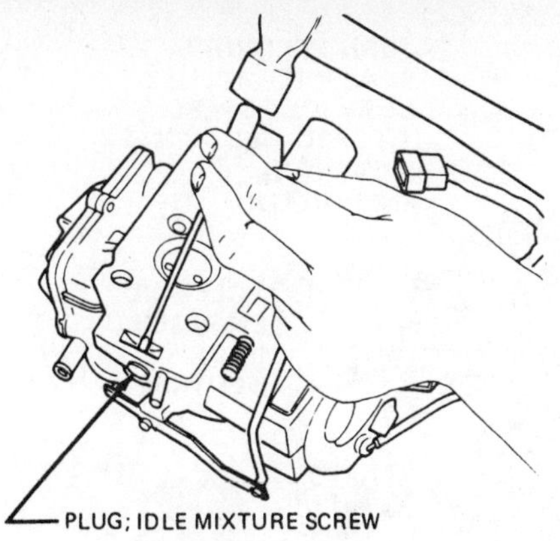

Removing the mixture screw plug — 1.9L engine

4. Reinstall the carburetor onto the engine. Start the engine and adjust the idle speed.

5. Allow the engine to reach normal operating temperatures, the choke must be Open and the air conditioning, if equipped, turned **OFF**. Disconnect and plug the distributor vacuum line, the EGR vacuum line and the idle compensator vacuum lines.

6. Turn the mixture screw all the way in, then back it out $1^{1}/_{2}$ turns.

NOTE: *After adjustment. Reset the throttle adjusting screw to 850 rpm for manual transmission or 950 rpm for automatic transmission.*

10. Turn the idle mixture screw (clockwise) until the engine speed is reduced to 800 rpm for manual transmission or 900 rpm for automatic transmission.

11. If equipped with air conditioning, perform the following procedures:

a. Turn the air conditioning to **MAX** Cold and the blower to **HIGH**.

b. Open the throttle to $1/3$ and allow it to close; this allows the speed-up solenoid to reach full travel.

c. Adjust the speed-up controller adjusting screw to set the idle to 900 rpm.

2.0L and 2.8L Engines

NOTE: *The idle mixture adjustments are factory set and sealed; no adjustment attempt should be made, except by an authorized GM dealer.*

WITHOUT AIR CONDITIONING

1. Refer to the emission control label on the vehicle and prepare the engine for adjustments.

2. Remove the air cleaner, set the parking brake and block the drive wheels.

3. Connect a tachometer to the distributor connector.

4. Place the transmission in **D** for automatic transmission or Neutral for manual transmission; make sure the solenoid is energized.

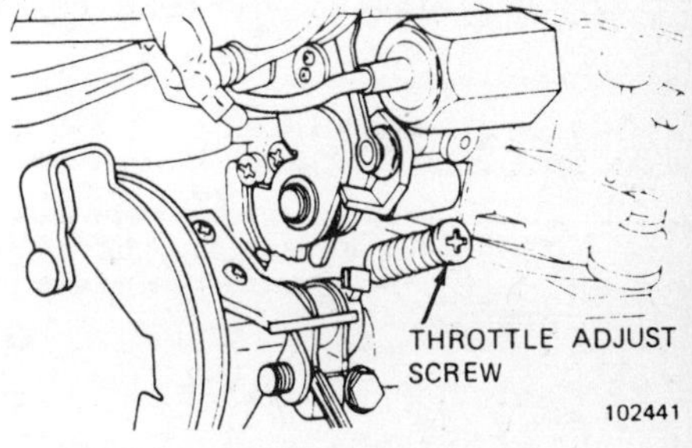

Adjusting the idle speed — 1.9L engine

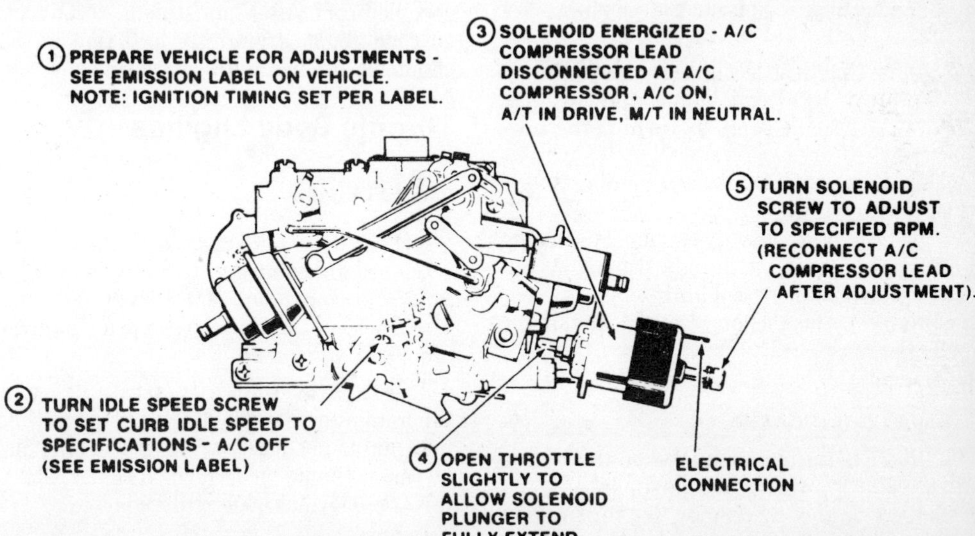

Adjusting the idle speed on E2SE carburetors without air conditioning — 2.0L and 2.8L engines

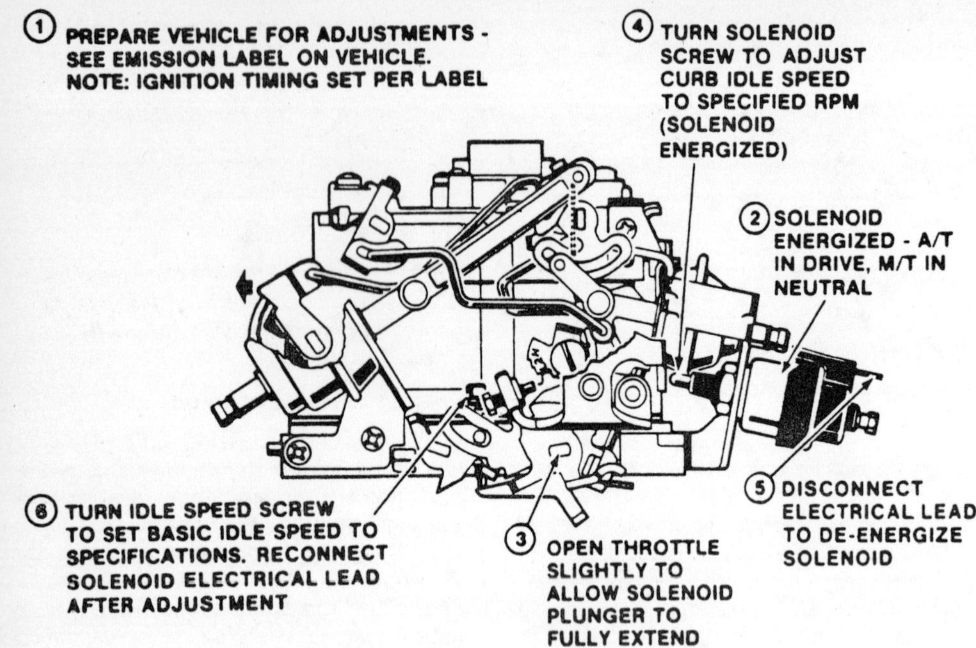

Adjusting the idle speed on E2SE carburetors with air conditioning — 2.0L and 2.8L engines

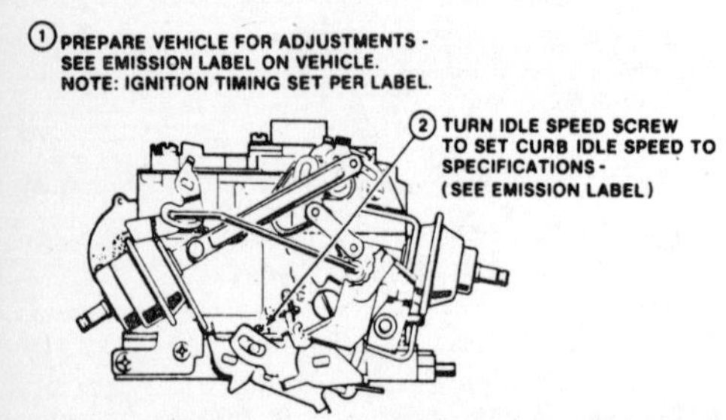

Adjusting the idle speed on the 2SE carburetor without air conditioning — 2.0L and 2.8L engines

5. Open the throttle slightly to allow the solenoid plunger to extend. Adjust the curb idle speed to the specified rpm by turning the solenoid screw.

6. De-energize the solenoid by disconnecting the electrical lead.

7. Set the basic idle speed rpm by turning the idle speed screw. After adjustment, reconnect the solenoid electrical lead.

8. Remove the tachometer and install the air cleaner.

WITH AIR CONDITIONING

1. Refer to the emission label on the vehicle and prepare the engine for adjustments.

2. Remove the air cleaner, set the parking brake and block the drive wheels.

3. Connect a tachometer to the distributor connector.

4. Place the transmission in **D** for automatic transmission or Neutral for manual transmission; make sure the solenoid is energized.

5. Turn the air conditioning **OFF** and set the curb idle speed by turning the idle speed screw.

6. Disconnect the air conditioning lead from the air conditioning compressor; make sure the solenoid is energized. Open the throttle slightly to allow the solenoid plunger to extend.

7. Turn the solenoid screw to adjust to the specified rpm. After adjustment, reconnect the air conditioning compressor lead, remove the tachometer and install the air cleaner.

Throttle Body Engines

2.5L EFI Engine

NOTE: *The following procedures require the use a tachometer, GM tool J-33047, BT-8207 or equivalent, GM Torx Bit 20, silicone sealant, a $\frac{5}{32}$ in. drill bit, a prick punch and a $\frac{1}{16}$ in. pin punch.*

The throttle stop screw, used in regulating the minimum idle speed, is adjusted at the factory and is not necessary to perform. This adjustment should be performed ONLY when the throttle body has been replaced.

NOTE: *The replacement of the complete throttle body assembly will have the minimum idle adjusted at the factory.*

1. Remove the air cleaner and the gasket. Be sure to plug the THERMAC vacuum port (air cleaner vacuum line-to-throttle body) on the throttle body.

2. Remove the throttle valve cable from the throttle control bracket to provide access to the minimum air adjustment screw.

3. Using the manufacturer's instructions, connect a tachometer to the engine.

4. Remove the electrical connector from the Idle Air Control (IAC) valve, located on the throttle body.

5. To remove the throttle stop screw cover, perform the following procedures:

   a. Using a prick punch, mark the housing at the top over the center line of the throttle stop screw.

   b. Using a $^5/_{32}$ in. drill bit, drill (on an angle) a hole through the casting to the hardened cover.

   c. Using a $^1/_{16}$ in. pin punch, place it through the hole and drive out the cover to expose the throttle stop screw.

6. Place the transmission in **P** for automatic transmission or Neutral for manual transmission, start the engine and allow the idle speed to stabilize.

7. Using the GM tool J-33047, BT-8207 or equivalent, install it into the idle air passage of the throttle body; be sure the tool is fully seated in the opening and no air leaks exist.

8. Using the GM Torx Bit 20, turn the throttle stop screw until the engine speed is 475–525 rpm for automatic transmission in **P** or 750–800 rpm for manual transmission in Neutral.

9. With the idle speed adjusted, stop the engine, remove the tool J-33047, BT-8207 or equivalent, from the throttle body.

10. Reconnect the Idle Air Control (IAC) electrical connector.

11. Using silicone sealant or equivalent, cover the throttle stop screw.

12. Reinstall the gasket and the air cleaner assembly.

2.8L EFI Engine

1. Remove the idle stop screw plug by piercing it with an awl.

2. With the idle air control motor connected, ground the diagnostic connector.

3. Turn the ignition **ON** and wait 30 seconds, do not start the engine.

4. Disconnect the idle air control connector with the ignition **ON**.

5. Remove the ground from the diagnostic connector and start the engine.

6. Adjust the idle stop screw to 700 rpm with the transmission in Neutral.

7. Turn the ignition **OFF** and reconnect the idle air control motor connector.

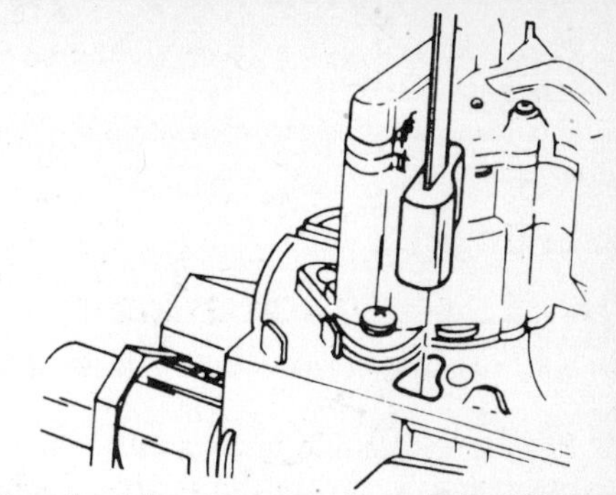

Plug the idle passages of each throttle body as shown

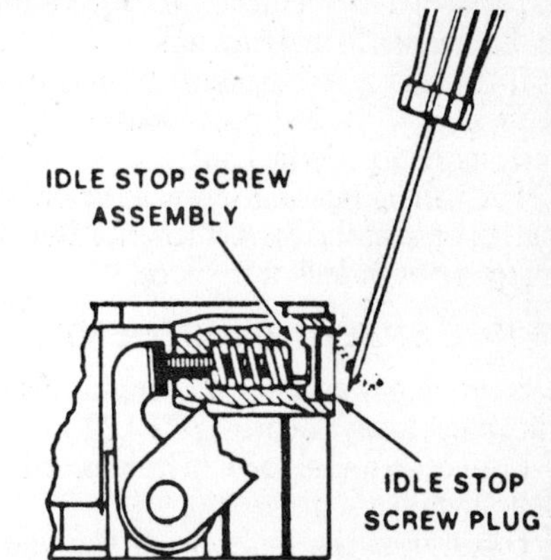

Removing the idle stop screw plug

8. Disconnect the electrical connector from the throttle position sensor (TPS), then install jumper wires between the TPS and the electrical connector.

9. Loosen the throttle position sensor screws.

10. With the ignition switch turned **ON**, check the voltage between terminals **B** and **C**; they should be 0.420V and 0.450V. If necessary, rotate the TPS to obtain the correct voltage.

11. With the voltage correct, tighten the mounting screws.

12. Reconnect the electrical connector and the air cleaner.

NOTE: *After installing the electrical connector to the TPS, it is a good idea to recheck the TPS voltage.*

FAST IDLE ADJUSTMENT

Carburetor Engines

2.0L AND 2.8L ENGINES

NOTE: *Following the adjustment of the idle speed, the fast idle speed may be adjusted.*

1. Place the transmission in **P** for automatic transmission or Neutral for manual transmission and refer to the recommendation on the emission label.

2. Place the fast idle screw on the highest step of the fast idle cam.

3. Turn the fast idle screw to obtain the specified fast idle rpm.

Diesel Engine

SLOW IDLE SPEED ADJUSTMENT

1. Set parking brake and block drive wheels.

2. Place transmission in Neutral.

3. Start and warm up the engine. Engine coolant temperature above 176°F (80°C).

4. Connect a diesel tachometer according to the manufacturer's instructions.

5. If the idle speed deviates from the specified range of 700–800 rpm, loosen the idle speed adjusting screw locknut.

6. Turn the adjusting screw in or out until the idle speed is in the correct range. After tightening the locknut, lock it in place.

FAST IDLE SPEED ADJUSTMENT

1. Start and warm up the engine. Engine coolant temperature above 176°F (80°).

2. Connect a diesel tachometer according to the manufacturer's instructions.

3. Disconnect the hoses from the vacuum

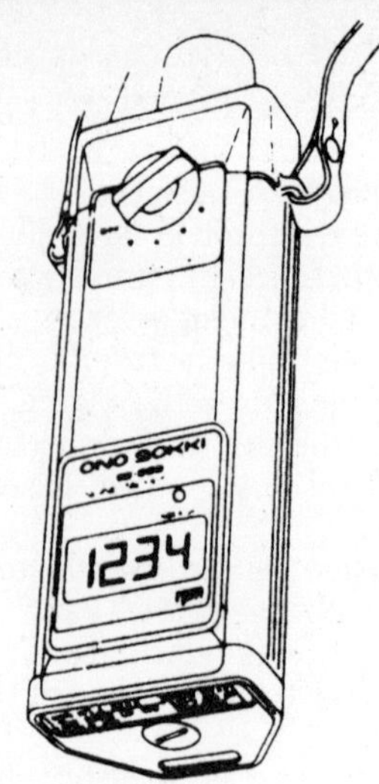

Diesel tachometer

switch valve, then connect a pipe (4mm dia.) in position between the hoses.

4. Loosen adjust nut and adjust engine idle speed by moving the nut. Fast idle should be 900–950 rpm.

5. Tighten the locknut.

6. Remove engine tachometer.

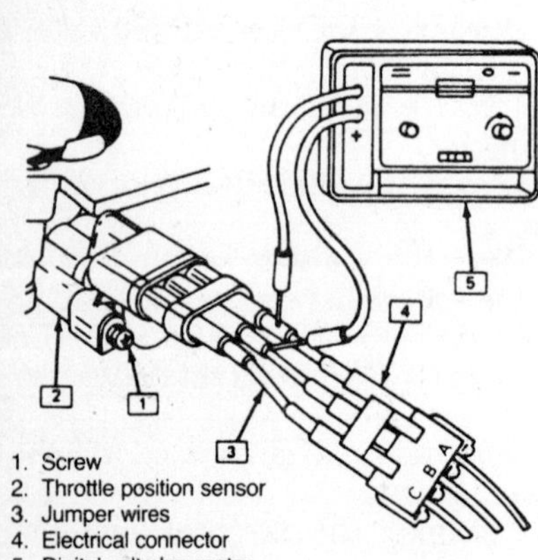

1. Screw
2. Throttle position sensor
3. Jumper wires
4. Electrical connector
5. Digital volt-ohm meter

Adjusting the throttle position sensor

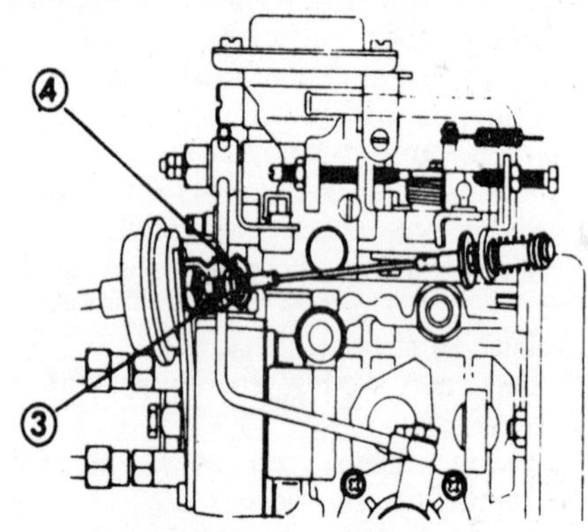

Fast idle adjustment 1983 2.2L diesel engine

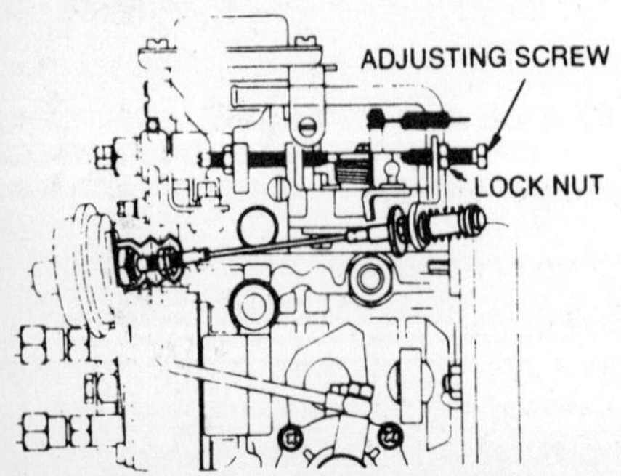

Fast idle adjustment 1984–85 2.2L diesel engine

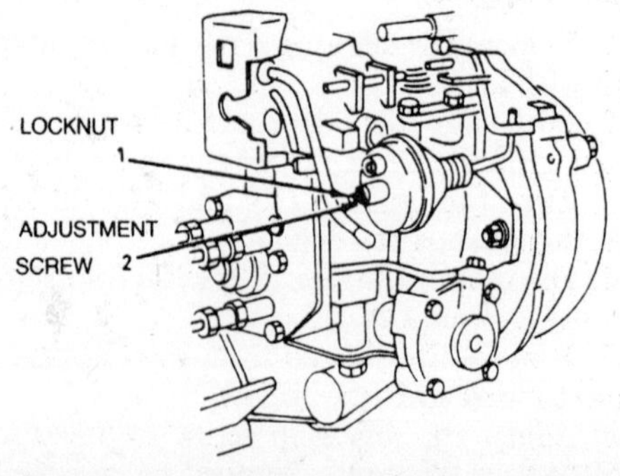

Idle speed adjustment points for the 1983 2.2L diesel engine

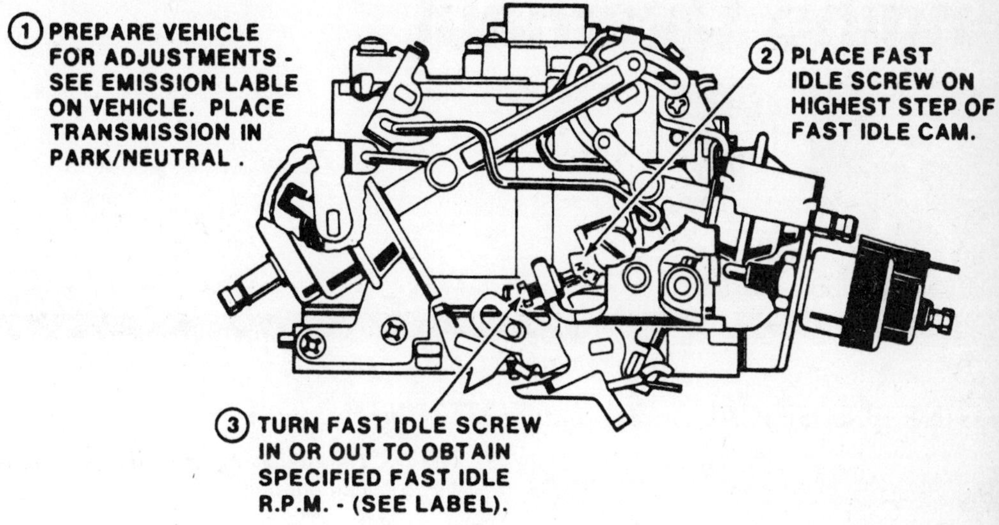

Fast idle adjustment procedure

ENGINE ELECTRICAL

Ignition Coil

The ignition coil on the 1.9L and 2.0L engines, are attached to bracket on the inner fender, located on the right side of the engine compartment; on the 2.5L engine, it is attached to the cylinder head, located on the right rear side of the engine; on the 2.8L engine, it is attached to a valve cover bracket, located on the right rear side of the engine; on the 4.3L engine, it is mounted on a bracket, attached to the rear of the intake manifold in front of the distributor.

TESTING

NOTE: *The following procedures require the use of an ohmmeter.*

1.9L and 2.0L Engines

For this procedure, the ignition coil may be removed from the vehicle or simply remove the electrical connectors and test it in the vehicle.

1. Remove the ignition coil from the vehicle.
2. Inspect the outer face of the coil for cracking, rusting and/or damage; be sure to inspect the high tension socket.
3. Using an ohmmeter, place one probe on the outer terminal of the electrical connector

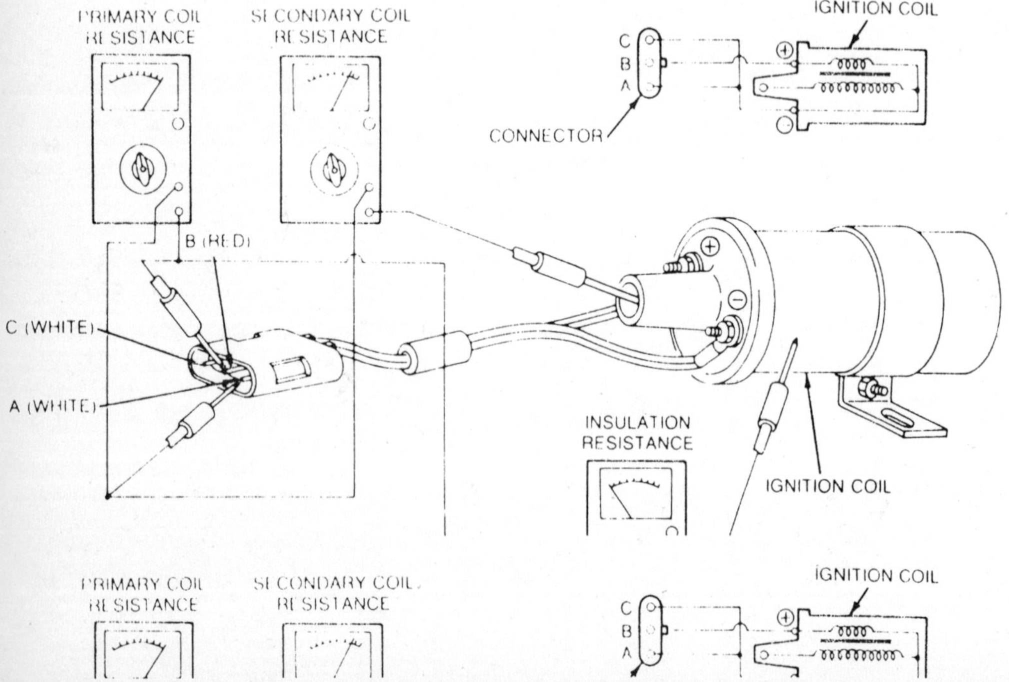

Testing the Non-EST ignition coil

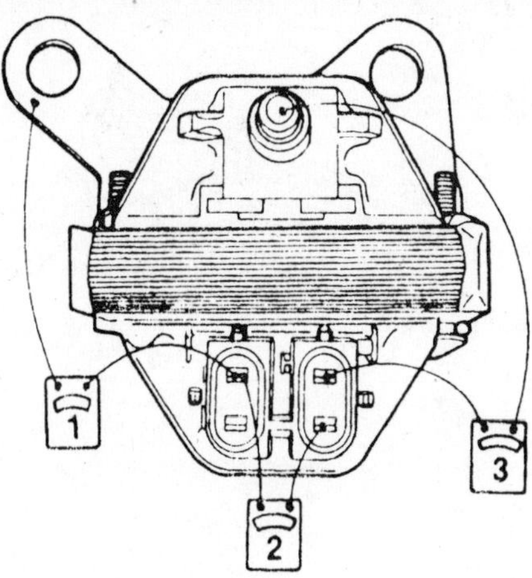

Testing the EST ignition coil

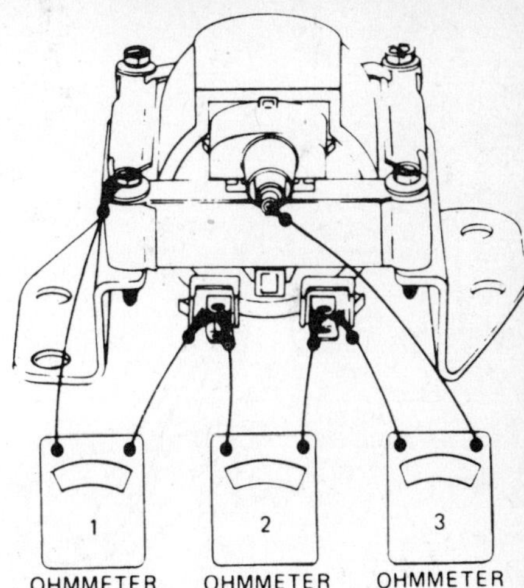

Using an ohmmeter to inspect the primary, secondary and insulation resistance of the ignition coil — 2.5L and 2.8L engines

and the other probe on the center terminal of the electrical connector, then inspect the primary coil resistance, it should be between 0.090–1.40 ohms.

4. Using an ohmmeter, place one probe on the outer terminal of the electrical connector and the other probe on the center terminal of the coil, then inspect the secondary coil resistance, it should be between 7,300–11,100 ohms.

5. Using an ohmmeter, place one probe on the outer terminal of the electrical connector and the other probe on the outer shell of the coil, then inspect the insulation resistance of the coil, it should be less than 1,000,000 ohms.

6. If the coil does not conform to these inspections, replace the coil.

2.5L, 2.8L and 4.3L Engines

For this procedure, the ignition coil may be removed from the engine or simply remove the electrical connectors and test it on the engine.

1. Using an ohmmeter (on the high scale), connect the probes between the primary (low voltage) terminal and coil ground; the reading should be very high or infinity, if not, replace the coil.

2. Using an ohmmeter (on the low scale), connect the probes between both primary (low voltage) terminals; the reading should be very low or zero, if not, replace the coil.

3. Using an ohmmeter (on the high scale), connect the probes between a primary (low voltage) terminal and the secondary (high voltage) terminal; the reading should be high (not infinite), if not, replace the coil.

REMOVAL AND INSTALLATION

1.9L and 2.0L Engines

1. Disconnect the negative battery terminal from the battery.

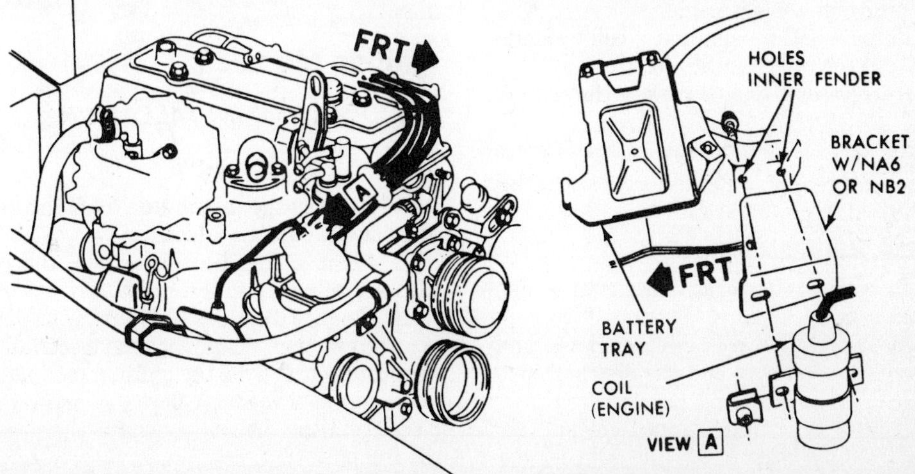

Ignition coil and distributor — 1.9L and 2.0L engine

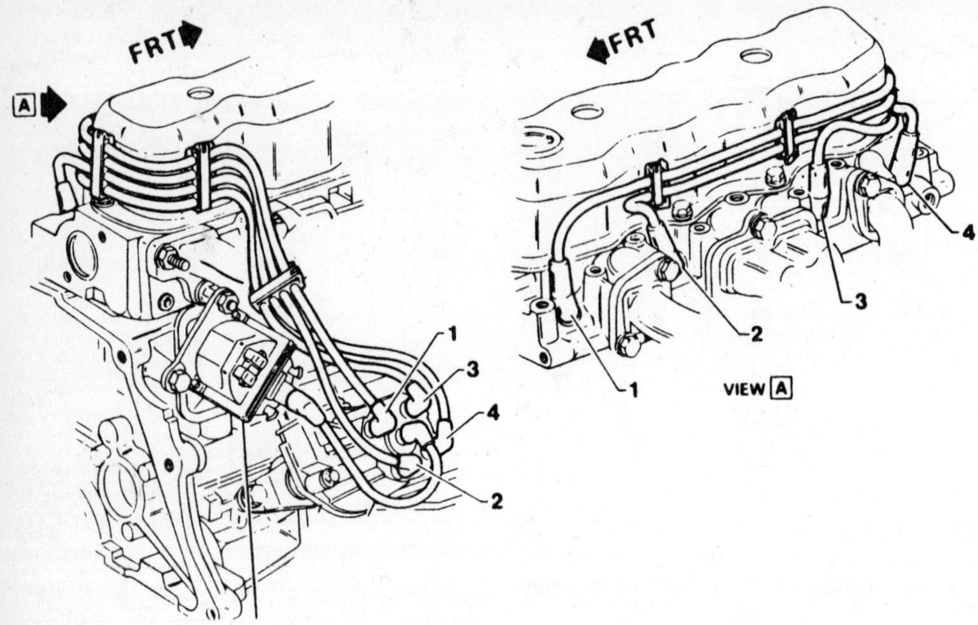

Ignition coil and distributor — 2.5L engine

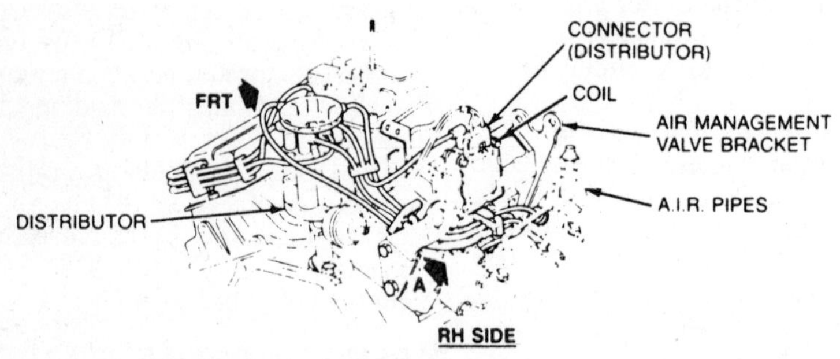

Ignition coil and distributor — 4.3L engine

2. From the ignition coil, disconnect the primary electrical wiring connector and the coil-to-distributor high tension cable.

3. Remove the ignition coil-to-fender screws and the coil from the vehicle.

4. If necessary, test or replace the ignition coil.

5. To install, reverse the removal procedures. Reinstall the wires and the battery terminal.

2.5L, 2.8L and 4.3L Engines

1. Disconnect the negative battery terminal from the battery.

2. At the ignition coil, disconnect the ignition switch-to-coil wire and the distributor-to-coil wires.

3. Remove the coil-to-engine nuts/bolts and the coil from the engine.

4. If necessary, test or replace the ignition coil.

5. To install, reverse the removal procedures. Reinstall the wires and the battery terminal.

Ignition Module

REMOVAL AND INSTALLATION

1.9L and 2.0L Engines

1. Remove the distributor from the engine and place it on a work bench.

2. Remove the distributor cap, the rotor, the packing ring and the cover.

3. Remove the electrical harness-to-distributor screw, then disconnect the electrical harness connectors from the ignition module.

4. Using 2 medium prybars, pry the pole piece from the distributor shaft, then remove the roll pin.

5. Using a Phillips Head screwdriver, remove the ignition module-to-breaker plate

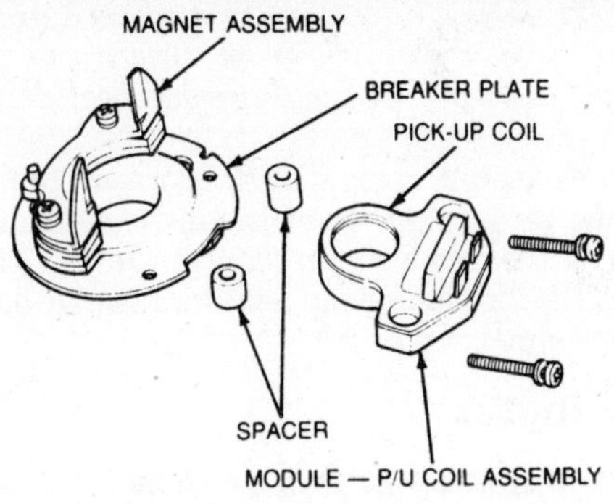

Exploded view of the ignition module and the breaker plate assembly

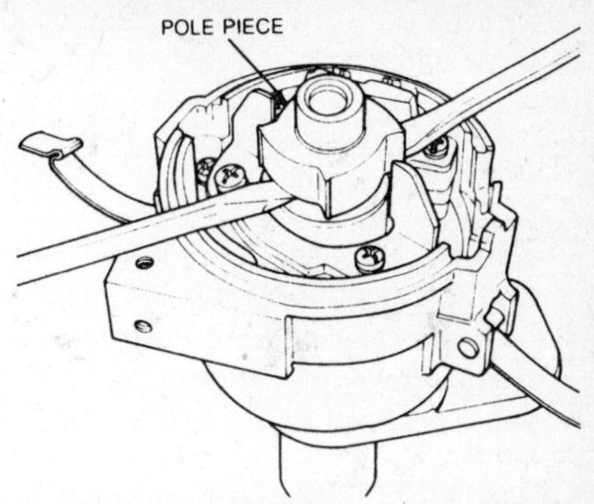

Using two pry bars to remove the pole piece from the distributor shaft on the Non-EST distributor

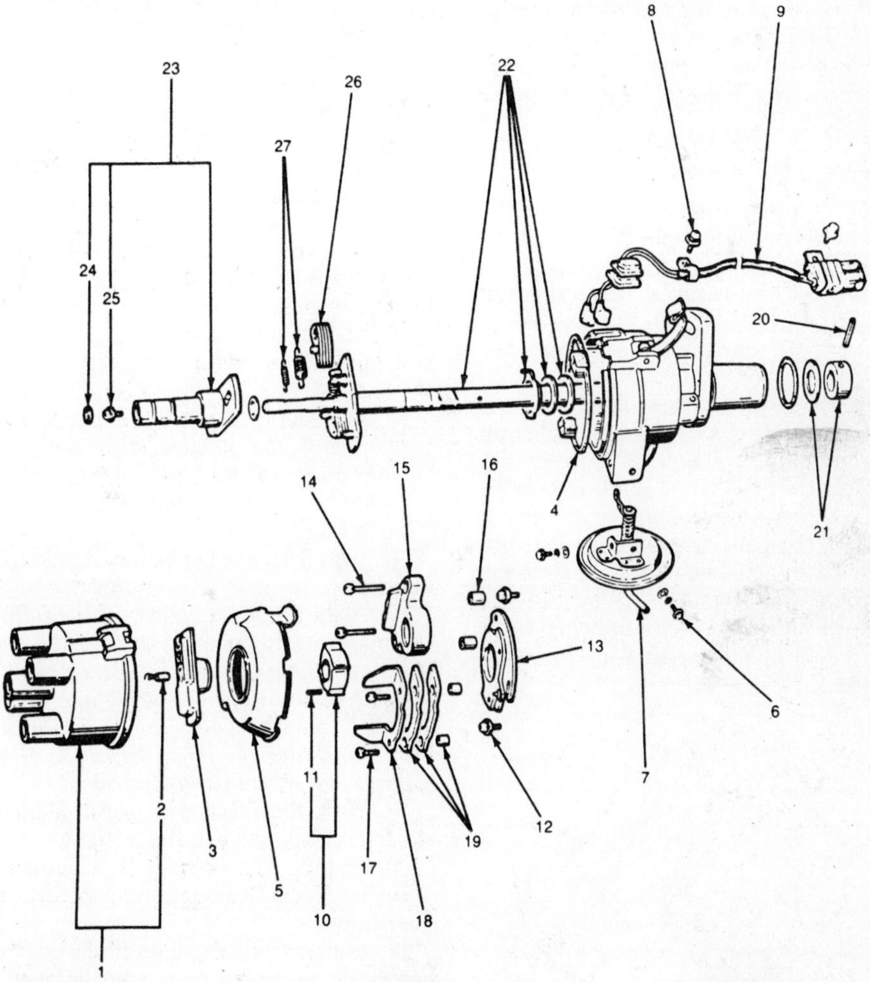

1. Cap assembly	10. Pole piece	19. Magnet set
2. Carbon point	11. Roll pin	20. Roll pin
3. Rotor head	12. Screw	21. Collar
4. Packing	13. Breaker plate assembly	22. Shaft assembly
5. Cover	14. Screw	23. Rotor shaft assembly
6. Screw	15. P/U coil module assembly	24. Packing
7. Vacuum control assembly	16. Spacer	25. Screw
8. Screw	17. Screw	26. Governor weight
9. Harness assembly	18. Stator	27. Governor spring

Exploded view of the Non-EST distributor

screws and lift the module from the distributor; be sure to remove the spacers from the module.

6. If the module is suspected as being defective, take it to a module testing machine and have it tested.

7. To install, replace the ignition module, spacers and screws onto the breaker plate.

NOTE: *When replacing the module, sure to coat the module-to-distributor surface with silicone lubricant that will provide heat dissipation.*

8. Install the pole piece onto the distributor shaft, followed by the new roll pin.

NOTE: *If the breaker plate was loosened, use a 0.12–0.20 in. (3–5mm) feeler gauge to measure the air gap between the pole piece and the breaker plate stator.*

9. To complete the installation, reverse the removal procedures. Reinstall the distributor onto the engine.

2.5L, 2.8L and 4.3L Engines

The ignition modules are located inside the distributor; they may be replaced without removing the distributor from the engine.

1. Disconnect the negative battery terminal.

2. Remove the distributor cap and the rotor.

3. If the flange, of the distributor shaft, is positioned above the module, place a socket on the crankshaft pulley bolt and rotate the crankshaft (turning the distributor shaft) to provide clearance to the ignition module.

4. Remove the ignition module-to-distributor screws, lift the module and disconnect the electrical connectors from it.

5. If the module is suspected as being defective, take it to a module testing machine and have it tested.

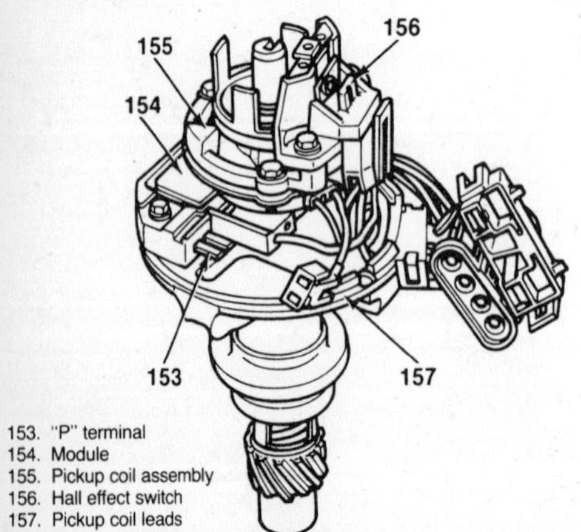

EST distributor used on the 2.5L 4-cylinder and all 6-cylinder engines

NOTE: *When replacing the module, sure to coat the module-to-distributor surface with silicone lubricant that will provide heat dissipation.*

6. To install, apply silicone lubricant to the module mounting area of the distributor and reverse the removal procedures. Install the rotor, the distributor cap and the negative battery terminal.

Distributor

REMOVAL AND INSTALLATION

Undisturbed Engine

This condition exists if the engine has not been rotated with the distributor removed.

1. Disconnect the negative battery terminal from the battery.

2. Tag and disconnect the electrical connector(s) from the distributor.

3. Remove the distributor cap (do not remove the ignition wires) from the distributor and move it aside.

4. Using a crayon or chalk, make locating marks (for installation purposes) on the rotor, the ignition module, the distributor housing and the engine.

5. Loosen and remove the distributor clamp bolt and clamp, then lift the distributor from the engine.

NOTE: *Noting the relative position of the rotor and the module alignment marks, make a second mark on the rotor to align it with the one mark on the module.*

To install:

6. Install a new O-ring on the distributor housing.

7. Align the second mark on the rotor with the mark on the module, then install the distributor, taking care to align the mark on the housing with the one on the engine.

NOTE: *It may be necessary to lift the distributor and turn the rotor slightly to align the gears and the oil pump driveshaft.*

8. With the respective marks aligned, install the clamp and bolt finger-tight.

9. Install and secure the distributor cap.

10. Connect the electrical connector(s) to the distributor.

11. Connect a timing light to the engine (following the manufacturer's instructions). Start the engine, then check and/or adjust the timing.

12. Turn the engine **OFF**, tighten the distributor clamp bolt and remove the timing light.

Disturbed Engine

This condition exists when the engine has been rotated with the distributor removed.

1. Disconnect the negative battery terminal from the battery.

2. Tag and disconnect the electrical connector(s) from the distributor.

3. Remove the distributor cap (do not remove the ignition wires) from the distributor and move it aside.

4. Using a crayon or chalk, make locating marks (for installation purposes) on the rotor, the ignition module, the distributor housing and the engine.

5. Loosen and remove the distributor clamp bolt and clamp, then lift the distributor from the engine.

NOTE: *Noting the relative position of the rotor and the module alignment marks, make a second mark on the rotor to align it with the one mark on the module.*

To install:

6. Install a new O-ring on the distributor housing.

7. Rotate the crankshaft to position the No. 1 cylinder on the TDC of it's compression stroke. This may be determined by inserting a rag into the No. 1 spark plug hole and slowly turn the engine crankshaft. When the timing mark on the crankshaft pulley aligns with the **0** degree mark on the timing scale and the rag is blown out by the compression, the No. 1 piston is at Top Dead Center (TDC).

8. Turn the rotor so it will point to the No. 1 terminal of the distributor cap.

9. Install the distributor into the engine block. It may be necessary to turn the rotor, a little in either direction, in order to engage the gears.

10. Tap the starter a few times to ensure that the oil pump shaft is mated to the distributor shaft.

11. Bring the engine to No. 1 TDC again and check to see that the rotor is indeed pointing toward the No. 1 terminal of the cap.

12. With the respective marks aligned, install the clamp and bolt finger-tight.

13. Install and secure the distributor cap.

14. Connect the electrical connector(s) to the distributor.

NOTE: *If equipped with a vacuum line, reconnect it.*

15. Connect a timing light to the engine (following the manufacturer's instructions). Start the engine, then check and/or adjust the timing.

16. Turn the engine **OFF**, tighten the distributor clamp bolt and remove the timing light.

Alternator

The alternators, used on the 1986–91 2.8L and 1988–91 4.3L engines, experienced engineering changes, which are: The elimination of the diode trio and the reduction of the external wiring connectors from 3-to-2 wires.

NOTE: *The new alternators are not serviceable and no periodic maintenance is required.*

ALTERNATOR PRECAUTIONS

To prevent damage to the on-board computer, alternator and regulator, the following precautionary measures must be taken when working with the electrical system.

• Never reverse the battery connections. Always check the battery polarity visually. This is to be done before any connections are made to be sure all of the connections correspond to the battery ground polarity.

• Booster batteries for starting must be connected properly. Make sure the positive cable of the booster battery is connected to the positive terminal of the battery that is getting the boost. This applies to both negative and ground cables.

• Make sure the ignition switch is OFF when connecting or disconnecting any electrical component, especially on trucks equipped with an on-board computer control system.

• Disconnect the battery cables before using a fast charger; the charger has a tendency to force current through the diodes in

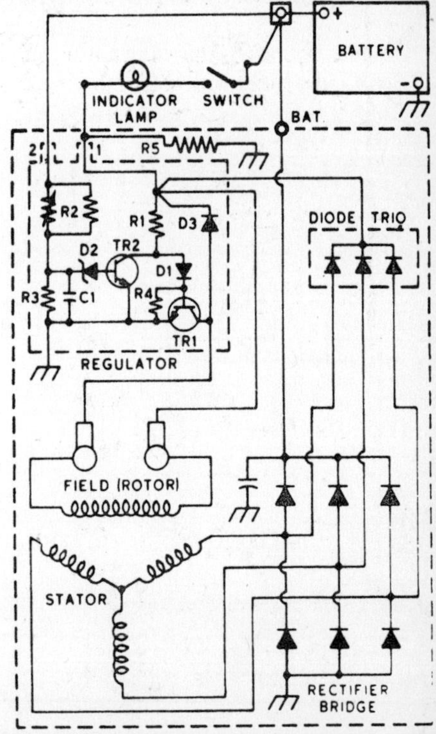

Schematic of the SI model alternator

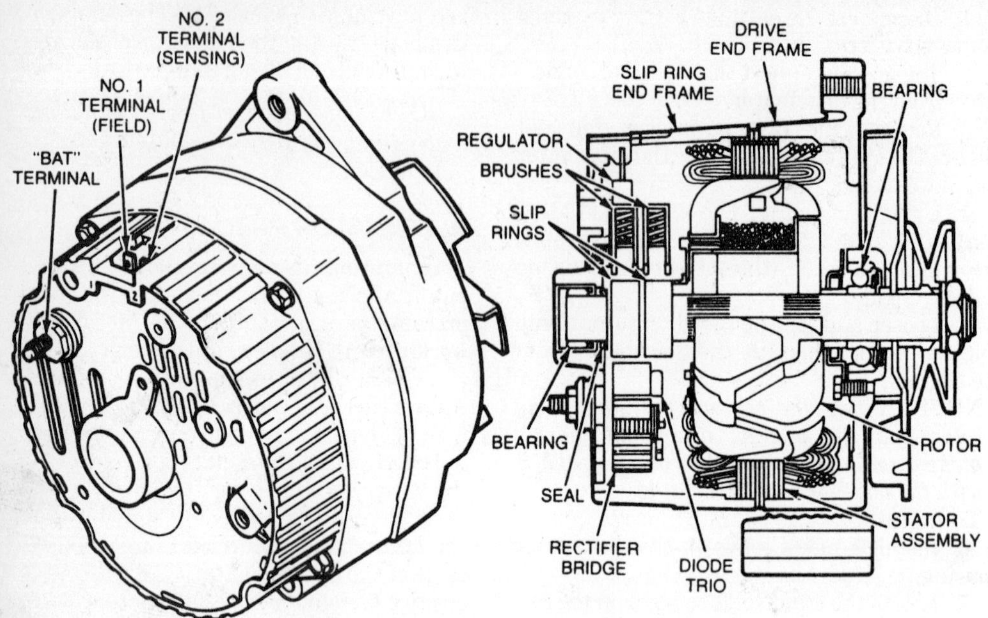

Sectional view of the SI model alternator

the opposite direction for which they were designed. This burns out the diodes.

• Never use a fast charger as a booster for starting the vehicle.

• Never disconnect the voltage regulator while the engine is running.

• Do not ground the alternator output terminal.

• Do not operated the alternator on an open circuit with the field energized.

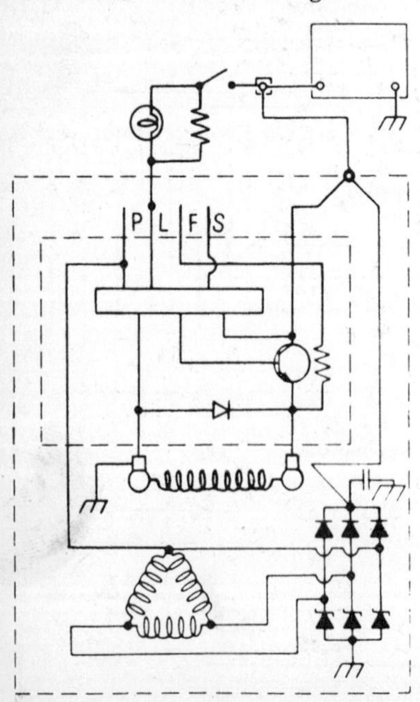

Schematic of the CS model alternator

• Do not attempt to polarize an alternator.

REMOVAL AND INSTALLATION

NOTE: *The following procedures require the use of GM belt tension gauge BT-33-95-ACBN (regular V-belts) or BT-33-97M (poly V-belts). The belt should deflect about $^1/_4$ in. (6mm) over a 7–10 in. (178–254mm) span or $^1/_2$ in. (12.7mm) over a 13–16 in. (330–406mm) span at this point.*

1. Disconnect the negative battery terminal from the battery.

2. If equipped, remove the air pump to gain access to the alternator.

3. Label and disconnect the alternator's electrical connectors.

4. Remove the alternator brace bolt and the drive belt.

5. Support the alternator, then remove the mounting bolts and the unit from the vehicle.

To install:

6. To install, reverse the removal procedures and adjust the drive belt tension. Torque the top mounting bolt to 22 ft. lbs. and the lower mounting bolt to 24–35 ft. lbs. Reconnect the negative battery terminal.

7. To adjust the drive belt, perform the following procedures:

a. If the belt is Cold, operate the engine (at idle speed) for 15 minutes; the belt will seat itself in the pulleys allowing the belt fibers to relax or stretch. If the belt is hot, allow it to cool, until it is warm to the touch.

NOTE: *A used belt is one that has been rotated at least one complete revolution on the pulleys. This begins the belt seating process and it must never be tensioned to the new belt specifications.*

b. Loosen the component-to-mounting bracket bolts.

c. Using a GM belt tension gauge BT-33-95-ACBN (standard V-belts) or BT-33-97M (poly V-belts), place the tension gauge at the center of the belt between the longest span.

d. Applying belt tension pressure on the component, adjust the drive belt tension to the correct specifications.

e. While holding the correct tension on the component, tighten the component-to-mounting bracket bolt.

f. When the belt tension is correct, remove the tension gauge.

Regulator

The voltage regulators are sealed units mounted within the alternator body and are nonadjustable.

REMOVAL AND INSTALLATION

NOTE: *This procedure is to be performed with the alternator removed from the vehicle. The new alternators—CS-130 models—on 1986–89 2.8L and 1988–91 4.3L engines, are non-serviceable; if the alternator proves to be defective, simply replace it.*

1. Mark scribe lines on the end-frames to make the reassembly easier.

2. Remove the 4 through-bolts and sepa-

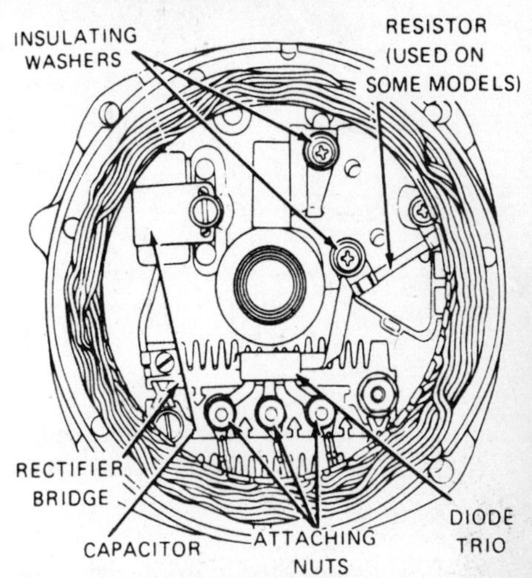

View of the alternator end frame — all except 1986–91 2.8L and 1988–91 4.3L engines

rate the drive end-frame assembly from the rectifier end-frame assembly.

3. Remove the 3 diode trio attaching nuts and the 3 regulator attaching screws.

4. Remove the diode trio and the regulator from the end frame.

NOTE: *Before installing the regulator, push the brushes into the brush holder and install a brush retainer or a tooth pick to hold the brushes in place.*

5. To install the regulator, reverse the removal procedures. After the alternator is assembled, remove the brush retainer.

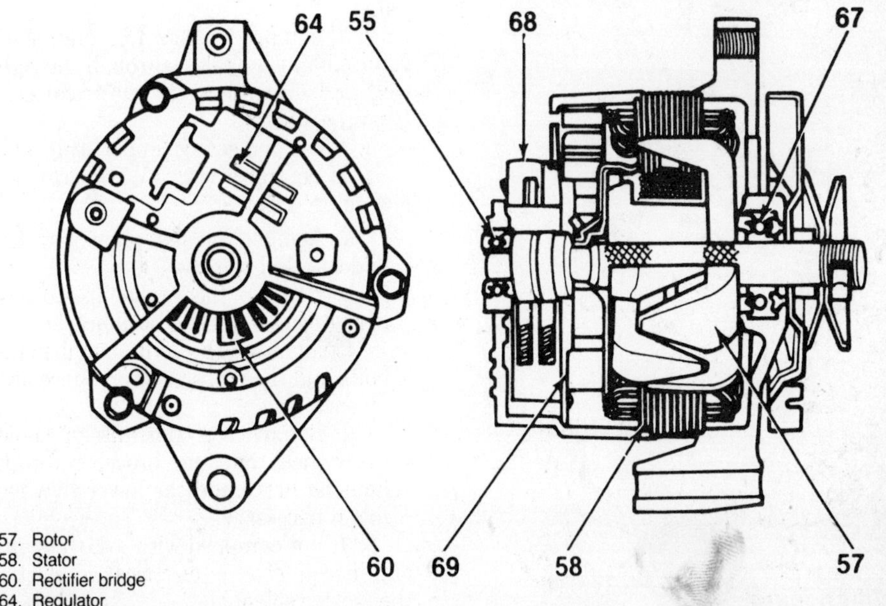

Sectional view of the CS model alternator

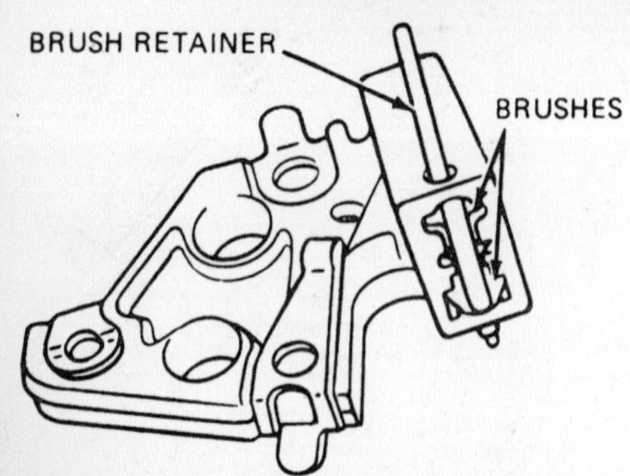

Voltage regulator with the brushes depressed — all except 1986–91 2.8L and 1988–91 4.3L engines

Battery

The battery is mounted in front, right side of the engine compartment. It is a non-tamperable type with side mounted terminals.

REMOVAL AND INSTALLATION

1. Disconnect the negative battery terminal, then the positive battery terminal.
2. Remove the battery hold-down retainer.
3. Remove the battery from the vehicle.
4. Inspect the battery, the cables and the battery carrier for damage.
5. To install, reverse the removal procedures. Torque the battery retainer to 11 ft. lbs., the top bar to 8 ft. lbs., if equipped, and the battery cable terminals to 10 ft. lbs.

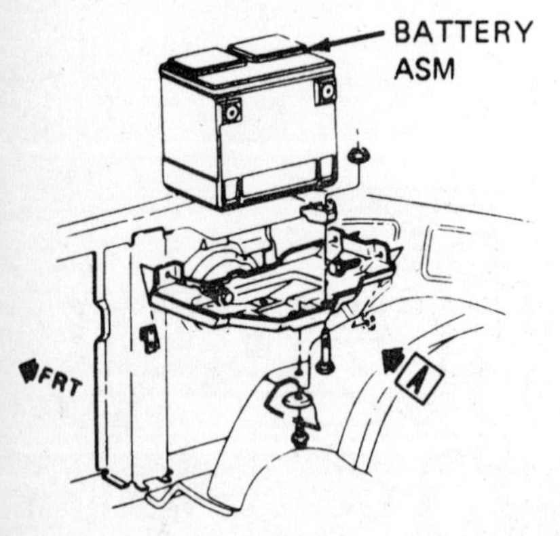

Replacing the battery

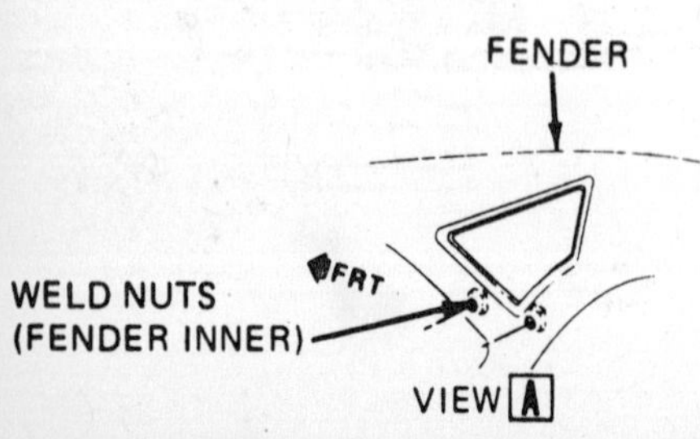

ADJUSTMENTS

No adjustments are necessary or possible. If the battery is determined to be defective (other than charging), discard it.

Starter

The gasoline starter is located on the lower right side (gasoline engines) or on the lower left side (diesel engine). The diesel engine starter is a gear reduction type.

REMOVAL AND INSTALLATION

1983–86

1. Disconnect the negative battery terminal from the battery.
2. Raise and safely support the vehicle.
3. If equipped, remove any starter braces or shields that may be in the way.
4. Label and disconnect the electrical connectors from the starter solenoid.
5. Remove the starter-to-engine bolts, nuts, washers and shims. Allow the starter to drop, then remove it from the engine.

NOTE: *Be sure to keep the shims in order so they may be reinstalled in the same order.*

6. To install, reverse the removal procedures. Torque the starter-to-engine bolts to 30 ft. lbs. Connect the wires to the starter solenoid and the negative battery cable.

1987–91

1. Disconnect the negative battery terminal.
2. If equipped with a 4.3L engine, raise the vehicle half way, reach through the right wheel well and disconnect the electrical connectors from the starter.
3. Raise and safely support the vehicle.
4. If equipped with 4WD, perform the following procedures:

   a. Remove the skid plate-to-chassis bolts and the skid plate.

   b. Remove the brake line-to-crossmember bracket bolts and both brackets.

   c. Remove the crossmember-to-chassis bolts and the crossmember; there are 3 bolts on each side.

   d. Remove the transmission cooler lines-to-flywheel housing brace, rod-to-flywheel housing brace and the lower flywheel housing, if necessary.

5. If not equipped with a 4.3L engine, label and disconnect the electrical connectors from the starter solenoid.
6. Remove the starter-to-engine bolts, nuts, washers and shim(s). Allow the starter to drop, then remove it from the engine.

STARTER SPECIFICATIONS

Years	Engine No. Cyl. (cu. in.) L	Series	Type	No-Load Test Amps	Volts	RPM
1983	4 (121) 2.0	5MT	—	50–75	10	6,000–11,900
	6 (173) 2.8	5MT	—	45–70	10	7,000–11,900
1984	4 (121) 2.0	5MT	—	50–75	10	6,000–11,900
	6 (173) 2.8	5MT	—	50–75	10	6,000–11,900
1985	4 (121) 2.0	5MT	—	50–75	10	6,000–11,900
	6 (173) 2.8	5MT	—	50–75	10	6,000–11,900
1986	4 (151) 2.5	5MT	101	50–75	10	6,000–11,900
	6 (173) 2.8	5MT	101	50–75	10	6,000–11,900
1987	4 (151) 2.5	5MT	101	50–75	10	6,000–11,900
	6 (173) 2.8	5MT	101	50–75	10	6,000–11,900
1988	4 (151) 2.5	5MT	101	50–75	10	6,000–11,900
	6 (173) 2.8	5MT	101	50–75	10	6,000–11,900
	6 (262) 4.3	PG-200	—	50–90	10	2,330–2,660
1989	4 (151) 2.5	SD200	—	50–75	10	6,000–11,900
	6 (173) 2.8	SD200	—	50–75	10	6,000–11,900
	6 (262) 4.3	PG-200	—	45–90	10	2,150–2,660
1990	6 (262) 4.3	PG-200	—	45–90	10	2,150–2,660
1991	6 (262) 4.3	SD260	—	50–62	10	8,500–10,700

NOTE: *Be sure to keep the shims in order so they may be reinstalled in the same order.*

7. To install, reverse the removal procedures. Torque the starter-to-engine bolts to 31 ft. lbs. for 2.5L engine or 33 ft. lbs. for 2.8L and 4.3L engines. Connect the wires to the starter solenoid and the negative battery cable.

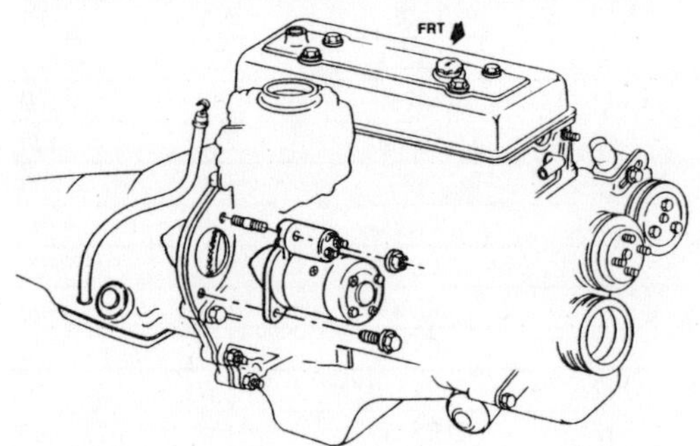

Starter mounting on the 1.9L and 2.0L engines

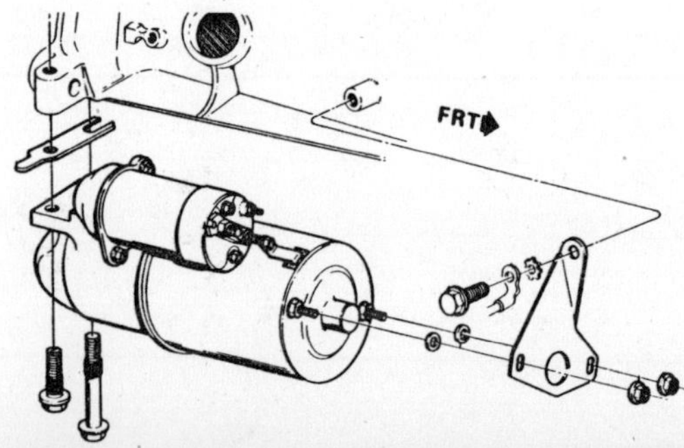

Starter mounting on the 2.5L engine; 2.8L and 4.3L engines are similar

SOLENOID REPLACEMENT

Direct Drive

1. Remove the starter, then place it on a workbench.

2. Remove the screw and the washer from the motor connector strap terminal.

3. Remove the 2 solenoid retaining screws.

4. Twist the solenoid housing clockwise to remove the flange key from the keyway in the housing, then remove the housing.

5. To install the unit, place the return spring on the plunger and place the solenoid body on the drive housing. Turn it counterclockwise to engage the flange key. Place the 2 retaining screws in position, then install the screw and washer which secures the strap terminal. Install the unit on the starter.

ENGINE MECHANICAL

Six engines and 3 fuel systems are used to power your S-10/S-15 vehicle, they are:

• 1983–85 Isuzu built 1.9L (118.9 cu. in.) 2-bbl.

• 1983–85 Chevy built 2.8L (173 cu. in.) 2-bbl.

• 1983–84 Chevy built 2.0L (121 cu. in.) 2-bbl.

• 1983–85 Isuzu built 2.2L (136.6 cu. in.) Diesel.

• 1985–89 Pontiac built 2.5L (151 cu. in.) TBI.

• 1986–89 Chevy built 2.8L (173 cu. in.)

ALTERNATOR AND REGULATOR SPECIFICATIONS

Years	Engine No. Cyl. (cu. in.) L	Alternator Field Current @ 12v (amps)	Output (amps)	Regulated Volts @ 75°F	Series	Rotation	Type
1983	4 (119) 1.9	4.0–5.0	37	12	10SI	CW	K85
		4.0–5.0	66	12	12SI	CW	K81
		4.0–5.0	78	12	12SI	CW	K64
	4 (121) 2.0	4.0–5.0	37	12	10SI	CW	K85
		4.0–5.0	66	12	12SI	CW	K81
		4.0–5.0	78	12	12SI	CW	K64
	6 (173) 2.8	4.0–5.0	37	12	10SI	CW	K85
		4.0–5.0	66	12	12SI	CW	K81
		4.0–5.0	78	12	12SI	CW	K64
1984	4 (119) 1.9	4.0–5.0	37	12	10SI	CW	K85
		4.0–5.0	66	12	12SI	CW	K81
		4.0–5.0	78	12	12SI	CW	K64
	4 (121) 2.0	4.0–5.0	37	12	10SI	CW	K85
		4.0–5.0	66	12	12SI	CW	K81
		4.0–5.0	78	12	12SI	CW	K64
	6 (173) 2.8	4.0–5.0	37	12	10SI	CW	K85
		4.0–5.0	66	12	12SI	CW	K81
		4.0–5.0	78	12	12SI	CW	K64
1985	4 (119) 1.9	4.0–5.0	37	12	10SI	CW	K85
		4.0–5.0	66	12	12SI	CW	K81
		4.0–5.0	78	12	12SI	CW	K64
	4 (151) 2.5	4.0–5.0	78	12	12SI	CW	100
	6 (173) 2.8	4.0–5.0	37	12	10SI	CW	K85
		4.0–5.0	66	12	12SI	CW	K81
		4.0–5.0	78	12	12SI	CW	K64
1986	4 (151) 2.5	4.0–5.0	78	12	12SI	CW	100
	6 (173) 2.8	5.4–6.4	85	12	CS130	CW	100
1987	4 (151) 2.5	4.0–5.0	78	12	12SI	CW	100
	6 (173) 2.8	5.4–6.4	85	12	CS130	CW	100
1988	4 (151) 2.5	4.8–5.7	85	12	CS130	CW	100
	6 (173) 2.8	4.8–5.7	85	12	CS130	CW	100
	6 (262) 4.3	5.7–7.1	85	12	CS130	CW	100
1989	4 (151) 2.5	6.0–7.5	96	12	CS130	CW	100
	6 (173) 2.8	4.8–5.7	85	12	CS130	CW	100
	6 (262) 4.3	5.7–7.1	85	12	CS130	CW	100
1990	6 (262) 4.3	5.7–7.1	85	12	CS130	CW	100
1991	6 (262) 4.3	5.7–7.1	85	12	CS130	CW	100
		6.0–7.5	100	12	CS130	CW	100

TBI.
• 1988–91 Chevy built 4.3L (262 cu. in.) TBI.

On the 1985, 2.5L EFI engine, the cylinder head and engine block are both constructed of cast iron. The valve guides are integral with the cylinder head and the rocker arms are retained by individual threaded shoulder bolts. Hydraulic roller lifters are incorporated to reduce the friction between the valve lifters and the camshaft lobes.

On the 1986–89, 2.5L EFI engine, a few changes appeared, such as: (1) the pistons were replaced with hypereutectic types (pistons embedded with silicone nodules in the walls to reduce the cylinder wall friction), (2) a reduced weight, high efficiency alternator and (3) a variable ratio air conditioner compressor.

The 2.8L engine utilizes a 2-bbl carburetor for 1983–85 or an EFI system for 1986–89 and the use of swirl chamber heads (to increase power and fuel efficiency). The engine block and cylinder heads are constructed of cast iron. Other major features are: a wider oil pan flange, raised rails inside the cylinder heads (to improve oil return control), machined rocker cover seal surfaces, a trough along the rocker cover rails (to channel oil away from the gasket) and even distribution of the clamping loads, to make this engine one of the most leak-resistant on the road today.

The 1988–91, 4.3L engine utilizes an EFI system and incorporates many of the design features used the 1986–89, 2.8L EFI engine. The engine is equipped with roller valve lifters instead of the standard flat bottom lifters. The roller lifter is still hydraulic, requiring no valve adjustment. The roller lifter incorporates a roller that rides along the cam lobe reducing friction and component wear. A roller lifter restrictor and retainer is needed to keep the lifter from turning in the bore while the engine is running.

Engine Overhaul Tips

Most engine overhaul procedures are fairly standard. In addition to specific parts replacement procedures and complete specifications for your individual engine, this Chapter also is a guide to accept rebuilding procedures. Examples of standard rebuilding practice are shown and should be used along with specific details concerning your particular engine.

Competent and accurate machine shop services will ensure maximum performance, reliability and engine life. Choose your machinist carefully. If the engine is not machined properly, engine failure will result within a short time period after installation.

On most instances it is more profitable for the do-it-yourself mechanic to remove, clean and inspect the component(s), buy the necessary parts and deliver these to a shop for actual machine work.

On the other hand, much of the rebuilding work (crankshaft, block, bearings, piston rods, and other components) is well within the scope of the do-it-yourself mechanic.

TOOLS

The tools required for an engine overhaul or parts replacement will depend on the depth of your involvement. With a few exceptions, they will be the tools found in a mechanic's tool kit (see Chapter 1). More in-depth work will require any or all of the following:
• A dial indicator (reading in thousandths) mounted on a universal base
• Micrometers and telescope gauges
• Jaw and screw-type pullers
• Scraper
• Valve spring compressor
• Ring groove cleaner
• Piston ring expander and compressor
• Ridge reamer
• Cylinder hone or glaze breaker
• Plastigage®
• Engine stand

Use of most of these tools is illustrated in this Chapter. Many can be rented for a one-time use from a local parts jobber or tool supply house specializing in automotive work.

Occasionally, the use of special tools is called for. See the information on Special Tools and Safety Notice in the front of this book before substituting another tool.

INSPECTION TECHNIQUES

Procedures and specifications are given in this Chapter for inspecting, cleaning and assessing the wear limits of most major components. Other procedures such as Magnaflux® and Zyglo® can be used to locate material flaws and stress cracks.

Magnaflux® is a magnetic process applicable only to ferrous materials. The Zyglo® process coats the material with a fluorescent dye penetrant and can be used on any material. Check for suspected surface cracks can be more readily made using spot check dye. The dye is sprayed onto the suspected area, wiped off and the area sprayed with a developer. Cracks will show up brightly.

OVERHAUL TIPS

Aluminum has become extremely popular for use in engines, due to its low weight. Observe the following precautions when handling aluminum parts:

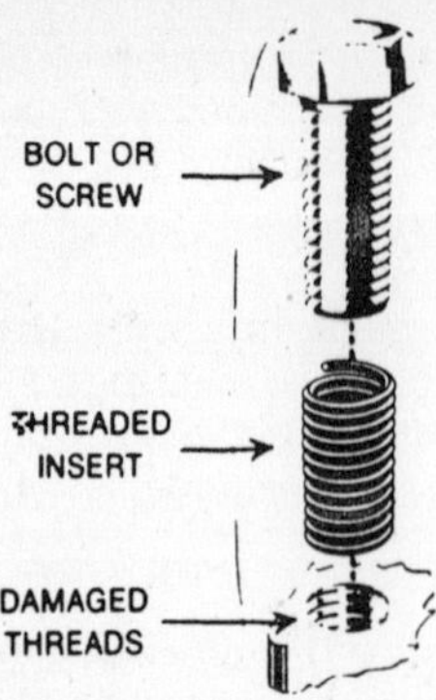

Using a thread insert to repair a damaged hole

• Never hot tank aluminum parts (the caustic hot tank solution will eat the aluminum.

• Remove all aluminum parts (identification tag, etc.) from engine parts prior to the tanking.

• Always coat threads lightly with engine oil or anti-seize compounds before installation, to prevent seizure.

• Never over-torque bolts or spark plugs especially in aluminum for you may strip the threads.

Stripped threads in any component can be repaired using any of several commercial repair kits (Heli-Coil®, Microdot®, Keenserts®, etc.).

When assembling the engine, any parts that will have frictional contact must be prelubed to provide lubrication at initial start-up. Any product specifically formulated for this purpose can be used, but engine oil is not recommended as a prelube.

When semi-permanent (locked, but removable) installation of bolts or nuts is desired, threads should be cleaned and coated with Loctite® or other similar, commercial non-hardening sealant.

REPAIRING DAMAGED THREADS

Several methods of repairing damaged threads are available. Heli-Coil® (shown here), Keenserts® and Microdot® are among the most widely used. All involve basically the same principle—drilling out stripped threads, tapping the hole and installing a prewound insert—making welding, plugging and oversize fasteners unnecessary.

Two types of thread repair inserts are usually supplied—a standard type for most Inch Coarse, Inch Fine, Metric Course and Metric Fine thread sizes and a spark plug type to fit most spark plug port sizes. Consult the individual manufacturer's catalog to determine exact applications. Typical thread repair kits will contain a selection of prewound threaded inserts, a

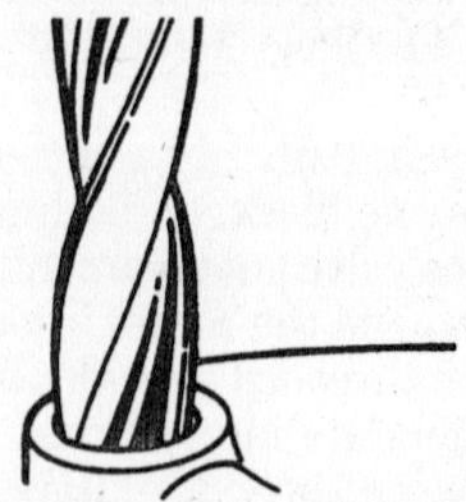

Using a specified drill bit to enlarge the damaged threads. Drill completely through the hole or to the bottom of a blind hole

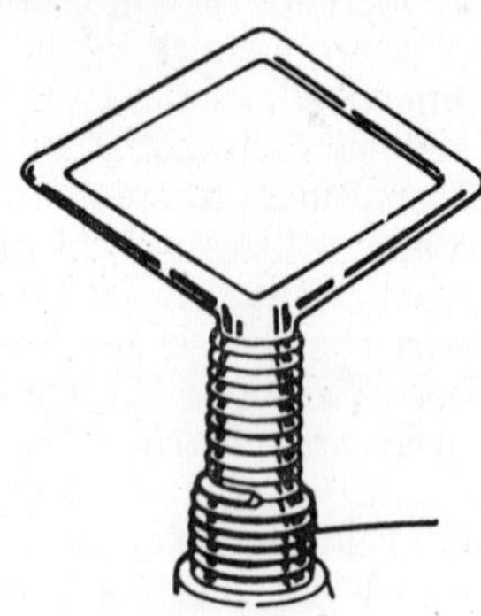

Screw the threaded insert onto the installation tool until the tang engages the slot. Screw the insert into the tapped hole until it is 1/4-1/2 turn below the top surface. After installation, break off the tang with a hammer and punch

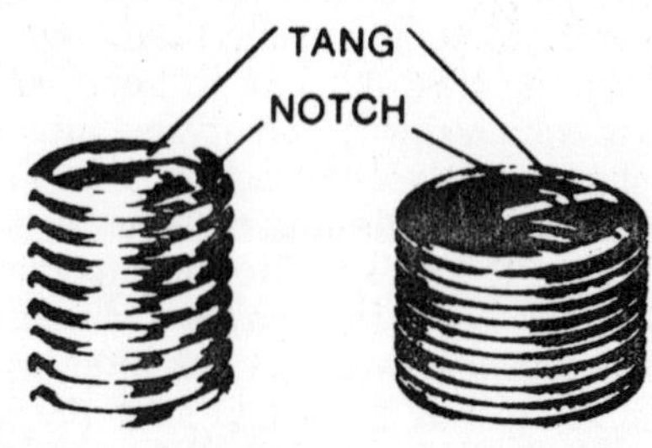

Standard thread repair insert (left) and the spark plug repair insert (right)

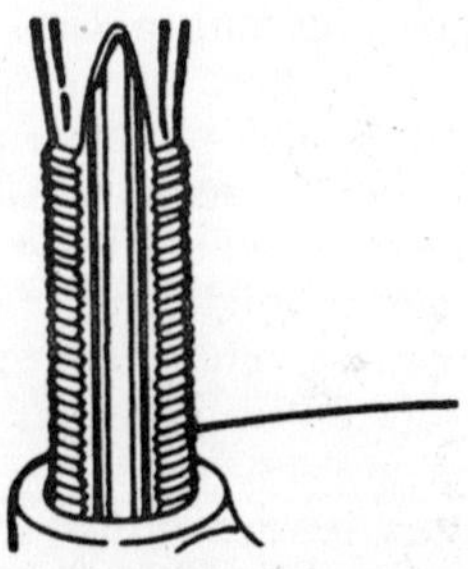

With the supplied tapping bit, tap the hole to receive the thread insert. Keep the tap well oiled and back it out frequently to avoid clogging the threads

tap (corresponding to the outside diameter threads of the insert) and an installation tool. Spark plug inserts usually differ because they require a tap equipped with pilot threads and a combined reamer/tap section. Most manufacturers also supply blister-packed thread repair inserts separately in addition to a master kit containing a variety of taps and inserts plus installation tools.

Before effecting a repair to a threaded hole, remove any snapped, broken or damaged bolts or studs. Penetrating oil can be used to free frozen threads; the offending item can be removed with locking pliers or with a screw or stud extractor. After the hole is clear, the thread can be repaired, as follows:

CHECKING ENGINE COMPRESSION

A noticeable lack of engine power, excessive oil consumption and/or poor fuel mileage measured over an extended period are all indicators of internal engine wear. Worn piston rings, scored or worn cylinder bores, blown head gaskets, sticking or burnt valves and worn valve seats are all possible culprits here. A check of each cylinder's compression will help you locate the problems.

As mentioned in the Tools and Equipment part of Chapter 1, a screw-in type compression gauge is more accurate that the type you simply hold against the spark plug hole, although it takes slightly longer to use. It's worth it to obtain a more accurate reading. Follow the procedures below.

Gasoline Engines

1. Warm up the engine to normal operating temperature.

2. Remove all spark plugs.

3. Disconnect the high tension lead from the ignition coil.

4. Fully open the throttle, either by operating the carburetor throttle linkage by hand or by having an assistant floor the accelerator pedal.

5. Screw the compression gauge into the No. 1 spark plug hole until the fitting is snug.

NOTE: *Be careful not to crossthread the plug hole. On aluminum cylinder heads use extra care, as the threads in these heads are easily ruined.*

6. Ask an assistant to depress the accelerator pedal fully on both carbureted and fuel injected vehicles. Then, while reading the compression gauge, ask the assistant to crank the engine 2–3 times in short bursts using the ignition switch.

7. Read the compression gauge at the end of each series of cranks and record the highest of these readings. Repeat this procedure for

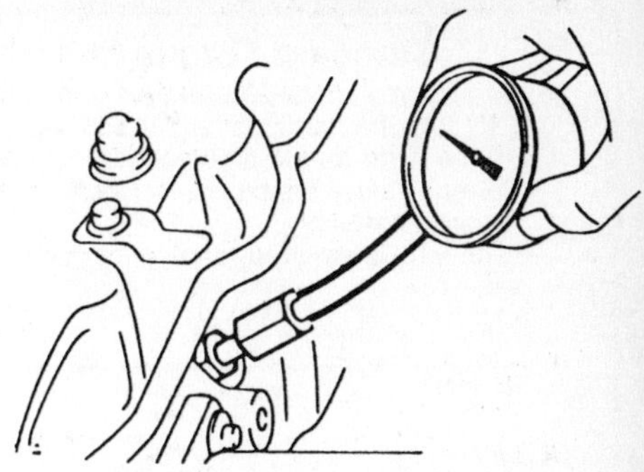

Screw-in type compression gauge

each of the engine's cylinders. Compare the highest reading of each cylinder to the compression pressure specification in the Tune-Up Specifications chart in Chapter 2. The specs in this chart are maximum values.

NOTE: *A cylinder's compression pressure is usually acceptable, if it is not less than 80 percent of maximum. The difference between each cylinder should be no more than 12–14 pounds.*

8. If a cylinder is unusually low, pour a tablespoon of clean engine oil into the cylinder through the spark plug hole and repeat the compression test. If the compression rises after adding the oil, it appears that the cylinder's piston rings or bore are damaged or worn. If the pressure remains low, the valves may not be seating properly (a valve job is needed) or the head gasket may be blown near that cylinder. If compression in any 2 adjacent cylinders is low and if the addition of oil doesn't help the compression, there is leakage past the head gasket. Oil and coolant water in the combustion chamber can result from this problem. There may be evidence of water droplets on the engine dipstick when a head gasket has blown.

NORMAL—Compression builds up quickly and evenly to the specified compression on each cylinder.

PISTON RINGS—Compression low on the first stroke, then tends to build up on the following strokes but does not reach normal. This reading should be tested with the addition of a few shots of engine oil into the cylinders. If the compression increases considerably, the rings are leaking compression.

VALVES—Low on the first stroke, does not tend to build up on following strokes. This reading will stay around the same with a few shots of engine oil in the cylinder.

HEAD GASKET—The compression reading is low between 2 adjacent cylinders. The head gasket between the 2 cylinders may be blown. If there are signs of white smoke coming from the exhaust, while the engine is running,

Standard Torque Specifications and Fastener Markings

In the absence of specific torques, the following chart can be used as a guide to the maximum safe torque of a particular size/grade of fastener.

- There is no torque difference for fine or coarse threads.
- Torque values are based on clean, dry threads. Reduce the value by 10% if threads are oiled prior to assembly.
- The torque required for aluminum components or fasteners is considerably less.

U.S. Bolts

SAE Grade Number	1 or 2			5			6 or 7		
Bolt Size (Inches)—(Thread)	**Ft./Lbs.**	**Kgm**	**Nm**	**Ft./Lbs.**	**Kgm**	**Nm**	**Ft./Lbs.**	**Kgm**	**Nm**
¼ — 20	5	0.7	6.8	8	1.1	10.8	10	1.4	13.5
— 28	6	0.8	8.1	10	1.4	13.6			
⁵/₁₆ — 18	11	1.5	14.9	17	2.3	23.0	19	2.6	25.8
— 24	13	1.8	17.6	19	2.6	25.7			
⅜ — 16	18	2.5	24.4	31	4.3	42.0	34	4.7	46.0
— 24	20	2.75	27.1	35	4.8	47.5			
⁷/₁₆ — 14	28	3.8	37.0	49	6.8	66.4	55	7.6	74.5
— 20	30	4.2	40.7	55	7.6	74.5			
½ — 13	39	5.4	52.8	75	10.4	101.7	85	11.75	115.2
— 20	41	5.7	55.6	85	11.7	115.2			
⁹/₁₆ — 12	51	7.0	69.2	110	15.2	149.1	120	16.6	162.7
— 18	55	7.6	74.5	120	16.6	162.7			
⅝ — 11	83	11.5	112.5	150	20.7	203.3	167	23.0	226.5
— 18	95	13.1	128.8	170	23.5	230.5			
¾ — 10	105	14.5	142.3	270	37.3	366.0	280	38.7	379.6
— 16	115	15.9	155.9	295	40.8	400.0			
⅞ — 9	160	22.1	216.9	395	54.6	535.5	440	60.9	596.5
— 14	175	24.2	237.2	435	60.1	589.7			
1 — 8	236	32.5	318.6	590	81.6	799.9	660	91.3	894.8
— 14	250	34.6	338.9	660	91.3	849.8			

Metric Bolts

Relative Strength Marking	4.6, 4.8			8.8		
Bolt Size Thread Size x Pitch (mm)	**Ft./Lbs.**	**Kgm**	**Nm**	**Ft./Lbs.**	**Kgm**	**Nm**
6 x 1.0	2–3	.2–.4	3–4	3–6	.4–.8	5–8
8 x 1.25	6–8	.8–1	8–12	9–14	1.2–1.9	13–19
10 x 1.25	12–17	1.5–2.3	16–23	20–29	2.7–4.0	27–39
12 x 1.25	21–32	2.9–4.4	29–43	35–53	4.8–7.3	47–72
14 x 1.5	35–52	4.8–7.1	48–70	57–85	7.8–11.7	77–110
16 x 1.5	51–77	7.0–10.6	67–100	90–120	12.4–16.5	130–160
18 x 1.5	74–110	10.2–15.1	100–150	130–170	17.9–23.4	180–230
20 x 1.5	110–140	15.1–19.3	150–190	190–240	26.2–46.9	160–320
22 x 1.5	150–190	22.0–26.2	200–260	250–320	34.5–44.1	340–430
24 x 1.5	190–240	26.2–46.9	260–320	310–410	42.7–56.5	420–550

this may indicate water leaking into the cylinder and being converted into steam. Check around the cylinder head-to-cylinder block area for signs of coolant and oil leakage, indicating a leaking head gasket.

Diesel Engines

Checking the cylinder compression on diesel engines is basically the same procedures as on gasoline engines, except for the following:

1. A special compression gauge adaptor suitable for diesel engines (because these engines have much greater compression pressures) must be used.

2. Remove the injector tubes and the injectors from each cylinder.

NOTE: *Don't forget to remove the washer beneath each injector; otherwise, it may get lost when the engine is cranked.*

3. When fitting the compression gauge adaptor to the cylinder head, make sure the bleeder of the gauge, if equipped, is closed.

4. When reinstalling the injector assemblies, install new washers under each injector.

NOTE: *The following procedures require the use of an engine hoist with sufficient capacity to safely lift and support 500–1000 lbs.*

Gasoline Engine

REMOVAL AND INSTALLATION

Except 4.3L Engine

1. Disconnect the negative battery terminal from the battery.

2. Using a scribing tool, mark the outline of the hood hinges on the hood, then remove the hinge bolts and the hood from the vehicle.

3. If equipped with power steering, disconnect the power steering reservoir from the fan shroud, then disconnect the power steering pump from it's brackets and lay it aside.

4. Remove the upper fan shroud and the fan. If equipped with an automatic transmission, disconnect the transmission oil cooler lines from the radiator.

5. Position a drain pan under the radiator, open the drain cock and drain the cooling system. Disconnect the upper and lower radiator hoses from the radiator, then remove the radiator from the vehicle.

GENERAL ENGINE SPECIFICATIONS

Year	VIN	No. Cylinder Displacement cu. in. (liter)	Fuel System Type	Net Horsepower @ rpm	Net Torque @ rpm (ft. lbs.)	Bore × Stroke (in.)	Compression Ratio	Oil Pressure @ rpm
1983	A	4-119 (1.9)	2bbl	84 @ 4600	101 @ 3000	3.43 × 3.23	8.4:1	57 @ 2000
	B	6-173 (2.8)	2bbl	110 @ 4800	148 @ 2000	3.50 × 2.99	8.5:1	45 @ 2000
	Y	4-121 (2.0)	2bbl	83 @ 4600	108 @ 2400	3.50 × 3.15	9.3:1	45 @ 2000
	S	4-136 (2.2)	Diesel	58 @ 4300	93 @ 2200	3.46 × 3.62	21.0:1	56 @ 2000
1984	A	4-119 (1.9)	2bbl	84 @ 4600	101 @ 3000	3.43 × 3.23	8.4:1	57 @ 2000
	B	6-173 (2.8)	2bbl	110 @ 4800	148 @ 2000	3.50 × 2.99	8.5:1	45 @ 2000
	Y	4-121 (2.0)	2bbl	83 @ 4600	108 @ 2400	3.50 × 3.15	9.3:1	45 @ 2000
	S	4-136 (2.2)	Diesel	58 @ 4300	93 @ 2200	3.46 × 3.62	21.0:1	56 @ 2000
1985	A	4-119 (1.9)	2bbl	84 @ 4600	101 @ 3000	3.43 × 3.23	8.4:1	57 @ 2000
	B	6-173 (2.8)	2bbl	110 @ 4800	148 @ 2000	3.50 × 2.99	8.5:1	45 @ 2000
	E	4-151 (2.5)	EFI	92 @ 4400	134 @ 2800	4.00 × 3.00	9.0:1	45 @ 2000
	S	4-136 (2.2)	Diesel	58 @ 4300	93 @ 2200	3.46 × 3.62	21.0:1	56 @ 2000
1986	E	4-151 (2.5)	EFI	92 @ 4400	134 @ 2800	4.00 × 3.00	9.0:1	45 @ 2000
	R	6-173 (2.8)	EFI	125 @ 4800	150 @ 2200	3.56 × 3.04	8.5:1	50 @ 2000
1987	E	4-151 (2.5)	EFI	92 @ 4400	134 @ 2800	4.00 × 3.00	9.0:1	45 @ 2000
	R	6-173 (2.8)	EFI	125 @ 4800	150 @ 2200	3.56 × 3.04	8.5:1	50 @ 2000
1988	E	4-151 (2.5)	EFI	92 @ 4400	130 @ 3200	4.00 × 3.00	8.3:1	41 @ 2000
	R	6-173 (2.8)	EFI	125 @ 4800	150 @ 2400	3.56 × 3.04	8.9:1	50 @ 2000
	Z	6-262 (4.3)	EFI	150 @ 4000	230 @ 2400	4.00 × 3.48	9.3:1	30 @ 2000
1989	E	4-151 (2.5)	EFI	92 @ 4400	130 @ 3200	4.00 × 3.00	8.3:1	41 @ 2000
	R	6-173 (2.8)	EFI	125 @ 4800	150 @ 2400	3.56 × 3.04	8.9:1	50 @ 2000
	Z	6-262 (4.3)	EFI	160 @ 4000	230 @ 2800	4.00 × 3.48	9.3:1	18 @ 2000
1990	Z	6-262 (4.3)	EFI	160 @ 4000	230 @ 2800	4.00 × 3.48	9.3:1	18 @ 2000
1991	Z	6-262 (4.3)	EFI	160 @ 4000	230 @ 2800	4.00 × 3.48	9.3:1	18 @ 2000

EFI—Electronic Fuel Injection

CRANKSHAFT AND CONNECTING ROD SPECIFICATIONS

All measurements are given in inches.

Year	VIN	No. Cylinder Displacement cu. in. (liter)	Crankshaft				Connecting Rod		
			Main Brg. Journal Dia.	Main Brg. Oil Clearance	Shaft End-play	Thrust on No.	Journal Diameter	Oil Clearance	Side Clearance
1983	A	4-119 (1.9)	2.2050	0.0008–0.0025	0.0117 max.	3	1.9290	0.0007–0.0030	0.0137 max.
	B	6-173 (2.8)	2.4940	0.0017–0.0030	0.0020–0.0067	3	1.9980	0.0014–0.0032	0.0062–0.0173
	Y	4-121 (2.0)	④	⑤	0.0020–0.0071	3	1.9990	0.0010–0.0031	0.0034–0.0240
	S	4-136 (2.2)	2.3590	0.0011–0.0033	0.0018	3	2.0837	0.0016–0.0047	0.0024
1984	A	4-119 (1.9)	2.2050	0.0008–0.0025	0.0117 max.	3	1.9290	0.0007–0.0030	0.0137 max.
	B	6-173 (2.8)	2.4940	0.0017–0.0030	0.0020–0.0067	3	1.9980	0.0014–0.0032	0.0063–0.0173
	Y	4-121 (2.0)	④	⑤	0.0020–0.0071	3	1.9990	0.0010–0.0031	0.0034–0.0240
	S	4-136 (2.2)	2.3590	0.0011–0.0033	0.0018	3	2.0837	0.0016–0.0047	0.0024
1985	A	4-119 (1.9)	2.2050	0.0008–0.0025	0.0117 max.	3	1.9290	0.0007–0.0030	0.0137 max.
	B	6-173 (2.8)	2.4940	0.0017–0.0030	0.0020–0.0067	3	1.9980	0.0014–0.0032–	0.0063–0.0173
	E	4-151 (2.5)	2.3000	0.0005–0.0022	0.0035–0.0085	5	2.000	0.0005–0.0026	0.0060–0.0220
	S	4-136 (2.2)	2.3590	0.0011–0.0033	0.0018	3	2.0837	0.0016–0.0047	0.0024
1986	E	4-151 (2.5)	2.3000	0.0005–0.0022	0.0035–0.0085	5	2.000	0.0005–0.0026	0.0060–0.0220
	R	6-173 (2.8)	①	0.0016–0.0032	0.0020–0.0070	3	1.9983–1.9993	0.0014–0.0035	0.0063–0.0173
1987	E	4-151 (2.5)	2.3000	0.0005–0.0022	0.0035–0.0085	5	2.000	0.0005–0.0026	0.0060–0.0220
	R	6-173 (2.8)	①	0.0016–0.0032	0.0020–0.0070	3	1.9983–1.9993	0.0014–0.0035	0.0063–0.0173
1988	E	4-151 (2.5)	2.3000	0.0005–0.0022	0.0035–0.0085	5	2.000	0.0005–0.0026	0.0060–0.0220
	R	6-173 (2.8)	①	0.0016–0.0032	0.0020–0.0070	3	1.9983–1.9993	0.0014–0.0035	0.0063–0.0173
	Z	6-262 (4.3)	②	③	0.0020–0.0060	3	2.2487–2.2497	0.0013–0.0035	0.0060–0.0140
1989	E	4-151 (2.5)	2.3000	0.0005–0.0022	0.0035–0.0085	5	2.000	0.0005–0.0026	0.0060–0.0220
	R	6-173 (2.8)	①	0.0016–0.0032	0.0020–0.0070	3	1.9983–1.9993	0.0014–0.0035	0.0063–0.0173
	Z	6-262 (4.3)	②	③	0.0020–0.0060	3	2.2487–2.2497	0.0013–0.0035	0.0060–0.0140
1990	Z	6-262 (4.3)	②	③	0.0020–0.0060	3	2.2487–2.2497	0.0013–0.0035	0.0060–0.0140
1991	Z	6-262 (4.3)	②	③	0.0020–0.0060	3	2.2487–2.2497	0.0013–0.0035	0.0060–0.0140

① Journals 1, 2, 4: 2.5336–2.5345
　Journal 3: 2.5332–2.5340
② Journal 1: 2.4484–2.4493
　Journal 2, 3: 2.4481–2.4490
　Journal 4: 2.4479–2.4488
③ Journal 1: 0.0008–0.0020
　Journal 2, 3: 0.0011–0.0023
　Journal 4: 0.0017–0.0032
④ Journals 1, 2, 3, 4: 2.4940–2.4950
　Journal 5: 2.4930–2.4950
⑤ Journals 1, 2, 3, 4: 0.0006–0.0019
　Journal 5: 0.0014–0.0027

VALVE SPECIFICATIONS

All measurements given in inches.

Year	VIN	No. Cylinder Displacement cu. in. (liter)	Seat Angle (deg.)	Face Angle (deg.)	Spring Test Pressure (lbs.)	Spring Installed Height (in.)	Stem-to-Guide Clearance (in.)		Stem Diameter (in.)	
							Intake	Exhaust	Intake	Exhaust
1983	A	4-119 (1.9)	45	45	①	NA	0.0009–0.0022	0.0015–0.0031	0.3102 min.	0.3091 min.
	B	6-173 (2.8)	46	45	195 @ 1.180	1.5748	0.0010–0.0027	0.0010–0.0027	0.3410–0.3416	0.3410–0.3416
	Y	4-121 (2.0)	46	45	182 @ 1.330	1.5984	0.0011–0.0026	0.0014–0.0031	0.3410–0.3416	0.3410–0.3416
	S	4-136 (2.2)	45	45	②	NA	0.0015–0.0027	0.0025–0.0037	0.3150–0.3100	0.3150–0.3090
1984	A	4-119 (1.9)	45	45	①	NA	0.0009–0.0022	0.0015–0.0031	0.3102 min.	0.3091 min.
	B	6-173 (2.8)	46	45	195 @ 1.180	1.5748	0.0010–0.0027	0.0010–0.0027	0.3410–0.3416	0.3410–0.3416
	Y	4-121 (2.0)	46	45	182 @ 1.330	1.5984	0.0011–0.0026	0.0014–0.0031	0.3410–0.3416	0.3410–0.3416
	S	4-136 (2.2)	45	45	②	NA	0.0015–0.0027	0.0025–0.0037	0.3150–0.3100	0.3150–0.3091
1985	A	4-119 (1.9)	45	45	①	NA	0.0009–0.0022	0.0015–0.0031	0.3102 min.	0.3091 min.
	B	6-173 (2.8)	46	45	195 @ 1.180	1.5748	0.0010–0.0027	0.0010–0.0027	0.3410–0.3416	0.3410–0.3416
	E	4-151 (2.5)	46	45	175 @ 1.26	1.69	0.0010–0.0025	0.0013–0.0030	0.3430–0.3420	0.3420–0.3430
	S	4-136 (2.2)	45	45	②	NA	0.0015–0.0027	0.0025–0.0037	0.3100–0.3150	0.3091–0.3150
1986	E	4-151 (2.5)	46	45	175 @ 1.26	1.69	0.0010–0.0025	0.0013–0.0030	0.3430–0.3420	0.3420–0.3430
	R	4-173 (2.8)	46	45	175 @ 1.26	1.94	0.0010–0.0002	0.0010–0.0002	0.3410–0.3420	0.3410–0.3420
1987	E	4-151 (2.5)	46	45	175 @ 1.26	1.69	0.0010–0.0025	0.0013–0.0030	0.3430–0.3420	0.3420–0.3430
	R	6-173 (2.8)	46	45	175 @ 1.26	1.94	0.0010–0.0002	0.0010–0.0002	0.3410–0.3420	0.3410–0.3420
1988	E	4-151 (2.5)	46	45	175 @ 1.26	1.69	0.0010–0.0025	0.0013–0.0030	0.3430–0.3420	0.3420–0.3430
	R	6-173 (2.8)	46	45	175 @ 1.26	1.94	0.0010–0.0002	0.0010–0.0002	0.3410–0.3420	0.3410–0.3420
	Z	6-262 (4.3)	46	45	194 @ 1.25	1.39	0.0010–0.0027	0.0010–0.0027	0.3410–0.3420	0.3410–0.3420
1989	Z	6-262 (4.3)	46	45	194 @ 1.25	1.39	0.0010–0.0027	0.0010–0.0027	0.3410–0.3420	0.3410–0.3420
1990	Z	6-262 (4.3)	46	45	194 @ 1.25	1.39	0.0010–0.0027	0.0010–0.0027	NA	NA
1991	Z	6-262 (4.3)	46	45	194 @ 1.25	1.39	0.0010–0.0027	0.0010–0.0027	NA	NA

NA—Not Available

① Outer: 35 @ 1.814
Inner: 20 @ 1.516
② Outer: 145 @ 1.535
Inner: 44 @ 1.457

CAMSHAFT SPECIFICATIONS

All measurements given in inches.

Year	VIN	No. Cylinder Displacement cu. in. (liter)	Journal Diameter					Lobe Lift		Bearing Clearance	Camshaft End Play
			1	2	3	4	5	In.	Ex.		
1983	A	4-119 (1.9)	1.3362–1.3370	1.3362–1.3370	1.3362–1.3370	1.3362–1.3370	1.3362–1.3370	NA	NA	0.0016–0.0035	0.0020–0.0059
	B	6-173 (2.8)	1.8677–1.8696	1.8677–1.8696	1.8677–1.8696	1.8677–1.8696	—	0.231	0.262	0.0010–0.0039	NA
	Y	4-121 (2.0)	1.8677–1.8696	1.8677–1.8696	1.8677–1.8696	1.8677–1.8696	1.8677–1.8696	0.262	0.262	0.0010–0.0039	NA
	S	4-136 (2.2)	1.8741–1.8898	1.8741–1.8898	1.8741–1.8898	—	—	NA	NA	0.0020–0.0097	0.0032–0.0079
1984	A	4-119 (1.9)	1.3362–1.3370	1.3362–1.3370	1.3362–1.3370	1.3362–1.3370	1.3362–1.3370	NA	NA	0.0016–0.0035	0.0020–0.0059
	B	6-173 (2.8)	1.8677–1.8696	1.8677–1.8696	1.8677–1.8696	1.8677–1.8696	—	0.231	0.262	0.0010–0.0039	NA
	Y	4-121 (2.0)	1.8677–1.8696	1.8677–1.8696	1.8677–1.8696	1.8677–1.8696	1.8677–1.8696	0.262	0.262	0.0010–0.0039	NA
	S	4-136 (2.2)	1.8741–1.8898	1.8741–1.8898	1.8741–1.8898	—	—	NA	NA	0.0020–0.0097	0.0032–0.0079
1985	A	4-119 (1.9)	1.3362–1.3370	1.3362–1.3370	1.3362–1.3370	1.3362–1.3370	1.3362–1.3370	NA	NA	0.0016–0.0035	0.0020–0.0059
	B	6-173 (2.8)	1.8677–1.8696	1.8677–1.8696	1.8677–1.8696	1.8677–1.8696	—	0.231	0.262	0.0010–0.0039	NA
	E	4-151 (2.5)	1.8690	1.8690	1.8690	—	—	0.398	0.398	0.0007–0.0027	0.0015–0.0050
	S	4-136 (2.2)	1.8741–1.8898	1.8741–1.8898	1.8741–1.8898	—	—	NA	NA	0.0020–0.0097	0.0032–0.0079
1986	E	4-151 (2.5)	1.8690	1.8690	1.8690	—	—	0.398	0.398	0.0007–0.0027	0.0015–0.0050
	R	6-173 (2.8)	1.8970–1.8990	1.8970–1.8990	1.8970–1.8990	1.8970–1.8990	—	0.234	0.266	0.0010–0.0040	—
1987	E	4-151 (2.5)	1.8690	1.8690	1.8690	—	—	0.398	0.398	0.0007–0.0027	0.0015–0.0050
	R	6-173 (2.8)	1.8970–1.8990	1.8970–1.8990	1.8970–1.8990	1.8970–1.8990	—	0.234	0.266	0.0010–0.0040	—
1988	E	4-151 (2.5)	1.8690	1.8690	1.8690	—	—	0.398	0.398	0.0007–0.0027	0.0015–0.0050
	R	6-173 (2.8)	1.8970–1.8990	1.8970–1.8990	1.8970–1.8990	1.8970–1.8990	—	0.234	0.266	0.0010–0.0040	—
	Z	6-262 (4.3)	1.8682–1.8692	1.8682–1.8692	1.8682–1.8692	1.8682–1.8692	—	0.357	0.390	0.0010–0.0030	0.004–0.012
1989	E	4-151 (2.5)	1.8690	1.8690	1.8690	—	—	0.232	0.232	0.0007–0.0027	0.0015–0.0050
	R	6-173 (2.8)	1.8970–1.8990	1.8970–1.8990	1.8970–1.8990	1.8970–1.8990	—	0.266	0.277	0.0010–0.0040	—
	Z	6-262 (4.3)	1.8682–1.8692	1.8682–1.8692	1.8682–1.8692	1.8682–1.8692	—	0.357	0.390	0.0010–0.0030	0.004–0.012
1990	Z	6-262 (4.3)	1.8682–1.8692	1.8682–1.8692	1.8682–1.8692	1.8682–1.8692	—	0.357	0.390	0.0010–0.0030	0.004–0.012
1991	Z	6-262 (4.3)	1.8682–1.8692	1.8682–1.8692	1.8682–1.8692	1.8682–1.8692	—	0.357 ①	0.390 ②	0.0010–0.0030	0.004–0.012

NA—Not Available   ① 0.234—Bravada   ② 0.257—Bravada

PISTON AND RING SPECIFICATIONS

All measurements are given in inches.

| Year | VIN | No. Cylinder Displacement cu. in. (liter) | Piston Clearance | Ring Gap | | | Ring Side Clearance | | |
				Top Compression	Bottom Compression	Oil Control	Top Compression	Bottom Compression	Oil Control
1983	A	4-119 (1.9)	0.0018–0.0026	0.012–0.020	0.008–0.016	0.008–0.035	0.0059 max.	0.0059 max.	0.0059 max.
	B	6-173 (2.8)	0.0017–0.0027	0.010–0.020	0.010–0.020	0.020–0.055	0.0012–0.0028	0.0016–0.0037	0.0078 max.
	Y	4-121 (2.0)	0.0008–0.0018	0.010–0.020	0.010–0.020	0.020–0.055	0.0012–0.0027	0.0012–0.0038	0.0078 max.
	S	4-136 (2.2)	0.0062–0.0070	0.008–0.016	0.008–0.016	0.008–0.016	0.0018–0.0028	0.0012–0.0021	0.0008–0.0021
1984	A	4-119 (1.9)	0.0018–0.0026	0.012–0.020	0.008–0.016	0.008–0.035	0.0059 max.	0.0059 max.	0.0059 max.
	B	6-173 (2.8)	0.0017–0.0027	0.010–0.020	0.010–0.020	0.020–0.055	0.0012–0.0028	0.0016–0.0037	0.0078 max.
	Y	4-121 (2.0)	0.0008–0.0018	0.010–0.020	0.010–0.020	0.020–0.055	0.0012–0.0027	0.0012–0.0038	0.0078 max.
	S	4-136 (2.2)	0.0062–0.0070	0.008–0.016	0.008–0.016	0.008–0.016	0.0018–0.0028	0.0012–0.0021	0.0008–0.0021
1985	A	4-119 (1.9)	0.0018–0.0026	0.012–0.020	0.008–0.016	0.008–0.035	0.0059 max.	0.0059 max.	0.0059 max.
	B	6-173 (2.8)	0.0017–0.0027	0.010–0.020	0.010–0.020	0.020–0.055	0.0012–0.0028	0.0016–0.0037	0.0078 max.
	E	4-151 (2.5)	0.0014–0.0022	0.010–0.020	0.010–0.020	0.020–0.060	0.0020–0.0030	0.0010–0.0030	0.0015–0.0055
	S	4-136 (2.2)	0.0062–0.0070	0.008–0.016	0.008–0.016	0.008–0.016	0.0018–0.0028	0.0012–0.0021	0.0008–0.0021
1986	E	4-151 (2.5)	0.0014–0.0022	0.010–0.020	0.010–0.020	0.020–0.060	0.0020–0.0030	0.0010–0.0030	0.0150–0.0550
	R	6-173 (2.8)	0.0007–0.0017	0.010–0.022	0.010–0.022	0.020–0.055	0.0012–0.0027	0.0015–0.0037	0.0078
1987	E	4-151 (2.5)	0.0014–0.0022	0.010–0.020	0.010–0.020	0.020–0.060	0.0020–0.0030	0.0010–0.0030	0.0150–0.0550
	R	6-173 (2.8)	0.0007–0.0017	0.010–0.022	0.010–0.022	0.020–0.055	0.0012–0.0027	0.0015–0.0037	0.0078
1988	E	4-151 (2.5)	0.0014–0.0022	0.010–0.020	0.010–0.020	0.020–0.060	0.0020–0.0030	0.0010–0.0030	0.0150–0.0550
	R	6-173 (2.8)	0.0007–0.0017	0.010–0.022	0.010–0.022	0.020–0.055	0.0012–0.0027	0.0015–0.0037	0.0078
	Z	6-262 (4.3)	0.0007–0.0017	0.010–0.020	0.010–0.025	0.015–0.055	0.0012–0.0032	0.0012–0.0032	0.0020–0.0070
1989	E	4-151 (2.5)	0.0010–0.0022	0.010–0.020	0.010–0.020	0.020–0.060	0.0020–0.0030	0.0010–0.0030	0.0150–0.0550
	R	6-173 (2.8)	0.0007–0.0017	0.010–0.022	0.010–0.022	0.020–0.055	0.0012–0.0027	0.0015–0.0037	0.078
	Z	6-262 (4.3)	0.0007–0.0017	0.010–0.020	0.010–0.025	0.015–0.055	0.0012–0.0032	0.0012–0.0032	0.0020–0.0070
1990	Z	6-262 (4.3)	0.0007–0.0017	0.010–0.020	0.010–0.025	0.015–0.055	0.0012–0.0032	0.0012–0.0032	0.0020–0.0070
1991	Z	6-262 (4.3)	0.0007–0.0017	0.010–0.020	0.010–0.025	0.015–0.055	0.0012–0.0032	0.0012–0.0032	0.0020–0.0070

TORQUE SPECIFICATIONS

All readings in ft. lbs.

Year	VIN	No. Cylinder Displacement cu. in. (liter)	Cylinder Head Bolts	Main Bearing Bolts	Rod Bearing Bolts	Crankshaft Pulley Bolts	Flywheel Bolts	Manifold		Spark Plugs
								Intake	Exhaust	
1983	A	4-119 (1.9)	72	75	43	87	76	17	16	18
	B	6-173 (2.8)	70	70	37	75	50	23	25	7–15
	Y	4-121 (2.0)	70	70	37	75	50	23	25	7–15
	S	4-136 (2.2)	60	116–130	65	125–150	70	15	15	22
1984	A	4-119 (1.9)	72	75	43	87	76	17	16	18
	B	6-173 (2.8)	70	70	37	75	50	23	25	7–15
	Y	4-121 (2.0)	70	70	37	75	50	23	25	7–15
	S	4-136 (2.2)	60	116–130	65	125–150	70	15	15	22
1985	A	4-119 (1.9)	72	75	43	87	76	17	16	18
	B	6-173 (2.8)	70	70	37	75	50	23	25	7–15
	E	4-151 (2.5)	90	70	39	160	55	30	①	7–15
	S	4-136 (2.2)	60	116–130	65	125–150	70	15	15	22
1986	E	4-151 (2.5)	90	70	32	160	55	30	①	7–15
	R	6-173 (2.8)	70	70	39	70	52	23	25	11
1987	E	4-151 (2.5)	90	70	32	160	55	30	①	7–15
	R	6-173 (2.8)	70	70	39	70	52	23	25	11
1988	E	4-151 (2.5)	③	70	32	160	55④	30	①	7–15
	R	6-173 (2.8)	⑤	70	39	70	52	23	25	11
	Z	6-262 (4.3)	65	80	45	70	75	35	②	11
1989	E	4-151 (2.5)	③	70	32	160	55④	30	①	7–15
	R	6-173 (2.8)	⑤	70	39	70	52	23	25	11
	Z	6-262 (4.3)	65	80	45	70	75	35	②	11
1990	Z	6-262 (4.3)	65	80	45	70	75	35	②	11
1991	Z	6-262 (4.3)	65	80	45	70	75	35	②	11

① Inner bolts: 36 ft. lbs.
Outer bolts: 32 ft. lbs.
② Center bolts: 26 ft.lbs.
Outer bolts: 20 ft. lbs.

③ Tighten in 3 stages:
1st to 18 ft. lbs.
2nd to 26 ft. lbs. (except studs—
tighten to 18 ft. lbs.)
3rd an additional 90 degrees (¼ turn)

④ With manual transmission 65 ft. lbs.
⑤ Tighten in 2 stages:
1st to 40 ft. lbs.
2nd an additional 90 degrees (¼ turn)

CAUTION: *When draining the coolant, keep in mind that cats and dogs are attracted by the ethylene glycol antifreeze, and are quite likely to drink any that is left in an uncovered container or in puddles on the ground. This will prove fatal in sufficient quantity. Always drain the coolant into a sealable container. Coolant should be reused unless it is contaminated or several years old.*

6. If equipped with air conditioning, remove the compressor from the engine and move it aside; do not disconnect the pressure lines from the compressor.

7. Remove the air cleaner, the fuel line bracket at the filter, the fuel line and the vacuum hoses from the engine.

8. Disconnect the accelerator, the TV and the cruise control cables from the engine. Disconnect the heater hoses from the engine.

9. Label and disconnect the electrical connectors from the O_2 sensor and other necessary electrical components.

10. Raise and support the front of the vehicle on jackstands.

11. On the 2WD models, disconnect the strut rod. On the 4WD models, disconnect the brake line clip from the crossmember, then remove the crossmember, the front drive shaft from the front axle and the automatic transmission cooler lines from the flywheel cover.

12. Disconnect the exhaust pipe from the catalytic converter hanger and the exhaust manifold(s).

13. Remove the drive belt splash shield, if equipped, and the starter. If equipped with an automatic transmission, remove the lower bell housing cover and the torque converter-to-flywheel bolts.

14. Remove the 2 left side outer air dam bolts, the lower fan shroud and the left side body (cab) mounting bolts, then raise and support (block) the left side of the body with wooden blocks.

15. Remove the upper transmission-to-engine bolts and the body-to-chassis wooden blocks, then lower the body.

16. Remove the lower transmission-to-engine bolts and engine-to-mount through bolts. Lower the vehicle and support the transmission.

17. Using a vertical lifting device, connect it to the engine, raise it slightly and move it forward.

18. From the rear of the engine, remove the wiring harness clips and the ground straps.

19. Lift the engine from the vehicle.

To install:

20. Lower the engine into the vehicle. Install the wiring harness clips and ground straps to the rear of the engine.

21. Install the upper transmission-to-engine bolts.

22. Raise and safely support the vehicle. Install the lower transmission-to-engine bolts and engine-to-mount through bolts. Torque the engine mount through bolts to 50 ft. lbs. for 4 cylinder engines or 85 ft. lbs. for V6 engines and the rear engine mount-to-crossmember nut to 24 ft. lbs.

23. Install the 2 left side outer air dam bolts, the lower fan shroud and the left side body (cab) mounting bolts.

24. If equipped with an automatic transmission, install the torque converter-to-flywheel bolts and the lower bell housing cover.

25. Install the drive belt splash shield, if equipped, and the starter.

26. Connect the exhaust pipe to the catalytic converter hanger and the exhaust manifold(s).

27. On the 2WD models, connect the strut rod. On the 4WD models, connect the automatic transmission cooler lines to the flywheel cover, the front driveshaft to the front differential. Install the crossmember and connect the brake line clip to the crossmember.

28. Lower the vehicle.

29. Connect the electrical connectors to the O_2 sensor and other necessary electrical components.

30. Connect the accelerator, the TV and the cruise control cables to the engine. Connect the heater hoses to the engine.

31. Install the air cleaner, the fuel line bracket at the filter, the fuel line and the vacuum hoses to the engine.

32. If equipped with air conditioning, install the compressor from the engine.

33. Install the radiator and connect the upper and lower radiator hoses to the radiator.

34. Install the upper fan shroud and the fan. If equipped with an automatic transmission, connect the transmission oil cooler lines to the radiator.

35. If equipped with power steering, connect the power steering reservoir to the fan shroud, then connect the power steering pump to it's brackets.

36. Install the hood. Connect the negative battery cable to the battery.

37. Start the engine, allow it to reach normal operating temperatures and check for leaks.

4.3L Engine

BRAVADA

1. Disconnect the negative battery cable.

2. Remove the underhood light.

3. Raise and safely support the vehicle. Drain the cooling system and the engine oil.

CAUTION: *When draining the coolant, keep in mind that cats and dogs are attracted by the ethylene glycol antifreeze, and are quite likely to drink any that is left in an uncovered container or in puddles on the ground. This will prove fatal in sufficient quantity. Always drain the coolant into a sealable container. Coolant should be reused unless it is contaminated or several years old.*

4. Disconnect the exhaust pipes from the exhaust manifold.

CAUTION: *The EPA warns that prolonged contact with used engine oil may cause a number of skin disorders, including cancer! You should make every effort to minimize your exposure to used engine oil. Protective gloves should be worn when changing the oil. Wash your hands and any other exposed skin areas as soon as possible after exposure to used engine oil. Soap and water, or waterless hand cleaner should be used.*

5. Remove the front driveshaft from the front differential.

6. Disconnect the electrical connectors from the starter. Remove the starter.

7. Remove the torque converter cover bolts and the cover. Matchmark the torque converter to flywheel. Remove the torque converter-to-flywheel bolts; it will be necessary to rotate the flywheel to access the other bolts.

8. Remove the engine mount through bolts.

9. Remove the oil filter adapter from the engine.

10. Remove the transmission-to-engine bolt at the strut rod, the transfer case bolt at the strut rod and the strut rod.

11. Remove the transmission-to-engine bolts. Disconnect the transmission cooler lines from the engine clips and lower the vehicle.

12. Remove the air cleaner assembly.

13. Remove the upper fan shroud and the accessory drive belt.

14. Remove the fan and fan clutch assembly. Remove the upper cooling inlet hose from the radiator and the engine.

15. Remove the air conditioner compressor

and lay it aside; do not disconnect the air conditioning hoses.

16. Remove the lower cooling outlet hose from the radiator and the engine.

17. Disconnect and drain the transmission and engine oil cooler lines from the radiator.

18. Disconnect the heater hoses from the engine. Remove the radiator-to-chassis bolts and the radiator.

19. Disconnect and plug the power steering hoses from the pump.

20. Label and disconnect the necessary electrical connectors from the engine.

21. Label and disconnect the necessary vacuum connectors from the engine.

22. Disconnect the accelerator cable, the TV cable and the cruise control cable from the engine.

23. Disconnect the electrical connectors and remove the alternator from the engine.

24. Disconnect and plug the fuel lines from the throttle body and remove the left side bracket.

25. Label and disconnect the wiring from the distributor cap and remove the distributor cap.

26. Using a floor jack, support the transmission.

27. Remove the oil bracket from the oil cooler.

28. Connect a vertical lifting device to the engine and lift the engine from the vehicle.

29. If necessary, remove the flywheel-to-crankshaft bolts and the flywheel.

To install:

30. If the flywheel was removed, install it and torque the bolts to 75 ft. lbs. (100 Nm).

31. Lower the engine into the vehicle, install the engine-to-engine mount bolts and torque the **A** bolts to 42 ft. lbs. (57 Nm) or nuts to 35 ft. lbs. (47 Nm), the **B** bolts to 35 ft. lbs. (47 Nm) and the **C** nut/bolt to 52 ft. lbs. (70 Nm).

32. Install the oil bracket from the oil cooler.

33. Install the distributor cap and connect the wiring to the distributor cap.

34. Install the left side bracket and connect and the fuel lines to the throttle body.

35. Install the alternator and connect the electrical connectors.

36. Connect the accelerator cable, the TV cable and the cruise control cable to the engine.

37. Connect the necessary vacuum connectors to the engine.

38. Connect the necessary electrical connectors to the engine.

39. Connect the power steering hoses to the pump.

40. Install the radiator and connect the heater hoses to the engine.

41. Connect the transmission and engine oil cooler lines to the engine.

42. Connect the lower cooling outlet hose to the radiator and the engine.

43. Install the air conditioner compressor.

44. Install the upper cooling inlet hose to the radiator and the engine. Install the fan clutch assembly and the fan.

45. Install the upper fan shroud and the accessory drive belt.

46. Install the air cleaner assembly.

47. Remove the floor jack from the transmission. Connect the transmission cooler lines to the engine clips. Raise and safely support the vehicle.

48. Install the transmission-to-engine bolts.

49. Install the strut rod, the transfer case bolt to strut rod and the transmission-to-engine bolt at the strut rod.

50. Install the oil filter adapter to the engine.

51. Align the flywheel to torque converter matchmarks and install the bolts.

52. Install the starter and connect the electrical connectors.

53. Install the front driveshaft to the front differential.

54. Connect the exhaust pipes to the exhaust manifold.

55. Lower the vehicle. Refill the cooling system and the engine crankcase.

56. Install the underhood light. Connect the negative battery cable.

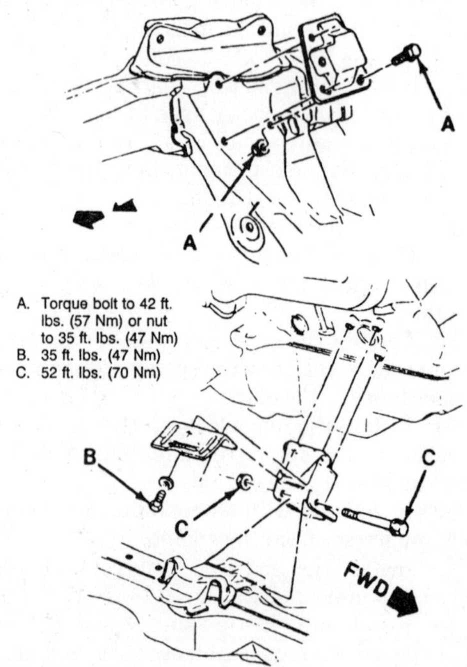

Install the engine mount bolts and nuts — 4.3L engine

57. Start the engine, allow it to reach normal operating temperatures and check for leaks.

2-WHEEL DRIVE BLAZER AND JIMMY

1. Disconnect the negative battery cable.

2. Raise and safely support the vehicle. Drain the cooling system and the engine oil.

CAUTION: *When draining the coolant, keep in mind that cats and dogs are attracted by the ethylene glycol antifreeze, and are quite likely to drink any that is left in an uncovered container or in puddles on the ground. This will prove fatal in sufficient quantity. Always drain the coolant into a sealable container. Coolant should be reused unless it is contaminated or several years old.*

3. Remove the upper cooling inlet hose from the radiator and the engine.

CAUTION: *The EPA warns that prolonged contact with used engine oil may cause a number of skin disorders, including cancer! You should make every effort to minimize your exposure to used engine oil. Protective gloves should be worn when changing the oil. Wash your hands and any other exposed skin areas as soon as possible after exposure to used engine oil. Soap and water, or waterless hand cleaner should be used.*

4. Remove the overflow hose.

5. Remove the upper fan shroud.

6. Disconnect the transmission cooler lines from the engine clips and lower the vehicle.

7. Remove the coolant hoses from the radiator and the radiator from the vehicle. Remove the fan.

8. Disconnect the heater hoses from the engine.

9. Remove the air cleaner assembly.

10. Label and disconnect the necessary vacuum connectors from the engine.

11. Label and disconnect the necessary electrical connectors from the engine.

12. Disconnect the accelerator cable and the cruise control cable from the engine.

13. Label and disconnect the wiring from the distributor cap and remove the distributor cap.

14. Raise and safely support the vehicle. Disconnect the converter-to-exhaust pipe bolts and the exhaust pipes from the exhaust manifold.

15. Remove the strut rods from the bell housing.

16. If equipped with an automatic transmission, remove the torque converter cover bolts and the cover. Matchmark the torque converter to flywheel. Remove the torque converter-to-flywheel bolts; it will be necessary to rotate the flywheel to access the other bolts.

17. Remove the shield from the rear of the catalytic converter.

18. Remove the converter hanger at the exhaust pipe.

19. Remove the lower fan shroud.

20. Disconnect and plug the fuel lines from the throttle body and remove the left side bracket.

21. Remove the 2 outer dam bolts.

22. Raise and safely support the vehicle. Remove the left body mounting bolts.

23. Lower the vehicle and remove the bell housing-to-engine bolts.

24. Remove the engine mount through bolts.

25. If equipped with air conditioning, remove the air conditioner compressor and lay it aside; do not disconnect the air conditioning hoses.

26. If equipped with power steering, remove the power steering pump and move it aside; do not disconnect the pressure hoses.

27. Using a floor jack, support the transmission.

28. Connect a vertical lifting device to the engine and lift the engine from the vehicle.

29. Lower the engine into the vehicle, install the engine-to-engine mount bolts and torque the **A** bolts to 42 ft. lbs. (57 Nm) or nuts to 35 ft. lbs. (47 Nm), the **B** bolts to 35 ft. lbs. (47 Nm) and the **C** nut/bolt to 52 ft. lbs. (70 Nm).

30. Raise and safely support the vehicle. Install the lower bell housing bolts.

31. Lower the vehicle and install the upper bell housing bolts.

32. Install the body mount bolts.

33. If equipped with power steering, install the power steering pump.

34. If equipped with air conditioning, install the air conditioner compressor.

35. Install the 2 outer dam bolts.

36. Install the fuel lines to the throttle body.

37. Install the lower fan shroud.

38. Install the converter hanger to the exhaust pipe. Install the shield to the rear of the catalytic converter.

39. If equipped with an automatic transmission, align the flywheel to torque converter matchmarks and install the bolts.

40. Install the strut rods to the bell housing.

41. Connect the exhaust pipes to the exhaust manifold. Connect the converter to the exhaust pipe and lower the vehicle.

42. Install the distributor cap.

43. Connect the accelerator cable and the cruise control cable to the engine.

44. Connect the necessary vacuum connectors to the engine.

45. Connect the necessary electrical connectors to the engine.

46. Install the air cleaner assembly.

47. Connect the heater hoses to the engine. Install the radiator.

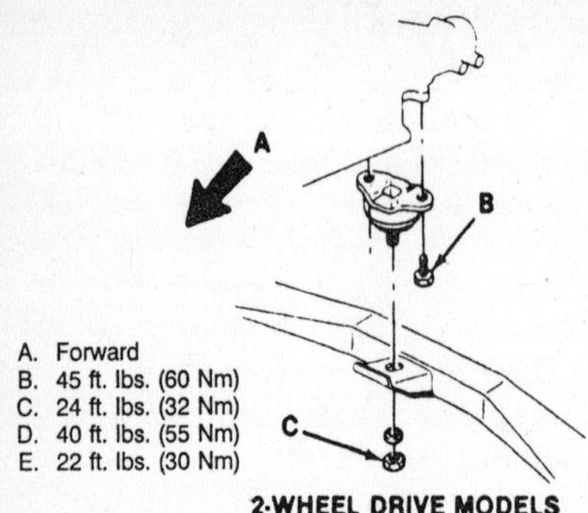

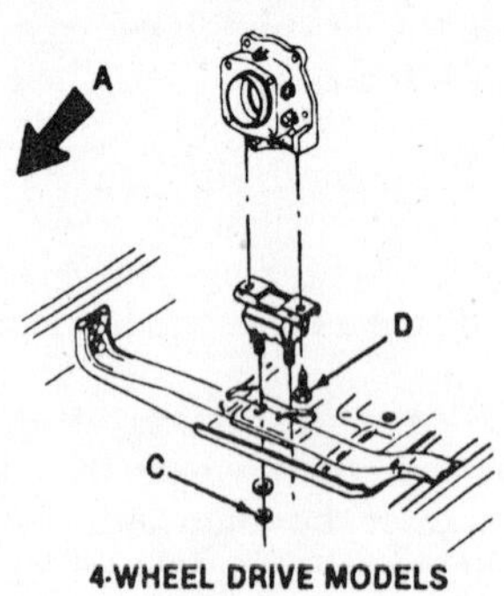

Exploded view of the rear engine mount — 4.3L engine

48. If equipped with an automatic transmission, connect the transmission and engine oil cooler lines to the engine.

49. Connect the lower cooling outlet hose to the radiator and the engine.

50. Install the upper cooling inlet hose to the radiator and the engine. Install the fan.

51. Install the upper fan shroud.

52. Lower the vehicle. Refill the cooling system and the engine crankcase.

53. Connect the negative battery cable.

54. Start the engine, allow it to reach normal operating temperatures and check for leaks.

4-WHEEL DRIVE

1. Disconnect the negative battery cable.

2. Remove the underhood light.

3. Raise and safely support the vehicle.

4. Remove the front air dam end bolts.

5. Remove the upper transmission-to-engine bolts and lower the vehicle.

6. Remove the remaining transmission-to-engine bolts.

7. Remove the 2nd crossmember.

8. Disconnect the exhaust pipes from the exhaust manifold.

9. Remove the catalytic converter hanger.

10. Remove the torque converter cover bolts and the cover. Matchmark the torque converter to flywheel. Remove the torque converter-to-flywheel bolts; it will be necessary to rotate the flywheel to access the other bolts.

11. Remove the front driveshaft from the front differential.

12. Disconnect the transmission cooler lines from the engine clips and lower the vehicle. Disconnect, drain and plug the transmission lines from the radiator.

13. Remove the engine mount through bolts. Remove the front splash shield-to-chassis bolts and the shield.

14. Remove the lower fan shroud bolts, lower the vehicle and drain the cooling system.

CAUTION: *When draining the coolant, keep in mind that cats and dogs are attracted by the ethylene glycol antifreeze, and are quite likely to drink any that is left in an uncovered container or in puddles on the ground. This will prove fatal in sufficient quantity. Always drain the coolant into a sealable container. Coolant should be reused unless it is contaminated or several years old.*

15. Remove the upper fan shroud bolts and the shroud.

16. Remove the radiator hoses from the radiator.

17. Remove the oil filter pipe and the remote oil filter.

18. Remove the radiator-to-chassis bolts and the radiator.

19. Remove the fan.

20. Remove the air cleaner assembly.

21. If equipped with air conditioning, remove the air conditioner compressor and lay it aside; do not disconnect the air conditioning hoses.

22. If equipped with power steering, the power steering pump and move it aside; do not disconnect the power steering hoses.

23. Disconnect and plug the fuel lines from the throttle body.

24. Label and disconnect the necessary electrical connectors from the engine.

25. Label and disconnect the necessary vacuum connectors from the engine.

26. Disconnect the accelerator cable, the TV cable and the cruise control cable from the engine.

27. Remove the electrical wiring harness from the bulkhead connector.

28. Disconnect the heater hoses from the engine. Using a floor jack, support the transmission.

29. Connect a vertical lifting device to the engine and lift the engine from the vehicle.

To install:

30. Lower the engine into the vehicle, install the engine-to-engine mount bolts and torque the **A** bolts to 42 ft. lbs. (57 Nm) or nuts to 35 ft. lbs. (47 Nm), the **B** bolts to 35 ft. lbs. (47 Nm) and the **C** nut/bolt to 52 ft. lbs. (70 Nm).

32. Install the rear engine mount-to-cross-

member bolts and torque the **A** bolts to 45 ft. lbs. (60 Nm), the **B** bolts to 24 ft. lbs. (32 Nm), the **C** bolts to 40 ft. lbs. (55 Nm) and the **E** bolts to 22 ft. lbs. (30 Nm).

33. Install the transmission-to-engine bolts.

34. Align the flywheel to torque converter matchmarks and install the bolts.

35. Install the front driveshaft to the front differential.

36. Install the catalytic converter to the hanger.

37. Connect the exhaust pipes to the exhaust manifolds.

38. Install the 2nd crossmember.

39. Install the lower fan shroud bolts and the splash shield.

40. Connect the transmission cooler lines to the engine clips.

41. Lower the vehicle and install the front air dam bolts.

42. Connect the electrical wiring harness to the bulkhead connector.

43. Connect the accelerator cable, the TV cable and the cruise control cable to the engine.

44. Connect the heater hoses to the engine.

45. Connect the necessary vacuum connectors to the engine.

46. Connect the necessary electrical connectors to the engine.

47. Connect and the fuel lines to the throttle body.

48. If equipped with power steering, connect the power steering pump.

49. If equipped with air conditioning, install the air conditioner compressor.

50. Install the fan and the radiator.

51. Using a new O-ring, install the oil filter pipe at the remote oil filter.

52. Install the radiator hoses.

53. Install the drive belts.

54. Install the fan shroud.

55. Lower the vehicle. Refill the cooling system.

56. Install the underhood light. Connect the negative battery cable.

57. Start the engine, allow it to reach normal operating temperatures and check for leaks.

Diesel Engine

REMOVAL AND INSTALLATION

2-Wheel Drive

1. Disconnect the negative battery terminal from the battery.

2. Using a scribing tool, mark the outline of the hood hinges on the hood, then remove the hinge bolts and the hood from the vehicle.

3. Remove the battery assembly.

CAUTION: *When draining the coolant, keep in mind that cats and dogs are attracted by the ethylene glycol antifreeze, and are quite likely to drink any that is left in an uncovered container or in puddles on the ground. This will prove fatal in sufficient quantity. Always drain the coolant into a sealable container. Coolant should be reused unless it is contaminated or several years old.*

4. Remove the splash shield, if equipped. Position a drain pan under the radiator, open the drain cock and drain the cooling system.

5. Remove the air cleaner assembly as follows:

    a. Remove the intake silencer.

    b. Remove the bolts fixing the air cleaner and loosen the clamp bolt.

    c. Lift the air cleaner slightly and disconnect the breather hose, then remove the air cleaner assembly.

6. Disconnect the upper radiator hose from the engine.

7. Loosen the air conditioner compressor drive belt(s) by moving the power steering oil pump or the idler, if equipped.

8. Remove the cooling fan and the fan shroud.

9. Disconnect the lower water hose the engine.

10. Remove the radiator grille and the radiator mounting bolts, then remove the radiator.

11. From the injection pump, disconnect the accelerator control cable and the fuel lines.

12. Disconnect the air conditioner compressor control cable, if equipped.

NOTE: *See the Chapter 5 for precautions and service procedures on the diesel engine injection pump and lines.*

13. Disconnect the battery cable from the cylinder block.

14. Disconnect the electrical connectors from the transmission, the fuel cut solenoid and the air conditioning compressor.

15. Disconnect the vacuum hose from the fast idle actuator.

16. From the cowl, disconnect the heater hoses at the heater unit.

17. If equipped with a vacuum pump, disconnect the master-vac hose and the vacuum hoses from the vacuum pump.

18. From the alternator, disconnect the electrical wiring connector(s).

19. From the exhaust manifold, disconnect the exhaust pipe. From the engine back plate, remove the exhaust pipe mounting brake.

20. Disconnect the electrical wiring connectors from the starter.

21. At the gearshift lever, slide the boot upwards, then remove the 2 gearshift lever mounting bolts and the lever.

22. Position an oil catch pan under the transmission, then remove the drain plug for manual transmission or the oil cooling lines for automatic transmission and drain the fluid from the transmission.

23. From the transmission, disconnect the speedometer cable and the ground cable.

24. Disconnect the drive shaft at differential side, then slide the driveshaft from the transmission and remove it from the vehicle.

25. If equipped with a manual transmission, remove the return spring from clutch fork and disconnect the clutch cable from the hooked portion of the clutch fork and pull it forward out through stiffener bracket.

26. Remove the transmission-to-rear bracket mount bolts and nuts.

27. Raise the engine/transmission assembly, as required, and remove the crossmember-to-frame bolts. Remove the mounting nuts from the transmission rear extension.

28. Disconnect the electrical connectors from the CRS switch and back-up lamp switch.

29. Be sure the engine is slightly lifted, then remove the engine mount nuts/bolts.

30. To remove the engine, perform the following procedures:

    a. Check that all of the parts have been removed or disconnected from the engine that are fastened to the frame side.

    b. Remove the engine toward the front of the vehicle, maneuvering the hose, so front part of the engine is lifted slightly.

31. To install, reverse the removal procedures. Torque engine mounting bolts to the following:

- Engine mount-to-engine: 35 ft. lbs.
- Engine mount-to-frame mount: 52 ft. lbs.
- Transmission mount-to-transmission: 45 ft. lbs.
- Transmission mount-to-crossmember: 24 ft. lbs.

4-Wheel Drive

1. Disconnect the negative battery terminal from the battery.

2. Using a scribing tool, mark the outline of the hood hinges on the hood, then remove the hinge bolts and the hood from the vehicle.

3. Remove the battery and the tray.

4. Remove the splash shield, if equipped. Position a drain pan under the radiator, open the drain cock and drain the cooling system.

CAUTION: *When draining the coolant, keep in mind that cats and dogs are attracted by the ethylene glycol antifreeze, and are quite likely to drink any that is left in an uncovered container or in puddles on the ground. This will prove fatal in sufficient quantity. Always drain the coolant into a sealable container. Coolant should be reused unless it is contaminated or several years old.*

5. Remove the air cleaner as follows:

    a. Remove the intake silencer.

    b. Remove the bolts fixing the air cleaner and loosen the clamp bolt.

    c. Lift the air cleaner slightly and disconnect the breather hose, then remove the air cleaner assembly.

6. From the engine, disconnect the upper radiator hose.

7. Loosen the compressor drive belts by moving the power steering oil pump or idler, if equipped.

8. Remove the cooling fan and fan shroud.

9. From the engine, disconnect the lower radiator hose.

10. Remove the radiator grille, the radiator mounting bolts and the radiator.

11. From the fuel injection pump, disconnect the accelerator control cable and the fuel hoses.

12. If equipped, disconnect the air conditioning compressor control cable.

13. Disconnect the battery cable from the cylinder block.

14. Disconnect the electrical wiring connectors from the transmission, the fuel cut solenoid and the air conditioning compressor.

15. Disconnect the vacuum hose(s) from the fast idle actuator and the master-vac hose from the vacuum pump.

16. At the cowl, disconnect the heater hoses from the heater unit.

17. From the alternator, disconnect the electrical wiring connectors.

18. From the exhaust manifold, disconnect the exhaust pipe, then remove the exhaust pipe mounting brake from the engine back plate.

19. From the starter, disconnect the electrical wiring connectors.

20. Slide the transmission and transfer gearshift lever boot upwards on each lever, remove the gearshift lever attaching bolts.

21. From the transfer case gearshift lever, remove the return spring, then the levers.

22. Remove the transmission.

23. Remove the engine mounting nuts/bolts; make sure the engine is slightly lifted before removing the mounting nuts/bolts.

24. To remove the engine, perform the following procedures:

    a. Check that all the parts have been removed or disconnected from the engine that are fastened to the frame side.

    b. Move the engine toward the front of the vehicle by maneuvering the hoist, so front part of the engine is lifted slightly, then remove the engine.

25. To install the engine, reverse the removal

procedures. Torque engine mounting bolts to the following:

- Engine mount-to-engine: 35 ft. lbs.
- Engine mount-to-frame mount: 52 ft. lbs.
- Transmission mount-to-transmission: 45 ft. lbs.
- Transmission mount-to-crossmember: 24 ft. lbs.

Rocker Arm Cover

REMOVAL AND INSTALLATION

1.9L Engine

1. Disconnect the negative battery terminal from the battery.
2. Remove the air cleaner assembly.
3. From the rocker arm cover, remove the spark plug wires, the evaporator pipe from the intake manifold-to-engine lift bracket.
4. Remove the rocker arm cover-to-engine nuts/washers.
5. Remove the rocker arm cover.
6. Using a putty knife, clean the gasket mounting surfaces.
7. To install, use a new gasket and reverse the removal procedures.

2.0L Engine

1. Disconnect the negative battery terminal from the battery.
2. Remove the air cleaner assembly and the distributor cap.

3. Remove the fuel vapor canister harness tubes from the rocker arm cover.
4. Remove the accelerator cable and the PCV valve.
5. Remove the rocker arm cover-to-cylinder head bolts and the cover.

NOTE: *If the cover sticks, use a rubber mallet to bump it or a prying tool to lift it from the cylinder head.*

6. Using a putty knife, clean the gasket mounting surfaces.
7. To install, use a new gasket, an $1/8$ in. bead of RTV sealant and reverse the removal procedures. Torque the rocker arm cover-to-cylinder head bolts to 8 ft. lbs.

2.2L Diesel Engine

1. Disconnect the negative battery terminal from the battery.
2. Remove the PCV valve from the rocker arm cover and the PCV valve hose.
3. Remove the air cleaner.
4. Remove the rocker arm cover-to-cylinder head bolts and the cover from the engine.
5. Using a putty knife, clean the gasket mounting surfaces.
6. To install, use a new gasket and reverse the removal procedures. Torque the rocker arm cover-to-cylinder head bolts to 9–13 ft. lbs.

2.5L Engine

1. Disconnect the negative battery cable from the battery.
2. Remove the air cleaner.
3. Disconnect the Positive Crankcase Ven-

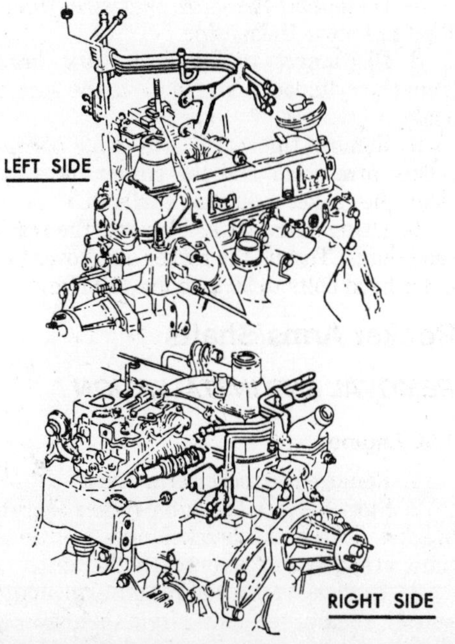

Removing the fuel evaporation tubes — 2.0L engine

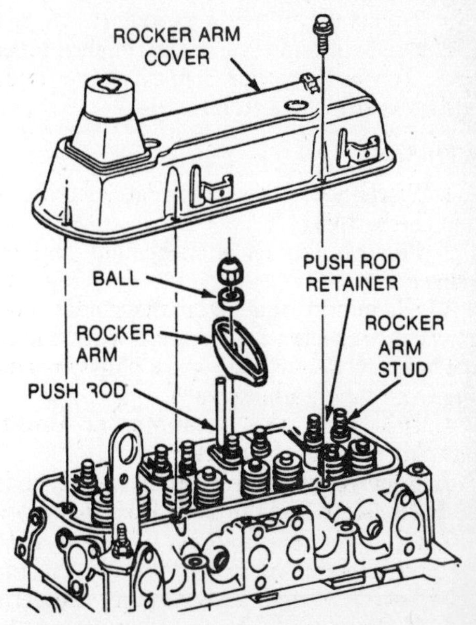

Exploded view of the rocker arm cover — 2.0L engine

tilation (PCV) valve hose, the ignition wires from the rocker arm cover.

4. Remove the Exhaust Gas Recirculation (EGR) valve.

5. From the intake manifold stud, label and disconnect the vacuum hoses.

6. Remove the rocker arm cover-to-cylinder head bolts and the cover.

7. Using a putty knife, clean the gasket mounting surfaces.

NOTE: *Be sure to use solvent to remove any oil or grease that may remain on the sealing surfaces.*

8. To install, use a new gasket, a $\frac{3}{16}$ in. (5mm) continuous bead of RTV sealant and reverse the removal procedures. Torque the valve cover-to-cylinder head bolts to 6 ft. lbs.

2.8L Engine

LEFT SIDE

1. Disconnect the negative battery terminal from the battery.

2. Disconnect the air management hose, the vacuum hose(s), the electrical wires and the pipe bracket. Remove the spark plug wires and clips from the retaining stubs.

3. Disconnect the fuel line(s) from the carburetor or throttle body.

4. Remove the rocker arm cover-to-cylinder head bolts/studs and the cover from the engine.

NOTE: *If the cover will not lift, use a rubber mallet to bump it loose from the cylinder head or use a small prybar to lift the cover.*

5. Using a putty knife, clean the gasket mounting surfaces.

6. To install, use a new gasket, a $\frac{1}{8}$ in. bead of RTV sealant and reverse the removal procedures. Torque the rocker arm cover-to-cylinder head bolts/studs to 8 ft. lbs.

RIGHT SIDE

1. Disconnect the negative battery terminal from the battery.

2. Remove the air management and coil brackets.

3. Disconnect the air management hose, the vacuum hose(s), the electrical wires and the pipe bracket. Remove the spark plug wires and clips from the retaining stubs.

4. Disconnect the carburetor or throttle body controls and the brackets.

5. Remove the rocker arm cover-to-cylinder head bolts/studs and the cover from the engine.

NOTE: *If the cover will not lift, use a rubber mallet to bump it loose from the cylinder head or use a small prybar to lift the cover.*

6. Using a putty knife, clean the gasket mounting surfaces.

7. To install, use a new gasket, a $\frac{1}{8}$ in. bead

of RTV sealant and reverse the removal procedures. Torque the rocker arm cover-to-cylinder head bolts/studs to 8 ft. lbs.

4.3L Engine

LEFT SIDE

1. Disconnect the negative battery cable.

2. Remove the air cleaner and the heat stove tube.

3. Remove the crankcase ventilation pipe.

4. Disconnect the fuel lines from the TBI and the retaining clips and move them aside.

5. Remove the alternator rear bracket.

6. Disconnect the spark plug wires from the clips and move them aside.

7. Disconnect the power brake vacuum line from the intake manifold and move it aside.

8. Remove the rocker arm cover bolts, the rocker arm cover and the gasket; be sure to clean the gasket mounting surfaces.

9. Using a new gasket, reverse the removal procedures. Torque the rocker arm cover-to-cylinder head bolts to 90 inch lbs. (10 Nm).

RIGHT SIDE

1. Disconnect the negative battery cable.

2. Remove the air cleaner.

3. Remove the PCV valve.

4. Disconnect the heater pipe from the intake manifold.

5. Remove the emission relays with the bracket and move the assembly aside.

6. Disconnect the electrical wiring harness from the clips move it aside.

7. Disconnect the spark plug wires from the clips and move them aside.

8. Disconnect the dipstick tube bracket from the cylinder head and move the assembly aside.

9. Remove the rocker arm cover bolts, the rocker arm cover and the gasket; be sure to clean the gasket mounting surfaces.

10. Using a new gasket, reverse the removal procedures. Torque the rocker arm cover-to-cylinder head bolts to 90 inch lbs. (10 Nm).

Rocker Arms/Shafts

REMOVAL AND INSTALLATION

1.9L Engine

1. Remove the rocker arm cover.

2. Starting with the outer rocker arm shaft bracket, loosen the bracket nuts a little at a time, in sequence, then remove the nuts.

3. To disassemble the rocker arm shaft assembly, remove the spring from the rocker arm shaft, then the rocker arm brackets and arms.

4. Inspect the rocker arm shafts for run-

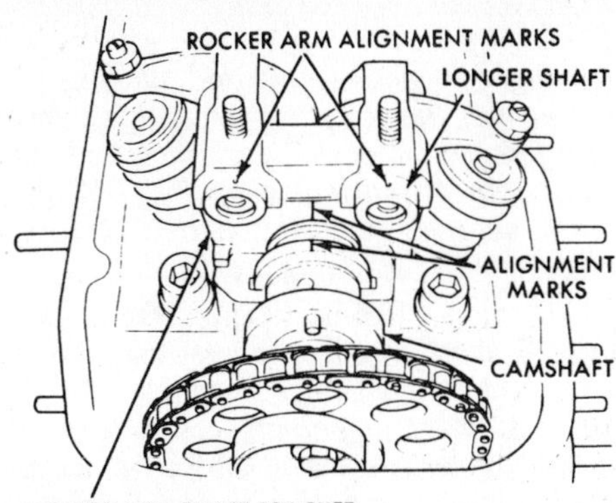

Rocker shaft removal/installation — 1.9L engine

nout, wear and/or damage, if necessary, replace the rocker arm shafts.

To install:

5. Using engine oil, lubricate all of the moving parts.

NOTE: *When installing the rocker arm shafts, position the longer shaft on the exhaust valve side with the shafts alignment mark facing the front side of the engine.*

6. Align the mark on the No. 1 rocker arm shaft bracket with the mark on the intake and exhaust valve side rocker arm shafts.

7. To complete the installation, torque the rocker arm shaft bracket stud nuts to 16 ft. lbs.

NOTE: *The valves are adjusted with the engine Cold.*

8. Using a wrench on the damper pulley bolt or a remote starter button, turn the engine's crankshaft until the No. 1 piston is at TDC of the compression stroke.

NOTE: *You can tell when the piston is coming up on the compression stroke by removing the spark plug and placing your thumb over the hole, then you will feel the air being forced out of the spark plug hole. Stop turning the crankshaft when the TDC timing mark on the crankshaft pulley is directly aligned with the timing mark pointer.*

9. Using a 0.006 in. (0.152mm) feeler gauge, set intake valves of cylinders No. 1 and 2. Using a 0.010 in. (0.254mm) feeler gauge, set the exhaust valves of cylinders No. 1 and 3.

10. Rotate the engine one complete revolution, so cylinder No. 4 is on the TDC of its compression stroke and the timing marks are aligned.

11. Using a 0.006 in. (0.152mm) feeler gauge, set intake valves of cylinders No. 3 and 4. Using a 0.010 in. (0.254mm) feeler gauge, set the exhaust valves of cylinders No. 2 and 4.

NOTE: *When adjusting the valve clearance, loosen the locknut with an open-end wrench,* then turn the adjuster screw with a screwdriver and retighten the locknut. The proper thickness feeler gauge should pass between the camshaft and the rocker with a slight drag when the clearance is correct.

12. To complete the installation, reverse the removal procedures.

2.0L Engine

1. Remove the rocker arm cover.

2. Remove the rocker arm nuts, the ball washers and the rocker arms off the studs, then lift out the pushrods.

NOTE: *Always keep the rocker arm assemblies together and install them on the same stud.*

To install:

3. Coat the bearing surfaces of the rocker arms and the rocker arm ball washers with Molykote® or its equivalent.

NOTE: *At time of installation, flanges must be free of oil. A bead of sealant must be applied to flanges and sealant must be wet to touch when bolts are torqued.*

4. Install the pushrods making sure they seat properly in the lifter.

5. Install the rocker arms, the ball washers and the nuts. Tighten the rocker arm nuts until all lash is eliminated.

6. Adjust the valves when the lifter is on the base circle of a camshaft lobe:

a. Crank the engine until the mark on the crankshaft pulley lines up with the **0** degree mark on the timing tab. Make sure the engine is in the No. 1 firing position. Place your fingers on the No. 1 rocker arms

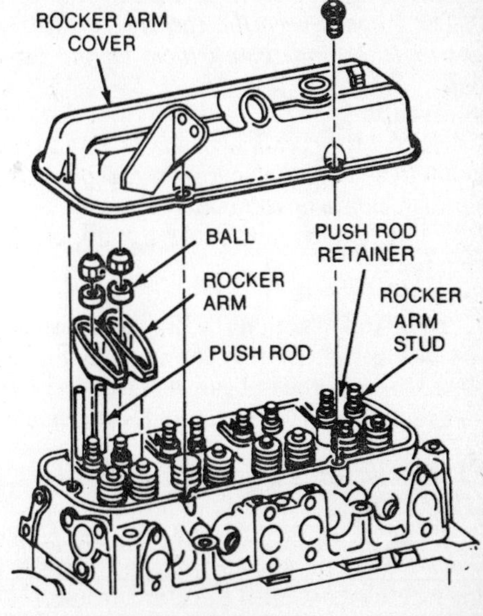

Rocker arm removal/installation — 2.0L engine

as the mark on the crank pulley comes near the **0** degree mark.

NOTE: *If the valves are not moving, the engine is in the No. 1 firing position. If the valves move, the engine is in the No. 4 firing position; rotate the engine one complete revolution and it will be in the No. 1 position.*

b. When the engine is on the No. 1 firing position, adjust the following valves:

- Exhaust – 1, 3
- Intake – 1, 2

c. Back the adjusting nut out until lash can be felt at the pushrod, then turn the nut until all lash is removed (this can be determined by rotating the pushrod while turning the adjusting nut). When all lash has been removed, turn the nut in 1½ additional turns, this will center the lifter plunger.

d. Crank the engine one complete revolution until the timing tab (**0** degree mark) and the crankshaft pulley mark are again in alignment. Now the engine is in the No. 4 firing position. Adjust the following valves:

- Exhaust – 2, 4
- Intake – 3, 4

7. After adjusting the valves, reverse the removal procedures. Start the engine, then check the timing and the idle speed.

2.2L Diesel Engine

1. Remove the rocker cover.

2. Remove the rocker arm bracket-to-cylinder head bolts in sequence, commencing with the outer ones.

3. Remove the rocker arm, the bracket and shaft assembly.

4. To disassemble, remove the snapring, the rocker arms, the springs and the brackets.

NOTE: *Always keep the rocker arm assemblies together and install them on the same stud.*

To install:

5. Inspect the rocker arm shafts for runout, wear and/or damage, if necessary, replace the rocker arm shafts or components.

6. Using engine oil, lubricate all of the moving parts.

To install:

7. To install, position the brackets with the marks facing the front of the engine. Torque the bracket-to-cylinder head bolts to 9–17 ft. lbs., working from the center and working outward.

NOTE: *The valves are adjusted with the engine Cold.*

8. Using a wrench on the damper pulley bolt or a remote starter button, turn the engine's crankshaft until the No. 1 piston is at TDC of the compression stroke.

NOTE: *You can tell when the piston is coming up on the compression stroke by removing the spark plug and placing your thumb over the hole, then you will feel the air being forced out of the spark plug hole. Stop turning the crankshaft when the TDC timing mark on the crankshaft pulley is directly aligned with the timing mark pointer.*

9. Using a 0.016 in. (0.4mm) feeler gauge, set the intake valves of cylinders No. 1, 2 and 3, then set the exhaust valve of cylinder No. 1.

10. Rotate the engine one complete revolution, so cylinder No. 4 is on the TDC of its compression stroke and the timing marks are aligned.

11. Using a 0.016 in. (0.4mm) feeler gauge, set the intake valve of cylinder No. 4, then the exhaust valves of cylinders No. 2, 3 and 4.

NOTE: *When adjusting the valve clearance, loosen the locknut with an open-end wrench, then turn the adjuster screw with a screwdriver and retighten the locknut. The proper thickness feeler gauge should pass between the camshaft and the rocker with a slight drag when the clearance is correct.*

12. To complete the installation, reverse the removal procedures.

2.5L Engine

The rocker arm opens and closes the valves through a very simple ball pivot type operation.

1. Remove the rocker arm cover.

2. Using a socket wrench, remove the rocker arm bolts, the ball washer and the rocker arm.

NOTE: *If only the pushrod is to be removed, back off the rocker arm bolt, swing the rocker arm aside and remove the pushrod. When removing more than one assembly, at the same time, be sure to keep them in order for reassembly purposes.*

To install:

3. Inspect the rocker arms and ball washers for scoring and/or other damage, replace them, if necessary.

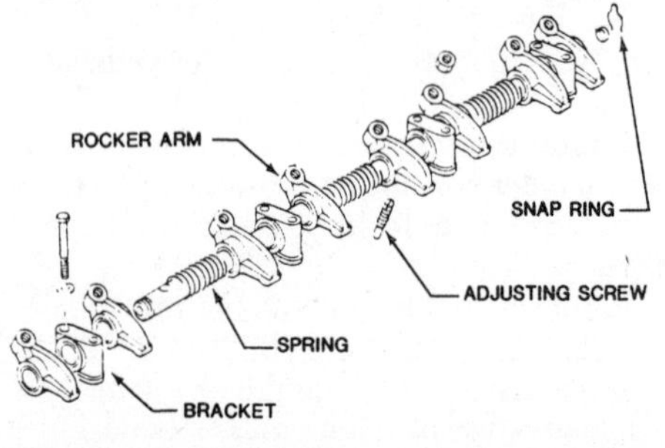

Rocker shaft assembly — 2.2L engine

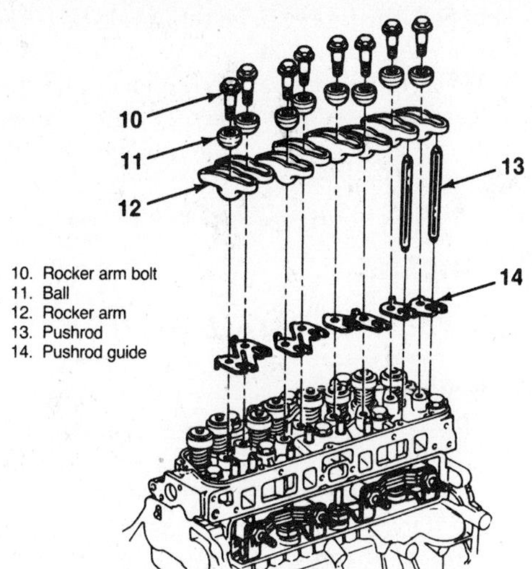

Rocker arm removal/installation — 2.5L engine

NOTE: *If replacing worn components with new ones, be sure to coat the new parts with Molykote® before installation.*

4. Torque the rocker arm-to-cylinder head bolts to 20 ft. lbs.; do not over tighten.

5. To complete the installation, reverse the removal procedures. Start the engine, the check for oil leaks and engine operation.

2.8L Engine

1. Remove the rocker arm cover.

2. Remove the rocker arm nut, the rocker arm and the ball washer.

NOTE: *If only the pushrod is to be removed, loosen the rocker arm nut, swing the rocker arm to the side and remove the pushrod.*

To install:

3. Inspect the part for damage, wear and/or scoring; if necessary, replace the damaged parts.

4. Before installation, coat all of the working parts with Molykote®.

5. To adjust the valves, rotate the crankshaft until the mark on the crankshaft pulley aligns with the **0** mark on the timing plate. Make sure the No. 1 cylinder is positioned on the compression stroke.

NOTE: *To determine the compression stroke, place your fingers on the No. 1 rocker arms, as the mark on the crankshaft pulley comes near the **0** mark on the timing plate. If the valves move, the engine is on the No. 4 firing position; rotate the crankshaft one complete revolution and realign the pulley mark with the timing plate **0** mark.*

6. Adjust the intake valves of cylinders No. 1, 5 and 6 and the exhaust valves of cylinders No. 1, 2 and 3.

7. To adjust the valves, back-out the adjust-

ing nut until lash can be felt at the pushrod, then turn the nut until all of the lash is removed.

NOTE: *To determine is all of the lash is removed, turn the pushrod with your fingers until the movement is removed.*

8. When all of the lash has been removed, turn the adjusting an additional 1½ turns; this will center the lifter plunger.

9. Rotate the crankshaft one complete revolution and realign the timing marks; the engine is now positioned on the No. 4 firing position.

10. Adjust the intake valves of cylinders No. 2, 3 and 4 and the exhaust valves of cylinders No. 4, 5 and 6. 11. To compete the installation, reverse the removal procedures.

NOTE: *Some engines are assembled using Room Temperature Vulcanizing (RTV) silicone sealant in place of rocker arm cover gasket. If the engine was assembled using RTV, never use a gasket when reassembling. Conversely, if the engine was assembled using a rocker arm cover gasket, never replace it with RTV. When using RTV, an ⅛ in. (3mm) inch bead is sufficient. Always run the bead on the inside of the bolt holes.*

Cylinder heads use threaded rocker arm studs. If the threads in the head are damaged or stripped, the head can be retapped and a helical type insert installed.

NOTE: *If the engine is equipped with the AIR exhaust emission control system, the interfering components of the system must be removed. Disconnect the lines of the air injection nozzles in the exhaust manifolds.*

4.3L Engine

1. Remove the rocker arm cover.

2. Remove the rocker arm nut, the rocker arm and the ball washer.

NOTE: *If only the pushrod is to be removed, loosen the rocker arm nut, swing the rocker arm to the side and remove the pushrod.*

To install:

3. Inspect the part for damage, wear and/or scoring; if necessary, replace the damaged parts.

4. Before installation, coat all of the working parts with Molykote®.

5. To adjust the valves, rotate the crankshaft until the mark on the crankshaft pulley aligns with the **0** mark on the timing plate. Make sure the No. 1 cylinder is positioned on the compression stroke.

NOTE: *To determine the compression stroke, place your fingers on the No. 1 rocker arms, as the mark on the crankshaft pulley comes near the "0" mark on the timing plate. If the valves move, the engine is on the No. 4 firing position; rotate the crankshaft one com-*

plete revolution and realign the pulley mark with the timing plate "0" mark.

6. Adjust the exhaust valves of cylinders No. 1, 5 and 6 and the intake valves of cylinders No. 1, 2 and 3.

7. To adjust the valves, back-out the adjusting nut until lash can be felt at the pushrod, then turn the nut until all of the lash is removed.

NOTE: *To determine is all of the lash is removed, turn the pushrod with your fingers until the movement is removed.*

8. When all of the lash has been removed, turn the adjusting an additional 1 turn; this will center the lifter plunger.

9. Rotate the crankshaft 1 complete revolution and realign the timing marks; the engine is now positioned on the No. 4 firing position.

10. Adjust the exhaust valves of cylinders No. 2, 3 and 4 and the intake valves of cylinders No. 4, 5 and 6. 11. To compete the installation, reverse the removal procedures.

NOTE: *Some engines are assembled using Room Temperature Vulcanizing (RTV) silicone sealant in place of rocker arm cover gasket. If the engine was assembled using RTV, never use a gasket when reassembling. Conversely, if the engine was assembled using a rocker arm cover gasket, never replace it with RTV. When using RTV, an $^1/_8$ in. (3mm) inch bead is sufficient. Always run the bead on the inside of the bolt holes.*

Cylinder heads use threaded rocker arm studs. If the threads in the head are damaged or stripped, the head can be retapped and a helical type insert installed.

NOTE: *If the engine is equipped with the AIR exhaust emission control system, the interfering components of the system must be removed. Disconnect the lines of the air injection nozzles in the exhaust manifolds.*

Thermostat

REMOVAL AND INSTALLATION

1.9L Engine

1. Place a drain pan under the radiator, open the drain cock and drain the cooling system to a level below the thermostat.

CAUTION: *When draining the coolant, keep in mind that cats and dogs are attracted by the ethylene glycol antifreeze, and are quite likely to drink any that is left in an uncovered container or in puddles on the ground. This will prove fatal in sufficient quantity. Always drain the coolant into a sealable container. Coolant should be reused unless it is contaminated or several years old.*

2. Disconnect the PCV hose, the ECS hose, the Air hose and the TCA hose.

3. Remove the air cleaner-to-carburetor bolts and loosen the clamp bolts, then lift the air cleaner and disconnect the TCA hose from the thermosenser (on the intake manifold). Remove the rubber hoses from the air cleaner-to-carburetor slow actuator and the air cleaner-to-vacuum control (California), then remove the air cleaner assembly.

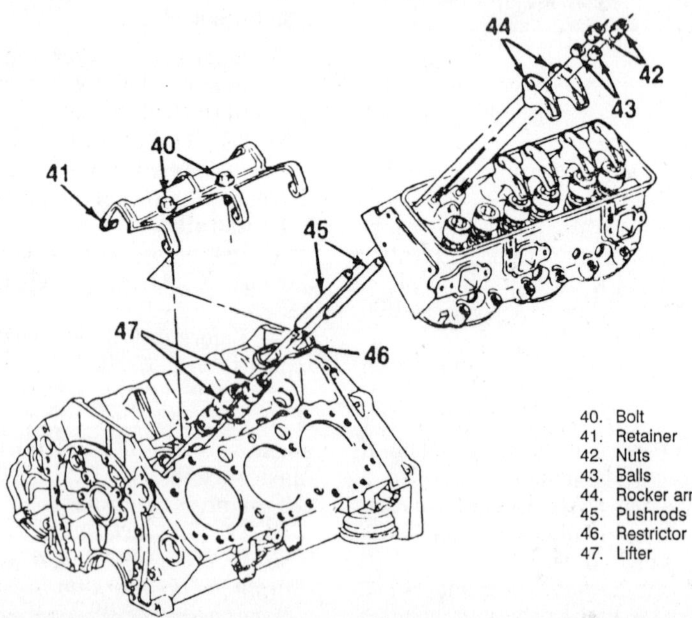

Exploded view of the rocker arm assembly — 4.3L engine

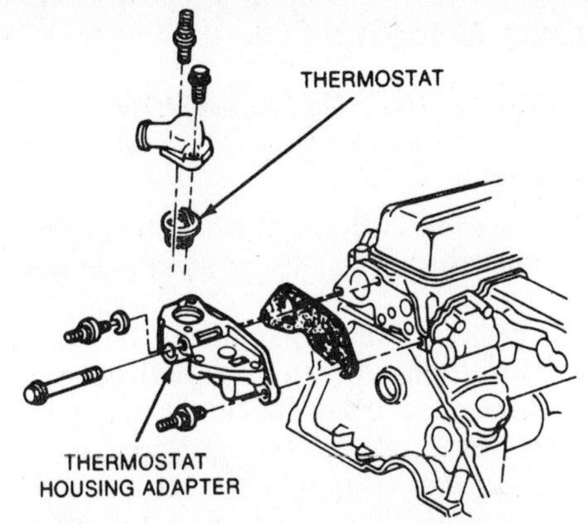

Thermostat replacement — 2.0L engine

4. Remove the outlet pipe-to-inlet manifold bolts, the outlet pipe (with the radiator hose attached) and the thermostat from the engine.

5. Using a putty knife, clean the gasket mounting surfaces.

6. To install, use a new gasket, RTV gasket sealant, the thermostat and reverse the removal procedures; install the outlet pipe while the sealant is wet. Torque the outlet pipe-to-intake manifold bolts to 21 ft. lbs. (28 Nm). Refill the cooling system with a 50 percent anti-freeze solution. Start the engine and check for leaks.

2.0L Engine

The thermostat is connected to the water outlet and the thermostat housing, located at the top front side of the engine.

1. Disconnect the negative battery terminal from the battery.

2. Place a drain pan under the radiator, open the drain cock and drain the cooling system to a level below the thermostat.

CAUTION: *When draining the coolant, keep in mind that cats and dogs are attracted by the ethylene glycol antifreeze, and are quite likely to drink any that is left in an uncovered container or in puddles on the ground. This will prove fatal in sufficient quantity. Always drain the coolant into a sealable container. Coolant should be reused unless it is contaminated or several years old.*

3. Remove the steel vacuum tubes.

4. Remove the water outlet-to-thermostat housing bolts, then lift the outlet from the thermostat housing and remove the thermostat.

5. Using a putty knife, clean the gasket mounting surfaces.

6. To install, use a new gasket, RTV gasket sealant, the thermostat and reverse the removal procedures; install the water outlet while the sealant is wet. Torque the water outlet-to-thermostat housing bolts to 17–22 ft.

lbs. Refill the cooling system with a 50 percent anti-freeze solution. Start the engine and check for leaks.

2.2L Diesel Engine

The thermostat is connected to the water outlet and the thermostat housing, located at the top front side of the engine.

1. Disconnect the negative battery terminal from the battery.

2. Place a drain pan under the radiator, open the drain cock and drain the cooling system to a level below the thermostat.

CAUTION: *When draining the coolant, keep in mind that cats and dogs are attracted by the ethylene glycol antifreeze, and are quite likely to drink any that is left in an uncovered container or in puddles on the ground. This will prove fatal in sufficient quantity. Always drain the coolant into a sealable container. Coolant should be reused unless it is contaminated or several years old.*

3. Disconnect the electrical wiring.

4. Remove the water outlet-to-thermostat housing bolts, then lift the outlet from the thermostat housing and remove the thermostat.

5. Using a putty knife, clean the gasket mounting surfaces.

6. To install, use a new gasket, RTV gasket sealant, the thermostat and reverse the removal procedures; install the water outlet while the sealant is wet. Torque the water outlet-to-thermostat housing bolts to 10–17 ft. lbs. Refill the cooling system with a 50 percent anti-freeze solution. Start the engine and check for leaks.

2.5L Engine

The thermostat is located inside the thermostat housing, which is attached to the front of the cylinder head.

1. Disconnect the negative battery cable from the battery.

2. Place a catch pan under the radiator, open the drain cock and drain the cooling system.

CAUTION: *When draining the coolant, keep in mind that cats and dogs are attracted by the ethylene glycol antifreeze, and are quite likely to drink any that is left in an uncovered container or in puddles on the ground. This will prove fatal in sufficient quantity. Always drain the coolant into a sealable container. Coolant should be reused unless it is contaminated or several years old.*

3. Remove the thermostat housing-to-engine bolts and the thermostat.

4. Using a putty knife, clean the gasket mounting surfaces.

5. Using RTV sealant or equivalent, place

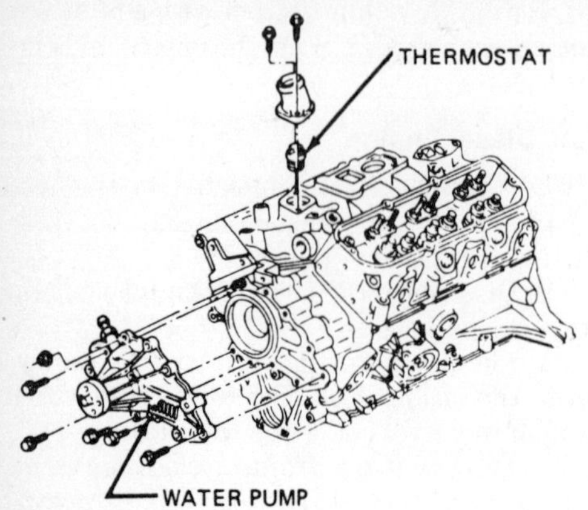

Exploded view of the thermostat and housing — 2.8L and 4.3L engines

an $^1/_8$ in. bead of sealant in the groove of the water outlet.

6. To install, use a new thermostat, if possible, a new gasket and reverse the removal procedures. Torque the thermostat housing-to-engine bolts to 21 ft. lbs. Refill the cooling system. Reconnect the battery cable, start the engine and check for leaks.

2.8L and 4.3L Engines

The thermostat is located between the water outlet and the front of the intake manifold.

1. Disconnect the negative battery terminal from the battery.
2. Place a drain pan under the radiator, open the drain cock and drain the cooling system to a level below the thermostat.

CAUTION: *When draining the coolant, keep in mind that cats and dogs are attracted by the ethylene glycol antifreeze, and are quite likely to drink any that is left in an uncovered container or in puddles on the ground. This will prove fatal in sufficient quantity. Always drain the coolant into a sealable container. Coolant should be reused unless it is contaminated or several years old.*

3. Remove the water outlet-to-intake manifold bolts, then lift the outlet from the intake manifold and remove the thermostat.
4. Using a putty knife, clean the gasket mounting surfaces.
5. To install, use RTV gasket sealant (place an $^1/_8$ in. bead in the groove on the outlet housing), the thermostat and reverse the removal procedures; install the water outlet housing while the sealant is wet. Torque the water outlet-to-intake manifold bolts to 21 ft. lbs. (28 Nm). Refill the cooling system with a 50 percent anti-freeze solution. Start the engine and check for leaks.

Intake Manifold

REMOVAL AND INSTALLATION

1.9L Engine

1. Disconnect the negative battery terminal from the battery. Remove the air cleaner assembly.
2. Position a drain pan under the radiator, open the drain cock and drain the cooling system to a level below the intake manifold.

CAUTION: *When draining the coolant, keep in mind that cats and dogs are attracted by the ethylene glycol antifreeze, and are quite likely to drink any that is left in an uncovered container or in puddles on the ground. This will prove fatal in sufficient quantity. Always drain the coolant into a sealable container. Coolant should be reused unless it is contaminated or several years old.*

3. From the intake manifold, disconnect the upper radiator hose, the vacuum hose, the heater hose (from the rear of the intake manifold).
4. From the carburetor, disconnect the accelerator control cable, then the automatic choke and the solenoid electrical connectors.
5. From the distributor, disconnect the vacuum advance hose and the thermo-unit wiring electrical connector.
6. Disconnect the PCV valve from the rocker arm cover, then remove the oil level gauge guide tube-to-intake manifold bolt.
7. Disconnect the EGR pipe from the EGR valve adapter, the EGR valve and the adapter. Remove the nut from under the EGR valve.
8. Disconnect the AIR vacuum hose from the 3-way connector.
9. Remove the intake manifold-to-cylinder head nuts and the intake manifold from the engine.
10. Using a putty knife, clean the gasket mounting surfaces. Inspect the manifold for cracks, damage or distortion; if necessary, replace the intake manifold.
11. To install, use a new gasket and reverse the removal procedures.

2.0L Engine

1. Disconnect the negative battery terminal from the battery.
2. Remove the air cleaner, then the distributor cap, the distributor hold-down nut and clamp.
3. Raise and support the vehicle on jackstands.
4. Position a drain pan under the radiator, open the drain cock and drain the cooling system to a level below the intake manifold.

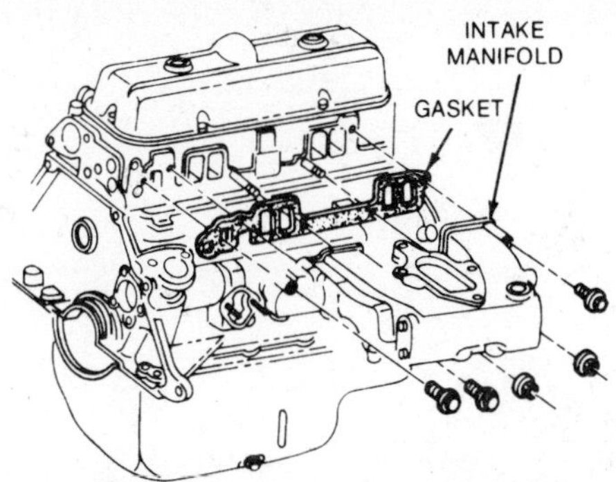

Intake manifold removal/installation — 2.0L engine

CAUTION: *When draining the coolant, keep in mind that cats and dogs are attracted by the ethylene glycol antifreeze, and are quite likely to drink any that is left in an uncovered container or in puddles on the ground. This will prove fatal in sufficient quantity. Always drain the coolant into a sealable container. Coolant should be reused unless it is contaminated or several years old.*

5. Tag and disconnect the vacuum hose and the primary wires from the coil.

6. Remove the fuel pump-to-engine bolts and allow the pump to hang.

7. Remove the jackstands and lower the vehicle.

8. Disconnect the accelerator cable, the fuel inlet line, then the necessary vacuum hoses and wires. Remove the carburetor-to-intake manifold nuts, the carburetor and lift off the Early Fuel Evaporation (EFE) heater grid.

9. Disconnect the fuel vapor harness pipes from the cylinder head.

10. From the intake manifold, disconnect the heater hose, the bypass hose, the necessary hoses and wires. Remove the intake manifold-to-cylinder head nuts/bolts, the intake manifold and the gasket.

11. Using a putty knife, clean the gasket mounting surfaces. Inspect the manifold for cracks, damage or distortion; if necessary, replace the intake manifold.

12. To install, use a new gasket and reverse the removal procedures. Torque the intake manifold-to-cylinder head nuts/bolts to 25 ft. lbs. Refill the cooling system. Adjust the drive belts. Check and/or adjust the engine timing and idle speed.

2.2L Diesel Engine

1. Disconnect the negative battery terminal from the battery.

2. Remove the air cleaner.

3. Disconnect the heater pipe bracket, the PCV valve hose, the necessary wires and clips from the intake manifold.

4. Remove the intake manifold-to-cylinder head bolts and the intake manifold.

NOTE: *If removing the intake/exhaust manifold gasket, it will be necessary to remove the exhaust manifold.*

5. If the exhaust manifold has been removed, perform the following procedures:

a. Using a putty knife, clean the gasket mounting surfaces.

b. Inspect the manifold for cracks, damage or distortion; if necessary, replace the intake manifold.

c. Using a new gasket, install it onto the cylinder head.

6. To install, reverse the removal procedures. Torque the intake manifold-to-cylinder head nuts/bolts to 10–17 ft. lbs., starting from the center and working outward.

2.5L Engine

The intake manifold is located on the right side of the cylinder head.

CAUTION: *Relieve the pressure on the fuel system before disconnecting any fuel line connection.*

1. Disconnect the negative battery cable from the battery.

2. Place a catch pan under the radiator, open the drain cock and drain the cooling fluid.

CAUTION: *When draining the coolant, keep in mind that cats and dogs are attracted by the ethylene glycol antifreeze, and are quite likely to drink any that is left in an uncovered container or in puddles on the ground. This will prove fatal in sufficient quantity. Always drain the coolant into a sealable container. Coolant should be reused unless it is contaminated or several years old.*

3. Remove the air cleaner assembly. Label and disconnect the vacuum hoses from the exhaust manifold, thermostat housing and etc.

4. Label and disconnect the electrical con-

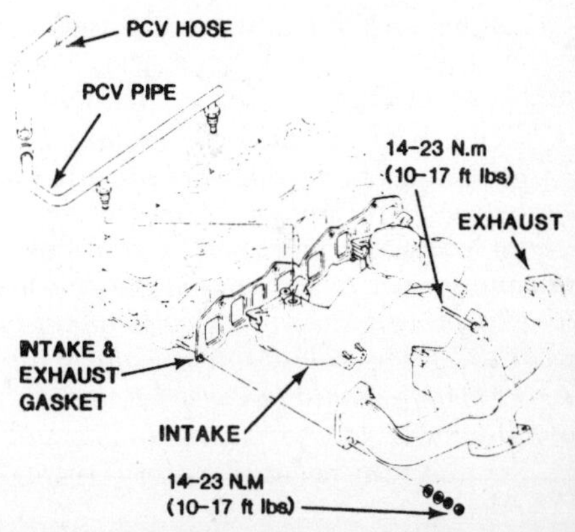

Intake manifold removal/installation — 2.2L engine

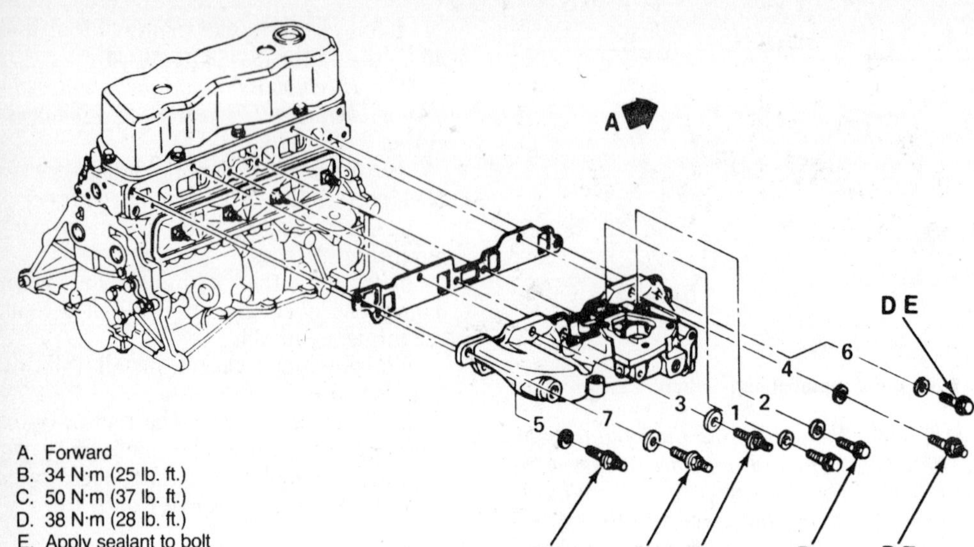

A. Forward
B. 34 N·m (25 lb. ft.)
C. 50 N·m (37 lb. ft.)
D. 38 N·m (28 lb. ft.)
E. Apply sealant to bolt

Intake manifold removal/installation — 2.5L engine

nectors that may be in the way. Disconnect the accelerator, the cruise control and TV cables.

5. Remove the coolant hoses from the intake manifold. Remove and plug the fuel line at the throttle body.

6. Remove the alternator bracket-to-engine bolts and move the alternator/bracket aside.

7. Remove the ignition coil-to-cylinder head/intake manifold bolts and the coil from the engine.

8. Remove the intake manifold-to-engine bolts and the manifold from the engine.

9. Using a putty knife, clean the gasket mounting surfaces.

10. To install, use a new gasket, sealant (for some bolts) and reverse the removal procedures. Torque the intake manifold-to-engine bolts to 25–37 ft. lbs. Refill the cooling system. Start the engine and check for leaks.

2.8L Engine

1. Position a drain pan under the radiator, open the drain cock and drain the cooling system to a level below the intake manifold.

CAUTION: *When draining the coolant, keep in mind that cats and dogs are attracted by the ethylene glycol antifreeze, and are quite likely to drink any that is left in an uncovered container or in puddles on the ground. This will prove fatal in sufficient quantity. Always drain the coolant into a sealable container. Coolant should be reused unless it is contaminated or several years old.*

2. Disconnect the negative battery terminal from the battery.

3. Remove the air cleaner. Remove the electrical connectors, the vacuum hoses, the fuel lines and the accelerator cables from the carburetor or TBI unit.

4. If equipped with an AIR management system, remove the hose and the mounting bracket.

5. Label and disconnect the spark plug wires from the spark plugs and the electrical connectors from the ignition coil. Disconnect the coolant switch electrical connectors on the intake manifold.

6. Remove the distributor cap (with the wires connected). Mark the position of the rotor-to-distributor body and the distributor body-to-engine relationships, then remove the distributor from the engine; do not crank the engine with the distributor removed.

7. Remove the heater and upper radiator hoses from the intake manifold.

8. If equipped, remove the evaporative canister and the power brake vacuum hoses from the intake manifold; remove the emission canister pipe bracket(s) from the rear of the rocker arm covers.

9. Remove the rocker arm covers.

10. Remove the intake manifold-to-engine nuts and bolts, then the intake manifold from the engine.

11. Using a putty knife, remove and discard the gaskets, then clean the gasket mounting surfaces. Since the manifold is made from aluminum, be sure to inspect it for warpage and/or cracks; if necessary, replace it.

12. To install, use new intake manifold-to-cylinder head gaskets, a $^3/_{16}$ in. (5mm) bead of RTV sealant, applied to the front and rear of the engine block.

NOTE: *The gaskets are marked "Right Side" and "Left Side"; do not interchange them. The gaskets will have to be cut slightly to fit past the center pushrods; do not cut any more material than necessary. Hold the gaskets in place by extending the ridge bead of sealer $^1/_4$ in. onto the gasket ends.*

13. To complete the installation, reverse the removal procedures. Torque the intake manifold-to-cylinder head nuts and bolts, in sequence, to 23 ft. lbs. Refill the cooling system with a 50 percent solution of ethylene glycol anti-freeze. Adjust the ignition timing, the idle speed, if possible, and check the coolant level after the engine has warmed up.

4.3L Engine

1. Position a drain pan under the radiator, open the drain cock and drain the cooling system to a level below the intake manifold.

CAUTION: *When draining the coolant, keep in mind that cats and dogs are attracted by the ethylene glycol antifreeze, and are quite likely to drink any that is left in an uncovered container or in puddles on the ground. This will prove fatal in sufficient quantity. Always drain the coolant into a sealable container. Coolant should be reused unless it is contaminated or several years old.*

2. Disconnect the negative battery cable from the battery.

3. Remove the air cleaner and the heat stove.

4. Remove the 2 braces from the rear of the fan belt tensioner.

5. Remove the radiator inlet hose.

6. Disconnect and remove the emission relays with the bracket.

7. Disconnect the electrical wiring harnesses from the clips and move them aside.

8. Disconnect the ground cable from the intake manifold stud.

9. Remove the power brake vacuum pipe

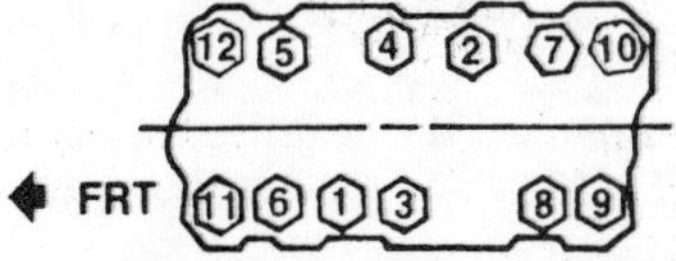

INITIAL TIGHTENING SEQUENCE

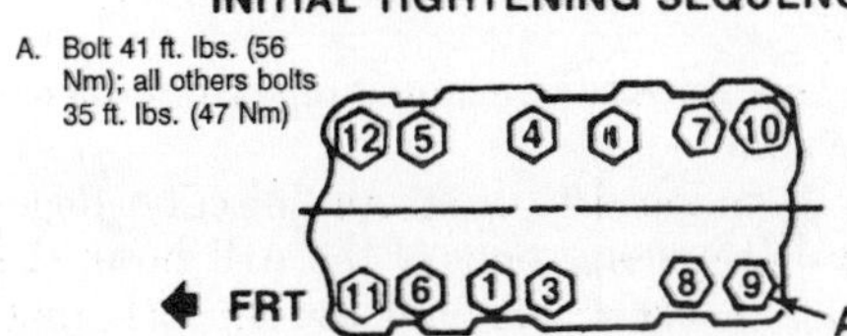

FINAL TIGHTENING SEQUENCE

View of the intake manifold torque sequence — 4.3L engine

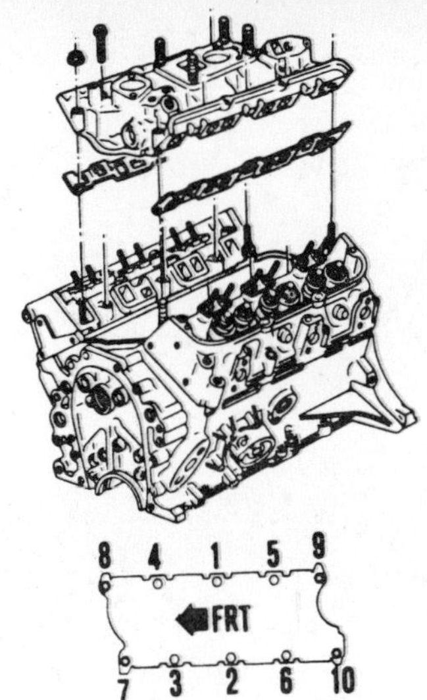

Intake manifold removal/installation with torque sequence — 2.8L engine

from the intake manifold.

10. Remove the heater hose from the intake manifold.

11. Disconnect and plug the fuel lines from the TBI.

12. Label and disconnect the electrical connectors from the ignition coil and remove the coil.

13. Label and disconnect the electrical connectors from the sensors on the manifold.

14. Label and disconnect the electrical connectors from the distributor and remove the distributor.

15. Label and disconnect the electrical connectors from the TBI unit.

16. Disconnect the EGR hose.

17. Disconnect the throttle cable, the TVS cable and the cruise control cable.

18. Remove the intake manifold-to-cylinder head bolts and the intake manifold.

19. Remove and discard the gaskets; be sure to clean the gasket mounting surfaces. Inspect the manifold for warpage and/or cracks; if necessary, replace it.

To install:

20. Using new gaskets, install the intake manifold. Apply a $^3/_{16}$ in. (5mm) bead of RTV sealant, applied to the front and rear of the engine block.

21. Torque the intake manifold-to-cylinder head nuts and bolts, in sequence, to 35 ft. lbs. (47 Nm), except for the rear left bolt which is 41 ft. lbs. (56 Nm).

22. Connect the throttle cable, the TVS and the cruise control cables.

23. Connect the EGR hose.

24. Connect the electrical connectors and hoses to the TBI unit.

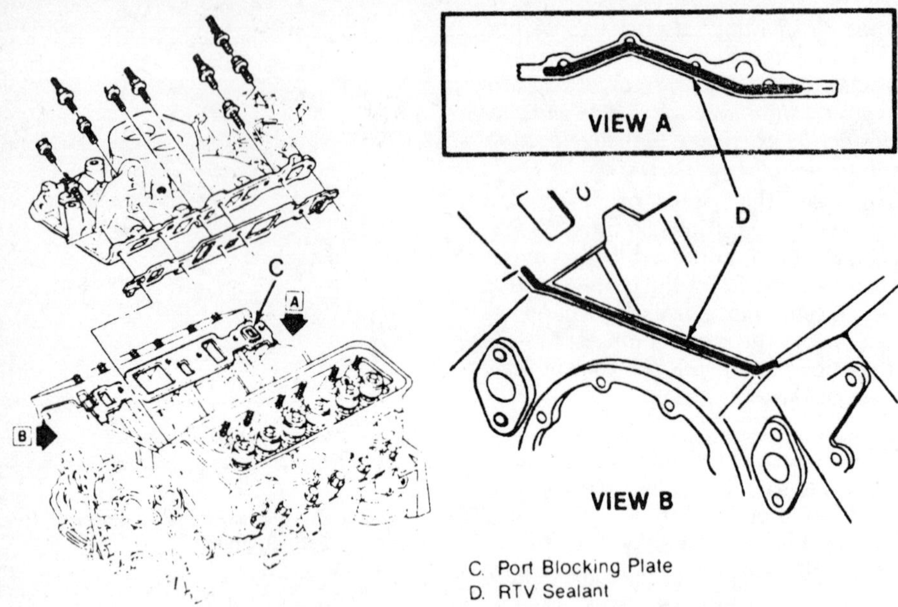

VIEW A

VIEW B

C. Port Blocking Plate
D. RTV Sealant

Intake manifold removal/installation — 4.3L engine

25. Install the distributor.

26. Connect the electrical connectors to the sensors on the intake manifold.

27. Install the ignition coil and connect the electrical connectors to it.

28. Connect the fuel lines. Connect the heater hoses.

29. Connect the power brake vacuum line. Connect the ground cable to the manifold stud.

30. Connect the electrical wiring harness to the clips. Install the emission relays with the bracket and connect the electrical connectors.

31. Install the radiator inlet hose and refill the cooling system.

32. Install the rear braces of the fan belt tensioner.

33. Install the air cleaner and the heat stove tube.

34. Connect the negative battery cable. Start the engine, allow it to reach normal operating temperatures and check for leaks. Adjust the ignition timing, the idle speed, if possible, and check the coolant level after the engine has warmed up.

Exhaust Manifold

REMOVAL AND INSTALLATION

1.9L Engine

1. Disconnect the negative battery terminal from the battery and remove the air cleaner assembly.

2. Raise and support the vehicle on jackstands.

3. Disconnect the exhaust pipe and the EGR pipe from the exhaust manifold, then lower the vehicle.

4. If equipped with an air conditioning compressor or a power steering pump, remove the drive belt(s), the compressor/pump (move them aside) and the mounting brackets.

5. Remove the exhaust manifold shield and the heat stove, if equipped.

6. Remove the exhaust manifold-to-cylinder head nuts and the manifold from the engine.

7. Using a putty knife, clean the gasket mounting surfaces. Inspect the exhaust manifold for distortion, cracks or damage; replace it, if necessary.

8. To install, use a new gasket and reverse the removal procedures. Torque the exhaust manifold-to-cylinder head nuts to 16 ft. lbs., in sequence, starting with the center and working outwards.

2.0L Engine

1. Disconnect the negative battery terminal from the battery and remove the air cleaner assembly.

2. Raise and support the vehicle on jackstands.

3. Disconnect the exhaust pipe from the exhaust manifold.

4. If equipped with an Air Injection Reaction (AIR) system, remove the AIR hose, the AIR pipe bracket bolt and the dipstick tube bracket.

5. From the front of the engine, remove the fuel vapor canister harness (steel) pipes.

6. Remove the exhaust manifold-to-cylin-

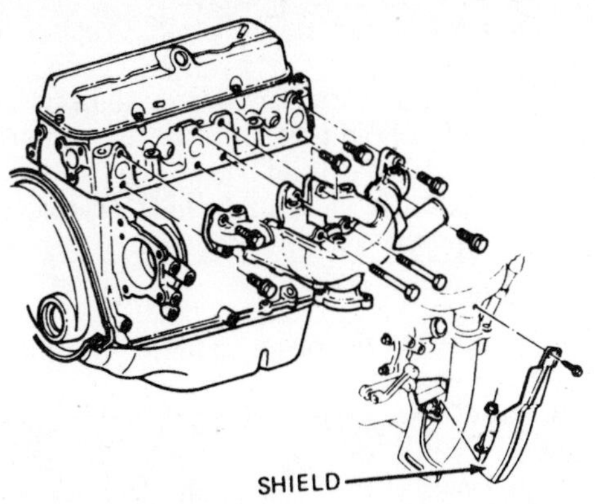

Exhaust manifold removal/installation — 2.0L engine

der head bolts and the manifold from the engine.

7. Using a putty knife, clean the gasket mounting surfaces. Inspect the exhaust manifold for distortion, cracks or damage; replace it, if necessary.

8. To install, use a new gasket and reverse the removal procedures. Torque the exhaust manifold-to-cylinder head bolts to 26 ft. lbs., in sequence, starting with the center and working outwards.

2.2L Diesel Engine

1. Disconnect the negative battery terminal from the battery.

2. Remove the air cleaner, then the PCV valve from the rocker arm cover.

3. Disconnect the exhaust pipe from the exhaust manifold at the flange.

4. Remove the exhaust manifold-to-cylin-

der head nuts and the exhaust manifold from the engine.

5. If the intake manifold has been removed, perform the following procedures:

    a. Using a putty knife, clean the gasket mounting surfaces.

    b. Inspect the manifold for cracks, damage or distortion; if necessary, replace the intake manifold.

    c. Using a new gasket, install it onto the cylinder head.

6. To install, reverse the removal procedures. Torque the exhaust manifold-to-cylinder head nuts/bolts to 10–17 ft. lbs., starting from the center and working outward.

2.5L Engine

The exhaust manifold is located on the left side of the engine.

1. Disconnect the negative battery terminal from the battery.

2. At the air conditioning compressor, if equipped, remove the drive belt, the compressor (lay it aside) and the rear adjusting bracket, if used.

3. Disconnect the exhaust pipe from the exhaust manifold, then lower the vehicle.

4. Remove the air cleaner and disconnect the electrical connector from the oxygen sensor.

5. Remove the exhaust manifold-to-engine bolts/washers and the manifold from the engine.

6. Using a putty knife, clean the gasket mounting surfaces.

7. To install, use a new gasket and reverse the removal procedures. Torque the exhaust

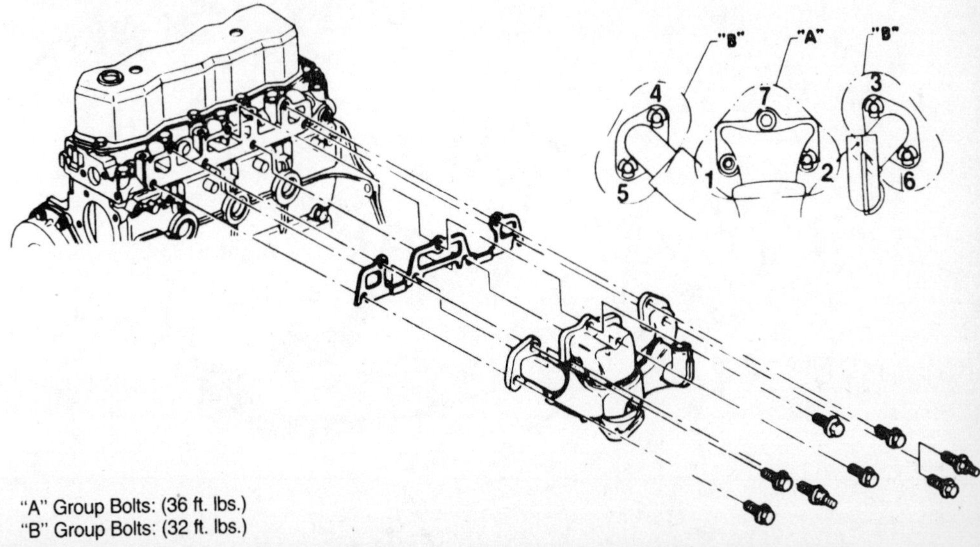

Exhaust manifold removal/installation — 2.5L engine

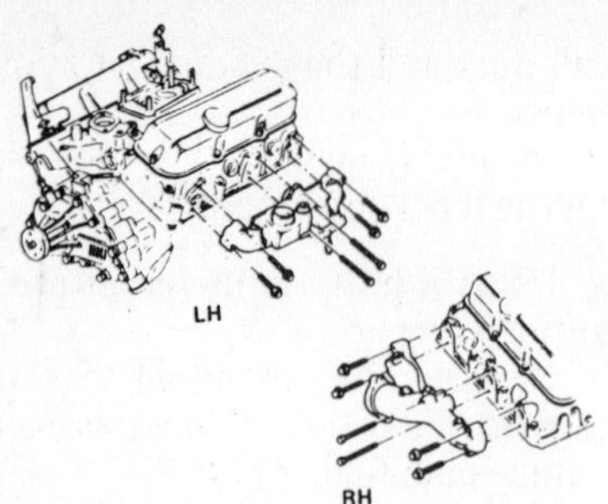

Exhaust manifold removal/installation — 2.8L engine

manifold-to-engine bolts to 36 ft. lbs. (center bolts) or 32 ft. lbs. (outer bolts).

2.8L Engine

LEFT SIDE

1. Disconnect the negative battery terminal from the battery.
2. Raise and support the vehicle on jackstands.
3. Disconnect the exhaust pipe from the exhaust manifold.
4. Remove the rear exhaust manifold-to-cylinder head bolts, then lower the vehicle.
5. Disconnect the air management hoses and wiring.
6. If equipped, remove the power steering pump and bracket; do not disconnect the power steering hoses.
7. Remove the front exhaust manifold-to-cylinder head bolts.
8. Using a putty knife, clean the gasket mounting surfaces. Inspect the exhaust manifold for distortion, cracks or damage; replace it, if necessary.
9. To install, use a new gasket and reverse the removal procedures. Torque the exhaust manifold-to-cylinder head bolts to 25 ft. lbs., in a circular pattern, working from the center to the outer ends.

RIGHT SIDE

1. Disconnect the negative battery terminal from the battery.
2. Raise and support the vehicle on jackstands.
3. Disconnect the exhaust pipe from the exhaust manifold.
4. Disconnect the air management hoses and wiring, then lower the vehicle.
5. Remove the exhaust manifold-to-cylinder head bolts.
6. Using a putty knife, clean the gasket mounting surfaces. Inspect the exhaust manifold for distortion, cracks or damage; replace it, if necessary.
7. To install, use a new gasket and reverse the removal procedures. Torque the exhaust manifold-to-cylinder head bolts to 25 ft. lbs., in a circular pattern, working from the center to the outer ends.

4.3L Engine

1. Disconnect the negative battery cable.
2. Raise and safely support the vehicle.
3. Disconnect the exhaust pipe(s) from the exhaust manifold(s). Lower the vehicle.
4. Label and disconnect the spark plug wires.

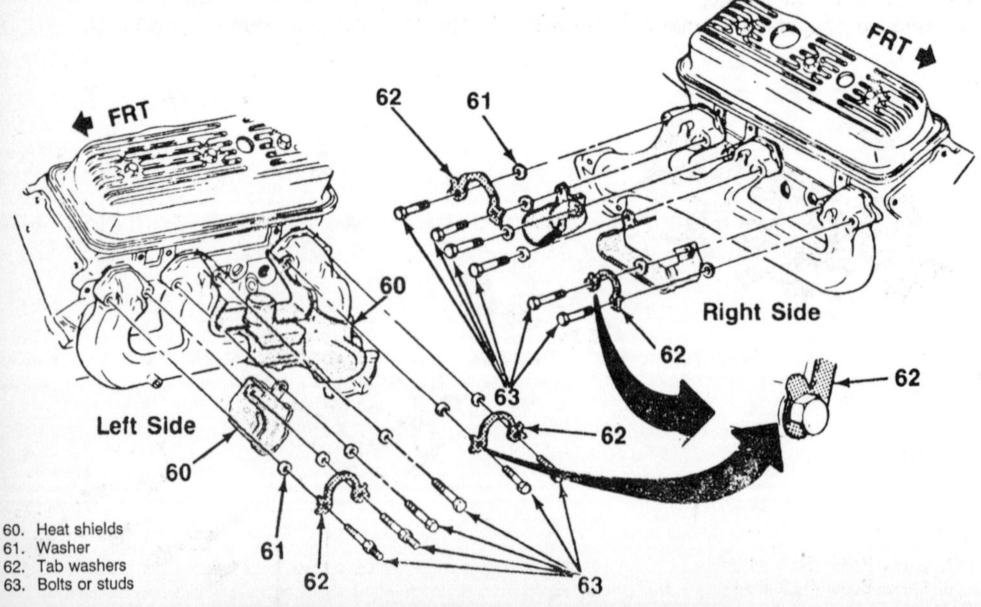

Exploded view of the exhaust manifold — 4.3L engine

5. From the left side of the engine, remove the following components:

a. The air cleaner with the heat stove pipe and the cold air intake pipe.

b. The power steering and the alternator brackets.

c. If necessary, disconnect the intermediate steering shaft from the steering gear and move it aside.

6. Remove the exhaust manifold(s)-to-engine bolts, washers and tab washers and the manifolds.

To install:

7. Using a new gasket(s), install the exhaust manifold(s).

8. Torque the center exhaust tube-to-engine bolts to 26 ft. lbs. (36 Nm), the front/rear exhaust tubes-to-engine manifold bolts to 20 ft. lbs. (28 Nm) and bend the tab washers over the bolt heads.

9. On the left side of the engine; perform the following procedures:

a. If the intermediate steering shaft was separated from the steering gear, connect it.

b. Install the alternator and power steering brackets.

c. Install the air cleaner with the heat stove pipe and the cold air intake pipe.

10. Install the spark plug wires.

11. Raise and safely support the vehicle.

12. Connect the exhaust pipes to the exhaust manifold.

13. Lower the vehicle and connect the negative battery cable.

Air Conditioning Compressor

REMOVAL AND INSTALLATION

4-Cylinder Engines

1. Have the system discharged by a professional shop.

2. Disconnect the negative battery terminal from the battery.

3. Disconnect the electrical connectors from the compressor.

4. At the rear of the compressor, remove the bracket from the exhaust manifold. If equipped, remove the power steering pump bracket.

5. Remove the compressor-to-front bracket bolts, the drive belt and the compressor from the vehicle.

6. To install, reverse the removal procedures. Torque the compressor-to-front bracket bolts to 68 ft. lbs., the manifold-to-rear compressor bolt to 47 ft. lbs. and the engine brace-to-compressor nut to 37 ft. lbs.

7. Refer to the Drive Belt Adjusting proce-

dures in Chapter 1 and adjust the air conditioning drive belt.

8. Refer to Charging The Air Conditioning System in Chapter 1 and charge the air conditioning system.

V6 Engines

1. Have the system discharged by a professional shop.

2. Disconnect the negative battery terminal from the battery.

3. Disconnect the electrical connectors from the compressor.

4. From the rear of the compressor, remove the intake manifold-to-compressor support bracket.

NOTE: *If the engine is equipped with a carburetor, disconnect the vacuum brake from the carburetor for access.*

5. Remove the drive belt idler bracket-to-intake manifold bolts, the drive belt and the bracket from the vehicle.

6. Remove the compressor-to-mounting bracket bolts and the compressor from the vehicle.

7. To install, reverse the removal procedures. Torque the compressor-to-front bracket bolts to 68 ft. lbs. and the manifold-to-compressor bolt to 47 ft. lbs.

8. Refer to the, Drive Belt Adjusting procedures in Chapter 1 and adjust the air conditioning drive belt.

9. Refer to Charging The Air Conditioning System in Chapter 1 and charge the air conditioning system.

Radiator

DIAGNOSIS

Test for restrictions in the radiator by warming the engine to operating temperature and then turning the engine off. Feel the radiator, it should be hot along the left side and warm along the right side. The temperature should rise evenly from right to left. If cold spots are felt, have the radiator tested for clogged sections.

REMOVAL AND INSTALLATION

1. Disconnect the negative battery terminal.

2. Using a drain pan, position it under the radiator, open the drain cock and drain the cooling system.

CAUTION: *When draining the coolant, keep in mind that cats and dogs are attracted by the ethylene glycol antifreeze, and are quite likely to drink any that is left in an uncovered container or in puddles on the ground. This will prove fatal in sufficient quantity.*

Always drain the coolant into a sealable container. Coolant should be reused unless it is contaminated or several years old.

3. From the radiator, remove the upper and lower radiator hoses, then the overflow hose.

4. If equipped with an automatic transmission, disconnect and plug the oil cooler lines at the radiator.

5. If equipped with air conditioning, remove the air conditioning hose retaining clip.

6. Remove the upper fan shroud, the radiator to chassis screws and the radiator.

7. To install, reverse the removal procedures. Refill the cooling system with a 50 percent solution of anti-freeze. Start the engine, allow it to reach normal operating temperatures and check for leaks.

Oil Cooler – Diesel Engine

REMOVAL AND INSTALLATION

1. Disconnect the negative battery terminal.

2. Using a drain pan, position it under the radiator, open the drain cock and drain the cooling system.

CAUTION: *When draining the coolant, keep in mind that cats and dogs are attracted by the ethylene glycol antifreeze, and are quite likely to drink any that is left in an uncovered container or in puddles on the ground. This will prove fatal in sufficient quantity. Always drain the coolant into a sealable container. Coolant should be reused unless it is contaminated or several years old.*

3. Remove the oil filter.

4. Disconnect the coolant hoses from the oil cooler.

5. Remove oil cooler nut and the cooler from the vehicle.

6. To install, reverse the removal procedures. Refill the cooling system with a 50 percent solution of anti-freeze. Start the engine, allow it to reach normal operating temperatures and check for leaks.

Air Conditioning Condenser

REMOVAL AND INSTALLATION

1. Have the system discharged by a professional shop.

2. Drain the cooling system.

CAUTION: *When draining the coolant, keep in mind that cats and dogs are attracted by the ethylene glycol antifreeze, and are quite likely to drink any that is left in an uncovered container or in puddles on the ground. This will prove fatal in sufficient quantity. Always drain the coolant into a sealable con-*

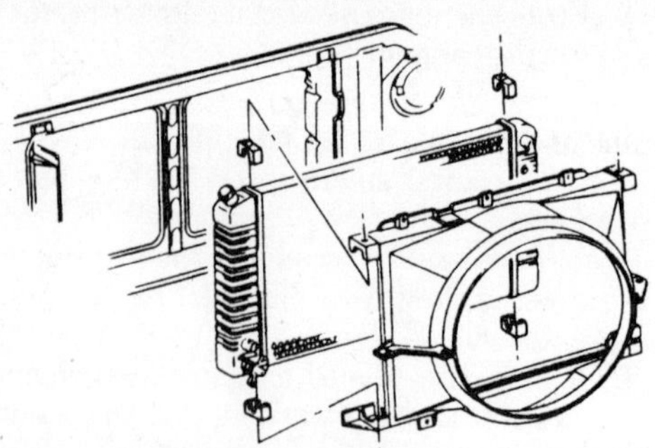
Radiator and shroud assembly

tainer. Coolant should be reused unless it is contaminated or several years old.

3. Remove the upper and lower radiator hoses.

4. Disconnect all coolant lines leading to the radiator.

5. Remove the radiator.

6. Remove the shields at both sides of the radiator support.

7. Remove the condenser retainers and lines. Remove the condenser.

8. Installation is the reverse of removal. Recharge the air conditioning system and fill the cooling system.

Engine Clutch Fan

DIAGNOSIS

Start the engine and listen for fan noise. Fan noise is usually evident during the first few minutes after start-up and when the clutch is engaged for maximum cooling (during idle). If fan noise is excessive, the fan cannot be rotated by hand or there is a rough grating feel as the fan is turned, replace the clutch.

Check a loose fan assembly for wear and re-

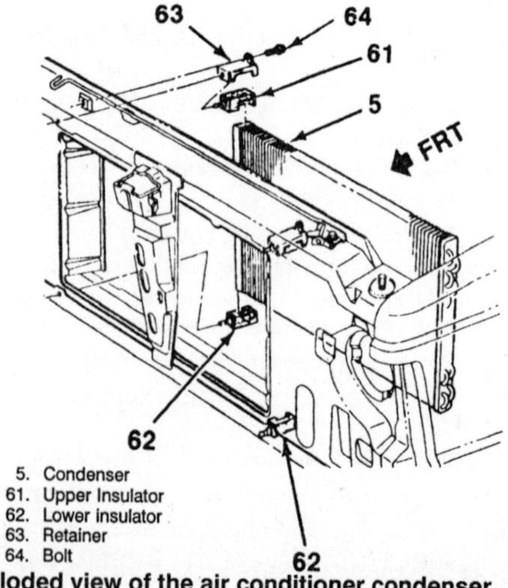

5. Condenser
61. Upper Insulator
62. Lower insulator
63. Retainer
64. Bolt

Exploded view of the air conditioner condenser

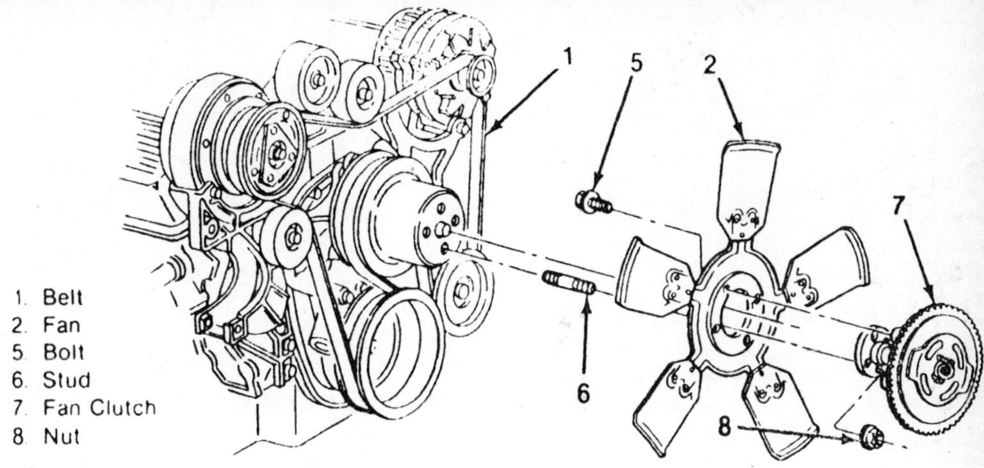

Replacing the fan and fan clutch

place as necessary. Under certain conditions, the fan may flex up to $1/4$ in. This is not cause for replacement.

The fan clutch is not affected by small fluid leaks which may occur in the area around the bearing assembly. If leakage appears excessive, replace the fan clutch.

If the fan clutch free-wheels with no drag (revolves more than 5 times when spun by hand), replace the clutch.

REMOVAL AND INSTALLATION

NOTE: *Do not use or repair a damaged fan assembly. An unbalanced fan assembly could fly apart and cause personal injury or property damage. Replace damaged assemblies with new ones.*

1. Remove the upper radiator shroud.
2. Remove the fan attaching nuts and remove the fan and clutch assembly from the engine.
3. Remove clutch from the fan by removing the attaching nuts.
4. To install, reverse the removal procedures. Torque bolts to the following torque:
- 2.5L and 2.8L clutch-to-fan bolts: 9 ft. lbs.
- 4.3L clutch-to-fan bolts: 25 ft. lbs.
- All others clutch-to-fan bolts: 11–16 ft. lbs.
- Fan-to-pulley nuts: 27–40 ft. lbs.

Water Pump

DIAGNOSIS

Check the water pump operation by running the engine while squeezing the upper radiator hose. When the engine warms (thermostat opens) a pressure surge should be felt. Check for a plugged vent hole at the pump snout.

REMOVAL AND INSTALLATION

1.9L Engine

1. Disconnect the negative battery terminal.
2. Raise and support the front of the vehicle on jackstands, then remove the lower fan shroud.
3. Position a drain pan under the radiator, open the drain cock and drain the coolant.

CAUTION: *When draining the coolant, keep in mind that cats and dogs are attracted by the ethylene glycol antifreeze, and are quite likely to drink any that is left in an uncovered container or in puddles on the ground. This will prove fatal in sufficient quantity. Always drain the coolant into a sealable container. Coolant should be reused unless it is contaminated or several years old.*

4. If not equipped with air conditioning, remove the fan-to-water pump nuts and the fan from the vehicle.
5. If equipped with air conditioning, perform the following procedures:
   a. Loosen the air pump and alternator adjusting bolts, pivot them toward the engine and remove the drive belt(s).
   b. Remove the fan-to-water pump nuts and the fan (with the fan and air pump drive pulley) from the vehicle.
   c. Remove the fan set plate/pulley-to-water pump bolts, then remove the set plate and the pulley.
6. Remove the water pump-to-engine bolts and the water pump from the engine.
7. Using a putty knife, clean the gasket mounting surfaces.
8. To install, use a new gasket, if equipped, RTV sealant, if necessary, and reverse the removal procedures. Refill the cooling system with a 50 percent solution of anti-freeze. Start

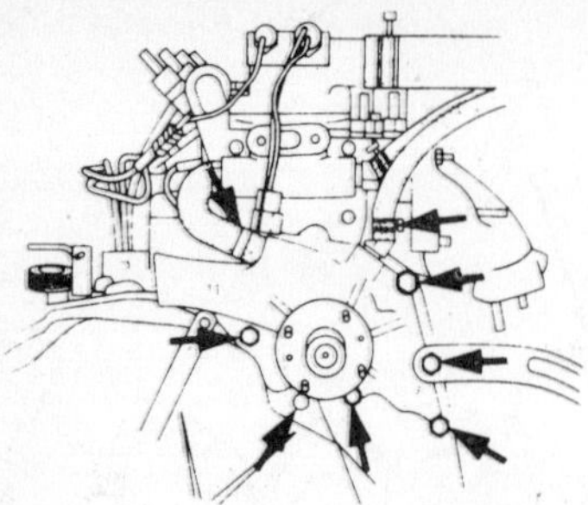

Water pump replacement — 1.9L engine

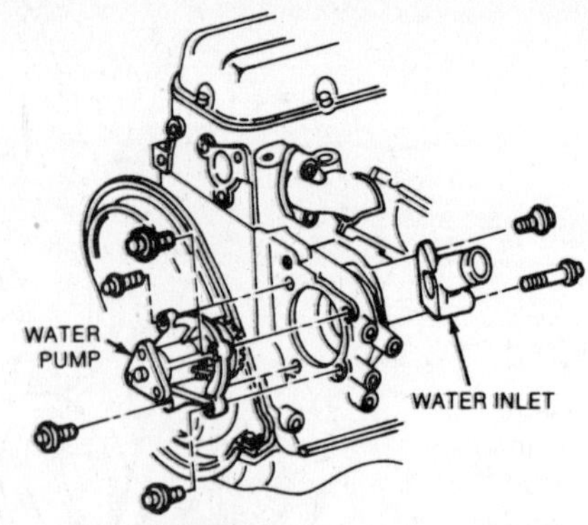

Water pump replacement — 2.0L engine

the engine, allow it to reach normal operating temperatures and check for leaks.

2.0L Engine

1. Disconnect the negative battery terminal.

2. Position a drain pan under the radiator, open the drain cock and drain the coolant.

CAUTION: *When draining the coolant, keep in mind that cats and dogs are attracted by the ethylene glycol antifreeze, and are quite likely to drink any that is left in an uncovered container or in puddles on the ground. This will prove fatal in sufficient quantity. Always drain the coolant into a sealable container. Coolant should be reused unless it is contaminated or several years old.*

3. Remove the upper fan shroud and all of the necessary drive belts.

4. Disconnect the radiator and heater hoses from the water pump.

5. Remove the water pump-to-engine bolts and the water pump from the vehicle.

6. Using a putty knife, clean the gasket mounting surfaces.

7. To install, use a new gasket, if equipped, RTV sealant, if necessary, and reverse the removal procedures. Refill the cooling system with a 50 percent solution of anti-freeze. Start the engine, allow it to reach normal operating temperatures and check for leaks.

2.2L Diesel Engine

1. Disconnect the negative battery terminal.

2. At the fan shroud, disconnect the power steering reservoir. Remove the upper fan shroud.

3. Position a drain pan under the radiator, open the drain cock and drain the coolant.

CAUTION: *When draining the coolant, keep in mind that cats and dogs are attracted by the ethylene glycol antifreeze, and are quite likely to drink any that is left in an uncovered container or in puddles on the ground. This will prove fatal in sufficient quantity. Always drain the coolant into a sealable con-*

tainer. Coolant should be reused unless it is contaminated or several years old.

4. Loosen the drive belts, the fan and the air conditioning compressor (move it aside).

5. Disconnect the front center radiator pipe.

6. From the right side of the water pump, disconnect the radiator and heater hoses.

7. Disconnect the PCV valve from the rocker cover. Remove the air cleaner and the heater pipe from the intake manifold.

8. Disconnect the heater hose from the left side of the water pump, then the alternator brace.

9. Remove the water pump-to-engine bolts and the water pump from the engine.

10. Using a putty knife, clean the gasket

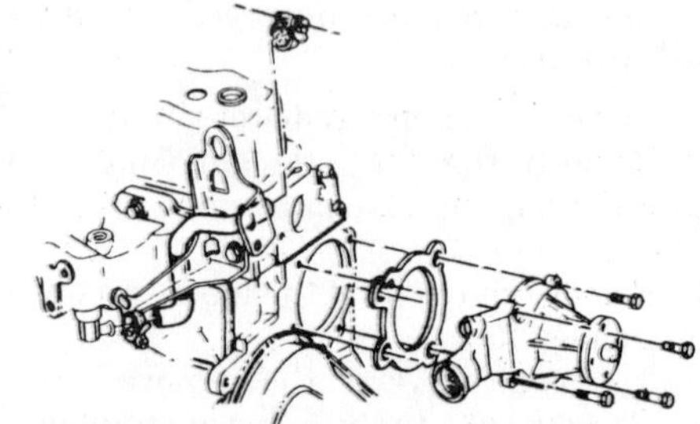

Water pump replacement — 2.5L engine

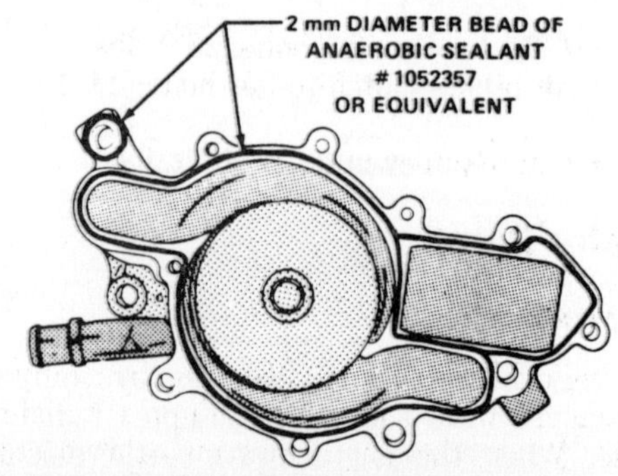

Applying sealer to the V6 water pump

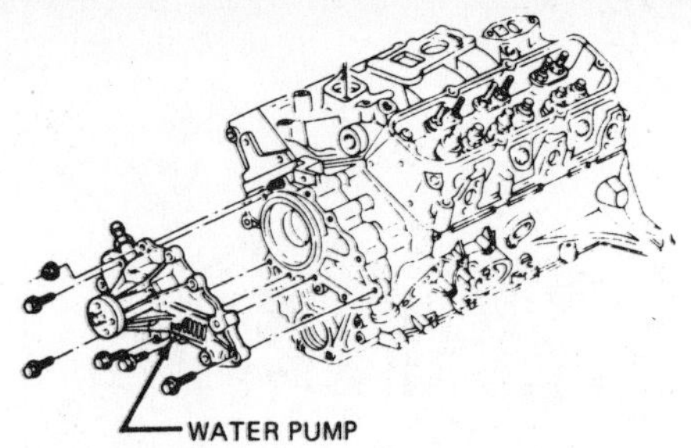

Water pump replacement — 4.3L engine

mounting surfaces.

11. To install, use a new gasket, RTV sealant, if necessary, and reverse the removal procedures. Torque the water pump-to-engine bolts to 10–17 ft. lbs. Refill the cooling system with a 50 percent solution of anti-freeze. Start the engine, allow it to reach normal operating temperatures and check for leaks.

2.5L Engine

1. Disconnect the negative battery terminal.

2. Place a catch pan under the radiator, open the drain cock and drain the cooling system.

CAUTION: *When draining the coolant, keep in mind that cats and dogs are attracted by the ethylene glycol antifreeze, and are quite likely to drink any that is left in an uncovered container or in puddles on the ground. This will prove fatal in sufficient quantity. Always drain the coolant into a sealable container. Coolant should be reused unless it is contaminated or several years old.*

3. At the front of the engine, loosen the accessory drive belt adjustments and remove the drive belts.

4. Remove the upper fan shroud. Remove the fan/clutch assembly-to-water pump bolts and the fan/clutch assembly from the water pump pulley.

5. Remove the drive belt pulley from the water pump.

6. Remove the clamps and the hoses from the water pump.

7. Remove the water pump-to-engine bolts and the water pump from the engine.

8. Using a putty knife, clean the gasket mounting surfaces.

9. To install, use new gasket(s), coat the bolt threads with sealant and reverse the removal procedures. Torque the water pump-to-engine bolts to 22 ft. lbs. Refill the cooling system with a 50 percent solution of anti-freeze. Start the engine, allow it to reach normal operating temperatures and check for leaks.

2.8L and 4.3L Engines

1. Disconnect the negative battery terminal.

2. Position a drain pan under the radiator, open the drain cock and drain the coolant from the engine.

CAUTION: *When draining the coolant, keep in mind that cats and dogs are attracted by the ethylene glycol antifreeze, and are quite likely to drink any that is left in an uncovered container or in puddles on the ground. This will prove fatal in sufficient quantity. Always drain the coolant into a sealable container. Coolant should be reused unless it is contaminated or several years old.*

3. Disconnect the radiator and heater hoses from the water pump.

4. At the front of the engine, loosen the accessory drive belt adjustments and remove the drive belts.

5. Remove the upper fan shroud. Remove the fan/clutch assembly-to-water pump bolts and the fan/clutch assembly from the water pump pulley.

6. Remove the water pump-to-engine bolts and the water pump from the engine.

7. Using a putty knife, clean the gasket mounting surfaces.

8. To install, use a new gaskets, RTV sealant, if necessary, and reverse the removal procedures. Torque the water pump-to-engine bolts to 22 ft. lbs. Refill the cooling system with a 50 percent solution of anti-freeze. Start the engine, allow it to reach normal operating temperatures and check for leaks.

NOTE: *Before installing the water pump, place a $^3/_{32}$ in. (2mm) bead of sealer on the water pump mating surface. Coat the bolt threads with pipe compound and mount the pump on the engine.*

Cylinder Head

REMOVAL AND INSTALLATION

1.9L Engine

1. Refer to the Rocker Arm Cover, Removal and Installation procedures in this Chapter and remove the rocker arm cover.

2. From the rear of the cylinder head, remove EGR pipe clamp bolt.

3. Raise and support the front of the vehicle on jackstands.

4. Disconnect the exhaust pipe from the exhaust manifold, then lower the vehicle.

5. Position a drain pan under the radiator, open the drain cock and drain the coolant from the engine.

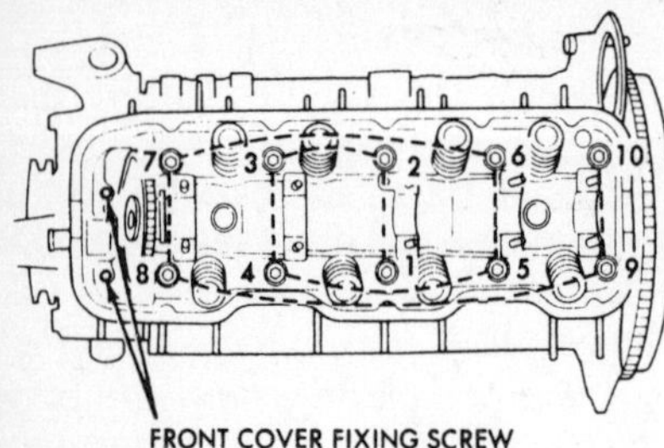

Cylinder head bolt torque sequence — 1.9L engine

CAUTION: *When draining the coolant, keep in mind that cats and dogs are attracted by the ethylene glycol antifreeze, and are quite likely to drink any that is left in an uncovered container or in puddles on the ground. This will prove fatal in sufficient quantity. Always drain the coolant into a sealable container. Coolant should be reused unless it is contaminated or several years old.*

6. From the intake manifold and the front of the cylinder head, disconnect the heater hoses.

7. If equipped with an air conditioning compressor and/or a power steering pump, disconnect them and lay them aside.

8. From the carburetor, disconnect the accelerator linkage, the fuel line, all necessary electrical connections, the spark plug wires and necessary vacuum lines.

9. Rotate the camshaft until the No. 4 cylinder is in the firing position. Remove the distributor cap and mark rotor-to-housing relationship, then remove the distributor.

10. Disconnect the fuel lines from the fuel pump and remove it.

11. Using 2 prybars, depress the adjuster lock lever to lock the automatic adjuster shoe in its fully retracted position.

12. From the camshaft, remove timing sprocket-to-camshaft bolt, the sprocket and the fuel pump drive cam. Keep the sprocket on the chain damper and tensioner—do not remove the sprocket from the chain.

13. Disconnect the AIR hose and check valve from the air manifold.

14. Remove the cylinder head-to-timing cover bolts.

15. Using the extension bar wrench tool J-24239-01 or equivalent, remove cylinder head-to-engine bolts; remove the bolts in a progressional sequence, beginning with the outer bolts and working inward.

16. Using an assistant, remove the cylinder head, intake and exhaust manifold as an assembly.

17. Using a putty knife, clean the gasket mounting surfaces.

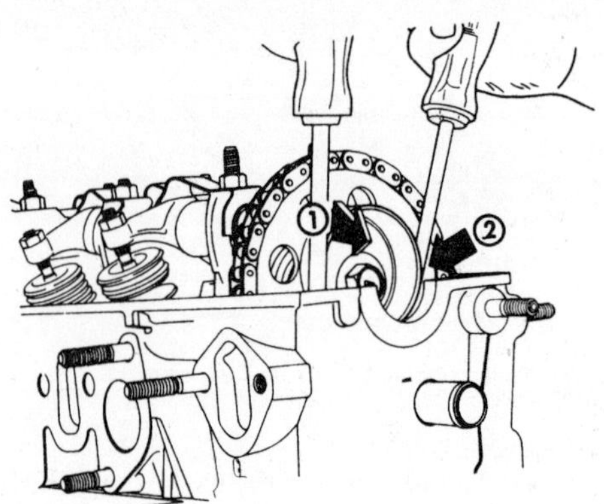

Using two pry bars to lock the automatic adjuster into position — 1.9L engine

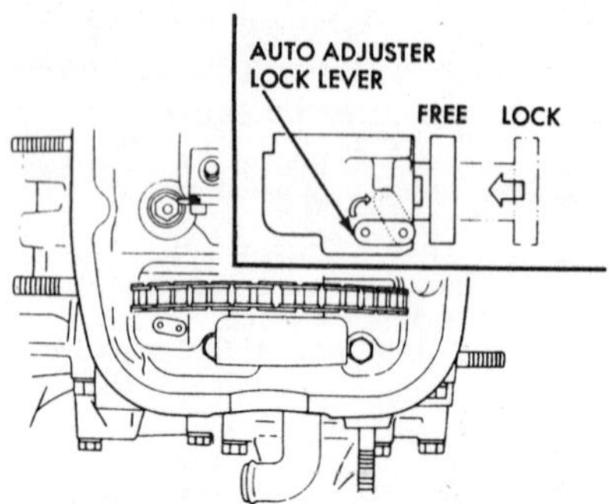

Locking the timing chain adjuster — 1.9L engine

NOTE: *The gasket surfaces on both the head and block must be clean of any foreign matter and free of nicks or heavy scratches. The cylinder bolt threads in the block and thread on the bolts must be cleaned (dirt will affect the bolt torque).*

18. To install, place the new gasket over dowel pins with **TOP** side of gasket up.

NOTE: *Be sure to lubricate the cylinder head bolts with engine oil before installing them.*

19. To complete the installation, reverse the removal procedures. Torque the cylinder head-to-engine bolts, a little at a time, in the sequence to 61 ft. lbs. and then retighten to 72 ft. lbs. Refill the cooling system. Start the engine, allow it to reach normal operating temperatures and check for leaks. Check and/or adjust the engine timing and idle speed.

2.0L Engine

NOTE: *The engine should be overnight cold before removing the cylinder head.*

1. Disconnect the negative battery terminal.

2. Position a drain pan under the radiator, open the drain cock and drain the coolant from the engine.

CAUTION: *When draining the coolant, keep in mind that cats and dogs are attracted by the ethylene glycol antifreeze, and are quite likely to drink any that is left in an uncovered container or in puddles on the ground. This will prove fatal in sufficient quantity. Always drain the coolant into a sealable container. Coolant should be reused unless it is contaminated or several years old.*

3. Remove the air cleaner, then raise and support the front of the vehicle on jackstands.

4. Remove the exhaust shield, then disconnect the exhaust pipe from the exhaust manifold. Lower the vehicle.

5. Disconnect the accelerator linkage, the necessary electrical wiring connectors and the vacuum lines.

6. From the top-front of the engine, remove the fuel vapor canister harness (steel) pipes.

7. Remove the distributor cap, then mark the rotor-to-distributor housing and the distributor housing-to-engine.

8. Remove the rocker arm cover, the rocker arms and the pushrods.

9. Remove the upper radiator hose, the heater hose, the upper fan shroud and the fan.

10. Remove the AIR management valve, the air pump and the upper AIR bracket.

11. Remove the fuel line from the fuel pump. Disconnect the wire from the rear of the cylinder head.

12. Remove the cylinder head-to-engine bolts and the cylinder head.

13. Using a putty knife, clean the gasket mounting surfaces.

NOTE: *To install, the gasket surfaces on both the head and the block must be clean of any foreign matter and free of any nicks or heavy scratches. Cylinder bolt threads in the block and the bolt must be clean.*

14. To install, use a new head gasket, sealing compound 10520026 (coat both sides of the gasket), position the gasket on the locating pins and reverse the removal procedures. Torque the cylinder head-to-engine bolts (in several steps, in sequence) to 65–75 ft. lbs. Refill the cooling system. Start the engine, allow it to reach normal operating temperatures and check for leaks. Check and/or adjust the engine timing and idle speed.

2.2L Engine

NOTE: *The injection timing must be reset after this procedure. See Chapter 5 for details and special tools required.*

1. Disconnect the negative battery terminal.

2. Position a drain pan under the radiator, open the drain cock and drain the coolant from the engine.

CAUTION: *When draining the coolant, keep in mind that cats and dogs are attracted by the ethylene glycol antifreeze, and are quite likely to drink any that is left in an uncovered container or in puddles on the ground. This will prove fatal in sufficient quantity. Always drain the coolant into a sealable container. Coolant should be reused unless it is contaminated or several years old.*

3. Remove the rocker arm cover, the rocker arm shaft and the pushrods.

4. From the cylinder head, remove the upper radiator hose and the heater hose.

5. Disconnect the heater tube and remove the exhaust pipe from the exhaust manifold.

6. Remove the vacuum pump and the air conditioning compressor, if equipped, move it aside.

7. Disconnect the heater hose/bracket, the necessary electrical wiring connectors. Disconnect the PCV valve hose from the pipe and move it aside.

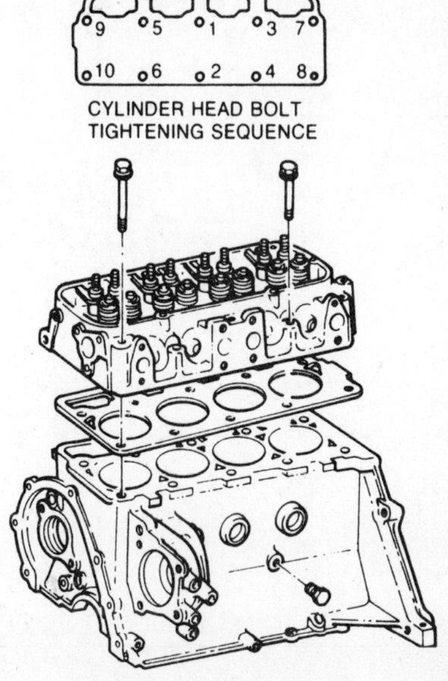

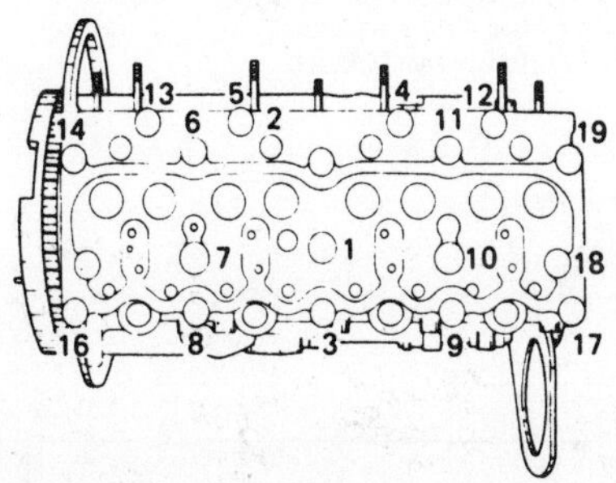

Cylinder head bolt torque sequence — 2.2L diesel engine

Cylinder head bolt torque sequence — 2.0L engine

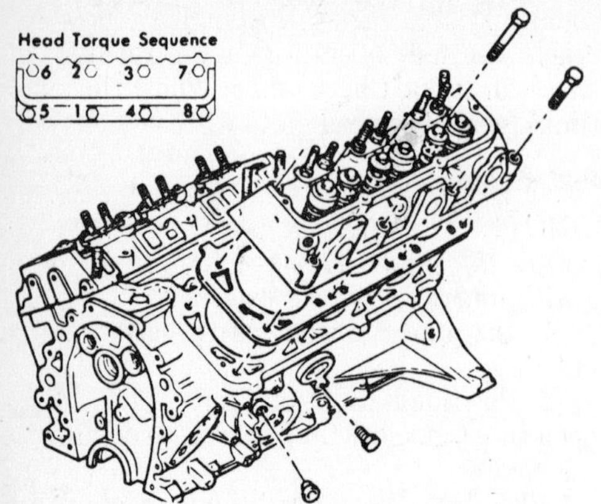

Cylinder head bolt torque sequence — 2.8L engine

8. Disconnect the dipstick tube bracket and dipstick, the breather pipe and the oil jet pipe.

9. Disconnect the fuel injection lines and cover them with protective caps.

10. Remove the air conditioning bracket and disconnect the return hose.

11. Remove the cylinder head-to-engine bolts and the cylinder head from the vehicle.

12. Using a putty knife, clean the gasket mounting surfaces. Inspect the cylinder head for distortion, cracks and/or damage.

NOTE: *To install, the gasket surfaces on both the head and the block must be clean of any foreign matter and free of any nicks or heavy scratches. The cylinder bolt threads in the block and the bolt must be clean.*

13. To install, use a new head gasket with the **TOP** side facing upward, position the gasket on the locating pins, apply engine oil to the cylinder head bolt threads and reverse the removal procedures. Torque the cylinder head-to-engine bolts, in sequence: First, to 40–47 ft. lbs. and then, to 54–61 ft. lbs. (new bolts) or 61–69 ft. lbs. (used bolts). Refill the cooling system. Start the engine, allow it to reach normal operating temperatures and check for leaks. Check and/or adjust the engine timing and idle speed.

2.5L Engine

NOTE: *Before disassembling the engine, make sure it is overnight cold.*

CAUTION: *Relieve the pressure on the fuel system before disconnecting any fuel line connection.*

1. Remove the rocker arm cover.

2. Place a catch pan under the radiator, open the drain cock and drain the cooling system.

CAUTION: *When draining the coolant, keep in mind that cats and dogs are attracted by the ethylene glycol antifreeze, and are quite likely to drink any that is left in an uncovered container or in puddles on the ground. This will prove fatal in sufficient quantity. Always drain the coolant into a sealable container. Coolant should be reused unless it is contaminated or several years old.*

3. Disconnect the accelerator, the cruise control and the TVS cables, if equipped.

4. From the intake manifold, remove the water pump bypass and heater hoses.

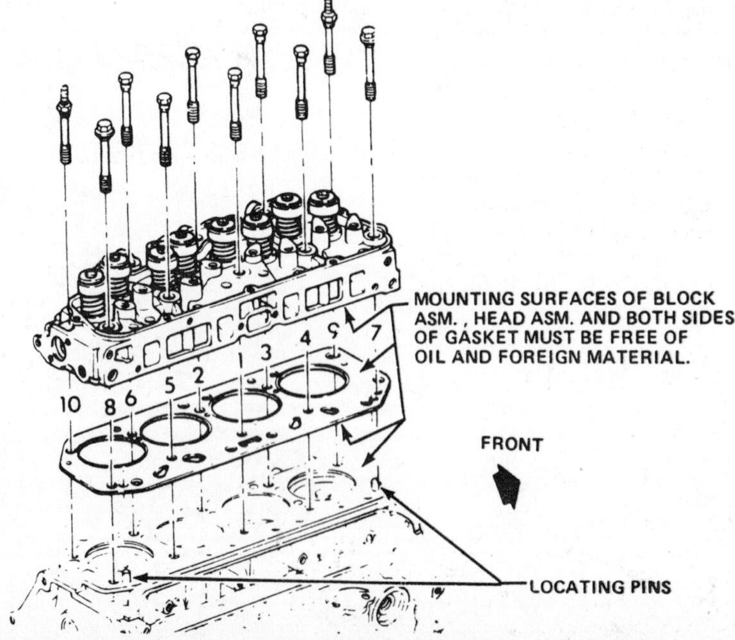

Cylinder head bolt torque sequence — 2.5L engine

5. From the alternator, remove the front and rear braces, then move it aside.

6. Disconnect the air conditioning compressor brackets and move the compressor aside.

7. Remove the thermostat housing-to-cylinder head bolts and the housing from the engine.

8. Remove the ground cable and any necessary electrical connectors from the cylinder head. Disconnect the wires from the spark plugs and the oxygen sensor. Disconnect and remove the ignition coil from the intake manifold and the cylinder head.

9. Remove the vacuum lines and fuel hoses from the intake manifold and the TBI unit.

10. Disconnect the exhaust pipe from the exhaust manifold.

11. Remove the rocker arm nuts, the washers, the rocker arms and the pushrods from the cylinder head.

12. Remove the cylinder head-to-engine bolts and the cylinder head from the engine (with the manifolds attached), then place the assembly on a workbench. If necessary, remove the intake and the exhaust manifolds from the cylinder head.

13. Using a putty knife, clean the gasket mounting surfaces. Using a wire brush, clean the carbon deposits from the combustion chambers.

14. Inspect the cylinder head and block for cracks, nicks, heavy scratches or other damage.

15. To install, use new gaskets, sealant, where necessary, and reverse the removal procedures. Torque the cylinder head bolts, in sequence, to 90 ft. lbs., in 3 steps. Adjust the rocker arms. Refill the cooling system, start the engine and check for leaks.

2.8L Engine

LEFT SIDE

1. Remove the intake manifold.

2. Raise and support the front of the vehicle on jackstands.

3. Position a drain pan under the radiator, open the drain cock and drain the coolant from the block.

CAUTION: *When draining the coolant, keep in mind that cats and dogs are attracted by the ethylene glycol antifreeze, and are quite likely to drink any that is left in an uncovered container or in puddles on the ground. This will prove fatal in sufficient quantity. Always drain the coolant into a sealable container. Coolant should be reused unless it is contaminated or several years old.*

4. Disconnect the exhaust pipe from the exhaust manifold and remove the exhaust manifold-to-cylinder block bolts.

5. Remove the dipstick tube from the engine.

6. Lower the vehicle.

7. Loosen the rocker arm nuts, turn the rocker arms and remove the pushrods. Keep the pushrods in the same order as removed.

8. Remove the cylinder head bolts in stages and in the reverse order of the tightening sequence.

9. Remove the cylinder head; do not pry on the head to loosen it.

10. Using a putty knife, clean the gasket mounting surfaces.

NOTE: *Coat the cylinder head bolts with sealer and torque to specifications in the sequence shown. Make sure the pushrods seat in the lifter seats and adjust the valves.*

11. To install, use a new gasket (position it on the dowel pins, with the words **This Side Up** facing upwards), use GM sealant 1052080 or equivalent and reverse the removal procedures. Torque the cylinder head-to-engine bolts, in sequence, to 70 ft. lbs. Refill the cooling system. Start the engine, allow it to reach normal operating temperatures and check for leaks. Check and/or adjust the ignition timing and idle speed, if possible.

RIGHT SIDE

1. Remove the intake manifold.

2. Raise and support the front of the vehicle on jackstands.

3. Position a drain pan under the radiator, open the drain cock and drain the coolant from the block.

CAUTION: *When draining the coolant, keep in mind that cats and dogs are attracted by the ethylene glycol antifreeze, and are quite likely to drink any that is left in an uncovered container or in puddles on the ground. This will prove fatal in sufficient quantity. Always drain the coolant into a sealable container. Coolant should be reused unless it is contaminated or several years old.*

4. Disconnect the exhaust pipe from the exhaust manifold and remove the exhaust manifold-to-cylinder block bolts.

5. Lower the vehicle.

6. Loosen the rocker arm nuts, turn the rocker arms and remove the pushrods. Keep the pushrods in the same order as removed.

7. Remove the alternator bracket.

8. Remove the cylinder head bolts in stages and in the reverse order of the tightening sequence.

9. Remove the cylinder head; do not pry on the head to loosen it.

10. Using a putty knife, clean the gasket mounting surfaces.

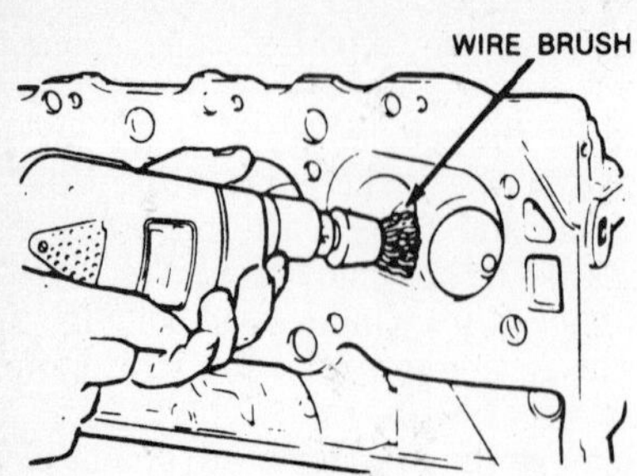

Remove the carbon from the cylinder head with a wire brush on an electric drill

NOTE: *Coat the cylinder head bolts with sealer and torque to specifications in the sequence shown. Make sure the pushrods seat in the lifter seats and adjust the valves.*

11. To install, use a new gasket (position it on the dowel pins, with the words **This Side Up** facing upwards), use GM sealant 1052080 or equivalent, and reverse the removal procedures. Torque the cylinder head-to-engine bolts, in sequence, to 70 ft. lbs. Refill the cooling system. Start the engine, allow it to reach normal operating temperatures and check for leaks. Check and/or adjust the ignition timing and idle speed, if possible.

4.3L Engine

NOTE: *Relieve the pressure on the fuel system before disconnecting any fuel line connection. See Chapter 5 for the proper procedures.*

1. Remove the negative battery cable.
2. Remove the rocker arm cover.
3. Drain the cooling system.

CAUTION: *When draining the coolant, keep in mind that cats and dogs are attracted by the ethylene glycol antifreeze, and are quite likely to drink any that is left in an uncovered container or in puddles on the ground. This will prove fatal in sufficient quantity. Always drain the coolant into a sealable container. Coolant should be reused unless it is contaminated or several years old.*

4. Remove the intake and exhaust manifolds.
5. Remove the following from the right cylinder head:

    a. Electrical connector at the sensor.

    b. Dipstick tube bracket.

    c. Air conditioning compressor (lay it aside).

    d. Air conditioning bracket and belt tensioner.

6. Remove the following from the left cylinder head:

    a. Alternator (lay it aside).

    b. Left side engine accessory bracket with

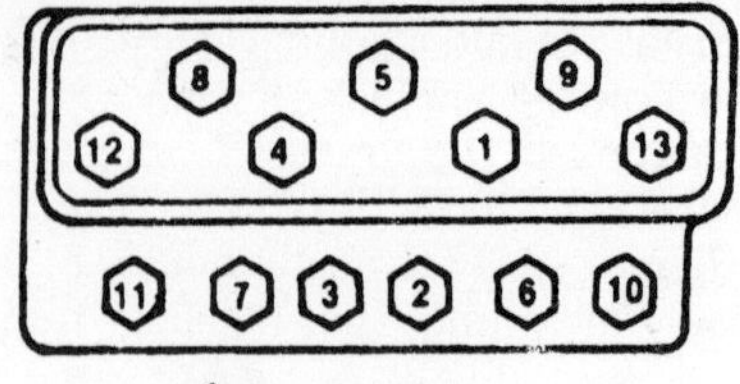

Cylinder head bolt torque sequence — 4.3L engine

power steering pump (lay it aside).

7. Remove the spark plug and wires.
8. Remove the rocker arms and pushrods.
9. Remove the cylinder head bolts by loosening them in sequence. Remove the cylinder head.
10. Using a putty knife, clean the gasket mounting surfaces.

NOTE: *If a steel head gasket is used, coat both sides with sealer. If a composition head gasket is used, do not use sealer.*

11. Installation is the reverse of removal. Using a new gasket, position it on the dowel pins, with the words **This Side Up** facing upwards. Torque the cylinder head-to-engine bolts in sequence to 65 ft. lbs. Use 3 steps when torquing.

CLEANING AND INSPECTION

1. Remove the valve assemblies from the cylinder head.
2. Using a small wire power brush, clean the carbon from the combustion chambers and the valve ports.
3. Inspect the cylinder head for cracks in the exhaust ports, combustion chambers or external cracks to the water chamber.
4. Thoroughly clean the valve guides using a suitable wire bore brush.

NOTE: *Excessive valve stem-to-bore clearance will cause excessive oil consumption and may cause valve breakage. Insufficient clearance will result in noisy and sticky functioning of the valve and disturb engine smoothness.*

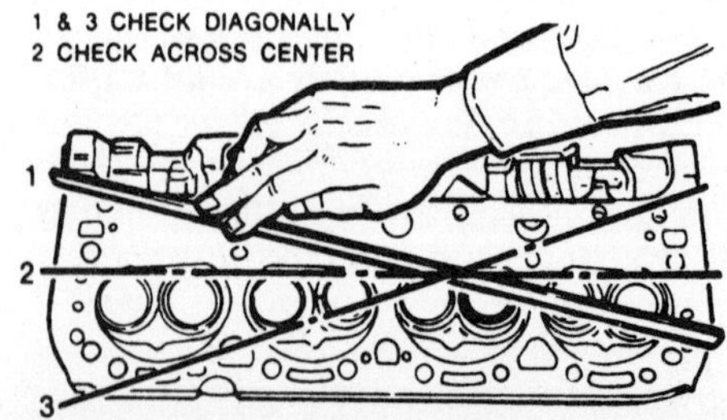

Measuring cylinder head warpage

5. Measure the valve stem clearance as follows:

a. Clamp a dial indicator on one side of the cylinder head rocker arm cover gasket rail.

b. Locate the indicator so movement of the valve stem from side to side (crosswise to the head) will cause a direct movement of the indicator stem. The indicator stem must contact the side of the valve stem just above the valve guide.

c. Prop the valve head about $\frac{1}{16}$ in. (1.6mm) off the valve seat.

d. Move the stem of the valve from side to side using light pressure to obtain a clearance reading. If the clearance exceeds specifications, it will be necessary to ream (for oversize valves) or knurl (raise the bore for original valves) the valve guides.

6. Inspect the rocker arm studs for wear or damage.

7. Install a dial micrometer into the valve guide and check the valve seat for concentricity.

RESURFACING

1. Using a straightedge, check the cylinder head for warpage.

2. If warpage exceeds 0.003 in. in a 6 in. span, or 0.006 in. over the total length, the cylinder head must be resurfaced. Resurfacing can be performed at most machine shops.

NOTE: *When resurfacing the cylinder head(s), the intake manifold mounting position is altered and must be corrected by machining a proportionate amount from the intake manifold flange.*

Valves

REMOVAL AND INSTALLATION

Cylinder Head Removed

NOTE: *The following procedures requires the use of a valve spring compressor tool J-15062 or equivalent.*

1. Remove the cylinder head.
2. Remove the rocker arm assemblies or the rocker arm nuts, the ball washers and the rocker arms, if not previously done.
3. Using a valve spring compressor tool J-15062 or equivalent, compress the valve springs and remove the stem keys. Release the compressor tool and the rotators or spring caps, the oil shedders, the springs and damper assemblies, then remove the oil seals and the valve spring shims.

Measuring valve stem clearance with a dial indicator

4. Remove the valve from the cylinder head and place them in a rack in their proper sequence so they can be reassembled in their original positions. Discard any bent or damaged valves.

5. To install, use new oil seals and reverse the removal procedures. Refer to the Rocker Arm, Removal and Installation procedures in this Chapter and adjust the valve lash.

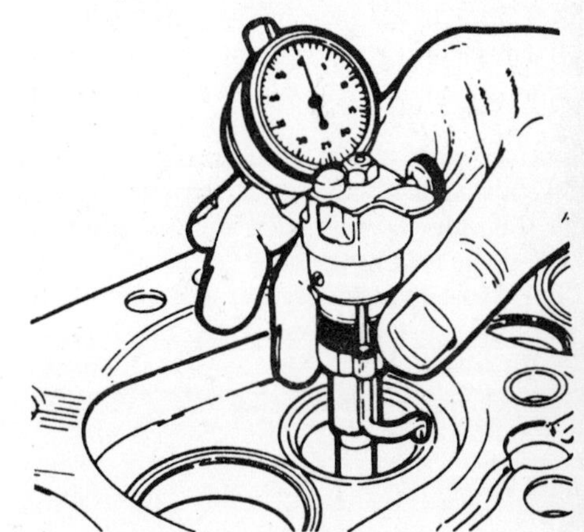

Checking valve seat concentricity with a run-out gauge

Removing the valve springs with the head off the engine

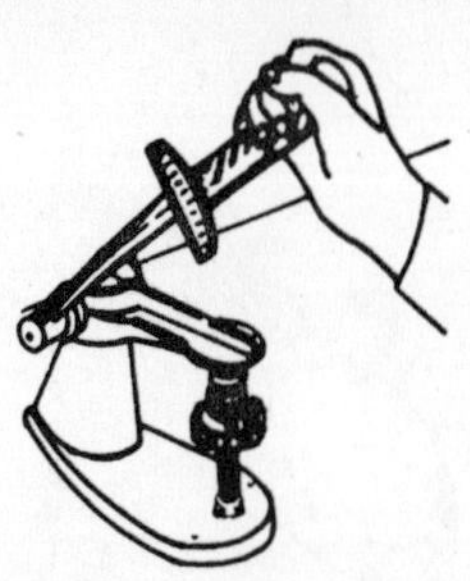

Checking the valve spring pressure

Cylinder Head Not Removed

NOTE: *The following procedures requires the use of GM air adapter tool J-23590 or equivalent, and spring compressor tool J-5892 or equivalent, a valve spring compressor tool J-5892 or equivalent, for 2.0L, 2.5L, 2.8L and 4.3L engines, tool J-26513 or equivalent for 1.9L engine or tool J-29760 or equivalent, for 2.2L engine.*

1. Remove the spark plug (in the cylinder being worked on).

NOTE: *The cylinder being worked on must be at the TDC of its compression stroke.*

2. Using an air pressure tool J-23590 and/or a valve spring compressor tool J-5892 or equivalent, for 2.0L, 2.5L, 2.8L and 4.3L engines, tool J-26513 or equivalent, for 1.9L engine or tool J-29760 or equivalent, for 2.2L engine, available at most auto parts stores, compress the valve spring, then remove the valve keys and the retaining ring.

3. Release the compressor and remove the spring and valve stem seal. Keep the valves in order for installation.

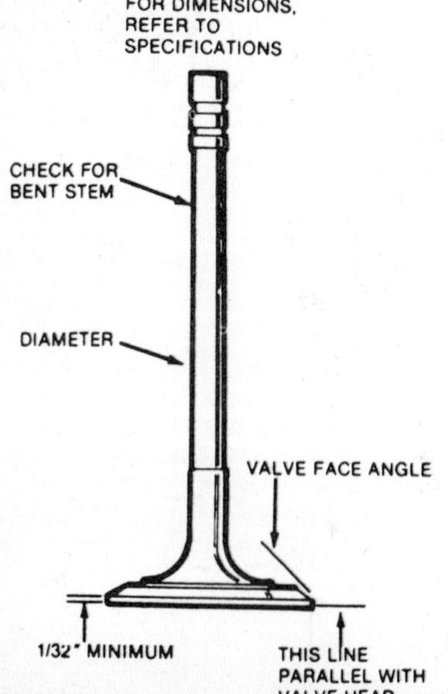

Valve inspection and head measurement

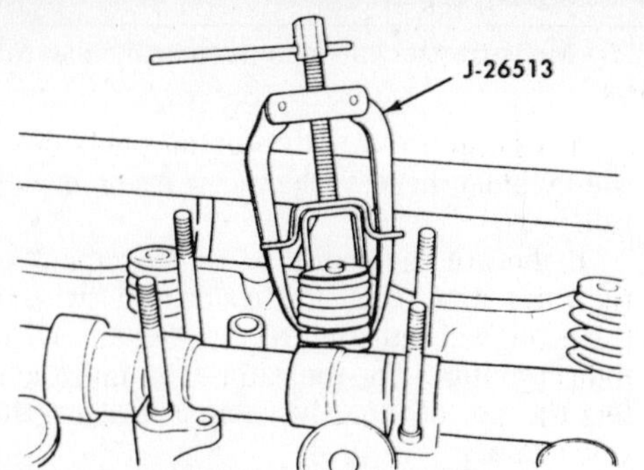

Valve Spring Compressor tool No. J-26513 — 1.9L engine

Lapping the valves

4. To install, reverse the removal procedures; be sure to use new seals.

NOTE: *Keep all parts in order so they may be assembled in their original locations.*

INSPECTION

Inspect the valve faces and seats (in the head) for pits, burned spots and other evidence of poor seating. If a valve face is in such bad shape that the head of the valve must be ground, in order to true up the face, discard the valve, because the sharp edge will run too hot. The correct angle for valve faces are 45 degrees. We recommend the refacing be performed by a reputable machine shop.

Check the valve stem for scoring and burned spots. If not noticeably scored or damaged, clean the valve stem with solvent to remove all gum and varnish. Clean the valve guides using

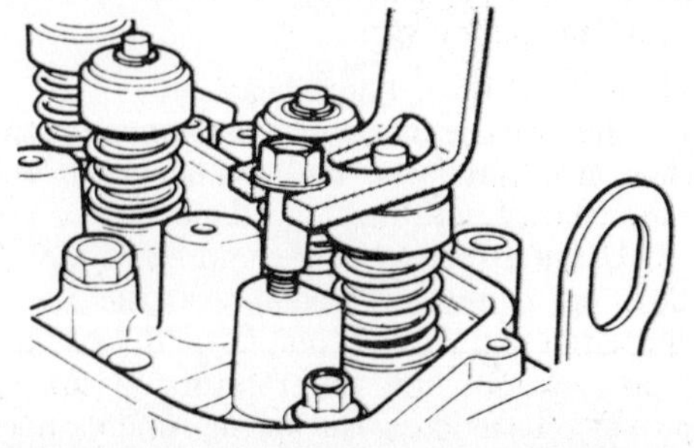

Valve Spring Compressor tool No. J-5892 — 2.0L, 2.5L, 2.8L and 4.3L engines

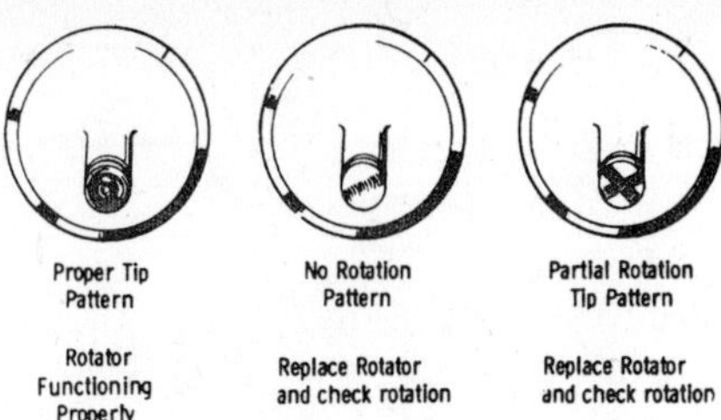

Valve stem wear patterns on engines using rotator cups

solvent and an expanding wire-type valve guide cleaner. If you have access to a dial indicator for measuring valve stem-to-guide clearance, mount it so the stem of the indicator is at 90 degrees to the valve stem and as close to the valve guide as possible. Move the valve off its seat, then measure the valve guide-to-stem clearance by rocking the stem back and forth to actuate the dial indicator. Measure the valve stem diameter using a micrometer and compare to specifications to determine whether the stem or guide wear is responsible for the excess clearance. If a dial indicator and micrometer are not available to you, take the cylinder head and valves to a reputable machine shop for inspection.

Some of the engines covered in this guide are equipped with valve rotators, which double as valve spring caps. In normal operation the rotators put a certain degree of wear on the tip of the valve stem; this wear appears as concentric rings on the stem tip. However, if the rotator is not working properly, the wear may appear as straight notches or **X** patterns across the valve stem tip. Whenever the valves are removed from the cylinder head, the tips should be inspected for improper pattern, which could indicate valve rotator problems. Valve stem tips will have to be ground flat if the rotator problems are severe.

REFACING

NOTE: *All valve grinding operations should be performed by a qualified machine shop; only the valve lapping operation is recommended to be performed by the inexperienced mechanic.*

Valve Lapping

When valve faces and seats have been refaced and/or recut, or if they are determined to be in good condition, the valves MUST BE lapped in to ensure efficient sealing when the valve closes against the seat.

1. Invert the cylinder head so the combustion chambers are facing upward.

2. Lightly lubricate the valve stems with clean engine oil and coat the valve seats with valve grinding compound. Install the valves in the cylinder head as numbered.

3. Attach the suction cup of a valve lapping tool to a valve head. You will probably have to moisten the cup to securely attach the tool to the valve.

4. Rotate the tool between the palms, changing position and lifting the tool often to prevent grooving. Lap the valve until a smooth polished seat is evident (you may have to add a bit more compound after some lapping is done).

5. Remove the valve and tool, then remove ALL traces of the grinding compound with a solvent-soaked rag or rinse the head with solvent.

NOTE: *Valve lapping can also be done by fastening a suction cup to a piece of drill rod in a hand egg-beater type drill. Proceed as above, using the drill as a lapping tool. Due to the higher speeds involved when using the hand drill, care must be exercised to avoid grooving the seat. Lift the tool and change direction of rotation often.*

Valve Springs

REMOVAL AND INSTALLATION

If the cylinder head is removed from the engine, refer to the Valve, Removal and Installation procedures in this Chapter and remove the valve spring.

NOTE: *The following procedures requires the use of GM air adapter tool J-23590 or equivalent, and spring compressor tool J-5892 for 2.0L, 2.5L, 2.8L and 4.3L engines, tool J-26513 for 1.9L engine, tool J-29760 or equivalent for 2.2L diesel engine.*

1. Remove the rocker arm nuts/bolts and the rocker arms.

2. Remove the spark plugs from the cylinders being worked on.

3. To remove the valve keepers, perform the following procedures:

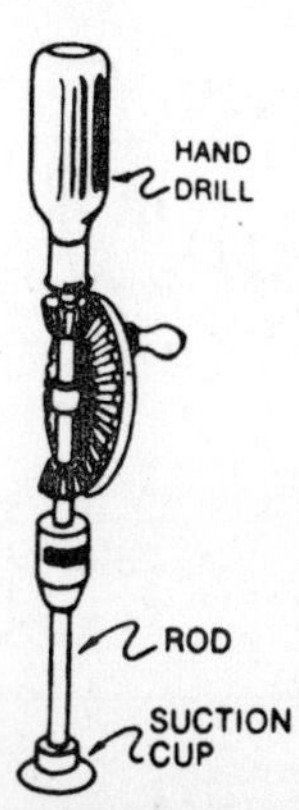

Home made valve lapping tool

a. Using the GM air adapter tool J-23590 or equivalent, install it into the spark plug hole.

b. Apply compressed air to the cylinder to hold the valves in place.

c. Install a rocker arm nut/bolt into the cylinder head.

d. Using the GM spring compressor tool J-5892 for 2.0L, 2.5L, 2.8L and 4.3L engines, tool J-26513 for 1.9L engine, tool J-29760 or equivalent for 2.2L diesel engine, compress the valve spring and remove the valve keepers.

e. Carefully release the spring pressure and remove the compressor tool.

4. Remove the valve cap, the shield and the spring.

5. Remove the O-ring seal and valve stem seal.

6. Inspect the valve spring, replace as necessary.

7. Lubricate the parts with engine oil, then install a new O-ring seal and valve stem seal onto each valve stem.

8. To complete the installation, adjust the valves and reverse the removal procedures. Start the engine, then check and/or adjust the timing.

INSPECTION

1. Position the valve spring on a flat, clean surface next to a square.

2. Measure the height of the spring and rotate it against the engine of the square to measure the distortion (out-of-roundness). If the spring height varies between the springs by more than $\frac{1}{16}$ in. (1.6mm) , replace the spring.

3. Using a valve spring tester, check the spring pressure at the installed and compressed height.

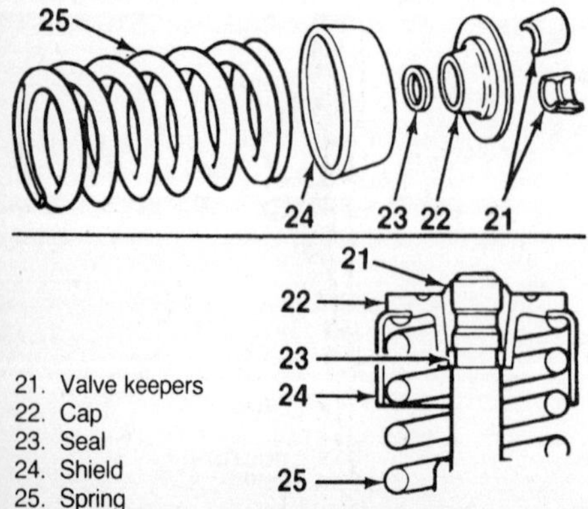

21. Valve keepers
22. Cap
23. Seal
24. Shield
25. Spring

Exploded view of the valve assembly

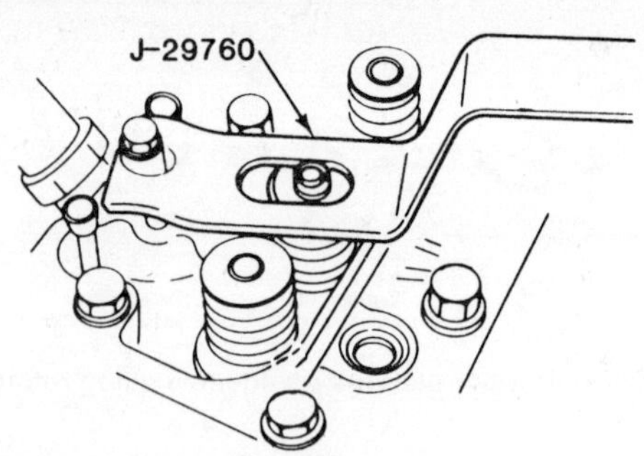

Valve Spring Compressor tool No. J-29760 — 2.2L engine

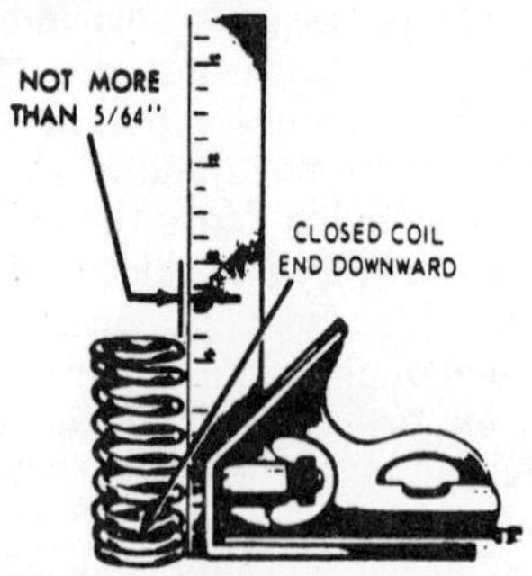

Checking the valve spring free length and squareness

Valve Seats

REMOVAL AND INSTALLATION

1.9L and 2.2L Engines

NOTE: *The following procedures requires the use of an arc welder, a wire brush, a slide hammer puller, dry ice and an arbor press.*

1. Weld pieces of welding rod to several points around the seat, then allow the head to cool for about 5 minutes.

2. Using a slide hammer puller, remove the valve seats attached to the welding rods.

3. Using a wire brush, clean the valve seat recess carefully.

4. Place the new valve seat in dry ice while heating the recess in the head with steam. Take about 5 minutes for this procedure. Perform the heating and cooling simultaneously.

5. Using protective gloves, insert the valve seat into the cylinder head recess. The seat depth below the combustion chamber face should be 0.0031–0.0047 in. (0.08–0.12mm).

6. Cut the valve seat to the angle shown in the valve specifications chart. Valve seat contact width should be 0.0472–0.0630 in. (1.2–1.6mm).

7. Polish the seat using lapping compound and a suction type lapper.

8. Smear the seat and the face of a correctly ground and cleaned valve with a dye such as Prussian blue. Turn the valve against the seat

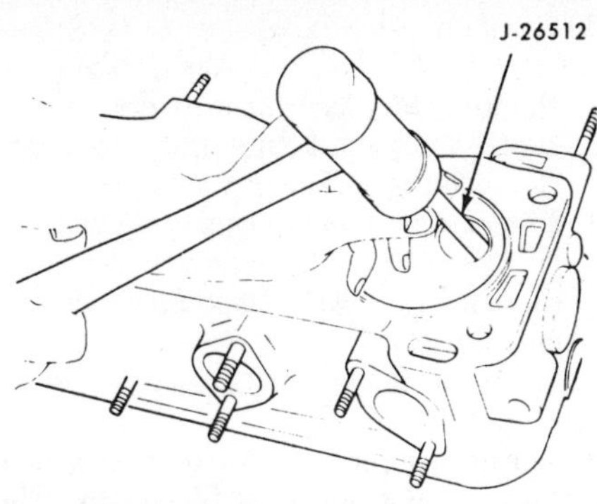

Valve guide removal

several times, remove the valve and check that the dye shows and even contact.

2.0L, 2.5L, 2.8L and 4.3L Engines

The valve seats used on these engines are an integral part of the cylinder head and are not replaceable; they should be refaced, cleaned and lapped, only. See the valve specifications chart for proper seat angle.

Valve Guides

REMOVAL AND INSTALLATION

1.9L and 2.2L Engines

NOTE: *The following procedures requires the use of valve guide removal and installation tool J-26512 or equivalent.*

1. Insert the guide remover such as tool J-26512 or equivalent, into the guide from the cylinder head's combustion chamber side. Drive the guide upward and out. Remove the lower valve spring seat.

2. Using clean engine oil, apply it to the outside of the new guide and position it on the head top side. Using opposite side of the tool J-26512 or equivalent, drive the guide in until it bottoms.

NOTE: *If the guides are replaced, the valves should be replaced also.*

3. The guide should protrude 0.4724 in. (12mm) above the head surface. Grind the end of the guide to achieve this height. Make certain that the guide has bottomed before grinding.

2.0L, 2.5L, 2.8L and 4.3L Engines

The valve guides are not replaceable. The guides should be reamed to accommodate valves with oversized stems. Oversized stems are available in 0.089mm, 0.394mm and 0.775mm.

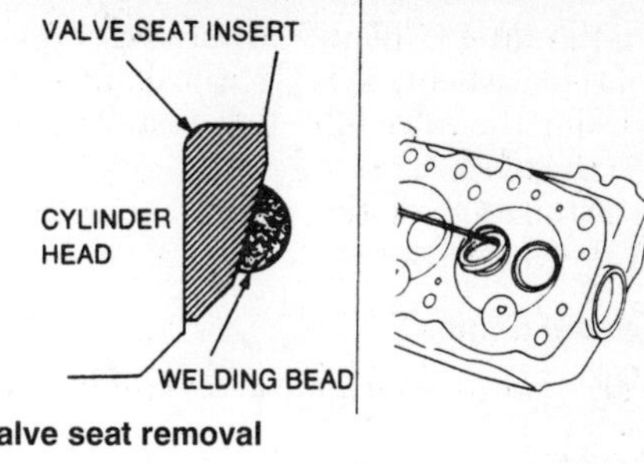

Valve seat removal

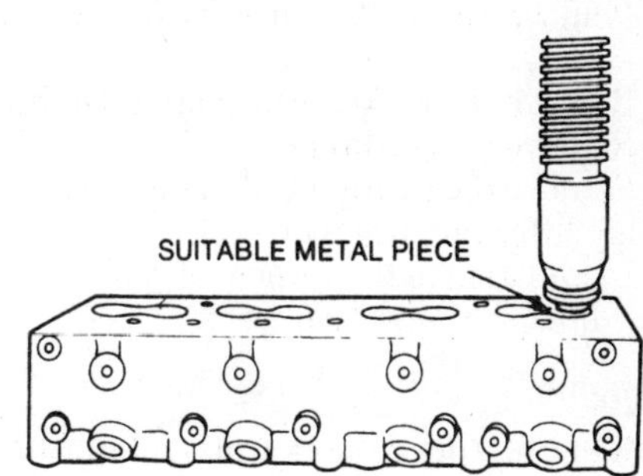

Valve seat installation using a bench press

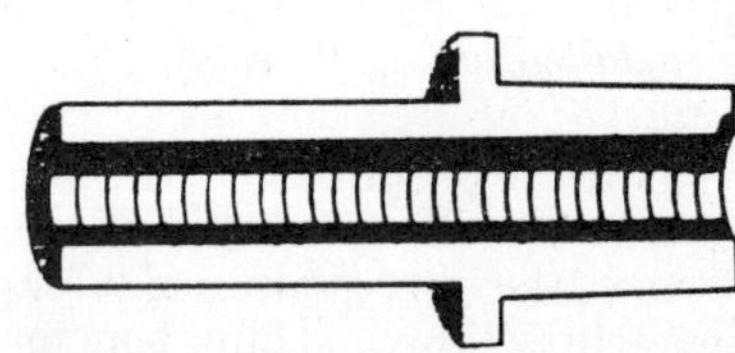

Cut-away view of a knurled valve guide

KNURLING

Valve guides which are not excessively worn or distorted may, in some cases, be knurled. knurling is a process in which metal is displaced and raised, thereby reducing clearance. Knurling also provides excellent oil control.

This procedure should only be performed by a qualified machine shop.

Valve Lifter

REMOVAL AND INSTALLATION

2.0L Engine

1. Remove the rocker arm covers.
2. Loosen the rocker arms and remove the pushrods and guide plates.
3. Using Valve Lifter Removal tool J-29834 or equivalent, remove the valve lifters.

NOTE: *Keep all components in order. If reusing components, install them into their original positions.*

4. For proper rotation during engine operation, the lifter bottom must be convex. Check the lifter bottom for proper shape using a straightedge. If the lifter bottom is not convex,

replace the lifter. Chances are if lifters are in need of replacement, so is the camshaft.

5. Using the valve lifter tool, install the lifters into the block.

6. Installation is the reverse of removal. Adjust the valve lash.

2.2L Diesel Engine

NOTE: *The diesel engine uses solid type lifters.*

1. Remove the rocker arm cover and side cover.

2. Remove the rocker arm shaft assembly.

3. Remove the pushrods.

4. Remove the hydraulic lifters using an appropriate lifter removal tool.

5. Installation is the reverse of removal.

6. Adjust the valve lash.

2.5L Engine

1. Remove the rocker arm and pushrod covers.

NOTE: *Keep all components in order. If reusing components, install them into their original positions. If a new hydraulic lifter is being installed, all sealer coating inside the lifter must be removed.*

2. Remove the pushrods.

3. Remove the lifter studs and retainers.

4. Remove the lifter guides and lifters.

5. Inspect the lifter and lifter bore for wear and scuffing. Examine the roller for freedom of movement and/or flat spots on the roller surface.

6. Installation is the reverse of removal.

2.8L Engine

Some engines have both standard size and 0.010 in. (0.25mm) oversize valve lifters. The cylinder block will be marked with a white paint mark and 0.25mm O.S. stamp where the oversize lifters are used. If lifters replacement is necessary, use new lifters with a narrow flat along the lower $^3/_4$ of the body length. This provides additional oil to the cam lobe and lifter surfaces.

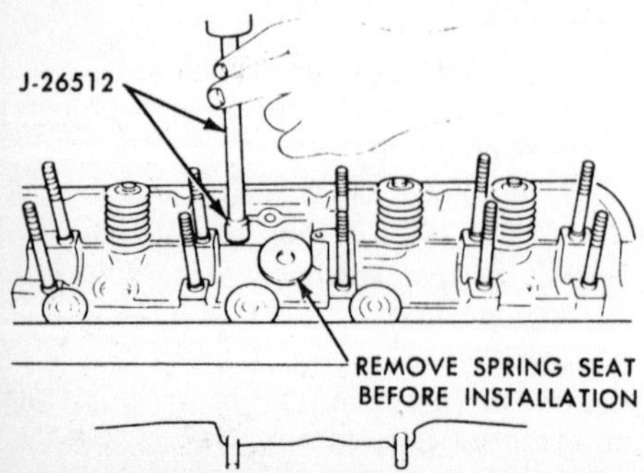

Valve guide installation

NOTE: *This procedure requires the use of a Hydraulic Lifter Remover tool J-9290-1.*

1. Remove the rocker arm covers.

2. Remove the intake manifold.

3. Remove the rocker arm nuts and balls.

4. Remove the rocker arms and pushrods.

NOTE: *Keep all components in order. If reusing components, install them into their original positions.*

5. Using the Hydraulic Lifter Remover tool, remove the lifters.

6. For proper rotation during engine operation, the lifter bottom must be convex. Check the lifter bottom for proper shape using a straightedge. If the lifter bottom is not convex, replace the lifter. Chances are if lifters are in need of replacement, so is the camshaft.

7. Lubricate and install the lifters.

8. Installation is the reverse of removal.

9. Adjust the valve lash.

4.3L Engine

1. Remove the rocker arm cover.

2. Remove the intake manifold.

NOTE: *Keep all components in order. If reusing components, install them into their original positions.*

3. Remove the rocker arms and pushrods.

4. Remove the hydraulic lifter retainer bolts, retainers and restrictors.

5. Inspect the lifter and lifter bore for wear and scuffing. Examine the roller for freedom of movement and/or flat spots on the roller surface.

6. Installation is the reverse of removal.

7. Adjust the valve lash.

Oil Pan

REMOVAL AND INSTALLATION

1.9L Engine

NOTE: *On 4WD, the engine must be removed before removing the oil pan.*

1. Disconnect the negative battery terminal.

2. Raise and support the vehicle on jack stands.

3. Position a catch pan under the oil pan, remove the drain plug and drain the oil.

CAUTION: *The EPA warns that prolonged contact with used engine oil may cause a number of skin disorders, including cancer! You should make every effort to minimize your exposure to used engine oil. Protective gloves should be worn when changing the oil. Wash your hands and any other exposed skin areas as soon as possible after exposure to used engine oil. Soap and water, or waterless hand cleaner should be used.*

4. If equipped, remove the front splash shield.

5. Remove the front crossmember, if necessary.

6. Disconnect the relay rod from the idler arm and lower the relay rod.

7. Remove the left side bell housing bracket and the vacuum line from the oil pan.

8. Remove the oil pan-to-engine bolts and the pan.

NOTE: *It may be necessary to remove the motor mounts and raise the engine in order to remove the oil pan.*

9. Using a putty knife, clean the gasket mounting surfaces.

10. To install, use a new gasket, seals, RTV sealant, if necessary, and reverse the removal procedures. Torque the oil pan-to-engine bolts to 43 inch lbs.

2.0L Engine

1. Disconnect the negative battery terminal.

2. Position a catch pan under the oil pan, remove the drain plug and drain the crankcase.

CAUTION: *The EPA warns that prolonged contact with used engine oil may cause a number of skin disorders, including cancer! You should make every effort to minimize your exposure to used engine oil. Protective gloves should be worn when changing the oil. Wash your hands and any other exposed skin areas as soon as possible after exposure to used engine oil. Soap and water, or waterless hand cleaner should be used.*

3. Raise and support the front of the vehicle on jackstands.

4. If equipped with air conditioning, remove the air conditioning compressor brace.

5. Remove the exhaust shield and disconnect the exhaust pipe from the exhaust manifold.

6. Remove the starter motor (position it out of the way) and the flywheel cover.

7. Remove the oil pan-to-engine bolts and the oil pan from the vehicle.

8. Using a putty knife, clean the gasket mounting surfaces. Make sure the sealing surfaces on the pan, cylinder block and front cover are clean and free of oil.

9. To install, use a new gasket, RTV sealant, apply an $1/8$ in. bead to the oil pan sealing surface, a new oil pan rear seal and reverse the removal procedures. Torque the oil pan-to-engine bolts to 9–13 ft. lbs. Refill the crankcase with clean engine oil. Start the engine and check for leaks.

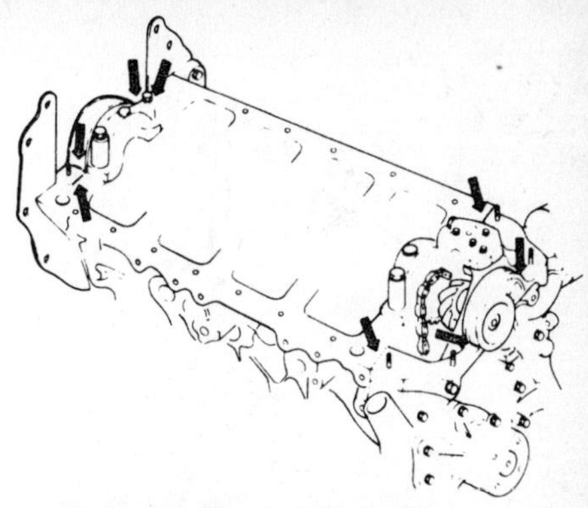

Oil pan sealer location — 1.9L engine

2.2L Diesel Engine

1. Refer to the Engine, Removal and Installation procedures in this Chapter and remove the engine and secure it to a workstand.

2. Remove the oil pan-to-crankcase bolts, the crankcase-to-engine bolts and the oil pans from the engine.

3. Using a putty knife, clean the gasket mounting surfaces.

4. Make sure the sealing surfaces on the pan, the cylinder block and the crankcase are clean and free of oil.

5. To install, use a new gasket, RTV sealant, apply an $1/8$ in. bead to the oil pan sealing surface, and reverse the removal procedures. Torque the oil pan-to-crankcase bolts to 5–9 ft. lbs. and/or the crankcase-to-engine bolts to 15 ft. lbs. Refill the crankcase with clean engine oil. Start the engine and check for leaks.

2.5L Engine

1. Disconnect the negative battery terminal.

2. Raise and support the front of the vehicle on jackstands.

3. Position a catch pan under the crankcase and drain the oil from the engine.

CAUTION: *The EPA warns that prolonged contact with used engine oil may cause a number of skin disorders, including cancer! You should make every effort to minimize your exposure to used engine oil. Protective gloves should be worn when changing the oil. Wash your hands and any other exposed skin areas as soon as possible after exposure to used engine oil. Soap and water, or waterless hand cleaner should be used.*

4. Remove the strut rods. Remove the flywheel/torque convertor dust cover from the bell housing.

5. Disconnect the electrical connectors from the starter, then remove the starter-to-engine bolts, the brace and the starter from the vehicle.

6. Disconnect the exhaust pipe(s) from the

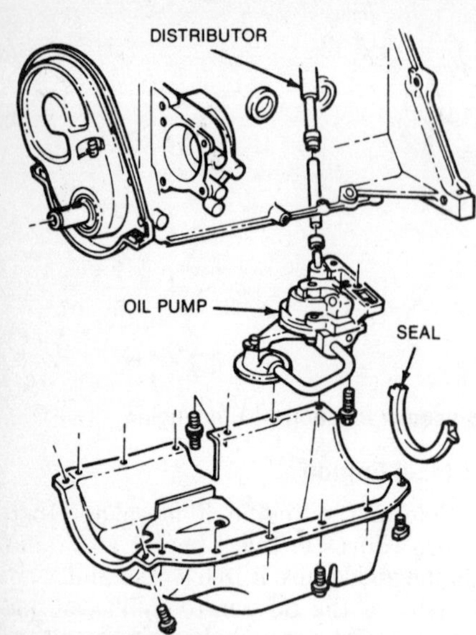

Oil pan — 2.0L engine

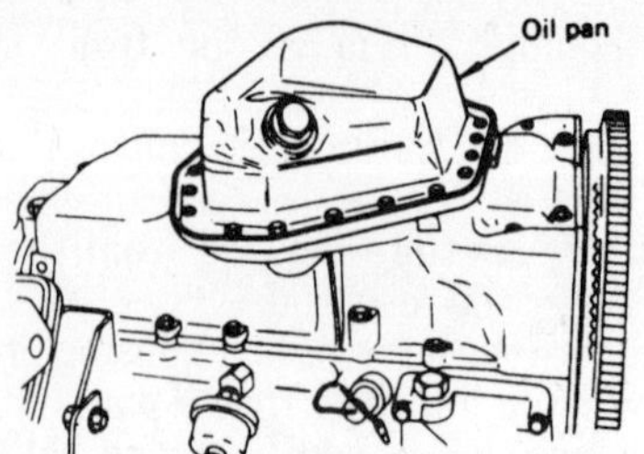

Oil pan — 2.2L diesel engine

exhaust manifold(s) and the exhaust pipe-to-catalytic converter hanger(s).

7. If necessary, remove the engine mount through bolts, then using an engine lifting device, raise the engine (enough) in order to make room for the oil pan removal.

8. Remove the oil pan-to-engine bolts and the oil pan from the engine.

9. Using a putty knife, clean the gasket mounting surfaces. Using solvent, clean the excess oil from the mounting surfaces.

10. Apply a $\frac{3}{16}$ in. (4.7mm) bead of RTV sealant to the oil pan flange (keep the bead inside the bolt holes), the rear main bearing, the timing gear cover and the engine block sealing surface. Refill the crankcase with fresh oil. Start the engine, establish normal operating temperatures and check for leaks.

2.8L and 4.3L Engines

2WD MODELS

1. Remove the engine and secure it to a work stand.

2. Remove the oil pan-to-engine bolts and the pan.

3. Using a putty knife, clean the gasket mounting surfaces. Make sure the sealing surfaces are free of oil and old RTV material.

NOTE: *The oil pan does not use a preformed gasket; it is sealed with RTV gasket material.*

4. Using RTV sealant, run an $\frac{1}{8}$ in. bead of sealer along the entire sealing surface of the pan.

5. Position the pan on the engine and finger tighten the bolts. Torque the smaller bolts to 10 ft. lbs.; the larger bolts to 22 ft. lbs. Refill

the crankcase with clean engine oil. Start the engine and check for leaks.

4WD MODELS

1. Disconnect the negative battery terminal.

2. Remove the dipstick.

3. Raise and support the front of the vehicle on jackstands.

4. Remove the drive belt splash pan, the front axle shield and the transfer case shield.

5. Remove the brake line clips from the crossmember and the 2nd crossmember from the vehicle.

6. If equipped with an automatic transmission, remove the hanger bolt and the exhaust pipe clamp from the catalytic converter, then disconnect the exhaust pipes from the exhaust manifolds and move the exhaust pipe rearward.

7. From the front drive pinion, remove the drive shaft-to-drive pinion nuts/bolts and the drive shaft from the vehicle.

8. Remove the flywheel cover-to-engine braces and the engine-to-chassis braces.

9. Remove the flywheel cover, the starter-to-engine bolts and the starter (lay it aside).

10. Remove the steering shock absorber

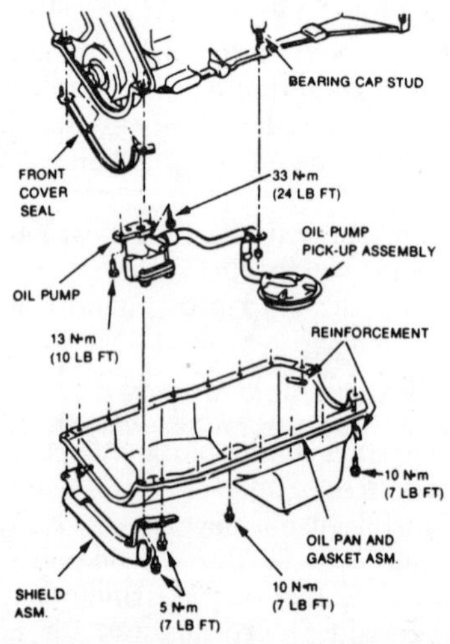

Exploded view of the oil pan and oil pump assembly — 2.5L engine

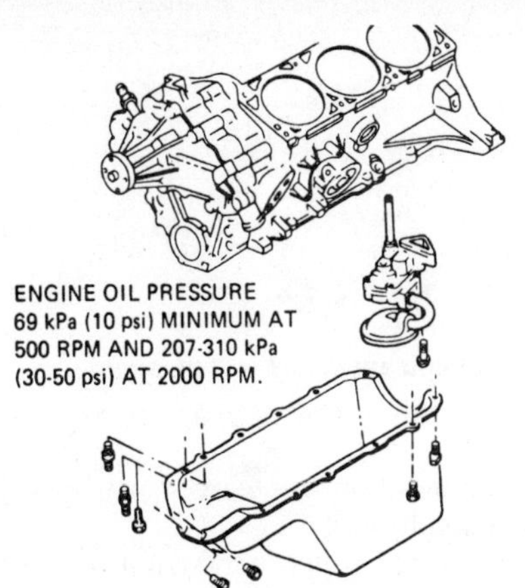

Exploded view of the oil pan and oil pump assembly — 2.8L and 4.3L engines

from the frame bracket. Using a scribing tool, mark the position of the idler arm-to-chassis, then remove the steering gear-to-chassis bolts, the steering gear, the idler arm-to-chassis bolts and the idler arm from the vehicle.

11. Remove the front differential-to-bracket bolts from the sides of the chassis, then pull the steering gear and linkage forward.

12. Remove the motor mount through bolts.

13. Position a catch pan under the oil pan, remove the drain plug and drain the crankcase.

CAUTION: *The EPA warns that prolonged contact with used engine oil may cause a number of skin disorders, including cancer! You should make every effort to minimize your exposure to used engine oil. Protective gloves should be worn when changing the oil. Wash your hands and any other exposed skin areas as soon as possible after exposure to used engine oil. Soap and water, or waterless hand cleaner should be used.*

14. Using a vertical lift, raise the engine slightly, then remove the oil pan-to-engine bolts and the oil pan from the engine.

15. Using a putty knife, clean the gasket mounting surfaces. Using solvent, clean the excess oil from the mounting surfaces.

16. Apply a $\frac{3}{16}$ in. (4.7mm) bead of RTV sealant to the oil pan flange (keep the bead inside the bolt holes), the rear main bearing, the timing gear cover and the engine block sealing surface. Torque the oil pan-to-engine bolts to 10 ft. lbs. (small bolts) or 22 ft. lbs. (large bolts). Refill the crankcase with fresh oil. Start the engine, establish normal operating temperatures and check for leaks.

Oil Pump

REMOVAL AND INSTALLATION

1.9L Engine

1. Remove the oil pan.

2. Disconnect the oil pump feed pipe-to-engine bolt and the pipe from the oil pump.

3. Remove the oil pump-to engine bolts and the oil pump from the engine.

4. To install, reverse the removal procedures.

2.0L Engine

1. Remove the oil pan.

2. Remove the oil pump-to-engine bolts and carefully lower the oil pump.

NOTE: *To ensure immediate oil pressure upon start-up, the oil pump gear cavity should be (primed) packed with petroleum jelly.*

3. To install, reverse the removal procedures. Torque the oil pump-to-engine bolts to 26–35 ft. lbs.

2.2L Diesel Engine

1. Refer to the Oil Pan, Removal and Installation procedures in this Chapter, then remove the crankcase-to-engine bolts and the crankcase together with the oil pan.

NOTE: *Pry off the crankcase by fitting a screwdriver into the slots in the crankcase.*

2. Remove the oil pipe sleeve nut.

3. Remove the oil pump-to-engine bolts and the oil pump with oil pipe from the engine.

4. To install, reverse the removal procedures and leave the joints semi-tight.

5. Fully tighten the oil pump fixing bolts and then the oil pipe joints.

6. To complete the installation, reverse the removal procedures.

2.5L Engine

1. Remove the oil pan.

2. Remove the oil pump-to-rear main bearing cap bolts, the pump and the extension shaft.

3. To install, assemble the oil pump and the extension shaft into the rear main bearing cap; be sure to align the slot (on top of the extension shaft) with the drive tang (on the lower end of the distributor driveshaft).

4. Torque the oil pump-to-bearing cap bolts to 22 ft. lbs. Refill the crankcase with fresh oil. Start the engine, establish normal operating temperatures and check for leaks.

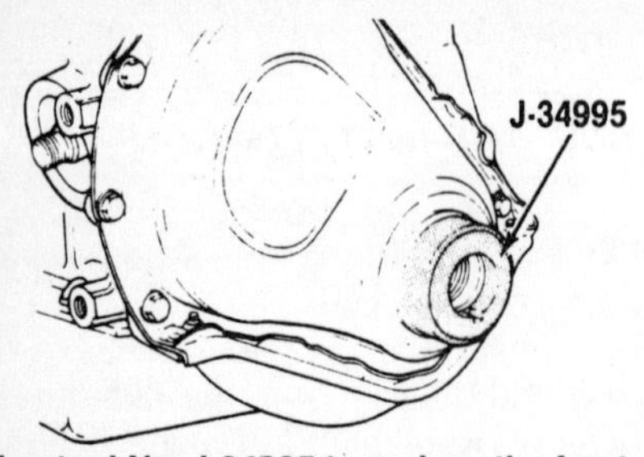

Using tool No. J-34995 to replace the front oil seal — 2.5L engine

2.8L and 4.3L Engine

1. Remove the oil pan.
2. Remove the oil pump-to-engine bolts and oil pump from the vehicle.
3. To install, reverse the removal procedures. Torque the oil pump-to-engine bolts to 26–35 ft. lbs. for 2.8L engine or 65 ft. lbs. for 4.3L engine.

Crankshaft Damper and Oil Seal

REMOVAL AND INSTALLATION

1.9L Engine

1. Disconnect the negative battery terminal.
2. Using a catch pan, place it under the radiator and drain the cooling system.

CAUTION: *When draining the coolant, keep in mind that cats and dogs are attracted by the ethylene glycol antifreeze, and are quite likely to drink any that is left in an uncovered container or in puddles on the ground. This will prove fatal in sufficient quantity. Always drain the coolant into a sealable container. Coolant should be reused unless it is contaminated or several years old.*

3. Remove the cooling fan-to-engine bolts and the fan from the engine.
4. Remove the upper and lower radiator hoses from the engine.
5. Remove the radiator-to-chassis screws and the radiator from the vehicle.
6. Remove the alternator and air conditioning compressor drive belts.
7. Remove the crankshaft pulley center bolt and the pulley/hub assembly from the crankshaft.
8. To install, reverse the removal procedures. Torque the crankshaft pulley center bolt to 87 ft. lbs. Adjust the drive belts.

2.0L Engine

NOTE: *The following procedure requires the use of the wheel puller tool J-24420 or equivalent, and the oil sealer installation tool J-23042 or equivalent.*

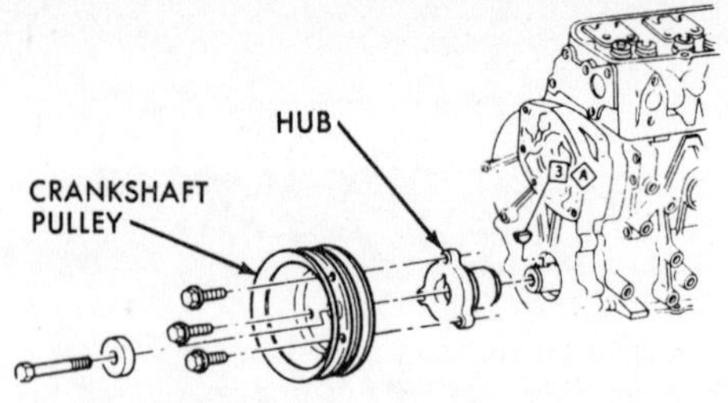

Pulley and hub assembly — 2.0L engine

1. Disconnect the negative battery terminal.
2. Remove the accessory drive belts from the crankshaft pulley.
3. Raise and support the front of the vehicle on jackstands.
4. Remove the damper pulley-to-hub bolts, the pulley and the hub-to-crankshaft bolt.
5. Using the wheel puller tool J-24420 or equivalent, pull the damper pulley hub from the crankshaft.

NOTE: *When the damper pulley hub is removed from the front cover, it is a good idea to replace the crankshaft oil seal.*

6. To replace the front oil seal, perform the following procedures:

   a. Using a medium prybar, pry the oil seal from the front timing cover; be careful not to damage the front timing cover.

   b. Using a new oil seal and the oil sealer installation tool J-23042 or equivalent, lubricate the seal lips with engine oil and drive the new seal into the timing cover, until it seats.

7. To complete the installation, reverse the removal procedures. Torque the hub-to-crankshaft bolt to 66–88 ft. lbs. and the damper pulley-to-hub bolts to 29–44 ft. lbs. Adjust the drive belts.

2.2L Diesel Engine

1. Disconnect the negative battery terminal.

NOTE: *If there is not enough room, it may be necessary to drain the cooling system and remove the radiator to provide enough room for the crankshaft pulley removal.*

2. Loosen the accessory drive belt adjustments and remove the drive belts from the crankshaft pulley.
3. Remove the crankshaft pulley-to-crankshaft pulley center and the crankshaft pulley from the engine.

NOTE: *To replace the front oil seal, it will be necessary to remove the timing belt and the crankshaft timing pulley.*

4. To install, reverse the removal procedures. Install and adjust the drive belt tensions.

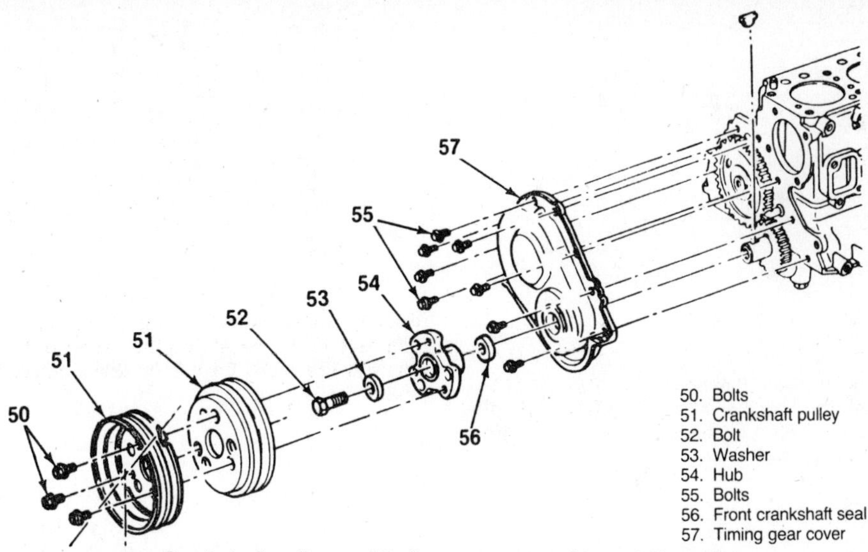

50. Bolts
51. Crankshaft pulley
52. Bolt
53. Washer
54. Hub
55. Bolts
56. Front crankshaft seal
57. Timing gear cover

Crankshaft pulley and timing cover assembly — 2.5L engine

2.5L Engine

NOTE: *The following procedure requires the use of the GM seal installer/centering tool J-34995 or equivalent.*

1. Disconnect the negative battery terminal.

2. If equipped, remove the upper fan shroud. Loosen and remove the accessory-to-damper pulley drive belts.

3. Remove the damper pulley/hub assembly-to-crankshaft bolt and washer, then the pulley/hub assembly from the crankshaft.

NOTE: *The damper pulley is connected to the damper pulley hub by 3 bolts; if necessary, remove the pulley-to-hub bolts and separate the pulley from the hub. When it becomes necessary to remove the damper pulley/hub assembly, always replace the front oil seal with a new one.*

4. Inspect the damper hub (oil seal surface) for rust or burrs; remove the roughness with fine emery cloth.

NOTE: *When installing the damper pulley hub to the crankshaft, be careful not to damage the front oil seal.*

5. To replace the timing cover oil seal, perform the following procedures:

a. Using a medium prybar, pry the oil seal from the timing cover.

b. Using the GM seal installer/centering tool J-34995 or equivalent, install the new oil seal into the timing cover, then remove the tool from the timing cover.

6. To install the damper hub, lubricate the it with engine oil, align it onto the keyway and reverse the removal procedures. Torque the damper pulley hub-to-crankshaft bolt to 160 ft.

lbs. Install the drive belts and adjust the belt tension.

2.8L and 4.3L Engines

NOTE: *The following procedure requires the use of the wheel puller tool J-23523-E, J-24420-A or equivalent, the torsional damper installer tool J-29113 or equivalent, and the oil seal installation tool J-35468 or equivalent.*

1. Disconnect the negative battery terminal.

2. Loosen the accessory drive belt adjustments and remove the drive belts.

3. Remove the damper pulley-to-crankshaft bolt.

4. Raise and support the vehicle on jackstands.

5. Using the wheel puller tool J-23523-E, J-24420-A or equivalent, pull the damper pulley from the crankshaft.

6. To remove the front oil seal, perform the following procedures:

a. Using a medium prybar, pry the oil seal from the front timing cover; be careful not to damage the front timing cover.

b. Using engine oil, lubricate the new seal.

c. Using the oil seal Installation tool J-35468 or equivalent, position it onto the timing cover and drive it into position, until it seats.

7. To complete the installation, reverse the removal procedures. Torque the damper pulley-to-crankshaft bolt to 70 ft. lbs. Adjust the drive belt tensions.

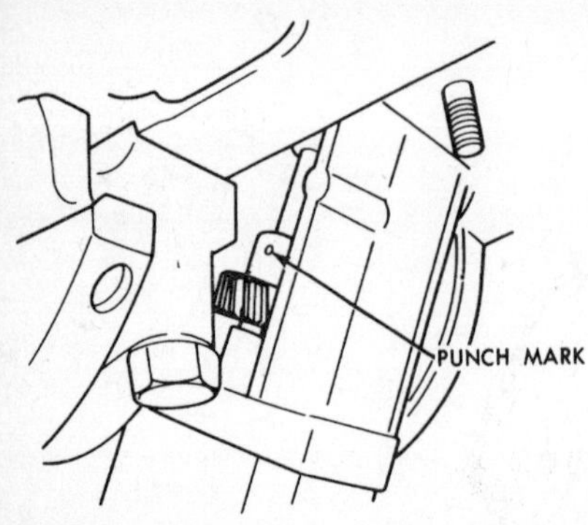

Checking that the punch mark on the oil pump drive gear is turned to the rear side as viewed through the clearance between the front cover and the cylinder block — 1.9L engine

Timing (Front) Covers

REMOVAL AND INSTALLATION

1.9L Engine

1. Remove the cylinder head and the oil pan from the engine.
2. Remove the oil pickup tube from the oil pump.
3. Remove the harmonic balancer from the crankshaft.
4. Remove AIR pump drive belt.
5. If equipped with air conditioning, remove the compressor and move it aside, then remove compressor mounting brackets. If equipped with power steering, remove the power steering pump, the bracket and move it aside.

CAUTION: *Do not remove any refrigerant lines from the air conditioning compressor.*

6. Remove the distributor cap. Mark the rotor-to-distributor housing and the distributor housing-to-engine relationships, then remove the distributor from the engine.
7. Remove the front cover-to-engine bolts and the front cover.
8. Remove and discard from cover to block gasket.
9. Using a putty knife, clean the gasket mounting surfaces. Be sure to wipe the mounting surfaces clean of all oil. Check the front cover for cracking or damage, replace it, if necessary.
10. Install a new gasket, RTV sealant, if necessary, onto the cylinder block.
11. Align the oil pump drive gear punch mark with the oil filter side of cover; then align the center of dowel pin with alignment mark on the oil pump case.
12. Rotate the crankshaft until the No. 1 and No. 4 cylinders are at TDC of the compression stroke.

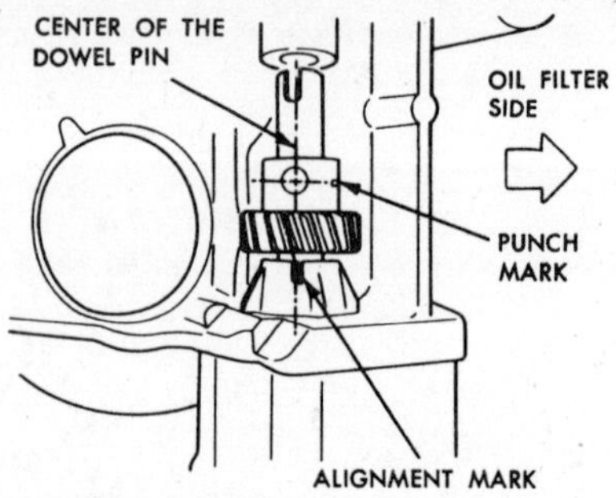

Aligning the oil pump drive gear mark with the oil filter side of the cover and the center of the dowel pin with the mark on the oil pump case — 1.9L engine

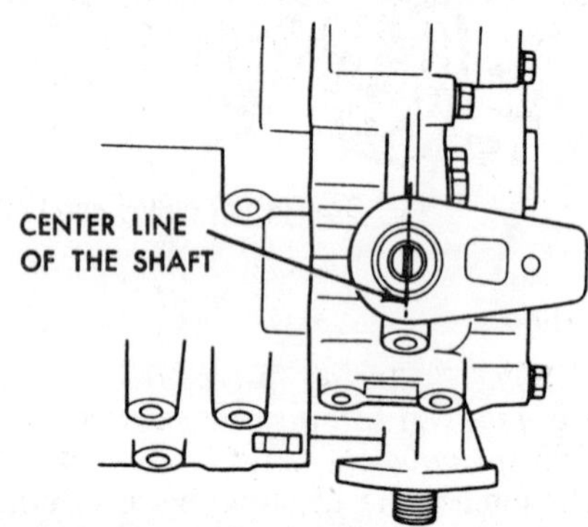

Checking that the slit at the end of the oil pump shaft is parallel with the front face of the block — 1.9L engine

13. Install the front cover by engaging the pinion gear with the oil pump drive gear on the crankshaft.
14. Check that the punch mark on the oil pump drive gear is turned to the rear side as viewed through clearance between front cover and cylinder block.
15. Check that the slit at the end of the oil pump shaft is parallel with front face of cylinder block and that it is offset forward.
16. With all parts correctly installed, reverse the removal procedures. Check and/or adjust the engine timing. Inspect for leaks.

2.0L Engine

NOTE: *The following procedure requires the use of the centering tool J-23042 or equivalent.*

1. Disconnect the negative battery terminal.
2. Position a catch pan under the radiator, open the drain cock and drain the cooling system.

CAUTION: *When draining the coolant, keep in mind that cats and dogs are attracted by the ethylene glycol antifreeze, and are quite likely to drink any that is left in an uncovered container or in puddles on the ground.*

This will prove fatal in sufficient quantity. Always drain the coolant into a sealable container. Coolant should be reused unless it is contaminated or several years old.

3. Remove the upper fan shroud.

4. Loosen the accessory drive belt adjusters and remove the drive belts from the crankshaft pulley.

5. Remove the cooling fan-to-water pump bolts and the pulley.

6. Remove the radiator hose and the heater hose from the water pump. Remove the water pump-to-engine bolts and the water pump from the engine.

7. Remove the crankshaft pulley-to-hub bolt and the pulley from the crankshaft.

8. Using the puller tool J-24420 or equivalent, pull the hub assembly from the crankshaft.

9. Remove the front cover-to-engine bolts and the cover from the engine.

10. Using a putty knife, clean the gasket mounting surfaces. Using solvent, clean the oil and grease from the gasket mounting surfaces.

11. The oil seal may be replaced with the cover removed or installed on the engine, by performing the following procedures:

a. Using a medium prybar, pry the oil seal from the front cover; be careful not to distort the seal mating surface.

b. Using engine oil, lubricate the new oil seal.

c. Install the new seal so the open side (helical side) is towards the engine.

d. Using the installation tool J-23042 or equivalent, drive the new seal into the front cover until it seats.

12. To complete the installation, apply an $^1/_8$ in. bead of RTV sealant to the front cover and reverse the removal procedures. Torque the hub-to-crankshaft bolt to 66–88 ft. lbs. and the damper pulley-to-hub bolts to 29–44 ft. lbs. Adjust the drive belts.

NOTE: *When applying RTV sealant to the front cover, be sure to keep it out of the bolt holes. The sealant must be wet to the touch when the bolts are torqued down.*

2.2L Diesel Engine

1. Disconnect the negative battery terminal.

NOTE: *If there is not enough room, it may be necessary to drain the cooling system and remove the radiator to provide room for the crankshaft pulley removal.*

2. Loosen the accessory drive belt adjustments and remove the drive belts from the crankshaft pulley.

3. Remove the crankshaft pulley-to-crank-

shaft pulley center and the crankshaft pulley from the engine.

NOTE: *To replace the front oil seal, it will be necessary to remove the timing belt and the crankshaft timing pulley.*

4. Remove the front cover housing-to-engine bolts and the covers.

5. To install, reverse the removal procedures. Install and adjust the drive belt tensions. If the radiator was removed, refill the cooling system.

2.5L Engine

NOTE: *The following procedure requires the use of the GM seal installer/centering tool J-34995 or equivalent.*

1. Refer to the Crankshaft Pulley, Damper and Oil Seal, Removal and Installation procedures in this Chapter and remove the damper from the crankshaft.

2. Remove the fan and the pulley. Remove the alternator and the brackets from the front of the engine.

3. Position a catch pan under the radiator, open the drain cock and drain the cooling system.

CAUTION: *When draining the coolant, keep in mind that cats and dogs are attracted by the ethylene glycol antifreeze, and are quite likely to drink any that is left in an uncovered container or in puddles on the ground. This will prove fatal in sufficient quantity. Always drain the coolant into a sealable container. Coolant should be reused unless it is contaminated or several years old.*

4. Remove the lower radiator hose clamp at the water pump.

5. Remove the timing cover-to-oil pan bolts, the timing cover-to-engine bolts and the timing cover from the engine.

6. Using a medium prybar, pry the oil seal from the timing cover.

7. Using a putty knife, clean the gasket mounting surfaces. Clean the surface with solvent to remove all traces of oil and grease.

NOTE: *The timing cover can become distorted very easily, so be careful when cleaning the gasket surface.*

8. Apply engine oil to the lips of the new oil seal. Using the GM seal installer/centering tool J-34995 or equivalent, install the new oil seal into the timing cover; leave the tool installed in the timing cover.

9. Using RTV sealant or equivalent, apply a $^1/_4$ in. (6mm) wide bead to the timing cover mounting surface and a $^3/_8$ in. (9.5mm) wide bead to the oil pan at the timing cover sealing surface.

10. Install the timing cover onto the engine and partially tighten the bolts.

11. First, torque the timing cover-to-engine bolts to 90 inch lbs.; secondly, torque the timing cover-to-oil pan bolts to 90 inch lbs. Remove the seal installer/centering tool J-34995 or equivalent, from the timing cover.

12. To complete the installation, reverse the removal procedures. Torque the damper pulley hub-to-crankshaft bolt to 160 ft. lbs. Adjust the drive belt(s) tension. Refill the cooling system and the power steering reservoir, if equipped.

2.8L Engine

NOTE: *The following procedure requires the use of the GM seal installer/centering tool J-34995 or equivalent.*

CAUTION: *The engines use a harmonic balancer. Breakage may occur if the balancer is hammered back onto the crankshaft; a press or special installation tool is necessary.*

1. Remove the water pump.

2. If equipped with air conditioning, remove the compressor and move it aside; do not remove any of the air conditioning lines.

3. Using a wheel puller, remove the harmonic balancer.

NOTE: *The outer ring (weight) of the harmonic balancer is bonded to the hub with rubber. The balancer must be removed with a puller which acts on the inner hub only. Pulling on the outer portion of the balancer will break the rubber bond or destroy the tuning of the torsional damper.*

4. Disconnect the lower radiator hose and heater hose.

5. Remove timing gear cover attaching screw, the cover and the gasket.

6. Using a putty knife, clean the gasket mounting surfaces on the front cover and block.

7. Apply a continuous $\frac{3}{32}$ in. (2mm) bead of sealant 1052357 or equivalent, to front cover sealing surface and around coolant passage parts and central bolt holes. Apply a bead of silicone sealer to the pan-to-cylinder block joint.

8. Using the GM seal installer/centering tool J-34995 or equivalent, position it in the crankcase snout hole in the front cover, then install the front cover.

9. Install the front cover bolts finger tight, remove the centering tools and tighten the cover bolts. Install the harmonic balancer, the pulley, the water pump, the drive belts, the radiator and all other parts. Adjust the drive belt(s) tension. Refill the cooling system and the power steering reservoir, if equipped.

4.3L Engine

1. Remove the torsional damper center bolts and the damper with suitable puller.

NOTE: *The outer ring (weight) of the torsional damper is bonded to the hub with rubber. The damper must be removed with a puller which acts on the inner hub only. Pulling on the outer portion of the damper will break the rubber bond or destroy the tuning of the unit.*

2. Drain the cooling system.

CAUTION: *When draining the coolant, keep in mind that cats and dogs are attracted by the ethylene glycol antifreeze, and are quite likely to drink any that is left in an uncovered container or in puddles on the ground. This will prove fatal in sufficient quantity. Always drain the coolant into a sealable container. Coolant should be reused unless it is contaminated or several years old.*

3. Remove the water pump.

4. Remove the oil pan.

5. Remove the upper radiator hose, air conditioner compressor (lay it aside) and right side engine accessory bracket.

6. Remove the front cover bolts and front cover.

7. If the front cover seal is to be replaced, it may be pryed front the front cover with a prybar. Use tool J-35468 to install the seal.

8. Clean all sealing surfaces and install a new gasket to the front cover. Use sealant to hold it in place.

9. Install the front cover and tighten the bolts to 10 ft. lbs.

10. Installation is the reverse of removal.

Timing Chains, Sprockets and Tensioners

REMOVAL AND INSTALLATION

1.9L Engine

NOTE: *The following procedure requires the use of the wheel puller tool J-25031 or equivalent, and timing sprocket installation tool J-26587 or equivalent.*

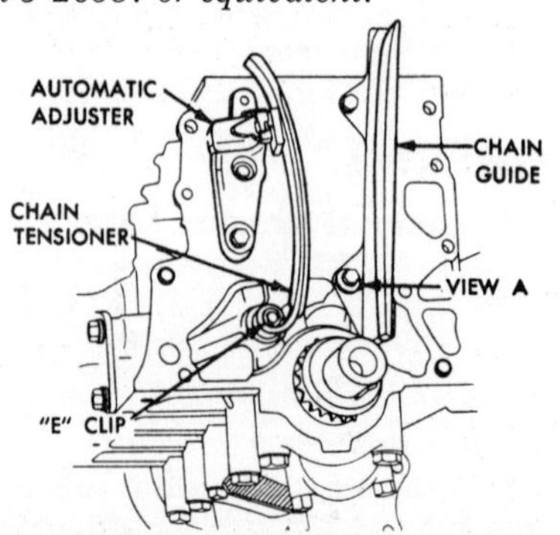

Timing chain guide and tensioner — 1.9L engine

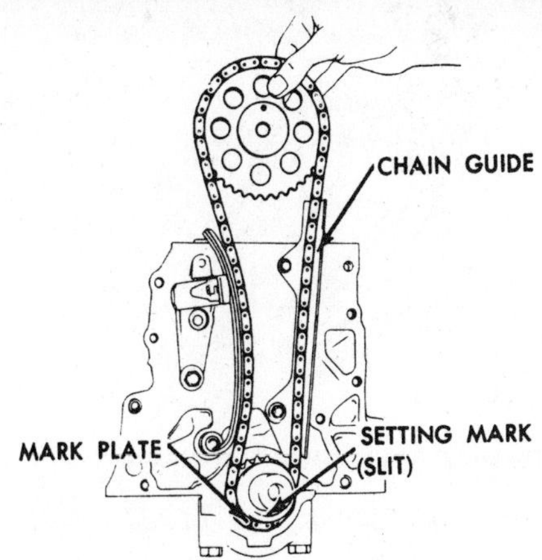

Timing chain alignment — 1.9L engine

1. Remove the timing cover.

2. At the shoe automatic adjuster, depress the adjuster lock lever to lock the shoe in the fully retracted position.

3. Remove timing chain from crankshaft sprocket.

NOTE: *To remove the timing chain, it may be necessary to remove the camshaft sprocket. Before removing the timing chain, be sure to align the timing marks.*

4. Check the timing sprockets for wear or damage. If crankshaft sprocket must be replaced, remove the sprocket and the pinion gear from crankshaft using the puller tool J-25031 or equivalent.

5. Check timing chain for wear or damage; replace as necessary. Measure distance (L) with chain stretched with a pull of approximately 22 lbs. (98N). Standard (L) valve is 15 in. (381mm); replace chain of (L) is greater than 15.16 in. (385mm).

6. Remove the automatic chain adjuster-to-engine bolt and the adjuster.

7. To check the operation of the automatic chain adjuster, push the shoe inwards, if it becomes locked, the adjuster is working properly. The adjuster assembly must be replaced if rack teeth are found to be worn excessively.

8. To remove the chain tensioner, remove the E-clip and the tensioner. Check the tensioner for wear or damage; if necessary, replace it.

9. Inspect the tensioner pin for wear or damage. If replacement is necessary, remove the pin from the cylinder block using a pair of locking pliers. Lubricate the NEW pin tensioner with clean engine oil. Start the pin into block, then place the tensioner over the appropriate pin. Position the E-clip onto the pin, then (using a hammer) tap it into the block until clip just clears tensioner. Check the ten-

sioner and adjuster for freedom of rotation on the pins.

10. Inspect the guide for wear or damage and plugged lower oil jet. If replacement or cleaning is necessary, remove the guide bolts, the guide and the oil jet. Install a new guide and upper attaching bolt. Install the lower oil jet and bolt, so the oil port is pointed toward crankshaft.

11. Install the timing sprocket and the pinion gear (groove side toward the front cover). Align the key groove with crankshaft key, then drive it into position using installing tool J-26587 or equivalent.

12. Turn the crankshaft so key is turned toward the cylinder head side (No. 1 and No. 4 pistons at TDC).

13. Install the timing chain, align the timing chain mark plate with the mark on the crankshaft timing sprocket. The side of the chain with the mark plate is on the front side and the side of chain with the most links between mark plates is on the chain guide side. Keep the timing chain engaged with the camshaft timing sprocket until the camshaft timing sprocket is installed on the camshaft.

14. Install the camshaft timing sprocket so it's marked side faces forward and it's triangular mark aligns with the chain mark plate.

15. Install the automatic chain adjuster.

16. Release the lock by depressing the shoe on adjuster by hand, and check to make certain the chain is properly tensioned when the lock is released.

17. Install from cover assembly as outlined previously.

2.0L Engine

NOTE: *The following procedure requires the use of the spring compressor tool J-33875 or equivalent, the gear puller tool J-22888-20 or equivalent.*

1. Refer to the Timing (Front) Cover, Removal and Installation procedures in this Chapter and remove the timing cover.

2. Rotate the crankshaft to position the No. 4 piston on TDC of the compression stroke; the marks on the camshaft and crankshaft sprockets are in alignment.

3. Loosen the timing chain tensioner nut, as far as possible, without actually removing it.

4. Remove the camshaft sprocket-to-camshaft bolts and the sprocket; remove the timing chain with the sprocket. If the sprocket does not slide from the camshaft easily, a light blow with a soft mallet at the lower edge of the sprocket will dislodge it.

5. Using the gear puller tool J-22888-20 or equivalent, remove the crankshaft sprocket.

6. Using a putty knife, clean the gasket

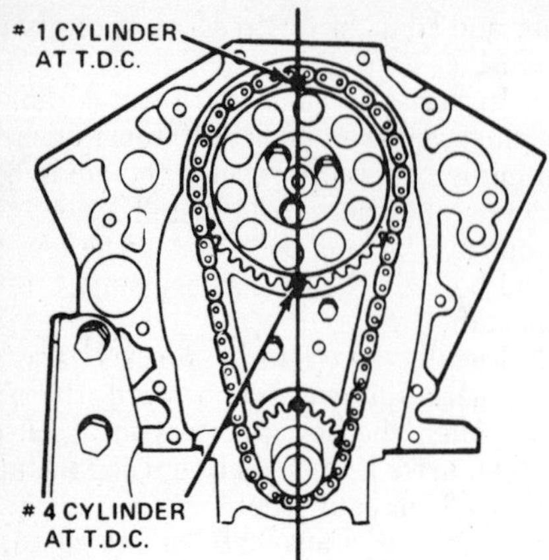

Timing chain alignment — 2.8L engine

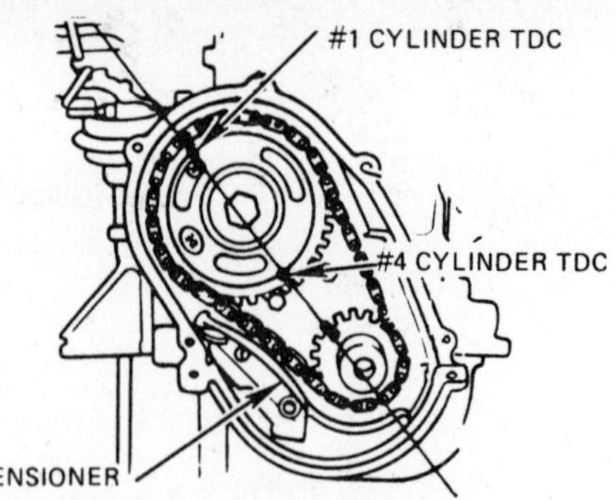

Timing chain alignment — 2.0L engine

mounting surfaces. Inspect the timing chain and the sprocket teeth for wear and/or damage; replace the parts, if necessary.

7. To install, press the crankshaft sprocket back onto the crankshaft, position the timing chain over the camshaft sprocket and then around the crankshaft sprocket. Make sure that the marks on the 2 sprockets are aligned. Lubricate the thrust surface with Molykote® or equivalent.

8. Align the dowel in the camshaft with the dowel hole in the sprocket and then install the sprocket onto the camshaft. Torque the camshaft sprocket-to-camshaft bolts to 27–33 ft. lbs.

9. Lubricate the timing chain with clean engine oil. Using the spring compressor tool J-33875 or equivalent, position the tangs under the sliding block and pull the tool to compress the spring. Tighten the chain tensioner.

10. To complete the installation, reverse the removal procedures.

2.8L and 4.3L Engines

NOTE: *The following procedure requires the use of the crankshaft sprocket removal tool J-5825 or equivalent, and the crankshaft*

Removing the crankshaft sprocket — 2.8L engine

sprocket installation tool J-5590 or equivalent.

1. Remove the timing cover.

2. Rotate the crankshaft until the No. 4 cylinder is on the TDC of its compression stroke and the camshaft sprocket mark (No. 4 cylinder) aligns with the mark on the crankshaft sprocket (facing each other) and in line with the shaft centers.

3. Remove the camshaft sprocket-to-camshaft bolts and the camshaft sprocket (with timing chain). If camshaft is difficult to remove, use a plastic mallet to bump the sprocket from the camshaft.

NOTE: *The camshaft sprocket (located by a dowel) is lightly pressed onto the camshaft and will come off readily. The chain comes off with the camshaft sprocket.*

4. Using the crankshaft sprocket removal tool J-5825 or equivalent, remove the timing sprocket from the crankshaft.

5. Inspect the timing chain and the timing sprockets for wear or damage, replace the damaged parts, if necessary.

6. Using a putty knife, clean the gasket mounting surfaces. Using solvent, clean the oil and grease from the gasket mounting surfaces.

7. Using the crankshaft sprocket installation tool J-5590 or equivalent, and a hammer, without disturbing the position of the engine, drive the crankshaft sprocket onto the crankshaft.

8. Position the timing chain over the camshaft sprocket. Arrange the camshaft sprocket in such a way that the timing marks will align between the shaft centers and the camshaft locating dowel will enter the dowel hole in the cam sprocket.

9. Place the cam sprocket, with its chain mounted over it, in position on the front of the camshaft and torque the camshaft sprocket-to-camshaft bolts to 17 ft. lbs.

10. With the timing chain installed, turn the crankshaft 2 complete revolutions, then check to make certain that the timing marks are in correct alignment between the shaft centers.

11. To complete the installation, use a bead of RTV sealant on the timing cover and reverse the removal procedures.

Timing Belt

REMOVAL AND INSTALLATION

2.2L Diesel Engine

NOTE: *The following procedure requires the use of the belt tension gauge tool J-29771 or equivalent.*

1. Remove the front cover.

2. From the injection pump timing pulley, remove the flange-to-pulley screws and the flange.

3. Remove the timing belt tension pulley spring.

NOTE: *When removing tension spring, avoid using excess force or distortion of spring will result.*

4. Remove the timing belt tension pulley-to-engine fixing nut, then the tension pulley and tension center.

5. Remove the timing belt. Avoid twisting or kinking the belt and keep it free from water, oil, dust and other foreign matter.

NOTE: *No attempt should be made to readjust belt tension. If the belt has been loosened through service of the timing system, it should be replaced with a new one.*

6. Check that the setting marks on the crank pulley, injection pump timing pulley, and camshaft pulley are in alignment, then install the timing belt in sequence of crankshaft

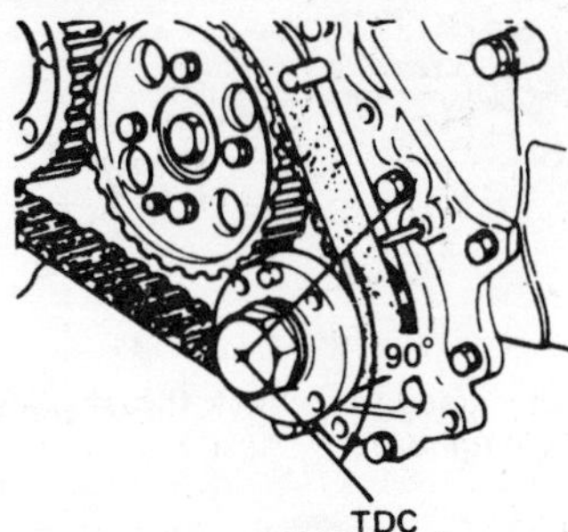

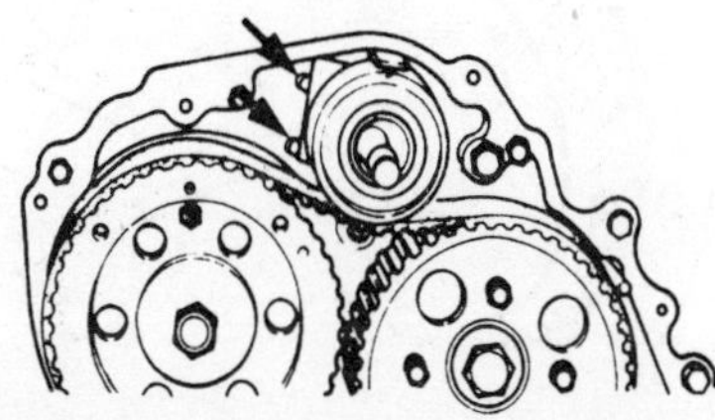

Aligning the tension pulley to make proper contact with the two housing pins — 2.2L diesel

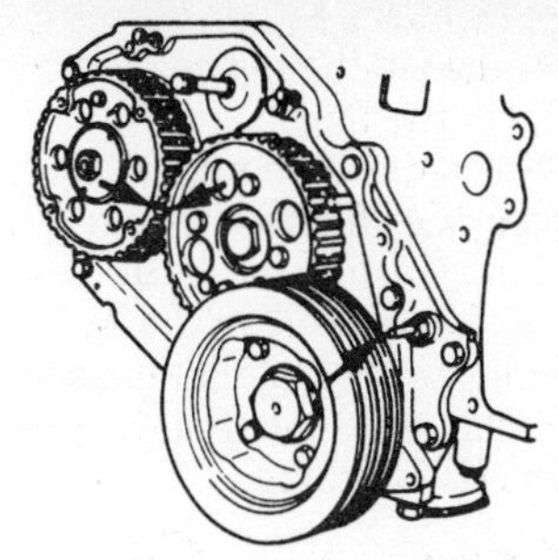

Aligning the timing marks — 2.2L diesel

timing pulley, camshaft timing pulley and injection pump timing pulley.

7. Make an adjustment, so slackness of the belt is taken up by the tension pulley. When installing the timing belt, care should be taken so as not to damage the belt.

8. Install the tension center and tension pulley, making certain the end of the tension center is in proper contact with 2 pins on the timing pulley housing.

9. Hand-tighten the nut, so tension pulley can slide freely.

10. Install the tension spring correctly and semi-tighten the tension pulley fixing nut.

11. Turn the crankshaft 2 turns in normal direction of rotation to permit seating of the belt. Further rotate the crankshaft 90 degrees beyond TDC to settle the injection pump. Never attempt to turn the crankshaft in reverse direction.

NOTE: *If the engine is turned past the timing marks, keep rotating the engine in the normal direction of rotation until the marks align properly.*

12. Loosen the tension pulley fixing nut completely, allowing the pulley to take up looseness of the belt. Then, tighten the nut to 78–95 ft. lbs.

13. Install the flange on the injection pump pulley. The hole in the outer circumference of the flange should be aligned with the timing mark **triangle** on the injection pump pulley.

14. Turn the crankshaft 2 (clockwise) turns to position the No. 1 cylinder on to TDC of it's compression stroke, then check that the **trian-**

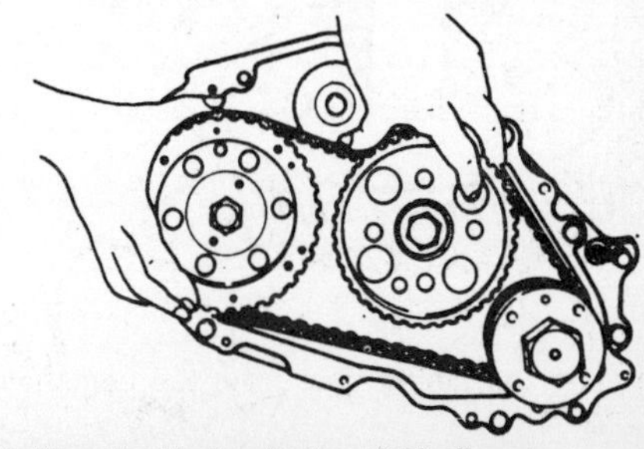

Installing the timing belt — 2.2L diesel

gle mark on the timing pulley is in alignment with the hole in the flange.

15. The belt tension should be checked at a point between the injection pump pulley and crankshaft pulley using tool J-29771 or equivalent, to 33–55 lbs. as read on the scale.

16. To complete the installation, adjust valve clearances and reverse the removal procedures. Check the injection timing.

Timing Gears

REMOVAL AND INSTALLATION

2.5L Engine

The timing gear is pressed onto the camshaft. To remove or install the timing gear, an arbor press must be used.

NOTE: *The following procedure requires the use of an arbor press, a press plate, the GM gear removal tool J-971 or equivalent, the GM gear installation tool J-21474-13, J-21795-1 or equivalent.*

1. Remove the camshaft from the engine.

2. Using an arbor press, a press plate and the GM gear removal tool J-971 or equivalent, press the timing gear from the camshaft.

NOTE: *When pressing the timing gear from the camshaft, be certain that the position of the press plate does not contact the woodruff key.*

3. To assembly, position the press plate to support the camshaft at the back of the front journal. Place the gear spacer ring and the thrust plate over the end of the camshaft, then install the woodruff key. Press the timing gear onto the camshaft, until it bottoms against the gear spacer ring.

NOTE: *The end clearance of the thrust plate should be 0.0015–0.005 in. (0.038–0.127mm). If less than 0.0015 in. (0.038mm), replace the spacer ring; if more than 0.005 in. (0.127mm), replace the thrust plate.*

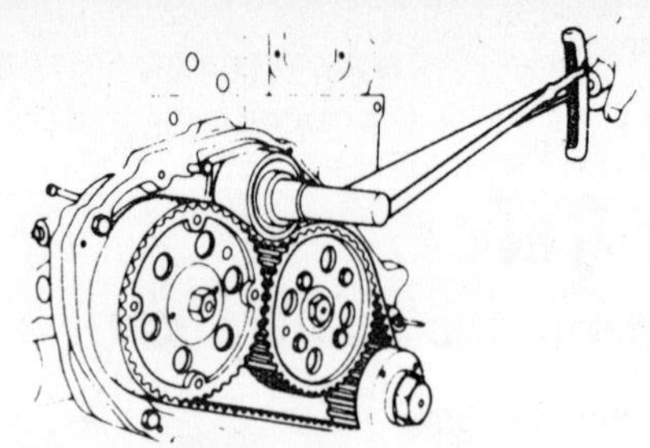
Torquing the tension pulley — 2.2L diesel

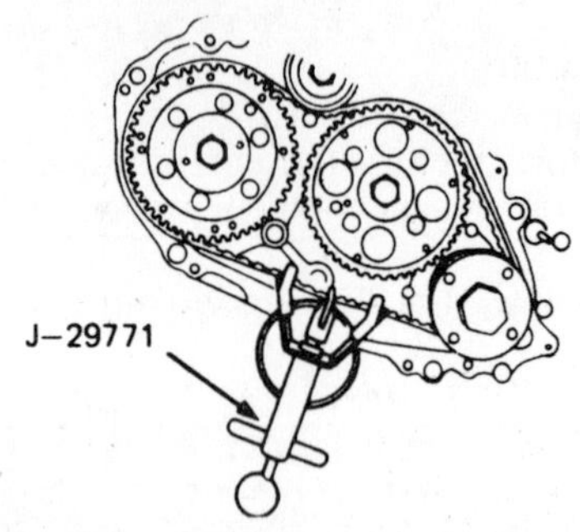

Using tool No. J-29771 to check the belt tension — 2.2L diesel

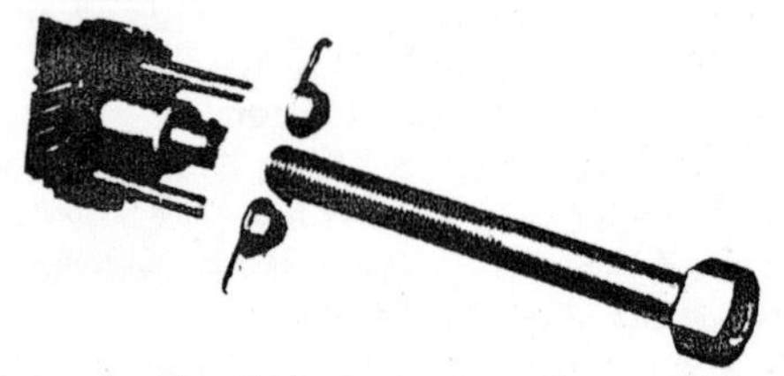
Removing the timing gear from the crankshaft — 2.5L engine

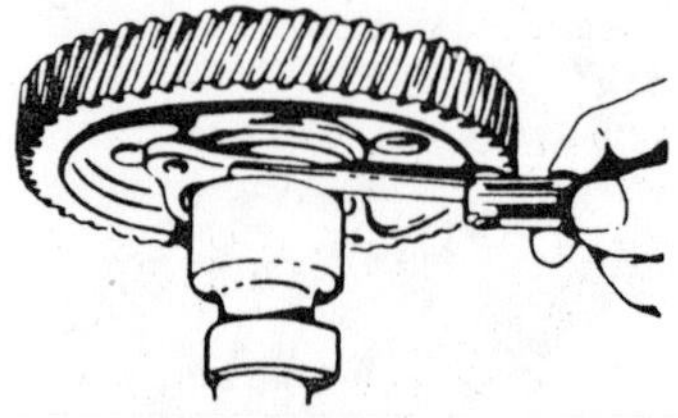
Using a feeler gauge to check thrust plate clearance — 2.5L engine

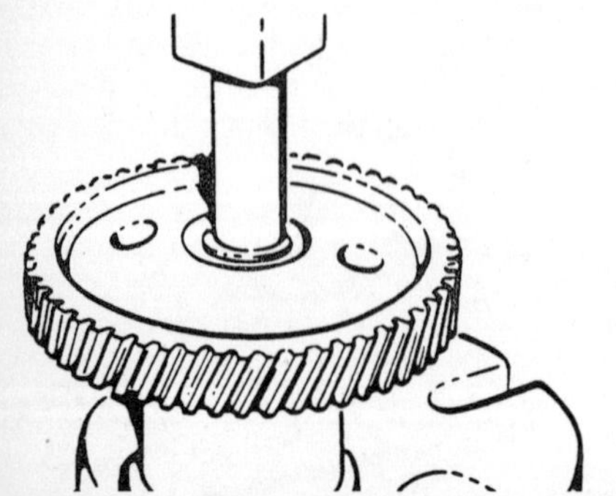
Separating the timing gear from the camshaft — 2.5L engine

Removing the camshaft thrust plate-to-engine screws — 2.5L engine

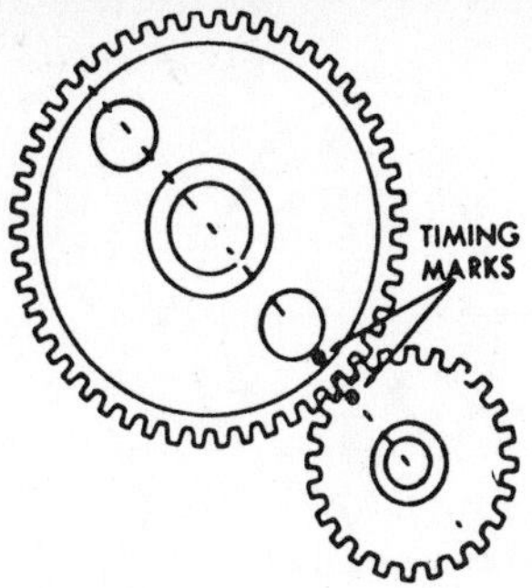

Timing mark alignment — 2.5L engine

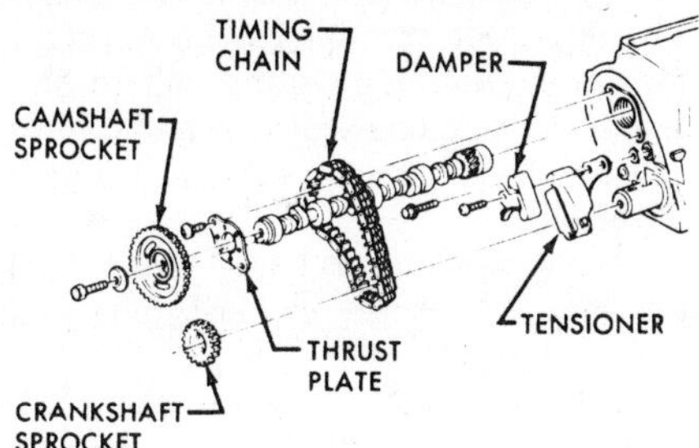

Timing chain and camshaft assembly — 2.0L engine

4. To complete the installation, align the marks on the timing gears and reverse the removal procedures.

Camshaft Sprocket — OHC Engine

REMOVAL AND INSTALLATION

1.9L Engine

1. Remove timing cover.
2. Rotate camshaft until No. 4 cylinder is on the TDC of it's compression stroke.
3. Remove the distributor cap. Using a marking tool, mark the rotor-to-housing and the housing-to-engine positions, then remove the distributor from the engine.
4. Disconnect the fuel lines and remove the fuel pump from the engine.
5. Using a screwdriver or equivalent, depress the automatic shoe adjuster lock lever into the fully retracted position. After locking the automatic adjuster, check that the chain is in free state.
6. Remove the timing sprocket-to-camshaft bolt, the sprocket and the fuel pump drive cam from the camshaft. Keep the timing sprocket on the chain damper and the tensioner without removing the chain from the sprocket.
7. Check that the mark on the No. 1 rocker arm shaft bracket is in alignment with the mark on the camshaft and that the crankshaft pulley groove is aligned with the TDC mark (**0** degree) on the front cover.
8. Assemble the timing sprocket to the camshaft by aligning it with the pin on the cam-

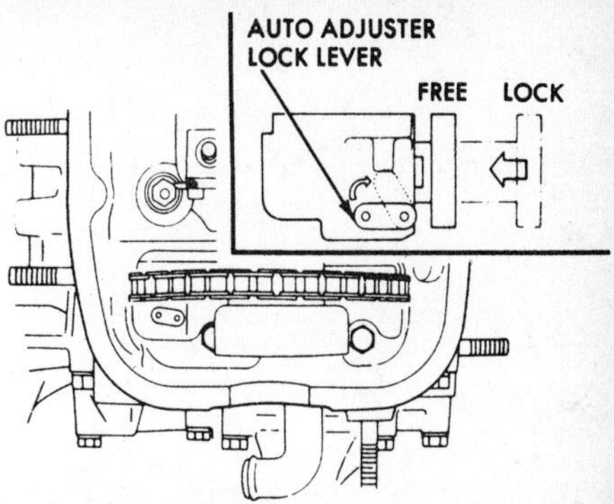

Depressing the adjuster lock lever — 1.9L engine

shaft; use care not to remove the chain from the sprocket.
9. Install the fuel pump drive cam, the sprocket retaining bolt and washer. Remove the 1/2 moon seal in from end of head; then install torque wrench and torque bolt to 58 ft. lbs; replace the 1/2 moon seal in cylinder head.
10. Using the alignment marks, install the distributor.
11. Using a medium prybar, depressing the adjuster shoe to release the lock, check the timing chain tension.
12. Check valve timing, the rotor and mark on distributor housing should be in alignment when the No. 4 cylinder on TDC. The timing mark on damper pulley should align with TDC mark (**0** degree mark) on front cover.
13. To complete the installation, reverse the removal procedures.

Camshaft and Bearings

REMOVAL AND INSTALLATION

1.9L Engine

1. Remove timing cover.
2. Rotate camshaft until No. 4 cylinder is on the TDC of it's compression stroke.
3. Remove the distributor cap. Using a marking tool, mark the rotor-to-housing and the housing-to-engine positions, then remove the distributor from the engine.

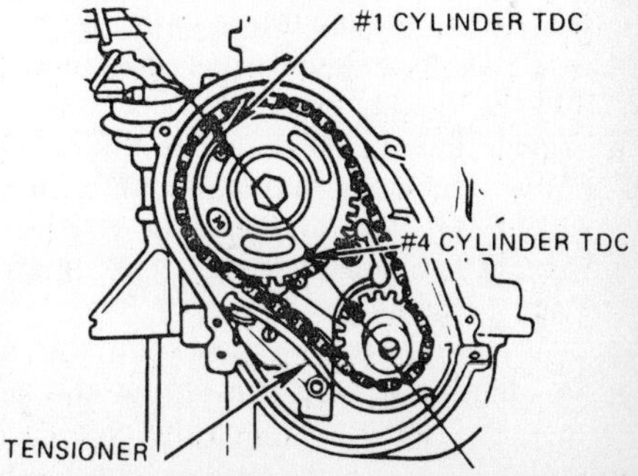

Timing mark alignment — 2.0L engine

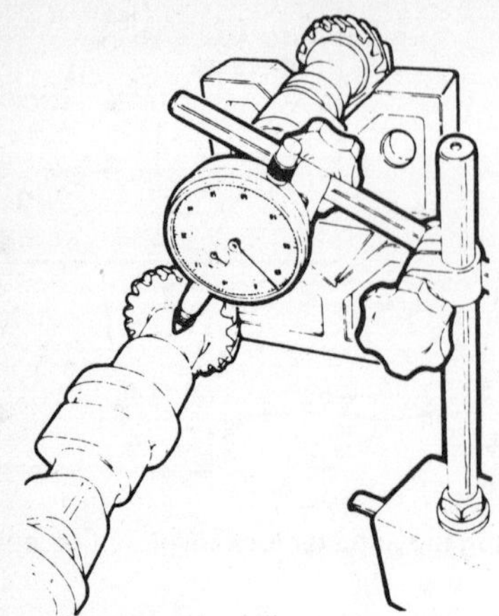

Checking the camshaft for straightness

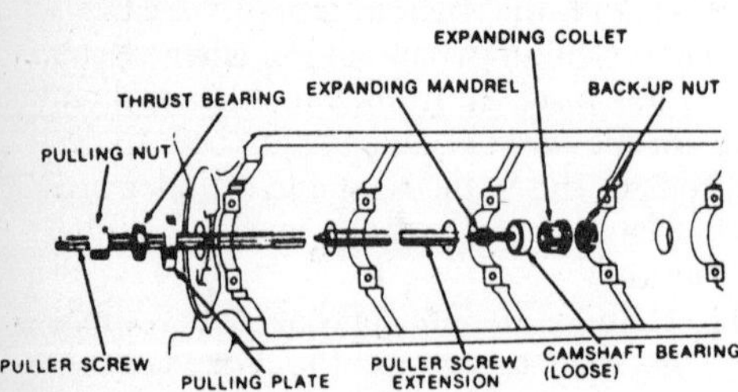

Camshaft bearing removal — OHV engines only

4. Disconnect the fuel lines and remove the fuel pump from the engine.

5. Using a screwdriver or equivalent, depress the automatic shoe adjuster lock lever into the fully retracted position. After locking the automatic adjuster, check that the chain is in free state.

6. Remove the timing sprocket-to-camshaft bolt, the sprocket and the fuel pump drive cam from the camshaft. Keep the timing sprocket on the chain damper and the tensioner without removing the chain from the sprocket.

7. Remove rocker arm, the shaft and the bracket assembly, the remove the camshaft assembly.

8. Using set of V-blocks and a dial indicator, inspect the camshaft for damage and/or wear; replace it, if necessary.

9. Using a generous amount of clean engine oil, lubricate the camshaft and journals.

10. Install the camshaft, the rocker arm, the shaft and the bracket assembly.

11. Check that the mark on the No. 1 rocker arm shaft bracket is in alignment with the mark on the camshaft and that the crankshaft pulley groove is aligned with the TDC mark (**0** degree) on the front cover.

12. Assemble the timing sprocket to the camshaft by aligning it with the pin on the camshaft; use care not to remove the chain from the sprocket.

13. Install the fuel pump drive cam, the

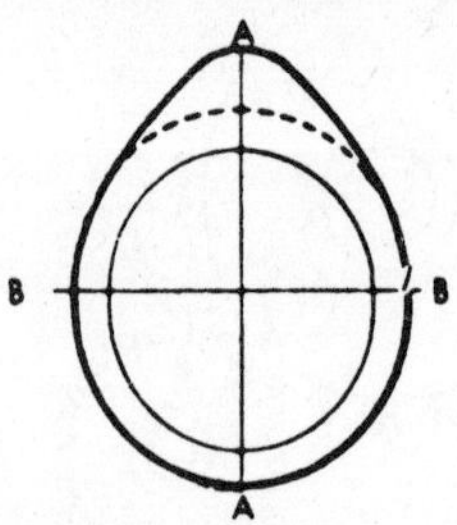

Camshaft lobe measurement

sprocket retaining bolt and washer. Remove the $^1/_2$ moon seal in from end of head; then install torque wrench and torque bolt to 58 ft. lbs; replace the $^1/_2$ moon seal in cylinder head.

14. Using the alignment marks, install the distributor.

15. Using a medium prybar, depressing the adjuster shoe to release the lock, check the timing chain tension.

16. Check valve timing, the rotor and mark on distributor housing should be in alignment when the No. 4 cylinder on TDC. The timing mark on damper pulley should align with TDC mark (**0** degree mark) on front cover.

17. To complete the installation, reverse the removal procedures. Adjust the drive belts. Refill the cooling system.

2.0L Engine

1. Remove the timing chain and the rocker arm assemblies.

2. Position a catch pan under the radiator, open the drain cock and drain the cooling system.

CAUTION: *When draining the coolant, keep in mind that cats and dogs are attracted by the ethylene glycol antifreeze, and are quite likely to drink any that is left in an uncovered container or in puddles on the ground. This will prove fatal in sufficient quantity. Always drain the coolant into a sealable container. Coolant should be reused unless it is contaminated or several years old.*

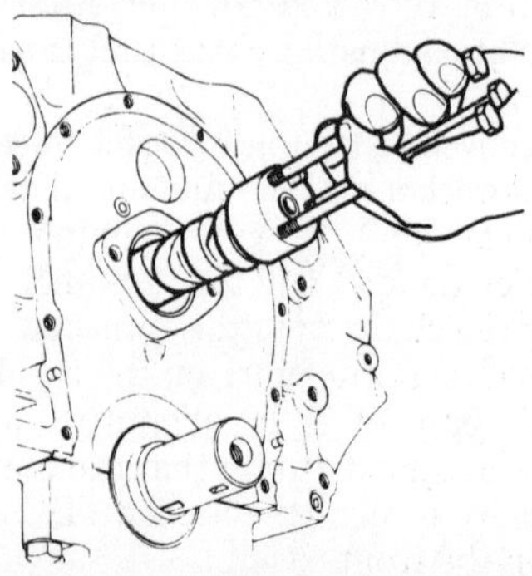

Using 3 long bolts to replace the camshaft — 2.8L and 4.3L engines

3. Remove the radiator hoses, the radiator-to-engine bolts and the radiator.

4. Remove the distributor cap, mark the rotor-to-housing and the housing-to-engine positions, then remove the distributor.

5. Raise and support the front of the vehicle on jackstands.

6. Disconnect the fuel lines and remove the fuel pump.

7. Lower the vehicle.

8. Remove the rocker arm studs and the pushrod guides.

9. Remove the valve lifters.

NOTE: *When removing the pushrods and the valve lifters, keep them in order.*

10. From the front of the engine, carefully pull the camshaft from the block, being sure the camshaft lobes do not contact the bearings.

11. Using set of V-blocks and a dial indicator, inspect the camshaft for damage, wear and/or out-of-round—0.0009 in. (0.0228mm) max; replace it, if necessary.

NOTE: *If installing a new camshaft, be sure to coat the lobes with GM part 1051396 or equivalent.*

12. Using a putty knife, clean the gasket mounting surfaces.

13. To install, lubricate the camshaft journals with clean engine oil and reverse the removal procedures. Lubricate the lobes with Molykote® or the equivalent. Install the camshaft into the engine, being extremely careful not to contact the bearings with the cam lobes. Adjust the valve lash after installing the engine. Adjust the drive belts. Refill the cooling system.

2.2L Diesel Engine

NOTE: *The following procedure requires the use of the camshaft bearing removal/installation tool J-29764 or equivalent.*

1. Remove the engine from the vehicle and mount it on a work stand.

2. Disconnect the PCV hoses from the rocker arm cover.

3. Remove the rocker arm cover, the rocker arm shaft and the pushrods.

4. Remove the upper timing housing cover. Turn the crankshaft to align the timing marks, then install a holding bolt into the injection pump gear.

5. Remove the crankshaft damper pulley and the lower timing housing cover.

6. Remove the injection pump timing gear flange, the timing belt tension spring and the pulley, then remove the timing belt.

7. Remove the camshaft sprocket, the hub and the camshaft oil seal retainer.

8. Remove the oil pump and the valve lifters.

9. From the front of the engine, pull the camshaft forward to remove it; be careful not to damage the camshaft bearings.

10. Using the camshaft bearing removal/installation tool J-29764 or equivalent, remove the camshaft bearings.

11. Inspect the inner bearing faces for damage. Using an inside micrometer, measure the inside diameter of the camshaft bearings; if bearing clearance is greater than 0.0047 in. (0.12mm), replace the bearing(s).

12. Using the camshaft bearing removal/installation tool J-29764 or equivalent, install the camshaft bearings into the engine block; be sure to align the oil ports in the bearings with those in the cylinder body.

13. To complete the installation, reverse the removal procedures.

2.5L Engine

1. Remove the pushrods and the valve lifters from the engine.

NOTE: *When removing the pushrods and the valve lifters, be sure to keep them in order for reassembly purposes.*

2. Place a catch pan under the radiator, open the drain cock and drain the cooling system.

CAUTION: *When draining the coolant, keep in mind that cats and dogs are attracted by the ethylene glycol antifreeze, and are quite likely to drink any that is left in an uncovered container or in puddles on the ground. This will prove fatal in sufficient quantity. Always drain the coolant into a sealable container. Coolant should be reused unless it is contaminated or several years old.*

3. Remove the power steering reservoir from the fan shroud, then the upper fan shroud, the radiator. Remove the grille, the headlight bezel and the bumper filler panel.

4. Remove the accessory drive belts, the cooling fan and the water pump pulley.

5. If equipped with air conditioning, disconnect the condenser baffles and the condenser, then raise the condenser and block it aside.

6. Remove the crankshaft drive belt pulley and the damper hub. Remove the timing gear cover-to-engine bolts and the cover.

7. Label and disconnect the distributor electrical connectors, then the hold-down bolt and the distributor from the engine. Remove the oil pump driveshaft.

8. Label and disconnect the vacuum lines from the intake manifold and the thermostat housing, then remove the Exhaust Gas Recirculation (EGR) valve from the intake manifold.

9. Remove the camshaft thrust plate-to-engine bolts. While supporting the camshaft (to prevent damaging the bearing or lobe surfaces), remove it from the front of the engine.

10. Inspect the camshaft for scratches, pitting and/or wear on the bearing and lobe surfaces. Check the timing gear teeth for damage.

11. To install, lubricate all of the parts with engine oil and reverse the removal procedures. Torque the camshaft thrust plate-to-engine bolts to 90 inch lbs. Refill the cooling system, start the engine, allow it to reach operating temperatures and check for leaks.

2.8L and 4.3L Engines

1. Remove the intake manifold, the timing chain and the sprocket.

2. Remove the radiator-to-vehicle bolts and the radiator from the vehicle.

3. Remove the rocker arm covers, the rocker arm assemblies, the pushrods and the valve lifters.

4. Using 3 long bolts, install them into the threaded holes in the end of the camshaft. Grasping the 3 bolts, pull the camshaft from the front of the engine block; be careful not to damage the bearing surfaces.

5. Using a putty knife, clean the gasket mounting surfaces.

6. Clean and inspect the related components.

7. To install, use new gaskets and seals, then reverse the removal procedures. Adjust the drive belt tensions. Refill the cooling system.

INSPECTION

Using solvent, degrease the camshaft and clean out all of the oil holes. Visually inspect the cam lobes and bearing journals for excessive wear. If a lobe is questionable, check all of the lobes as indicated. If a journal or lobe is worn, the camshaft must be reground or replaced.

NOTE: *If a journal is worn, there is a good chance that the bushings are worn and need replacement.*

If the lobes and journals appear intact, place the front and rear journals in V-blocks and rest a dial indicator on the center journal. Rotate the camshaft to check the straightness. If deviation exceeds 0.001 in. (0.0254mm), replace the camshaft.

Check the camshaft lobes with a micrometer, by measuring the lobes from the nose to the base and again at 90 degrees, see illustration. The lobe lift is determined by subtracting the second measurement from the first. If all of the exhaust and intake lobes are not identical, the camshaft must be reground or replace.

Pistons and Connecting Rods

REMOVAL

1. Remove the engine from the vehicle.

2. Remove the intake manifold and the cylinder head(s).

3. Remove the oil pan and the oil pump assembly.

4. Stamp the cylinder number on the machined surfaces of the bolt bosses of the connecting rod and cap for identification when reinstalling. If the pistons are to be removed from the connecting rod, mark the cylinder number

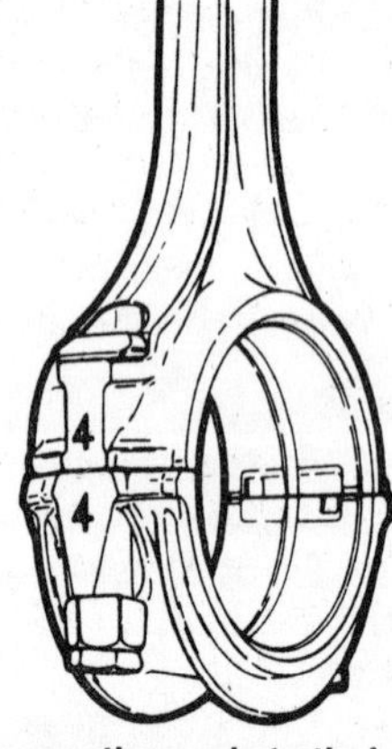

Match the connecting rods to their cylinders with a number stamp

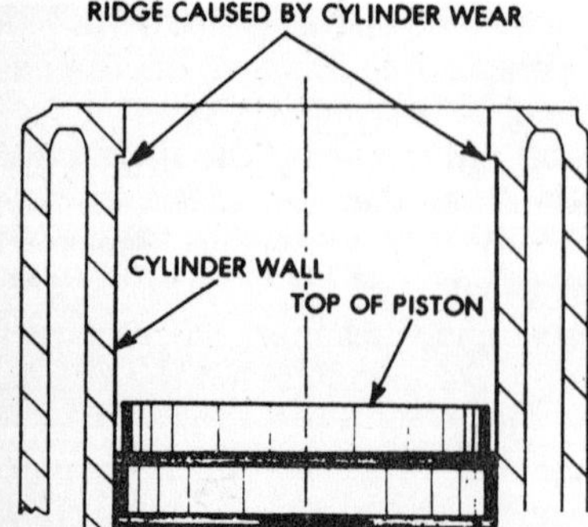

The ridge at the top of the cylinder wall must be removed prior to removing the piston

Carefully tap the piston and rod assembly out of the cylinder with a wooden hammer handle

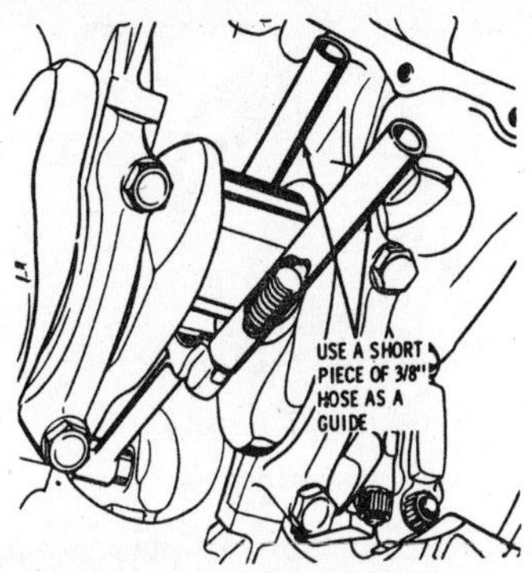

Install a short piece of rubber hose over the connecting rod bolts to protect the crankshaft journals during removal/installation

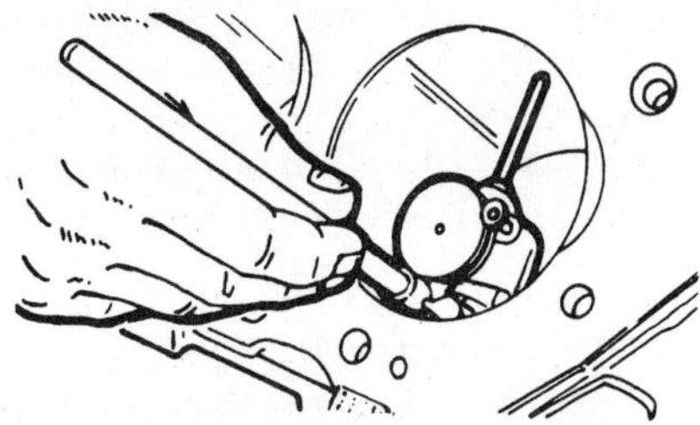

Measuring the cylinder bore with a dial gauge

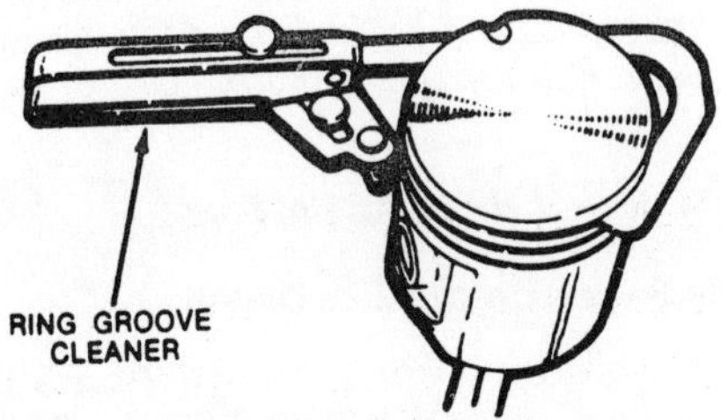

Clean the piston ring grooves using a ring groove cleaner

on the piston with a silver pencil or quick drying paint for proper cylinder identification and cap to rod location.

NOTE: *The cylinders on a 4-cylinder engine are numbered 1–2–3–4 (front-to-rear); on the V6 (2.8L) engine, are numbered 1–3–5 (front-to-rear) on the right side and 2–4–6 (front-to-rear) on the left side.*

5. Examine the cylinder bore above the ring travel. If a ridge exists, remove it with a ridge

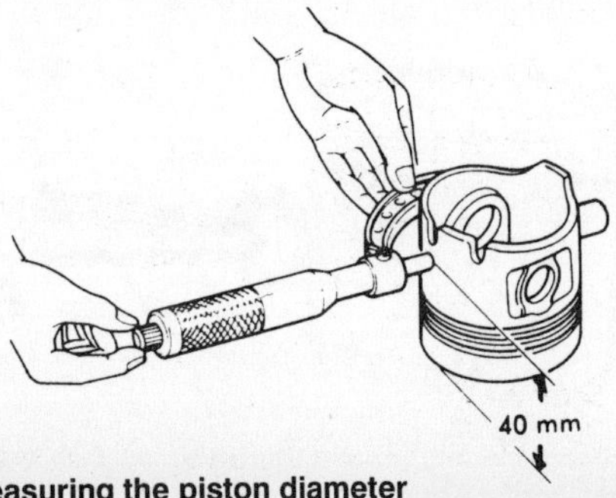

Measuring the piston diameter

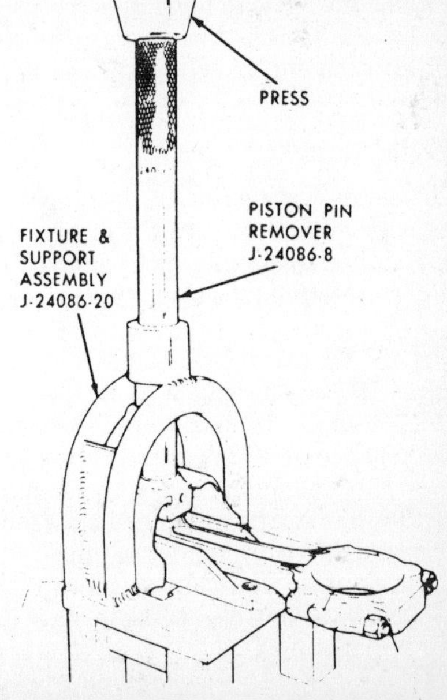

Cylinder bore cross-hatch pattern after honing

reamer before attempting to remove the piston and rod assembly.

6. Remove the connecting rod bearing cap and bearing.

7. Install a $^3/_8$ in. rubber guide hose over the rod bolt threads; this will prevent damage to the bearing journal and rod bolt threads.

8. Remove the rod and piston assembly through the top of the cylinder bore; remove the other rod and piston assemblies in the same manner.

9. Clean and inspect the engine block, the crankshaft, the pistons and the connecting rods.

CLEANING AND INSPECTION

Using a piston ring expanding tool, remove the piston rings from the pistons; any other method (screwdriver blades, pliers, etc.) usu-

Removing the piston pin from the piston assembly

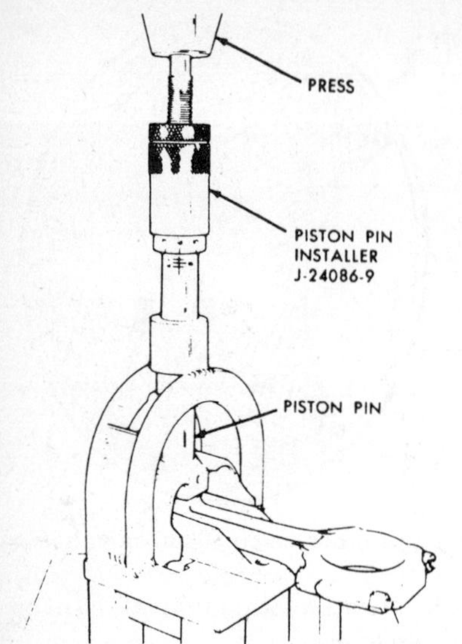

Installing the piston pin into the piston assembly

ally results in the rings being bent, scratched or distorted and/or the piston itself being damaged.

Pistons

Clean the varnish from the piston skirts and pins with a cleaning solvent. Do not wire brush any part of the piston. Clean the ring grooves with a groove cleaner and make sure the oil ring holes and slots are clean.

Inspect the piston for cracked ring lands, scuffed or damaged skirts, eroded areas at the top of the piston. Replace the pistons that are damaged or show signs of excessive wear.

Inspect the grooves for nicks of burrs that might cause the rings to hang up.

Measure the piston skirt, across the center line of the piston pin, and check the piston clearance.

Connecting Rods

Wash the connecting rods in cleaning solvent and dry with compressed air. Check for twisted or bent rods and inspect for nicks or cracks. Replace the connecting rods that are damaged.

Cylinder Bores

Using a telescoping gauge or an inside micrometer, measure the diameter of the cylinder bore, perpendicular (90 degrees) to the piston pin, at $2^1/2$ in. (63.5mm) below the surface of the cylinder block. The difference between the 2 measurements is the piston clearance.

If the clearance is within specifications or slightly below, after the cylinders have been bored or honed, finish honing is all that is necessary, If the clearance is excessive, try to obtain a slightly larger piston to bring the clear-

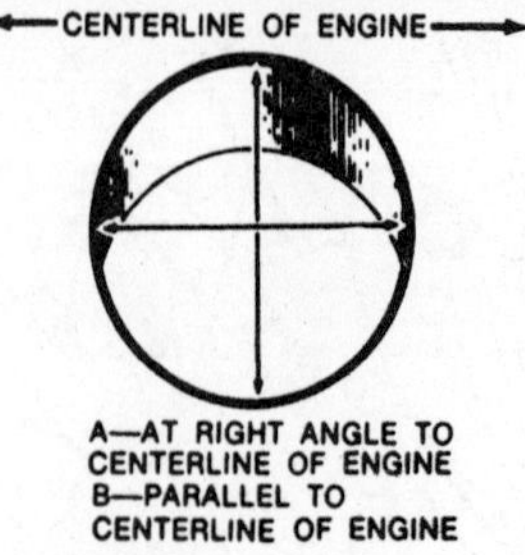

Cylinder bore measuring points

ance within specifications. If this is not possible obtain the first oversize piston and hone the cylinder or, if necessary, bore the cylinder to size. Generally, if the cylinder bore is tapered more than 0.005 in. (0.127mm) or is out-of-round more than 0.003 in. (0.0762mm), it is advisable to rebore for the smallest possible oversize piston and rings. After measuring, mark the pistons with a felt-tip pen for reference and for assembly.

NOTE: *Boring of the cylinder block should be performed by a reputable machine shop with the proper equipment. In some cases, clean-up honing can be done with the cylinder block in the vehicle, but most excessive honing and all cylinder boring must be done with the block stripped and removed from the vehicle.*

PISTON PIN REPLACEMENT

All Engines—Except 2.2L Diesel

NOTE: *The following procedure requires the use of the GM fixture/support assembly tool J-24086-20 or equivalent, the GM piston pin removal tool J-24086-8 or equivalent, and the GM piston pin installation tool J-24086-9 or equivalent.*

Use care at all times when handling and servicing the connecting rods and pistons. To prevent possible damage to these units, do not clamp the rod or piston in a vise since they may become distorted. Do not allow the pistons to strike one another, against hard objects or bench surfaces, since distortion of the piston contour or nicks in the soft aluminum material may result.

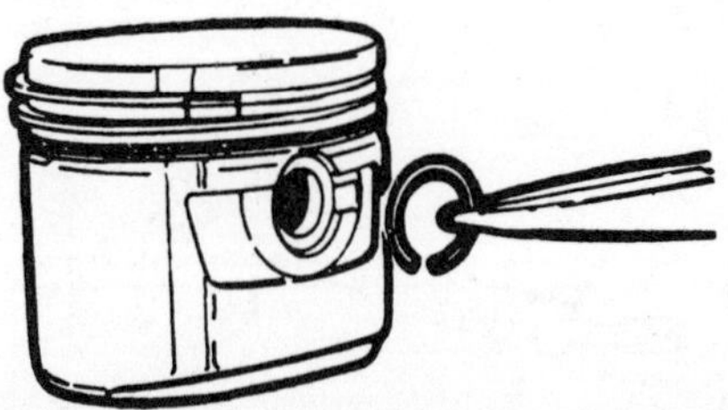

Replacing the piston pin snapring — 2.2L diesel engine

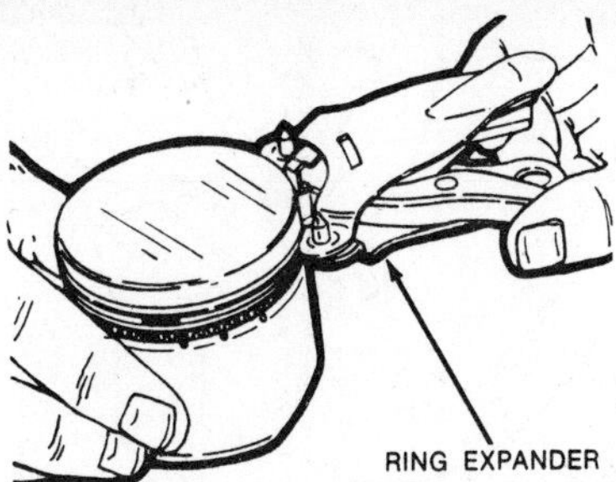

Removing the piston rings with a piston ring expander

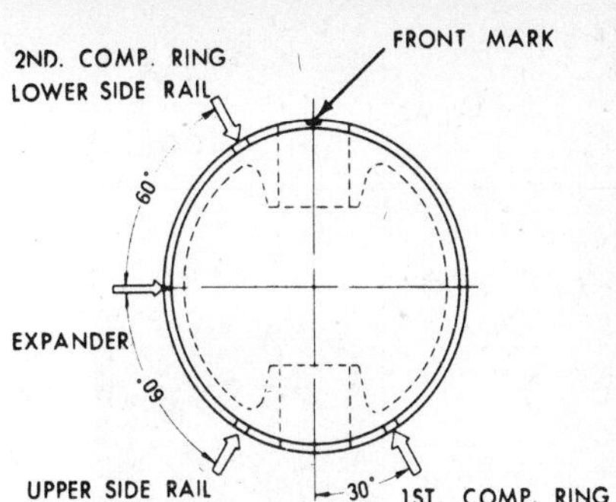

Piston ring positioning — 1.9L engine

1. Using an arbor press, the GM fixture/support assembly tool J-24086-20 or equivalent, and the GM piston pin removal tool J-24086-8 or equivalent, place the piston assembly in the fixture/support tool and press the pin from the piston assembly.

NOTE: *The piston and the piston pin are a matched set which are not serviced separately.*

2. Using solvent, wash the varnish and oil from the parts, then inspect the parts for scuffing or wear.

3. Using a micrometer, measure the diameter of the piston pin. Using a inside micrometer or a dial bore gauge, measure the diameter of the piston bore.

NOTE: *If the piston pin-to-piston clearance is in excess of 0.001 in. (0.0254mm), replace the piston and piston pin assembly.*

4. Before installation, lubricate the piston pin and the piston bore with engine oil.

5. To install the piston pin into the piston assembly, use an arbor press, the GM fixture/support assembly tool J-24086-20 or equivalent, and the GM piston pin installation tool J-24086-9 or equivalent, then press the piston pin into the piston/connecting rod assembly.

NOTE: *When installing the piston pin into the piston/connecting rod assembly and the installation tool bottoms onto the support assembly, do not exceed 5000 lbs. of pressure for structural damage may occur to the tool.*

6. After installing the piston pin, make sure that the piston has freedom of movement with the piston pin. The piston/connecting rod assem-

bly is ready for installation into the engine block.

2.2L Diesel Engine

1. Using a pair of snapring pliers, remove the piston pin snapring from the piston.

2. Slide the piston pin from the connecting rod and piston assembly.

NOTE: *When separating the piston from the connecting rod, be sure to mark them for reassembly purposes.*

3. Clean and inspect the piston and the connecting rod bearing surfaces for damage and/or wear; if necessary, replace the damaged part.

4. To install, lubricate the piston pin and bearing surfaces with clean engine oil, then reverse the removal procedures.

PISTON RING REPLACEMENT AND SIDE CLEARANCE MEASUREMENT

Check the pistons to see that the ring grooves and oil return holes have been properly cleaned. Slide a piston ring into its groove and check the side clearance with a feeler gauge. Make sure the feeler gauge is inserted between the ring and its lower land (lower edge of the groove), because any wear that occurs forms a step at the inner portion of the lower land. If the piston grooves have been worn to the extent that relatively high steps exist on the lower land, the piston should be replaced, because these will interfere with the operation of the new rings and ring clearances will be exces-

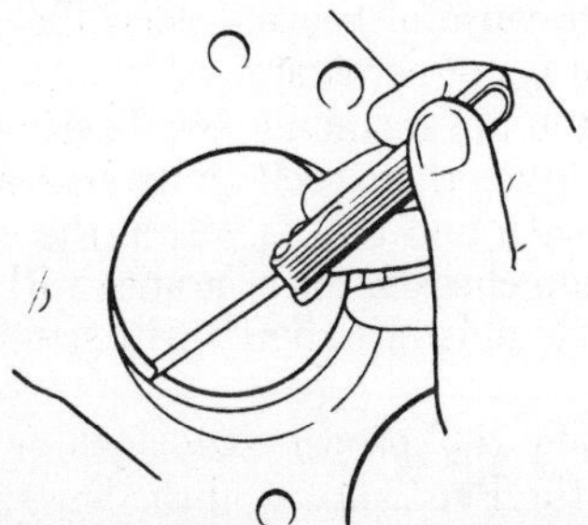

Checking piston ring end gap with a feeler gauge

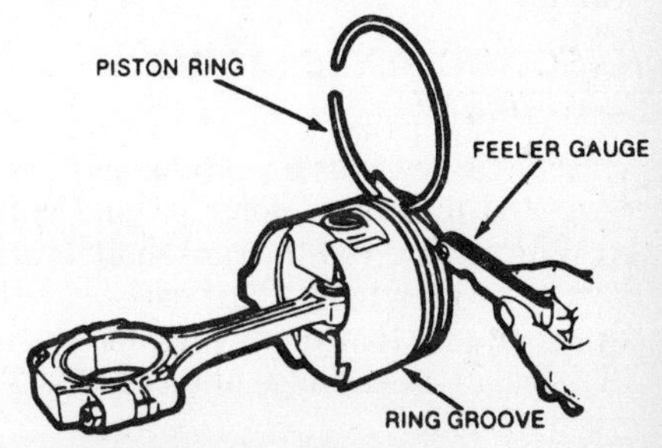

Checking piston ring side clearance

Undersize mark are stamped on the bearing shells. The tang fits in the notch on the connecting rod and cap

sive. Piston rings are not furnished in oversize widths to compensate for ring groove wear.

Install the rings on the piston, bottom ring first, using a piston ring expander. There is a high risk of breaking or distorting the rings and/ or scratching the piston, if the rings are installed by hand or other means.

Position the rings on the piston as illustrated; spacing of the various piston ring gaps is crucial to the proper oil retention and cylinder wear. When installing the new rings, refer to the installation diagram furnished with the new parts.

CHECKING RING END GAP

The piston ring end gap should be checked while the rings are removed from the pistons. Incorrect end gap indicates that the wrong size rings are being used; **ring breakage could result.**

1. Compress the new piston ring into a cylinder (one at a time).

2. Squirt some clean oil into the cylinder so the ring and the top 2 in. (51mm) of the cylinder wall are coated.

3. Using an inverted piston, push the ring approximately 1 in. (25.4mm) below the top of the cylinder.

4. Using a feeler gauge, measure the ring gap and compare it to the Ring Gap chart in this Chapter. Carefully remove the ring from the cylinder.

CONNECTING ROD BEARING REPLACEMENT

Replacement bearings are available in standard size and undersize (for reground crankshafts). Connecting rod-to-crankshaft bearing clearance is checked using Plastigage® at either the top or the bottom of each crank journal. The Plastigage® has a range of 0.001–0.003 in. (0.0254–0.0762mm).

1. Remove the rod cap with the bearing shell. Completely clean the bearing shell and

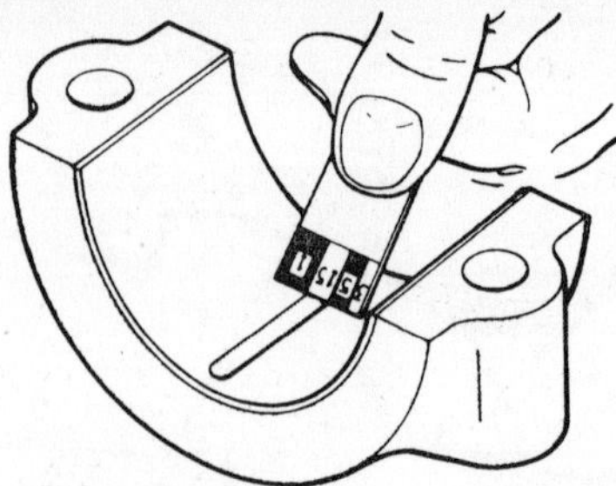

Measuring Plastigage® to determine main bearing clearance

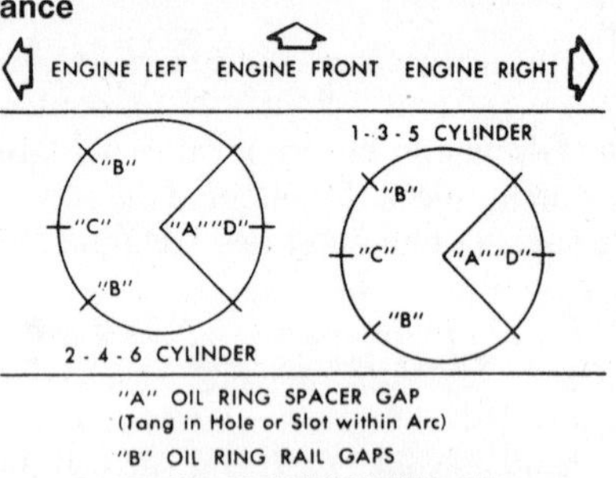

Piston ring positioning — 2.0L and 2.5L engine

the crank journal, blow any oil from the oil hole in the crankshaft; place the Plastigage® lengthwise along the bottom center of the lower bearing shell, then install the cap with the shell and torque the bolt or nuts to specification. Do not turn the crankshaft with the Plastigage® on the bearing.

2. Remove the bearing cap with the shell. The flattened Plastigage® will be found sticking to either the bearing shell or the crank journal. Do not remove it yet.

3. Use the scale printed on the Plastigage® envelope to measure the flattened material at its widest point. The number within the scale which most closely corresponds to the width of the Plastigage® indicates the bearing clearance in thousandths of an inch.

4. Check the specifications chart in this Chapter for the desired clearance. It is advisable to install a new bearing if the clearance exceeds 0.003 in. (0.0762mm); however, if the bearing is in good condition and is not being checked because of bearing noise, bearing replacement is not necessary.

5. If you are installing new bearings, try a standard size, then each undersize in order until one is found that is within the specified limits when checked for clearance with Plastigage®; each undersize shell has its size stamped on it.

6. When the proper size shell is found, clean off the Plastigage®, oil the bearing thoroughly, reinstall the cap with its shell and torque the rod bolt nuts to specifications.

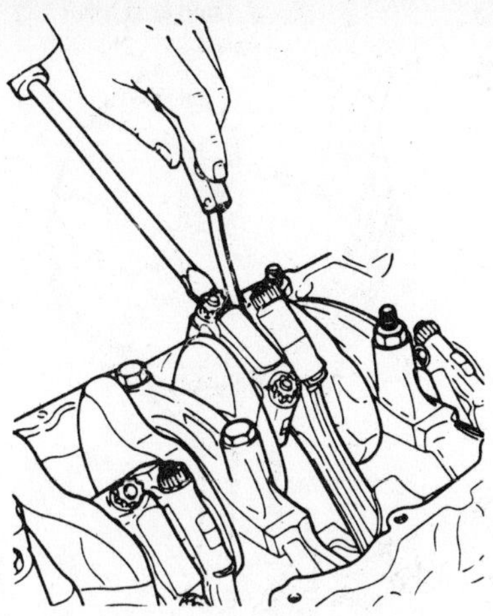

Check the connecting rod side clearance with a feeler gauge. Use a small pry bar to carefully spread the rods to specified clearance

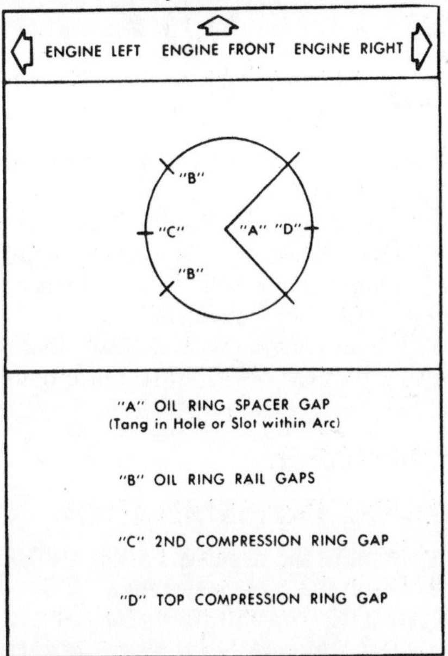

Piston ring positioning — 2.8L engine

NOTE: *With the proper bearing selected and the nuts torqued, it should be possible to move the connecting rod back and forth freely on the crank journal as allowed by the specified connecting rod end clearance. If the rod cannot be moved, either the rod bearing is too far undersize or the rod is misaligned.*

INSTALLATION

NOTE: *The following procedure requires the use of the ring compressor tool J-8037 or equivalent, and the ring installation tool.*

Position the rings on the piston; **spacing of the various piston ring gaps is crucial to proper oil retention and even cylinder wear.** When installing new rings, refer to the

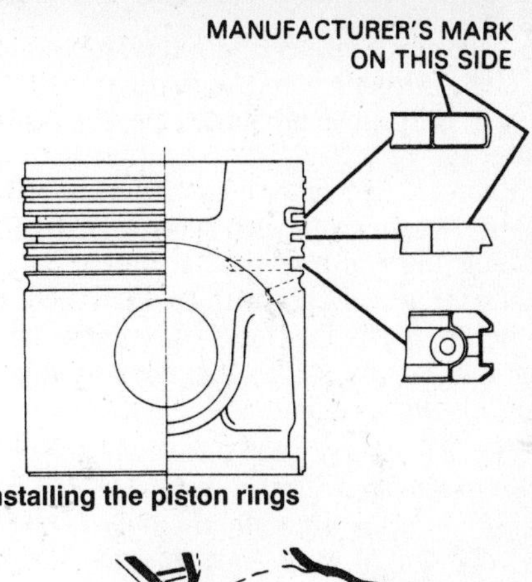

Installing the piston rings

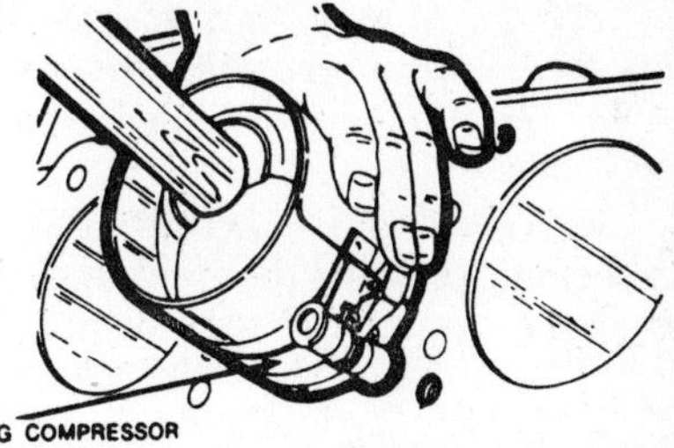

Install the piston ring compressor, then tap the piston into the cylinder bore with a wooden hammer handle

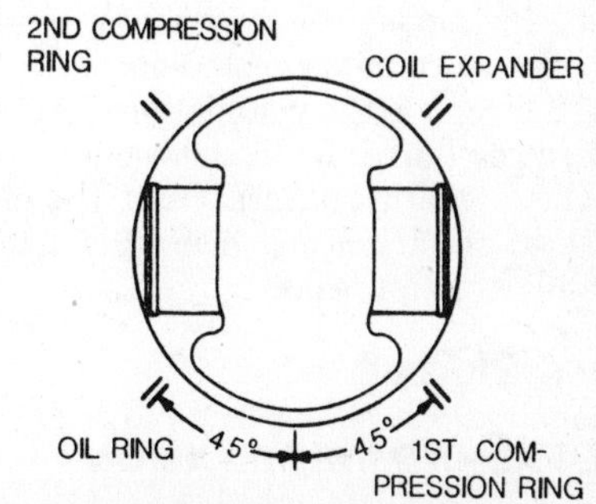

Piston ring positioning — 2.2L engine

installation diagram furnished with the new parts.

Install the connecting rod to the piston, making sure the piston installation notches and marks, if any, on the connecting rod are in proper relation to one another.

1. Make sure the connecting rod big-end bearings (including the end cap) are of the correct size and properly installed.

2. Fit rubber hoses over the connecting rod bolts to protect the crankshaft journals, as in the Piston Removal procedure. Lubricate the connecting rod bearings with clean engine oil.

3. Using the ring compressor tool J-8037 or equivalent, compress the rings around the piston head. Insert the piston assembly into the cylinder, so the notch (on top of the piston) faces the front of the engine.

4. Working under the engine, coat each crank journal with clean oil. Using a hammer

handle, drive the connecting rod/piston assembly into the cylinder bore. Align the connecting rod (with bearing shell) onto the crankshaft journal.

5. Remove the rubber hoses from the studs. Install the bearing cap (with bearing shell) onto the connecting rod and the cap nuts. Torque the connecting rod cap nuts to 43 ft. lbs. for 1.9L engine, 36 ft. lbs. for 2.0L engine, 62 ft. lbs. for 2.2L engine, 32 ft. lbs. for 2.5L engine or 39 ft. lbs. for 2.8L and 4.3L engines.

NOTE: *When more than one connecting rod/ piston assembly are being installed, the connecting rod cap nuts should only be tightened enough to keep each rod in position until the all have been installed. This will ease the installation of the remaining piston assemblies.*

6. Check the clearance between the sides of the connecting rods and the crankshaft using a feeler gauge. Spread the rods slightly with a small prybar to insert the feeler gauge. If the clearance is below the minimum tolerance, the rod may be machined to provide adequate clearance. If the clearance is excessive, substitute an unworn rod and recheck. If clearance is still outside specifications, the crankshaft must be welded and reground or replaced.

7. To complete the installation, reverse the removal procedures. Refill the cooling system. Refill the engine crankcase. Start the engine, allow it to reach normal operating temperatures and check for leaks.

Freeze Plugs

REMOVAL AND INSTALLATION

1. Remove the negative battery cable.
2. Drain the cooling system.

CAUTION: *When draining the coolant, keep in mind that cats and dogs are attracted by the ethylene glycol antifreeze, and are quite likely to drink any that is left in an uncovered container or in puddles on the ground. This will prove fatal in sufficient quantity. Always drain the coolant into a sealable container. Coolant should be reused unless it is contaminated or several years old.*

3. If equipped, remove the engine coolant drain plugs (located at the bottom of the block near the oil pan rail) and drain the coolant from the block. If the engine is not equipped with coolant drain plugs, drill a small hole in the leaking freeze plug and allow the coolant to drain.

4. Remove any components that restrict access to the freeze plug.

5. Using a chisel, tap the bottom edge of the freeze plug to cock it in the bore. Remove the plug using pliers. An alternate method is to

Install the pistons with the notch facing the front of the engine

drill an ⅛ in. hole in the plug and remove it using a dent puller.

6. Clean the freeze plug hole and using an appropriate driver tool or socket, install the freeze plug into the hole. Coat the freeze plug with sealer before installation.

7. Fill the engine with coolant, install the negative battery cable, start the engine and check for leaks.

Block Heater

REMOVAL AND INSTALLATION

1. Remove the negative battery cable.
2. Drain the cooling system.

CAUTION: *When draining the coolant, keep in mind that cats and dogs are attracted by the ethylene glycol antifreeze, and are quite likely to drink any that is left in an uncovered container or in puddles on the ground. This will prove fatal in sufficient quantity. Always drain the coolant into a sealable container. Coolant should be reused unless it is contaminated or several years old.*

3. If equipped, remove the engine coolant drain plugs (located at the bottom of the block near the oil pan rail) and drain the coolant from the block. If the engine is not equipped with coolant drain plugs, be ready to catch the coolant that will drain from the block when the block heater is removed.

4. Disconnect the block heater electrical connector.

5. Loosen the block heater retaining screw and remove the block heater from the engine.

6. Coat the block heater O-ring with engine

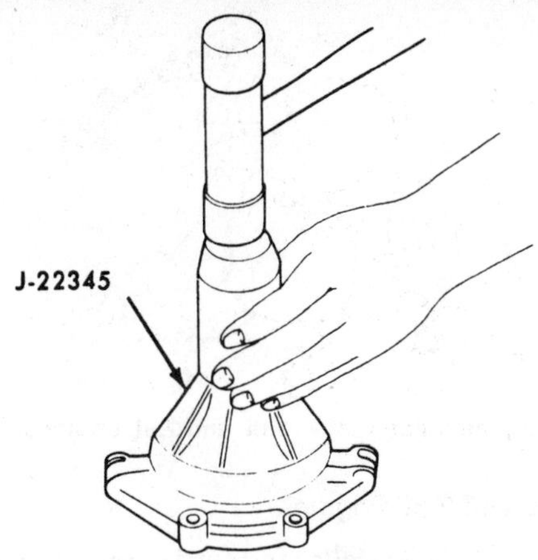

Rear main seal installation — 1.9L engine

oil and clean the block heater hole of rust.

7. Install the block heater and tighten the retaining screw.

8. Fill the engine with coolant, install the negative battery cable, start the engine and check for leaks.

Rear Main Oil Seal

REPLACEMENT

1.9L Engine

NOTE: *The following procedure requires the use of the seal installer tool J-22928-A or equivalent*

1. Disconnect the negative battery terminal.

2. Raise and support the front of the vehicle on jackstands.

3. Position a catch pan under the oil pan, remove the drain plug and drain the crankcase. Remove the oil pan-to-engine bolts and the oil pan from the engine.

CAUTION: *The EPA warns that prolonged contact with used engine oil may cause a number of skin disorders, including cancer! You should make every effort to minimize your exposure to used engine oil. Protective gloves should be worn when changing the oil. Wash your hands and any other exposed skin areas as soon as possible after exposure to used engine oil. Soap and water, or waterless hand cleaner should be used.*

4. Remove driveshaft from the differential and slide it from the transmission. Remove the torque converter-to-flywheel bolts for automatic transmission, the transmission-to-engine bolts, the crossmember and the transmission.

CAUTION: *Before removing the transmission, be sure to secure the engine.*

NOTE: *On manual transmissions, remove the clutch assembly.*

5. Unbolt the starter and support it out of the way.

6. Remove the flywheel-to-crankshaft bolts and the flywheel.

7. Remove the rear main seal retainer from the engine.

8. Using a medium prybar, remove the rear main oil seal from the retainer and discard it.

9. To install, lubricate the seal lips, fill the space between the seal and the crankshaft with grease. Using the seal installer tool J-22928-A or equivalent, drive the new rear main oil seal into it's housing.

10. To complete the installation, reverse the removal procedures. Refill the crankcase.

2.2L Diesel Engine

NOTE: *The following procedure requires the use of the seal installation tool J-22928 or equivalent.*

1. Refer to the Engine, Removal and Installation procedures in this Chapter and remove the engine from the vehicle.

2. Remove the flywheel-to-crankshaft bolts and the flywheel.

3. Using a medium prybar, pry the rear main seal from the rear of the engine.

4. Using clean engine oil, lubricate the lips of the new seal.

5. Using the seal installation tool J-22928 or equivalent, drive the new seal into the rear of the engine until it seats.

6. To complete the installation, reverse the removal procedures.

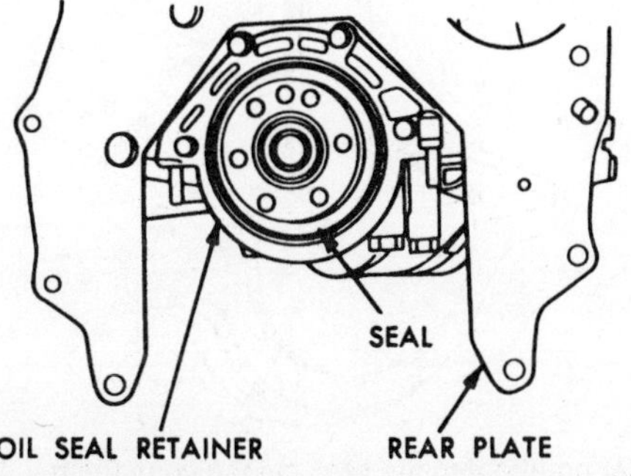

Rear main seal — 1.9L engine

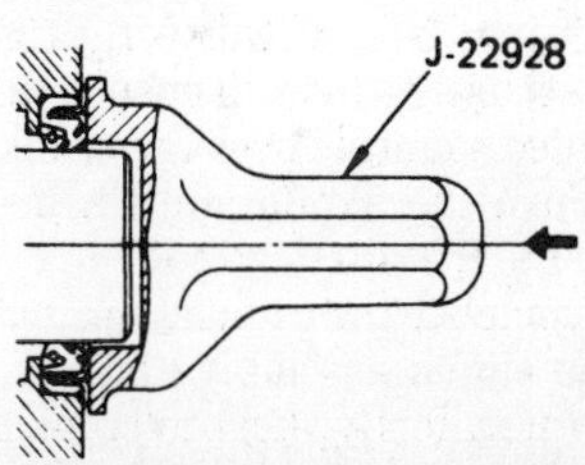

Rear main seal installation — 2.2L diesel

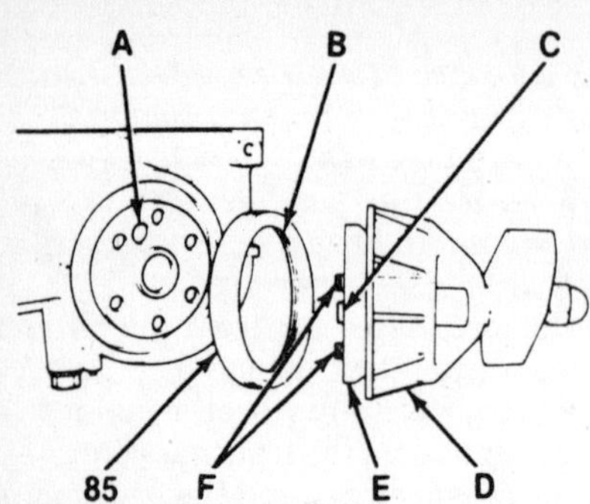

A. Alignment hole in crankshaft
B. Dust lip
C. Dowel pin
D. Collar
E. Mandrel
F. Screws
85. Crankshaft rear oil seal

Installing the 11mm one-piece rear main seal

2.5L and 4.3L Engines

The rear main oil seal is a one piece unit. It can be removed or installed without removing the oil pan or the crankshaft.

NOTE: *The following procedure requires the use of the GM oil seal installation tool J-34924 or equivalent.*

1. Refer to the Transmission, Removal and Installation procedures in Chapter 7 and remove the transmission from the vehicle.

2. If equipped with a manual transmission, remove the clutch assembly, the flywheel-to-crankshaft bolts and the flywheel from the crankshaft.

3. Using a small prybar, pry the oil seal from the rear of the crankshaft.

NOTE: *When removing the oil seal, be careful not to damage the crankshaft sealing surface.*

4. To install the new oil seal into the rear retainer, perform the following procedures:

a. Using new engine oil, lubricate the inner and outer diameter of the seal.

b. Using the GM oil seal installation tool J-34924 or equivalent, install the new oil seal onto it, position the assembly against the crankshaft.

c. Align the dowel with the alignment hole in the crankshaft and thread the attaching screws into the tapped holes in the crankshaft.

d. Using a screwdriver, tighten the screws securely; this will ensure that the seal is installed squarely over the crankshaft.

e. Turn the handle until it bottoms and remove the installation tool.

5. To complete the installation, install the flywheel, the clutch assembly and the transmission. Torque the flywheel-to-crankshaft bolts to 55 ft. lbs. and the bell housing-to-engine bolts to 46 ft. lbs.

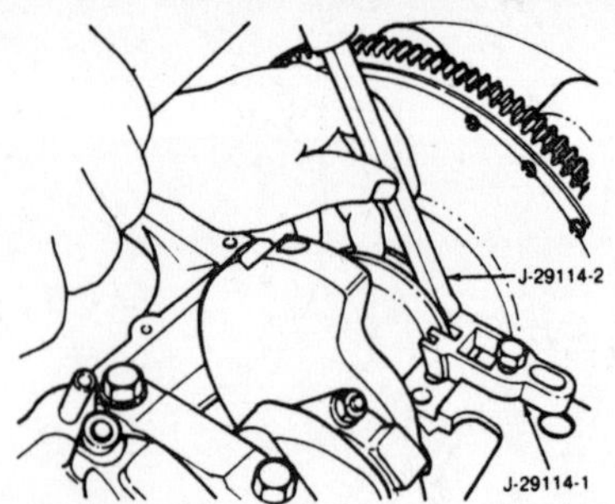

Using the guide tool — 2.0L and 2.8L engines

2.0L and 2.8L Engines

NOTE: *The following procedure requires the use of the upper seal packing tool J-29114-2 or equivalent, and the lower seal packing tool J-29590 or equivalent.*

1. Refer to the Oil Pump, Removal and Installation procedures in this Chapter and remove the oil pump.

2. Remove the rear main bearing cap.

3. Using the upper seal packing tool J-29114-2 or equivalent, gently pack the upper seal into the groove approximately $^1/_4$ in. on each side.

4. Measure the amount the seal was driven in on one side and add $^1/_{16}$ in. (1.6mm). Cut this length from the old lower cap seal. Be sure to get a sharp cut. Repeat this procedure for the other side.

5. Place a piece of cut seal into the groove and pack the seal into the block; repeat this procedure for each side.

NOTE: *GM makes a guide tool J-29114-l or equivalent, which bolts to the block via an oil*

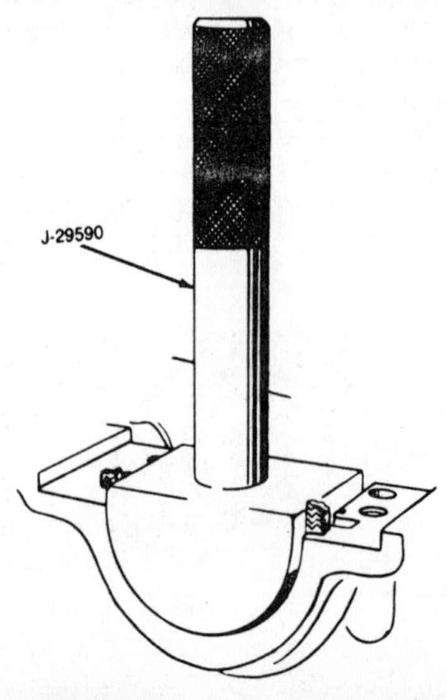

After positioning the seal, cut the ends flush — 2.0L and 2.8L engines

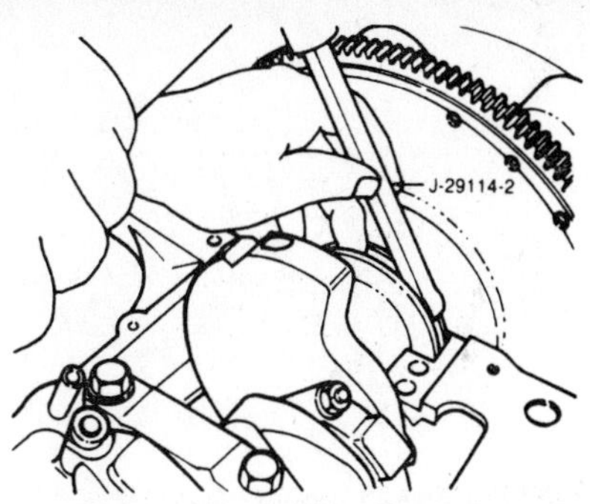

Using the packing tool — 2.0L and 2.8L engines

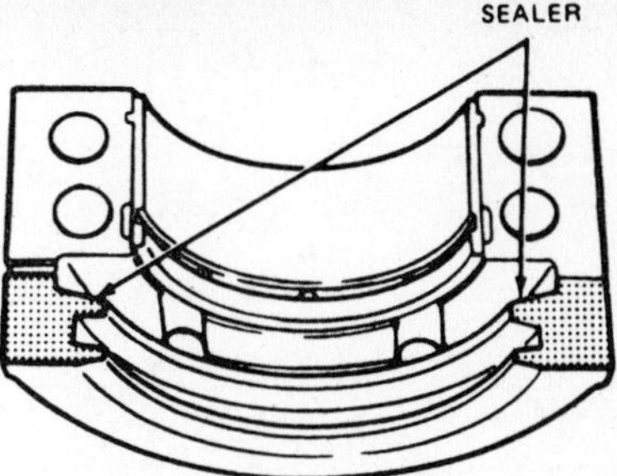

Applying sealer to the rear main cap — 2.0L and 2.8L engines

pan bolt hole and are machined to provide a built-in stop for the installation of the short cut pieces. Using the packing tool, work the short pieces of seal onto the guide tool, then pack them into the block.

6. Install a new lower seal in the rear main cap.

7. Install a piece of Plastigage® or equivalent, on the bearing journal. Install the rear cap and tighten to 70 ft. lbs. Remove the cap and check for gauge for bearing clearance. If out of specification, the ends of the seal may be frayed or not flush, preventing the cap from proper seating. Correct as required.

8. Clean the journal, and apply a thin film of sealer to the mating surfaces of the cap and tighten to 70 ft. lbs. Install the pan and pump.

9. Clean the journal, and apply a thin film of sealer to the mating surfaces of the cap and block. Do not allow any sealer to get onto the journal or bearing. Install the bearing cap and tighten to 70 ft. lbs.

10. To complete the installation, reverse the removal procedures.

Crankshaft and Main Bearings

REMOVAL AND INSTALLATION

NOTE: *The following procedure requires the use of the main bearing removal/installation tool J-8080, a fabricated cotter pin or equivalent.*

1. Refer to the Engine, Removal and Installation procedures in this Chapter and remove the engine from the vehicle.

NOTE: *If removing the crankshaft from the 1.9L engine, it will be necessary to remove the timing sprocket from the rocker arm shaft to disconnect the timing chain from the crankshaft sprocket.*

2. If equipped with a flywheel, remove it and mount the engine onto a work stand.

3. Disconnect the spark plug wires from the plugs, then remove the spark plugs.

4. Remove the drive belt pulley from the damper pulley/hub, the damper pulley/hub-to-crankshaft bolt, the damper pulley/hub from the crankshaft and the timing cover from the engine.

NOTE: *After removing the damper pulley/hub from the crankshaft, be sure to remove the woodruff key from the crankshaft. When removing the damper pulley/hub from the crankshaft, the oil seal should be replaced.*

5. Rotate the crankshaft, until the timing marks on the timing gears or sprockets align with each other, then remove the timing gear or sprocket from the crankshaft.

NOTE: *After removing the timing gear or sprocket from the crankshaft, be sure to remove the woodruff key from the crankshaft.*

6. Place a catch pan under the engine, remove the oil pan plug and drain the oil into the pan. Invert the engine and remove the oil pan from the engine.

CAUTION: *The EPA warns that prolonged contact with used engine oil may cause a number of skin disorders, including cancer! You should make every effort to minimize your exposure to used engine oil. Protective gloves should be worn when changing the oil. Wash your hands and any other exposed skin areas as soon as possible after exposure to used engine oil. Soap and water, or waterless hand cleaner should be used.*

7. On the 2.0L, 2.2L (diesel), 2.8L and 4.3L engines, it will be necessary to remove the oil pump.

8. Inspect the connecting rods and bearing caps for identification marks (numbers); if there are none, mark them for reassembly purposes.

9. Remove the connecting rod nuts and caps, then store them in the order of removal. Be sure to place short pieces of rubber hose on the connecting rod studs to prevent damaging the crankshaft bearing surfaces.

NOTE: *When installing the rubber hoses onto the connecting rod studs, position the long tool so it may be used to push the connecting rod up into the bore.*

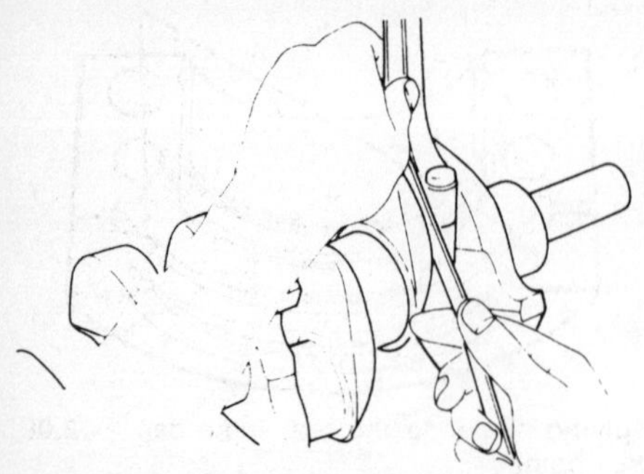

Measuring connecting rod side clearance

10. Check the main bearing caps for identification marks, if not identified, mark them. Remove the main bearing caps and store them in order, for reassembly purposes; the caps must be reinstalled in their original position.

11. Remove the crankshaft, the main bearing inserts and the rear main oil seal, the rear main oil seal/retainer or the rear main oil shell sections.

NOTE: *When removing the bearing shells, it is recommended to replace them with new ones.*

12. Using solvent, clean all of the parts for inspection purposes. If necessary, replace any part that may be questionable.

13. To install, use new bearing shell inserts and check the bearing clearances using the Plastigage® method.

NOTE: *If necessary, deliver the crankshaft to an automotive machine shop, have the crankshaft journals ground and new bearing shells matched.*

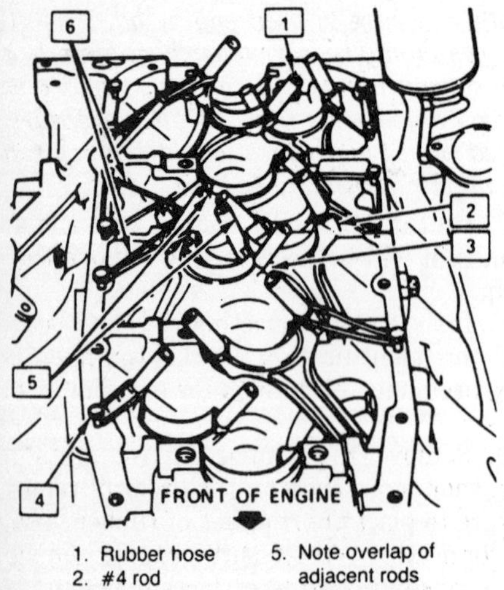

1. Rubber hose
2. #4 rod
3. #3 rod
4. Oil pan bolt
5. Note overlap of adjacent rods
6. Rubber bands

Support the connecting rods with rubber bands and install rubber rod bolt caps to protect the crankshaft during removal/installation

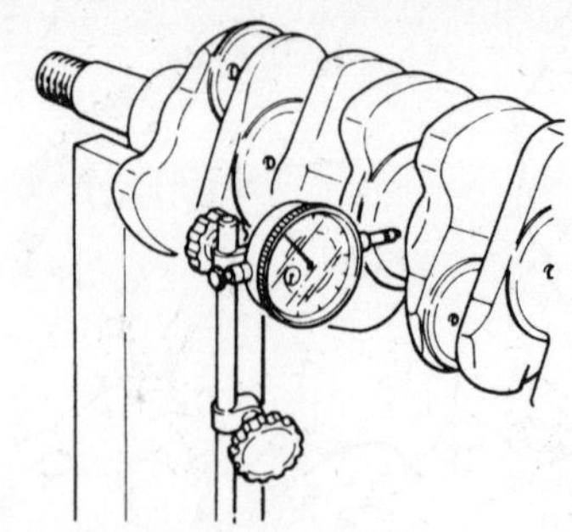

Checking crankshaft runout

14. Lubricate all of the parts and oil seals with clean engine oil.

15. Using a feeler gauge and a medium prybar, move the crankshaft forward-and-rearward, then the feeler gauge to check the crankshaft end play.

16. To complete the installation, use new gaskets (sealant if necessary) and reverse the re-

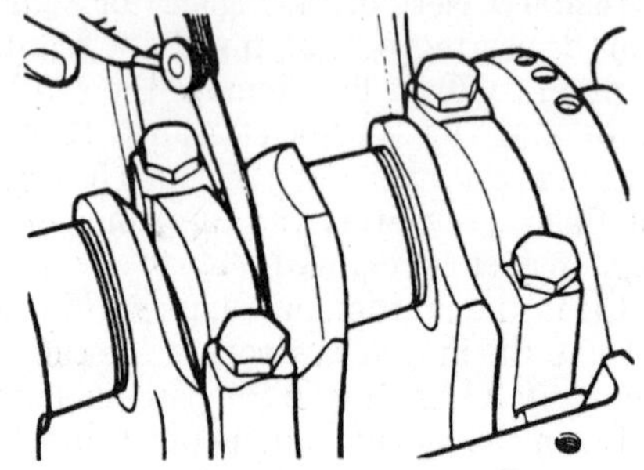

Checking crankshaft endplay with a feeler gauge

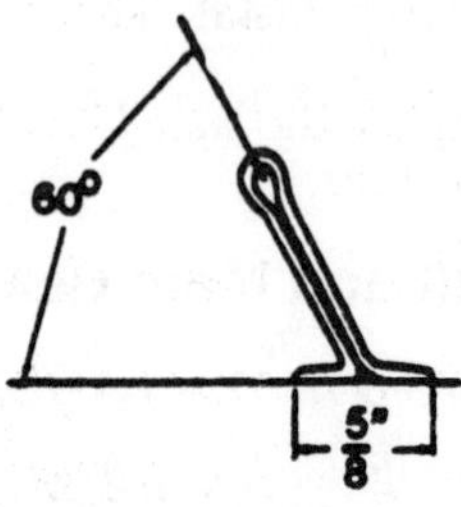

Fabricate a roll-out pin as illustrated, if necessary

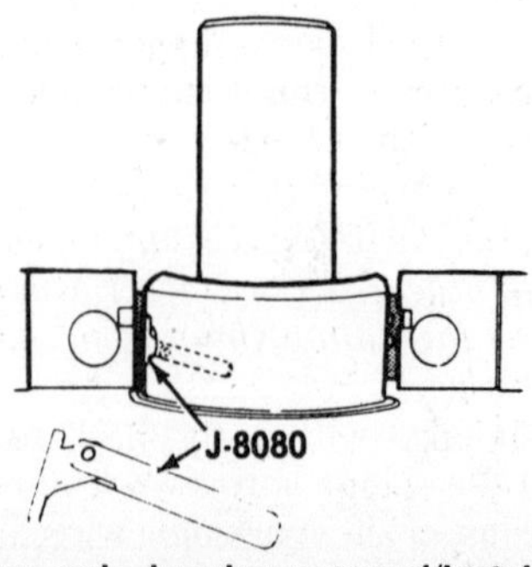

Using the main bearing removal/installation tool No. J-8080

moval procedures. Torque the main bearing cap-to-engine bolts to 70 ft. lbs. for all engines,except 2.2L diesel or 124 ft. lbs. for 2.2L diesel engine. Refill the cooling system (with the saved coolant) and the crankcase (with new oil). Start the engine, allow it to reach normal operating temperatures and check for leaks.

CLEANING AND INSPECTION

NOTE: *The following procedure requires the use of a set of V-blocks, a dial indicator, an outside micrometer, an inside micrometer and Plastigage®.*

1. Remove the bearing cap and wipe the oil from the crankshaft journal and outer/inner surfaces of the bearing shell.

2. To inspect the crankshaft bearing journals, perform the following procedures:

a. Using a set of V-blocks and a dial indicator, inspect the main bearing journals for runout; if necessary, regrind the bearing journals.

b. Using an outside micrometer, measure the main bearing journals for diameter and out-of-round conditions; if necessary, regrind the bearing journals.

c. Install the main bearing caps and torque the nuts/bolts to specifications. Using an inside micrometer, inspect the main bearing journals in the engine block; if necessary, rebore the bearing seats in the engine block.

3. To inspect the main bearing surfaces, using the Plastigage® method, perform the following procedures:

a. Using a piece of Plastigage® material, position it in the center of the main bearing surface(s).

b. Install the main bearing cap(s) and torque the cap nuts/bolts to specifications.

NOTE: *When the Plastigage® material is installed on the bearing surfaces, do not rotate the crankshaft.*

c. Remove the bearing caps and determine the bearing clearance by comparing the width of the flattened Plastigage® material at

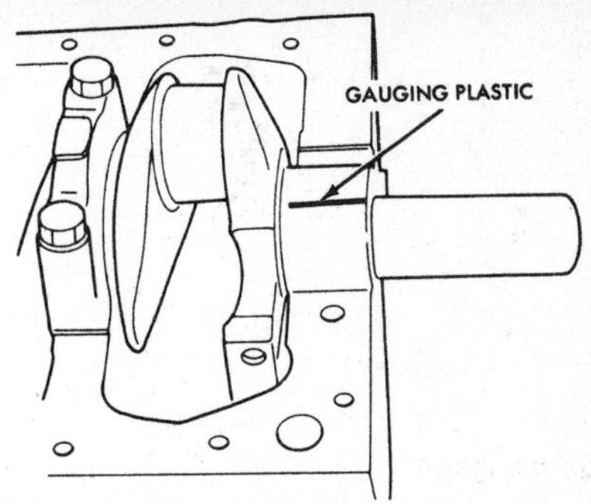

Position Plastigage® on the bearing surface. The surface must be clean and dry

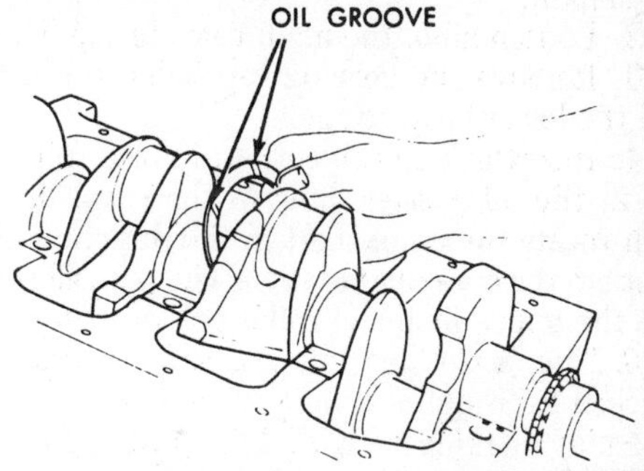

Thrust bearing location

its widest point with the graduations on the gauging material container.

NOTE: *The number within the graduation on the envelope indicates the clearance in millimeters or thousandths of an inch. If the clearance is greater than allowed. Replace both bearing shells as a set. Recheck the clearance after replacing the shells. Refer to the Main Bearing Replacement in this Chapter.*

MAIN BEARING REPLACEMENT

Main bearing clearances must be corrected by the use of selective upper and lower shells. Under no circumstances should the use of shims behind the shells to compensate for wear be attempted. To install the main bearing shells, proceed as follows:

1. Refer to the Oil Pan, Removal and Instal-

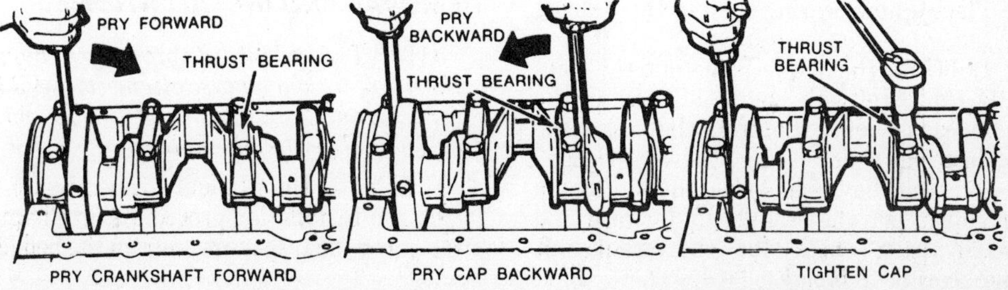

Aligning the thrust bearings and torquing the main caps

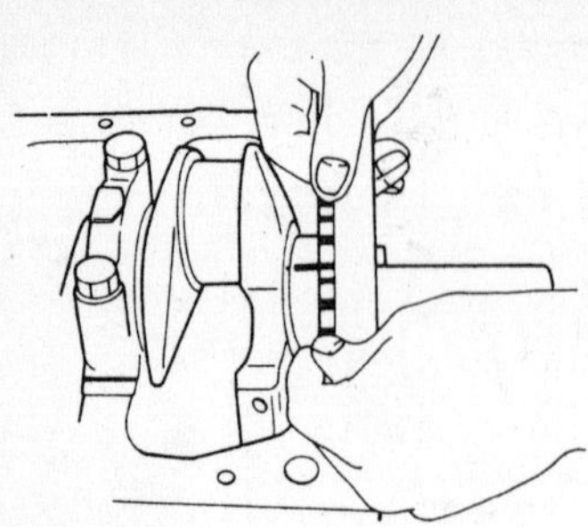

Using Plastigage®

lation procedures in this Chapter and remove the oil pan.

2. Loosen all of the main bearing cap bolts.

3. Remove the bearing cap bolts, the caps and the lower bearing shell.

4. Insert a flattened cotter pin or a roll out pin in the oil passage hole in the crankshaft, then rotate the crankshaft in the direction opposite to the cranking rotation. The pin will contact the upper shell and roll it out.

5. The main bearing journals should be checked for roughness and wear. Slight roughness may be removed with a fine grit polishing cloth, saturated with engine oil. Burrs may be removed with a fine oil stone. If the journals are scored or ridged, the crankshaft must be replaced.

NOTE: *The journals can be measured for out-of-round with the crankshaft installed by using a crankshaft caliper and inside micrometer or a main bearing micrometer. The upper bearing shell must be removed when measuring the crankshaft journals. Maximum out-of-round of the crankshaft journal must not exceed 0.0015 in. (0.038mm).*

6. Clean the crankshaft journals and bearing caps thoroughly before installing the new main bearings.

7. Apply special lubricant, GM 1050169 or equivalent, to the thrust flanges of the bearing shells.

8. Place the new upper shell on the crankshaft journal with the locating tang in the correct position and rotate the shaft to turn it into place using a cotter pin or a roll out pin as during removal.

9. Place a new bearing shell in the bearing cap.

10. Lubricate the new bearings and the main bearing cap bolts with engine oil. Install the main bearing shells, the crankshaft and the main bearing caps. Using the Plastigage® method, check the bearing clearances. Using a feeler gauge, pry the crankshaft forward and rearward, then check for the crankshaft (thrust bearing) end play.

NOTE: *In order to prevent the possibility of cylinder block and/or main bearing cap*

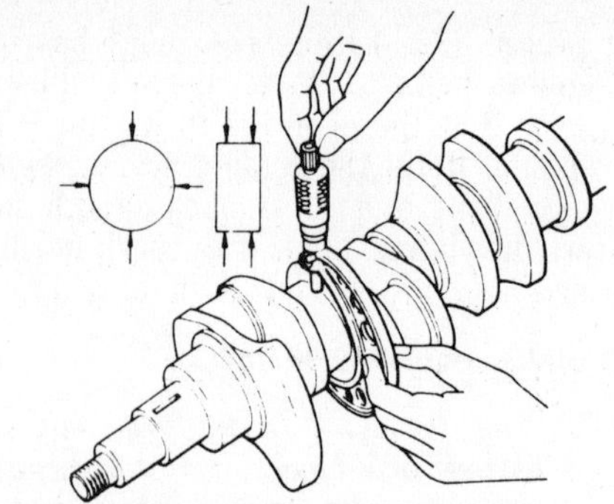

Checking main bearing journal diameter

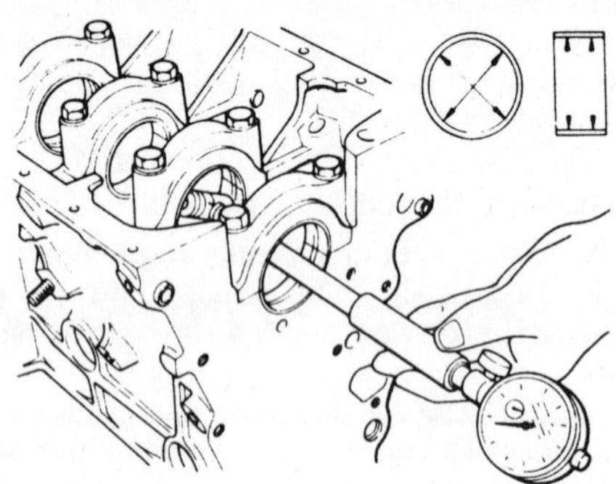

Checking main bearing bore diameter with bearings installed

damage, the main bearing caps are to be tapped into their cylinder block cavity, using a brass or leather mallet before the bolts are installed. Do not use the bolts to pull the main bearing caps into their seats. Failure to observe this procedure may damage the cylinder block or bearing cap.

11. To complete the installation, use new oil seals, gaskets (sealant, if necessary) and reverse the removal procedures. Torque the main bearing cap-to-engine bolts to 70 ft. lbs. for all, engines—except 2.2L diesel or 124 ft. lbs. for 2.2L diesel engine.

Flywheel

The flywheel and the ring gear are machined from one piece of metal and cannot be separated.

REMOVAL AND INSTALLATION

NOTE: *The following procedure requires the use of the clutch disc aligner tool J-33169 for 2.5L and 2.8L engines or J-33034 for all, except 2.5L and 2.8L engines.*

1. Refer to the Manual Transmission, Removal and Installation procedures in Chapter 7 and remove the transmission from the bell housing.

2. Remove the slave cylinder-to-bell housing bolts and move the slave cylinder aside; do

not disconnect the hydraulic line from the cylinder.

3. Remove the bell housing-to-engine bolts and the bell housing from the engine. When removing the bell housing, slide the clutch fork from the ball stud.

NOTE: *The clutch fork ball stud is threaded into the bell housing and can easily be replaced, if necessary.*

4. Using the clutch disc aligner tool J-33169 for 2.5L, 2.8L and 4.3L engines or J-33034 for all, except 2.5L, 2.8L and 4.3L engines, position it in the pilot bushing (to support the clutch disc).

5. Inspect the flywheel/pressure plate assembly for matchmarks, a stamped or a painted **X** mark; if no mark exists, mark the flywheel and the pressure plate.

6. Loosen the clutch-to-flywheel bolts, evenly (one turn at a time), until the spring tension is relieved, then remove the retaining bolts, the pressure plate and the clutch assembly.

7. Remove the flywheel-to-crankshaft bolts and the flywheel from the engine.

8. Clean the clutch disc (use a stiff brush), the pressure plate and the flywheel of all dirt, oil and grease. Inspect the flywheel, the pressure plate and the clutch disc for scoring, cracks, heat checking and/or other defects.

NOTE: *When the flywheel is removed, it is a good idea to replace the rear main oil seal, the pilot bushing and/or the clutch plate, if necessary.*

9. To install, align flywheel with the crankshaft, then torque the flywheel-to-crankshaft bolts to 50 ft. lbs. for 2.0L, 2.5L, 2.8L and 4.3L engines or 70 ft. lbs. for 1.9L and 2.2L engines.

10. Using the clutch disc aligner tool J-33169 for 2.5L, 2.8L and 4.3L engines or J-33034 for all, except 2.5L, 2.8L and 4.3L engines, position it in the pilot bushing (to support the clutch disc), then assemble the clutch disc (the damper springs facing the transmission), the pressure plate and the retaining bolts onto the flywheel.

NOTE: *When installing the pressure plate onto the flywheel, be sure to align the **X** marks.*

11. Tighten the pressure plate-to-flywheel bolts gradually and evenly (to prevent clutch plate distortion) to 20 ft. lbs., then remove the alignment tool.

12. To complete the installation, lubricate the pilot bushing and the clutch release lever, then reverse the removal procedures. Torque the bell housing-to-engine bolts to 55 ft. lbs., the transmission-to-bell housing bolts to 25 ft. lbs. and the clutch slave cylinder-to-bell housing bolts to 13 ft. lbs.

EXHAUST SYSTEM

Two types of pipe connections are used on the exhaust system, they are: the ball joint (to allow angular movement for alignment purposes) and the slip joint. Gaskets are used with the ball joint type connections.

The system is supported by free hanging rubber mountings which permit some movement of the exhaust system but do not allow the transfer of noise and vibration into the passenger compartment. Any noise vibrations or rattles in the exhaust system are usually caused by misalignment of the parts.

CAUTION: *Before performing any operation on the exhaust system, be sure to allow it to cool down.*

Front Pipe

REMOVAL AND INSTALLATION

NOTE: *The following procedure requires the use of GM sealing compound 1051249 or equivalent, at the slip joint connection.*

1. Raise and support the front of the vehicle on jackstands.

2. Remove the front pipe(s)-to-manifold(s) nuts and separate (pry, if necessary) the front pipe (ball joint) from the exhaust manifold(s).

3. At the catalytic converter, loosen the front pipe-to-converter clamp nuts, then slide the clamp away from the converter and separate the front pipe from the converter.

NOTE: *Use a twisting motion to separate the front pipe-to-converter slip joint connection. If the front pipe cannot be removed from the catalytic converter, use a hammer (to loosen the connection) or wedge tool to separate the connection.*

4. Inspect the pipe for holes, damage or deterioration; if necessary, replace the front pipe.

5. To install, lubricate the front pipe-to-manifold(s) studs/nuts and the front pipe-to-converter clamp threads, then reverse the removal procedures. Torque the front pipe-to-exhaust manifold bolts to 15 ft. lbs. and the front pipe-to-converter clamp nuts to 35 ft. lbs.

6. Start the engine and check for exhaust leaks.

Catalytic Converter

The catalytic converter is an emission control device added to the exhaust system to reduce the emission of hydrocarbon and carbon monoxide pollutants.

NOTE: *The following procedure requires the use of GM sealing compound 1051249 or equivalent, at the slip joint connection.*

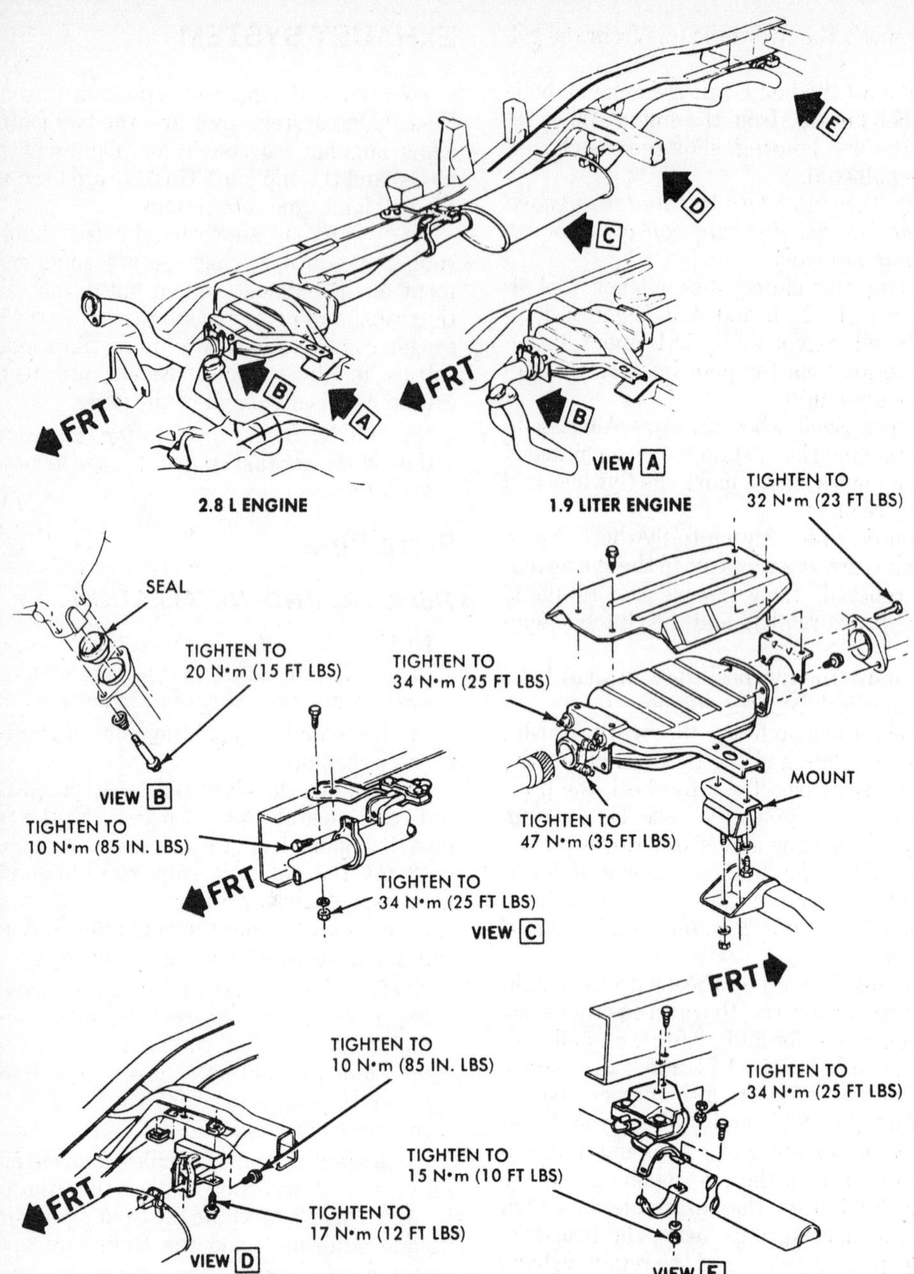

Exhaust system components — typical

REMOVAL AND INSTALLATION

1. Raise and support the front of the vehicle on jackstands.

2. Remove the catalytic converter-to-muffler bolts and separate the muffler from the converter.

NOTE: *The connection between the converter and the muffler is a ball joint type, which can be easily separated.*

3. Remove the catalytic converter-to-front pipe clamp nuts and move the clamp forward.

4. Remove the converter-to-mounting bracket bolts, then twist the converter to separate it from the front pipe.

5. Inspect the condition of the catalytic converter for physical damage, replace it, if necessary.

NOTE: *When installing the catalytic converter, be sure it is installed with adequate clearance from the floor pan, to prevent overheating of the vehicle floor.*

6. To install, align the components and reverse the removal procedures. Torque the con-

verter-to-mounting bracket bolts to 25 ft. lbs., the converter-to-front pipe clamp nuts to 35 ft. lbs. and the converter-to-muffler bolts to 23 ft. lbs. Be careful not to damage the pipe sealing surfaces when tightening the retaining clamps. Start the engine and check for exhaust leaks.

Muffler

REMOVAL AND INSTALLATION

1. Remove the catalytic converter-to-muffler flange bolts and separate the items.

2. Remove the intermediate and rear tail pipe-to-bracket clamp nuts/bolts.

3. Remove the muffler bracket-to-chassis bolts and lower the muffler from the vehicle.

4. To install, coat the slip joints with GM sealing compound 1051249 or equivalent, and loosely install the components onto the vehicle.

5. After aligning the components, tighten the connecting bolts and clamps. Torque the muffler bracket-to-chassis bolts 12 ft. lbs., the rear tail pipe-to-bracket clamp nuts/bolts to 25 ft. lbs., the intermediate pipe-to-chassis bracket bolt to 85 inch lbs. and the muffler-to-converter bolts to 23 ft. lbs.

NOTE: *When torquing the exhaust system connectors, be careful not to tighten the pipe clamps too tight, for deformation of the pipes may occur.*

6. Start the engine and check for exhaust leaks.

TROUBLESHOOTING

Engine Speed Oscillates at Idle

When the engine idle speed will not remain constant, replace or repair the following items or systems, as necessary:
- A faulty fuel pump.
- A leaky Exhaust Gas Recirculation (EGR) valve.
- A blown head gasket.
- A worn camshaft.
- Worn timing gears, chain or sprockets.
- Leaking intake manifold-to-engine gasket.
- A blocked Positive Crankcase Ventilation (PCV) valve.
- Overheating of the cooling system.

Low Power Output of Engine

When the engine power output is below normal, replace or repair the following items or systems, as necessary:
- Overheating of the cooling system.
- Leaks in the vacuum system.
- Leaking of the fuel pump or hoses.
- Unadjusted valve timing.
- A blown head gasket.
- A slipping clutch disc or mis-adjusted pedal.
- Excessive piston-to-bore clearance.
- Worn piston rings.
- A worn camshaft.
- Sticking valve(s) or weak valve spring(s).
- A poorly operating diverter valve.
- A faulty pressure regulator valve for automatic transmission.
- Low fluid level for automatic transmission.

Poor High Speed Operation

When the engine cannot maintain high speed operations, replace or repair the following items or systems, as necessary:
- A faulty fuel pump producing low fuel volume.
- A restriction in the intake manifold.
- A worn distributor shaft.
- Unadjusted valve timing.
- Leaking valves or worn valve springs.

Poor Acceleration

When the engine experiences poor acceleration characteristics, replace or repair the following items or systems, as necessary:
- Incorrect ignition timing.
- Poorly seated valves.
- Improperly adjusted accelerator pump stroke (carburetor equipped).
- Worn accelerator pump diaphragm or piston (carburetor equipped).

Backfire — Intake Manifold

When the engine backfires through the intake manifold, replace or repair the following items or systems, as necessary:
- Incorrect ignition timing.
- Incorrect operation of the choke (carburetor equipped).
- Choke setting (initial clearance) too large (carburetor equipped).
- Defective Exhaust Gas Recirculation (EGR) valve.
- A very lean air/fuel mixture (carburetor equipped).

Backfire — Exhaust Manifold

When the engine backfires through the exhaust manifold, replace or repair the following items or systems, as necessary:
- Leaks in the vacuum hose system.
- Leaks in the exhaust system.
- Faulty choke adjustments or operation (carburetor equipped).
- Faulty vacuum diverter valve.

Engine Detonation (Dieseling)

When the engine operates beyond the controlled limits, replace or repair the following items or systems, as necessary:
- Faulty ignition electrical system components.
- The ignition timing may be too far advanced.
- Inoperative Exhaust Gas Recirculation (EGR) valve.
- Inoperative Positive Crankcase Ventilation (PCV) valve.
- Faulty or loose spark plugs.
- Clogged fuel delivery system.
- Sticking, leaking or broken valves.
- Excessive deposits in the combustion chambers.
- Leaks in the vacuum system.

Excessive Oil Leakage

When large amounts of oil are noticed under the engine after each operation, replace or repair the following items or systems, as necessary:
- Damaged or broken oil filter gasket.
- Leaking oil pressure sending switch.
- Worn rear main oil seal gasket.
- Worn front main oil seal gasket.
- Damaged or broken fuel pump gasket (mechanical pump).
- Damaged or loose valve cover gasket.
- Damaged oil pan gasket or bent oil pan.
- Improperly seated oil pan drain plug.
- Broken timing chain cover gasket.
- Blocked camshaft bearing drain hole.

Heavy Oil Consumption

When the engine is burning large amounts of oil, replace or repair the following items or systems, as necessary:
- The engine oil level may be to high.
- The engine oil may be to thin.
- Wrong size of piston rings.
- Clogged piston ring grooves or oil return slots.
- Insufficient tension of the piston rings.
- Piston rings may be sticking in the grooves.
- Excessively worn piston ring grooves.
- Reversed (upside down) compression rings.
- Non-staggered piston ring gaps.
- Improper Positive Crankcase Ventilation (PCV) valve operation.
- Damaged valve O-ring seals.
- Restricted oil drain back holes.

- Worn valve stem or guides.
- Damaged valve stem oil deflectors.
- Too long intake gasket dowels.
- Mismatched rail and expander of the oil ring.
- Excessive clearance of the main and connecting rods.
- Scored or worn cylinder walls.

Negative Oil Pressure

When the engine presents no oil pressure, replace or repair the following items or systems, as necessary:
- Low oil level in the crankcase.
- Broken oil pressure gauge or sender.
- Blocked oil pump passages.
- Blocked oil pickup screen or tube.
- Malfunctioning oil pump.
- Sticking oil pressure relief valve.
- Leakage of the internal oil passages.
- Worn (loose) camshaft bearings.

Low Oil Pressure

When the engine presents low oil pressure, replace or repair the following items or systems, as necessary:
- Low oil level in the crankcase.
- Blocked oil pickup screen or tube.
- Malfunctioning or excessive clearance of the oil pump.
- Sticking oil pressure relief valve.
- Very thin engine oil.
- Worn (loose) main, rod or camshaft bearings.

High Oil Pressure

When the engine presents high oil pressure, replace or repair the following items or systems, as necessary:
- Sticking (closed) oil pressure relief valve.
- Wrong grade of oil.
- Faulty oil pressure gauge or sender.

Knocking Main Bearings

When the main bearings are constantly making noise, replace or repair the following items or systems, as necessary:
- Oval shaped crankshaft journals.
- Loose torque converter or flywheel mounting bolts.
- Loose damper pulley hub.
- Excessive clearance of the main bearings.
- Excessive belt tension.
- Low oil supply to the main bearings.
- Extreme crankshaft end play.

Knocking Connecting Rods

When the connecting rod bearings are constantly making noise, replace or repair the following items or systems, as necessary:
- Misaligned connecting rod or cap.
- Missing bearing shell or excessive bearing clearance.
- Incorrectly torqued connecting rod bolts.
- Connecting rod journal of the crankshaft is out-of-round.

Knocking Pistons and Rings

When the pistons and/rings are constantly making noise, replace or repair the following items or systems, as necessary:
- Misaligned connecting rods.
- Out-of-round or tapered cylinder bore.
- Loose or tight ring side clearance.
- Build-up of carbon on the piston(s).
- Piston-to-cylinder bore clearance is excessive.
- Broken piston rings.
- Loose or seized piston pin(s).

Knocking Valve Train

When the valve train is constantly making noise, replace or repair the following items or systems, as necessary:
- Retighten any loose rocker arms.
- Remove any dirt or chips in the valve lifters.
- Excessive valve stem-to-guide clearance.

- Remove restrictions from valve lifter oil holes.
- Incorrect valve lifter may be installed in the engine.
- Valve lock(s) may be missing.
- Valve lifter check ball may be faulty.
- Valve lifter leak down may be excessive.
- Rocker arm nut may be reversed (installed upside down).
- Camshaft lobes may be excessively worn.
- Bent or worn pushrods.
- Excessively worn bridged pivots or rocker arms.
- Cocked or broken valve springs.
- Bent valve(s).
- Worn valve lifter face(s).
- Damaged lifter plunger or pushrod seat.

Knocking Valves

When the valves are constantly noisy, replace or repair the following items or systems, as necessary:
- Unadjusted valve lash.
- Valve springs may be broken.
- Pushrods may be bent.
- Camshaft lobes may be excessively worn.
- Dirty or worn valve lifters.
- Valve guides may be worn.
- Valve seat or face runout may be excessive.
- Loose rocker arm studs.

EMISSION CONTROLS

Crankcase Ventilation System

OPERATION

The crankcase vapors are drawn into the intake manifold to be burned in the combustion chambers, instead of merely venting the crankcase vapors into the atmosphere. An added benefit to engines equipped with this system is that the engine oil will tend to stay cleaner for a longer period of time; therefore, if you notice that the oil in your engine becomes dirty very easily, check the functioning of the PCV valve. Engines which use a PCV system are calibrated to run richer, to compensate for the added air which accompanies the crankcase vapors to be combustion chambers. If the PCV valve or line is clogged, the engine idle will tend to be rough due to excessively rich mixture. Maintenance is covered in Chapter 1.

On the 1.9L engine, the blow by gases are forced back into the intake manifold through a closed loop system which consists of a baffle plate and an orifice mounted in the intake manifold.

SERVICE

NOTE: *Inspect the PCV system hose(s) and connections at each tune-up and replace any deteriorated hoses. Check the PCV valve at*

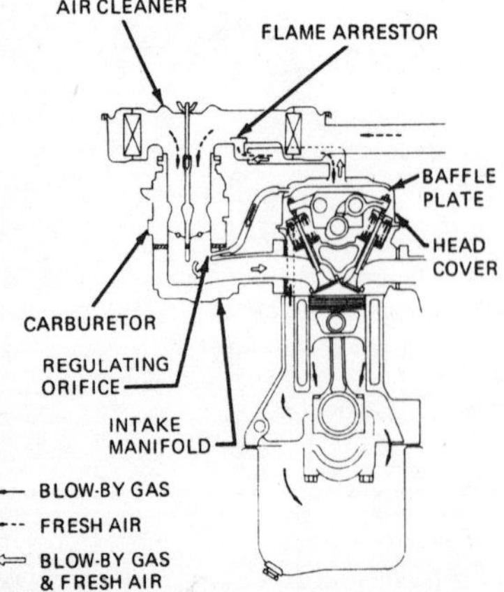

Exploded view of the positive Crankcase ventilation (PCV) valve — 2.8L engine

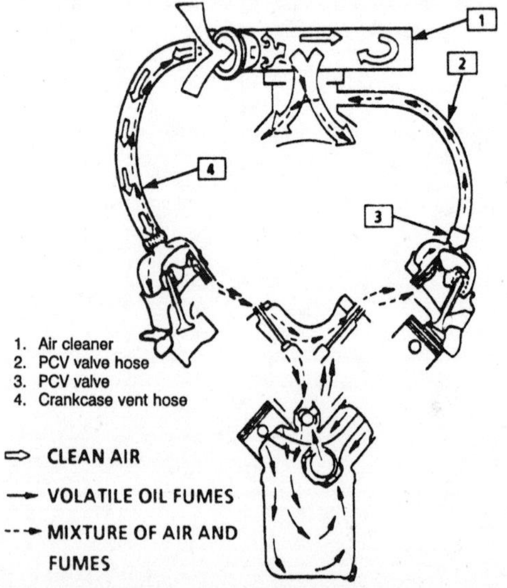

View of the PCV flow — V6 engines

View of the positive crankcase ventilation system — 1.9L engine

every tune-up and replace it at 30,000 mile intervals.

1. Remove the PCV valve from the rocker arm cover.

2. Operate the engine at idle speed.

3. Place your thumb over the end of the valve to check for vacuum. If no vacuum exists, check the valve, the hoses or the manifold port for a plugged condition.

4. Remove the valve from the hose(s), then

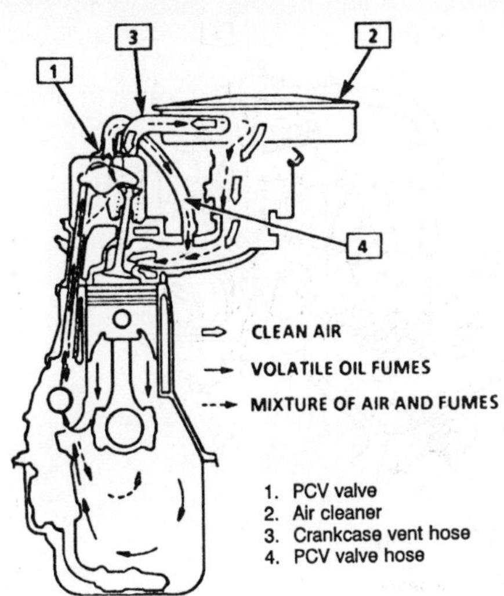

View of the PCV flow — 4 cylinder engines

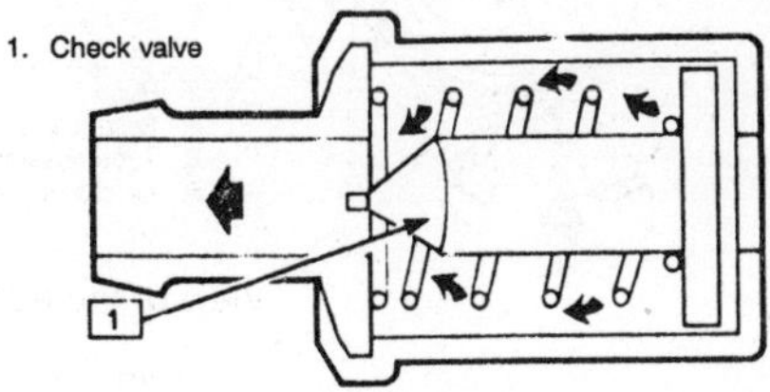

Cross-sectional view of a PCV valve

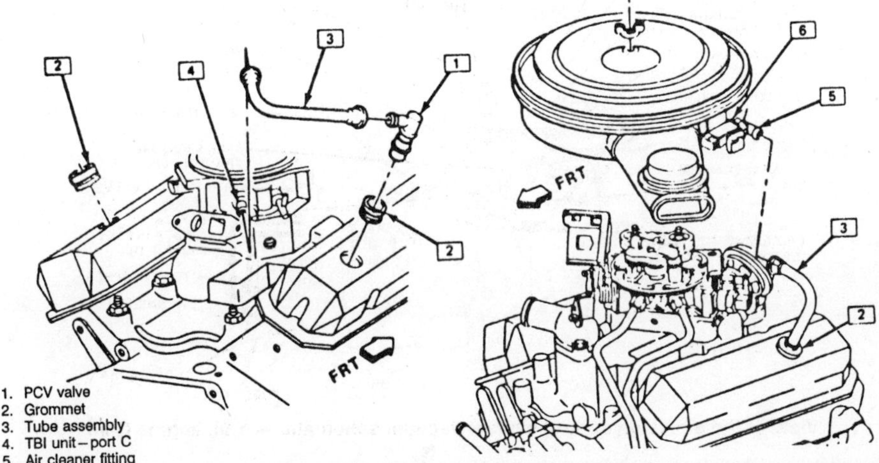

View of the PCV system — 2.8L engine

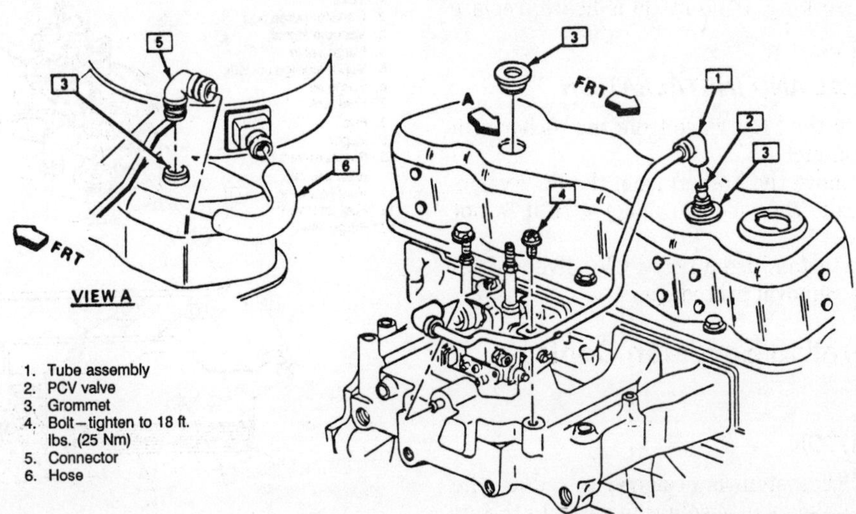

View of the PCV system — 2.5L engine

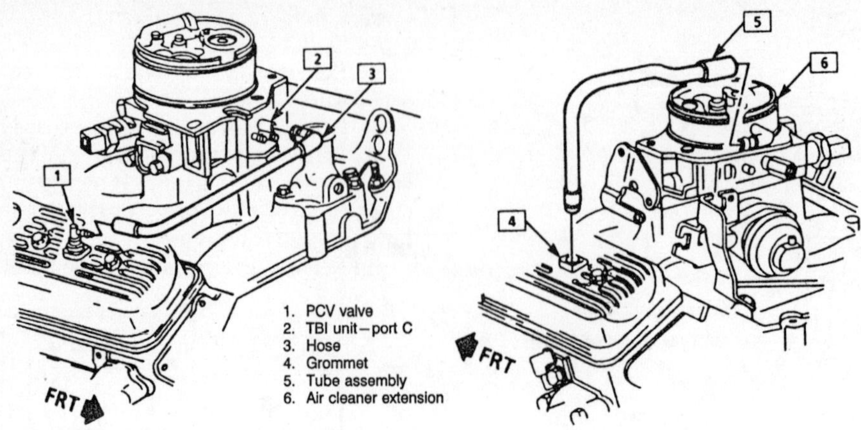

1. PCV valve
2. TBI unit—port C
3. Hose
4. Grommet
5. Tube assembly
6. Air cleaner extension

View of the PCV system — 4.3L engine

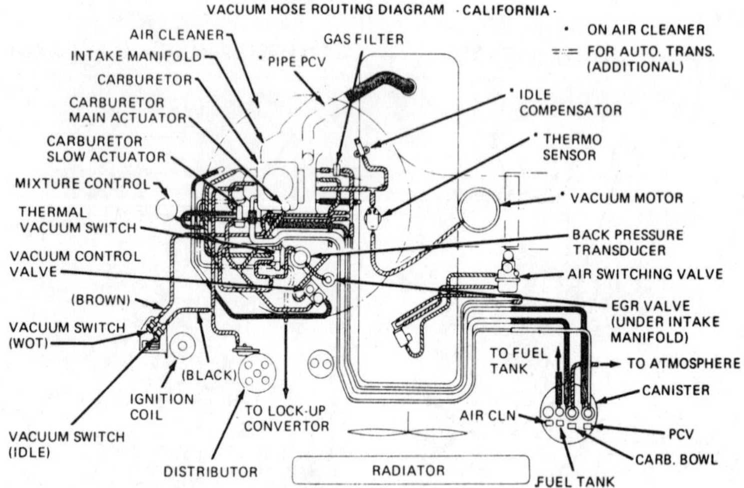

View of the emission control system vacuum schematic — 1.9L engine Calif.

shake it and listen for a rattling of the check needle (inside the valve); the rattle means the valve is working. If no rattle is heard, replace the valve.

REMOVAL AND INSTALLATION

1. Pull the PCV valve from the rocker arm cover grommet.
2. Remove the hose(s) from the PCV valve.
3. Shake the valve to make sure it is not plugged.
4. To install, use a new PCV valve and reverse the removal procedures.

Evaporative Emission Controls (EEC)

OPERATION

The EEC system is designed to reduce the amount of escaping gasoline vapors into the atmosphere. Fuel vapors are directed through lines to a canister containing an activated char-

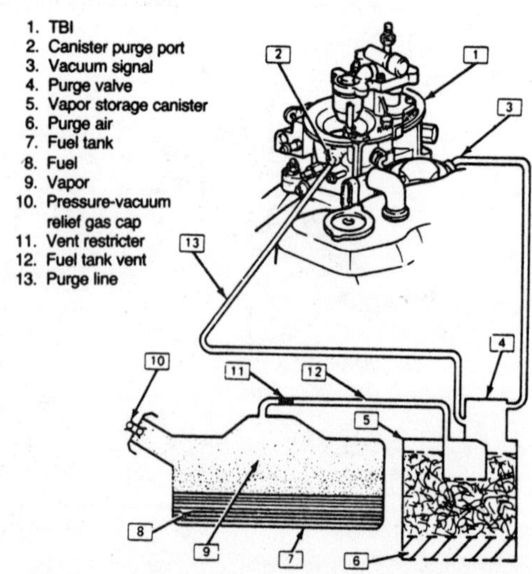

1. TBI
2. Canister purge port
3. Vacuum signal
4. Purge valve
5. Vapor storage canister
6. Purge air
7. Fuel tank
8. Fuel
9. Vapor
10. Pressure-vacuum relief gas cap
11. Vent restricter
12. Fuel tank vent
13. Purge line

View of the emission control system vacuum schematic — 2.0L, 2.8L and 4.3L engines

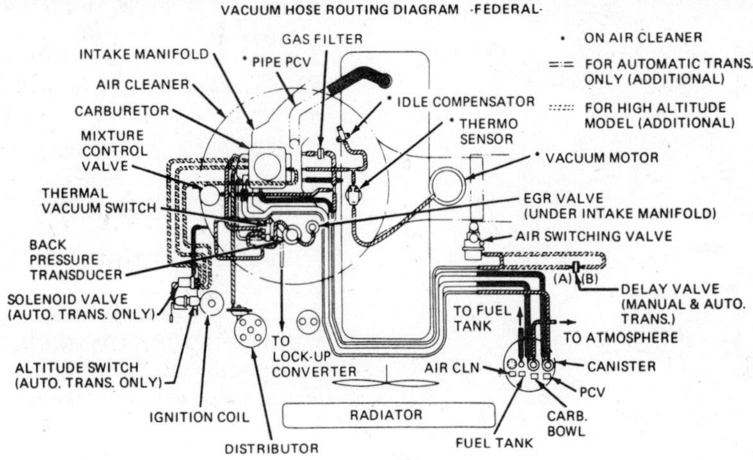

View of the emission control system vacuum schematic — 1.9L engine, except Calif.

1. Carburetor
2. Top view of canister
3. Fuel tank
4. Canister
5. TVS
6. PVC
7. Carburetor bowl vent line
8. Fuel tank vapor line
9. Ported vacuum line
10. Fuel vapor purge line
11. Canister purge valve
12. Control vacuum tube (ported vac)
13. Purge tube (PCV)
14. Canister vent
15. Vapor vent valve
16. Vapor from carburetor tube
17. Control vacuum tube (manifold vac)
18. Sealed fuel tank cap
19. Fuel tank vapor line restriction

View of the emission control system vacuum schematic — 2.5L engine

coal filter; unburned fuel vapor is trapped here until the engine is started. When the engine is running above idle speed, the canister is purged by air drawn in by the manifold vacuum. The air/fuel vapor mixture is drawn into the engine and burned.

SERVICE

Charcoal Canister

NOTE: *The 2.2L (diesel) engines is not equipped with a charcoal canister.*

ALL CARBURETED AND 2.5L (TBI) ENGINES

1. Remove the lower tube of the canister (purge valve) and install a short length of tube, then try to blow through it (little or no air should pass).

2. Using a vacuum source, apply 15 in. Hg to the upper tube of the canister (purge valve).

The diaphragm should hold the vacuum for at least 20 seconds, if not replace the canister.

3. While holding the vacuum on the upper tube, blow through the lower tube (air should now pass); if not, replace the canister.

Thermostatic Vacuum Switch (TVS)

NOTE: *The number stamped on the base of the switch (valve) is the calibration temperature.*

CARBURETED ENGINES

1. If the TVS is hot, allow it to cool to a level below the calibration temperature.

2. Make sure the switch is in good condition.

3. Using a vacuum gauge, connect it to the output ports of the TVS and check the vacuum readings.

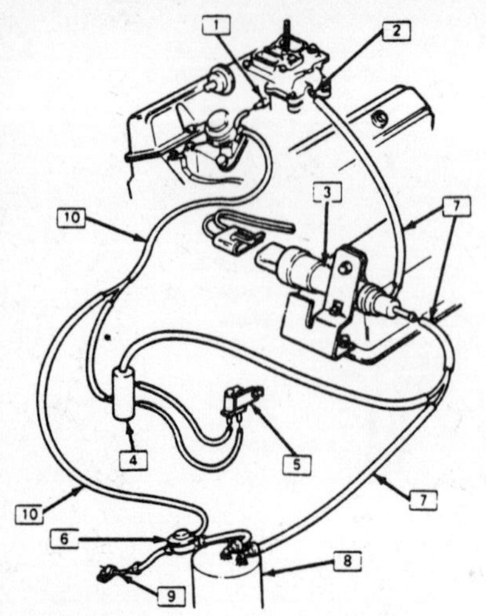

1. Port "B" ported vacuum
2. Port "F" bowl vent
3. Fuel bowl vent solenoid
4. Fuel vapor connector
5. Fuel vapor purge solenoid
6. Tank pressure control valve
7. Vent/purge hose
8. Canister
9. Tank vapor vent pipe
10. Ported vacuum line

View of the emission control system vacuum schematic — 2.8L and 4.3L engines

NOTE: *A leakage of up to 2 in. Hg vacuum/2 min. is allowable and does not mean that the valve is defective.*

4. Using boiling water, heat the TVS to a level above the calibration temperature; the valve should open, if not, replace it.

REMOVAL AND INSTALLATION

Charcoal Canister

ALL ENGINES
EXCEPT 2.2L DIESEL

1. Label and disconnect the hoses from the canister.
2. Loosen the retaining bolt and remove the canister from the vehicle.
NOTE: *If necessary to replace the canister filter, simply pull the filter from the bottom of the charcoal filter and install a new one.*
3. To install, reverse the removal procedures.

Thermostatic Vacuum Switch (TVS)

The TVS is located near the engine coolant outlet housing.

ALL ENGINES
EXCEPT TBI AND 2.2L DIESEL

1. Place a drain pan under the radiator, open the drain cock and drain the coolant to a level below the TVS.
CAUTION: *When draining the coolant, keep in mind that cats and dogs are attracted by the ethylene glycol antifreeze, and are quite likely to drink any that is left in an uncov-*

ered container or in puddles on the ground. This will prove fatal in sufficient quantity. Always drain the coolant into a sealable container. Coolant should be reused unless it is contaminated or several years old.

2. Disconnect the vacuum hoses from the TVS.
3. Using a wrench, remove the TVS from the engine.
4. Inspect and test the TVS; if defective, replace it.
5. Using soft setting sealant, apply it to the TVS threads and reverse the removal procedures. Torque the TVS-to-engine to 120 inch lbs. Reconnect the vacuum hoses. Refill the cooling system.
NOTE: *When applying sealant, be sure the sensor end of the TVS does not become covered.*

Exhaust Gas Recirculation (EGR) System

The EGR valves are mounted on the intake manifold and is connected, through a pipe to the exhaust manifold.

OPERATION

All engines are equipped with an exhaust gas recirculation (EGR) system. This system consists of a metering valve, a vacuum line to the intake manifold and cast-in exhaust gas passages in the intake manifold.

On the 1.9L engine, the vacuum diaphragm of the EGR valve is connected to a signal port at the carburetor flange through a Back Pressure Transducer (BPT) which is responsive to the exhaust pressure to modulate the vacuum signal and a thermal vacuum valve which operates for the EGR cold override.

On the 2.5L engine, the EGR is controlled by manifold vacuum which accordingly opens and closes to admit exhaust gases into the fuel/air mixture. The exhaust gases lower the combustion temperature and reduce the amount of

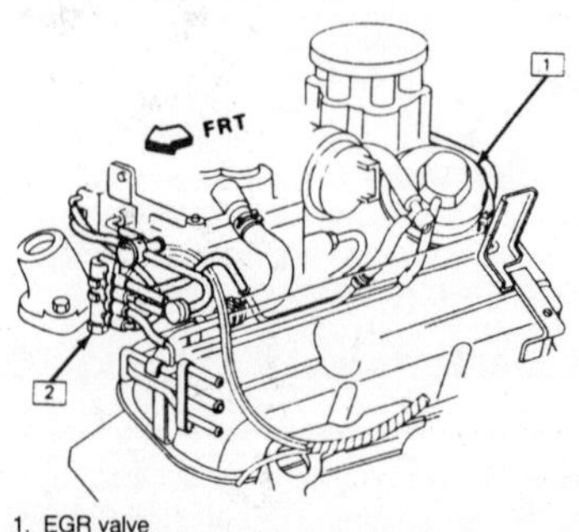

1. EGR valve
2. TVS

View of the Thermostatic Vacuum Switch (TVS) — 2.8L and 4.3L engines

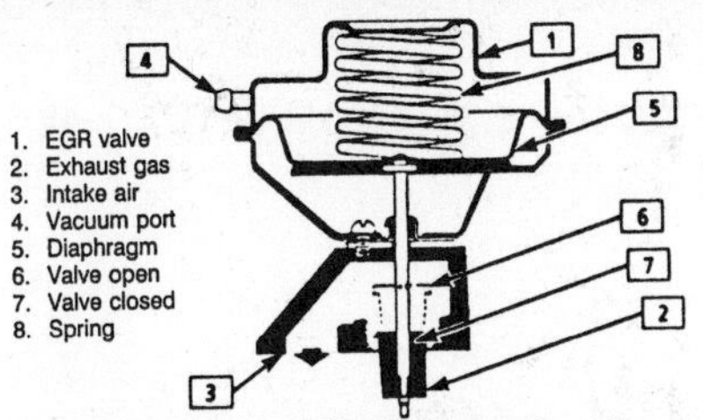

Cross-sectional view of the Exhaust Gas Recycling (EGR) valve — 2.8L and 4.3L engines

oxides of nitrogen (NOx) produced. The valve is closed at idle between the two extreme throttle positions.

On the 2.0L and 2.8L carbureted engines, the vacuum to the EGR valve is controlled by a Thermal Vacuum Switch (TVS). On the 2.8L and 4.3L(TBI) engines, the vacuum to the EGR valve is controlled by EGR solenoid (controlled by the ECM). Vacuum to the EGR valve is restricted until the engine is hot. This prevents the stalling and lumpy idle conditions which would result if the EGR occurred when the engine was cold.

SERVICE

EGR Valve

1. Check hose routing (Refer to Vehicle Emission Control Information Label).

2. Check the EGR valve signal tube orifice for obstructions.

3. Connect a vacuum gauge between EGR valve and carburetor, then check the vacuum; the engine must be at operating temperature of 195°F (90°C). With the engine running at approximately 3000 rpm there should be at least 5 in. Hg vacuum.

4. Check the EGR solenoid for correct operation.

5. To check the valve, perform the following procedures:

    a. Depress the valve diaphragm.

    b. With the diaphragm still depressed hold finger over source tube and release the diaphragm.

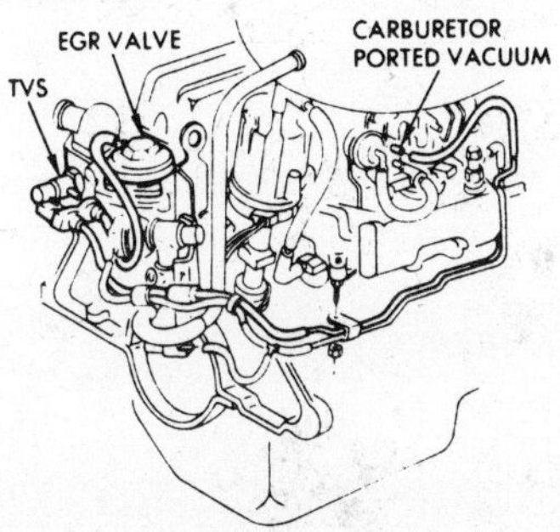

View of the Exhaust Gas Recirculation (EGR) system — 2.0L engine

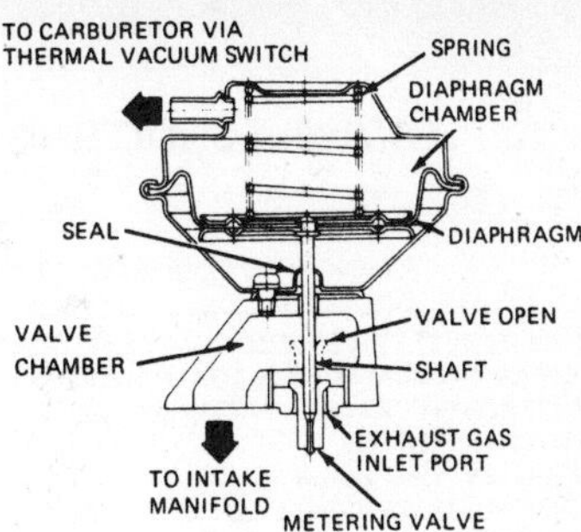

Cross-sectional view of the Exhaust Gas Recycling (EGR) valve — 1.9L engine

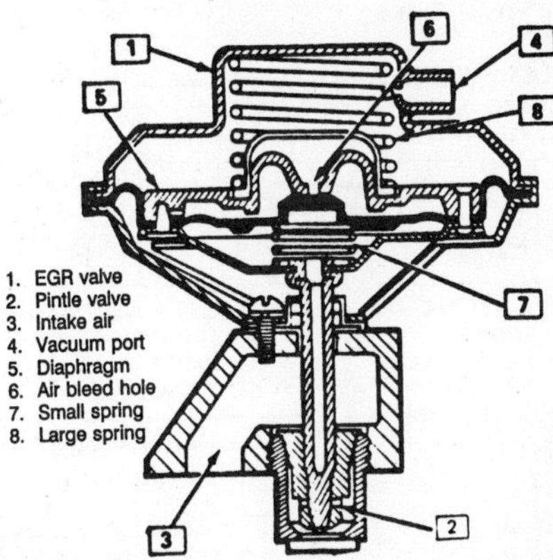

Cross-sectional view of the Exhaust Gas Recycling (EGR) valve with negative backpressure — 2.5L engine

    c. Check the diaphragm and seat for movement. The valve is good if it takes over 20 seconds for the diaphragm to move to the seated position (valve closed).

    d. Replace the EGR valve if it takes less than 20 seconds to move to the seated position.

EGR Solenoid

2.8L AND 4.3L TBI ENGINES

1. Disconnect the electrical connector from the solenoid.

2. Using an ohmmeter, measure the solenoid's resistance, it should be more than 20Ω. If less than 20Ω, replace the solenoid and/or possibly the ECM.

Thermostatic Vacuum Switch (TVS)

If the thermostatic vacuum switch is not working, a Code 32 will store in the ECM memory and a "Service Engine Soon" lamp will light on the instrument panel.

1. Remove the TVS from the engine.

2. Using a vacuum gauge, connect it to one of the hose connections and apply 10 in. Hg vacuum.

TROUBLESHOOTING THE EGR SYSTEM — 2.8L AND 4.3L

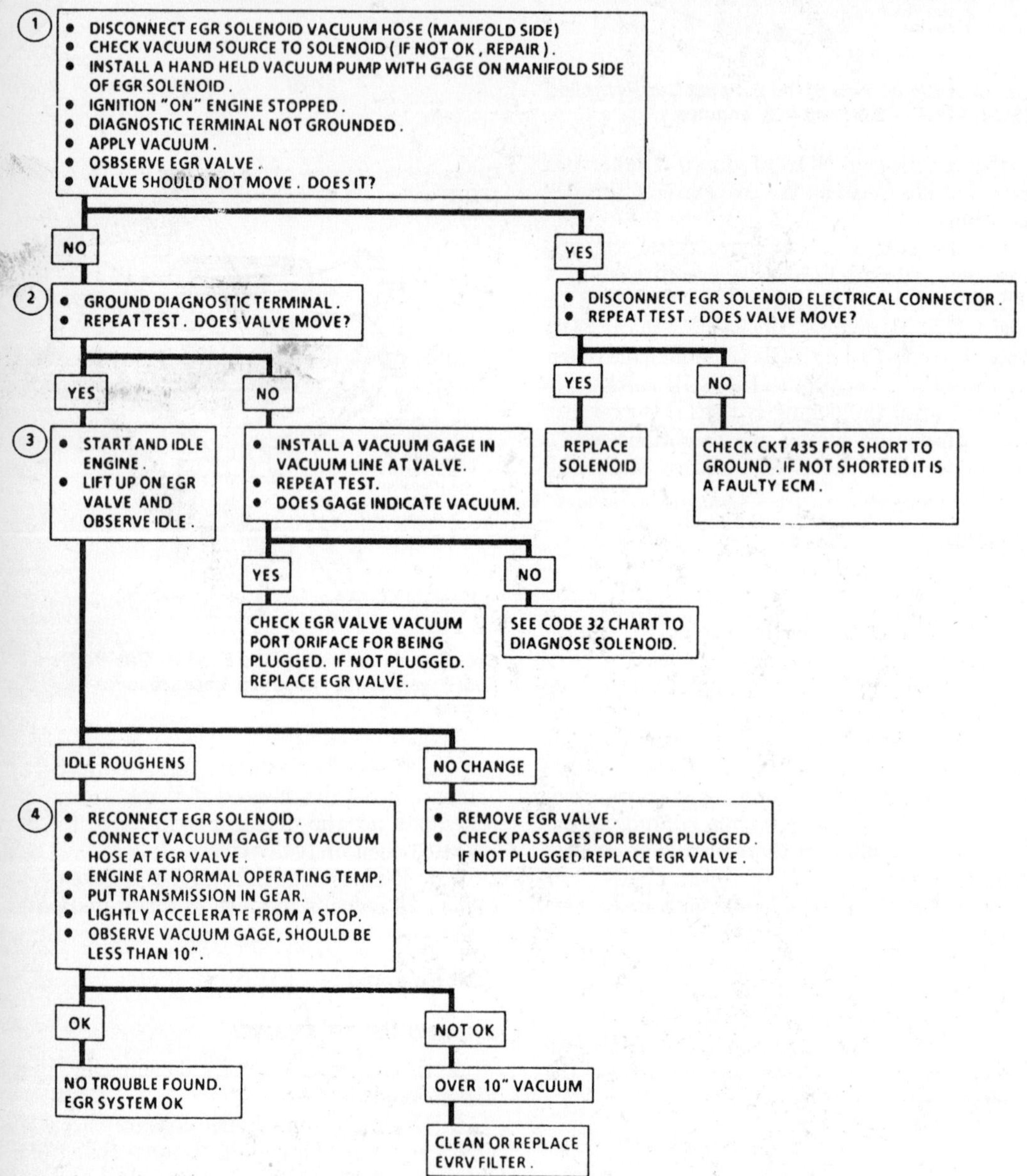

TROUBLESHOOTING THE EGR SYSTEM — 2.5L ENGINE

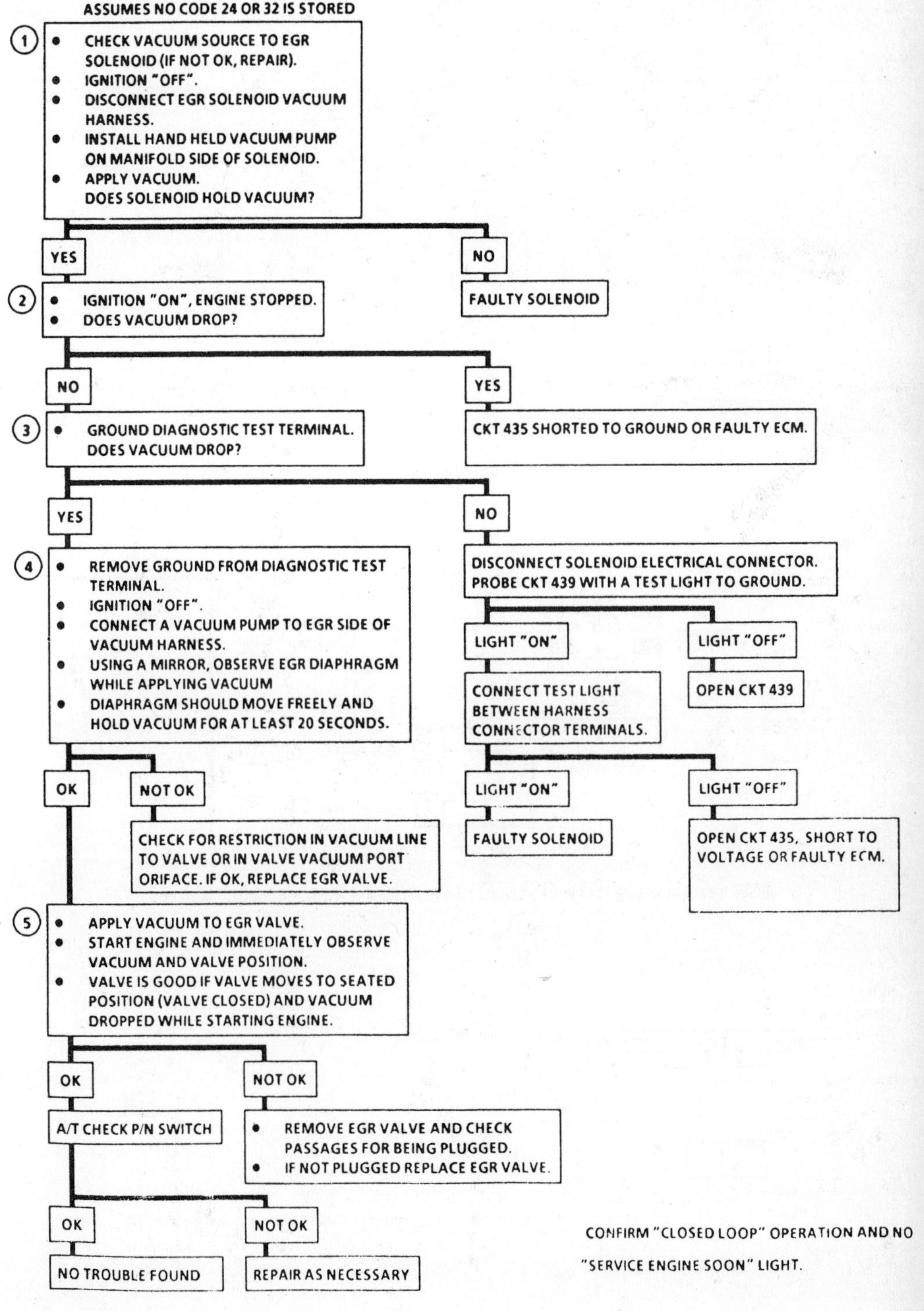

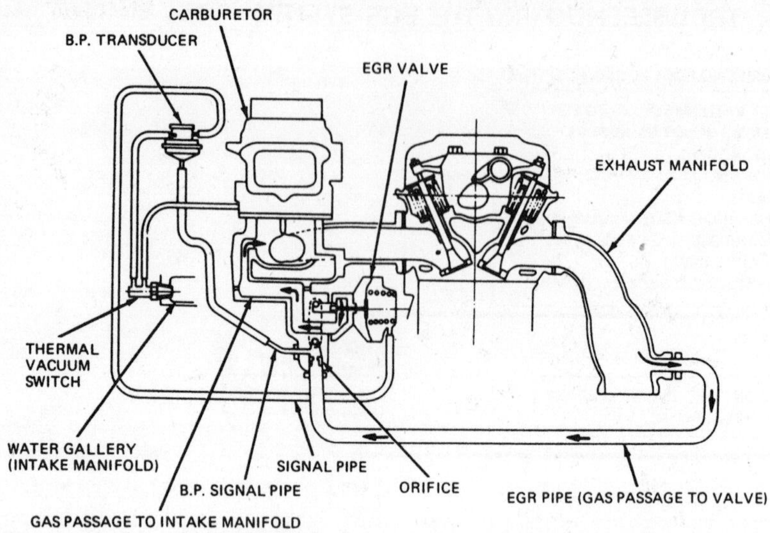

View of the Exhaust Gas Recycling (EGR) system — 1.9L engine

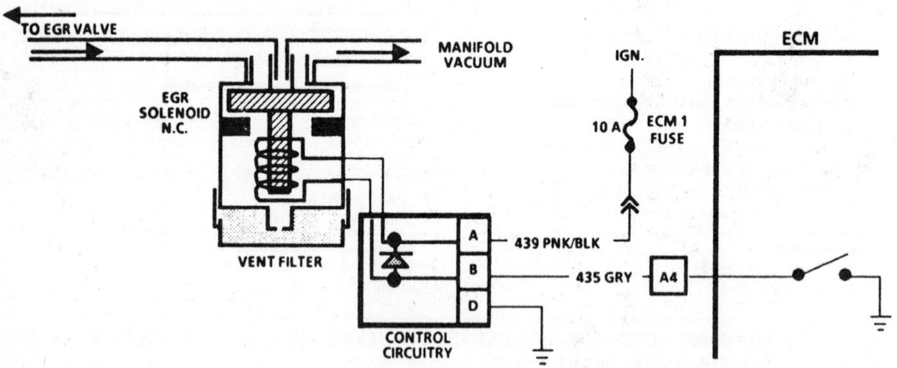

EGR system electrical and vacuum schematic — 2.8L and 4.3L engines

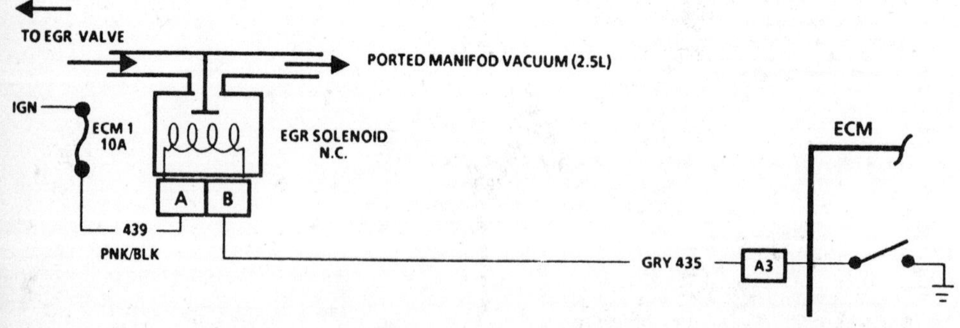

EGR system electrical and vacuum schematic — 2.5L engine

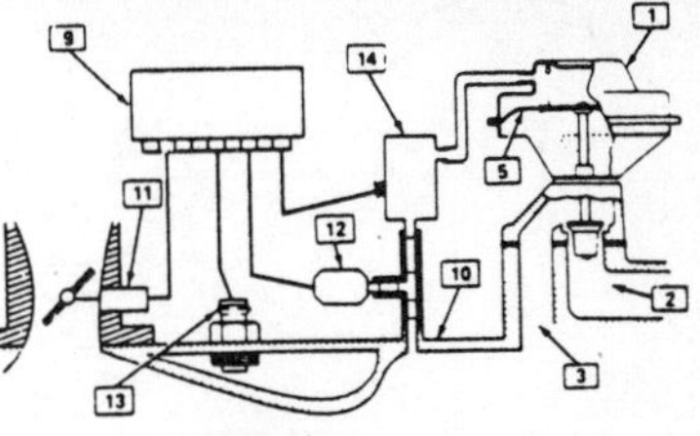

1. EGR valve
2. Exhaust gas
4. Intake flow
6. Vacuum port
7. Throttle valve
8. Vacuum chamber
9. Valve return spring
10. Thermal vacuum switch
11. Coolant
12. Diaphragm

View of the Termostatic Vacuum Switch (TVS) controlled EGR system — 2.8L engine

NOTE: *A vacuum drop of 2 in. Hg vacuum/2 minutes is allowable.*

3. Place the tip of the switch in boiling water. When the switch reaches 195°F (91°C), the valve should open and the vacuum will drop; if not, replace the switch.

RESETTING ECM

To clear the codes stored in the ECM, turn the ignition **OFF** and disconnect the negative battery terminal or the ECM **B** fuse for 10 seconds.

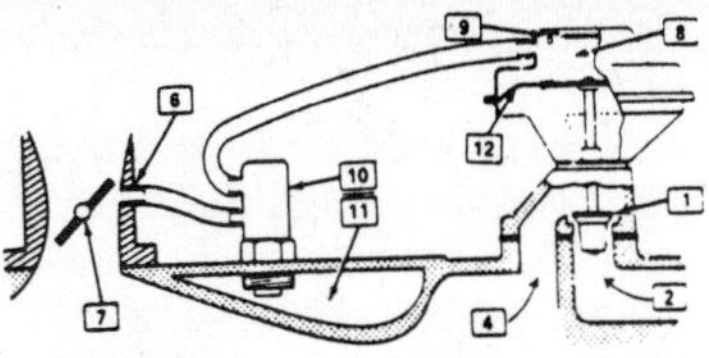

1. EGR valve
2. Vacuum harness
3. EGR solenoid
4. Manifold vacuum

View of the EGR valve and solenoid — 2.8L engine

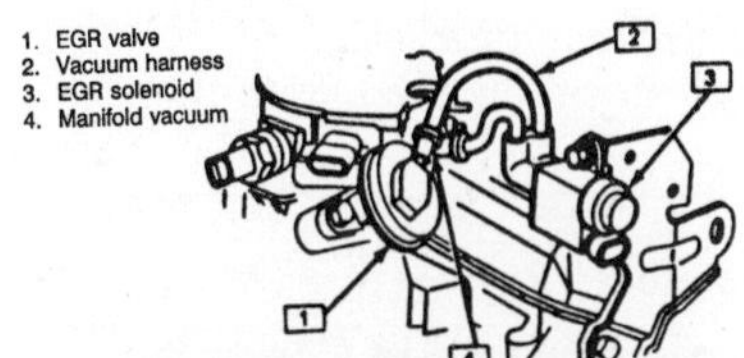

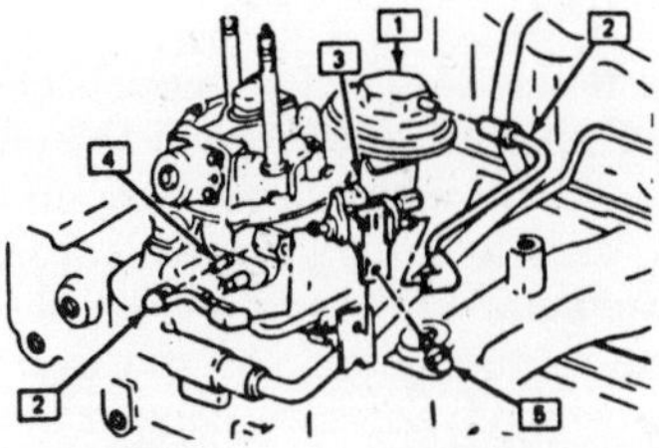

1. EGR valve
2. Vacuum harness
3. EGR solenoid
4. Ported manifold vacuum (port F)
5. Bolt—torque to 35 inch lbs. (4 Nm)

View of the EGR valve and solenoid — 2.5L engine

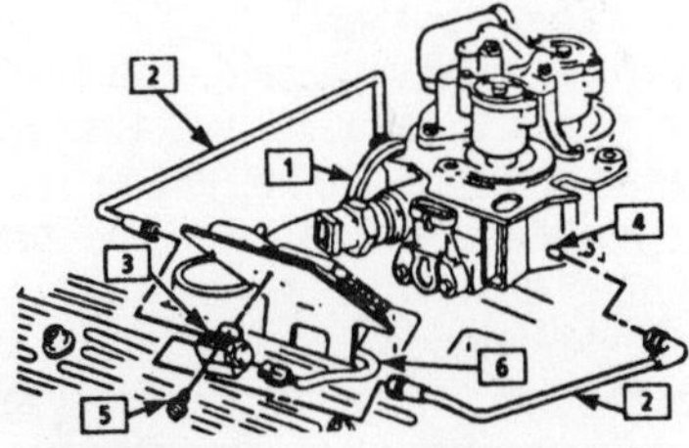

1. EGR valve
2. Vacuum harness
3. EGR solenoid
4. Manifold vacuum (port J)
5. Bolt—torque to 18 inch lbs. (2 Nm)
6. Harness connector

View of the EGR valve and solenoid — 4.3L engine

1. EGR valve
2. Exhaust gas
3. Intake air
5. Diaphragm
9. Electronic control module
10. Manifold vacuum
11. Throttle position sensor
12. Manifold pressure sensor
13. Coolant temperature sensor
14. EGR control solenoid

View of the Electronic Control Module (ECM) controlled EGR system — 2.8L and 4.3L TBI engines

EGR VALVE CLEANING

NOTE: *Do not wash valve assembly in solvents or degreaser — permanent damage to valve diaphragm may result. Also, sand blasting of the valve is recommended since this can affect the operation of the valve.*

1. Remove the EGR valve-to-intake manifold bolts and the valve, discard the gasket.

2. With a wire brush, buff the exhaust deposits from the mounting surface and around the valve.

3. Depress the valve diaphragm and look at the valve seating area through the valve outlet for cleanliness. If the valve and/or seat are not completely clean, repeat Step 2.

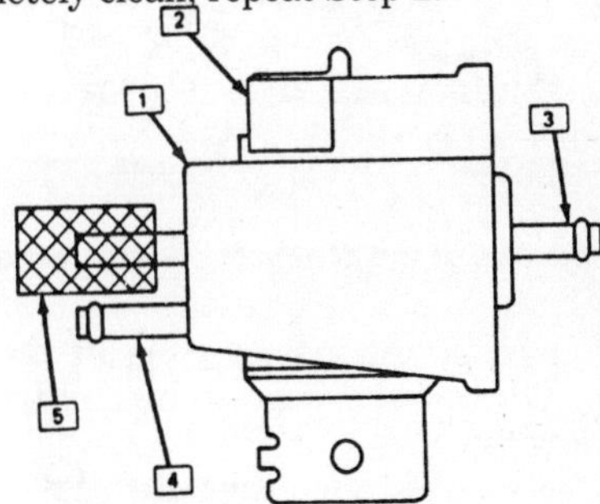

1. EGR control solenoid assembly
2. Electrical connector
3. Vacuum connector from source
4. Vacuum connector to EGR valve
5. Vent

Exploded view of the EGR control solenoid — 2.5L engine

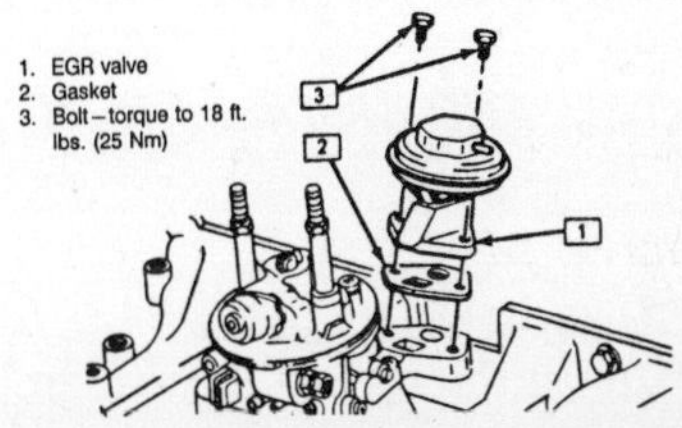

1. EGR valve
2. Gasket
3. Bolt—torque to 18 ft. lbs. (25 Nm)

Exploded view of the EGR valve — 2.5L engine

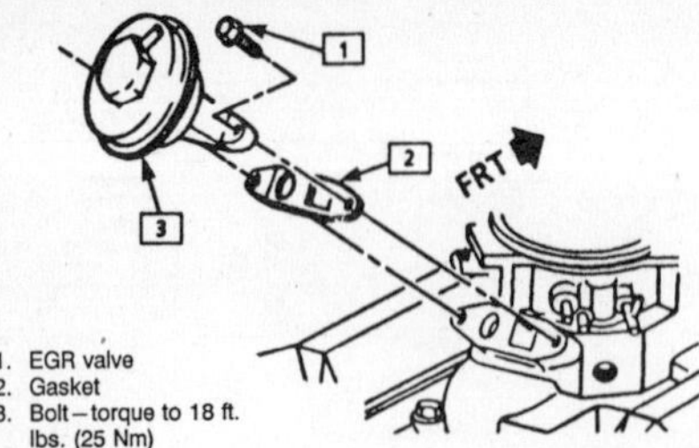

1. EGR valve
2. Gasket
3. Bolt—torque to 18 ft.
   lbs. (25 Nm)

Exploded view of the EGR valve — 2.8L engine

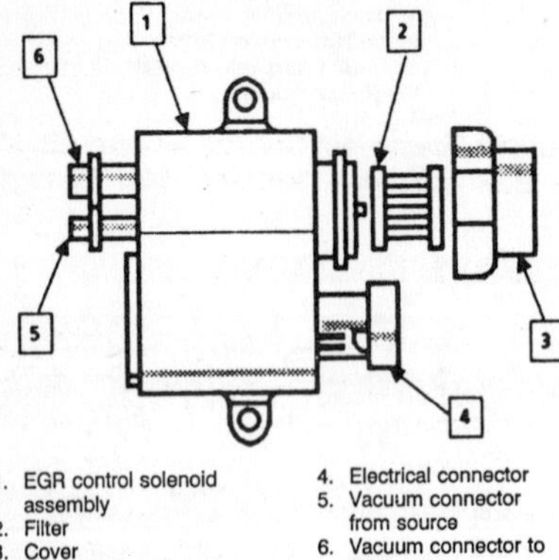

1. EGR control solenoid
   assembly
2. Filter
3. Cover
4. Electrical connector
5. Vacuum connector
   from source
6. Vacuum connector to
   EGR valve

Exploded view of the EGR control solenoid (EVRV) — 2.8L and 4.3L engines

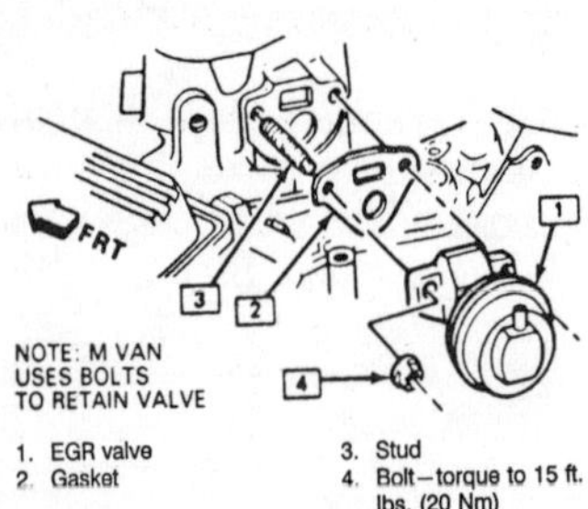

1. EGR valve
2. Gasket
3. Stud
4. Bolt—torque to 15 ft.
   lbs. (20 Nm)

Exploded view of the EGR valve — 4.3L engine

4. Look for exhaust deposits in the valve outlet. Remove the deposit build-up with a small scraper.

5. Clean the mounting surfaces of the intake manifold and the valve assembly, then using a new gasket install the valve assembly to the intake manifold. Torque the bolts to 35 inch lbs. (4 Nm) for 2.5L engine or 18 inch lbs. (2 Nm) for 2.8L and 4.3L engines.

6. Connect the vacuum hoses.

REMOVAL AND INSTALLATION

EGR Valve

1. Remove the air cleaner.
2. Detach the vacuum hose from the EGR valve.
3. On the 2.8L and 4.3L TBI engines, dis-connect the temperature switch from the EGR valve.

4. Remove the EGR valve-to-intake manifold bolts and the valve from the manifold.

5. To install, use a new gasket and reverse the removal procedures. Torque the EGR valve-to-manifold bolts to 18 ft. lbs. (25 Nm) for 2.5L and 2.8L engines or 15 ft. lbs. (20 Nm) for 4.3L engine.

EGR Solenoid

2.8L TBI ENGINE

1. Disconnect the negative battery cable from the battery.
2. Remove the air cleaner.
3. Disconnect the electrical connector and the vacuum hoses from the solenoid.
4. Remove the mounting nut and the solenoid.
5. To install, reverse the removal procedures. Torque the solenoid mounting nut to 17 ft. lbs. (24 Nm).

Back Pressure Transducer

1. Remove the back pressure transducer from the clamp bracket.
2. Remove the hoses from the transducer.
3. Inspect and/or replace the transducer.
4. To install, reverse the removal procedures.

Thermostatic Air Cleaner (THERMAC)

OPERATION

This system is designed to improve driveability and exhaust emissions when the engine is cold. Components added to the basic air cleaner assembly include a temperature sensor (connected to a manifold vacuum source), a vacuum diaphragm motor (connected to the temperature sensor) and an inlet damper door (installed in the air cleaner inlet snorkel). Additional components of the system include a hot idle compensator (1.9L) and a hot air duct running from the heat source to the underside of the air cleaner snorkel.

When the engine is cold, the temperature sensor allows vacuum to pass through to the vacuum diaphragm motor. The vacuum acting on the vacuum motor causes the motor to close the damper door, which prohibits the introduction of cold, outside air to the air cleaner. The intake vacuum then pulls hot air, generated by the exhaust manifold, through the hot air duct and into the air cleaner. This heated air supply helps to more effectively vaporize the fuel mixture entering the engine. As the engine warms, the temperature sensor bleeds off vacuum to

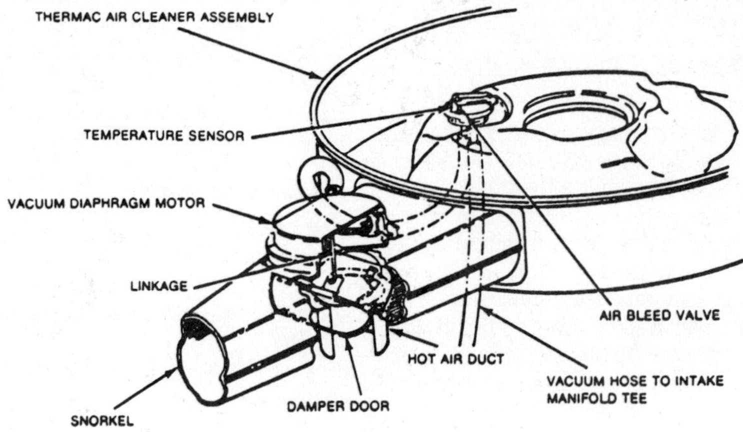

View of a thermostatic air cleaner — typical

the vacuum motor, allowing the damper door to gradually open.

The usual problems with this system are leaking vacuum lines (which prevent proper operation of the sensor and/or motor); torn or rusted through hot air ducts and/or rusted through heat stoves (either condition will allow the introduction of too much cold air to the air cleaner). Visually check and replace these items as necessary. Should the system still fail to operate properly, disconnect the vacuum line from the vacuum motor and apply at least 7 in. Hg vacuum directly to the motor from an outside vacuum source; the damper door should close. If the door does not close, either the vacuum motor is defective or the damper door and/or linkage is binding. If the door closes, but then gradually opens (with a steady vacuum source), the vacuum motor is defective.

SERVICE

Vacuum Motor

1. With the engine Off, disconnect the hose from the vacuum diaphragm motor.

2. Using a vacuum source, apply 7 in. Hg vacuum to the vacuum motor; the door should close and block off the outside air, completely.

3. Bend the vacuum hose (to trap the vacuum in the motor) and make sure the door stays closed; if not, replace the vacuum motor.

NOTE: *Before replacing the vacuum motor (if defective), be sure to check the motor linkage, for binding.*

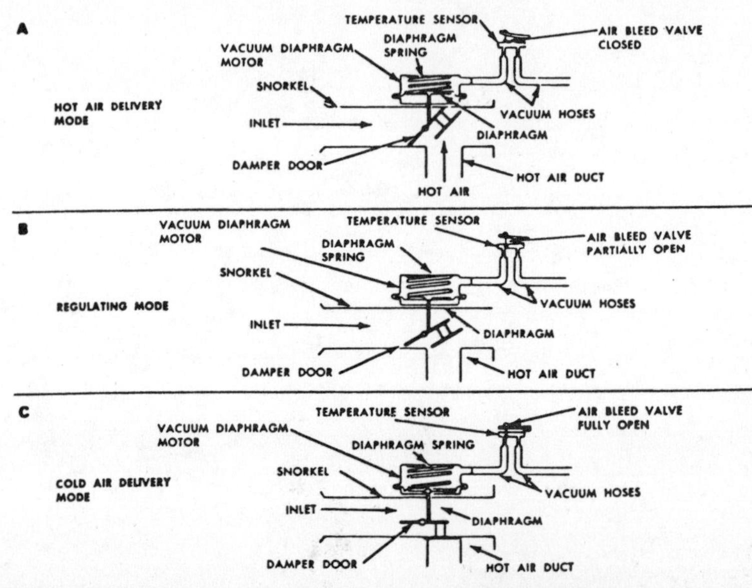

Thermostatic air cleaner operation schematic — typical

4. If the vacuum motor is OK and the problem still exists, check the temperature sensor.

Temperature Sensor

1. Remove the air cleaner cover and place a thermometer near the temperature sensor; the temperature must be below 86°F (30°C). When the temperature is OK, replace the air cleaner.

2. Start the engine and allow it to idle. Watch the vacuum motor door, it should close immediately (if the engine is cool enough).

3. When the vacuum motor door starts to open, remove the air cleaner cover and read the thermometer, it should be about 131°F (55°C).

4. If the door does not respond correctly, replace the temperature sensor.

REMOVAL AND INSTALLATION

Vacuum Motor

1. Remove the air cleaner.

2. Disconnect the vacuum hose from the motor.

3. Using a 1/8 in. drill bit, drill out the spot welds, then enlarge as necessary to remove the retaining strap.

4. Remove the retaining strap.

5. Lift up the motor and cock it to one side to unhook the motor linkage at the control damper assembly.

6. Install the new vacuum motor as follows:

a. Using a 7/64 in. drill bit, drill a hole in the snorkel tube at the center of the vacuum motor retaining strap.

b. Insert the vacuum motor linkage into the control damper assembly.

c. Use the motor retaining strap and a sheet metal screw to secure the retaining strap and motor to the snorkel tube.

NOTE: *Make sure the screw does not interfere with the operation of the damper assembly; shorten the screw, if necessary.*

Temperature Sensor

1. Remove the air cleaner.

2. Disconnect the hoses from the sensor.

3. Pry up the tabs on the sensor retaining clip and remove the clip and sensor from the air cleaner.

4. To install, reverse the removal procedures.

Air Injection Reactor (AIR) 1.9L, 2.0L and 2.8L Engines

OPERATION

The AIR system uses an air pump, air check valve(s), a mixture control (deceleration) valve, an air switching (diverter) valve, an air mani-

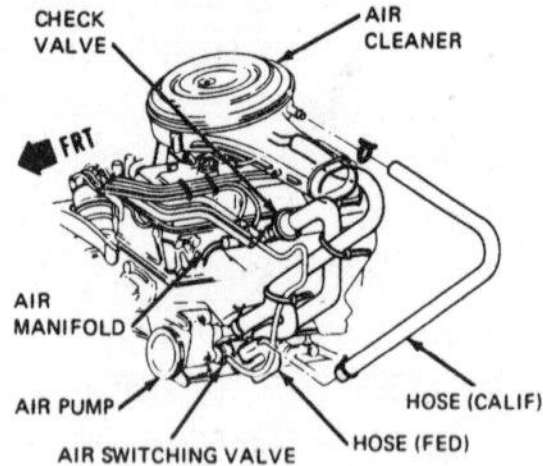

Exploded view of the Air Injection Reaction (AIR) system — 1.9L engine

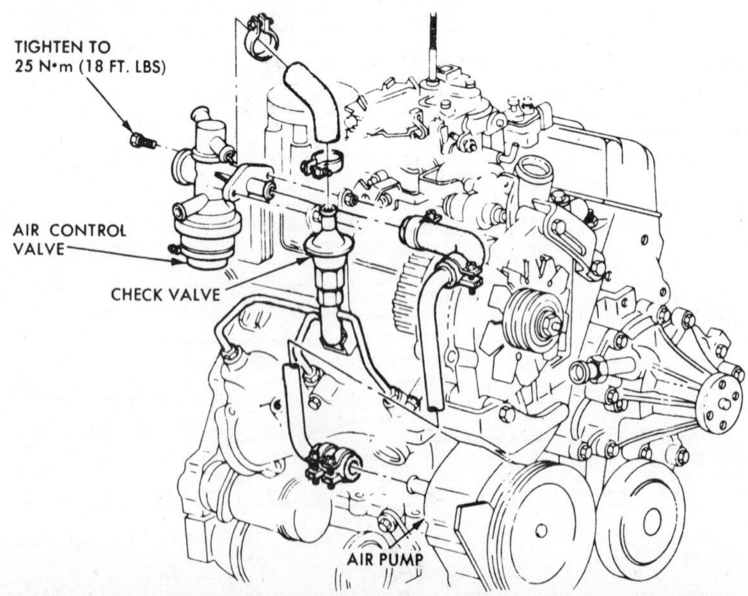

Exploded view of the Air Injection Reaction (AIR) system — 2.8L engine

fold (with air injector nozzles) and an electric air control valve on 2.8L TBI — 1986–87 California.

On the Federal, 1.9L engine models, the air switching (diverter) valve, directs the air flow from the AIR pump to the exhaust manifolds (during normal operation) and away from the exhaust manifolds (during engine deceleration).

On the 1.9L engine for California and the 2.8L TBI engine models, the Electronic Control Module (ECM) operates the electric air control valve which directs the air flow to the engine exhaust manifold ports or the air cleaner. When the engine is cold or in wide-open throttle, the ECM energizes the solenoid to direct the air flow into the exhaust manifold check valves. When the engine warms, operating at high speeds or deceleration, the ECM de-energizes the electric air control valve, changing the air flow from the exhaust manifold to the air cleaner. The diversion of the air flow to the air cleaner acts as a silencer.

A check valve(s) prevents back flow of the exhaust gases into the air pump, if there is an exhaust backfire or pump drive belt failure.

The deceleration valve (if equipped) helps to prevent backfiring during periods of high vacuum (deceleration) by allowing large quantities of air to flow into the intake manifold.

SERVICE

Air Injection Pump

Accelerate the engine to approximately 1500 rpm and observe the air flow from hose(s). If the air flow increases as the engine is accelerated, the pump is operating satisfactorily. If the air flow does not increase or is not present, proceed as follows:

1. Check for proper drive belt tension. The Air Management System is not completely noiseless. Under normal conditions, noise rises in pitch as the engine speed increases. To determine if excessive noise is the present, operate the engine with the pump drive belt removed. If excessive noise does not exist with the belt removed, proceed as follows:

2. Check for a seized Air Injection Pump. Do not oil the air pump.

3. Check the hoses, the pipes and all connections for leaks and proper routing.

4. Check the air control valve.

5. Check air injection pump for proper mounting and bolt torque.

6. Repair irregularities in these components, as necessary.

7. If no irregularities exist and the air injection pump noise is still excessive, replace the pump.

Check Valves

1. The check valve should be inspected whenever the hose is disconnected from the check valve or whenever check valve failure is suspected (A pump that had become inoperative and had shown indications of having exhaust gases in the pump would indicate check valve failure).

2. Blow through the check valve (toward the cylinder head) then attempt to suck back through check valve. The flow should only be in one direction (toward the exhaust manifold). Replace the valve which does not function correctly.

Air Hoses and Injection Pipes

1. Inspect all hoses for deterioration or holes.

2. Inspect all air injection pipes for cracks of holes.

3. Check all hose and pipe connections.

4. Check pipe and hose routing; interference may cause wear.

5. If a leak is suspected on the pressure side of the system or any hose has been disconnected on the pressure-side, the connection should be checked for leaks with a soapy water solution.

6. If a hose, manifold and/or pipe assembly replacement is required, note the routing, then replace the item as required.

7. When installing the new item, be sure to connect the hoses correctly.

Air Switching (Diverter) Valve (ASV)

The diverter valve will act like the electric air control valve, except, that it is not controlled by an ECM. Air is directed to the exhaust ports, unless there is a sudden rise of manifold vacuum due to throttle deceleration.

If the air switching valve is normal, the secondary air continues to blow out from the valve for a few seconds when the accelerator pedal is depressed all the way to floor and released quickly. If the secondary air continues to blow out for more than 5 seconds, replace the air switching valve.

Electric Air Control Valve
2.8L TBI Engine

1. Perform the following inspection checks:

a. The engine coolant must be at operating temperatures.

b. Disconnect the air cleaner-to-electric air control valve hose.

c. Start the engine and operate it at idle (under 2000 rpm). Within the first 5 seconds, the air should be directed to the exhaust ports and then change to the air cleaner.

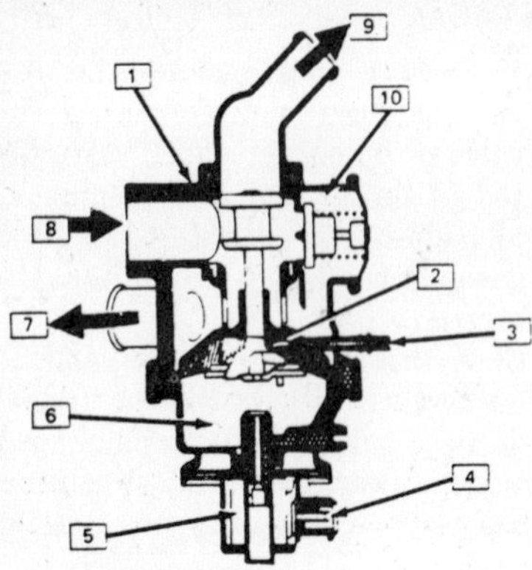

1. Electrical air control (EAC) valve
2. Decel timing assembly
3. Manifold vacuum signal tube
4. Electrical terminal
5. EAC solenoid
6. Decel Timing chamber
7. Air to air cleaner
8. Air from air pump
9. Air to exhaust ports or manifold
10. Pressure relief assembly

Cross-sectional view of the Electric Air Control (EAC) valve — 2.8L TBI engine

d. If the system checks OK, the electric air control valve is working.

2. If inspections in Step 1 were not satisfactory, perform the following procedures:

a. Turn the engine Off but allow the ignition switch to remain On.

b. Reconnect the air cleaner-to-electric air control valve hose.

c. Disconnect the electrical connector from the electric air control valve solenoid and connect a test light between the harness connector terminals.

d. If the test light is On, check for a ground between the solenoid-to-ECM wire(Circuit 436) or replace the ECM (if not grounded).

3. If the test light is Off, perform the following procedures:

a. Using a jumper wire, connect it between the ECM diagnostic (C2) terminal and ground.

b. If the test light turns On, replace the electric air control valve.

c. Remove the jumper wire.

4. If the test light still remains Off, perform the following procedures:

a. Connect one probe of the test light to terminal **A** of the solenoid's connector and the other probe to a ground.

b. If the light still remains Off, check for a blown fuse or an broken ignition (pink) wire.

5. If the light turns On, check for the following problems:

a. A broken solenoid-to-ECM (Circuit 436) wire or check the solenoid's resistance of the air control valve.

b. If the resistance of the solenoid is above 20Ω, replace the ECM.

c. If the resistance of the solenoid is below 20Ω, replace the electric air control valve and the ECM.

Mixture Control (Deceleration) Valve

1. Install a tachometer to the engine and allow the engine to establish normal operating temperatures.

2. Remove the air cleaner and plug the air cleaner vacuum hose(s).

3. Operate the engine at idle speed, then remove the deceleration valve-to-intake manifold (diaphragm) hose.

4. Reconnect the hose and listen for a noticeable air flow (hiss) through the air cleaner-to-deceleration valve hose; there should also be a noticeable drop in idle speed.

5. If the air flow does not continue for at least one second or the engine speed does not drop, check the hoses (of the deceleration valve) for restrictions or leaks.

6. If no restrictions are found, replace the deceleration valve.

REMOVAL AND INSTALLATION

Air Injection Pump

NOTE: *The air pump is non-serviceable, it must be replaced as an assembly, if defective.*

1. Compress the drive belt to keep the pump pulley from turning, then loosen the pump pulley bolts.

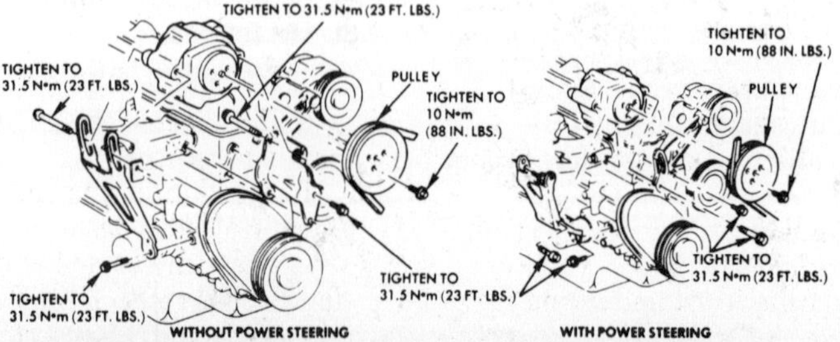

Exploded view of the air pump assembly — 2.0L engine

2. Loosen the pump-to-mounting brackets, release the tension on the drive belt and remove the drive belt.

3. Unscrew the mounting bolts and then remove the pump pulley.

4. If necessary, use a pair of needle nose pliers to pull the fan filter from the hub.

5. Remove the hoses, the vacuum lines, the electrical connectors, if equipped, and the air control or diverter valve.

6. Unscrew the pump mounting bolts and then remove the pump.

7. To install, reverse the removal procedures. Torque the pump pulley bolts to 90 inch lbs. and the pump-to-bracket nuts/bolts to 25 ft. lbs. Adjust the drive belt tension after installation.

Air Pump Drive Belt Adjustment and Replacement

1. Inspect the drive belt for wear, cracks or deterioration.

2. Loosen the pump adjustment and the pivot bolts.

3. Replace the drive belt, if necessary.

4. Move the air pump until the drive belt is at proper tension, then retighten bolts.

5. Check the drive belt tension using a belt tension gauge.

Air Pump Pulley Replacement

1. Hold the pump pulley from turning by compressing the drive belt, then loosen the pump pulley bolts.

2. Loosen the pump through bolt and the adjusting bolt.

3. Remove the drive belt, the pump pulley and the pulley spacer.

4. Install the pump pulley and spacer with the retaining bolts hand tight.

5. Install the drive belt and adjust to proper tension.

6. Hold the pump pulley from turning by compressing the drive belt, then torque the pump pulley bolts to 24 ft. lbs.

7. Recheck drive belt tension and adjust it, if necessary.

Air Pump Filter Fan Replacement

Before starting this operation, note the following:

• Do not allow any filter fragments to enter the air pump intake hole.

• Do not remove the filter fan by inserting a screwdriver between pump and filter fan. Air damage to the sealing lip pump will result.

• Do not remove the metal drive hub from the filter fan.

• It is seldom possible to remove the filter fan without destroying it.

1. Remove the drive belt, the pump pulley and spacer.

2. Insert needle nose pliers and pull the filter fan from hub.

3. Position a new filter fan onto the pump hub.

4. Position the spacer and the pump pulley against the centrifugal filter fan.

5. Install the pump pulley bolts and torque them equally to 80 inch lbs. This will compress the centrifugal filter fan into the pump hole. Do not drive the filter fan on with a hammer.

A slight amount of interference with the housing bore is normal. After a new filter fan has been installed, it may squeal upon initial operation or until O.D. sealing lip has worn in. This may require a short period of pump operation at various engine speeds.

6. To complete the installation, replace the pump drive belt and adjust it.

Check Valve(s)

1. Remove the clamp(s) and disconnect the hose from the valve(s).

2. Unscrew the valve(s) from the air injection pipe(s).

3. To test the valve(s), air should pass only in one direction only.

4. To install, reverse the removal procedures.

Air Control Valve

1. Disconnect the negative battery cable.

2. Disconnect the air inlet and outlet hoses from the valve.

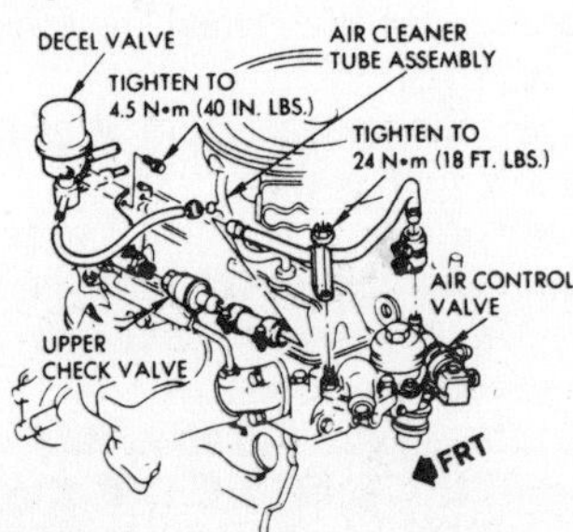

Exploded view of the upper check valve and hoses — 2.0L engine

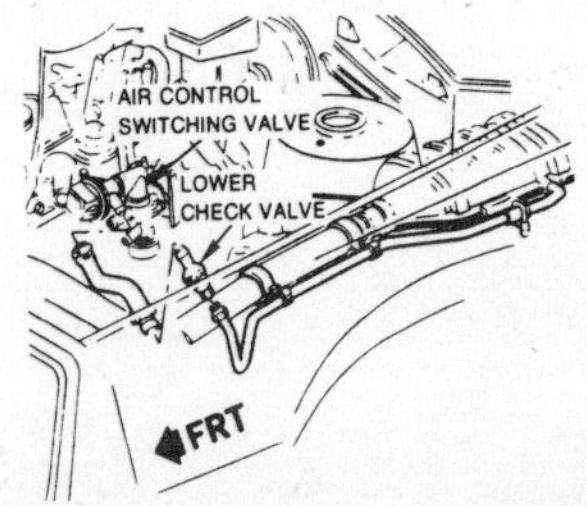

Exploded view of the lower check valve and hoses — 2.0L engine

3. Disconnect the electrical connector, if equipped, and the vacuum hoses at the valve. Remove the electric air control or the diverter valve.

4. To install, reverse the removal procedures. For California models, check the system operation.

Air Switching (Diverter) Valve

The switching valve is replaced in basically the same manner as the air control valve.

Mixture Control (Deceleration) Valve

1. Remove the vacuum hoses from the valve.

2. Remove the deceleration valve-to-engine bracket screws.

3. Remove the deceleration valve.

4. To install, reverse the removal procedures. Torque the deceleration valve-to-engine bracket screws to 30 inch lbs.

Vacuum Switching Valve (VSV)

1. Disconnect the electrical wiring connector.

2. Remove the hoses from the valve.

3. Remove the vacuum switching valve.

4. To install, reverse the removal procedures.

Early Fuel Evaporation System Carbureted Engines

OPERATION

The early fuel evaporation system provides a rapid heating source to the engine induction system during cold drive-away conditions, thus, providing quick fuel evaporation and more uniform fuel distribution. When reducing the length of carburetor choking time, the exhaust emissions are also reduced.

The system consists of a ceramic heater grid (located between the carburetor and the intake manifold) and a temperature switch (non-ECM models) or a relay (ECM models) which activates the heater during cold operation. The relay, located under the right fender, is operated by the ECM.

As the coolant temperature increases, the temperature switch (non-ECM models) or the relay (ECM models) turns Off the current to the ceramic heater, allowing the engine to operate on it's own.

NOTE: *Operational checks should be made at normal maintenance intervals.*

SERVICE

Temperature Switch

1. Disconnect the electrical connector from temperature switch.

2. Connect a 12 volt test lamp across the connector terminals.

3. If the lamp glows when the ignition switch is **ON** and engine **OFF**, the EFE heater is good.

4. If the lamp does not glow, reconnect the heater switch connector. With the engine temperature below 140°F (60°C), measure the voltage across the EFE heater by inserting the test probes into the rear of the connector body (black wire is Negative). The voltage should be approximately 11–13 volts.

5. If the voltage is not 11–13 volts across the heater terminals, check the black wire voltage-to-ground. If the voltage is not 0 volts, the black (ground) wire is an open circuit; repair it.

6. If the voltage is 0 volts, check the voltage-to-vehicle ground from each heater switch terminal — the voltage should be 11–13 volts at each switch terminal.

7. If 11–13 volts is measured at one switch terminal but low or 0 volts at the other, inspect the connector for deformed terminals and repair, as required.

8. If the connector is making proper contact, replace heater switch.

9. If the voltage is not 11–13 volts at both switch terminals, inspect the wiring circuit between the heater switch and the ignition switch, then repair, as required.

10. Start the engine and allow it to warm up to above 170°F (76.7°C). Check the voltage across the EFE heater terminals. The voltage should be 0 volts. If the voltage is not 0 volts, replace the temperature switch.

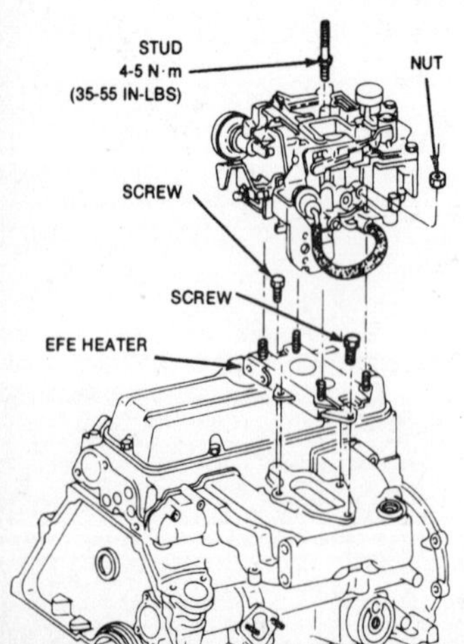

Exploded view of the Early Fuel Evaporation (EFE) system — 2.0L engine

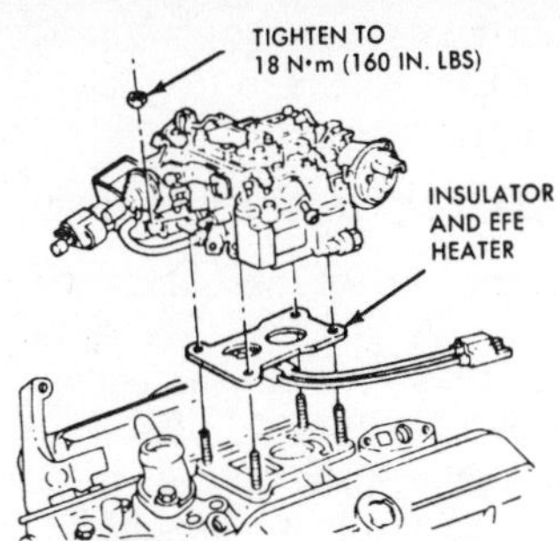

Exploded view of the Early Fuel Evaporation (EFE) heater — 2.8L carbureted engine

REMOVAL AND INSTALLATION

EFE Heater

1. Remove the air cleaner.
2. Disconnect all electrical, vacuum and fuel connections from carburetor.
3. Disconnect the EFE Heater electrical connector.
4. Remove the carburetor-to-intake manifold nuts/bolts and the carburetor.
5. Remove the EFE Heater isolator assembly.
6. To install, reverse the removal procedures.
7. Start the engine and check for leaks.

Temperature Switch
Non-ECM Models

The temperature switch is located on the rear, for 2.0L engine, of the intake manifold coolant outlet housing or behind the engine coolant housing, for 2.8L engine.

1. Disconnect the electrical connector from the temperature switch.
2. Place a catch pan under the radiator, open the drain cock and drain the coolant to a level below the intake manifold coolant housing.

CAUTION: *When draining the coolant, keep in mind that cats and dogs are attracted by the ethylene glycol antifreeze, and are quite likely to drink any that is left in an uncovered container or in puddles on the ground. This will prove fatal in sufficient quantity. Always drain the coolant into a sealable container. Coolant should be reused unless it is contaminated or several years old.*

NOTE: *If replacing the temperature switch, refer to the calibration number stamped on the base.*

3. To install, apply soft setting sealant to the male threads of the temperature switch and reverse the removal procedures. Torque the temperature switch-to-intake manifold coolant housing to 10 ft. lbs. Refill the cooling

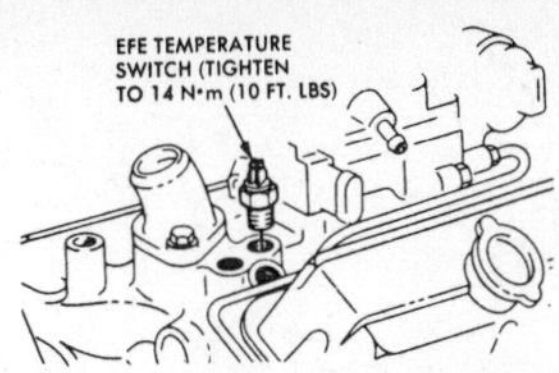

Exploded view of the Early Fuel Evaporation (EFE) temperature switch — 2.8L carbureted engine

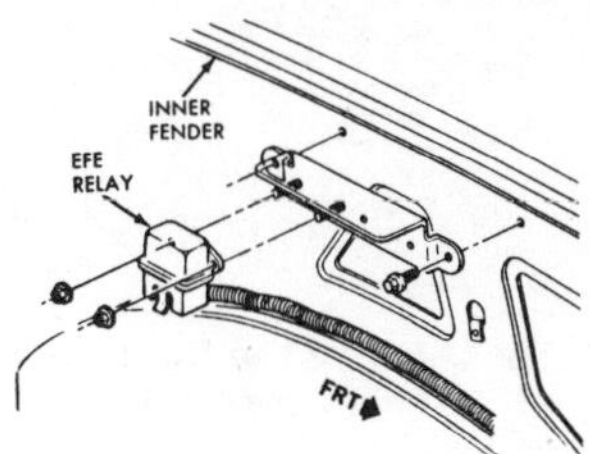

Exploded view of the Early Fuel Evaporation (EFE) relay — 2.8L engine

system. Start the engine, run the engine to normal operating temperatures and check the operation.

NOTE: *When applying sealant to the temperature switch, be sure not to coat the sensor end with sealant.*

Relay — ECM Models

1. Disconnect negative battery terminal from the battery.
2. Disconnect electrical connector from the relay.
3. Remove relay-to-bracket bolts and the relay.
4. To install, reverse the removal procedures.

Oxygen Sensor

The oxygen sensor protrudes into the exhaust stream and monitors the oxygen content of the exhaust gases. The difference between the oxygen content of the exhaust gases and that of the outside air generates a voltage signal to the ECM. The ECM monitors this voltage and depending upon the value of the signal received, issues a command to adjust for a rich or a lean condition.

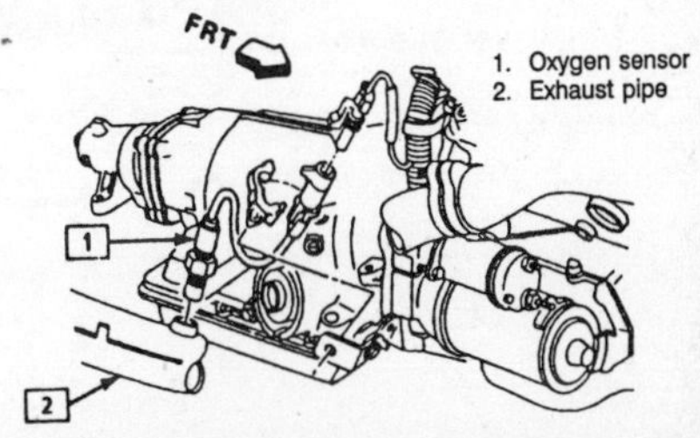

Location of the O_2 sensor in the exhaust pipe — 2.8L and 4.3L engines

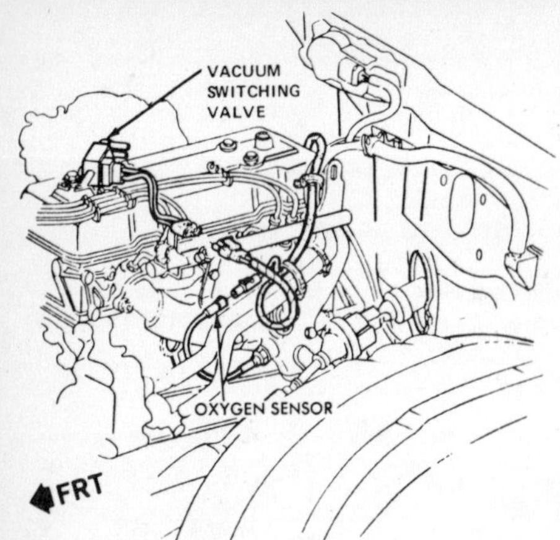

Location of the O$_2$ sensor in the exhaust manifold — 1.9L engine — others are similar

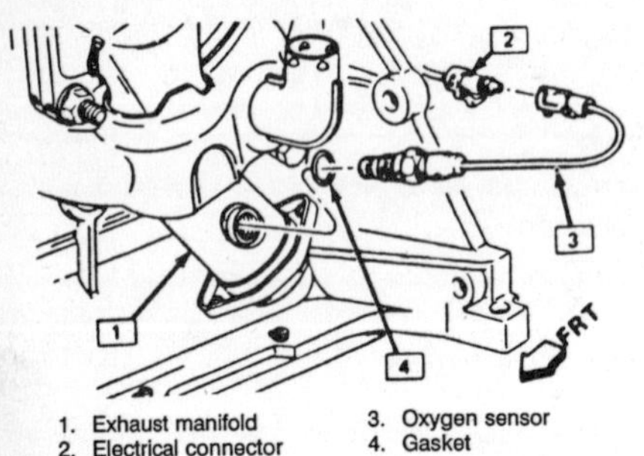

1. Exhaust manifold
2. Electrical connector
3. Oxygen sensor
4. Gasket

Location of the O$_2$ sensor in the exhaust manifold — 2.5L engine

No attempt should ever be made to measure the voltage output of the sensor. The current drain of any conventional voltmeter would be such that it would permanently damage the sensor. No jumpers, test leads or any other electrical connections should ever be made to the sensor. Use these tools only on the ECM side of the wiring harness connector after disconnecting it from the sensor.

REMOVAL AND INSTALLATION

The oxygen sensor must be replaced every 30,000 miles (48,000 km). The sensor may be difficult to remove when the engine temperature is below 120°F (48°C). Excessive removal force may damage the threads in the exhaust manifold or pipe; follow the removal procedure carefully.

1. Locate the oxygen sensor.

NOTE: *It protrudes from the exhaust manifold on the left side for 4 cylinder engines, the right side for 2.8L engine — 1982–85, the left exhaust pipe for 2.8L engine — 1986–87, Federal, the right exhaust pipe for 2.8L engine — 1986–87, Calif. or the exhaust pipe for 2.8L engine — 1988 and 4.3L engines.*

2. Disconnect the electrical connector from the oxygen sensor.

3. Spray a commercial solvent onto the sensor threads and allow it to soak in for at least five minutes.

4. Carefully remove the sensor.

5. To install, first coat the new sensor's threads with GM Anti-Seize Compound No. 5613695 or equivalent. This is not a conventional anti-seize paste. The use of a regular compound may electrically insulate the sensor, rendering it inoperative. You must coat the threads with an electrically conductive anti-seize compound.

6. Torque the sensor to 30 ft. lbs. (42 Nm). Be careful not to damage the electrical pigtail; check the sensor boot for proper fit and installation.

VACUUM DIAGRAMS

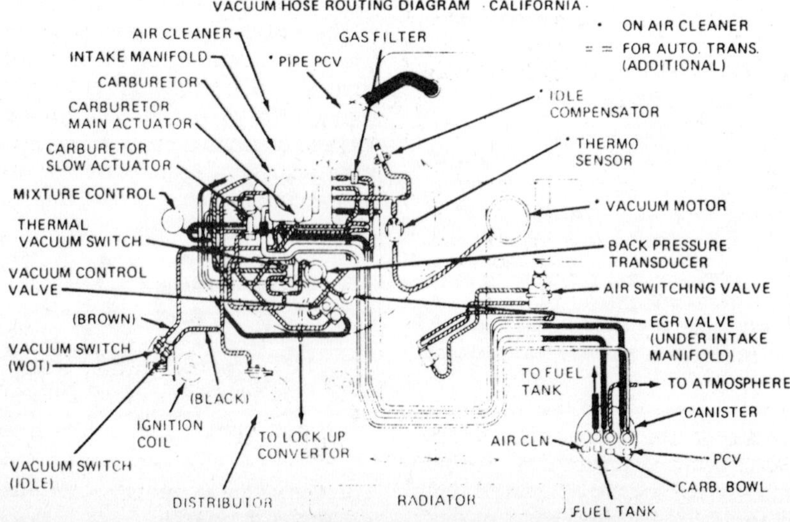

Vacuum hose routing for the 1.9L engine, California

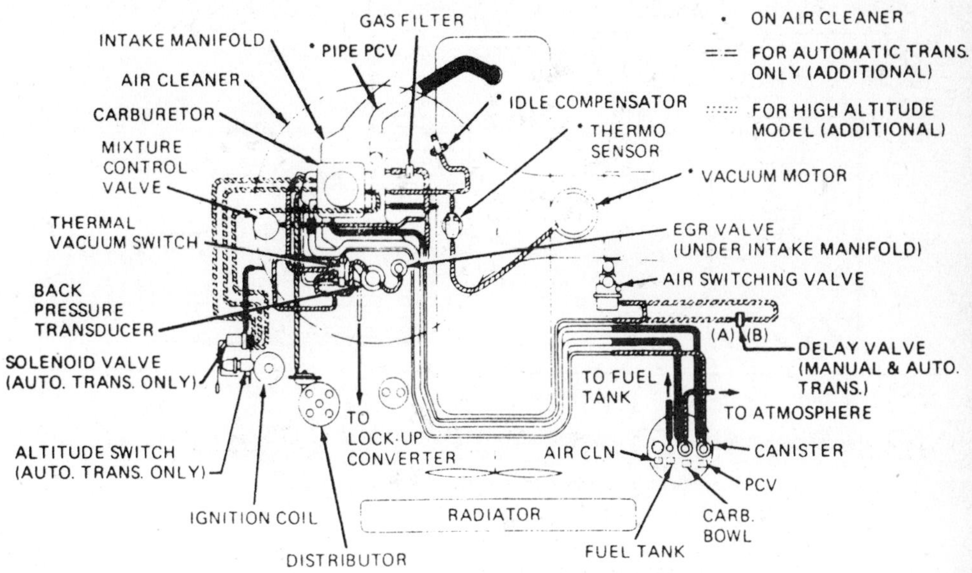

Vacuum hose routing for the 1.9L engine, exc. California

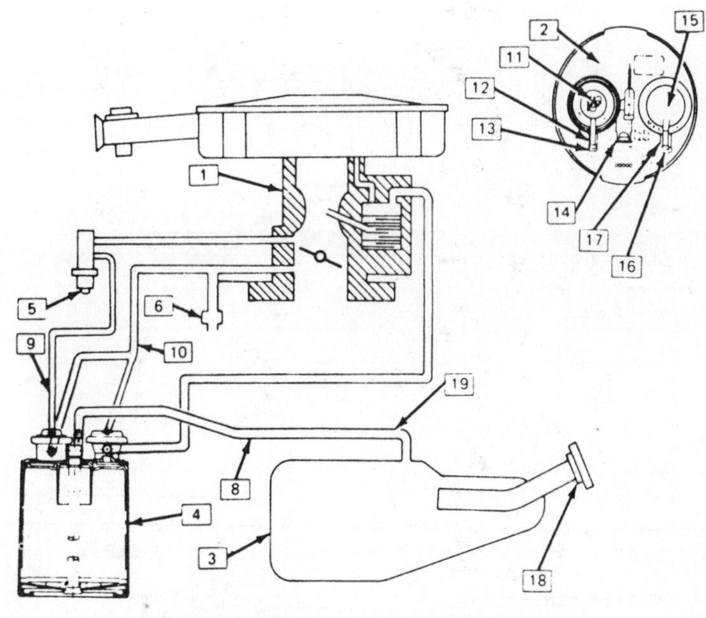

1. Carburetor	8. Fuel tank vapor line	15. Vapor vent valve
2. Top view of canister	9. Ported vacuum line	16. Vapor from carburetor tube
3. Fuel tank	10. Fuel vapor purge line	17. Control vacuum tube (manifold vac)
4. Canister	11. Canister purge valve	18. Sealed fuel tank cap
5. TVS	12. Control vacuum tube (ported vac)	19. Fuel tank vapor line restriction
6. PVC	13. Purge tube (PCV)	
7. Carburetor bowl vent line	14. Canister vent	

Vacuum hose routing for the 2.0L and 2.8L carbureted engines

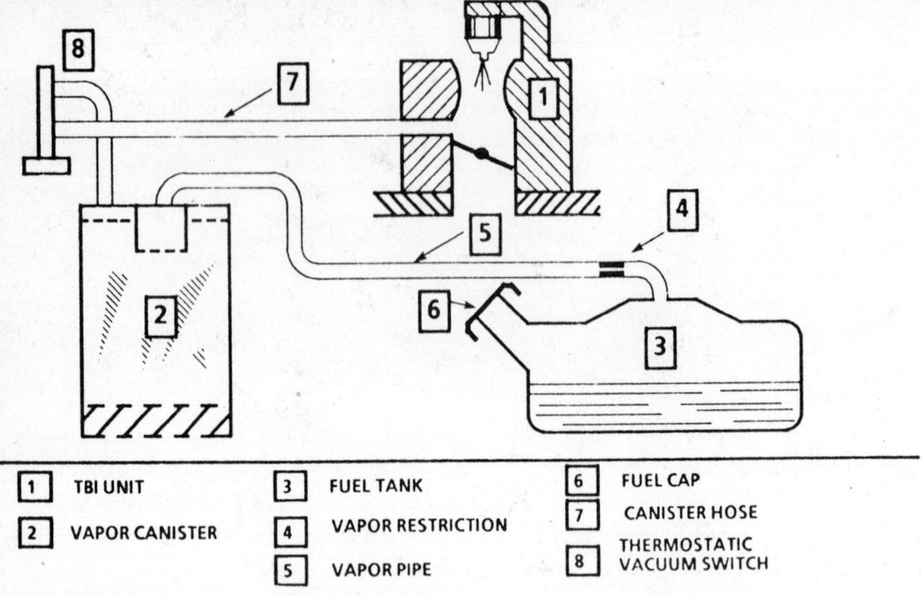

1	TBI UNIT	3	FUEL TANK	6	FUEL CAP
2	VAPOR CANISTER	4	VAPOR RESTRICTION	7	CANISTER HOSE
		5	VAPOR PIPE	8	THERMOSTATIC VACUUM SWITCH

Vacuum hose routing for the 2.8L TBI engine

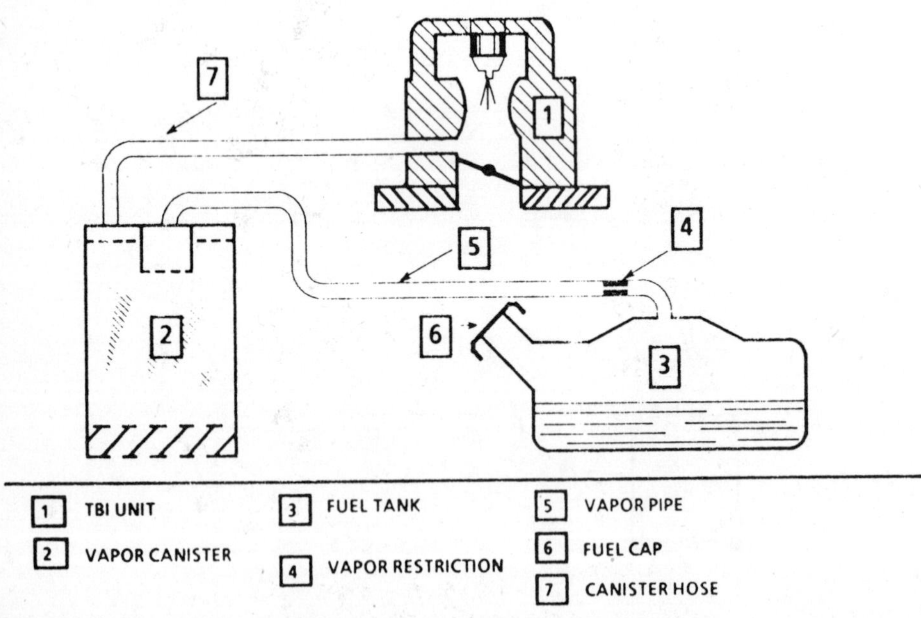

1	TBI UNIT	3	FUEL TANK	5	VAPOR PIPE
2	VAPOR CANISTER	4	VAPOR RESTRICTION	6	FUEL CAP
				7	CANISTER HOSE

Vacuum hose routing for the 2.5L and 4.3L TBI engines

CARBURETED FUEL SYSTEM

Mechanical Fuel Pump

All engine use a mechanical fuel pump, driven off the camshaft and located on the engine block.

REMOVAL AND INSTALLATION

1.9L and 2.0L Engines

The fuel pump is located near the front right side of the engine.

1. Disconnect the negative battery terminal from the battery.
2. Remove the distributor.
3. Disconnect the fuel hoses from the fuel pump.
4. Remove the engine lifting hook.
5. Remove the fuel pump-to-engine bolts and the fuel pump, then discard the gasket.

NOTE: *Before installing the fuel pump, rotate the crankshaft so the cam lobe is on the down stroke.*

6. To install, use a new gasket, RTV sealant and reverse the removal procedures. Torque the fuel pump-to-engine bolts to 15 ft. lbs. Check and/or adjust the timing.

2.8L Engine

The fuel pump is located near the front left side of the engine.

1. Disconnect the negative battery terminal from the battery.
2. Disconnect the fuel hoses the from pump.
3. Remove the fuel pump-to-engine bolts and the fuel pump from the engine, then discard the gasket.

NOTE: *Before installing the fuel pump, rotate the crankshaft so the cam lobe is on the down stroke.*

4. To install, use a new gasket, RTV sealant and reverse the removal procedures. Torque the fuel pump-to-engine bolts to 15 ft. lbs.

TESTING

To determine if the pump is in good condition, tests for both volume and pressure should be performed. The tests are made with the pump installed, and the engine at normal operating temperature and idle speed. Never replace a fuel pump without first performing these simple tests.

Be sure the fuel filter has been changed at

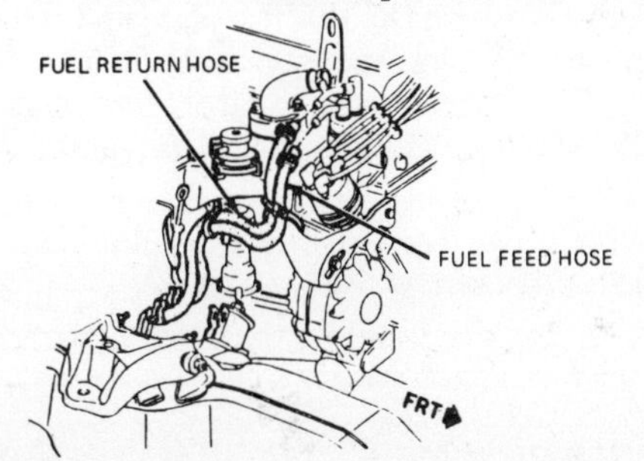

Mechanical fuel pump and hoses — 1.9L and 2.0L engines

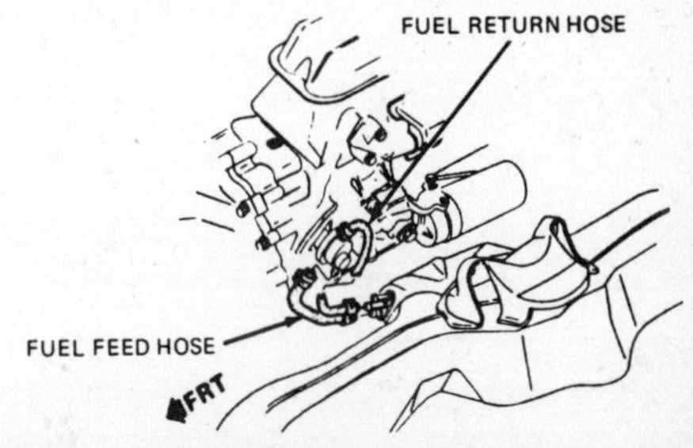

Mechanical fuel pump — 2.8L engine

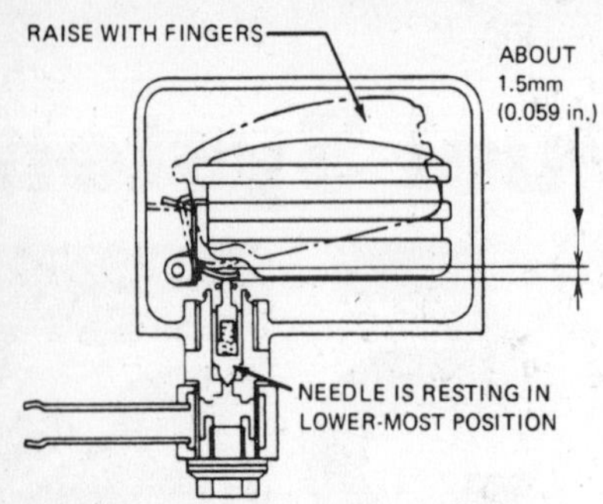

Adjusting the float level — 1.9L engine

the specified interval. If in doubt, install a new filter first.

Pressure Test

1. Disconnect the fuel line from the carburetor and connect a fuel pump pressure gauge.

2. Start the engine and check the pressure with the engine at idle. If the pump has a vapor return hose, squeeze it off so an accurate reading can be obtained. Pressure should not be below 4.5 psi.

3. If the pressure is incorrect, replace the pump. It if is OK, perform the volume test.

Volume Test

1. Disconnect the fuel line from the carburetor and connect a fuel pump pressure gauge.

2. Place the fuel line into a graduated container.

3. Run the engine at idle until one pint of gasoline has been pumped. One pint should be delivered in 30 seconds or less. There is normally enough fuel in the carburetor float bowl to perform this test, but refill it, if necessary.

4. If the delivery rate is below the minimum, check the lines for restrictions or leaks, then replace the pump.

Carburetor

ADJUSTMENTS

NOTE: *Refer to the "Idle Speed and Mixture Adjustment" procedures in Chapter 2 and adjust the idle speed and fuel mixture.*

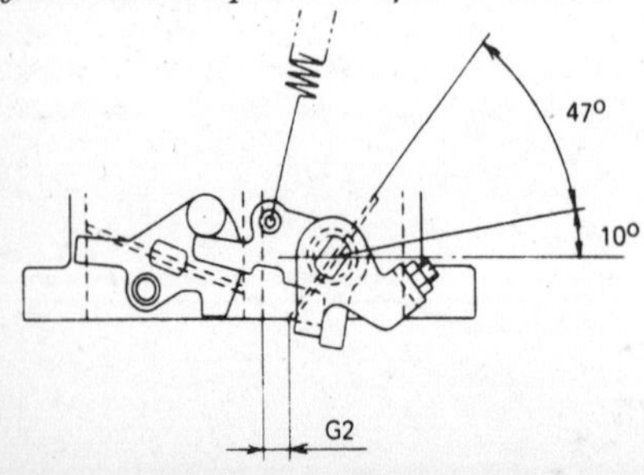

Adjusting the throttle linkage — 1.9L engine

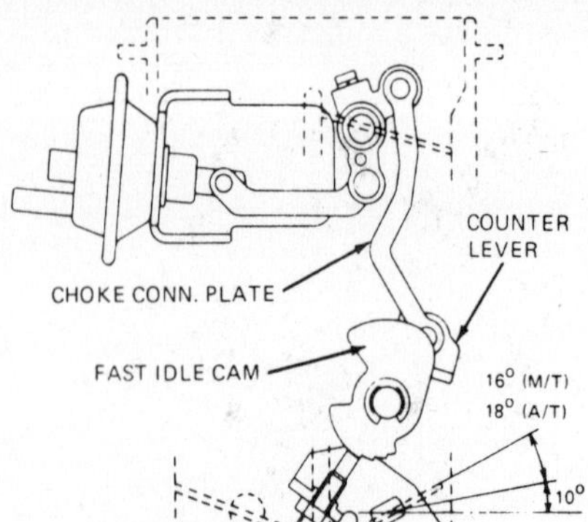

Adjusting the primary throttle valve — 1.9L engine

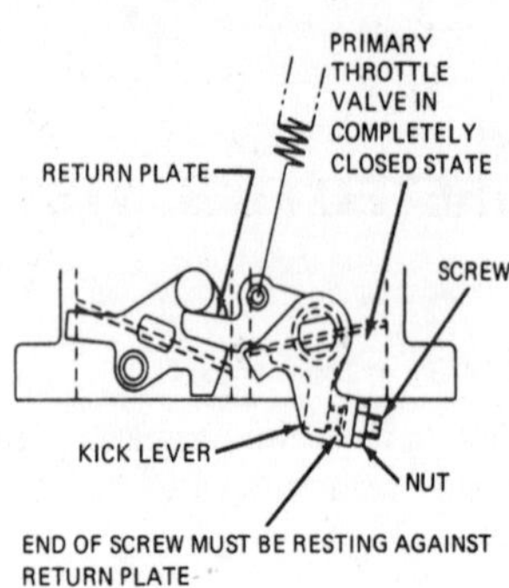

Adjusting the kickdown lever — 1.9L engine

1.9L Engine

FLOAT LEVEL

The fuel level is normal if it is seen to be within the mark on the float bowl window. If not, Remove the top of the carburetor and bend the float seat to regulate the level.

PRIMARY THROTTLE VALVE

When the choke plate is completely closed, the primary throttle valve should be opened by the fast idle screw to an angle of 16 degrees for manual transmission or 18 degrees for automatic transmission. To check this adjustment, perform the following procedures:

1. Close the choke plate completely, then measure between the throttle plate and the air horn wall; the clearance should be 0.050–0.059 in. (1.27–1.49mm) for manual transmission or 0.059–0.069 in. (1.49–1.75mm) for automatic transmission.

NOTE: *The measurement should be made at the center point of the choke plate.*

2. If necessary, adjust the opening by turning the fast idle screw.

THROTTLE LINKAGE

1. Turn the primary throttle valve plate until the adjustment plate is in contact with

the kickdown lever. This is a primary throttle plate opening of about 47 degrees.

2. Measure the clearance between the center point of the primary throttle plate and the air horn wall; the clearance should be 0.24–0.30 in. (6.1–7.6mm), if not, bend the kickdown lever tab.

KICKDOWN LEVER ADJUSTMENT

1. Turn the primary throttle lever until the plate is completely closed. Back off the throttle adjustment screw, if necessary.

2. Loosen the locknut on the kickdown lever screw and turn the screw until it just contacts the return plate, then tighten the locknut.

2.0L and 2.8L Engines

FLOAT LEVEL

1. With the engine Cold, remove the top of the carburetor.

2. While holding a finger lightly but firmly, on the float retainer, press down lightly on the float tab to seat the needle valve.

3. Measure the distance between the float bowl gasket surface and the point on the float farthest from the needle valve.

4. If the measurement is not correct, remove the float and bend the tab.

PUMP

1. With the throttle plate in the Closed position and the fast idle screw off the steps of the fast idle cam, measure the distance from the air horn casting to the top of the pump stem.

2. To adjust, remove the retaining screw, the washer and the pump lever. Bend the end of the lever to correct the stem height. Do not twist the lever or bend it sideways.

3. Install the lever, washer and screw, then check the adjustment. When correct, open and close the throttle a few times to check the linkage movement and alignment.

FAST IDLE

1. Set the ignition timing and curb idle speed, then disconnect and plug the hoses as directed on the emission control decal.

2. Position the fast idle screw on the highest step of the fast idle cam.

3. Start the engine and adjust the engine speed to specification with the fast idle screw.

CHOKE COIL LEVER

NOTE: *The following procedure requires the use of the Choke Valve Angle Gauge tool J-26701 or BT-7704 or equivalent.*

1. Remove the 3 retaining screws, the choke cover and coil. On models with a riveted choke cover, drill out the 3 rivets, then remove the cover and the choke coil.

NOTE: *A choke stat cover retainer kit is required for reassembly.*

2. Place the fast idle screw on the high step of the fast idle cam.

3. Close the choke plate by pushing in on the intermediate choke lever.

4. Insert a drill or plug gauge, of the specified size, into the hole in the choke housing. The choke lever in the housing should be up against the side of the gauge.

5. If the lever does not just touch the gauge, bend the intermediate choke rod to adjust.

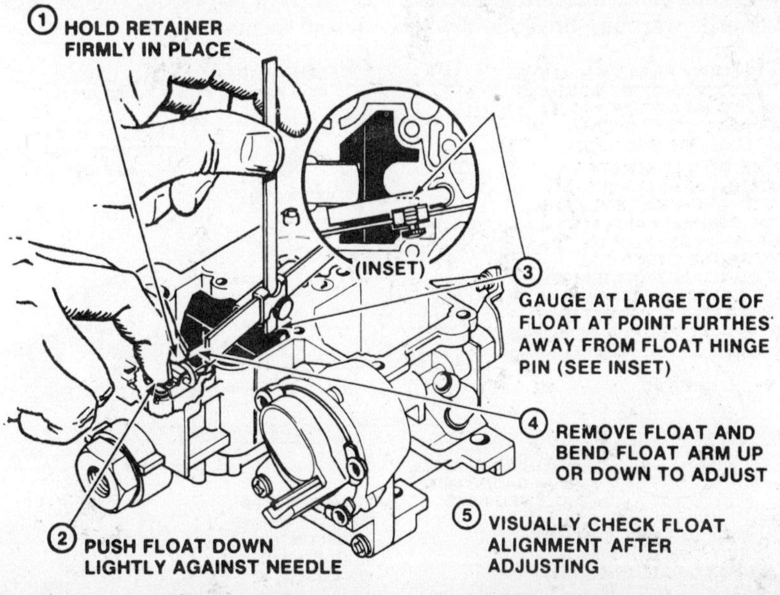

Adjusting the float level — 2.0L and 2.8L engines

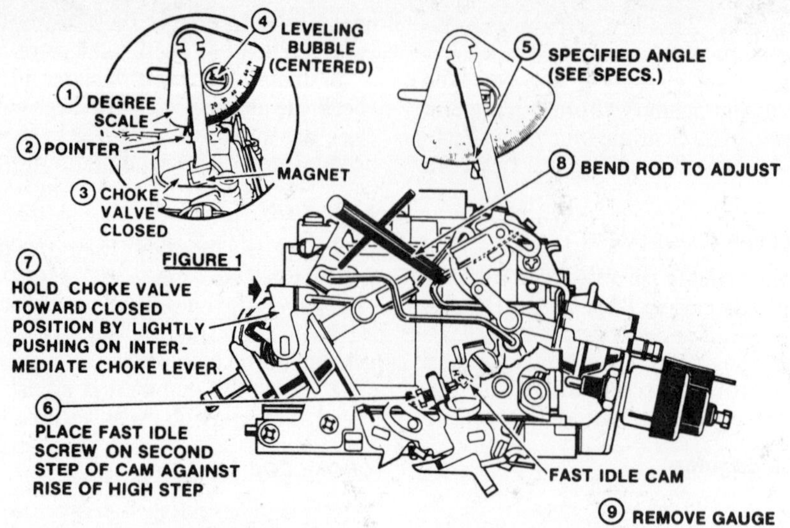

Adjusting the choke rod — 2.0L and 2.8L engines

FAST IDLE CAM (CHOKE ROD)

NOTE: *The following procedure requires the use of the Choke Valve Angle Gauge tool J-26701 or BT-7704 or equivalent.*

1. First, adjust the choke coil lever and fast idle speed.
2. Rotate the degree scale until it is zeroed.
3. Close the choke and install the degree scale onto the choke plate. Center the leveling bubble.
4. Rotate the scale so the specified degree is opposite the scale pointer.
5. Place the fast idle screw on the second step of the cam (against the high step). Close the choke by pushing in the intermediate lever.
6. Push on the vacuum break lever, to

Open the choke, until the lever is against the rear tang on the choke lever.
7. Bend the fast idle cam rod at the U to adjust the angle to specifications.

AIR VALVE ROD

NOTE: *The following procedure requires the use of the Choke Valve Angle Gauge tool J-26701 or BT-7704 or equivalent.*

1. Align the 0 degree mark with the pointer on an angle gauge.
2. Close the air valve and place a magnet on top of it.
3. Rotate the bubble until it is centered.
4. Rotate the degree scale until the specified degree mark is aligned with the pointer.
5. Seat the vacuum diaphragm using an external vacuum source.

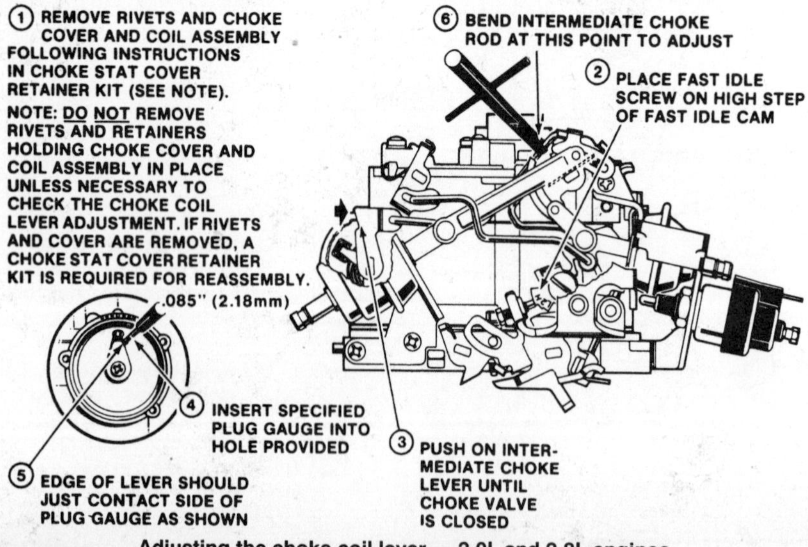

Adjusting the choke coil lever — 2.0L and 2.8L engines

6. On 4 cylinder models plug the end cover. Unplug after adjustment.

7. Apply a light pressure to the air valve shaft in the direction to open the air valve until all the slack is removed between the air link and plunger slot.

8. Bend the air valve link until the bubble is centered.

PRIMARY SIDE VACUUM BREAK

NOTE: *The following procedure requires the use of the Choke Valve Angle Gauge tool J-26701 or BT-7704 or equivalent.*

1. Rotate the degree scale on the measuring gauge until the 0 degree is opposite the pointer.

NOTE: *Prior to adjustment, remove the vacuum break from the carburetor. Place the bracket in a vise and using the proper safety precautions, grind off the adjustment screw cap then reinstall the vacuum break.*

2. Seat the choke vacuum diaphragm by applying an external vacuum source of over 5 in. Hg vacuum to the vacuum break.

NOTE: *If the air valve rod is restricting the vacuum diaphragm from seating, it may be necessary to bend the air valve rod slightly to gain clearance. Make the air valve rod adjustment after the vacuum break adjustment.*

3. Read the angle gauge while lightly pushing on the intermediate choke lever so the choke valve is toward the Closed position.

4. Using an $1/8$ in. hex wrench, turn the screw in the rear cover until the bubble is centered. Apply a silicone sealant over the screw head to seal the setting.

ELECTRIC CHOKE

This procedure is only for those carburetors with choke covers retained by screws. Riveted choke covers are preset and nonadjustable.

1. Loosen the 3 retaining screws.

2. Place the fast idle screw on the high step of the cam.

3. Rotate the choke cover to align the cover

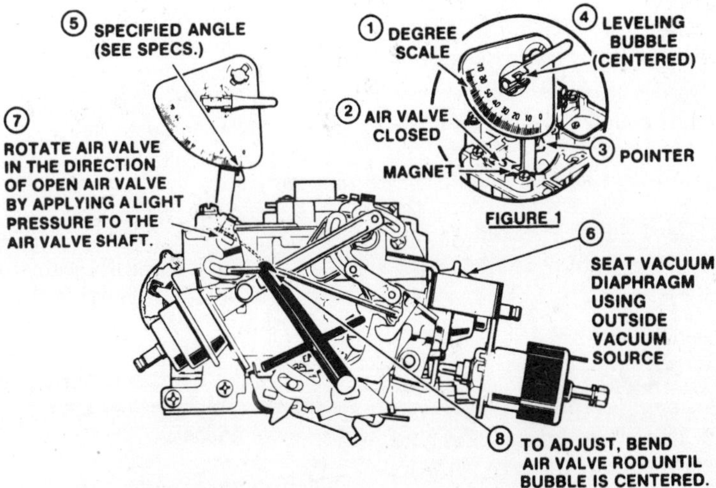

Adjusting the air valve rod — 2.0L and 2.8L engines

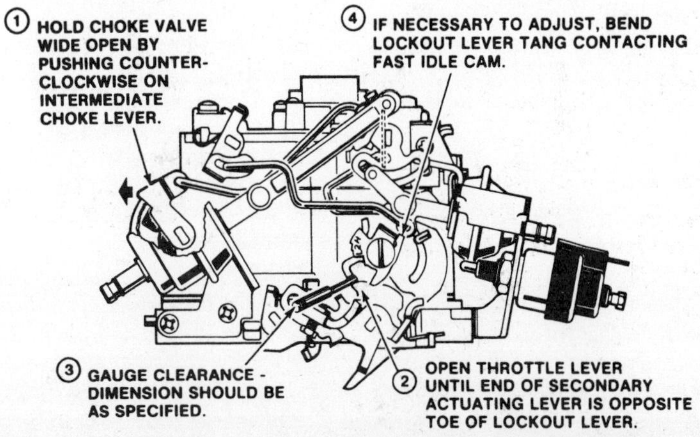

Adjusting the secondary lockout — 1.9L engine

mark with the specified housing mark.

SECONDARY VACUUM BREAK

NOTE: *The following procedure requires the use of the Choke Valve Angle Gauge tool J-26701, BT-7704 or equivalent.*

1. Rotate the degree scale on the measuring gauge until the 0 degree is opposite the pointer.

NOTE: *Prior to adjustment, remove the vacuum break from the carburetor. Place the bracket in the vise and using the proper safety precautions, grind off the adjustment screw cap then reinstall the vacuum break. Plug the end cover using an accelerator pump plunger cup or equivalent. Remove the cup after the adjustment.*

2. Seat the choke vacuum diaphragm by applying an external vacuum source of over 5 in. Hg vacuum to the vacuum break.

NOTE: *If the air valve rod is restricting the vacuum diaphragm from seating it may be necessary to bend the air valve rod slightly to gain clearance. Make an air valve rod adjustment after the vacuum break adjustment.*

3. Read the angle gauge while lightly pushing on the intermediate choke lever so the choke valve is toward the Closed position.

4. Using an $1/8$ in. hex wrench, turn the screw in the rear cover until the bubble is centered. Apply silicone sealant over the screw head to seal the setting.

CHOKE UNLOADER

1. Follow Steps 1–4 of the Fast Idle Cam Adjustment.

2. If removed, install the choke cover and the coil, then align the housing marks with the cover marks, as specified.

3. Hold the primary throttle valve Wide Open.

4. If the engine is Warm, push inward on the intermediate choke lever to close the choke valve.

5. Bend the unloader tang until the bubble is centered.

SECONDARY LOCKOUT

1. Place the choke in the Wide Open position by pushing outward on the intermediate choke lever.

2. Open the throttle valve until the end of the secondary actuating lever is opposite the toe of the lockout lever.

3. Gauge the clearance between the lockout lever and secondary lever, as specified.

4. To adjust, bend the lockout lever where it contacts the fast idle cam.

REMOVAL AND INSTALLATION

1.9L Engine

1. Remove the PCV valve from the rocker arm cover.

2. Disconnect the ECS hose from the air cleaner.

3. Disconnect the AIR hose from the pump.

4. On California models, disconnect the air hose from the slow carburetor.

5. Unbolt the air cleaner, lift it slightly, disconnect the hoses and remove the unit.

6. Disconnect the rubber piping from the TVS switch.

7. Disconnect the vacuum advance hose, if equipped, from the distributor.

8. If equipped with an automatic transmission, disconnect the vacuum hose from the converter housing.

9. On California models, disconnect the vacuum hoses from the slow and main actuator.

10. Disconnect the carburetor solenoid lead wire, the accelerator control cable and the cruise control cable.

11. On automatic transmission models, disconnect the control cable.

12. Disconnect the fuel line(s) from the carburetor.

13. Disconnect the ECS hose from the carburetor.

14. Remove the carburetor-to-intake manifold bolts and the carburetor; discard the mounting gasket.

15. To install, reverse the removal procedures. Make sure all of the linkage is properly adjusted and operates smoothly. Check that there are no leaks.

2.0L Engine

1. Remove the air cleaner and the gasket.

2. Disconnect the fuel pipe and all of the vacuum lines.

3. Label and disconnect all of the electrical connections.

4. Disconnect the downshift cable.

5. If equipped with cruise control, disconnect the linkage.

6. Remove the carburetor-to-intake manifold bolts and the carburetor, then discard the mounting gasket.

NOTE: *Before installing the carburetor, fill the float bowl with gasoline to reduce the battery strain and the possibility of backfiring when the engine is started again.*

7. Inspect the EFE heater for damage. Using a putty knife, clean the gasket mounting surfaces. Be sure the throttle body and EFE mating surfaces are clean.

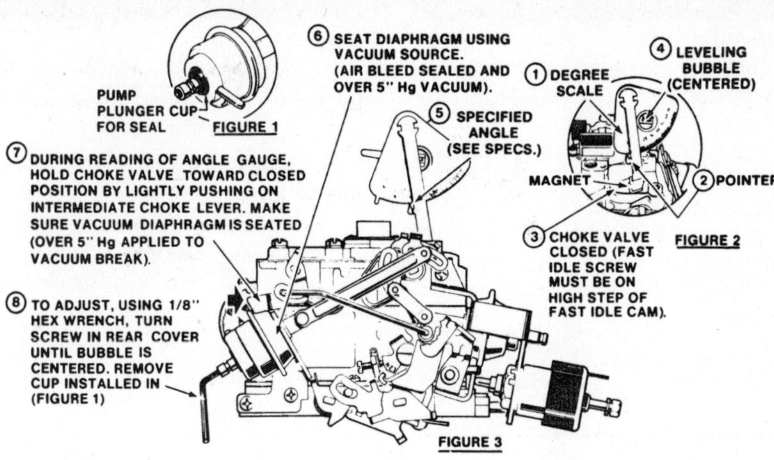

Adjusting the secondary vacuum break — 2.0L and 2.8L engines

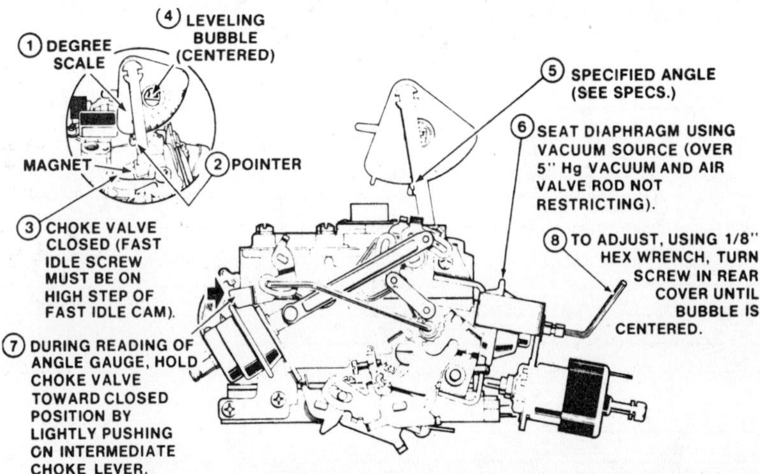

Adjusting the primary vacuum break — 2.0L and 2.8L engines

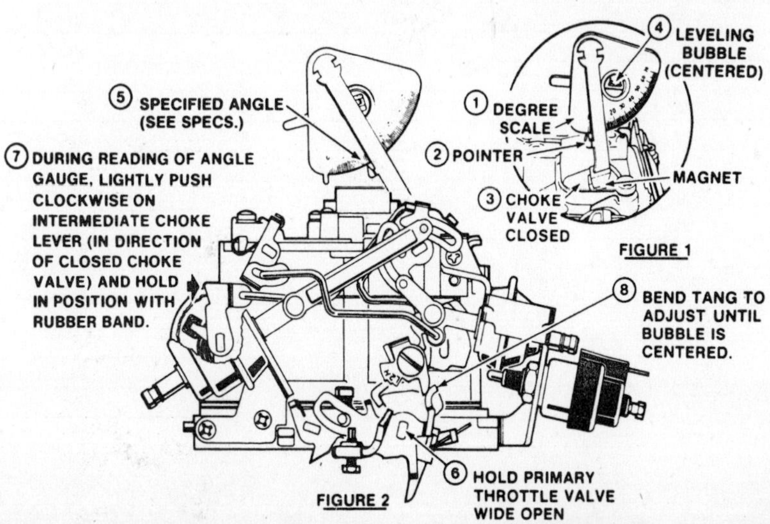

Adjusting the choke unloader — 2.0L and 2.8L engines

8. To install, use a new gasket and the carburetor; tighten the nuts alternately.

9. To complete the installation, reverse the removal procedures.

2.8L Engine

1. Remove the air cleaner.

2. Disconnect the fuel and vacuum lines from the carburetor.

3. Disconnect all of the electrical connectors from the carburetor.

4. Disconnect all of the linkage from the carburetor.

5. Remove the carburetor-to-intake manifold nuts or bolts and the carburetor from the vehicle; discard the gasket.

6. Using a putty knife, clean the gasket mounting surfaces.

7. To install, use a new gasket and reverse the removal procedures. Check that the linkage works smoothly and is properly adjusted. Make sure there are no leaks.

CARBURETOR SPECIFICATIONS

Type 2SE 6-2.8L (Code B) (excluding California)

Carb. Number	Float Level (in.)	Fast Idle Cam. (deg.)	Primary Vacuum Break (deg.)	Air Valve Rod (deg.)	Secondary Vacuum Break (deg.)	Choke Unloader (deg.)
17082348	$7/16$	22	26	1	32	40
17082349	$7/16$	22	28	1	32	40
17082350	$7/16$	22	26	1	32	40
17082351	$7/16$	22	28	1	32	40
17082353	$7/16$	22	28	1	35	30
17082355	$7/16$	22	28	1	35	30
17083348	$7/16$	22	30	1	32	40
17083349	$7/16$	22	30	1	32	40
17083350	$7/16$	22	30	1	32	40
17083351	$7/16$	22	30	1	32	40
17083352	$7/16$	22	30	1	35	40
17083353	$7/16$	22	30	1	35	40
17083354	$7/16$	22	30	1	35	40
17083355	$7/16$	22	30	1	35	40
17083360	$7/16$	22	30	1	32	40
17083361	$7/16$	22	28	1	32	40
17083362	$7/16$	22	30	1	32	40
17083363	$7/16$	22	28	1	32	40
17083364	$7/16$	22	30	1	35	40
17083365	$7/16$	22	30	1	35	40
17083366	$7/16$	22	30	1	35	40
17083367	$7/16$	22	30	1	35	40
17083390	$13/32$	28	30	1	35	38
17083391	$13/32$	28	30	1	35	38
17083392	$13/32$	28	30	1	35	38
17083393	$13/32$	28	30	1	35	38
17083394	$13/32$	28	30	1	35	38
17083395	$13/32$	28	30	1	35	38
17083396	$13/32$	28	30	1	35	38
17083397	$13/32$	28	30	1	35	38
17084410	$11/32$	15	23	1	38	42
17084412	$11/32$	15	23	1	38	42
17084425	$11/32$	15	26	1	36	40
17084427	$11/32$	15	26	1	36	40
17084560	$11/32$	15	24	1	34	38
17084562	$11/32$	15	24	1	34	38
17084569	$11/32$	15	24	1	34	38

CARBURETOR SPECIFICATIONS
Type DCH340 4-1.9L Engine

Primary Throttle Plate Gap (in.)	Primary Main Jet Number	Secondary Main Jet Number	Primary Slow Jet Number	Secondary Slow Jet Number	Power Jet Number	Primary Main Air Bleed Number	Secondary Main Air Bleed Number	Slow Air Bleed Number
.050–.059 (MT)	114 Fed.	170	50 Fed.	100	50	120 Fed.	70 Fed.	150 Fed.
.059–.069 (AT)	85 Cal.		54 Cal.			110 Cal.	90 Cal.	130 Cal.

Type E2SE 6-2.8L (Code B) (California)

Carb. Number	Float Level (in.)	Fast Idle Cam. (deg.)	Primary Vacuum Break (deg.)	Air Valve Rod (deg.)	Secondary Vacuum Break (deg.)	Choke Unloader (deg.)
17082356	13/32	22	25	1	30	30
17082357	13/32	22	25	1	32	30
17082358	13/32	22	25	1	30	30
17082359	13/32	22	25	1	32	30
17072683	9/32	28	25	1	35	45
17074812	9/32	28	25	1	35	45
17084356	9/32	22	25	1	30	30
17084357	9/32	22	25	1	30	30
17084358	9/32	22	25	1	30	30
17084359	9/32	22	25	1	30	30
17084368	1/8	22	25	1	30	30
17084370	1/8	22	25	1	30	30
17084430	11/32	15	26	1	38	42
17084431	11/32	15	26	1	38	42
17084434	11/32	15	26	1	38	42
17084435	11/32	15	26	1	38	42
17084452	5/32	28	25	1	35	45
17084453	5/32	28	25	1	35	45
17084455	5/32	28	25	1	35	45
17084456	5/32	28	25	1	35	45
17084458	5/32	28	25	1	35	45
17084532	5/32	28	25	1	35	45
17084534	5/32	28	25	1	35	45
17084535	5/32	28	25	1	35	45
17084537	5/32	28	25	1	35	45
17084538	5/32	28	25	1	35	45
17084540	5/32	28	25	1	35	45
17084542	1/8	28	25	1	35	45
17084632	9/32	28	25	1	35	45
17084633	9/32	28	25	1	35	45
17084635	9/32	28	25	1	35	45
17084636	9/32	28	25	1	35	45

GASOLINE FUEL INJECTION SYSTEM

NOTE: *This book contains simple testing and service procedures for your vehicle's fuel injection system.*

Electric Fuel Pump

The electric fuel pump is attached to the fuel sending unit, located in the fuel tank.

REMOVAL AND INSTALLATION

NOTE: *The following procedure requires the use of the GM Fuel Gauge Sending Unit Retaining Cam tool J-24187 or equivalent, a brass drift and a hammer.*

1. If the 2.8L TBI or 4.3L TBI engine has been in use, turn the ignition switch Off and allow the system time to reduce the fuel pressure.

2. To relieve the fuel pressure on the 2.5L

TBI engine, perform the following procedures:

a. From the fuse block, located in the passenger compartment, remove the fuel pump fuse.

b. Start the engine and allow it to Run until the fuel, in the system is used up.

c. After the engine stops, crank the engine a few times to make sure all of the fuel is removed from the system.

3. Disconnect the negative battery terminal from the battery.

NOTE: *Be sure to keep a Class B (dry chemical) fire extinguisher nearby.*

CAUTION: *Due to the possibility of fire or explosion, never drain or store gasoline in an open container.*

4. Using a hand pump or a siphon hose, drain the gasoline into an approved container.

5. Raise and support the vehicle on jackstands.

6. Support the fuel tank and remove the fuel tank-to-vehicle straps.

7. Lower the tank slightly, then remove the sender unit wires, the hoses and the ground strap.

8. Remove the fuel tank from the vehicle.

9. Using the GM Fuel Gauge Sending Unit Retaining Cam tool J-24187 (or equivalent) or a brass drift and a hammer, remove the cam locking ring (fuel sending unit) counterclockwise, then lift the sending unit from the fuel tank.

10. Remove the fuel pump from the fuel sending unit, by performing the following procedures:

a. Pull the fuel pump up into the mounting tube, while pulling outward (away) from the bottom support.

NOTE: *When removing the fuel pump from the sending unit, be careful not to damage the rubber insulator and the strainer.*

b. When the pump assembly is clear of the bottom support, pull it out of the rubber connector.

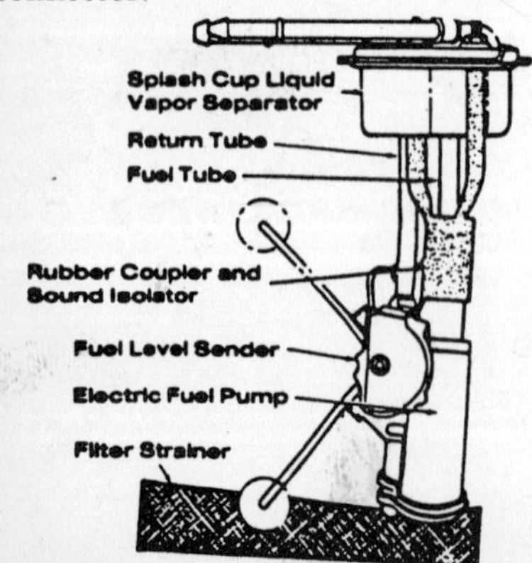

TBI fuel pump and fuel gauge sender assembly

11. Inspect the fuel pump hose and bottom sound insulator for signs of deterioration, then replace it, if necessary.

12. Push the fuel pump onto sending tube.

13. Using a new sending unit-to-fuel tank O-ring, install the sending unit into the fuel tank.

NOTE: *When installing the sending unit, be careful not to fold or twist the fuel strainer, for it will restrict the fuel flow.*

14. Using the GM Fuel Gauge Sending Unit Retaining Cam tool J-24187 (or equivalent) or a brass drift and a hammer, turn the sending unit-to-fuel tank locking ring clockwise.

15. To install the fuel tank, align the insulator strips and reverse the removal procedures. Torque the inner fuel tank strap-to-vehicle bolts to 26 ft. lbs. and the outer fuel tank strap-to-vehicle nuts/bolts to 26 ft. lbs.

TESTING AND ADJUSTMENTS

Flow Test

1. Remove the fuel pump-to-throttle body line from the throttle body.

2. Place the fuel line in a clean container.

3. Turn the ignition switch On; approximately 1/2 pint of the fuel should be delivered in 15 seconds.

4. If the fuel flow is below minimum, inspect the fuel system for restrictions; if no restrictions are found, replace the fuel pump.

Pressure Test

NOTE: *The following procedure requires the use of a GM Fuel Pressure Gauge tool J-29658-A or equivalent.*

1. If equipped with an EFI equipped engine, refer to the "Fuel Pressure Relief" procedures in this Chapter and relieve the fuel pressure.

2. Remove the air cleaner, then disconnect and plug the THERMAC vacuum port on the throttle body unit.

3. Place a rag (to catch excess fuel) under the fuel line-to-throttle body connection. Disconnect the fuel line from the throttle body.

NOTE: *When disconnecting the fuel line, use a back-up wrench to hold the fuel nut on the throttle body.*

4. Using a GM Fuel Pressure Gauge tool J-29658-A or equivalent, install it into the fuel line.

5. Start the engine and observe the fuel pressure, it should be 9–13 psi.

NOTE: *If the fuel pressure does not meet specifications, inspect the fuel system for restrictions or replace the fuel pump.*

6. Turn the engine **OFF**, relieve the fuel pressure and remove the GM Fuel Pressure Gauge tool J-29658-A or equivalent.

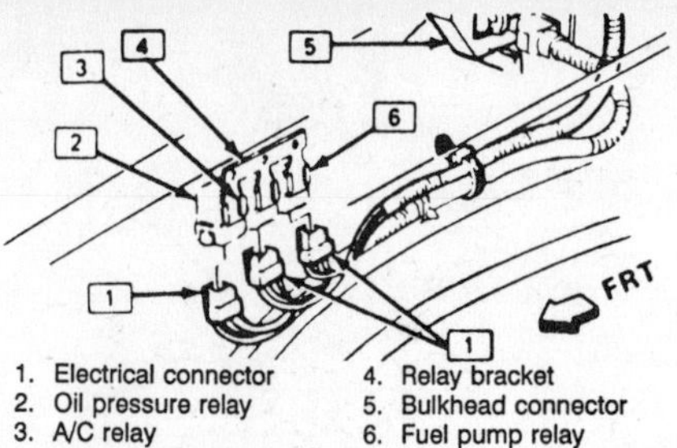

1. Electrical connector
2. Oil pressure relay
3. A/C relay
4. Relay bracket
5. Bulkhead connector
6. Fuel pump relay

View of the fuel pump relay — all 1983–90 TBI engines

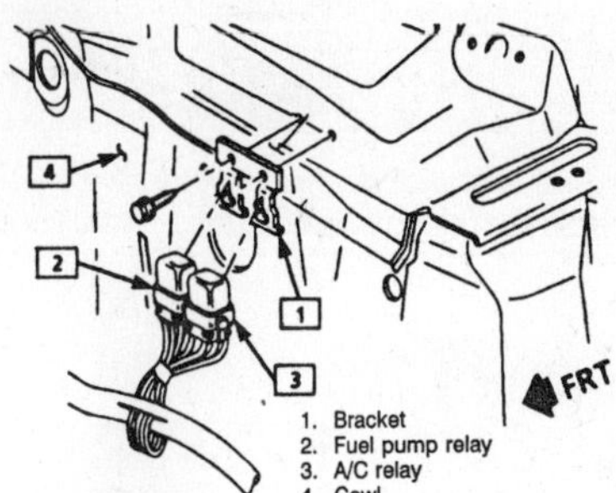

1. Bracket
2. Fuel pump relay
3. A/C relay
4. Cowl

View of the fuel pump relay — 4.3L TBI engine for 1991

7. Install a new fuel line-to-throttle body O-ring and reverse the removal procedures. Unplug from the THERMAC vacuum port. Start the engine and check for fuel leaks.

Fuel Pump Relay

The fuel pump relay is mounted on the left-front fender in the engine compartment. Check for loose electrical connections; no other service is possible, except replacement.

REMOVAL AND INSTALLATION

1. Disconnect the negative battery terminal from the battery.
2. Disconnect the relay/electrical connector assembly from the bracket.
3. Pull the fuel pump relay from the electrical connector.
4. If necessary, use a new fuel pump and reverse the removal procedures.

FUEL PRESSURE RELIEF

2.5L TBI Engine

1. From the fuse block, located in the passenger compartment, remove the fuse labeled, Fuel Pump.
2. Start the engine.
NOTE: *The engine will start and run, for a short period of time, until the remaining fuel is used up.*
3. Engage the starter, a few more times, to relieve any remaining pressure.
4. Turn the ignition switch **OFF** and install the Fuel Pump fuse into the fuse block.

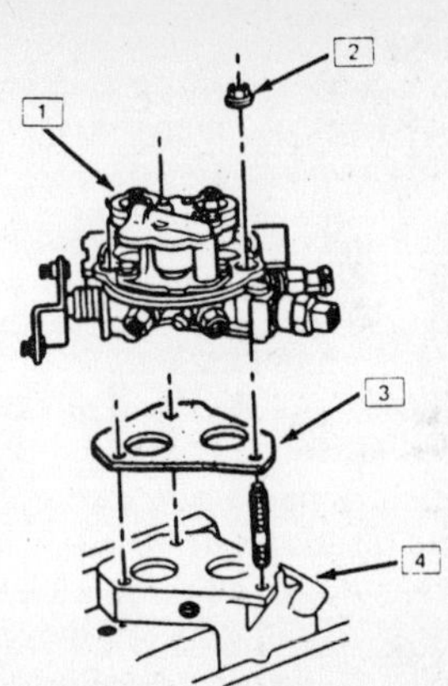

1. TBI unit
2. Nut-tighten to 25 N·m (18 ft. lbs.)
3. Gasket
4. Engine inlet manifold

Removing the model 220 TBI unit — 2.8L and 4.3L engine

2.8L TBI and 4.3L Engines

1. Disconnect the negative battery cable.
2. Loosen the fuel tank filler cap to relieve the fuel pressure.
3. Allow the engine to set for 5–10 minutes; this will allow the orifice (in the fuel system) to bleed off the pressure.

Throttle Body

The Model 300 throttle body, used on the 2.5L engine for 1985–86, is a single barrel, single injector type. The Model 700 throttle body, used on the 2.5L engine for 1987–88, is a single barrel, single injector type. The Model 220 throttle body, used on the 2.8L engine (1986–89) and the 4.3L engine for 1988–91, is a dual barrel, twin injector type. The operation of both types are basically the same.

Both throttle bodies are constantly monitored by the ECM to produce a 14.7:1 air/fuel ratio, which is vital to the catalytic converter operation.

REMOVAL AND INSTALLATION

1. Relief the fuel pressure in the fuel system.
2. Remove the air cleaner. Disconnect the negative battery cable from the battery.
3. Disconnect the electrical connectors from the idle air control valve, the throttle position sensor and the fuel injector(s).
4. Remove the throttle return spring(s), the cruise control, if equipped, and the throttle linkage.
5. Label and disconnect the vacuum hoses from the throttle body.
6. Place a rag (to catch the excess fuel) under the fuel line-to-throttle body connection, then disconnect the fuel line from the throttle body.

7. Remove the attaching hardware, the throttle body-to-intake manifold bolts, the throttle body and the gasket.

NOTE: *Be sure to place a cloth in the intake manifold to prevent dirt from entering the engine.*

8. Using a putty knife, if necessary, clean the gasket mounting surfaces.

9. To install, use a new gasket and reverse the removal procedures. Torque the throttle body-to-intake manifold nuts/bolts to 13 ft. lbs. (18 Nm) for 2.5L and 4.3L engines or 18 ft. lbs. (25 Nm) for 2.8L engine. Depress the accelerator pedal to the floor and release it, to see if the pedal returns freely. Turn the ignition switch On and check for fuel leaks.

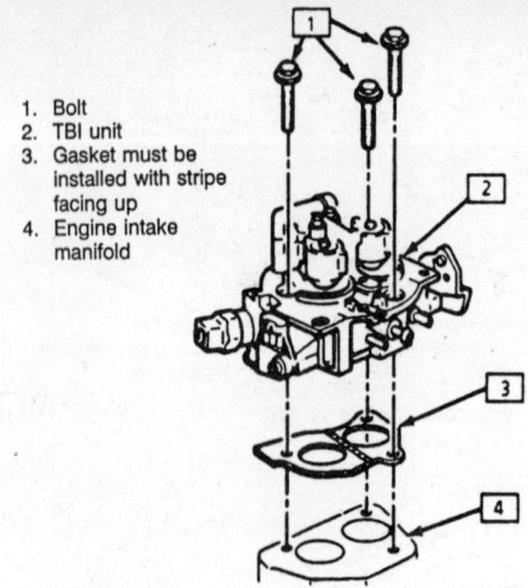

Removing the model 220 TBI unit — 4.3L TBI engine

1. Screw assembly—fuel meter cover attaching—long
2. Screw assembly—fuel meter cover attaching—short
3. Fuel meter cover assembly
4. Gasket—fuel meter cover
5. Gasket—fuel meter outlet
6. Seal—pressure regulator
7. Pressure regulator
10. Injector—fuel
11. Filter—fuel injector inlet
12. O-ring—fuel injector—lower
13. O-ring—fuel injector—upper
14. Washer—fuel injector
20. Screw assembly—fuel meter body—throttle body attaching
21. Fuel meter body assembly
22. Gasket—throttle body to fuel meter body
23. Gasket—air filter
30. O-ring—fuel return line
31. Nut—fuel outlet
37. O-ring—fuel inlet line
38. Nut—fuel inlet
40. Gasket—fuel outlet nut
41. Gasket—fuel inlet nut
50. Screw—TPS lever attaching
51. Lever—TPS
52. Screw assembly—TPS attaching
55. Retainer—TPS attachingscrew
58. Sensor—throttle position (TPS)
60. Plug—idle stop screw
61. Screw assembly—idle stop
62. Spring—idle stop screw
65. Throttle body assembly
70. Gasket—flange
75. Valve assembly—idle air control (IAC)
76. Gasket—idle air control valve assembly

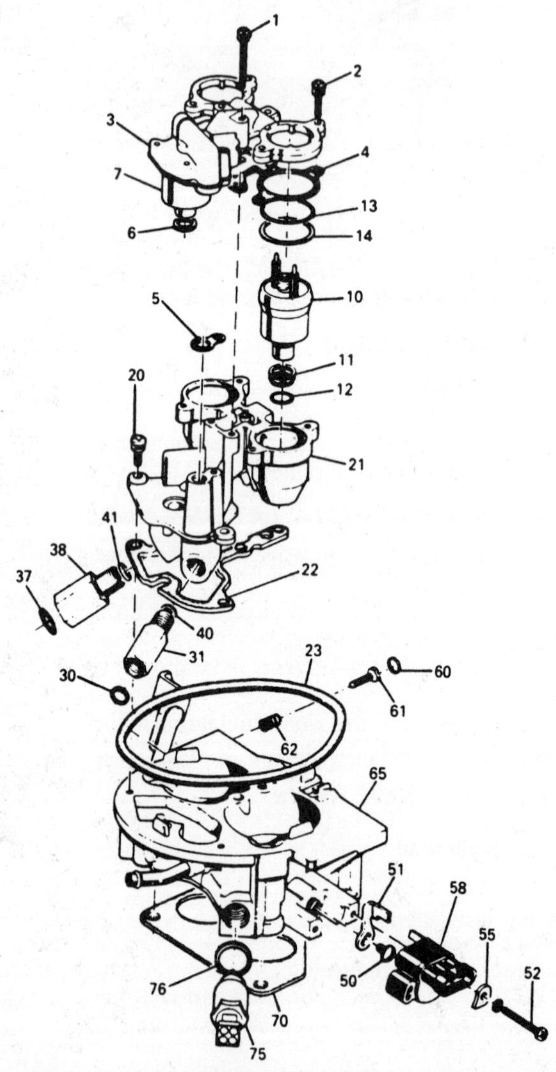

Exploded view of the model 220 TBI unit — 2.8L TBI and 4.3L engines

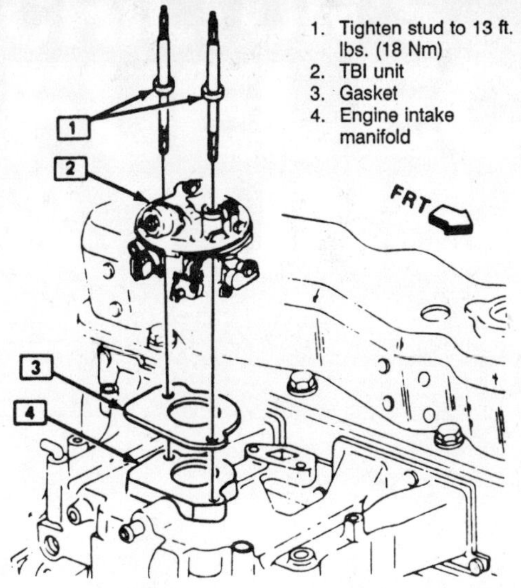

Removing the model 700 TBI unit — 2.5L TBI engine for 1987–89

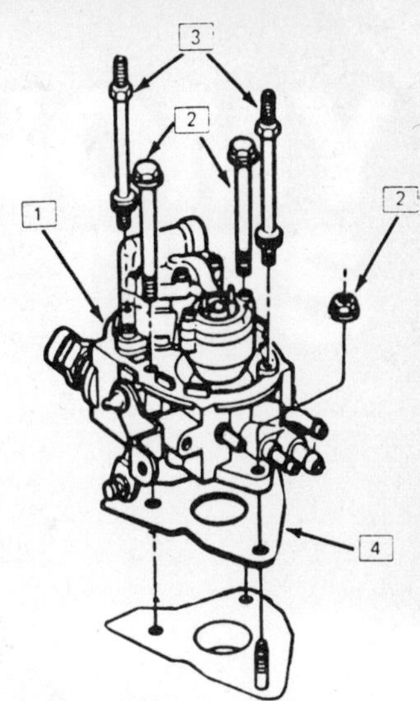

Removing the model 300 TBI unit — early 2.5L engine

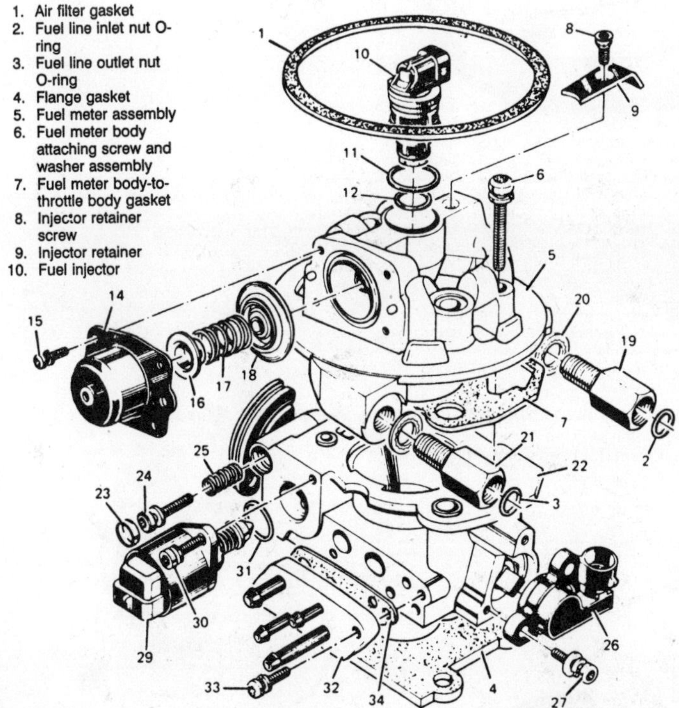

Exploded view of the model 700 TBI unit — 2.5L TBI engine for 1987–89

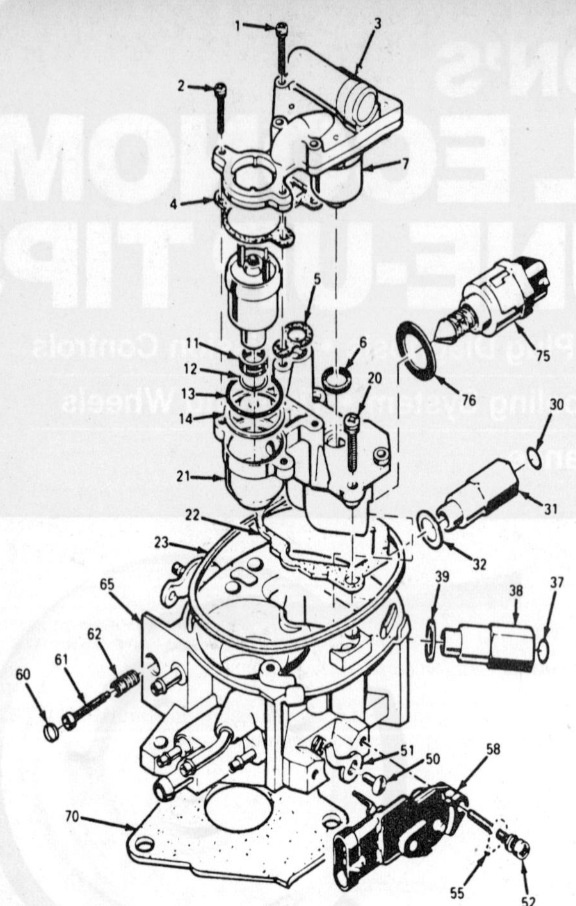

1. Screw & washer assembly	32. Gasket—fuel return nut
2. Screw & washer assembly	37. Fuel inlet line "O" ring
3. Fuel meter cover assembly	38. Nut—fuel inlet
4. Gasket—fuel meter cover	39. Gasket—fuel inlet nut
5. Gasket—fuel meter outlet	50. Screw—TPS lever attaching
6. Dust seal—pressure regulator	51. Lever—TPS
7. Pressure regulator	52. Screw & washer assembly
11. Filter—fuel injector nozzle	55. Retainer—TPS attaching screw
12. Lower "O" ring	58. Sensor—throttle position
13. Upper "O" ring	60. Plug—idle stop screw
14. Back-up washer—fuel injector	61. Screw—throttle stop
20. Screw & washer assembly	62. Spring—throttle stop screw
21. Fuel meter body assembly	65. Throttle body assembly
22. Gasket—fuel meter body	70. Gasket—flange mounting
23. Gasket—air filter	75. Idle air control assembly
30. Fuel return line "O" ring	76. Gasket—IAC to throttle body
31. Nut—fuel return	

Exploded view of the model 300 TBI unit — early 2.5L engines

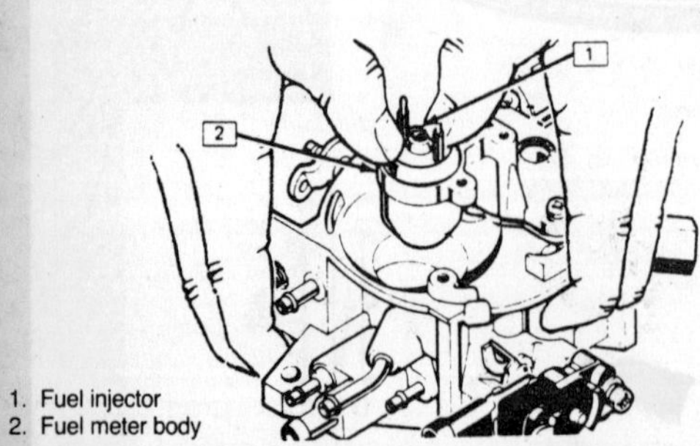

1. Fuel injector
2. Fuel meter body

Installing the Model 300 fuel injector — 2.5L TBI engine for 1985–86 — 2.8L and 4.3L TBI engines are similar

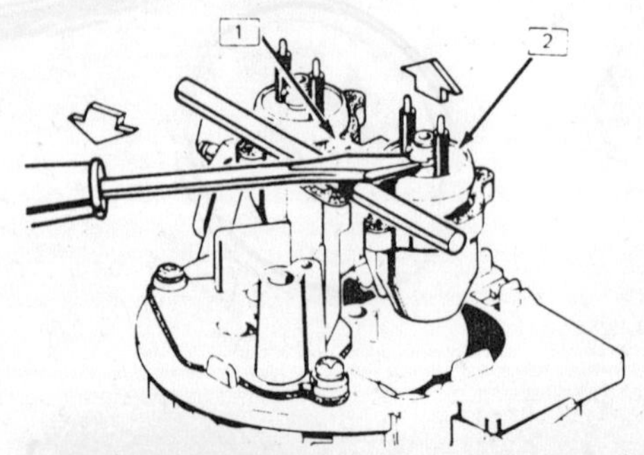

1. Fuel meter cover gasket
2. Removing fuel injector

Fuel injector removal — model 220

CHILTON'S
FUEL ECONOMY
& TUNE-UP TIPS

Tune-up • Spark Plug Diagnosis • Emission Controls

Fuel System • Cooling System • Tires and Wheels

General Maintenance

CHILTON'S FUEL ECONOMY & TUNE-UP TIPS

Fuel economy is important to everyone, no matter what kind of vehicle you drive. The maintenance-minded motorist can save both money and fuel using these tips and the periodic maintenance and tune-up procedures in this Repair and Tune-Up Guide.

There are more than 130,000,000 cars and trucks registered for private use in the United States. Each travels an average of 10-12,000 miles per year, and, and in total they consume close to 70 billion gallons of fuel each year. This represents nearly $2/3$ of the oil imported by the United States each year. The Federal government's goal is to reduce consumption 10% by 1985. A variety of methods are either already in use or under serious consideration, and they all affect you driving and the cars you will drive. In addition to "down-sizing", the auto industry is using or investigating the use of electronic fuel delivery, electronic engine controls and alternative engines for use in smaller and lighter vehicles, among other alternatives to meet the federally mandated Corporate Average Fuel Economy (CAFE) of 27.5 mpg by 1985. The government, for its part, is considering rationing, mandatory driving curtailments and tax increases on motor vehicle fuel in an effort to reduce consumption. The government's goal of a 10% reduction could be realized — and further government regulation avoided — if every private vehicle could use just 1 less gallon of fuel per week.

How Much Can You Save?

Tests have proven that almost anyone can make at least a 10% reduction in fuel consumption through regular maintenance and tune-ups. When a major manufacturer of spark plugs sur-

TUNE-UP

1. Check the cylinder compression to be sure the engine will really benefit from a tune-up and that it is capable of producing good fuel economy. A tune-up will be wasted on an engine in poor mechanical condition.

2. Replace spark plugs regularly. New spark plugs alone can increase fuel economy 3%.

3. Be sure the spark plugs are the correct type (heat range) for your vehicle. See the Tune-Up Specifications.

Heat range refers to the spark plug's ability to conduct heat away from the firing end. It must conduct the heat away in an even pattern to avoid becoming a source of pre-ignition, yet it must also operate hot enough to burn off conductive deposits that could cause misfiring.

The heat range is usually indicated by a number on the spark plug, part of the manufacturer's designation for each individual spark plug. The numbers in bold-face indicate the heat range in each manufacturer's identification system.

Periodically, check the spark plugs to be sure they are firing efficiently. They are excellent indicators of the internal condition of your engine.

Manufacturer	Typical Designation
AC	R **45** TS
Bosch (old)	WA **145** T30
Bosch (new)	HR **8** Y
Champion	RBL **15** Y
Fram/Autolite	**415**
Mopar	P-**62** PR
Motorcraft	BRF-**42**
NGK	BP **5** ES-15
Nippondenso	W **16** EP
Prestolite	14GR **5** 2A

On AC, Bosch (new), Champion, Fram/Autolite, Mopar, Motorcraft and Prestolite, a higher number indicates a hotter plug. On Bosch (old), NGK and Nippondenso, a higher number indicates a colder plug.

4. Make sure the spark plugs are properly gapped. See the Tune-Up Specifications in this book.

5. Be sure the spark plugs are firing efficiently. The illustrations on the next 2 pages show you how to "read" the firing end of the spark plug.

6. Check the ignition timing and set it to specifications. Tests show that almost all cars have incorrect ignition timing by more than 2°.

veyed over 6,000 cars nationwide, they found that a tune-up, on cars that needed one, increased fuel economy over 11%. Replacing worn plugs alone, accounted for a 3% increase. The same test also revealed that 8 out of every 10 vehicles will have some maintenance deficiency that will directly affect fuel economy, emissions or performance. Most of this mileage-robbing neglect could be prevented with regular maintenance.

Modern engines require that all of the functioning systems operate properly for maximum efficiency. A malfunction anywhere wastes fuel. You can keep your vehicle running as efficiently and economically as possible, by being aware of your vehicle's operating and performance characteristics. If your vehicle suddenly develops performance or fuel economy problems it could be due to one or more of the following:

PROBLEM	POSSIBLE CAUSE
Engine Idles Rough	Ignition timing, idle mixture, vacuum leak or something amiss in the emission control system.
Hesitates on Acceleration	Dirty carburetor or fuel filter, improper accelerator pump setting, ignition timing or fouled spark plugs.
Starts Hard or Fails to Start	Worn spark plugs, improperly set automatic choke, ice (or water) in fuel system.
Stalls Frequently	Automatic choke improperly adjusted and possible dirty air filter or fuel filter.
Performs Sluggishly	Worn spark plugs, dirty fuel or air filter, ignition timing or automatic choke out of adjustment.

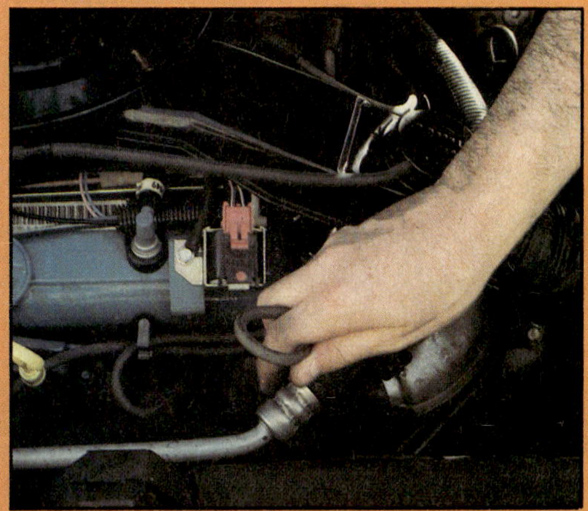

Check spark plug wires on conventional point type ignition for cracks by bending them in a loop around your finger.

Be sure that spark plug wires leading to adjacent cylinders do not run too close together. (Photo courtesy Champion Spark Plug Co.)

7. If your vehicle does not have electronic ignition, check the points, rotor and cap as specified.

8. Check the spark plug wires (used with conventional point-type ignitions) for cracks and burned or broken insulation by bending them in a loop around your finger. Cracked wires decrease fuel efficiency by failing to deliver full voltage to the spark plugs. One misfiring spark plug can cost you as much as 2 mpg.

9. Check the routing of the plug wires. Misfiring can be the result of spark plug leads to adjacent cylinders running parallel to each other and too close together. One wire tends to pick up voltage from the other causing it to fire "out of time".

10. Check all electrical and ignition circuits for voltage drop and resistance.

11. Check the distributor mechanical and/or vacuum advance mechanisms for proper functioning. The vacuum advance can be checked by twisting the distributor plate in the opposite direction of rotation. It should spring back when released.

12. Check and adjust the valve clearance on engines with mechanical lifters. The clearance should be slightly loose rather than too tight.

SPARK PLUG DIAGNOSIS

Normal

APPEARANCE: This plug is typical of one operating normally. The insulator nose varies from a light tan to grayish color with slight electrode wear. The presence of slight deposits is normal on used plugs and will have no adverse effect on engine performance. The spark plug heat range is correct for the engine and the engine is running normally.

CAUSE: Properly running engine.

RECOMMENDATION: Before reinstalling this plug, the electrodes should be cleaned and filed square. Set the gap to specifications. If the plug has been in service for more than 10-12,000 miles, the entire set should probably be replaced with a fresh set of the same heat range.

Oil Deposits

APPEARANCE: The firing end of the plug is covered with a wet, oily coating.

CAUSE: The problem is poor oil control. On high mileage engines, oil is leaking past the rings or valve guides into the combustion chamber. A common cause is also a plugged PCV valve, and a ruptured fuel pump diaphragm can also cause this condition. Oil fouled plugs such as these are often found in new or recently overhauled engines, before normal oil control is achieved, and can be cleaned and reinstalled.

RECOMMENDATION: A hotter spark plug may temporarily relieve the problem, but the engine is probably in need of work.

Incorrect Heat Range

APPEARANCE: The effects of high temperature on a spark plug are indicated by clean white, often blistered insulator. This can also be accompanied by excessive wear of the electrode, and the absence of deposits.

CAUSE: Check for the correct spark plug heat range. A plug which is too hot for the engine can result in overheating. A car operated mostly at high speeds can require a colder plug. Also check ignition timing, cooling system level, fuel mixture and leaking intake manifold.

RECOMMENDATION: If all ignition and engine adjustments are known to be correct, and no other malfunction exists, install spark plugs one heat range colder.

Carbon Deposits

APPEARANCE: Carbon fouling is easily identified by the presence of dry, soft, black, sooty deposits.

CAUSE: Changing the heat range can often lead to carbon fouling, as can prolonged slow, stop-and-start driving. If the heat range is correct, carbon fouling can be attributed to a rich fuel mixture, sticking choke, clogged air cleaner, worn breaker points, retarded timing or low compression. If only one or two plugs are carbon fouled, check for corroded or cracked wires on the affected plugs. Also look for cracks in the distributor cap between the towers of affected cylinders.

RECOMMENDATION: After the problem is corrected, these plugs can be cleaned and reinstalled if not worn severely.

MMT Fouled

APPEARANCE: Spark plugs fouled by MMT (Methycyclopentadienyl Maganese Tricarbonyl) have reddish, rusty appearance on the insulator and side electrode.

CAUSE: MMT is an anti-knock additive in gasoline used to replace lead. During the combustion process, the MMT leaves a reddish deposit on the insulator and side electrode.

RECOMMENDATION: No engine malfunction is indicated and the deposits will not affect plug performance any more than lead deposits (see Ash Deposits). MMT fouled plugs can be cleaned, regapped and reinstalled.

High Speed Glazing

APPEARANCE: Glazing appears as shiny coating on the plug, either yellow or tan in color.

CAUSE: During hard, fast acceleration, plug temperatures rise suddenly. Deposits from normal combustion have no chance to fluff-off; instead, they melt on the insulator forming an electrically conductive coating which causes misfiring.

RECOMMENDATION: Glazed plugs are not easily cleaned. They should be replaced with a fresh set of plugs of the correct heat range. If the condition recurs, using plugs with a heat range one step colder may cure the problem.

Ash (Lead) Deposits

APPEARANCE: Ash deposits are characterized by light brown or white colored deposits crusted on the side or center electrodes. In some cases it may give the plug a rusty appearance.

CAUSE: Ash deposits are normally derived from oil or fuel additives burned during normal combustion. Normally they are harmless, though excessive amounts can cause misfiring. If deposits are excessive in short mileage, the valve guides may be worn.

RECOMMENDATION: Ash-fouled plugs can be cleaned, gapped and reinstalled.

Detonation

APPEARANCE: Detonation is usually characterized by a broken plug insulator.

CAUSE: A portion of the fuel charge will begin to burn spontaneously, from the increased heat following ignition. The explosion that results applies extreme pressure to engine components, frequently damaging spark plugs and pistons.

Detonation can result by over-advanced ignition timing, inferior gasoline (low octane) lean air/fuel mixture, poor carburetion, engine lugging or an increase in compression ratio due to combustion chamber deposits or engine modification.

RECOMMENDATION: Replace the plugs after correcting the problem.

EMISSION CONTROLS

13. Be aware of the general condition of the emission control system. It contributes to reduced pollution and should be serviced regularly to maintain efficient engine operation.

14. Check all vacuum lines for dried, cracked or brittle conditions. Something as simple as a leaking vacuum hose can cause poor performance and loss of economy.

15. Avoid tampering with the emission control system. Attempting to improve fuel econ-

FUEL SYSTEM

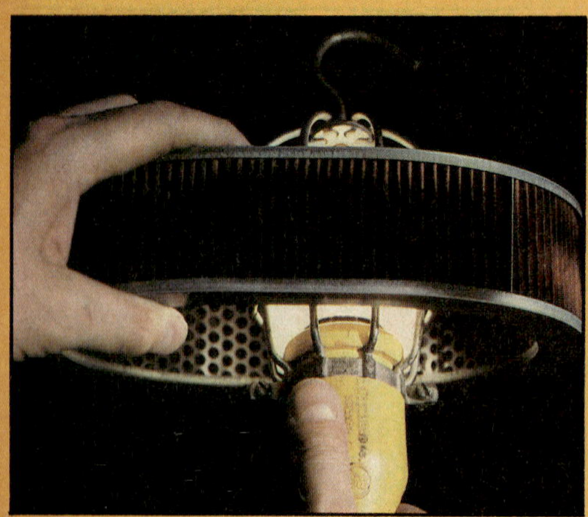

Check the air filter with a light behind it. If you can see light through the filter it can be reused.

Extremely clogged filters should be discarded and replaced with a new one.

18. Replace the air filter regularly. A dirty air filter richens the air/fuel mixture and can increase fuel consumption as much as 10%. Tests show that ⅓ of all vehicles have air filters in need of replacement.

19. Replace the fuel filter at least as often as recommended.

20. Set the idle speed and carburetor mixture to specifications.

21. Check the automatic choke. A sticking or malfunctioning choke wastes gas.

22. During the summer months, adjust the automatic choke for a leaner mixture which will produce faster engine warm-ups.

COOLING SYSTEM

29. Be sure all accessory drive belts are in good condition. Check for cracks or wear.

30. Adjust all accessory drive belts to proper tension.

31. Check all hoses for swollen areas, worn spots, or loose clamps.

32. Check coolant level in the radiator or expansion tank.

33. Be sure the thermostat is operating properly. A stuck thermostat delays engine warm-up and a cold engine uses nearly twice as much fuel as a warm engine.

34. Drain and replace the engine coolant at least as often as recommended. Rust and scale

TIRES & WHEELS

38. Check the tire pressure often with a pencil type gauge. Tests by a major tire manufacturer show that 90% of all vehicles have at least 1 tire improperly inflated. Better mileage can be achieved by over-inflating tires, but never exceed the maximum inflation pressure on the side of the tire.

39. If possible, install radial tires. Radial tires deliver as much as ½ mpg more than bias belted tires.

40. Avoid installing super-wide tires. They only create extra rolling resistance and decrease fuel mileage. Stick to the manufacturer's recommendations.

41. Have the wheels properly balanced.

omy by tampering with emission controls is more likely to worsen fuel economy than improve it. Emission control changes on modern engines are not readily reversible.

16. Clean (or replace) the EGR valve and lines as recommended.

17. Be sure that all vacuum lines and hoses are reconnected properly after working under the hood. An unconnected or misrouted vacuum line can wreak havoc with engine performance.

23. Check for fuel leaks at the carburetor, fuel pump, fuel lines and fuel tank. Be sure all lines and connections are tight.

24. Periodically check the tightness of the carburetor and intake manifold attaching nuts and bolts. These are a common place for vacuum leaks to occur.

25. Clean the carburetor periodically and lubricate the linkage.

26. The condition of the tailpipe can be an excellent indicator of proper engine combustion. After a long drive at highway speeds, the inside of the tailpipe should be a light grey in color. Black or soot on the insides indicates an overly rich mixture.

27. Check the fuel pump pressure. The fuel pump may be supplying more fuel than the engine needs.

28. Use the proper grade of gasoline for your engine. Don't try to compensate for knocking or "pinging" by advancing the ignition timing. This practice will only increase plug temperature and the chances of detonation or pre-ignition with relatively little performance gain.

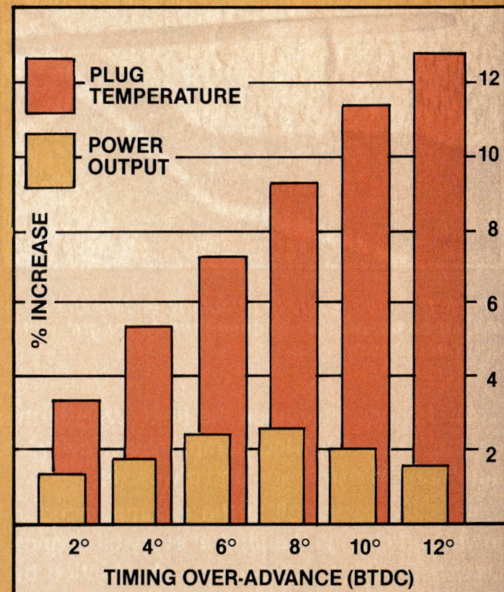

Increasing ignition timing past the specified setting results in a drastic increase in spark plug temperature with increased chance of detonation or preignition. Performance increase is considerably less. (Photo courtesy Champion Spark Plug Co.)

that form in the engine should be flushed out to allow the engine to operate at peak efficiency.

35. Clean the radiator of debris that can decrease cooling efficiency.

36. Install a flex-type or electric cooling fan, if you don't have a clutch type fan. Flex fans use curved plastic blades to push more air at low speeds when more cooling is needed; at high speeds the blades flatten out for less resistance. Electric fans only run when the engine temperature reaches a predetermined level.

37. Check the radiator cap for a worn or cracked gasket. If the cap does not seal properly, the cooling system will not function properly.

42. Be sure the front end is correctly aligned. A misaligned front end actually has wheels going in differed directions. The increased drag can reduce fuel economy by .3 mpg.

43. Correctly adjust the wheel bearings. Wheel bearings that are adjusted too tight increase rolling resistance.

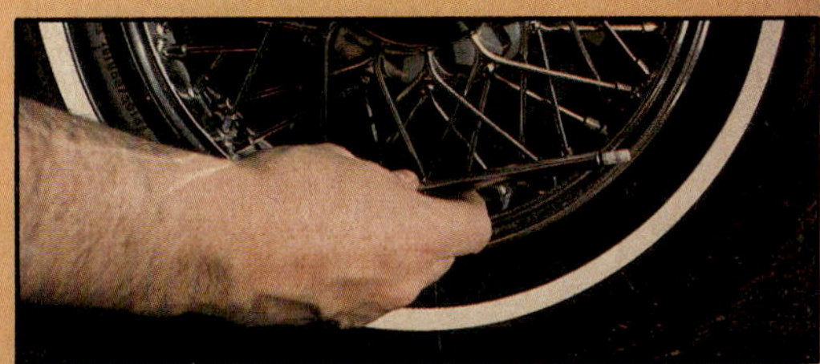

Check tire pressures regularly with a reliable pocket type gauge. Be sure to check the pressure on a cold tire.

GENERAL MAINTENANCE

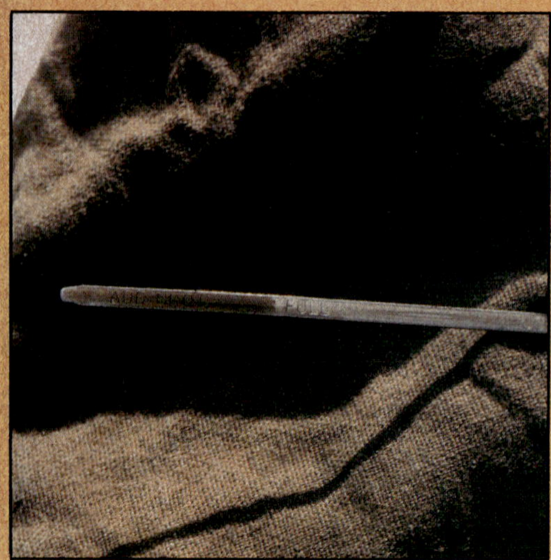

Check the fluid levels (particularly engine oil) on a regular basis. Be sure to check the oil for grit, water or other contamination.

A vacuum gauge is another excellent indicator of internal engine condition and can also be installed in the dash as a mileage indicator.

44. Periodically check the fluid levels in the engine, power steering pump, master cylinder, automatic transmission and drive axle.

45. Change the oil at the recommended interval and change the filter at every oil change. Dirty oil is thick and causes extra friction between moving parts, cutting efficiency and increasing wear. A worn engine requires more frequent tune-ups and gets progressively worse fuel economy. In general, use the lightest viscosity oil for the driving conditions you will encounter.

46. Use the recommended viscosity fluids in the transmission and axle.

47. Be sure the battery is fully charged for fast starts. A slow starting engine wastes fuel.

48. Be sure battery terminals are clean and tight.

49. Check the battery electrolyte level and add distilled water if necessary.

50. Check the exhaust system for crushed pipes, blockages and leaks.

51. Adjust the brakes. Dragging brakes or brakes that are not releasing create increased drag on the engine.

52. Install a vacuum gauge or miles-per-gallon gauge. These gauges visually indicate engine vacuum in the intake manifold. High vacuum = good mileage and low vacuum = poorer mileage. The gauge can also be an excellent indicator of internal engine conditions.

53. Be sure the clutch is properly adjusted. A slipping clutch wastes fuel.

54. Check and periodically lubricate the heat control valve in the exhaust manifold. A sticking or inoperative valve prevents engine warm-up and wastes gas.

55. Keep accurate records to check fuel economy over a period of time. A sudden drop in fuel economy may signal a need for tune-up or other maintenance.

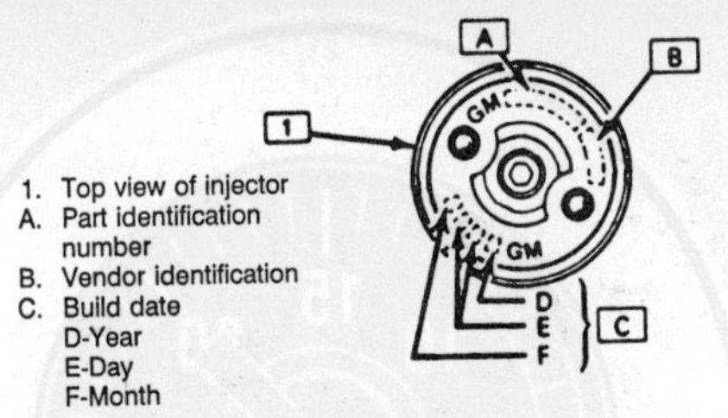

Exploded view of the Model 220 fuel meter body assembly — 2.8L and 4.3L TBI engines

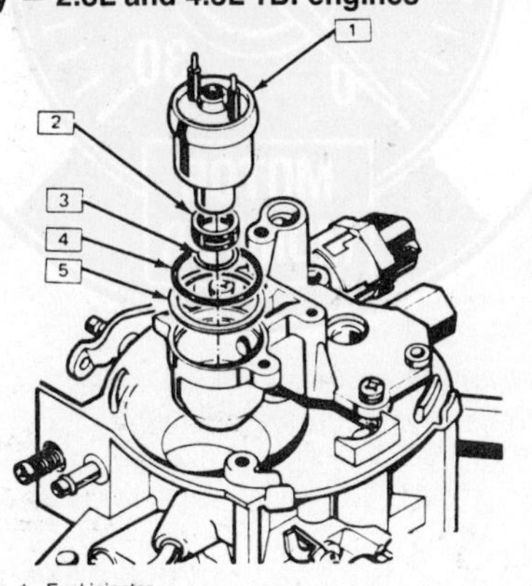

Fuel injector removal — model 300

INJECTOR REPLACEMENT

Model 300 for 2.5L TBI Engine (1985–86) and Model 220 for 2.8L and 4.3L TBI Engines

NOTE: *When removing the injector(s), be careful not to damage the electrical connector pins (on top of the injector), the injector fuel filter and the nozzle. The fuel injector is serviced as a complete assembly only, it is an electrical component and should not be immersed in any kind of cleaner.*

1. Remove the air cleaner. Disconnect the negative battery terminal.

2. Relieve the fuel pressure.

3. At the injector connector, squeeze the 2 tabs together and pull it straight up.

4. Remove the fuel meter cover and leave the cover gasket in place.

5. Using a small prybar or tool J-26868, carefully lift the injector until it is free from the fuel meter body.

6. Remove the small O-ring form the nozzle end of the injector. Carefully rotate the injec-

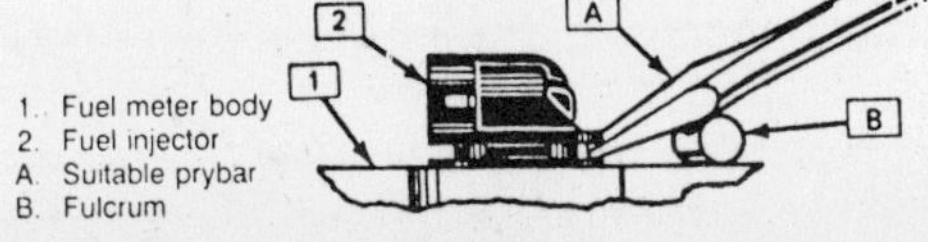

Fuel injector removal — model 700

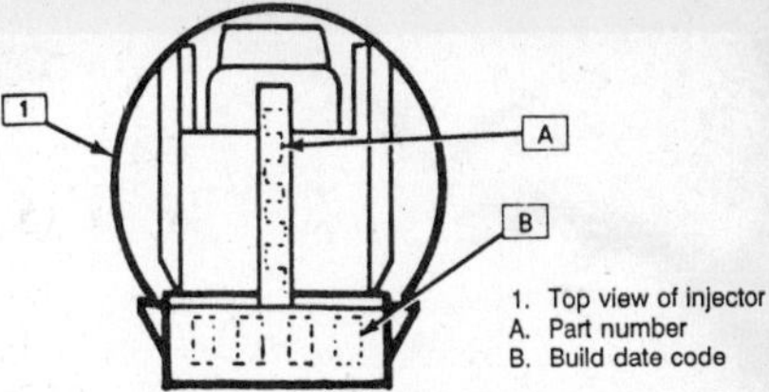

View of the Model 700 fuel injector part number — 2.5L TBI engine for 1987–89

tor's fuel filter back-and-forth to remove it from the base of the injector.

7. Discard the fuel meter cover gasket.

8. Remove the large O-ring and back-up washer from the top of the counterbore of the fuel meter body injector cavity.

9. To install, lubricate the O-rings with automatic transmission fluid and push it into the fuel injector cavity. To complete the installation, reverse the removal procedures. Start the engine and check for fuel leaks.

Model 700 for 2.5L TBI Engine (1987–89)

1. Relieve the fuel pressure in the system.

2. Disconnect the negative battery cable.

3. Remove the air cleaner and gasket; discard the gasket.

4. Disconnect the electrical connector from the fuel injector.

5. Remove the injector retainer screw and the retainer.

6. Using a small prybar and a fulcrum, place the prybar under the ridge opposite the fuel injector and pry it carefully from the housing.

7. Remove the upper and lower O-rings from the fuel injector and/or cavity; discard them.

To install:

8. Inspect the fuel injector for dirt and/or other contaminants. If necessary, replace the fuel injector with an identical part.

9. Using new O-rings, lubricate them with automatic transmission fluid and install them onto the fuel injector; make sure the upper O-ring is in the groove and the lower 1 is flush against the filter.

10. Install the injector by pushing it straight into the fuel injector cavity.

NOTE: *Be sure the electrical connector end, of the injector, is facing in the general direction to the cut-out in the fuel meter body for the wire grommet.*

11. Apply thread locking compound to the retainer screw and install the injector retainer. Torque the screw to 27 inch lbs. (3.0 Nm).

12. With the engine **OFF**, turn the ignition switch **ON** and check for fuel leaks.

13. Install the air cleaner with a new gasket.

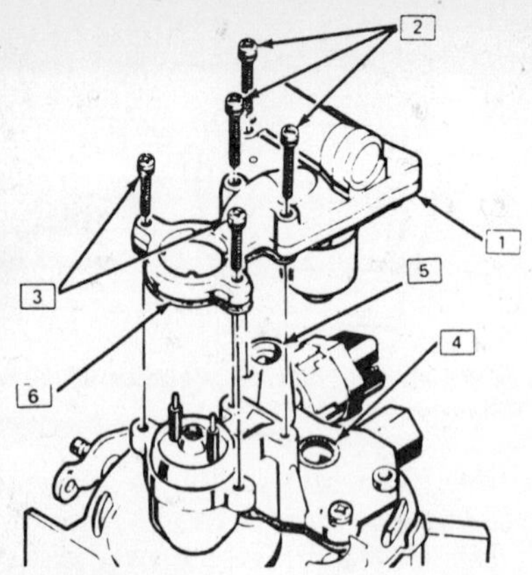

1. Fuel meter cover
2. Screws—long
3. Screws—short
4. Dust seal
5. Outlet gasket
6. Cover gasket

Exploded view of the Model 300 fuel meter cover — 2.5L TBI engine for 1985–86 — 2.8L and 4.3L TBI engines are similar

FUEL METER COVER REPLACEMENT

1. Remove the air cleaner. Disconnect the negative battery terminal from the battery.

2. At the injector electrical connector, squeeze the 2 tabs together and pull it straight up.

3. Remove the fuel meter-to-fuel meter body screws and lock washers.

NOTE: *When removing the fuel meter cover screws, note the location of the 2 short screws.*

4. Remove the fuel meter cover and discard the gasket.

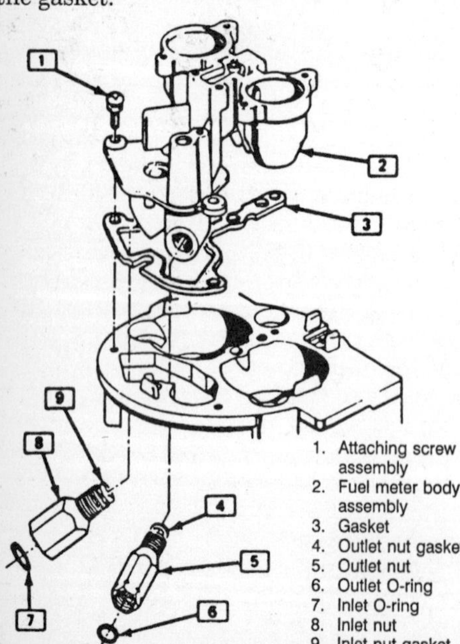

1. Attaching screw assembly
2. Fuel meter body assembly
3. Gasket
4. Outlet nut gasket
5. Outlet nut
6. Outlet O-ring
7. Inlet O-ring
8. Inlet nut
9. Inlet nut gasket

View of the Model 220 fuel injector part number location — 2.8L and 4.3L TBI engines

5. To install, use a new gasket and reverse the removal procedures.

FUEL INJECTOR ASSEMBLY — MODEL 220

1. Relieve the fuel pressure from the fuel system.

2. Disconnect the negative battery cable.

3. Remove the air cleaner and gasket.

4. Disconnect the electrical connectors from the fuel meters, squeeze the 2 tabs together and pull the injector(s) straight up.

5. Remove the fuel meter cover.

6. Remove the fuel injectors.

7. Remove the fuel inlet and outlet nuts and gaskets from the fuel meter body assembly; discard the gaskets.

8. Remove the fuel meter body-to-throttle body screws.

9. Remove the fuel meter body from the throttle body and discard the gasket.

10. Using a new fuel meter assembly-to-throttle body gasket, lubricate the screws with locking compound and torque the fuel meter assembly screws to 30 inch lbs. (4.0 Nm).

11. Using new gaskets, install the fuel meter inlet and outlet nuts and torque to the outlet nut to 21 ft. lbs. (29 Nm) and the inlet nut to 30 ft. lbs. (40 Nm).

12. Using new O-rings and a back-up wrench, install the fuel inlet and outlet lines; torque the fuel lines to 17 ft. lbs. (23 Nm).

13. Using new fuel injector O-rings, lubricate them with automatic transmission fluid; install them into the fuel injector body assembly.

14. Install the fuel meter cover assembly.

15. Coat the screws with locking compound and torque the screws to 27 inch lbs. (3.0 Nm).

16. Connect the electrical connectors to the fuel injectors. Connect the negative battery cable.

17. With the engine **OFF**, turn the ignition switch **ON** and check for fuel leaks.

PRESSURE REGULATOR ASSEMBLY MODEL 700 TBI UNIT

NOTE: *To prevent leaks, the pressure regulator diaphragm assembly must be replaced whenever the cover is removed.*

1. Relieve the fuel pressure from the fuel system.

2. Disconnect the negative battery cable.

3. While keeping the pressure regulator spring compressed, remove the pressure regulator-to-throttle body screws.

CAUTION: *The pressure regulator contains a large spring under heavy compression pressure. Use care when removing the screw to prevent personal injury.*

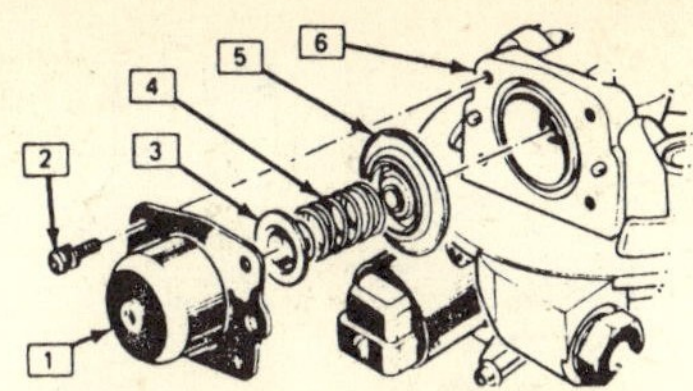

1. Pressure regulator cover
2. Screw assembly
3. Spring seat
4. Spring
5. Diaphragm
6. Fuel meter assembly

Exploded view of the pressure regulator assembly — Model 700 2.5L TBI engine

4. Remove the pressure regulator cover assembly.

5. Remove the pressure regulator spring.

6. Remove the spring seat.

7. Remove the pressure regulator diaphragm assembly.

To install:

8. Inspect the pressure regulator seat in the fuel meter body for pitting, nicks or irregularities; use a magnifying glass, if necessary. If any problem exists, replace the whole fuel body.

9. Using a new pressure regulator diaphragm, make sure it is seated in the groove in the fuel meter body.

10. Install the regulator spring seat and spring into the cover assembly.

11. Install the cover assembly of the diaphragm, while aligning the mounting holes; be careful not to misalign the pressure regulator, for leaks may exists.

12. While maintaining the regulator spring pressure, coat the screws with locking compound and install. Torque the screws to 22 inch lbs. (2.5 Nm).

13. With the engine **OFF** and the engine **ON**; check for fuel leaks.

14. To complete the installation, reverse the removal procedures.

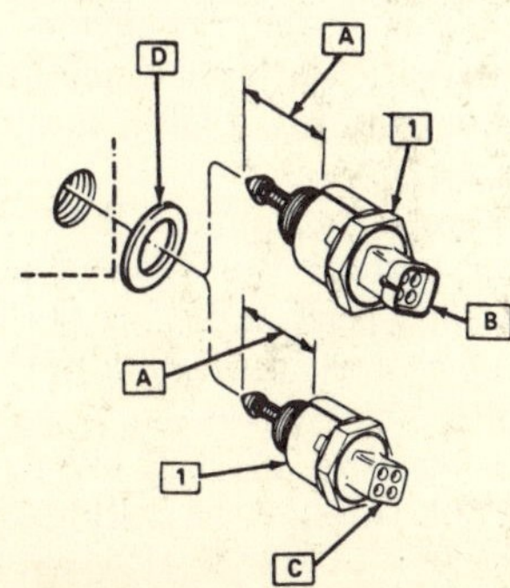

1. Idle air control valve
A. Less than 28mm (1⅛ in.)
B. Type I (with collar)
C. Type II (without collar)
D. Gasket (part of IAC valve service kit)

Idle air control valve

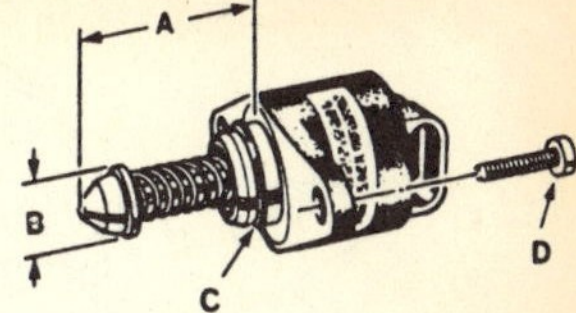

A. Distance of pintle extension
B. Diameter of pintle
C. IAC valve O-ring
D. IAC valve attaching screw

Exploded view of the Idle Air Control (IAC) valves — Model 700 throttle body

IDLE AIR CONTROL (IAC) VALVE REPLACEMENT

Model 220 and 300 Throttle Bodies

1. Remove the air cleaner. Disconnect the negative battery terminal from the battery.

2. Disconnect the electrical connector from the Idle Air Control (IAC) valve.

3. Remove the idle air control valve and discard the O-ring.

NOTE: *Before installing a new idle air control valve, measure the distance that the valve extends (from the motor housing to the end of the cone); the distance should be no greater than 1⅛ in. (28mm). If it extends to far, damage will occur to the valve when it is installed.*

4. To install, use a new gasket, lubricate it with automatic transmission fluid and reverse the removal procedures. Torque the IAC to 13 ft. lbs. (18 Nm). Start the engine and allow it to reach normal operating temperatures; then, turn it **OFF**.

NOTE: *The ECM will reset the idle Air Control (IAC) valve after the engine has normal operating temperatures.*

Model 700 Throttle Body

1. Remove the air cleaner. Disconnect the negative battery terminal from the battery.

2. Disconnect the electrical connector from the Idle Air Control (IAC) valve.

3. Remove the idle air control valve and discard the O-ring.

NOTE: *Before installing a new idle air control valve, measure the distance that the valve extends (from the motor housing to the end of the cone); the distance should be no greater than 1⅛ in. (28mm). If it extends to*

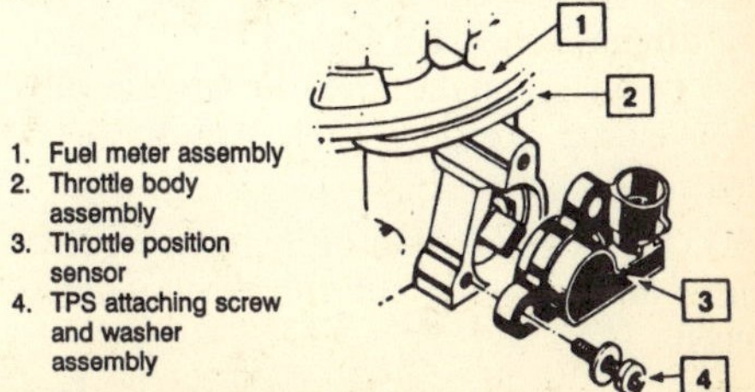

1. Fuel meter assembly
2. Throttle body assembly
3. Throttle position sensor
4. TPS attaching screw and washer assembly

Exploded view of the Throttle Position Sensor (TPS) — Model 700 throttle body

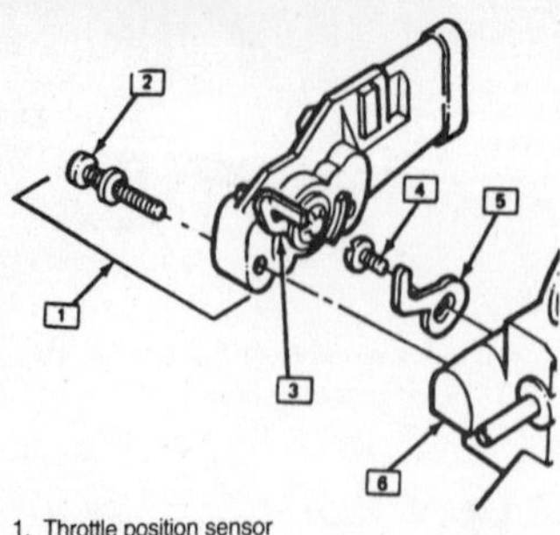

1. Throttle position sensor
2. Screw & washer
3. TPS pick up lever
4. Screw
5. Lever
6. Throttle body assembly

Throttle position sensor — 2.5L engine

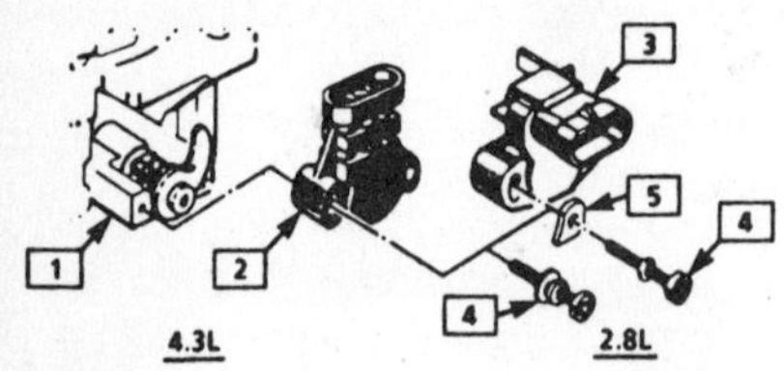

4.3L

1. Throttle body assembly
2. Throttle position sensor — non-adjustable

2.8L

3. Throttle position sensor — adjustable
4. Screw assembly
5. Retainer

Exploded view of the Throttle Position Sensor (TPS) — Model 220 throttle body

far, damage will occur to the valve when it is installed.

4. To install, use a new gasket, lubricate it with automatic transmission fluid and reverse the removal procedures. Torque the IAC to 28 inch lbs. (3.2 Nm). Start the engine and allow it to reach normal operating temperatures; then, turn it **OFF**.

NOTE: *The ECM will reset the idle Air Control (IAC) valve after the engine has normal operating temperatures.*

THROTTLE POSITION SENSOR (TPS)

1. Remove the air cleaner.
2. Disconnect the electrical connector from the throttle position sensor (TPS).
3. Remove the TPS mounting screws, the lock washers and the retainers.
4. Remove the TPS sensor.
5. To install, make sure the throttle valve is in the closed position, then install the TPS sensor.

NOTE: *Make sure the TPS pickup lever is located above the tang on the throttle actuator lever.*

6. To complete the installation, lubricate the mounting screws with Loctite® (thread locking compound) No. 262 or equivalent, then re-

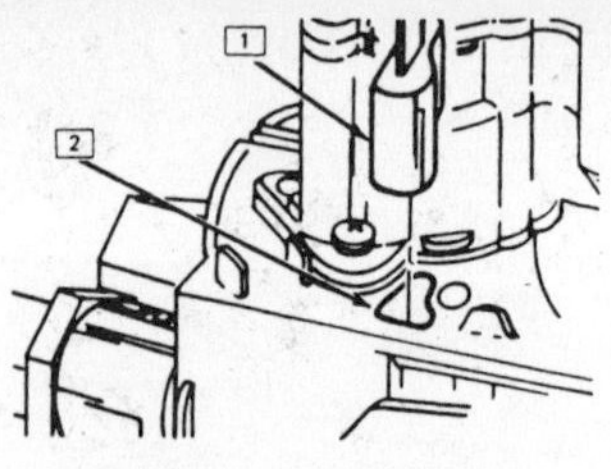

1. Idle air passage plug (J33047/BT 8207-A)
2. Idle air passage

Plug the idle passages of each throttle body as illustrated

verse the removal procedures. Torque the screws to 18 inch lbs. (2.0 Nm).

ADJUSTMENTS

Idle Speed and Mixture Adjustment

2.5L TBI ENGINE

Model 300 Throttle Body—1985–86

NOTE: *The following procedures require the use a tachometer, GM tool J-33047, BT-8207 or equivalent, GM Torx Bit No. 20, silicone sealant, a $5/32$ in. drill bit, a prick punch and a $1/16$ in. pin punch.*

The throttle stop screw, used in regulating the minimum idle speed, is adjusted at the factory and is not necessary to perform. This adjustment should be performed only when the throttle body has been replaced.

NOTE: *The replacement of the complete throttle body assembly will have the minimum idle adjusted at the factory.*

1. Remove the air cleaner and the gasket. Be sure to plug the THERMAC vacuum port (air cleaner vacuum line-to-throttle body) on the throttle body.
2. Remove the throttle valve cable from the throttle control bracket to provide access to the minimum air adjustment screw.
3. Using the manufacturer's instructions, connect a tachometer to the engine.
4. Remove the electrical connector from the Idle Air Control (IAC) valve, located on the throttle body.
5. If necessary to remove the throttle stop screw cover, perform the following procedures:

    a. Using a prick punch, mark the housing at the top over the center line of the throttle stop screw.

    b. Using a $5/32$ in. drill bit, drill (on an angle) a hole through the casting to the hardened cover.

    c. Using a $1/16$ in. pin punch, place it through the hole and drive out the cover to expose the throttle stop screw.

6. Place the transmission in **P** for automatic transmission or Neutral for manual transmis-

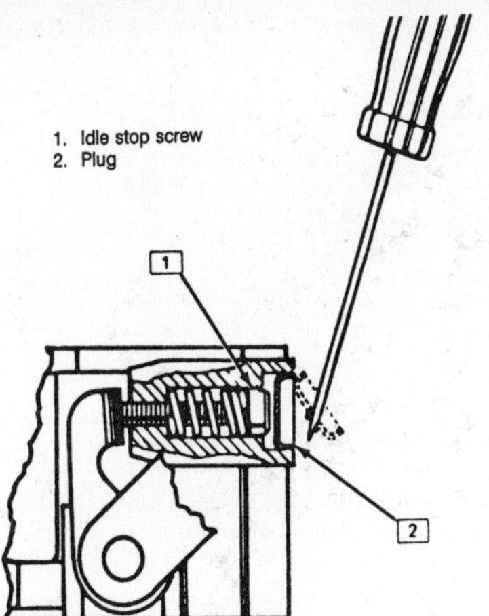

Unpluging the idle stop screw plug — Model 220 throttle body

sion, start the engine and allow the idle speed to stabilize.

7. Using the GM tool J-33047, BT-8207 or equivalent, install it into the idle air passage of the throttle body; be sure the tool is fully seated in the opening and no air leaks exist.

8. Using the GM Torx Bit No. 20, turn the throttle stop screw until the engine speed is 475–525 rpm in **P** or **N** for automatic transmission or 750–800 rpm in Neutral for manual transmission.

9. With the idle speed adjusted, stop the engine, remove the tool J-33047, BT-8207 or equivalent, from the throttle body.

10. Reconnect the Idle Air Control (IAC) electrical connector.

11. Using silicone sealant or equivalent, cover the throttle stop screw.

12. Reinstall the gasket and the air cleaner assembly.

Model 700 Throttle Body — 1987–89

1. Remove the air cleaner and discard the gasket.

2. Plug any vacuum line ports, as necessary.

3. With the IAC connected, ground the diagnostic terminal (ALDL connector).

4. Turn the ignition switch to the **START** position; do not start the engine. This allows the IAC valve pintle to extend and seat in the throttle body.

5. With the ignition switch **ON**, disconnect the IAC valve electrical connector.

6. Remove the ground from the diagnostic terminal and start the engine.

7. Remove the plug, by first piercing it with an awl, then apply leverage to remove it.

8. Adjust the idle stop screw to obtain 650 rpm ± 25 rpm in Neutral.

9. Turn the ignition switch **OFF** and reconnect the IAC valve electrical connector.

10. Unplug any plugged vacuum line ports and install the air cleaner and a new gasket.

2.8L TBI AND 4.3L ENGINES

NOTE: *The following procedure requires the use of a tachometer, a prick punch, a $\frac{5}{32}$ in. drill bit, a $\frac{1}{16}$ in. pin punch, a grounding wire and silicone sealant.*

1. Remove the air cleaner and the gasket.

2. If necessary to remove the throttle stop screw cover, perform the following procedures:

   a. Using a prick punch, mark the housing at the top over the center line of the throttle stop screw.

   b. Using a $\frac{5}{32}$ in. drill bit, drill (on an angle) a hole through the casting to the hardened cover.

   c. Using a $\frac{1}{16}$ in. pin punch, place it through the hole and drive out the cover to expose the throttle stop screw.

NOTE: *The following adjustment should be performed only when the throttle body assembly has been replaced; the engine should be at normal operating temperatures before making this adjustment.*

3. With the Idle Air Control (IAC) connected, ground the diagnostic terminal of the Assembly Line Communications Link (ALCL) connector.

NOTE: *The Assembly Line Communications Link (ALCL) connector is located in the engine compartment on the left side firewall.*

4. Turn the ignition switch **ON** but do not start the engine. Wait 30 seconds, this will allow the IAC valve pintle to extend and seat in the throttle body.

5. With the ignition switch turned **ON**, disconnect the Idle Air Control (IAC) valve electrical connector.

6. Remove the ground from the Diagnostic Terminal ALCL connector and start the engine.

7. Adjust the idle stop screw to obtain 700 rpm ± 25 rpm for the 2.8L engine, to 600–650 rpm, in Neutral, for manual transmission for 4.3L engine or 500–550 rpm, in **D** for automatic transmission for 4.3L engine.

8. Turn the ignition switch **OFF** and reconnect the IAC valve electrical connector.

9. Using silicone sealant or equivalent, cover the throttle stop screw.

10. Reinstall the gasket and the air cleaner assembly.

Throttle Position Sensor (TPS)

2.5L AND 2.8L TBI ENGINES

The throttle position sensor is non-adjustable but a test should be performed only when throttle body parts have been replaced or AFTER the minimum idle speed has been adjusted.

NOTE: *The following procedure requires the use of the Digital Voltmeter tool J-29125-A or equivalent.*

1. Using the Digital Voltmeter tool J-29125-A or equivalent, set it on the 0–5.0V scale, then connect the probes to the center terminal **B** and the outside terminal **C**.

NOTE: *To attach probes to the TPS electrical connector, disconnect the TPS electrical connector, install thin wires into the sockets and reconnect the connector.*

2. Turn the ignition **ON** (engine stopped).

3. On the 2.5L TBI engine, the output voltage should be 1.25V. If the voltage is more that 1.25V, replace the TPS.

4. On the 2.8L TBI engine, the output voltage should be 0.420–0.450V; if not, rotate the TPS to obtain the correct voltage.

5. Remove the voltmeter and the jumper wires.

DIESEL ENGINE FUEL SYSTEM – 2.2L ENGINE

CAUTION: *The following procedures should not be attempted unless all tools necessary to adjust the injection pump timing are available.*

Fuel Injectors

The primary function of the nozzles is to distribute the fuel in the combustion chamber, which effects the combustion efficiency and engine performance.

REMOVAL AND INSTALLATION

1. Disconnect the negative battery terminal from the battery.

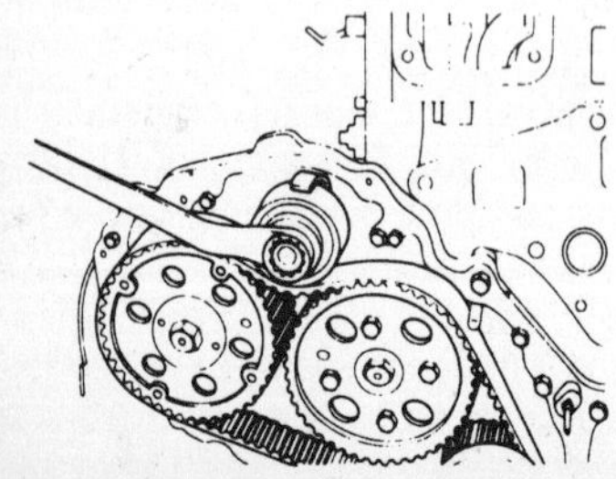

Loosen the tension pulley

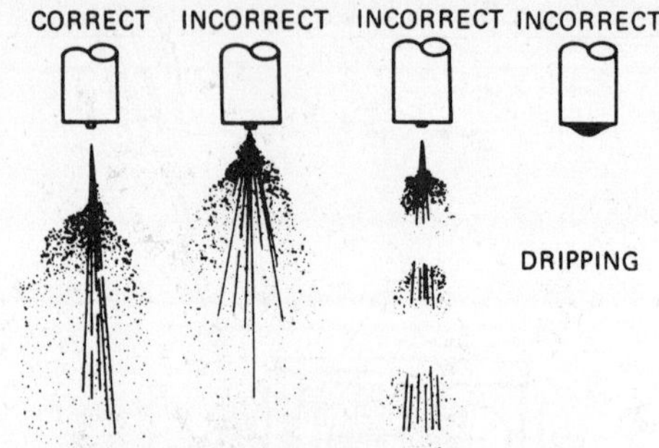

Description of the fuel nozzle spray pattern — 2.2L Diesel engine

2. From the fuel injector nozzle(s), disconnect the fuel return line(s).

3. From the fuel injector nozzle(s), disconnect the fuel injection line(s).

4. Remove the fuel injector nozzle(s) from the engine.

5. Inspect and test the fuel injector nozzle(s).

6. To install, reverse the removal procedures.

TESTING

NOTE: *The following procedure requires the use of a reliable pressure tester and Calibrating Oil SAE J9670 or equivalent (70°F).*

CAUTION: *Do not use diesel fuel; it is unstable with the respect to corrosion inhibition and may cause skin problems.*

Opening Pressure

1. Using a reliable pressure tester, connect the test line to a fuel nozzle and tighten the fittings.

CAUTION: *Exercise extreme care, when using the pressure tester, not to damage the gauge with excessive pressure during the test procedure. When testing the nozzle(s), be sure not to position your hands or arms near the nozzle tip. The atomized high pressure fuel spray has enough penetrating power to puncture the flesh and destroy tissue and may also cause blood poisoning. The nozzle tip should always be enclosed in a transparent receptacle, to contain the spray.*

2. Close the gauge valve and operate the handle several times, then check for proper nozzle spray pattern.

3. Open the gauge valve and operate the handle slowly to determine the injector opening pressure. Observe the gauge reading just before the oil is sprayed from the tip; a buzzing noise will occur when the spray is injected. The minimum opening pressure is 1493 psi.

9. If the reading of the dial indicator is not as described, hold the crankshaft in position (15 degrees) before TDC and loosen 2 nuts on the injection pump flange. Move the injection pump to a point where the dial indicator gives reading of 0.020 in. (0.5mm), then tighten pump flange nuts.

10. Recheck the dial indicator reading and re-adjust the injection pump as necessary. Remove the dial indicator from the pump.

11. Install the distributor screw and washer into injection pump, then tighten.

12. Install the injection lines; do not over tighten the connections.

13. To complete the installation, reverse the removal procedures. Adjust the idle speed and the fast idle speed as described in Chapter 2. Check for leaks in the fuel system and correct, if necessary.

FUEL TANK

REMOVAL AND INSTALLATION

1. Drain the tank.

2. Raise and support the vehicle on jack-stands.

3. Disconnect the wiring and ground strap at the tank.

4. Disconnect the filler neck hose and vent hose from the tank.

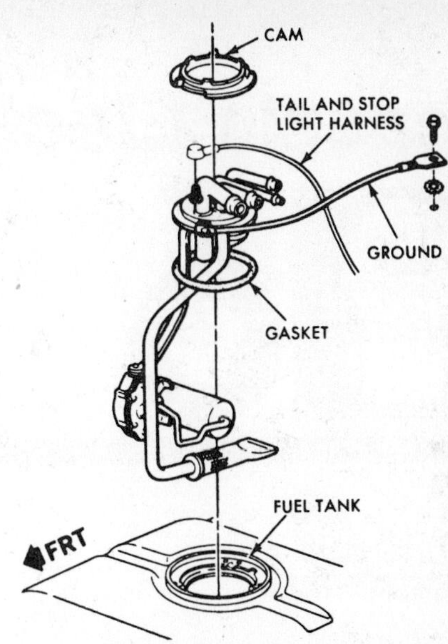

Fuel pump and fuel sender unit assembly

5. Disconnect the fuel feed line and vapor line at the tank.

6. Place a floor jack under the tank to take up its weight.

7. Remove the fuel tank support bolts and lower the tank.

8. To install, reverse the removal procedures.

HEATING AND AIR CONDITIONING

Blower Motor

REMOVAL AND INSTALLATION

1. Disconnect the negative battery cable from the battery.

2. Disconnect the electrical connectors from the blower motor.

NOTE: *On some earlier models equipped with air conditioning, it may be necessary to remove the air conditioning vacuum tank and move it aside.*

3. Remove the blower motor-to-case screws, then lift the blower motor from the case.

4. To install, reverse the removal procedures. Torque the blower motor-to-case screws to 18 ft. lbs.

Heater Core

REMOVAL AND INSTALLATION

1. The heater core is removable from under the right-side of the instrument panel. Disconnect the negative battery cable from the battery.

2. Position a drain pan under the radiator, open the drain cock and drain the cooling system to a level below the heater core.

CAUTION: *When draining the coolant, keep in mind that cats and dogs are attracted by the ethylene glycol antifreeze, and are quite likely to drink any that is left in an uncovered container or in puddles on the ground. This will prove fatal in sufficient quantity. Always drain the coolant into a sealable container. Coolant should be reused unless it is contaminated or several years old.*

3. Disconnect the heater-to-engine coolant hoses from the core tubes on the fire wall, in the engine compartment.

NOTE: *Plug the heater core tubes to avoid spilling coolant in the passenger compart-*

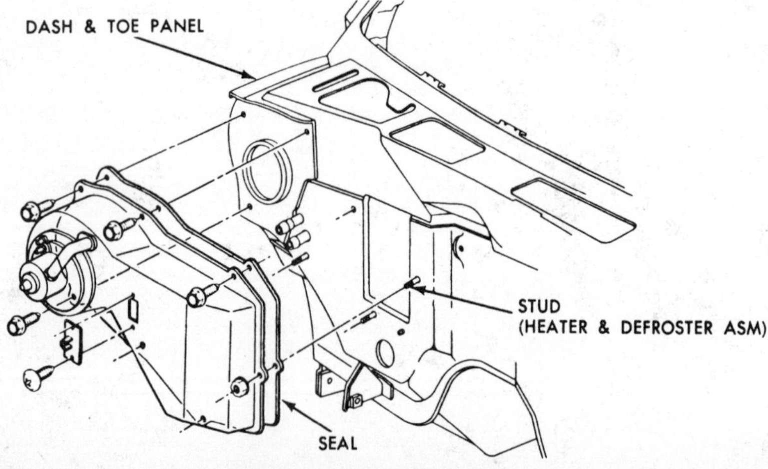

Heater case and blower motor

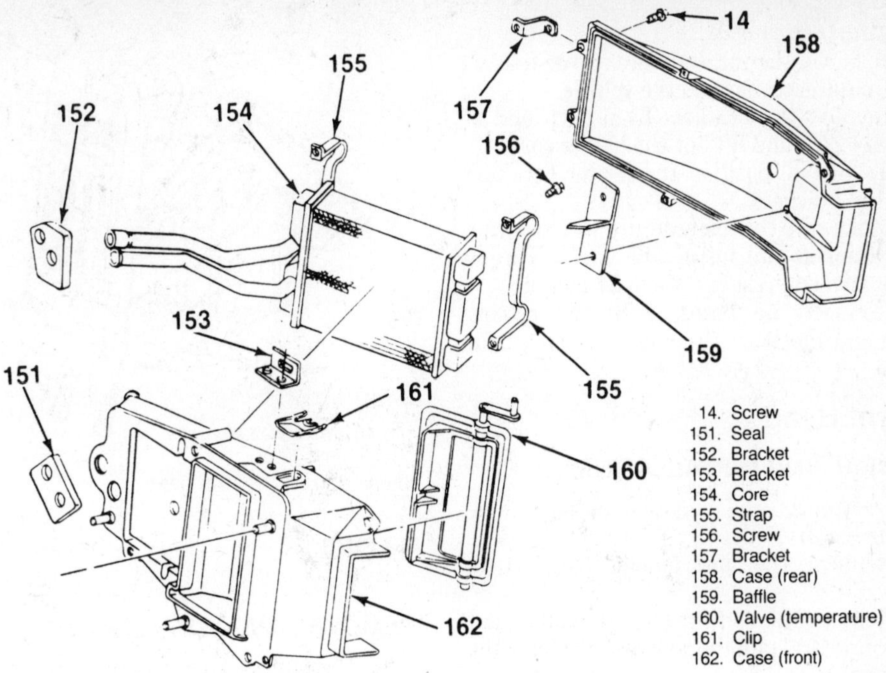

14. Screw
151. Seal
152. Bracket
153. Bracket
154. Core
155. Strap
156. Screw
157. Bracket
158. Case (rear)
159. Baffle
160. Valve (temperature)
161. Clip
162. Case (front)

Exploded view of the heater core assembly

4. Accumulator
108. Inlet line (accumulator)
130. Plate
131. Washer
132. Fan
133. Nut
134. Gasket
135. Wire
136. Screw
137. Seal
138. Tube
139. Screw
140. Case
141. Seal
142. Orifice
143. Core
144. Screw
145. Resistor
146. Case
147. Nut
148. Screw
149. Clamp
150. Clamp
151. Seal
152. Relay
153. Gasket
154. Switch
155. Motor
156. Screw
157. Inlet (evaporator)

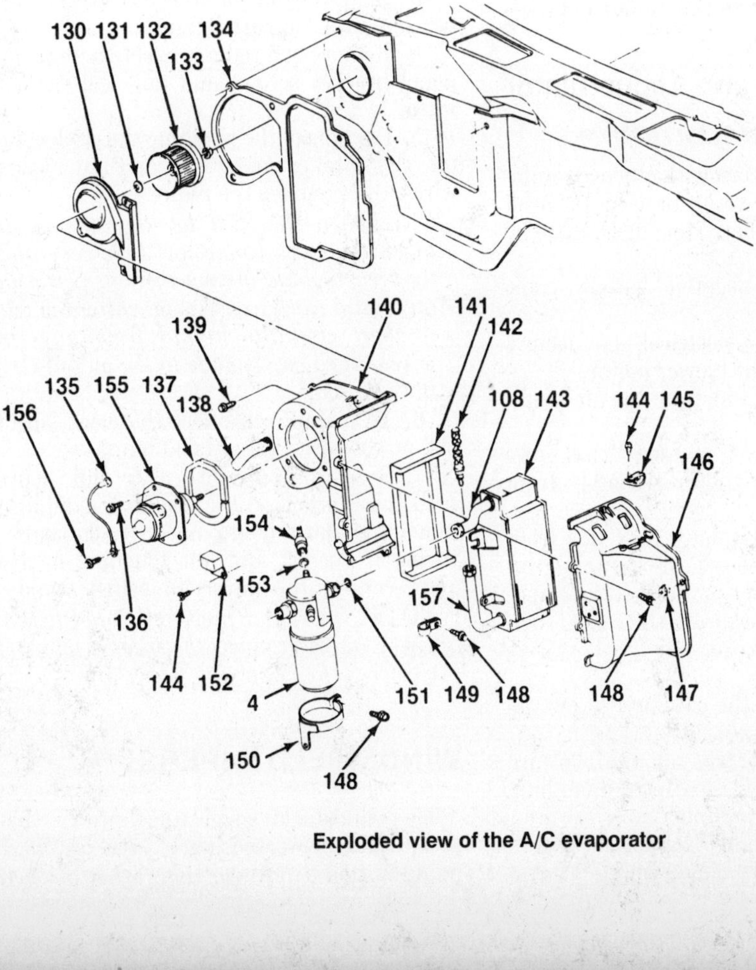

Exploded view of the A/C evaporator

ment during removal.

4. Remove the heater core cover-to-cowl screws and the cover from the vehicle.

5. Remove the brackets from each end of the heater core and lift out the heater core.

6. To install, position the heater core and secure the brackets.

7. Make sure the temperature valve is properly positioned and install the cover. Torque the rear cover-to-case screws to 27 inch lbs.

8. Connect the hoses, refill the cooling system and the start the engine to check for leaks.

Control Head

REMOVAL AND INSTALLATION

1. Disconnect the negative battery cable from the battery.

2. Remove the instrument panel trim bezel(s).

3. Remove the control head-to-instrument panel screws and pull the control head from the instrument panel.

4. Disconnect the vacuum hoses, the electrical connectors and the control cables and remove the control head.

5. To install, reverse the removal procedures.

Evaporator Core and Accumulator

REMOVAL AND INSTALLATION

1. The evaporator core with the accumulator can be removed separately or as a unit from under the hood. Have the system discharged by a professional shop.

2. Disconnect the negative battery cable from the battery.

3. Disconnect the electrical connectors from the resistor and the blower motor.

4. Remove the inlet line from the air conditioning evaporator.

5. Remove the blower motor-to-case nuts/screws and the blower motor assembly from the vehicle.

6. Remove the accumulator inlet line from the evaporator and if desired, the accumulator.

7. Remove the blower motor case-to-evaporator case screws and separate the cases, then remove the evaporator core.

To install:

8. Fit the core into the case and screw the case halves together.

9. If the accumulator was removed, be sure to use a new gasket and seal when installing the accumulator and/or switch.

10. Attach the lines and assemble the case.

11. Recharge the air conditioning system and check for leaks.

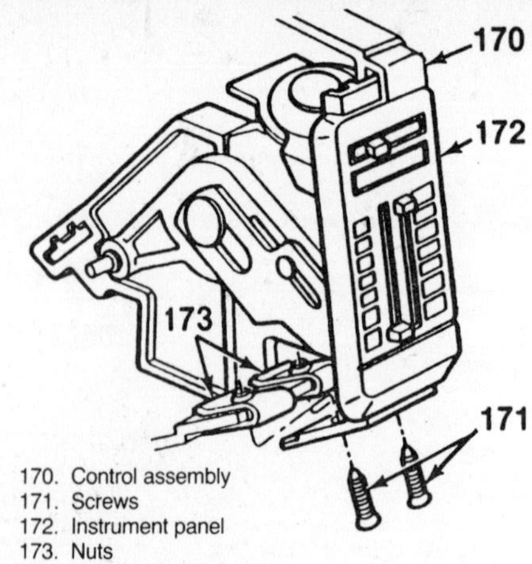

170. Control assembly
171. Screws
172. Instrument panel
173. Nuts

Heater and A/C control head

RADIO

REMOVAL AND INSTALLATION

1. Disconnect the negative battery cable from the battery.

2. Remove the ash tray and any necessary wires.

3. Remove the instrument panel center bezel and the support clip nuts.

4. Remove the radio bracket-to-instrument panel bracket screws and pull the radio forward.

5. Disconnect the antenna, the clock connector, the speaker connectors and any electrical wires, then remove the radio.

CAUTION: *DO NOT let the antenna cable touch the clock connector! It is very important when changing speakers or performing any radio work to avoid pinching the wires. A short circuit-to-ground from any radio wire will cause damage to the output circuit in the radio.*

6. To install, reconnect the clock, speaker and power wires, then the antenna.

7. Slide the radio into place and secure it with the bracket screws. Before installing the remaining dash board parts, make sure all wiring is correct and not touching anything and reconnect the battery to test the radio.

NOTE: *In order to prevent damage to the receiver, always connect the speaker wire to the receiver before applying power to it.*

WINDSHIELD WIPERS

The windshield wiper units are of the 2-speed, non-depressed park type. A washer pump is mounted under the washer bottle and a single turn signal type wiper/washer switch incorporates all controls. A single wiper motor operates both wiper blades. Rotating the switch to either **LO** or **HI** speed position completes the circuit and the wiper motor runs at that speed.

The pulse/demand wash functions are controlled by a plug-in printed circuit board enclosed in the wiper housing cover.

Blade and Arm

REMOVAL AND INSTALLATION

NOTE: *The following procedure requires the use of GM Windshield Wiper Blade/Arm Removal tool J-8966 or equivalent.*

If the wiper assembly has a press type release tab at the center, simply depress the tab and remove the blade. If the blade has no release tab, use a screwdriver to depress the spring at the center; this will release the assembly. To install the assembly, position the blade over the pin, at the tip of the arm, and press until the spring retainer engages the groove in the pin.

To remove the element, either depress the release button or squeeze the spring type retainer clip, at the outer end, together and slide the blade element out. To install, slide the new element in until it latches.

1. Remove the wiper arm as described above. If equipped, disconnect the washer hose from the arm.

2. To install, operate the wiper motor (momentarily) to position the pivot shafts into the

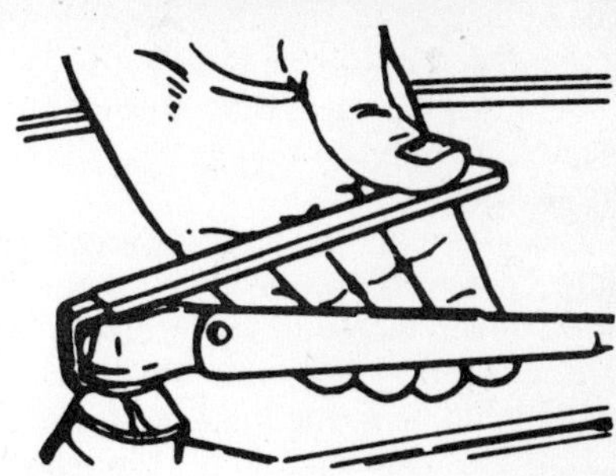

Using the GM Windsheild Wiper Blade/Arm Removal tool No. J-8966 to remove the wiper arms

Park position and reverse the removal procedures. The proper Park position for the arms is with the blades approximately 2 in. (51mm) on the driver's side, or $2^{3}/_{4}$ in. (70mm) on the passenger's-side, above the lower windshield molding.

Wiper Motor

REMOVAL AND INSTALLATION

1. Disconnect the negative battery cable from the battery.

2. Remove the cowl grille.

3. Loosen but DO NOT remove the nuts which hold the drive link to the motor crank arm.

4. Detach the drive link from the crank arm.

5. Disconnect the wiring from the wiper motor.

1. Arm, windshield wiper
2. Blade
    insert
3. Nozzle
4. Spacer, nozzle
5. Nut, type R stamped (M16)
6. Transmission, left hand
    transmission, right hand
7. Lever
8. Module
9. Lens, pulse switch
10. Knob, pulse switch
11. Nut, pulse module retaining
12. Reserovir
13. Bolt, (M6 × 1 × 25)
14. Hose, (5/32″ ID)
15. Strap
16. Connector
17. Motor assembly
18. Bolt (M5 × .8 × 28)
19. Screw, (M6.3 × 1.69 × 20)
20. Pump

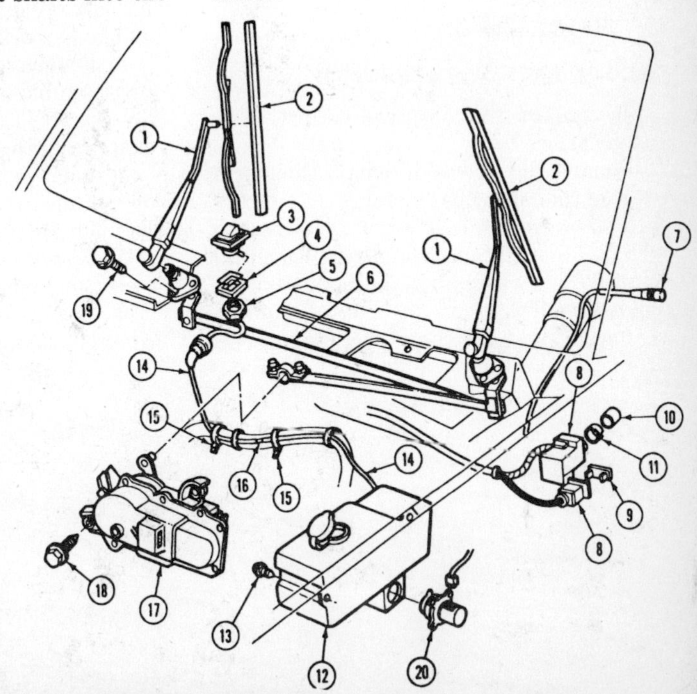

Windshield wiper motor

6. Remove the wiper motor-to-cowl screws. Turn the motor upward, then move it outward and remove it from the vehicle.

To install:

7. Make sure the wiper motor is in the Park position. To do this, connect the motor wiring and operate the motor in low speed. Turn the wiper switch OFF and wait until the motor stops. It should be in the Park position.

8. Position the motor to the cowl and loosely attach the linkage. Torque the wiper motor-to-cowl screws to 50–75 inch lbs.

9. Place the wiper arms into the Park position and secure the linkage to the motor. Test the system before installing the remaining body parts.

Wiper Linkage

REMOVAL AND INSTALLATION

1. Disconnect the negative battery cable from the battery.

2. Using the GM Windshield Wiper Blade/Arm Removal tool J-8966 or equivalent, remove the wiper arms.

3. Remove the cowl grille.

4. Remove the wiper linkage-to-motor clamp.

5. Remove the wiper linkage-to-cowl panel screws.

6. To install, reverse the removal procedures. Torque the wiper linkage-to-panel screws to 50–80 inch lbs.

Rear Wiper Motor

REMOVAL AND INSTALLATION

1. Disconnect the negative battery cable from the battery.

2. Remove the screws to remove the plastic cover from the rear wiper motor.

3. To remove the rear wiper arm, insert a $^1/_8$ inch (3mm) drift pin through the hole in the arm hinge. This will depress the detent and the arm should pull right off.

4. Carefully pry off the support arm socket from the ball on the glass and support the glass.

5. One of the wiper motor bolts also holds the hinge to the glass. Make sure the glass is properly supported and unbolt the motor to remove it.

To install:

6. When installing the motor, replace all rubber sealing parts.

7. Install the beveled washer and inner seal grommet to the motor and install the motor to the glass.

8. Fit the flat seal, spacer and nut to the motor but do not tighten the nut yet.

9. Install the hinge bolt, make sure glass is properly aligned and torque the motor nut and hinge bolt both to 54 inch lbs. (6 Nm).

10. Pop the support strut onto the ball and attach the washer hose.

11. Install the wiper arm and cover.

INSTRUMENTS AND SWITCHES

Instrument Cluster

REMOVAL AND INSTALLATION

1. Disconnect the negative battery cable from the battery.

2. Remove the lamp switch trim plate-to-instrument panel screws and the trim plate, then disconnect the electrical connector from the lamp switch.

3. Remove the air conditioning/heater control assembly-to-instrument panel screws and the assembly, the disconnect the electrical connector from the lamp switch.

4. Remove the filler panel (under the steering column) to instrument panel screws and the filler panel.

5. Remove the instrument cluster-to-instrument panel nuts and the instrument cluster.

6. Disconnect the speedometer drive cable from the instrument cluster.

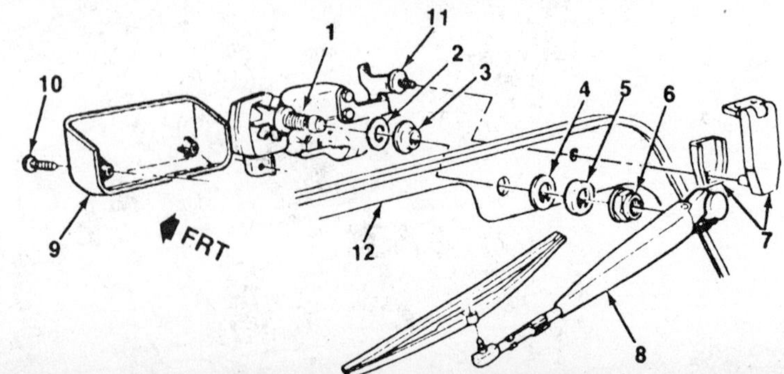

Rear wiper motor assembly: a hinge bolt also holds the motor

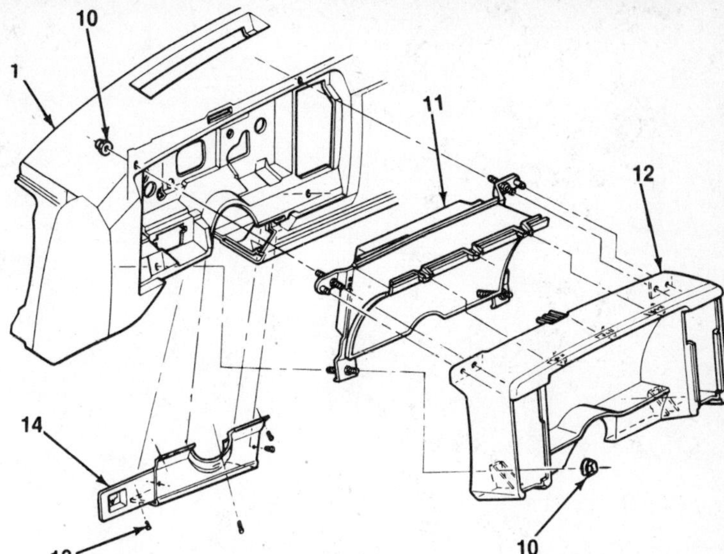

Exploded view of the instrument panel

7. Disconnect the cluster electrical connectors and remove the instrument cluster.

8. To install, reconnect the instrument wiring and speedometer drive cable.

9. Install the cluster and filler panel under the steering column.

10. Connect the wiring and install the air conditioner/heater controls.

11. Install the trim plate and reconnect the battery.

Windshield Wiper Switch

REMOVAL AND INSTALLATION

The wiper switch is part of the combination switch that includes the turn signal, the windshield wiper/washer, the dimmer and the cruise control switches.

Removal and installation of this switch is covered in Chapter 8, Suspension and Steering.

Headlight and Rear Wiper Switch

The headlight switch, a push button switch to turn the lights On and Off, is located on the left-side of the instrument panel. A rheostat dial, located just above the headlight/parking light switch, is used to control the illumination of the instrument panel.

A dimmer switch (part of the combination switch), to control the **HI** and **LO** beam operation, is located on the steering column; the lights are changed by pulling the combination switch lever toward the driver.

REMOVAL AND INSTALLATION

1. Disconnect the negative battery cable from the battery.

2. From under the headlight switch assembly, remove the switch assembly-to-instrument panel screws and pull the switch and trim plate from the instrument panel.

3. Disconnect the electrical wiring connectors from the rear of the headlight switch assembly.

4. Installation is the reverse of removal.

Back-Up Light Switch

REMOVAL AND INSTALLATION

Automatic Transmission

1. Disconnect the negative battery cable from the battery.

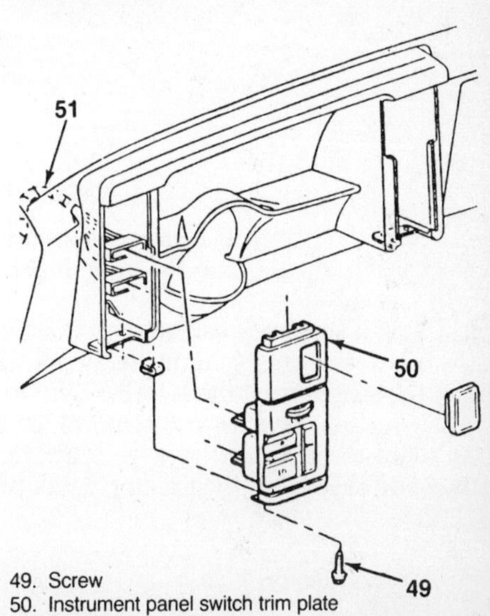

49. Screw
50. Instrument panel switch trim plate
51. Instrument panel harness

Headlight switch assembly

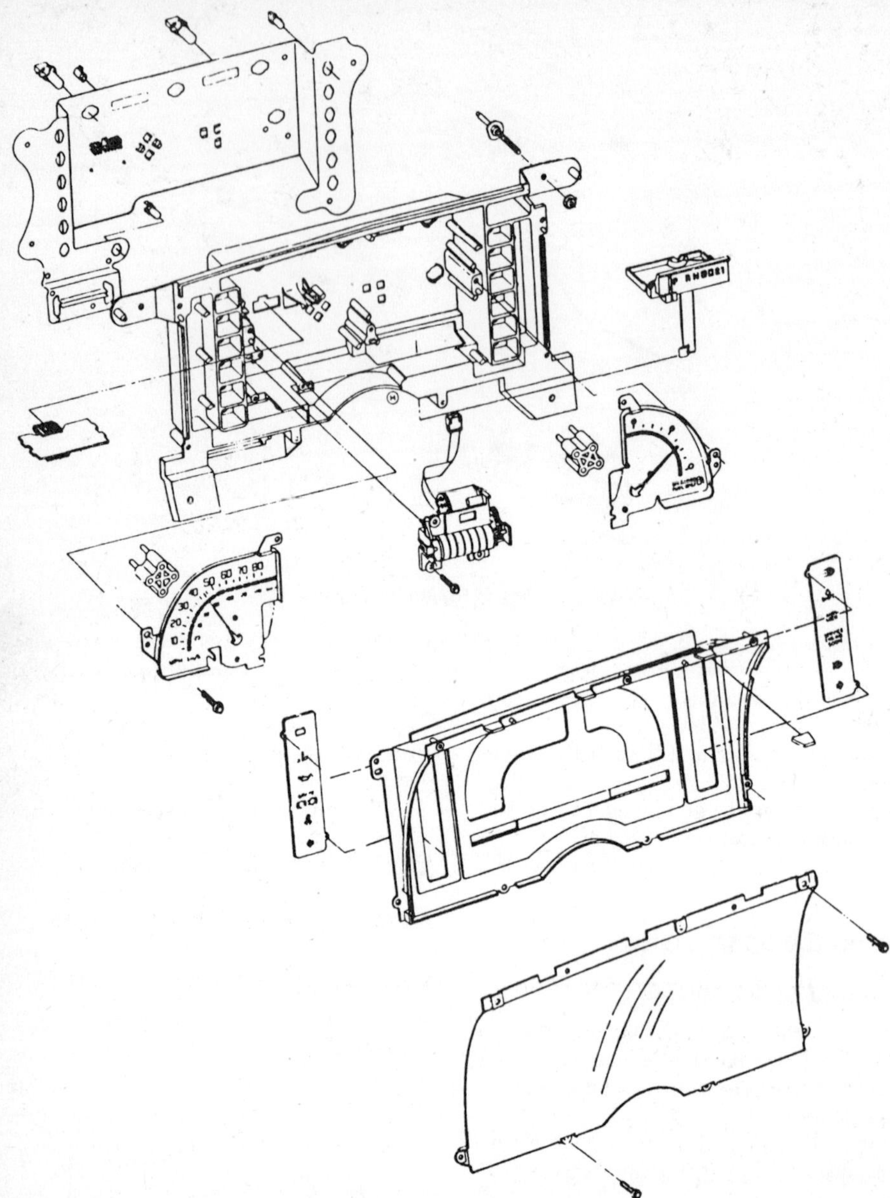

Instrument panel components

2. From the steering column, disconnect the electrical harness connector from the back-up light switch.

3. Using a small pry bar, expand the back-up switch-to-steering column retainers and remove the switch from the steering column.

4. To install, reverse the removal procedures. Place the gear shift lever in the reverse position and check that the back-up lights turn On.

Manual Transmission

To replace the back-up light switch, refer to the Back-Up Light Switch, Removal and Installation procedures in Chapter 7.

Speedometer Cable

REMOVAL AND INSTALLATION

1. Refer to the "Instrument Cluster, Removal and Installation" procedures in this Chapter and remove the instrument cluster.

2. From the rear of the instrument cluster, remove the speedometer cable-to-head fitting.

3. If replacing ONLY the speedometer cable, perform the following procedures:

  a. Disconnect the speedometer casing from the speedometer head.

  b. Pull the speedometer cable from the speedometer casing.

  c. Using lubricant Part Number 6478535

or equivalent, lubricate a new speedometer cable and install the cable into the casing.

4. If replacing the speedometer cable and the speedometer casing, perform the following procedures:

    a. Disconnect the speedometer casing from the speedometer head.

    b. Disconnect the speedometer casing from the transmission.

    c. Remove the various speedometer cable/casing retaining clips.

    d. Remove the speedometer cable/casing assembly from the vehicle.

5. To install the speedometer cable, reverse the removal procedures.

LIGHTING

Headlights

REMOVAL AND INSTALLATION

1. Disconnect the negative battery cable from the battery.

2. Remove the headlight-to-fender bezel and the retaining spring.

3. Rotate the headlight to the right and remove it from the adjusters.

4. Disconnect the electrical harness connector from the rear of the headlight and remove the headlight from the vehicle.

5. To install, reverse the removal procedures.

Signal and Marker Lights

REMOVAL AND INSTALLATION

Front Turn Signal/Marker Lights

1. Disconnect the negative battery cable from the battery.

2. Remove the headlight bezel-to-fender screws and the bezel; allow the bezel to hang by the turn signal/marker light wires.

3. At the rear of the headlight bezel, turn the turn signal/marker bulb socket $\frac{1}{4}$ turn and remove it from the headlight bezel.

4. Remove the bulb from the turn signal/marker bulb socket; if necessary, replace the bulb.

5. To install, use a new bulb, if necessary, and reverse the removal procedures. Check the turn signal/marker light operations.

Parking Lights

1. Disconnect the negative battery cable from the battery.

2. At the rear of the front bumper, turn the

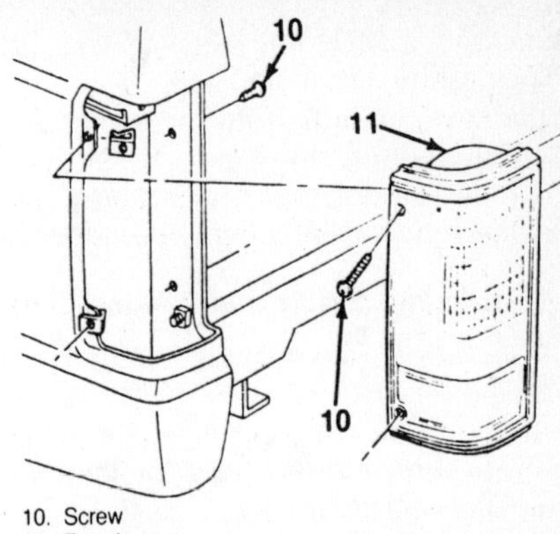
10. Screw
11. Rear lamp

Rear turn signal/brake/parking light assembly

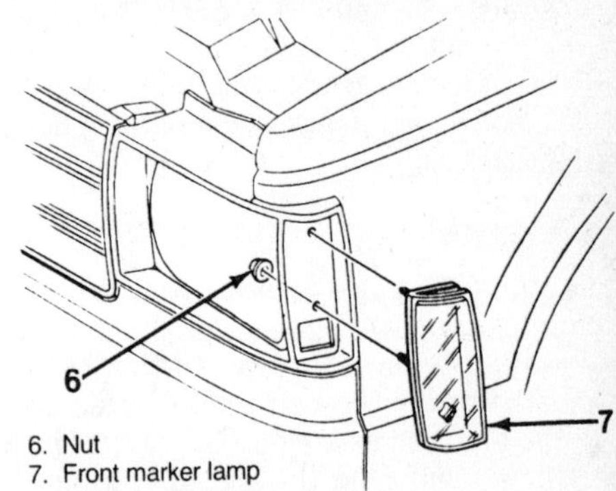
6. Nut
7. Front marker lamp

Turn signal/marker light assembly

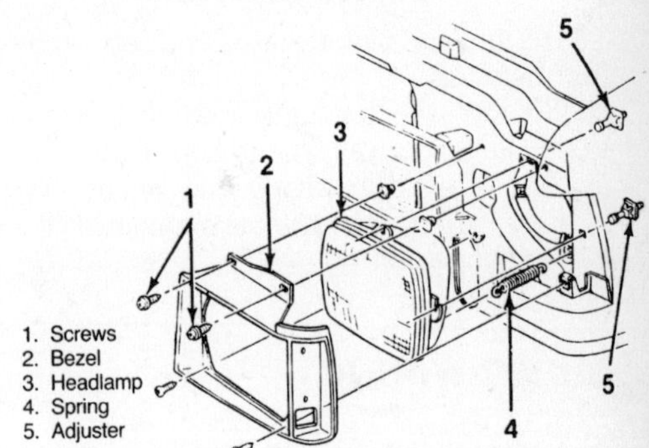
1. Screws
2. Bezel
3. Headlamp
4. Spring
5. Adjuster

Exploded view of the headlight assembly

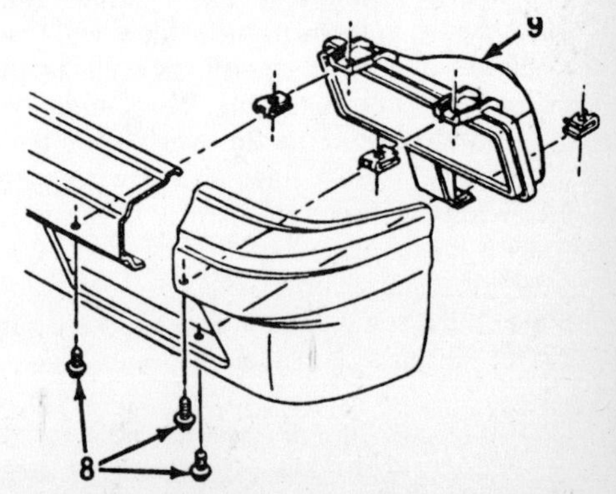

Parking light assembly

bulb socket $1/4$ turn and remove the socket from the parking brake housing.

3. Remove the bulb from the socket; if necessary, replace the bulb.

4. To install, reverse the removal procedures. Check the parking light operations.

Rear Turn Signal, Brake and Parking Lights

1. Disconnect the negative battery cable from the battery.

2. Remove the rear turn signal/brake/parking lamp-to-vehicle screws and the lamp housing from the vehicle.

3. Turn the bulb socket $1/4$ turn and remove the socket from the lamp housing.

4. Remove the bulb from the bulb socket; if necessary, replace the bulb.

5. To install, reverse the removal procedures. Check the turn signal/brake/parking light operations.

Fog Lights

The optional fog lights operate only when the parking lights or low beam headlights are on. A relay is used to supply power to the fog light switch. Power for the relay coil is interrupted when the high beams are on. The relay is in the instrument panel near the fog light switch.

REMOVAL AND INSTALLATION

1. Disconnect the negative battery cable from the battery.

2. Remove the fog light retaining screws and pull the light away from the air dam.

3. Disconnect the wiring and remove the light. Installation is the reverse of removal. The lights cannot be aimed.

TRAILER WIRING

Wiring the truck for towing is fairly easy. There are a number of good wiring kits available and these should be used, rather than trying to design your own. All trailers will need brake lights and turn signals as well as tail lights and side marker lights. Most states require extra marker lights for overly wide trailers. Also, most states have recently required back-up lights for trailers, and most trailer manufacturers have been building trailers with back-up lights for several years.

Additionally, some Class I, most Class II and just about all Class III trailers will have electric brakes.

Add to this number an accessories wire, to operate trailer internal equipment or to charge the trailer's battery, and you can have as many as seven wires in the harness.

Determine the equipment on your trailer and buy the wiring kit necessary. The kit will contain all the wires needed, plus a plug adapter set which included the female plug, mounted on the bumper or hitch, and the male plug, wired into, or plugged into the trailer harness.

When installing the kit, follow the manufacturer's instructions. The color coding of the wires is standard throughout the industry.

One point to note: some domestic vehicles, and most imported vehicles, have separate turn signals. On most domestic vehicles, the brake lights and rear turn signals operate with the same bulb. For those vehicles with separate turn signals, you can purchase an isolation unit so the brake lights won't blink whenever the turn signals are operated, or you can go to your local electronics supply house and buy 4 diodes to wire in series with the brake and turn signal bulbs. Diodes will isolate the brake and turn signals. The choice is yours. The isolation units are simple and quick to install, but far more expensive than the diodes. The diodes, however, require more work to install properly, since they require the cutting of each bulb's wire and soldering in place of the diode.

One, final point, the best kits are those with a spring loaded cover on the vehicle mounted socket. This cover prevents dirt and moisture from corroding the terminals. Never let the vehicle socket hang loosely; always mount it securely to the bumper or hitch.

CIRCUIT PROTECTION

Fuses

The fuses are of the miniaturized (compact) size and are located on a fuse block, they provide increased circuit protection and reliability. Access to the fuse block is gained through a swing-down unit at the far left-side of the dash panel. Each fuse receptacle is marked as to the circuit it protects and the correct amperage of the fuse.

REPLACEMENT

1. Pull the fuse from the fuse block.

2. Inspect the fuse element (through the clear plastic body) to the blade terminal for defects.

NOTE: *When replacing the fuse, do not use one of a higher amperage.*

3. To install, reverse the removal procedures.

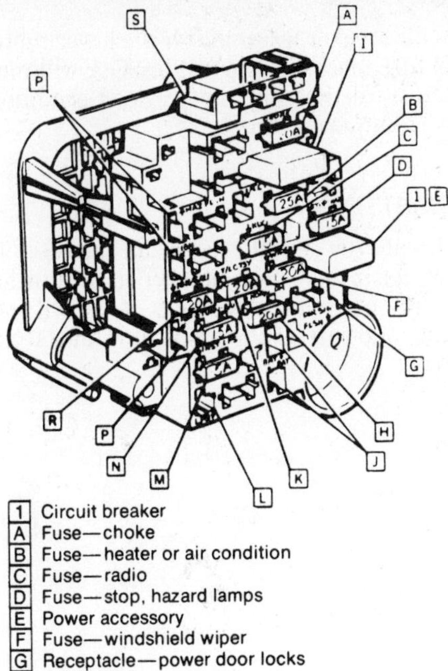

1	Circuit breaker
A	Fuse—choke
B	Fuse—heater or air condition
C	Fuse—radio
D	Fuse—stop, hazard lamps
E	Power accessory
F	Fuse—windshield wiper
G	Receptacle—power door locks
H	Fuse—horn
J	Receptacle—clock, courtesy lamp, dome lamp, I/P compt lamp & hdlp wrng buzzer
K	Fuse—tail & ctsy lamps
L	Receptacle—headlamp on warning
M	Fuse—instrument panel lamps
N	Fuse—turn & back up lamps
P	Receptacle—cruise control & auto trans
R	Fuse—ignition & gauges
S	Connector—seat belt warning buzzer & timer

Fuse box

Convenience Center

The Convenience Center is a swing-down unit located on the underside of the instrument panel, near the steering column. The swing-down feature provides central location and easy access to buzzers, relays and flasher units. All units are serviced by plug-in replacement.

Fusible Links

In addition to fuses, the wiring harness incorporates fusible links (in the battery feed cir-

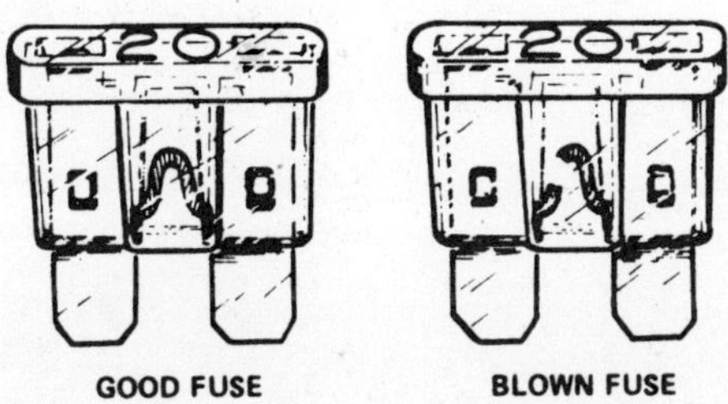

Remove and inspect the fuse to determine if the element is broken or burned. If so, determine the reason why the fuse blew and replace the fuse with one of the same rating

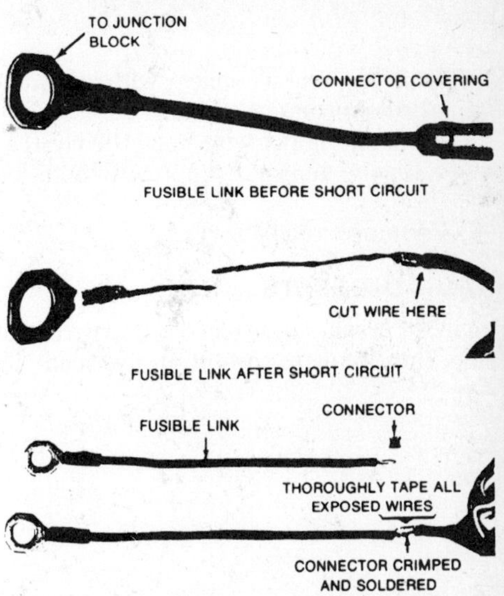

New fusible links are spliced into the wire

cuits) to protect the wiring. Fusible links are 4 in. (102mm) sections of copper wire, 4 gauges smaller than the circuit(s) they are protecting, designed to melt under electrical overload. There are 4 different gauge sizes used. The fusible links are color coded so they may be installed in their original positions.

REPLACEMENT

1. Disconnect the negative battery cable from the battery.

2. Locate the burned out link.

3. Strip away the melted insulation and cut the burned link ends from the wire.

4. Strip the wire back 1/2 in. (13mm) to allow soldering of the new link.

5. Using a new fusible link 4 gauges smaller than the protected circuit, approximately. 10 in. (254mm) long, solder it into the circuit.

NOTE: *Whenever splicing a new wire, always bond the splice with rosin core solder,*

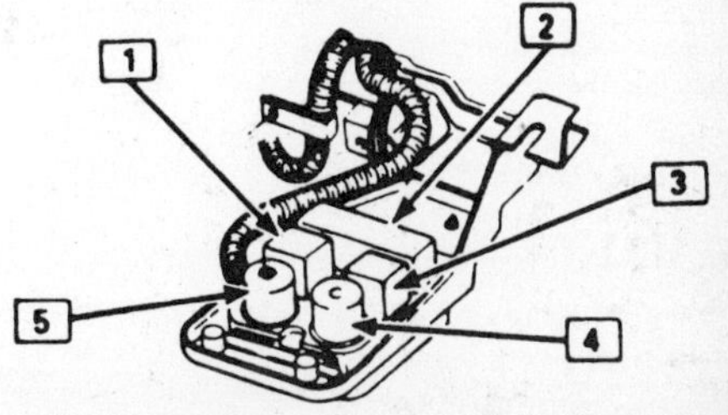

1. Horn relay
2. Seat belt–ignition key–headlight buzzer
3. Choke relay (vacant w/EFI)
4. Hazard flasher
5. Signal flasher

Convenience center and components

then cover with electrical tape. Using acid core solder may cause corrosion.

6. Tape and seal all splices with silicone to weatherproof repairs.

7. After taping the wire, tape the electrical harness leaving an exposed 5 in. (127mm) loop of wire.

8. Reconnect the battery.

Circuit Breakers

A circuit breaker is an electrical switch which breaks the circuit in case of an overload. The circuit breaker is located on the lower center of the fuse block. The circuit breaker will remain open until the short or overload condition in the circuit is corrected.

RESETTING

Locate the circuit breaker on the fuse block, then push the circuit breaker in until it locks. If the circuit breaker kicks itself Off again, locate and correct the problem in the electrical circuit.

MANUAL TRANSMISSION

Identification

Manual transmissions are officially identified by using the following descriptions:

a. The number of forward gears.

b. The measured distance between the center lines of the mainshaft and the countergear.

The 4-speed (77.5mm) transmission is a fully synchronized unit with blocker ring synchronizers and a sliding mesh reverse gear. It is contained in an aluminum alloy case with an integral clutch housing, a center support and an extension housing, which houses some of the gears, bearings and shafts. The shift lever is mounted on top of the extension housing. This transmission is used with the 2.8L 6-cylinder and the 1.9L 4-cylinder engines. The easiest way to identify the 77.5mm transmission is that the gear box and bell housing are one casting.

The 4-speed (77mm) and 5-speed (77mm) model transmissions are fully synchronized units with blocker ring synchronizers and a sliding mesh reverse gear. They have the more familiar aluminum gear box type of transmission case that houses the various gears, bearings and shafts. The floor-mounted gearshift lever assembly is located on top of the extension housing. The ML2 model is used with the 2.5L 4-cylinder engine; the ML3 model is used with the V6 engine. The easiest way to identify 77mm transmissions is that the gear box can be removed from the bell housing.

Adjustments

CLUTCH SWITCH

A clutch switch is located under the instrument panel and attached to the top of the clutch pedal. Its function is to prevent starter operation unless the clutch pedal is depressed. On some vehicles, the switch must be adjusted for reliable starter operation.

1. Remove the lower steering column-to-instrument panel cover.

2. Disconnect the electrical connector from the clutch switch.

3. Be sure to leave any carpets and floor mats in place when making the adjustment.

4. At the clutch switch, move the slider (A) rearward (towards the clutch switch) on the clutch switch shaft (B).

5. Push the clutch pedal to the floor. A clicking noise will be heard as the switch adjusts itself.

6. Release the clutch pedal; the adjustment is complete.

7. Reconnect the switch and test it.

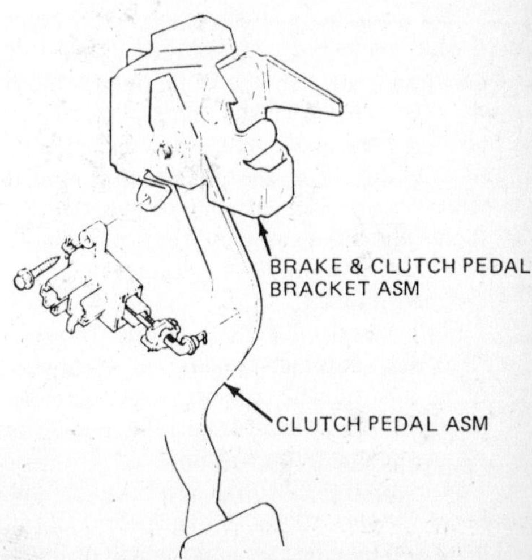

On some models the clutch safety start switch is adjustable

Shift Lever

REMOVAL AND INSTALLATION

1. With the transmission in Neutral, loosen the lock nut under the shift knob and unscrew the knob from the lever.

2. Unscrew and remove the shifter boot.

3. On 1984–91 models, there is another lock nut which can be loosened to remove upper portion of the lever.

4. Remove the bolts to remove the shift lever from the housing assembly.

5. When reassembling, lightly lubricate the shifter with molybdenum-disulphide grease and use a new gasket or silicone sealer. Torque the bolts to 10 ft. lbs. (13 Nm).

Back-Up Light Switch

REMOVAL AND INSTALLATION

1. Disconnect the negative battery terminal from the battery.

2. At the left-rear of the transmission, the back-up light switch is threaded into the transmission case. The speed sensor is held in with a separate bracket. Disconnect the electrical connector from the back-up light switch.

3. Remove the back-up light switch from the transmission.

4. To install, reverse the removal procedures. Place the gear shift lever in the reverse position and check the back-up lights work.

Extension Housing Seal

REMOVAL AND INSTALLATION

2-Wheel Drive

This seal controls transmission oil leakage around the driveshaft. Continued failure of this seal usually indicates a worn output shaft bushing. If so, there will be signs of the same wear on the driveshaft where it contacts the seal and bushing. The seal is available and is fairly simple to install, with the proper tool.

1. Raise and safely support rear of the vehicle to minimize transmission oil loss when the driveshaft is removed.

2. Unbolt the driveshaft from the differential and center support bearing, if equipped. Wrap tape around the bearing cups to keep them in place on the universal joint and slide the shaft out of the transmission.

3. Use a small pry tool to carefully pry out the old seal. Be careful not to insert the tool too far into the housing or the bushing will be damaged.

4. Use an oil seal installation tool to evenly drive the new seal into the housing. Make sure

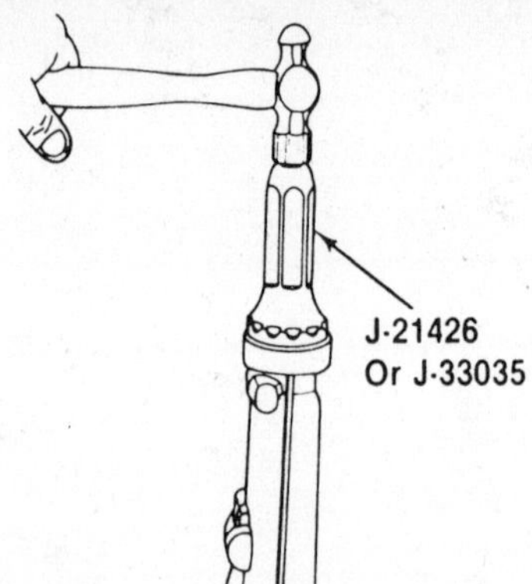

Using an oil seal installation tool on the extension housing seal

the tool only contacts the outer metal portion of the seal.

5. Install the driveshaft. Torque the universal bearing cup retainer bolts to 15 ft. lbs. Torque the center bearing bolts to 25 ft. lbs.

Transmission

REMOVAL AND INSTALLATION

2-Wheel Drive

1. Disconnect the negative battery terminal from the battery.

2. If the bell housing is being removed with the transmission (77.5mm 4-speed) remove the starter. The 77mm 4- and 5-speed can be removed without removing the bell housing.

3. Shift the transmission into Neutral. Remove the shift lever boot-to-console screws and slide the boot up the shift lever.

4. Remove the shift lever.

5. Raise and safely support the truck on jackstands. Remove the drain plug and drain the oil. Dispose of old oil properly at a reclamation center, such as a gas station or parts retailer.

6. Disconnect the speedometer cable and/or the electrical wiring connectors from the transmission.

7. Remove the driveshaft(s). Refer to the Driveline section if necessary.

8. Disconnect the exhaust pipe-to-exhaust manifold nuts and separate the exhaust pipe from the manifold.

9. On the 1982–83 models, disconnect the clutch cable from the clutch lever. On the 1984–91 models, remove the clutch slave cylinder from the clutch release lever. It can be secured out of the way without disconnecting the hydraulic line.

10. Position a floor jack under the transmission and support the transmission. Secure the jack to the transmission so it won't slip

11. Remove the transmission-to-crossmember mount bolts.

12. Remove the catalytic converter-to-chassis hanger bolts.

13. Remove the crossmember-to-chassis bolts and the crossmember from the vehicle.

14. If the bell housing is being removed, remove the clutch cover from the front of the housing.

15. Unbolt the bell housing from the engine, or the transmission from the bell housing and carefully roll the floor jack straight back away from the engine. Carefully lower it from the vehicle.

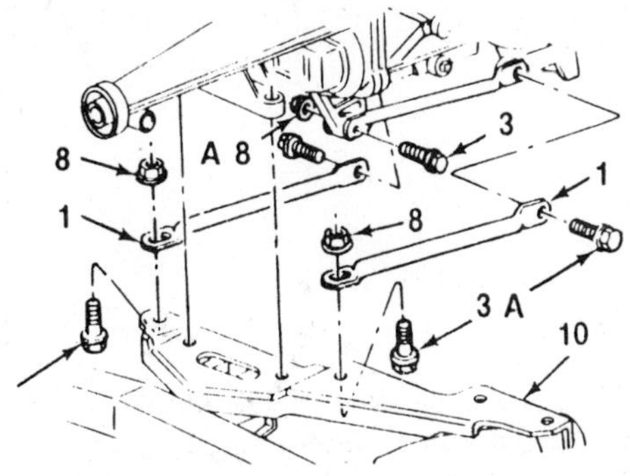

Catalytic converter hanger assembly under transmission

To install

16. Lightly coat the input shaft spline with high temperature or molyebdenum-disulphide grease. Don't use too much or the clutch disc will be ruined.

17. If the clutch was removed, make sure it is properly aligned or it will be impossible to install the transmission.

18. Put the transmission into high gear.

19. With the transmission properly placed behind the engine, turn the output shaft slowly to engage the splines of the input shaft into the clutch while pushing the transmission forward into place. Don't force it, the transmission will easily fall into place when everything is properly aligned.

20. On 4-cylinder engines with the 77.5mm transmission, torque the bell housing-to-engine bolts to 25 ft. lbs. On all others, torque all the bolts to 55 ft. lbs.

21. Install the cross member and torque the bolts to 25 ft. lbs.

22. Install the support braces and catalyst hanger and torque the nuts and bolts to 35 ft. lbs.

23. Install the clutch inspection cover and starter.

24. On 1984–91 models, install the slave cylinder and if necessary, attach the hydraulic line and bleed the system.

25. On earlier models, attach the clutch cable and push the pedal to test its operation.

26. Install the shift lever and boot.

27. Reassemble the exhaust system.

28. Install the driveshaft and refill the transmission with the proper oil.

20. Connect the wiring for the back-up lights and speed sensor, or the speedometer cable.

30. Lower the vehicle to the ground and reconnect the battery.

4-Wheel Drive

1. Shift the transfer case into **4H**.

2. Disconnect the negative battery cable.

3. Raise and support the vehicle safely. Remove the skid plate.

4. Drain the lubricant from the transfer case.

5. Mark the transfer case front output shaft yoke and driveshaft for assembly reference. Disconnect the front driveshaft from the transfer case.

6. Mark the rear axle yoke and driveshaft for assembly reference. Remove the rear driveshaft.

7. Disconnect the speedometer cable and vacuum harness at the transfer case. Remove the shift lever from the transfer case.

8. Remove the catalytic converter hanger bolts at the converter.

9. Raise the transmission and transfer case and remove the transmission mount attaching bolts. Remove the mount and catalytic converter hanger and lower the transmission and transfer case.

10. If the bell housing is being removed, remove the clutch cover from the front of the housing.

11. Unbolt the bell housing from the engine, or the transmission from the bell housing and carefully roll the floor jack straight back away from the engine. Carefully lower it from the vehicle.

To install

12. Lightly coat the input shaft spline with high temperature or molyebdenum-disulphide grease. Don't use too much or the clutch disc will be ruined.

13. If the clutch was removed, make sure it is properly aligned or it will be impossible to install the transmission.

14. Put the transmission into high gear.

15. With the transmission properly placed behind the engine, turn the output shaft slowly to engage the splines of the input shaft into the clutch while pushing the transmission forward into place. Don't force it, the transmission will easily fall into place when everything is properly aligned.

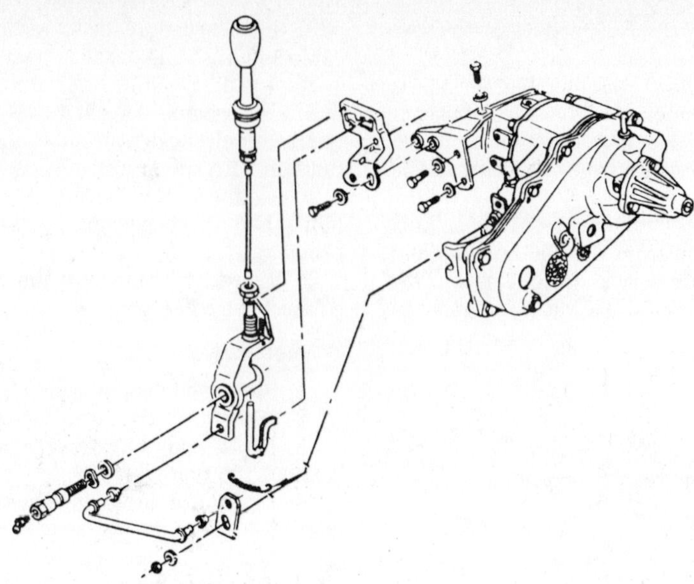

Transfer case shift linkage

16. On 4-cylinder engines with the 77.5mm transmission, torque the bell housing-to-engine bolts to 25 ft. lbs. On all others, torque all the bolts to 55 ft. lbs.

17. Install the cross member and torque the bolts to 25 ft. lbs.

18. Install the support braces and catalyst hanger and torque the nuts and bolts to 35 ft. lbs.

19. Install the clutch inspection cover and starter.

20. On 1984–91 models, install the slave cylinder and if necessary, attach the hydraulic line and bleed the system.

21. On earlier models, attach the clutch cable and push the pedal to test its operation.

22. Install the transmission shift lever and transfer case shift linkage.

23. Reassemble the exhaust system.

24. Install the driveshafts. Note the alignment marks and make sure the

shafts are installed the same way.

25. Refill the transmission and transfer case with the proper fluids.

26. Connect the wiring for the back-up lights and speed sensor, or the speedometer cable. Connect the transfer case vacuum lines.

27. Lower the vehicle to the ground and re-connect the battery.

CLUTCH

The 1984–91 trucks use a hydraulic clutch system which consists of a master and a slave cylinder. When pressure is applied to the clutch pedal (pedal depressed), the push rod contacts the plunger and pushes it up the bore of the master cylinder. In the first $\frac{1}{32}$ in. (0.8mm) of movement, the center valve seal closes the port to the fluid reservoir tank and as the plunger continues to move up the bore of the cylinder, the fluid is forced through the outlet line to the slave cylinder mounted on the clutch housing. As fluid is pushed down the pipe from the master cylinder, this in turn forces the piston in the slave cylinder outward. A push rod is connected to the slave cylinder and rides in the pocket of the clutch fork. As the slave cylinder piston moves rearward the push rod forces the clutch fork and the release bearing to disengage the pressure plate from the clutch disc. On the return stroke (pedal released), the plunger moves back as a result of the return pressure of the clutch. Fluid returns to the master cylinder and the final movement of the plunger lifts the valve seal off the seat, allowing an unrestricted flow of fluid between the system and the reservoir.

A piston return spring in the slave cylinder preloads the clutch linkage and assures contact of the release bearing with the clutch release fingers at all times. As the driven disc wears, the diaphragm spring fingers move rearward forcing the release bearing, fork and push rod to move. This movement forces the slave cylinder piston forward in its bore, displacing hydraulic fluid up into the master cylinder reservoir, thereby providing the self-adjusting feature of the hydraulic clutch linkage system.

Before attempting to repair the clutch, transmission, hydraulic system or related linkages for any reason other than an obvious failure,

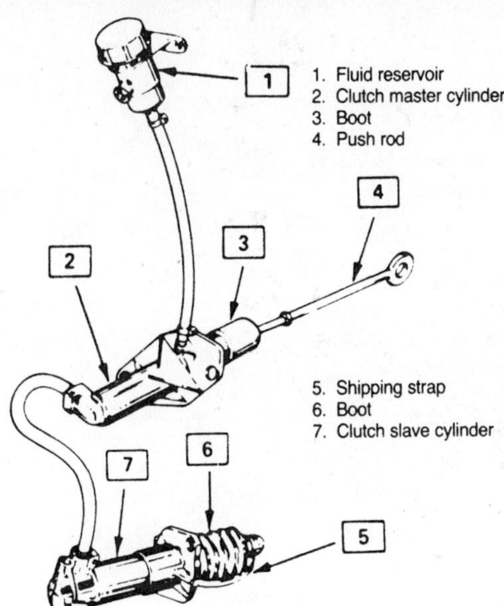

Hydraulic clutch system

the problem and probable cause should be identified. A large percentage of clutch and manual transmission problems are manifested by shifting difficulties such as high shift effort, gear clash and grinding or transmission blockout. When any of these problems occur, a careful analysis of these difficulties should be made, then the basic checks and adjustments performed before removing the clutch or transmission for repairs. Run the engine at a normal idle with the transmission in Neutral (clutch engaged). Disengage the clutch, wait about 10 seconds and shift the transmission into Reverse (no grinding noise should be heard). A grinding noise indicates incorrect clutch travel, lost motion, clutch misalignment or internal problems such as failed dampers, facings, cushion springs, diaphragm spring fingers, pressure plate drive straps, pivot rings or etc.

Adjustment

Since the hydraulic system provides automatic clutch adjustment, no adjustment of the clutch linkage or pedal height is required.

CLUTCH CABLE — 1982–83

1. Lift up on the pedal to allow the self adjuster to adjust the cable length.

2. Depress the pedal several times to set the pawl into mesh with the detent teeth.

3. Check the linkage for lost motion caused by loose or worn swivels, mounting brackets or a damaged cable.

Clutch Plate and Pressure Plate

REMOVAL AND INSTALLATION

CAUTION: *The clutch plate contains asbestos, which has been determined to be a cancer causing agent. Never clean the clutch surfaces with compressed air! Avoid inhaling any dust from any clutch surface! When cleaning clutch surfaces, use a commercially available brake cleaning fluid.*

1. Refer to the "Transmission, Removal and Installation" procedures in this Chapter and remove the transmission.

NOTE: *If equipped with a clutch cable (1982–83), disconnect the cable from the clutch lever and move it aside. If equipped with a hydraulic clutch system (1984–91), disconnect the slave cylinder from the clutch release fork and move it aside.*

2. If the bell housing was not removed with the transmission, remove it.

3. Remove the clutch fork from the ball stud and the dust boot.

4. Using the Clutch Alignment tool No. J-33169 (V6) or J-33034 (4-cyl), insert it into the crankshaft pilot bearing to support the clutch assembly.

5. Check for an "X" or other painted mark on the pressure plate and flywheel. If there

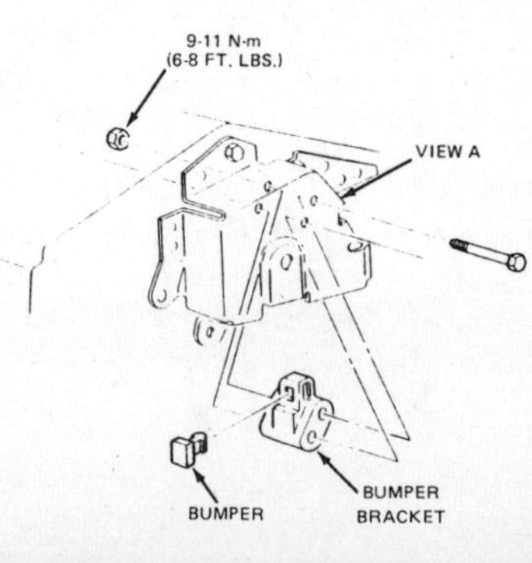

Clutch pedal on hydraulic systems

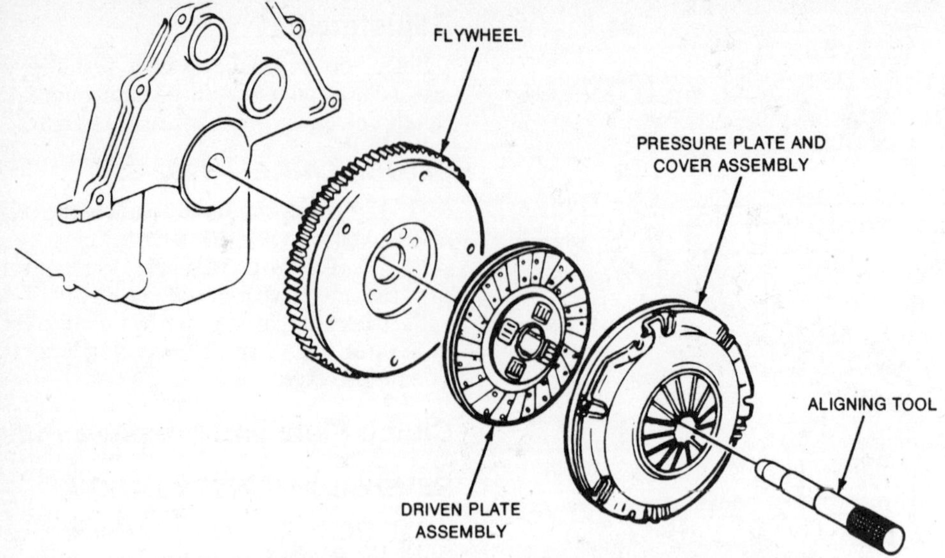

Clutch alignment tool is required to install the clutch assembly

isn't a mark, mark the assembly for installation purposes.

6. Loosen the pressure plate-to-flywheel bolts, evenly and alternately, a little at a time, until the spring tension is released. Remove the pressure plate and the driven clutch plate.

7. Check the flywheel for cracks, wear, scoring or other damage. Check the pilot bearing for wear. Replace it by removing it with a slide-type bearing puller and driving in a new one with a wood or plastic hammer.

8. To install, use the clutch assembly alignment tool and reverse the removal procedures. The raised hub of the driven plate faces the transmission. Align the mating marks and torque the pressure plate-to-flywheel bolts (evenly and alternately) to 20 ft. lbs.

NOTE: *If equipped with a clutch cable (1982–83), install and/or adjust the clutch cable.*

Master Cylinder

The clutch master cylinder is located in the engine compartment, on the left-side of the firewall, above the steering column.

REMOVAL AND INSTALLATION

1. Disconnect negative battery terminal from the battery.
2. Remove hush panel from under the dash.
3. Disconnect push rod from clutch pedal.
4. Disconnect hydraulic line from the clutch master cylinder.
5. Remove the master cylinder-to-cowl

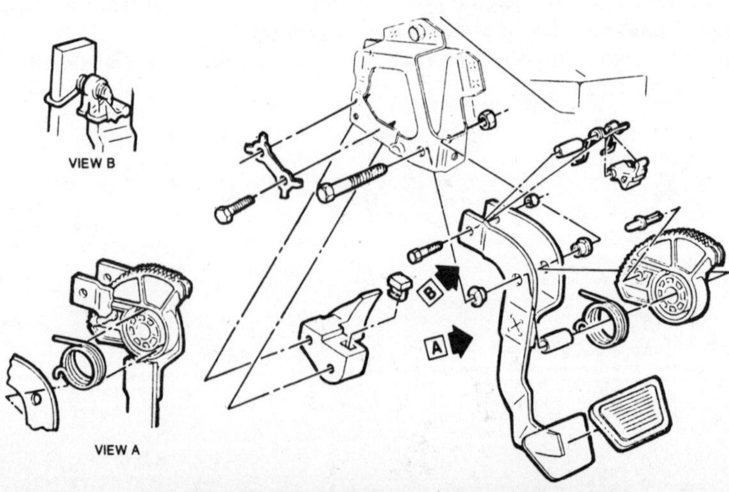

Pedal assembly and adjuster on cable clutch

brace nuts. Remove master cylinder and overhaul (if necessary).

6. Using a putty knife, clean the master cylinder and cowl mounting surfaces.

7. To install, reverse the removal procedures. Torque the master cylinder-to-cowl brace nuts to 10–15 ft. lbs. (14–20 Nm). Fill master cylinder with new hydraulic fluid conforming to Dot 3 specifications. Bleed and check the hydraulic clutch system for leaks.

OVERHAUL

1. Remove the filler cap and drain fluid from the master cylinder.

2. Remove the reservoir and seal from the master cylinder. Pull back the dust cover and remove the snapring.

3. Remove the push rod assembly. Using a block of wood, tap the master cylinder on it to eject the plunger assembly from the cylinder bore.

4. Remove the seal (carefully) from the front of the plunger assembly, ensuring no damage occurs to the plunger surfaces.

5. From the rear of the plunger assembly, remove the spring, the support, the seal and the shim.

6. Using clean brake fluid, clean all of the parts.

7. Inspect the cylinder bore and the plunger for ridges, pitting and/or scratches, the dust cover for wear and cracking; replace the parts if any of the conditions exist.

8. To install, use new seals, lubricate all of the parts in clean brake fluid, fit the plunger seal to the plunger and reverse the removal procedures.

9. Insert the plunger assembly, valve end leading into the cylinder bore (easing the entrance of the plunger seal).

10. Position the push rod assembly into the cylinder bore, then install a new snapring to retain the push rod. Install dust cover onto the master cylinder. Lubricate the inside of the dust cover with Girling® Rubber Grease or equivalent.

NOTE: *Be careful not to use any lubricant that will deteriorate rubber dust covers or seals.*

Slave Cylinder

The slave cylinder is located on the left side of the bell housing and controls the clutch release fork operation.

REMOVAL AND INSTALLATION

1. Disconnect the negative battery cable.

2. Raise and safely support the front of the vehicle on jackstands.

3. Disconnect the hydraulic line from clutch master cylinder. Remove the hydraulic line-to-chassis screw and the clip from the chassis.

NOTE: *Be sure to plug the line opening to keep dirt and moisture out of the system.*

4. Remove the slave cylinder-to-bell housing nuts.

5. Remove the push rod and the slave cylinder from the vehicle, then overhaul it (if necessary).

6. To install, reverse the removal procedures. Lubricate leading end of the slave cylinder with Girling® Rubber Lube or equivalent. Torque the slave cylinder-to-bell housing nuts to 10–15 ft. lbs. (14–20 Nm). Fill the master cylinder with new brake fluid conforming to Dot 3 specifications. Bleed the hydraulic system.

OVERHAUL

1. Remove the shield, the pushrod and dust cover from the slave cylinder, then inspect the cover for damage or deterioration.

2. Remove the snapring from the end of the cylinder bore.

3. Using a block of wood, tap the slave cylinder on it to eject the plunger, then remove the seal and the spring.

4. Using clean brake fluid, clean all of the parts.

5. Inspect the cylinder bore and the plunger for ridges, pitting and/or scratches, the dust cover for wear and cracking; replace the parts if any of the conditions exist.

6. To install, use new seals and lubricate all of the parts in clean brake fluid. Install the spring, the plunger seal and the plunger into the cylinder bore, then install a new snapring.

7. Lubricate the inside of the dust cover with Girling® Rubber Grease or equivalent, then install it into the slave cylinder.

NOTE: *Be careful not to use any lubricant that will deteriorate the rubber dust covers or seals.*

BLEEDING THE HYDRAULIC CLUTCH

Bleeding air from the hydraulic clutch system is necessary whenever any part of the system has been disconnected or the fluid level (in the reservoir) has been allowed to fall so low, that air has been drawn into the master cylinder.

1. Fill master cylinder reservoir with new brake fluid conforming to Dot 3 specifications.

CAUTION: *Never, under any circumstances, use fluid which has been bled from a system to fill the reservoir as it may be aerated, have too much moisture content and possibly be contaminated.*

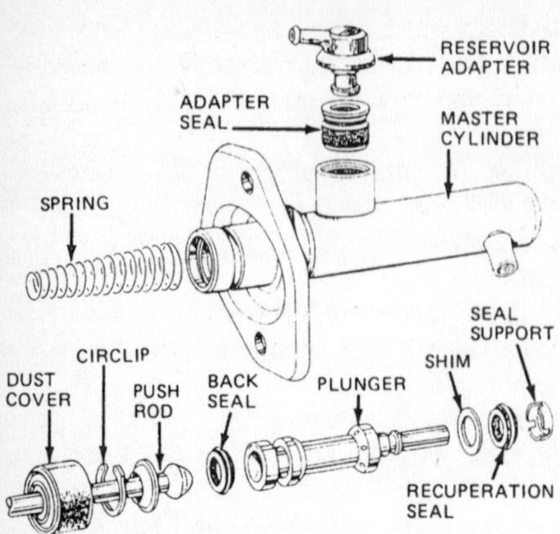

Clutch master cylinder assembly

2. Raise and safely support the front of the vehicle on jackstands.

3. Remove the slave cylinder attaching bolts.

4. Hold slave cylinder at approximately 45° with the bleeder at highest point. Fully depress clutch pedal and open the bleeder screw.

5. Close the bleeder screw and release clutch pedal.

6. Repeat the procedure until all of the air is evacuated from the system. Check and refill master cylinder reservoir as required to prevent air from being drawn through the master cylinder.

NOTE: *Never release a depressed clutch pedal with the bleeder screw open or air will be drawn into the system.*

AUTOMATIC TRANSMISSION

Identification

The Turbo Hydra-Matic (THM) 180C and 200C transmission is a fully automatic transmission which provides 3 forward gears and a reverse gear.

The Turbo Hydra-Matic (THM) 700-R4 and 4L60 transmission is a fully automatic transmission which provides 4 forward gears and a reverse gear. The oil pressure and shifting points are controlled by the throttle opening, via a Throttle Valve (TV) cable.

Fluid Pan

REMOVAL AND INSTALLATION

NOTE: *The fluid should be drained when the transmission is warm.*

1. Raise and safely support the front of the vehicle with jackstands.

2. Place a drain catch pan under the transmission oil pan.

3. Remove the pan bolts from the front and sides of the pan, then loosen the rear bolts 4 turns.

4. Using a small pry bar, pry the oil pan loose and allow the pan to partially drain. Remove the remaining pan bolts and carefully lower the pan away from the transmission.

NOTE: *If the transmission fluid is dark or has a burnt smell, transmission damage is indicated. Have the transmission checked professionally. If the pan sticks, carefully tap sideways on the pan with a rubber or plastic mallet to break it loose; DO NOT dent the pan.*

5. Empty and wash the pan in solvent, then blow dry with compressed air.

6. Using a putty knife, clean the gasket mounting surfaces.

7. To install, use a new filter, a new gasket and reverse the removal procedures. Torque the pan-to-transmission bolts to 12–14 ft. lbs. (in a criss-cross pattern). Recheck the bolt torque after all of the bolts have been tightened once. Add Dexron®II automatic transmission fluid through the filler tube.

CAUTION: *DO NOT OVERFILL the transmission; foaming of the fluid and subsequent transmission damage due to slippage will result.*

8. With the gear selector lever in the Park position, start the engine and let it idle; DO NOT race the engine.

9. Move the gear selector lever through each position, holding the brakes. Return the lever to Park and check the fluid level with the engine idling. The level should be between the two dimples on the dipstick, about 1/4 in. (6mm) below the ADD mark. Add fluid, if necessary.

10. Check the fluid level after the vehicle has been driven enough to thoroughly warm the transmission. Details are given under "Fluid Level Checks" earlier in Chapter 1. If the transmission is overfilled, the excess must be drained off. Use a suction pump, if necessary.

FILTER SERVICE

1. Refer to the "Fluid Pan, Removal and Installation" procedures in this Chapter and remove the fluid pan.

2. Remove the transmission filter screws or clips and the filter from the valve body. The filter may have either a fibrous or screen filtering element and is retained by one or two fasteners.

NOTE: *If the transmission uses a filter having a fully exposed screen, it may be cleaned and reused.*

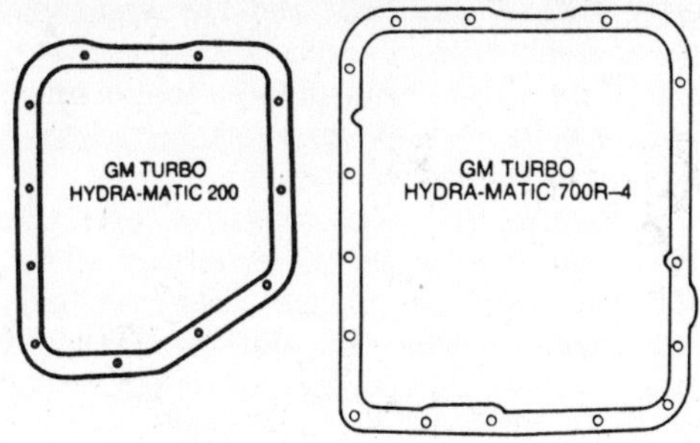

Three speed and four speed transmission pans

3. To install, use a new filter, a new gasket and reverse the removal procedures. Torque the pan-to-transmission bolts to 12–14 ft. lbs. (in a criss-cross pattern). Recheck the bolt torque after all of the bolts have been tightened once. Add Dexron®II automatic transmission fluid through the filler tube.

Adjustments

SHIFT LINKAGE

The shift linkage should be adjusted so that the engine will start when the transmission is in the Park and Neutral positions.

1. Firmly apply the parking brake and chock the rear wheels.

2. Raise and safely support the front of the vehicle on jackstands.

3. At the left-side of the transmission, loosen the shift rod swivel-to-equalizer lever nut.

4. Rotate the transmission shift lever clockwise (forward) to the last detent (Park) position, then turn it counterclockwise (rearward) to the rear of the 2nd detent (Neutral) position.

5. At the steering column, place the gear selector lever into the Neutral position.

NOTE: *When positioning the gear selector lever, DO NOT use the steering column indicator to find the Neutral position.*

6. Tightly, hold the shifting rod (swivel) against the equalizer lever, then torque the adjusting nut to 11 ft. lbs.

7. Using the gear selector lever (on the steering column), place it in the Park position and check the adjustment. Move the gear selector lever into the various positions; the engine must start in the Park and the Neutral positions.

NOTE: *If the engine will not start in the Neutral and/or Park positions, refer to Back-Up Light Switch adjustment procedures in Chapter 5 and adjust the switch.*

CAUTION: *With the gear selector lever in the Park position, the parking pawl should*

engage the rear internal gear lugs or output ring gear lugs to prevent the vehicle from rolling and causing personal injury.

8. Align the gear selector lever indicator, if necessary. Lower the vehicle and release the parking brake.

THROTTLE VALVE (TV) CABLE

If the TV cable is broken, sticking, misadjusted or using an incorrect part for the model, the vehicle may exhibit various malfunctions, such as: delayed or full throttle shifts.

Preliminary Checks

1. Inspect and/or correct the transmission fluid level.

2. Make sure that the brakes are not dragging and that the engine is operating correctly.

3. Make sure that the cable is connected at both ends.

4. Make sure that the correct cable is installed.

Adjustment

1. If necessary, remove the air cleaner.

2. If the cable has been removed and installed, check to see that the cable slider is in the zero or the fully adjusted position; if not, perform the following procedures:

   a. Depress and hold the readjust tab.

   b. Move the slider back through the fitting (away from the throttle lever) until it stops against the fitting.

   c. Release the readjust tab.

3. Rotate the throttle lever to the Full Throttle Stop position to obtain a minimum of 1 click.

4. Release the throttle lever.

Neutral Safety Switch

The Neutral Safety Switch is a part of the Back-Up Light Switch. For the replacement or adjustment procedures, refer to the "Back-Up Light Switch, Removal and Installation" procedures in Chapter 6, Chassis Electrical.

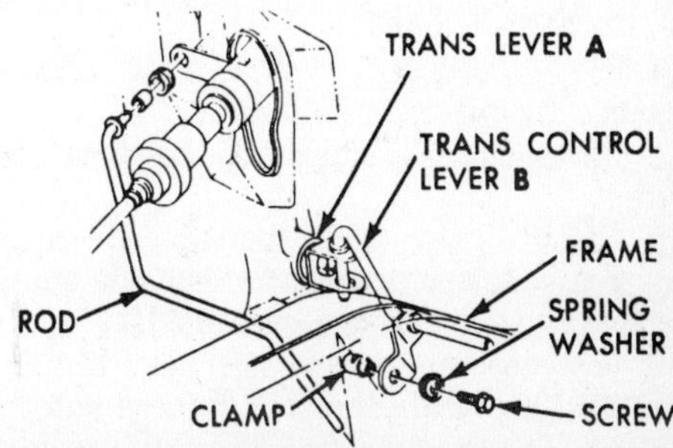

Transmission shift linkage adjustment

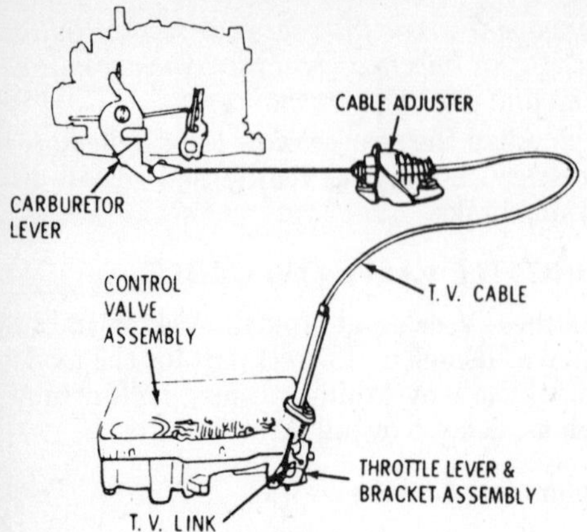

Throttle valve (TV) cable

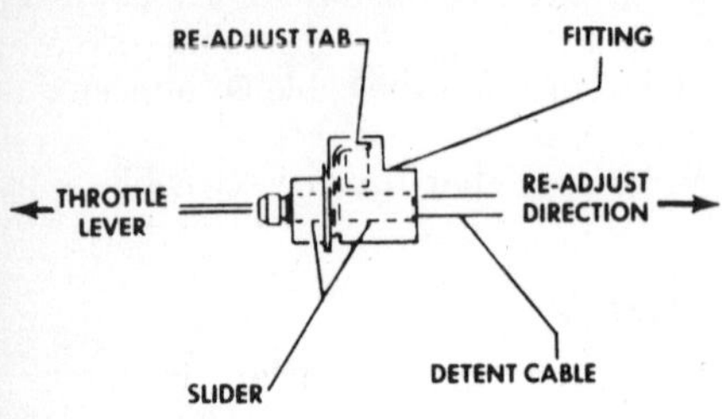

TV cable adjustment

Back-Up Light Switch

NOTE: *The back-up light switch is located on the steering column. To replace the back-up light switch, refer to the "Back-Up Light Switch, Removal and Installation" procedures in Chapter 6, Chassis Electrical.*

Transmission

REMOVAL AND INSTALLATION

NOTE: *The following procedure requires the use of the Torque Converter Holding Strap tool No. J-21366 or equivalent.*

1. Disconnect the negative battery terminal from the battery.
2. Remove the air cleaner assembly.
3. Disconnect the Throttle Valve (TV) cable from the throttle linkage.

NOTE: *If equipped with a 4-cyl engine, remove the upper starter bolt.*

4. Raise and safely support the truck on jackstands.
5. Remove the driveshaft-to-differential bolts, the slide the driveshaft from the transmission (2WD) or transfer case (4WD).
6. Disconnect the speedometer cable, the dipstick tube (and seal), the shift linkage and the electrical wiring connectors from the transmission.
7. Remove the transmission-to-catalytic con-

verter support brackets and the engine-to-transmission support brackets, if equipped.

8. Remove the transmission-to-crossmember nuts/bolts, slide the crossmember rearward and remove it from the vehicle.
9. Remove the torque converter cover, then match-mark the torque converter-to-flywheel.
10. Remove the torque converter-to-flywheel bolts. Using the Converter Holding Strap tool No. J-21366 or equivalent, secure the torque converter to the transmission.
11. Using a transmission jack, position and secure it to the underside of the transmission, then to take up its weight.
12. Remove the transmission-to-engine mount bolts and the mounts from the vehicle.
13. Lower the transmission slightly to gain access to the fluid cooler lines, then disconnect and cap the fluid lines.
14. Disconnect the Throttle Valve (TV) cable from the transmission.
15. Position a floor jack or jackstand under the engine and support it.
16. Remove the transmission-to-engine bolts and then the transmission from the engine; pull the transmission rearward to disengage it and lower it from the truck.

NOTE: *When removing the transmission, be careful not to allow the transmission to hang from the pilot shaft, for it could become bent.*

To install:

17. Carefully position the transmission behind the engine and push it forward to engage the pilot shaft.
18. Install the transmission-to-engine bolts. On 4-cylinder engines, torque the bolts to 25 ft. lbs. (30 Nm). On V6 engines, torque the bolts to 55 ft. lbs. (75 Nm).
19. Connect the fluid coolant lines and the TV cable.
20. Install the transmission mount bolts and torque to 25 ft. lbs. Make sure the torque converter turns freely by hand.
21. Install the crossmember bolts and torque to 25 ft. lbs. (35 Nm).
23. Install all the converter-to-flywheel bolts finger tight, then torque to 35 ft. lbs. (50 Nm). Install the converter cover.
24. Install the transmission-to-engine bracket bolts, if equipped and torque to 41 ft. lbs. (55 Nm) at the transmission end and 52 ft. lbs. (70 Nm) at the engine end.
25. Install the catalyst support bracket and torque to 50 Ft. lbs. (68 Nm).
26. Install the dipstick tube, speedometer cable and wiring.
27. Attach and adjust the shift linkage as required.
28. Install the driveshaft(s). Torque the shaft bearing cap retainer bolts on both 2WD

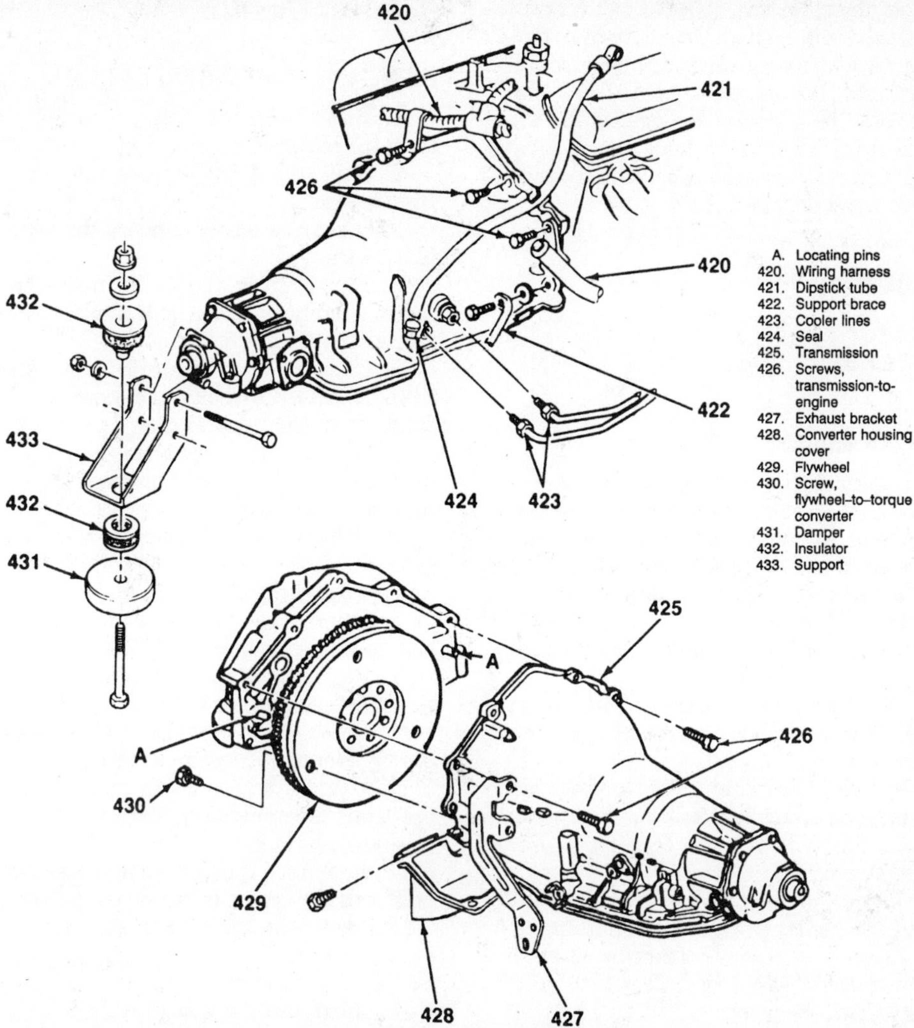

A. Locating pins
420. Wiring harness
421. Dipstick tube
422. Support brace
423. Cooler lines
424. Seal
425. Transmission
426. Screws,
       transmission-to-
       engine
427. Exhaust bracket
428. Converter housing
       cover
429. Flywheel
430. Screw,
       flywheel–to–torque
       converter
431. Damper
432. Insulator
433. Support

Removal of automatic transmission

and 4WD shafts to 17 ft. lbs. (23 Nm). On two piece shafts, torque the center bearing mount bolts to 25 ft. lbs. (39 Nm).

29. On 4-cylinder engines, install the starter bolt.

30. Lower the vehicle and connect the TV cable. Adjust as necessary.

31. Refill the transmission with fluid and check as described in Filter Service.

TRANSFER CASE

Identification

An identification tag, which is attached to the rear half of the case, gives the model number, low range reduction ratio and assembly number. The vehicles use one of three units: the New Process 207, New Process 231 or on Bravada, the Borg Warner 4472.

The Model 207 transfer case is an aluminum case, chain drive, 4 position unit providing 4WD High and Low ranges, a 2WD High range and a Neutral position. The 207 is a part-time 4WD unit. Range positions are selected by a floor mounted shift lever. Dexron® II automatic transmission fluid, or equivalent, is the recommended lubricant.

The Model 231 is a part-time transfer case with a built in low range gear reduction system. A front axle disconnect mechanism is used for 2-wheel drive operation. The 231 has three operating ranges – 2-wheel drive High and 4-wheel drive High and Low, plus Neutral. The 4-wheel drive operating ranges are undifferentiated. Dexron® II automatic transmission fluid, or equivalent, is used as a lubricant.

The Model 4472 used on the Bravada is an

all–wheel drive system. It has a two piece aluminum case and a chain driven viscous clutch that in turn drives a planetary gear set. The gear set splits the torque $1/3$ to the front and $2/3$ to the rear. This system is engaged full time, there is no neutral or high/low range and no control lever or switch. The clutch pack is sealed and not serviceable.

Adjustment

SHIFT LEVER

Model 207 and 231

1. Loosen the switch-to-transfer case bolt and the shift lever-to-transfer case pivot bolt.
2. Using the shift lever, shift the transfer case to the 4WD High position.
3. Remove the console and slide the upper boot Up the shift lever.
4. Loosen the lower transfer case shift lever-to-transfer case lock bolt.
5. Using a $3/16$ in. (5mm) drill bit, insert it through the shift lever and into the switch bracket.
6. Install the lower transfer case shift lever-to-transfer case lock bolt to lock the lever into position; this will lock the transfer case into 4WD High position.
7. Torque the switch bracket bolt to 30 ft. lbs. and the shifter pivot bolt to 96 ft. lbs.
8. Remove the lower transfer case shift lever-to-transfer case lock bolt, which was installed to lock the lever.
9. Remove the drill bit and check the shifting action.

Transfer Case

REMOVAL AND INSTALLATION

1. Disconnect the negative battery cable from the battery.
2. Shift the transfer case into the 4WD High range.
3. Raise and safely support the vehicle on jackstands.
4. From under the transmission/transfer case assembly, remove the skid plate bolts and the skid plate.
5. Remove the front/rear driveshaft-to-transfer case nuts/bolts and lower the driveshafts from the transfer case.
6. Remove the speedometer cable, the vacuum harness and/or the electrical connectors from the transmission.
7. Remove console cover from the console; slide the upper boot up the shift lever and remove the shift boot.
8. Remove the shift lever-to-transfer case bolt and shift lever from the case.
9. Remove the catalytic converter hanger-to-catalytic converter bolts.
10. Remove the transmission/transfer case assembly mount-to-crossmember bolts.
11. Using a transmission jack, secure it to the transmission/transfer case assembly, then raise the assembly.
12. Remove the crossmember-to-chassis bolts and the crossmember from the vehicle.
13. Lower the transmission/transfer case assembly, then remove transfer case-to-transmission bolts, the transfer case from the adapter (A/T) or extension housing (M/T).
To install:
14. Use a new transfer case-to-transmission

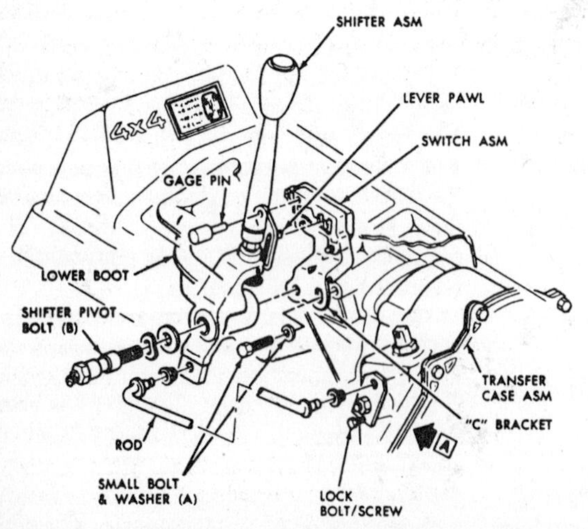

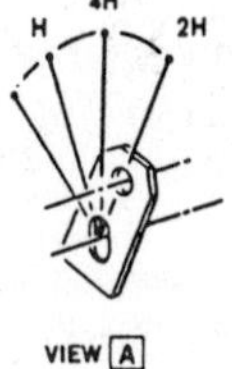

ADJUSTMENT PROCEDURE

1. Loosen bolt (A) and pivot bolt (B).
2. Shift transfer case shifter to 4 Hi.
3. Remove console and raise boot up shifter.
4. Install a gage pin 8mm or 5/16 drill bit through shifter into bracket (C).
5. Install a bolt at the transfer case shift lever as shown in View A. This will lock the transfer case in 4 HI.
6. Tighten bolt (A) to 34-48 N·m (25-35 FT. LBS.) next tighten pivot bolt (B) to 120-140 N·m (88-103 FT. LBS.).
7. Remove the bolt at the transfer case lever and the gage pin at the shifter.
8. Install shifter boot retaining screws and install console.

Shift lever adjustment on Model 207 and 231 transfer case

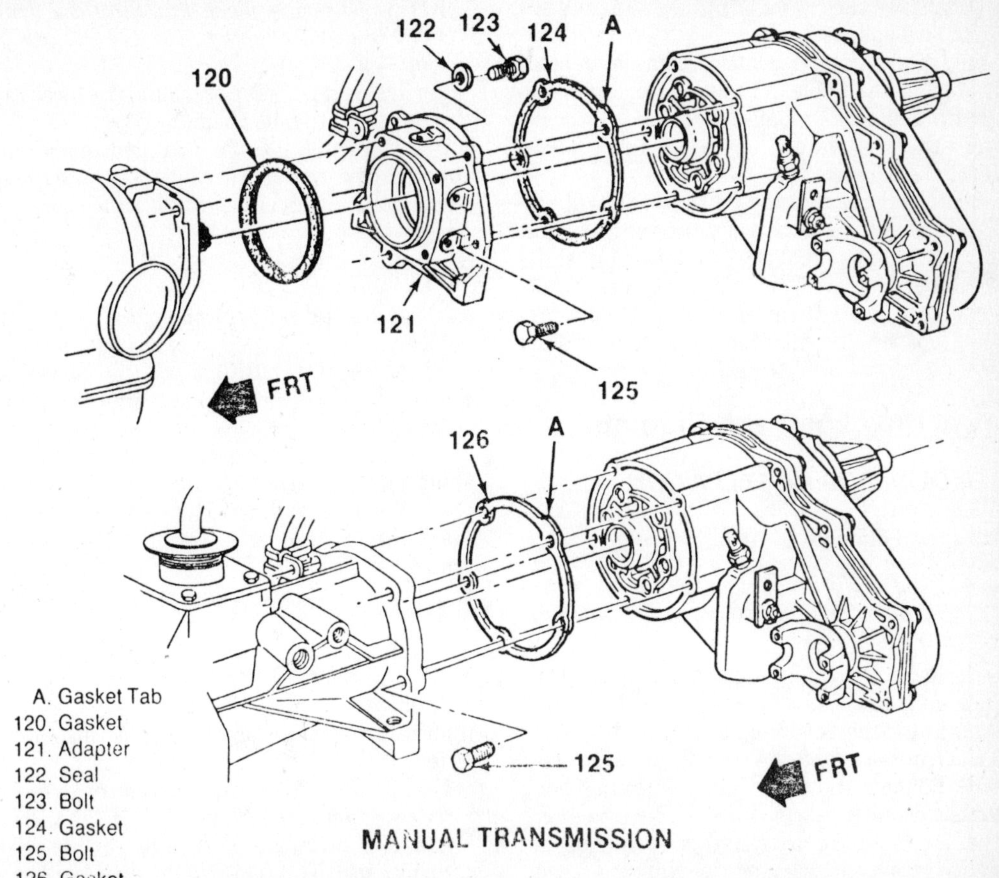

Removing transfer case from manual and automatic transmission

gasket and mount the unit to the transmission. Torque the bolts to 23 ft. lbs. (31 Nm), or 38 ft. lbs. (52 Nm) on Bravada.

15. Lower the transmission enough to install the shift lever bracket bolts, if removed.

16. Raise the transmission to install the catalytic converter hanger and crossmember. Torque the crossmember and the converter hanger–to–transmission bolts to 22 ft. lbs. (30 Nm). Torque the converter bolts to 40 ft. lbs. (53 Nm).

17. Install the driveshafts and torque the bearing cap retainer bolts to 15 ft. lbs. (20 Nm).

18. Connect the speedometer cable and shift linkage. Adjust as required.

19. Install the skid plate if equipped, fill the transfer case with Dexron II transmission fluid and road test the vehicle.

DRIVELINE

On all models, conventional, open type driveshafts are used. Located at either end of the driveshaft is a universal joint (U-joint), which allows the driveshaft to move up and down to match the motion of the rear axle.

Since the truck can be obtained in 2WD and 4WD, three types of driveshafts may be employed. On the 2WD model, a one-piece driveshaft is used. On some 4WD models is a two-piece rear driveshaft with a center bearing, and the front shaft is a two piece telescope type with internal splines.

On the front of the one-piece driveshaft (2WD) or the two-piece driveshaft (4WD), the U-joints connect the driveshaft to a slip-jointed yoke. This yoke is internally splined and allows the driveshaft to move in and out on the transmission splines.

On the rear of the one-piece driveshaft (2WD) or the two-piece driveshaft (4WD), the U-joint is clamped to the rear axle pinion. It is attached to the rear axle pinion by use of bolted straps.

On the front driveshaft (4WD), the U-joints are secured to the transfer case and the front differential by the use of bolted straps. Located in the center of the driveshaft is a slip-joint, which allows the driveshaft to move in and out on its own splines.

On production U-joints, nylon is injected through a small hole in the yoke during manufacture and flows along a circular groove between the U-joint and the yoke, creating a non-metallic snapring.

Bad U-joints, requiring replacement, will produce a clunking sound when the vehicle is put into gear and when the transmission shifts from gear-to-gear. This is due to worn needle bearings or scored trunnion ends. U-joints require no periodic maintenance and therefore have no lubrication fittings.

Front driveshaft and U-Joints

REMOVAL AND INSTALLATION

Blazer and Jimmy

NOTE: *DO NOT pound on the original driveshaft ears or the injected nylon U-joints may fracture.*

1. Raise and safely support the front of the truck on jackstands.
2. Mark the relationship of the driveshaft to the front axle and the transfer case flanges.
3. Remove the driveshaft-to-retainer bolts and the retainers.
4. Collapse the driveshaft so it may be disengaged from the transfer case flange.
5. Move the driveshaft rearward (between the transfer case and the chassis) to disengage it from the front axle.

NOTE: *Use care when handling the driveshaft to avoid dropping the U-joint cap assemblies.*

6. Using tape, wrap it around the loose caps (if necessary) to hold them in place.
7. To install, use the alignment marks and reverse the removal procedures. Torque the retainer-to-transfer case/front axle bolts to 12−17 ft. lbs.

Bravada

1. Raise and safely support the front of the vehicle.
2. Mark the position of the driveshaft flanges to the transfer case and front axle flanges.
3. Unbolt the flanges and lower the driveshaft out of the truck.
4. When installing, make sure the match marks line up properly. Torque the front axle flange bolts to 53 ft. lbs. (72 Nm). Torque the transfer case flange bolts to 92 ft. lbs. (125 Nm).

U-JOINT OVERHAUL

A universal type U-joint is used: it uses an internal snapring (production is plastic injected).

NOTE: *The following procedure requires the use of an Arbor Press, the GM Cross Press tool No. J-9522-3 or equivalent, the GM Spacer tool No. J-9522-5 or equivalent, and a 1^{1}/$_{8}$ in. (29mm) socket.*

1. While supporting the driveshaft, in the horizontal position, position it so that the lower

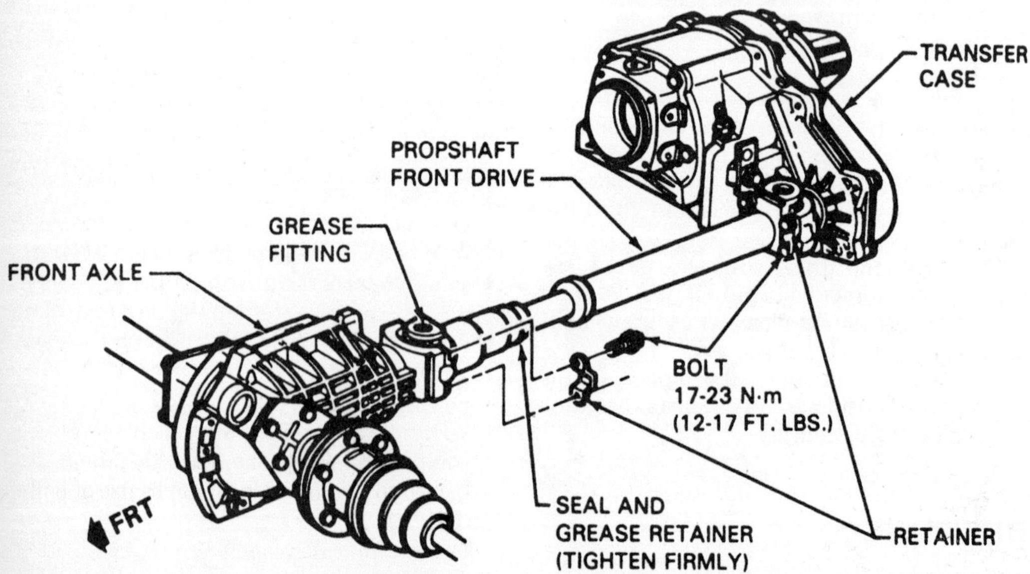

Front drive shaft assembly on Blazer and Jimmy; Bravada similar

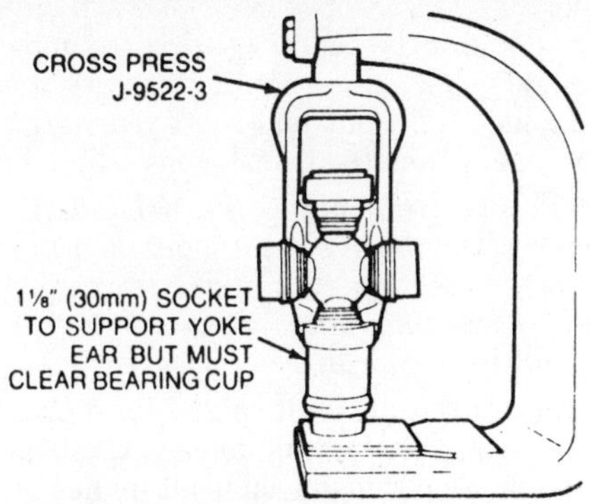

Pressing out the old U-joint

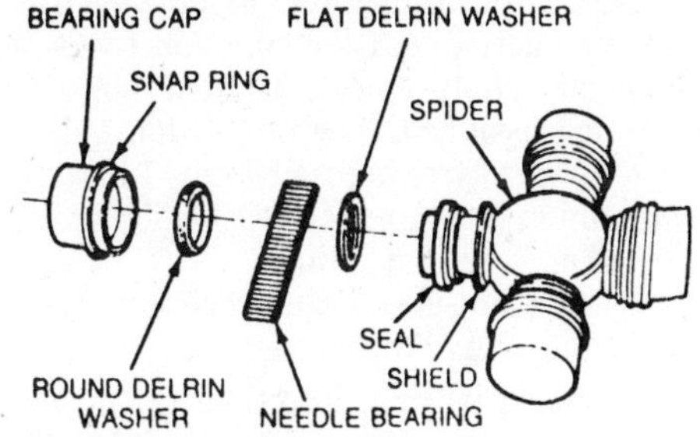

Internal snapring U-joint assembly

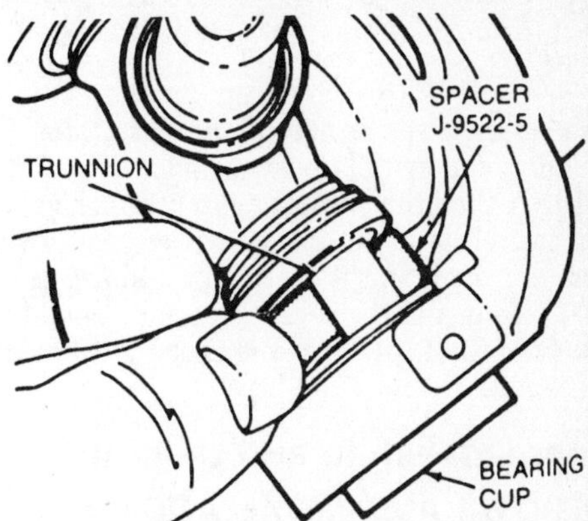

Spacer tool used to push the cup out all the way

NOTE: *When the front universal joint has been disassembled, it must be discarded and replaced with a service kit joint, for the production joint is not equipped with bearing retainer grooves on the bearing cups.*

6. Clean (remove any remaining plastic particles) and inspect the slip yoke and driveshaft for damage, wear or burrs.

NOTE: *The universal joint service kit includes: A pregreased cross assembly, four bearing cups with seals, needle rollers, washers, four bearing retainers and grease. Make sure that the bearing cup seals are installed to hold the needle bearings in place for handling.*

7. To install, position one bearing cup assembly part way into the yoke ear (turn the ear to the bottom), insert the bearing cross (into the yoke) so that the trunnion seats freely into the bearing cup. Turn the yoke 180° and install the other bearing cup assembly.

NOTE: *When installing the bearing cup assemblies, make sure the trunnions are started straight and true into the bearing cups.*

8. Using the arbor press, press the bearing cups onto the cross trunnion, until they seat.

NOTE: *While installing the bearing cups, twist the cross trunnion to work it into the bearings. If there seems to be a hangup, stop*

ear of the front universal joint's shaft yoke is supported on a 1^1/$_8$ in. (29mm) socket.

NOTE: *DO NOT clamp the driveshaft tube in a vise, for the tube may become damaged.*

2. Using the GM Cross Press tool No. J-9522-3 or equivalent, place it on the horizontal bearing cups and press the lower bearing cup out of the yoke ear; the pressing action will shear the plastic retaining ring from the lower bearing cup. If the bearing cup was not completely removed, insert the GM Spacer tool No. J-9522-5 or equivalent, onto the universal joint, then complete the pressing procedure to remove the joint.

3. Rotate the driveshaft and shear the plastic retainer from the opposite side of the yoke.

4. Disengage the slip yoke from the driveshaft.

5. To remove the universal joint from the slip yoke, perform the procedures used in Steps 1–4.

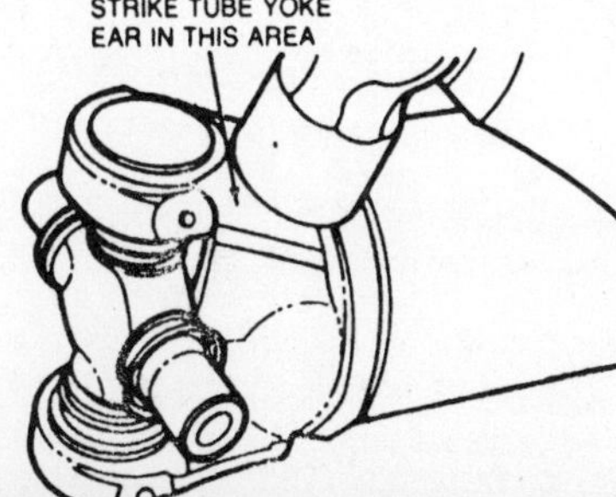

Seating the snapring

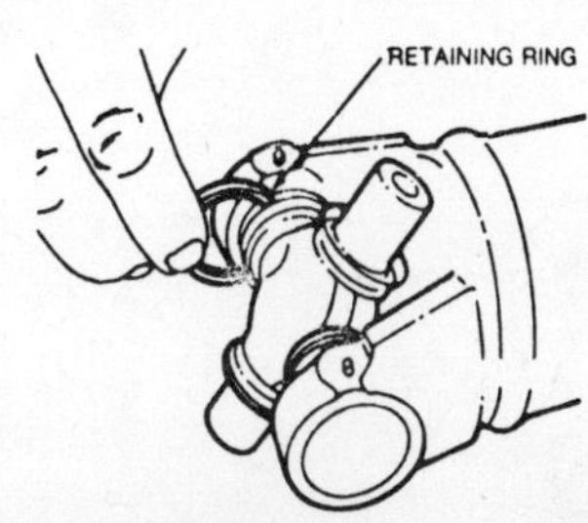

Installing the snapring

the pressing and recheck the needle roller alignment.

9. Once the bearing cup retainer grooves have cleared the inside of the yoke, stop the pressing and install the snaprings.

10. If the other bearing cup retainer groove has not cleared the inside of the yoke, use a hammer to aid in the seating procedure.

11. To install the yoke/universal assembly to the driveshaft, perform the Steps 7–10 of this procedure.

Rear Driveshaft and U-Joints

REMOVAL AND INSTALLATION

NOTE: *DO NOT pound on the original propeller shaft yoke ears for the injected nylon joints may fracture.*

1. Raise and safely support the rear of the vehicle on jackstands.

2. Mark relationship of the driveshaft-to-pinion flange and disconnect the rear universal joint by removing retainers. If the bearing cups are loose, tape them together to prevent dropping and loss of bearing rollers.

3. If equipped with a one-piece driveshaft, perform the following procedures:

a. Slide the driveshaft forward to disengage it from the rear axle flange.

b. Move the driveshaft rearward to disengage it from the transmission slip-joint, passing it under the axle housing.

4. If equipped with a two-piece driveshaft, perform the following procedures:

a. Slide the driveshaft forward to disengage it from the rear axle flange.

b. Slide the driveshaft rearward to disengage it from slip-joint of the front half-shaft, passing it under the axle housing.

c. Remove the center bearing-to-support nuts and bolts.

d. Slide the front half-shaft rearward to disengage it from the transfer case slip-joint.

NOTE: *DO NOT allow the driveshaft to drop or allow the universal joints to bend to extreme angles, as this might fracture injected joint internally. Support propeller shaft during removal.*

5. Inspect the slip-joint splines for damage, burrs or wear, for this will damage the transmission seal. Apply engine oil to all splined propeller shaft yokes.

6. DO NOT use a hammer to force the driveshaft into place. Check for burrs on transmission output shaft spline, twisted slip yoke splines or possibly the wrong U-joint. Make sure the splines agree in number and fit. To prevent trunnion seal damage, DO NOT place any tool between yoke and splines.

7. If installing a one-piece driveshaft, perform the following procedures:

a. Slide driveshaft into the transmission.

b. Align the rear universal joint-to-rear axle pinion flange, make sure the bearings are properly seated in the pinion flange yoke.

c. Install the rear driveshaft-to-pinion fasteners. Torque the fasteners to 15 ft. lbs. (20 Nm).

8. If installing a two-piece driveshaft, perform the following procedures:

a. Install the front half-shaft into the transmission and bolt the center bearing-to-support. Torque the center bearing to support nuts and bolts to 25 ft. lbs. (34 Nm).

NOTE: *The front half-shaft yoke must be bottomed out in the transmission (fully forward) before installation to the support.*

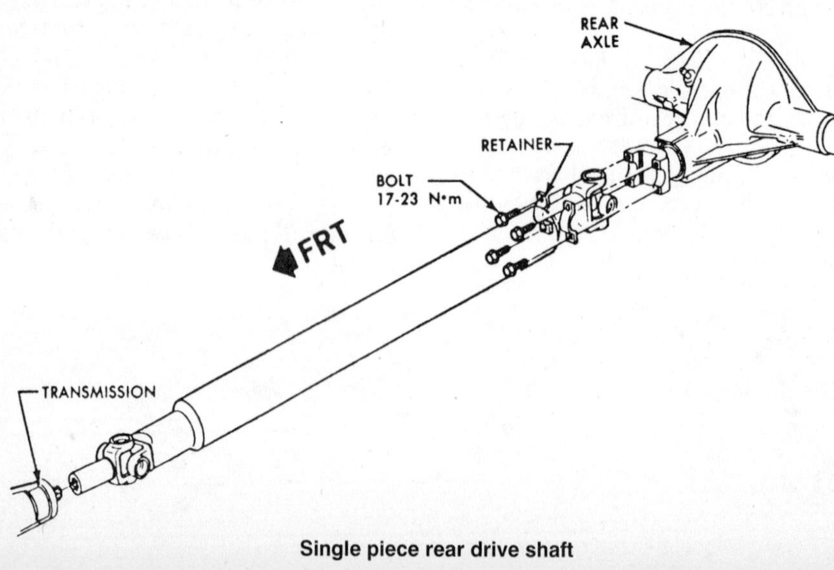

Single piece rear drive shaft

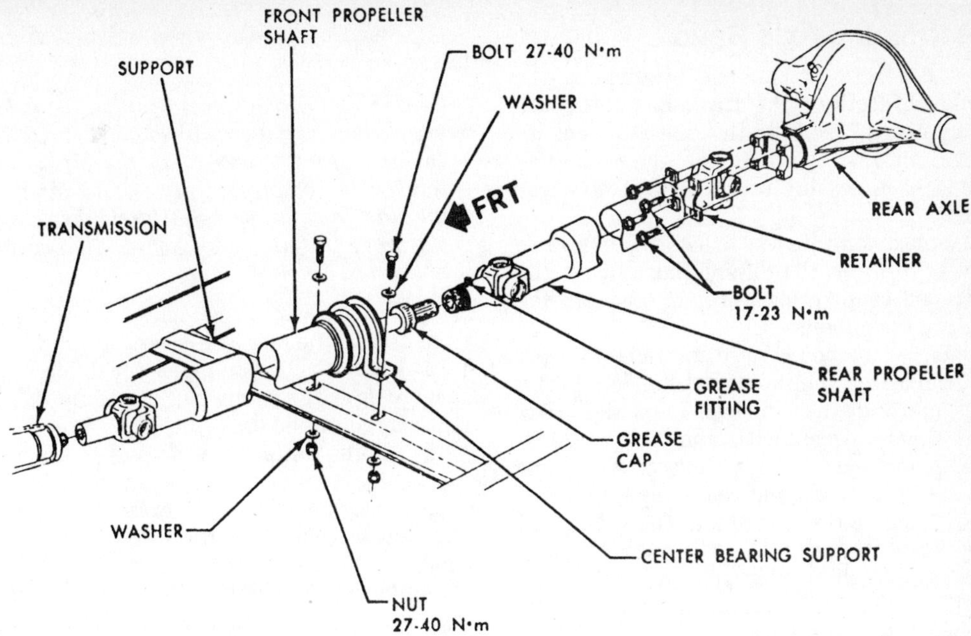

Two-piece rear drive shaft

b. Rotate the shaft so that the front U-joint trunnion is in the correct position.

NOTE: *Before installing the rear driveshaft, align the U-joint trunnions (a "key" in the output spline of the front half-shaft will align with a missing spline in the rear yoke).*

c. Attach the rear U-joint to axle. Torque the retainers to 15 ft. lbs. (20 Nm).

9. Road test the vehicle.

Center Support Bearing

REMOVAL AND INSTALLATION

1. Refer to the "Rear Driveshaft, Removal and Installation" procedures in this Chapter and remove the driveshaft.

2. Remove the strap retaining the rubber cushion from the bearing support.

3. Pull the support bracket from the rubber cushion and the cushion from the bearing.

4. Press the bearing assembly from half-shaft.

5. To assemble the bearing support, perform the following procedures:

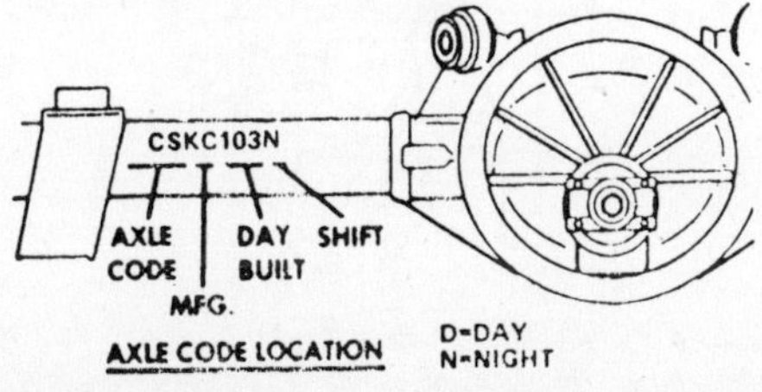

Axle data on the rear axle housing

a. If removed, install the inner deflector onto the half-shaft and prick punch the deflector at 2 opposite points to make sure it is tight on the shaft.

b. Fill the space between the inner dust shield and bearing with lithium soap grease.

c. Start the bearing and slinger assembly straight onto the shaft journal. Support the half-shaft and using a length of pipe over the splined end of the shaft, press the bearing and inner slinger against the shoulder of the half-shaft.

d. Install the bearing retainer, the rubber cushion onto bearing, the bracket onto the cushion and the retaining strap.

6. To install driveshaft, reverse the removal procedures. Torque the center bearing-to-support nuts/bolts to 20–30 ft. lbs. and the driveshaft-to-pinion retainer bolts to 12–17 ft. lbs.

REAR AXLE

Identification

The rear axle identification code and manufacturer's code must be known before attempting to adjust or repair axle shafts or rear axle case assembly. Rear axle ratio, differential type, manufacturer, and build date information is stamped on the right axle tube on the forward side. Any reports made on rear axle assemblies must include the full code letters and build date numbers.

Determining Axle Ratio

An axle ratio is obtained by dividing the number of teeth on the drive pinion gear into the number of teeth on the ring gear. For instance, on a 4.11:1 ratio, the driveshaft will turn 4.11 times for every turn of the rear wheels.

The most accurate way to determine the axle ratio is to drain the differential, remove the cover and count the number of teeth on the ring and the pinion.

An easier method is raise and safely support the rear of the vehicle on jackstands. Make a chalk mark on the rear wheel and the driveshaft. Block the front wheels and put the transmission in Neutral. Turn the rear wheel one complete revolution and count the number of turns made by the driveshaft. The number of driveshaft rotations is the axle ratio. More accuracy can be obtained by going more than one tire revolution and dividing the result by the number of tire rotations.

The axle ratio is also identified by the axle serial number prefix on the axle; the axle ratios are listed in the dealer's parts books according to the prefix number.

Axle Shaft, Bearing and Seal

REMOVAL AND INSTALLATION

NOTE: *The following procedures requires the use of the GM Slide Hammer tool No. J-2619 or equivalent, the GM Adapter tool No. J-2619-4 or equivalent, the GM Axle Bearing Puller tool No. J-22813-01 or equivalent, the GM Axle Shaft Seal Installer tool No. J-33782, J-23771 or equivalent and the Axle Shaft Bearing Installer tool No. J-34974, J-23765 or equivalent.*

1. Raise and support the rear of the vehicle on jackstands.

2. Remove the rear wheel assemblies and the brake drums.

CAUTION: *Brake shoes contain asbestos, which has been determined to be a cancer causing agent. Never clean the brake surfaces with compressed air! Avoid inhaling any dust from any brake surface! When cleaning brake surfaces, use a commercially available brake cleaning fluid.*

3. Using a wire brush, clean the dirt/rust from around the rear axle cover.

4. Place a catch pan under the differential, then remove the drain plug (if equipped) or rear axle cover and drain the oil.

5. At the differential, remove the rear pinion shaft lock bolt and the pinion shaft.

6. Push the axle shaft inward and remove the C-lock from the button end of the axle shaft.

7. Remove the axle shaft from the axle housing, be careful not to damage the oil seal.

8. Using a putty knife, clean the gasket mounting surfaces.

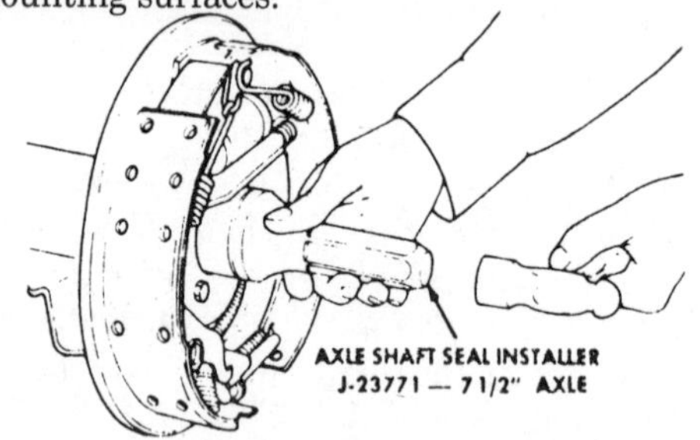

Installing the axle seal

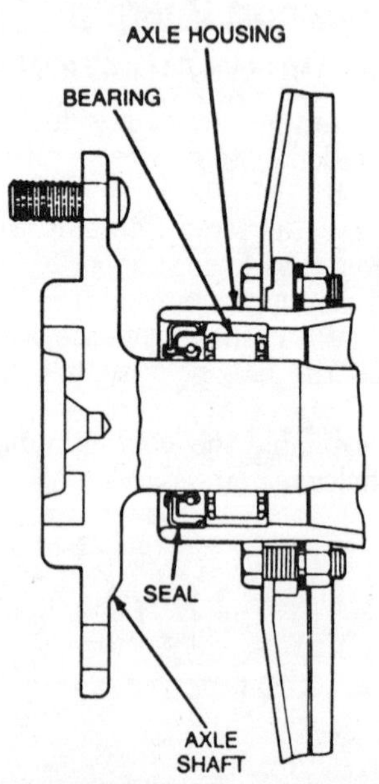

Axle bearing and seal

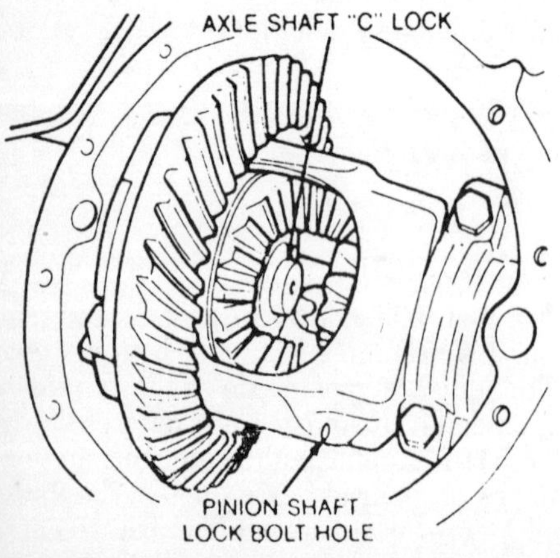

Removing the axle shaft C-lock

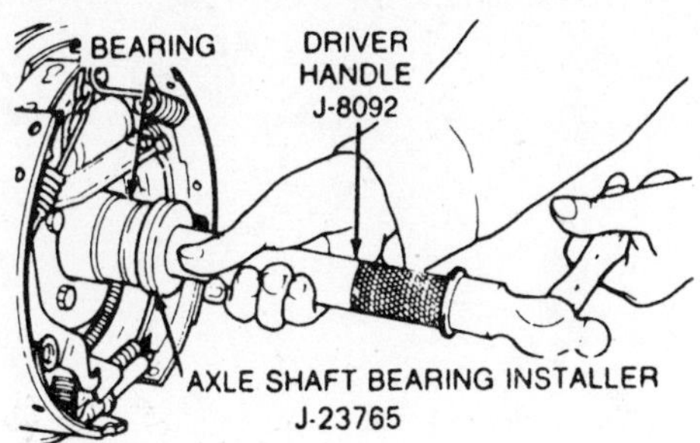

Installing the axle bearing

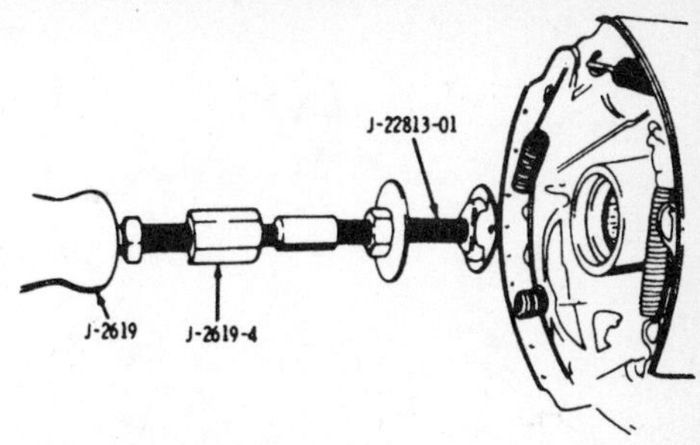

Removing the axle bearing

NOTE: *It is recommended, when the axle shaft is removed, to replace the oil seal.*

9. To replace the oil seal, perform the following procedures:

a. Using a medium pry bar, pry the oil seal from the end of the rear axle housing; DO NOT damage the housing oil seal surface.

b. Clean and inspect the axle tube housing.

c. Using the GM Axle Shaft Seal Installer tool No. J-33782, J-23771 or equivalent, drive the new seal into the housing until it is flush with the axle tube.

d. Using gear oil, lubricate the new seal lips.

10. If replacing the wheel bearing, perform the following procedures:

a. Using the GM Slide Hammer tool No. J-2619 or equivalent, the GM Adapter tool No. J-2619-4 or equivalent and the GM Axle Bearing Puller tool No. J-22813-01 or equivalent, install the tool assembly so that the tangs engage the outer race of the bearing.

b. Using the action of the slide hammer, pull the wheel bearing from the axle housing.

c. Using solvent, thoroughly clean the wheel bearing, then blow dry with compressed air. Inspect the wheel bearing for excessive wear or damage. If it feels rough, replace it.

d. With a new or the reused bearing, place a blob of heavy grease in the palm of your hand, then work the bearing into the grease until it is thoroughly lubricated.

e. Using the Axle Shaft Bearing Installer tool No. J-34974, J-23765 or equivalent, drive the bearing into the axle housing until it bottoms against the seat. Install a new seal.

11. To install, slide the axle shaft into the rear axle housing and engage the splines of the axle shaft with the splines of the rear axle side gear, then install the C-lock retainer on the axle shaft button end. After the C-lock is installed,

pull the axle shaft outward to seat the C-lock retainer in the counterbore of the side gears.

NOTE: *When installing the axle shaft(s), be careful not to cut the oil seal lips.*

12. Install the pinion shaft through the case and the pinions, then install a new pinion shaft lock bolt. Torque the new lock bolt to 25 ft. lbs. (34 Nm).

13. To complete the installation, use a new rear axle cover gasket and reverse the removal procedures. Torque the carrier cover-to-rear axle housing bolts to 20 ft. lbs. (27 Nm). Refill the housing with SAE-80W or SAE-80W-90 GL-5 oil to a level 3/8 in. (10mm) below the filler plug hole.

NOTE: *When adding oil to the rear axle, be aware that some locking differentials require the use of a special gear lubricant additive GM No. Seal Replacement*

Pinion Oil Seal Replacement

REMOVAL AND INSTALLATION

NOTE: *The following procedure requires the use of the Pinion Holding tool No. J-8614-10 or equivalent, the Pinion Flange Removal tool No. J-8614-1, J-8614-2, J-8614-3 or equivalent, and the Pinion Oil Seal Installation tool No. J-23911 or equivalent.*

1. Mark the driveshaft and pinion flange so they can be reassembled in the same position.

2. Disconnect the driveshaft from rear axle pinion flange and support the shaft up in body

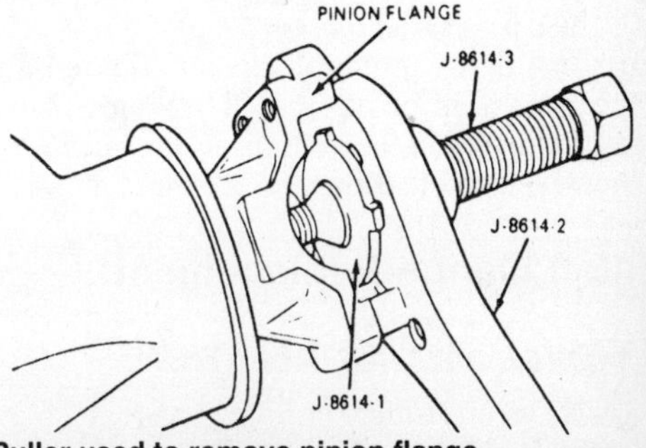

Puller used to remove pinion flange

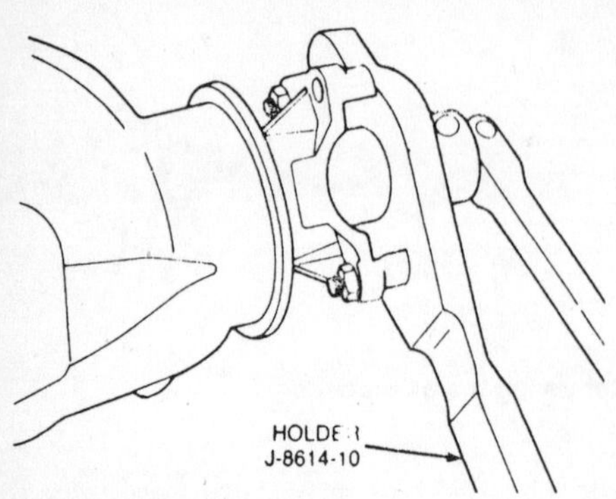

Special tools used to remove the pinion nut

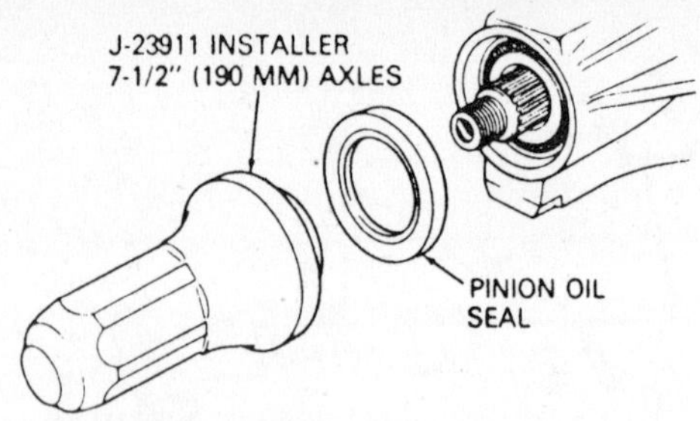

Installing pinion oil seal

tunnel by wiring the driveshaft to the exhaust pipe. If the U-joint bearings are not retained by a retainer strap, use a piece of tape to hold bearings on their journals.

3. Mark the position of the pinion flange, the pinion shaft and nut so the proper pinion bearing pre-load can be maintained.

4. Using the Pinion Holding tool No. J-8614-10 or equivalent, the Pinion Flange Removal tool No. J-8614-1, J-8614-2, J-8614-3 or equivalent, remove the pinion flange nut and washer.

5. With suitable container in place to hold any fluid that may drain from rear axle, remove the pinion flange.

6. Remove the oil seal by driving it out of the differential with a blunt chisel; DO NOT damage the carrier.

7. Examine the seal surface of pinion flange for tool marks, nicks or damage, such as a groove worn by the seal. If damaged, replace flange as outlined under PINION FLANGE RE-PLACEMENT.

8. Examine the carrier bore and remove any burrs that might cause leaks around the O.D. of the seal.

9. To install a new seal, apply GM Seal Lubricant No. 1050169 or equivalent, to the outside diameter of the pinion flange and sealing lip of new seal. Drive the new seal into place with the correct size tool.

10. Install the pinion flange and tighten nut to the same position as marked in Step 4. While holding the pinion flange tighten the nut $^1/_{16}$ in. (1.5mm) beyond the alignment marks.

Pinion Flange Replacement

REMOVAL AND INSTALLATION

1. Raise and safely support the rear of the truck on jackstands. Remove both rear wheels and drums.

2. Mark the driveshaft and pinion flange, then disconnect the rear U-joint and support the driveshaft out of the way. If the U-joint bearings are not retained by a retainer strap, use a piece of tape to hold bearing caps on their journals.

3. The pinion rides against a tapered roller bearing. Check the pre-load by reading how much torque is required to turn the pinion. Use an inch pound torque wrench on the pinion flange nut and record the reading. This will give combined pinion bearing, carrier bearing, axle bearing and seal pre-load.

4. Remove pinion flange nut and washer.

5. With a suitable container in place to hold any fluid that may drain from the rear axle, remove the pinion flange.

6. Apply the GM Seal lubricant No. 1050169 or equivalent, to the outside diameter of the new pinion flange, then install the pinion flange, washer and pinion flange nut finger tight.

7. While holding the pinion flange, tighten the nut a little at a time and turn the drive pinion several revolutions after each tightening to set the rollers. Check the pre-load of bearings each time with an inch pound torque wrench until pre-load is 3–5 inch lbs. more than the reading obtained in Step 3.

8. Install the driveshaft-to-rear axle pinion flange and torque the retainer bolts to 15 ft. lbs. (20 Nm).

9. To complete the installation, reverse the removal procedures. Check and/or add correct lubricant as necessary.

Axle Housing

REMOVAL AND INSTALLATION

1. Refer to the "Driveshaft, Removal and Installation" procedures in this Chapter and disconnect the driveshaft from the rear axle housing; the driveshaft may either be removed or supported on a wire. Using a floor jack, position it under and support the rear axle housing.

NOTE: *When supporting the rear of the vehicle, be sure to place the jackstands under the frame.*

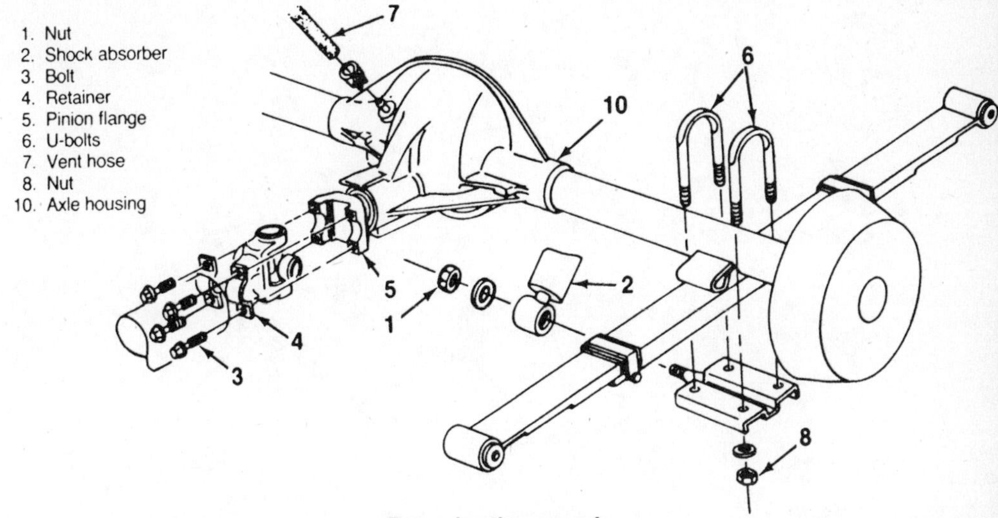

Removing the rear axle

2. Remove the rear wheel assemblies.

3. Remove the shock absorber-to-axle housing nuts/bolts, then swing the shock absorbers away from the axle housing.

4. Disconnect the brake lines from the axle housing clips and the backing plates (wheel cylinders).

NOTE: *When disconnecting the brake lines from the wheel cylinders, be sure to plug the lines to keep dirt from entering the lines.*

5. Disconnect the axle housing-to-spring U-bolt nuts, the U-bolts and the anchor plates.

6. Remove the vent hose from the top of the axle housing.

7. The axle can either be moved to the side to clear the leaf spring or, if desired, the leaf springs can be disconnected from the frame at the rear end to lower the axle down and back.

8. When installing the axle, be sure the housing is properly positioned on the leaf spring. Tighten the U-bolt nuts in a cross pattern to 18 ft. lbs. (25 Nm) to made sure everything is evenly seated. Then torque the nuts in steps to 41 ft. lbs. (55 Nm), then to 85 ft. lbs. (115 Nm).

9. Torque the lower shock mount nuts to 74 ft. lbs. (100 Nm) and the U-joint-to-pinion flange retainer bolts to 15 ft. lbs. (20 Nm).

10. Reconnect the rear brake lines and bleed the system as described in the Chapter 9. Check the fluid level in the axle before test driving: it should be almost even with the filler plug hole.

FRONT DRIVE AXLE

Identification

The front axle assembly, used on the 4WD models, utilizes a central disconnect type front axle/transfer case system which allows shifting in and out of 4WD when the vehicle is moving under most driving conditions. The axle has an aluminum carrier which includes a vacuum activated center lock feature.

The drive axles employ completely flexible assemblies which consist of inner and outer constant velocity (CV) joints connected by an axle shaft. The inner CV joint is a "tri-pot" design, which is completely flexible and can move in and out. The outer CV joint is a "Rzeppa" design which is also flexible but cannot move in or out.

Axle Tube and Shaft Assembly
REMOVAL AND INSTALLATION

NOTE: *The following procedure requires the use of the Shift Cable Housing Seal Installer tool No. J-33799 or equivalent.*

1. Disconnect the negative battery terminal from the battery.

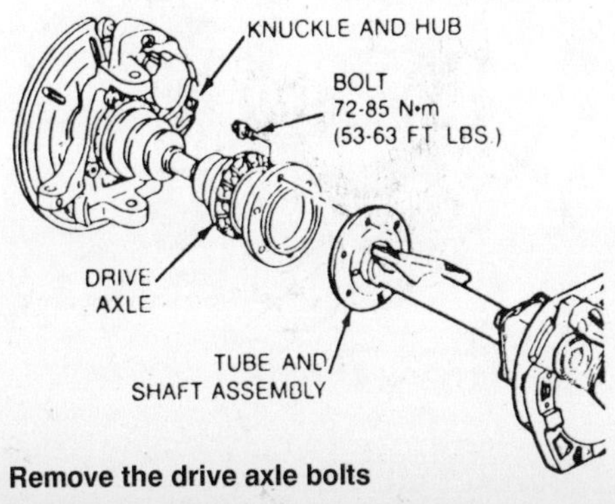

Remove the drive axle bolts

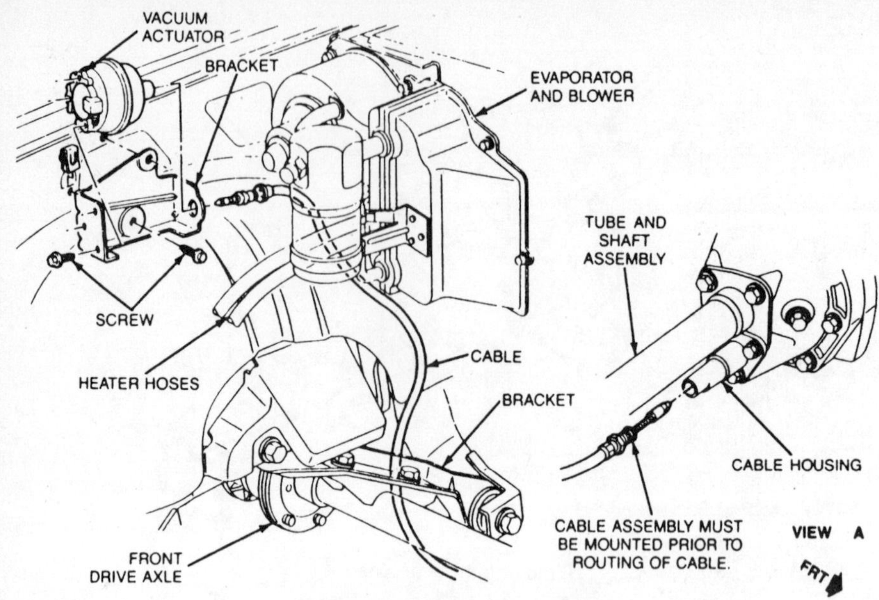

Disconnect the vacuum actuator

2. Disconnect the shift cable from the vacuum actuator by disengaging the locking spring. Then push the actuator diaphragm in to release the cable.

3. Unlock the steering wheel at steering column so the linkage is free to move.

4. Raise and safely support the front of the truck on jackstands.

NOTE: *If a twin post hoist is used, place the jackstands under frame and lower front post hoist.*

5. Remove the front wheel assemblies, the engine drive belt shield and the front axle skid plate (if equipped).

6. Place a support under right-side lower control arm and disconnect right-side upper ball joint, then remove the support so the control arm will hang free.

NOTE: *To keep the axle from turning, insert a drift through the opening in the top of the brake caliper, into the corresponding vane of the brake rotor.*

7. Remove the right-side drive axle shaft-to-tube assembly bolts and separate the drive axle from the tube assembly, then remove the drift from the brake caliper and rotor.

8. Disconnect the four wheel drive indicator lamp electrical connector from the switch.

9. Remove the three bolts securing the cable and switch housing-to-carrier and pull the housing away to gain access to the cable locking spring. DO NOT unscrew the cable coupling nut unless the cable is being replaced.

10. Disconnect the cable from the shift fork shaft by lifting spring over slot in shift fork.

11. Remove the two bolts securing the tube

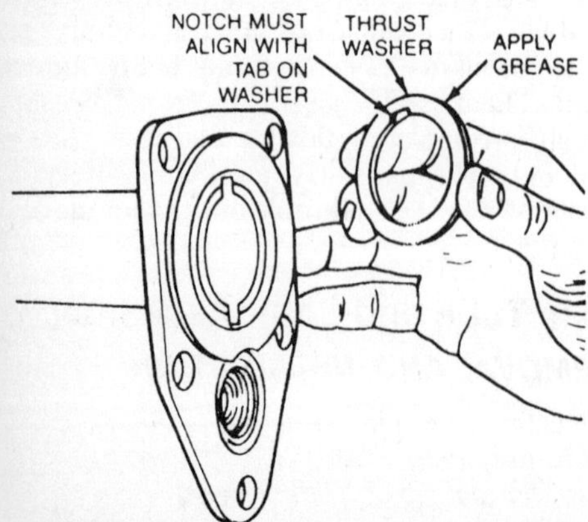

Thrust washer

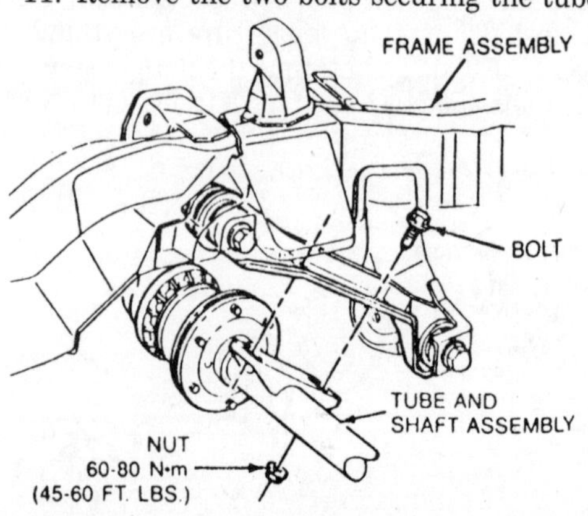

Tube-to-frame attachment

bracket to the frame.

12. Remove the remaining upper bolts securing the tube assembly to the carrier.

13. Remove the tube assembly by working around the drive axle. Be careful not to allow the sleeve, thrust washers, connector and output shaft to fall out of carrier or be damaged when removing the tube.

To install:

14. Install the sleeve, thrust washers, connector and output shaft in carrier. Apply Sealant No. 1052357, Loctite® 514 or equivalent, on the tube-to-carrier surface. Be sure to install the thrust washer. Apply grease to the washer to hold it in place during assembly.

15. Install the tube and shaft assembly-to-carrier and install a bolt at one o'clock position but DO NOT torque. Pull the assembly down, then install the cable/switch housing and the remaining bolts. Torque the bolts to 55 ft. lbs. (75 Nm).

16. Install the tube-to-frame nuts/bolts and torque to the bolts to 36 ft. lbs. (48 Nm) and the nuts to 55 ft. lbs. (75 Nm).

17. Using the Shift Cable Housing Seal Installer tool No. J-33799 or equivalent, check the operation of the 4WD mechanism. Insert tool into the shift fork and check for the rotation of the axle shaft.

18. Remove the Shift Cable Housing Seal Installer tool No. J-33799 or equivalent, and install the shift cable switch housing by pushing the cable through into fork shaft hole. The cable will automatically snap into place (Refer to Shift Cable Replacement).

19. Connect 4WD indicator light electrical connector to the switch.

20. Install the support under the right-side lower control arm to raise arm and connect upper ball joint.

21. Install right-side drive axle-to-axle tube by installing one bolt first, then, rotate the axle to install remaining bolts. Torque the bolts to 60 ft. lbs. (80 Nm).

NOTE: *To hold the axle from turning, insert a drift through the opening in the top of the*

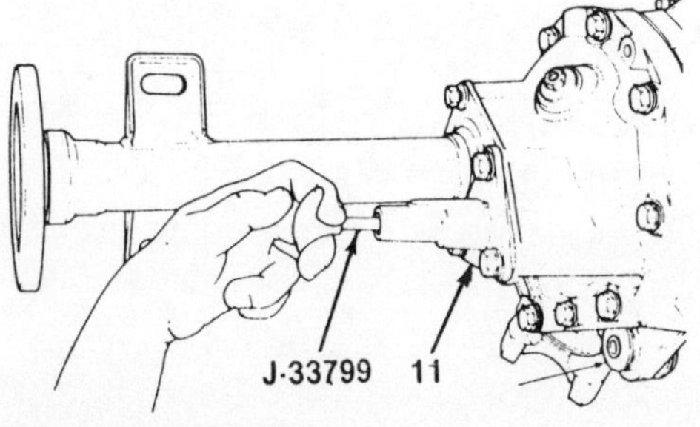

Checking the shift mechanism on the front axle

brake caliper into the corresponding vane of the brake rotor.

22. To complete the installation, reverse the removal procedures. Connect the shift cable-to-vacuum actuator by pushing the cable end into the vacuum actuator shaft hole. The cable will snap into place, automatically; Refer to the Shift Cable Replacement.

Differential Output Shaft Pilot Bearing

REMOVAL AND INSTALLATION

NOTE: *The following procedures requires the use of the Pilot Bearing Remover tool No. J-34011 or equivalent, and the Pilot Bearing Installer tool No. J-33842 or equivalent.*

1. Refer to the "Tube and Shaft Assembly, Removal and Installation" procedures in this Chapter and remove the tube and shaft.

2. Using the Pilot Bearing Remover tool No. J-34011 or equivalent, remove the pilot bearing.

3. Using axle fluid, lubricate the new bearing.

4. Using the Pilot Bearing Installer tool No. J-33842 or equivalent, install the new pilot bearing.

Differential Carrier

REMOVAL AND INSTALLATION

1. Raise and safely support the front of the truck on jackstands.

NOTE: *If a twin post hoist is used, place jackstands under the frame and lower front post.*

2. Refer to the "Tube and Shaft Assembly, Removal and Installation" procedures in this Chapter and remove the tube and shaft assembly.

3. Remove the stabilizer-to-frame bolts.

4. Using a scribing tool, mark the location of the steering idler arm-to-frame, then remove the steering arm-to-frame bolts.

5. Push the steering linkage towards the front of the truck.

6. Remove the axle vent hose from the carrier fitting.

7. Remove the left-side drive axle shaft-to-carrier bolts and the drive axle shaft.

NOTE: *To keep the axle from turning, insert a drift through top opening of the brake caliper, then through the corresponding vane of the brake rotor.*

8. Disconnect the front driveshaft.

9. Remove the differential carrier-to-frame bolts; use an 18mm combination wrench to hold the upper nut from turning, by holding it through the frame.

10. To remove the differential carrier, tip it counterclockwise while lifting it up to gain clearance from the mounting ears.

11. To install, reverse the removal procedures. Torque the left-side drive axle shaft-to-differential carrier bolts to 60 ft. lbs. (80 Nm). Check and/or add axle lubricant, fill to level of fill plug hole. Lower vehicle, test drive and recheck the lubricant.

Shift Cable

REMOVAL AND INSTALLATION

1. Disengage the shift cable from the vacuum actuator by disengaging the locking spring, then, push the actuator diaphragm in to release the cable. Using a pair of pliers, squeeze the two cable locking fingers, then pull the cable out of the bracket hole.

2. Raise and safely support the front of the truck on jackstands, then remove cable/switch housing-to-carrier bolts and pull housing away to gain access to the cable locking spring. Disconnect the cable from the shift fork shaft by lifting the spring over shift fork slot.

3. Unscrew the cable from the housing.

4. Remove the cable from the truck.

5. To install the cable, observe the proper routing.

6. Install the cable/switch housing-to-carrier bolts. Torque the bolts to 36 ft. lbs. (48 Nm).

7. Guide the cable through the switch housing into the fork shaft hole and push the cable inward; the cable will automatically snap into place. Start turning the coupling nut by hand, to avoid cross threading, then torque the nut to 71–106 inch lbs. DO NOT over torque the nut as this will cause thread damage to the plastic housing.

8. Lower the vehicle.

9. Connect the shift cable-to-vacuum actuator by pressing the cable into the bracket hole. The cable and housing will snap into place, automatically.

10. Check the cable operation.

WHEELS

2- and 4-Wheel Drive

REMOVAL AND INSTALLATION

These vehicles use a variety of wheel styles, but from the factory they are all one piece rims with 5 bolt holes in a $4^3/4$ in. (120.65mm) bolt circle. Standard sizes are 14×6 in. (152.4mm) and 15×7 in. (177.8mm). A space saver spare for emergency use only comes in a 16×4 in. (101.6mm) size.

1. When removing a wheel, loosen all the lug nuts with the wheel on the ground, then raise and safely support the vehicle.

2. If the wheel is stuck or rusted on the hub, make all the lug nuts finger tight, then back each one off 2 turns. Put the truck back on the ground and rock it side to side. Get another person to help if necessary. This is far safer than hitting a stuck wheel with the vehicle on a jack or lift.

3. When installing a wheel, tighten the lug nuts in a rotation, skipping every other one. If the nuts are numbered 1 through 5 in a circle, the tightening sequence will be 1–3–5–2–4.

4. Always use a torque wrench to avoid uneven tightening, which will distort the brake drum or disc. On steel wheels, torque the nuts to 73 ft. lbs. (100Nm). On aluminum alloy wheels, torque the nuts to 90 ft. lbs. (120Nm).

INSPECTION

Wheels can be distorted or bent and not effect dry road handling to a noticeable degree. Out of round wheels will show up as uneven tire wear, or will make it difficult to balance the tire. Runout can be checked with the wheel on or off the truck, with the tire on or off the rim, but off is better.

1. If the tire is on the wheel, set a dial indicator to touch the wheel in position "A" in the illustration to measure lateral runout.

2. To measure radial runout, set the dial indicator to position "B".

3. If the tire is not on the wheel, use the same positions on the inside of the rim. This is usually more accurate and easier to get a clean surface for the indicator stem.

4. For steel wheels, the radial runout limit is 1mm (0.040 in.), the lateral runout limit is 1.1mm (0.045 in.).

5. For aluminum alloy wheels, the limit for both runout directions is 0.8mm (0.030 in.).

Wheel Lug Studs

REMOVAL AND INSTALLATION

2-Wheel Drive Front Wheels

1. Raise and safely support the vehicle and remove the wheel.

2. Remove the brake pads and caliper. Refer to the Chapter 9.

3. Remove the outer wheel bearing and lift

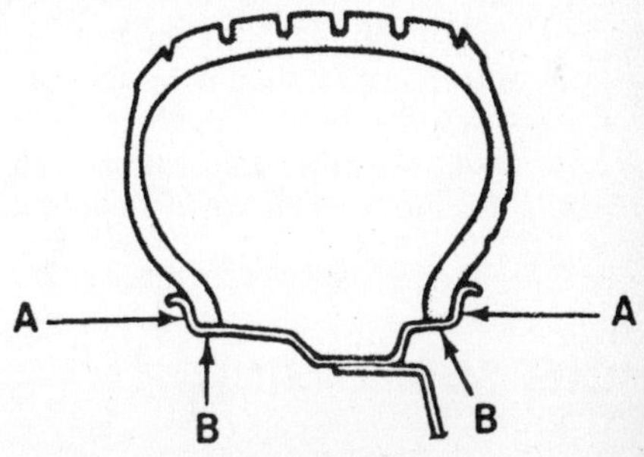

Use a dial indicator to measure radial and lateral runout with or without the tire on the rim

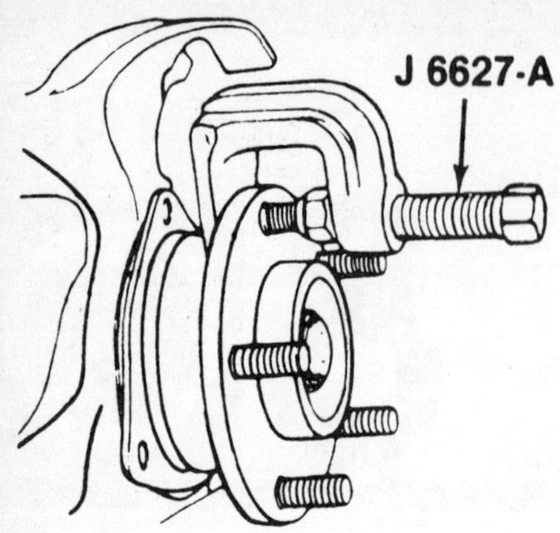

Pressing the old stud off

the rotor off the axle. Refer to **Front Wheel Bearings** later in this Chapter, if necessary.

4. Properly support the rotor and press the stud out.

5. Clean the stud hole with a wire brush and start the new stud with a hammer and drift pin. Do not use any lubricant or thread sealer.

6. Finish installing the stud with the press.

7. Install the rotor, adjust the wheel bearing and install the brake caliper and pads.

4-Wheel Drive Front
2- and 4-Wheel Drive Rear

1. Raise and safely support the vehicle and remove the wheel.

2. On front wheels, remove the brake, caliper and rotor. On rear wheels, remove the brake drum. Refer to the Chapter 9.

3. Do not hammer the wheel stud to remove it. This will ruin the wheel bearing. Use the stud press tool J6627A or equivalent to press the stud out of the hub.

4. Clean the hole with a wire brush and start the new stud into the hole. Do not use any lubricant or thread sealer.

5. Stack 4 or 5 washers onto the stud and then put the nut on. Tighten the nut to draw the stud into place.It should be easy to feel when the stud is seated.

6. Reinstall the rotor and caliper or drum and use a torque wrench when installing the wheel.

FRONT SUSPENSION

Coil Spring—2WD
REMOVAL

NOTE: *The following procedure requires the use of the Coil Spring Removal and In-*

stallation tool No. J-23028 or equivalent.

1. Raise and safely support the front of the vehicle so that the front wheels hang free.

2. Remove the shock absorber-to-lower control arm bolts, then push the shock up through the control arm and into the spring.

3. Using the Coil Spring Removal and Installation tool No. J-23028 or equivalent, secured to the end of a jack, cradle the inner control arm bushings.

4. Remove the stabilizer bar link from the lower control arm.

5. To remove the lower control arm pivot bolts, perform the following procedures:

    a. Raise the jack to remove the tension from the lower control arm pivot bolts.

    b. Install a chain around the spring and through the control arm as a safety measure.

    c. Remove the lower control arm-to-frame pivot nuts and bolts—remove the rear pivot bolt first.

    d. Lower the control arm by slowly lowering the jack.

6. When all of the compression is removed from the spring, remove the safety chain and the spring.

NOTE: *DO NOT apply force to the lower control arm and/or ball joint to remove the spring. Proper maneuvering of the spring will allow for easy removal.*

7. To install, properly position the spring on the control arm, make sure the spring insulator is in place.

8. Using the Coil Spring Removal and Installation tool No. J-23028 or equivalent, raise the control arm and spring assembly into position.

9. To complete the installation, align the control arm with the frame and install the pivot bolts (front bolt first) and nuts, then reverse the removal procedures. Torque the lower control arm-to-frame pivot nuts/bolts to 45 ft. lbs., the stabilizer bar-to-lower control

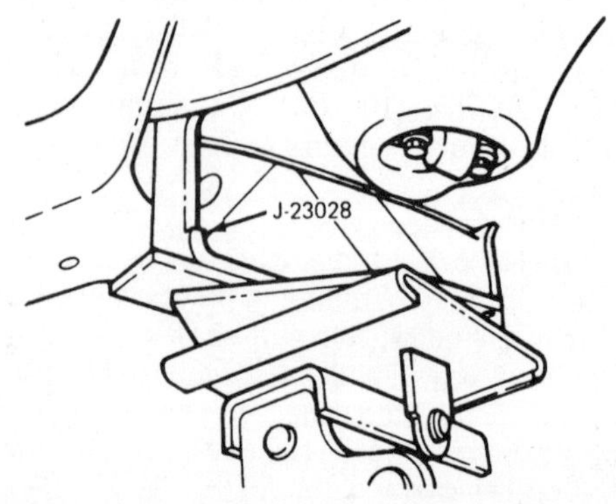

With the spring compressor secured to the jack, lift the control arm to take the tension off the spring

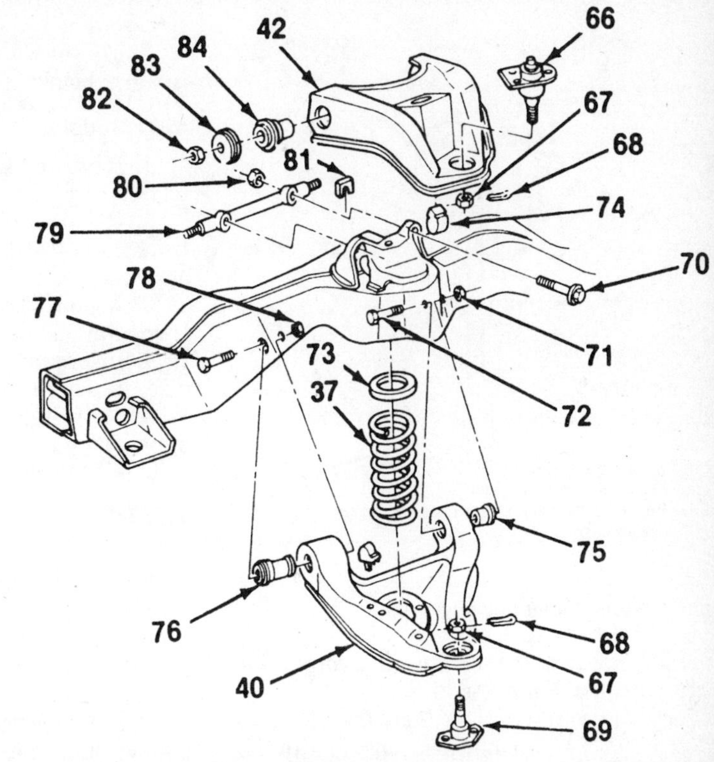

37. Coil spring
40. Lower control arm
42. Upper control arm
66. Upper ball joint
67. Nut
68. Cotter pin
69. Lower ball joint
70. Bolt
71. Nut
72. Bolt
73. Insulator
74. Bumper
75. Bushing
76. Bushing
77. Bolt
78. Nut
79. Shaft
80. Nut
81. Shim
82. Nut
83. Retainer
84. Bushing

Front control arms and components on 2WD

arm link to 13 ft. lbs. and the shock absorber-to-lower control arm bolts to 20 ft. lbs. Road test the vehicle.

Torsion Bar — 4WD

REMOVAL AND INSTALLATION

NOTE: *The following procedure requires the use of the Torsion Bar Unloader tool No. J-22517-C or equivalent.*

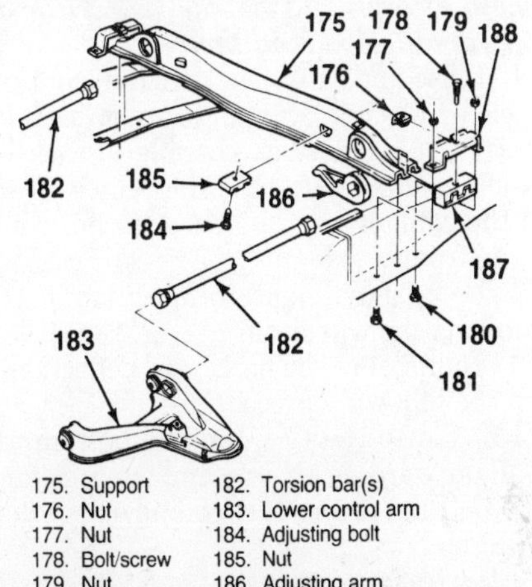

175. Support		182. Torsion bar(s)	
176. Nut		183. Lower control arm	
177. Nut		184. Adjusting bolt	
178. Bolt/screw		185. Nut	
179. Nut		186. Adjusting arm	
180. Bolt		187. Insulator	
181. Bolt		188. Retainer	

Torsion bar front suspension on 4WD

1. Raise and safely support the front of the vehicle on jackstands.

2. Using the Torsion Bar Unloader tool No. J-22517-C or equivalent, attach it and apply pressure (to relax the tension) to the torsion bar adjusting arm screw; remove the adjusting screw by counting the number of turns necessary to remove the screw.

3. Remove the torsion support-to-insulator nut/bolt, the support insulator-to-frame nuts/bolts, the insulator retainer and the insulator from the support.

4. Slide the torsion bar(s) forward into the control arm(s) to clear the support.

5. Remove the adjusting arm, the adjusting arm screw and the nut from the support.

6. Remove the torsion bar from the control arm and the support.

7. To install the support insulator, reverse the removal procedures. Torque the insulator-to-frame nuts/bolts to 26 ft. lbs. and the torsion support-to-insulator nut/bolt to 25 ft. lbs.

8. To install the torsion bar, perform the following procedures:

a. Slide the torsion bar into the lower control arm.

b. Raise and slide the torsion bar into the adjusting arm.

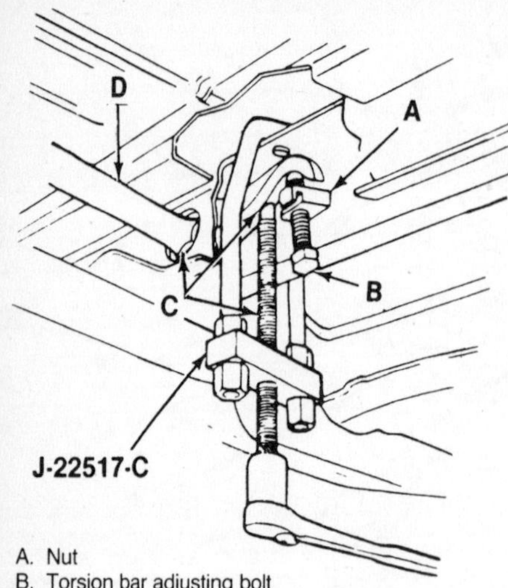

J-22517-C

A. Nut
B. Torsion bar adjusting bolt
C. Apply lubricant at points to ease installation
D. Torsion bar

Using the torsion bar unloader tool

NOTE: *Be sure the torsion bar clearance at the support is 6mm (0.236 in.).*

c. Using the Torsion Bar Unloader tool No. J-22517-C or equivalent, install it to the adjusting arm, then turn the adjusting arm screw the same number of turns which were necessary to remove it.

d. After the adjustment is complete, remove the Torsion Bar Unloader tool No. J-22517-C or equivalent.

9. Lower the truck. Refer to the "Front End Alignment" in this Chapter and adjust the final "Z" trim height.

Shock Absorbers

REMOVAL AND INSTALLATION

2WD Models

1. Raise and safely support the front of the truck.
2. Using an open end wrench, hold the shock absorber upper stem from turning, then remove the upper stem retaining nut, the retainer and rubber grommet.
3. Remove the shock absorber-to-lower control arm bolts and lower the shock absorber assembly from the bottom of the control arm.
4. Inspect and test the shock absorber; replace it, if necessary.
5. To install the shock absorber, fully extend the shock absorber stem, then push it up through the lower control arm and spring, so that the upper stem passes through the mounting hole in the upper control arm frame bracket.
6. Torque the upper shock absorber nut to 8 ft. lbs. If desired, use the old nut as a jam nut. Be careful not to crush the rubber bushing.
7. Torque the shock absorber-to-lower control arm bolts to 20 ft. lbs.

4WD Models

1. Raise and safely support the front of the truck.
2. Remove the shock absorber-to-lower control arm nut and bolt, then collapse the shock absorber.
3. Remove the upper shock absorber-to-frame nut and bolt.
4. Inspect and test the shock absorber; replace it, if necessary.
5. To install, reverse the removal procedures. Torque the upper and lower mounting bolts to 54 ft. lbs.

TESTING

Visually inspect the shock absorber. If there is evidence of leakage and the shock absorber is covered with oil, the shock is defective and should be replaced.

If there is no sign of excessive leakage (a small amount of weeping is normal) bounce the truck at one corner by pressing down on the bumper and releasing it. When you have the truck bouncing as much as you can, release the bumper. The truck should stop bouncing after the first rebound. If the bouncing continues past the center point of the bounce more than once, the shock absorbers are worn and should be replaced.

Upper Ball Joint

INSPECTION

NOTE: *Before performing this inspection, make sure that the wheel bearings are adjusted correctly and that the control arm bushings are in good condition.*

1. Raise and safely support the front of the vehicle by placing jackstands under each lower control arm as close as possible to each lower ball joint. Make sure that the vehicle is stable and the control arm bumpers are not contacting the frame.
2. Using a dial indicator, position it so that it contacts the wheel rim.
3. To measure the horizontal deflection, perform the following procedures:

a. Grasp the tire (top and bottom), then pull outward on the top and push inward on the bottom; record the reading on the dial indicator.

b. Grasp the tire (top and bottom), then pull outward on the bottom and push inward on the top; record the reading on the dial indicator.

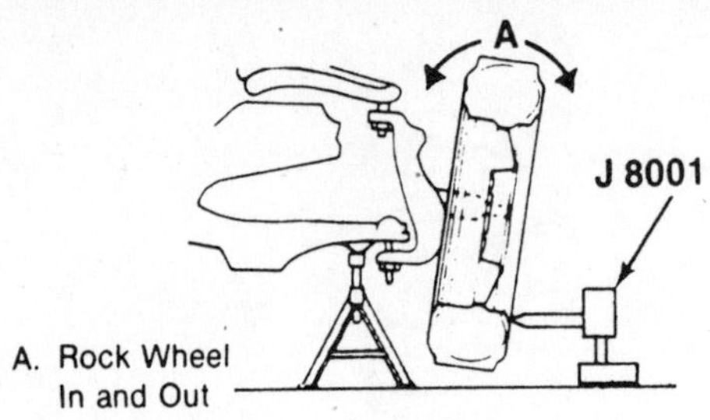

Using a dial indicator to determine ball joint ware

    c. If the difference in the dial indicator reading is more than 3mm (0.12 in.), or if the rubber seal is cut or appears damaged, the ball joint must be replaced.

REMOVAL AND INSTALLATION

NOTE: *The following procedure requires the use of the GM Ball Joint Remover tool No. J-23742 or equivalent.*

    1. Raise and safely support the front of the vehicle by placing jackstands under the frame, not the lower control arms.

    2. Place the floor jack under the lower control arm spring seat and raise it slightly to retain the spring and the lower control arm in position.

CAUTION: *With the ball joint nut removed, the floor jack is holding the lower control arm in place against the coil spring. Make sure the jack is firmly engaged with the spring seat and cannot move, or personal injury could result.*

    3. Remove the wheel and brake caliper. Without disconnecting the hydraulic line, hang

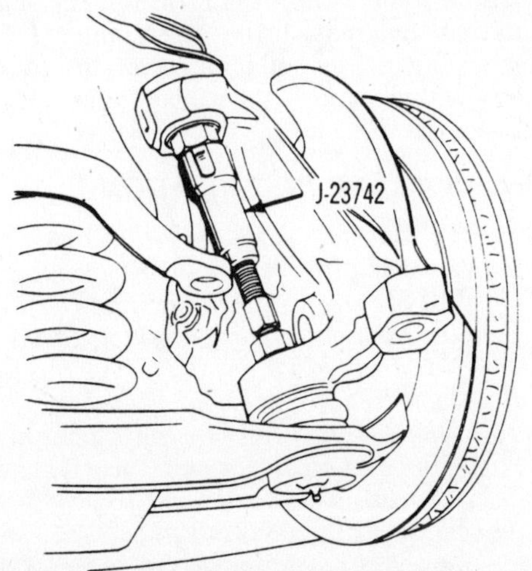

Use a ball joint removal tool to press the ball joint out of the steering knuckle

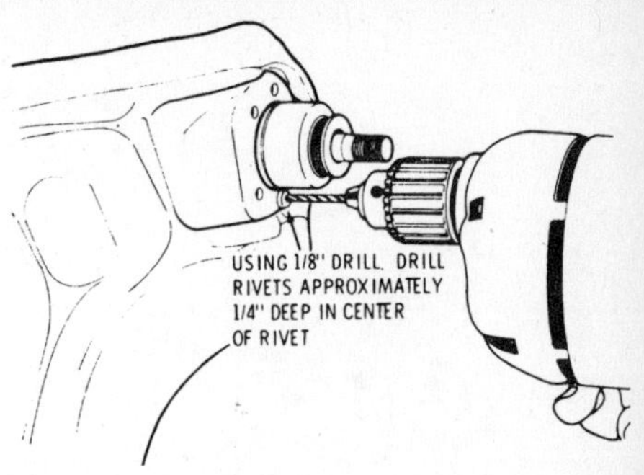

Drill the upper ball joint rivets

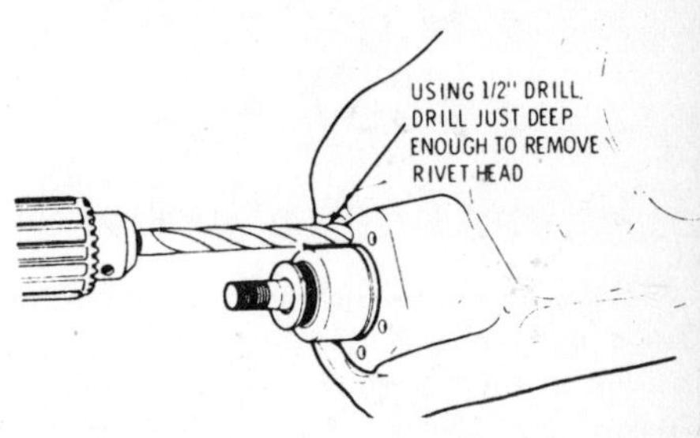

Drill the rivet heads

the caliper from the body with wire so it does not hang on the line.

    5. From the upper ball joint, remove the cotter pin, the nut and the grease fitting.

    6. Using the GM Ball Joint Remover tool No. J-23742 or equivalent, separate the upper ball joint from the steering knuckle. Pull the steering knuckle free of the ball joint after removal.

NOTE: *After separating the steering knuckle from the upper ball joint, be sure to support the steering knuckle/hub assembly to prevent damaging the brake hose.*

    7. To remove the upper ball joint from the upper control arm, perform the following procedures:

    a. Using a $^1/_8$ in. (3mm) drill bit, drill a $^1/_4$ in. (6mm) deep hole into each rivet.

    b. Using a $^1/_2$ in. (13mm) drill bit, drill off the rivet heads.

    c. Using a pin punch and the hammer, drive the rivets from the upper ball joint-to-upper control arm assembly and remove the upper ball joint.

    8. Clean and inspect the steering knuckle hole. Replace the steering knuckle if the hole is out of round.

    To install:

    9. When installing the new joint, put the bolts up through the control arm and install the joint down onto the bolts. Torque the nuts to 17 ft. lbs.

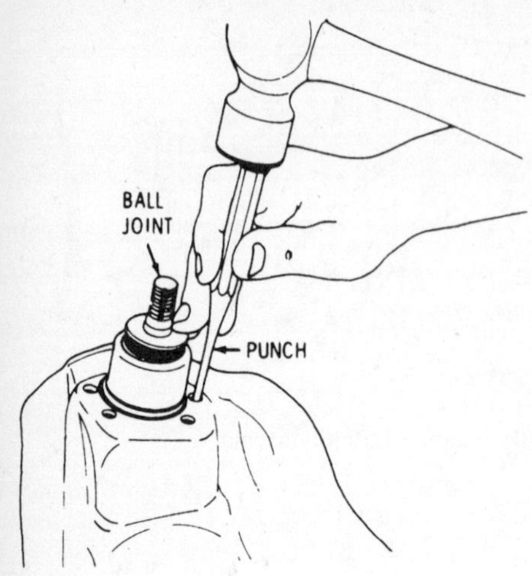

Punch the rivets out to remove the ball joint

10. To complete the installation, seat the upper ball joint into the steering knuckle and install the nut. Torque the upper ball joint-to-steering knuckle nut to 65 ft. lbs. and install a new cotter pin.

NOTE: *When installing the cotter pin, never loosen the castle nut to expose the cotter pin hole.*

11. Use a grease gun to lubricate the upper ball joint.
12. Install the brake caliper and pads and the wheel. When a ball joint is replaced, a front end alignment is strongly recommended.

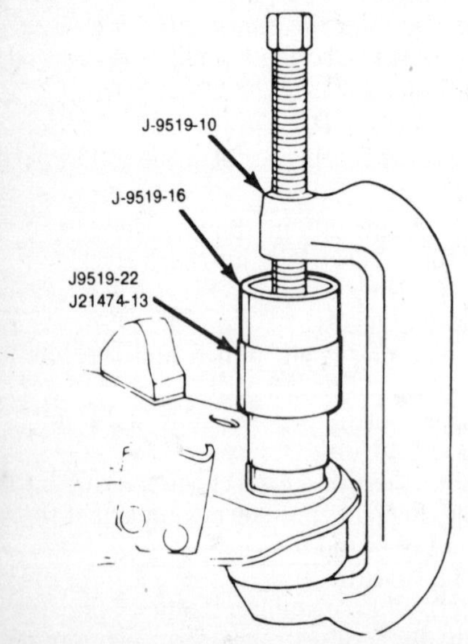

Pressing the lower ball joint out of the control arm

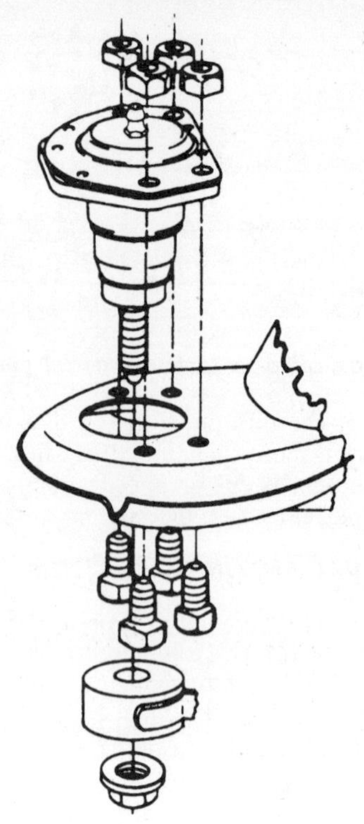

Install the new joint down onto the bolts, nuts touching the joint

Lower Ball Joint

INSPECTION

NOTE: *Before performing this inspection, make sure that the wheel bearings are adjusted correctly and that the control arm bushings are in good condition.*

Visually check the wear indicator, the small nub that the grease fitting screws into. If it is flush or inside the ball joint cover surface, replace the ball joint. If the rubber grease seal is broken, the ball joint must be replaced.

REMOVAL AND INSTALLATION

NOTE: *The following procedure requires the use of the GM Ball Joint Separator tool No. J-23742 or equivalent, the GM Front and Rear Lower Control Arm Bushing Installer tool No. J-21474-13 or equivalent, the GM Ball Joint Installer tool No. J-9519-9 or equivalent, the GM Ball Joint Installer tool No. J-9519-16 or equivalent, and the GM Ball Joint Fixture tool No. J-9519-10 (1982–85) or J-9519-30 (1986–91) or equivalent.*

1. Raise and safely support the front of the vehicle on jackstands. Remove the wheel and brake caliper.
2. Using a floor jack, place it under the

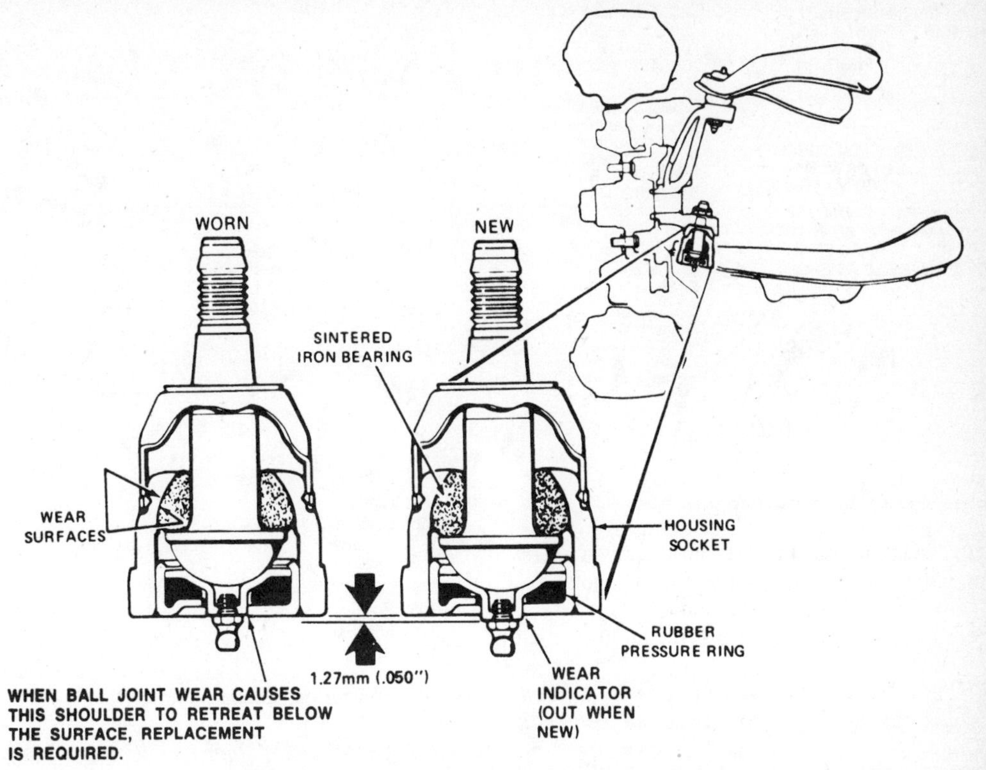

The grease fitting mounting is also the wear indicator

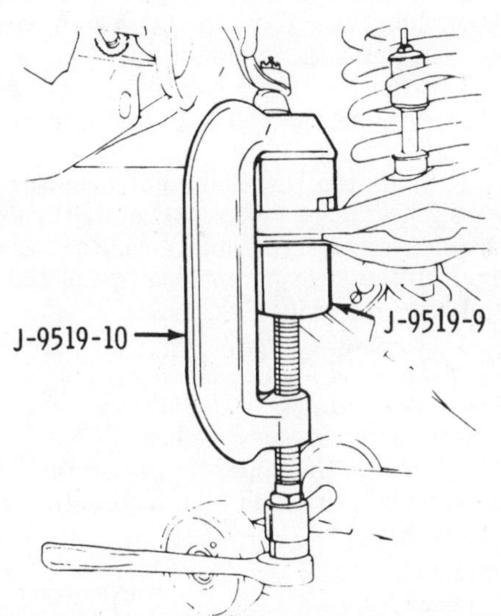

Installing the new ball joint

spring seat of the lower control arm, then raise the jack to support the arm.

NOTE: *The floor jack MUST remain under the lower control arm, during the removal and installation procedures, to retain the arm and spring positions.*

3. Remove the cotter pin (discard it) and the ball joint nut.

4. Using the GM Ball Joint Separator tool No. J-23742 or equivalent, disconnect the lower ball joint from the steering knuckle. Pull the steering knuckle away from the lower control arm, place a block of wood between the frame and the upper control arm; make sure that the brake hose is free of tension.

5. From the lower ball joint, remove the rubber grease seal and the grease fitting.

6. Using the GM Ball Joint Installer tool No. J-9519-16 or equivalent, the GM Front and Rear Lower Control Arm Bushing Installer tool No. J-21474-13 or equivalent, and the GM Ball Joint Fixture tool No. J-9519-10 (1982–85) or J-9519-30 (1986–91) or equivalent, remove the lower ball joint from the lower control arm.

7. To install, position the new lower ball joint into the lower control arm. Using the GM Ball Joint Installer tool No. J-9519-9 or equivalent, and the GM Ball Joint Fixture tool No. J-9519-10 (1982–85) or J-9519-30 (1986–91) or equivalent, press the new lower ball joint into the lower control arm.

8. Install the grease fitting and the grease seal onto the lower ball joint; the grease seal MUST BE fully seated on the ball joint and the grease purge hole MUST face inboard.

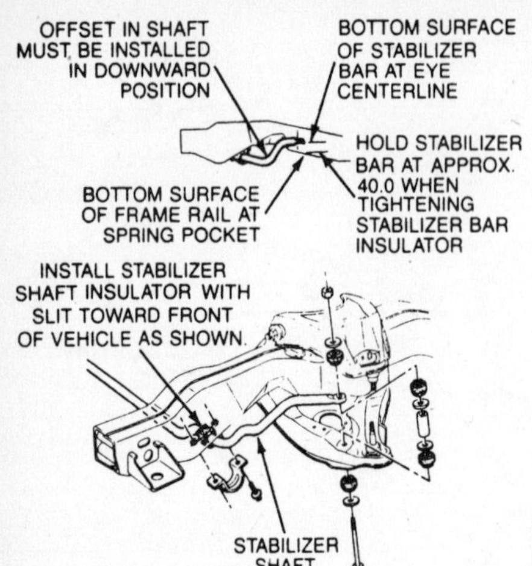

Front stabilizer bar mounting on 4WD

9. To complete the installation, reverse the removal procedures. Torque the ball joint-to-steering knuckle nut to 90 ft. lbs.

10. Install a new cotter pin to the lower ball joint stud.

NOTE: *When installing the cotter pin, never loosen the castle nut to expose the cotter pin hole.*

11. Use a grease gun to lubricate the ball joint.

12. Install the brake caliper and pads and the wheel. When a ball joint is replaced, a front end alignment is strongly recommended.

Stabilizer Bar

REMOVAL AND INSTALLATION

1. Raise and safely support the front of the vehicle on jackstands. Remove the wheels.

2. Disconnect the stabilizer bar link nuts from the lower control arms.

3. Remove the stabilizer bar-to-frame clamps.

4. Remove the stabilizer bar from the vehicle.

5. To install, reverse the removal procedures. Torque the stabilizer bar link-to-lower control arm nuts/bolts to 13 ft. lbs. (2WD) or 24 ft. lbs. (4WD) and the stabilizer retainer-to-frame nuts/bolts to 24 ft. lbs. (2WD) or 35 ft. lbs. (4WD).

Upper Control Arm

REMOVAL AND INSTALLATION

NOTE: *The following procedure requires the use of the GM Ball Joint Remover tool No. J-23742 or equivalent.*

1. Raise and safely support the front of the vehicle by placing jackstands under the frame.

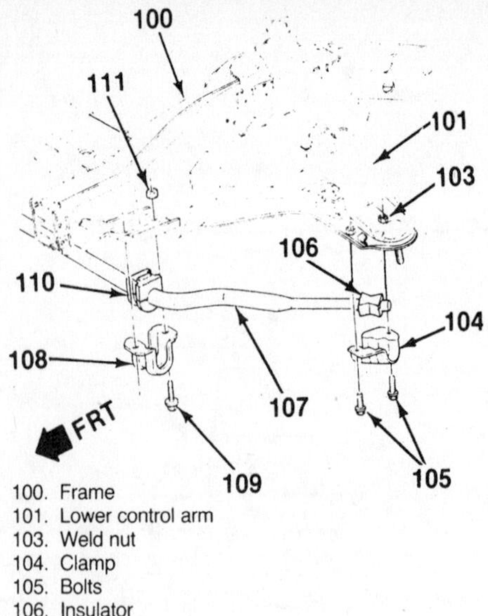

100. Frame
101. Lower control arm
103. Weld nut
104. Clamp
105. Bolts
106. Insulator
107. Stabilizer shaft
108. Clamp
109. Bolt
110. Insulator
111. Nut

Front stabilizer bar mounting on 2WD

NOTE: *Allow the floor jack to remain under the lower control arm seat, to retain the spring and the lower control arm position.*

2. Remove the wheels and brake caliper. Hang the caliper from the body with wire to avoid straining the hydraulic line.

3. From the upper ball joint, remove the cotter pin and the ball joint-to-upper control arm nut.

4. Using the GM Ball Joint Remover tool No. J-23742 or equivalent, separate the upper ball joint from the steering knuckle/hub assembly. Pull the steering knuckle free of the ball joint after removal.

NOTE: *After separating the steering knuckle from the upper ball joint, be sure to support steering knuckle/hub assembly to prevent damaging the brake hose.*

5. Remove the upper control arm-to-frame nuts and bolts, then lift and remove the upper control arm from the vehicle.

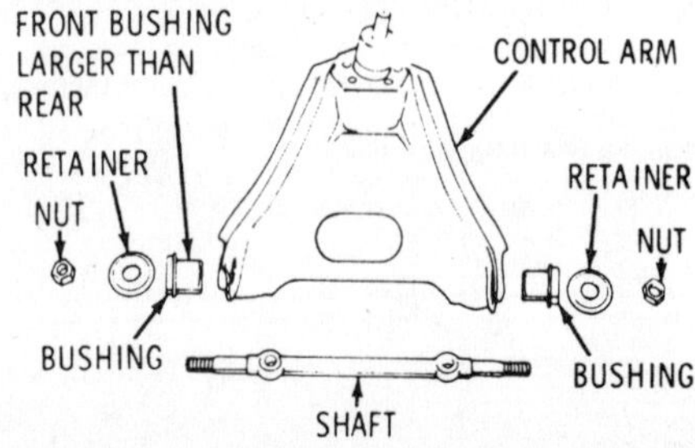

Upper control arm components

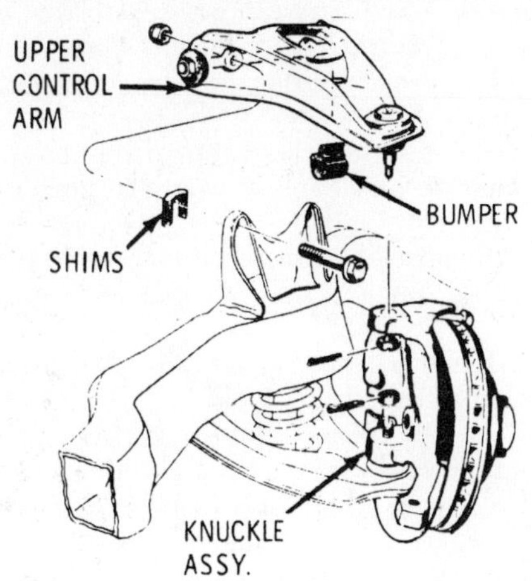

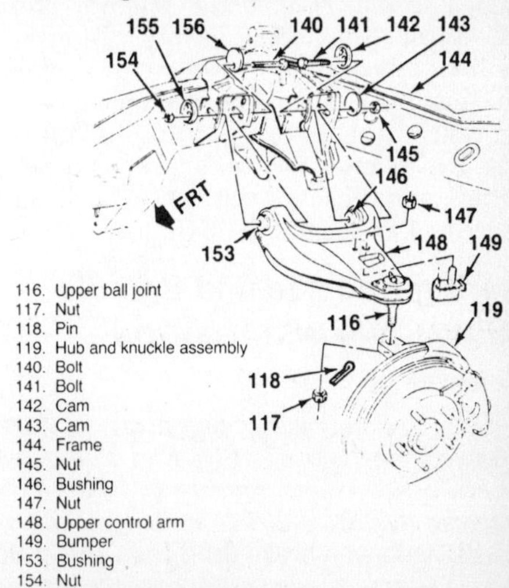

Upper control arm removal

NOTE: *On 2WD, tape the shims together and identify them so that they can be re-installed in the same place.*

6. Clean and inspect the steering knuckle hole. Replace the steering knuckle, if any out of roundness is noted.

To install

7. Attach the upper control arm to the frame, insert the shims in their proper positions, and torque the upper control arm bolts to 45 ft. lbs. (2WD) or 70 ft. lbs. (4WD).

8. Seat the upper ball joint into the steering knuckle, install the nut and torque it to 61 ft. lbs.

9. Install a new cotter pin to the upper ball joint stud.

NOTE: *When installing the cotter pin, never loosen the castle nut to expose the cotter pin hole.*

10. Use a grease gun to lubricate the upper ball joint.

Pivot bolt installation

11. Install the brake caliper and pads and the wheel. On 4WD, when a control arm is removed, a front end alignment is essential.

Lower Control Arm

REMOVAL AND INSTALLATION

2WD Models

NOTE: *The following procedure requires the use of the GM Ball Joint Remover tool No. J-23742 or equivalent.*

1. Refer to the "Coil Spring, Removal and Installation" procedures in this Chapter and remove the coil spring.

2. Remove the cotter pin (discard it) and the ball joint nut.

3. Using the GM Ball Joint Remover tool

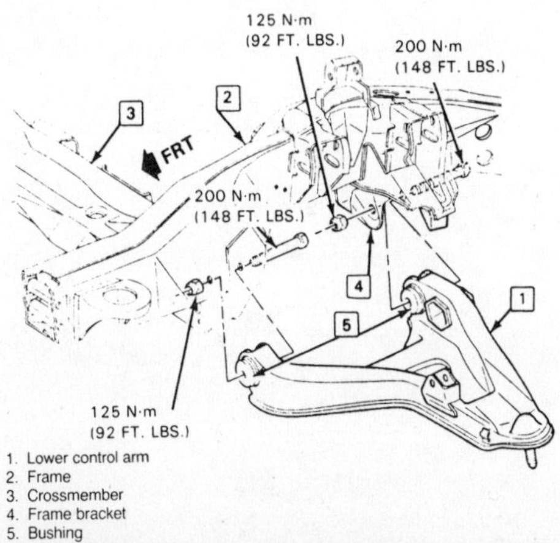

Upper control arm installation on 2WD

Upper control arm assembly on 4WD vehicles

No. J-23742 or equivalent, disconnect the lower ball joint from the steering knuckle and the lower control arm from the vehicle.

NOTE: *Place a block of wood between the frame and the upper control arm; make sure that the brake hose is free of tension.*

4. To install, position the lower ball joint stud into the steering knuckle and finger tighten it for now.

5. Install the control arm bolts, making sure the bolt goes in from the front of the vehicle. Torque the front nut and bolt to 94 ft. lbs., and the rear nut and bolt to 66 ft. lbs. Torque the ball joint-to-steering knuckle nut to 81 ft. lbs.

6. Install a new cotter pin to the lower ball joint stud.

NOTE: *When installing the cotter pin, never loosen the castle nut to expose the cotter pin hole.*

7. Pull the shock absorber down, then install the shock absorber-to-lower control arm nuts/bolts. Torque the nuts and bolts to 20 ft. lbs.

9. Remove the lower control arm support and lower the vehicle.

4WD Models

1. Refer to the "Torsion Bar, Removal and Installation" procedures in this Chapter, then remove the torsion bar and support assembly.

2. Remove the stabilizer bar-to-lower control arm nuts/bolts.

3. Remove the shock absorber-to-lower control arm nuts/bolts and push the shock absorber upward.

4. Remove the lower control arm-to-frame nuts/bolts and the lower control arm from the truck.

5. To install, reverse the removal procedures. Torque the lower control arm-to-frame bolts to 148 ft. lbs., the lower control arm-to-frame nuts to 92 ft. lbs., the shock absorber-to-lower control arm nut/bolt to 54 ft. lbs., the stabilizer bar-to-lower control arm nuts/bolts to 24 ft. lbs. and the lower control arm ball joint-to-steering knuckle nut to 83 ft. lbs.

Steering Knuckle and Spindle
REMOVAL AND INSTALLATION

2WD Model

NOTE: *The following procedure requires the use of the GM Tie Rod End Puller tool J-6627 or equivalent, and the GM Ball Joint Remover tool No. J-23742 or equivalent.*

1. Siphon some brake fluid from the brake master cylinder.

2. Raise and safely support the front of the vehicle on jackstands. Remove the wheels.

NOTE: *When supporting the vehicle on jackstands, DO NOT place the jackstands under the lower control arms. Place them under the frame.*

3. Remove the brake caliper from the steering knuckle and hang it from the body on a wire.

4. Remove the grease cup, the cotter pin, the castle nut and the hub–and–rotor assembly.

5. Remove the splash shield-to-steering knuckle bolts and the shield.

6. At the tie rod end-to-steering knuckle stud, remove the cotter pin and the nut. Using the GM Tie Rod End Puller tool J-6627 or equivalent, separate the tie rod end from the steering knuckle.

7. Using a floor jack, place it under the spring seat of the lower control arm and support the arm.

8. From the upper and lower ball joint studs, remove the cotter pins and the nuts.

9. Using the GM Ball Joint Remover tool No. J-23742 or equivalent, separate the upper ball joint from the steering knuckle.

10. Raise the upper control arm to separate it from the steering knuckle.

11. Using the GM Ball Joint Remover tool No. J-23742 or equivalent, separate the lower ball joint from the steering knuckle, then lift the steering knuckle from the lower control arm.

12. Clean and inspect the steering knuckle and spindle for signs of wear or damage; if necessary, replace the steering knuckle.

13. To install the steering knuckle, position it onto the lower ball joint stud, then lift the upper control arm to insert the upper ball joint

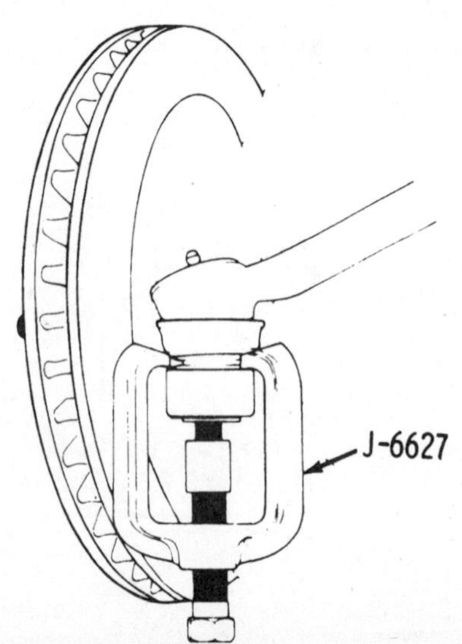

Removing the tie rod end from the steering knuckle

stud into the steering knuckle. Torque the upper ball joint-to-steering knuckle nut to 65 ft. lbs. and the lower ball joint-to-steering knuckle nut to 90 ft. lbs. Remove the floor jack from under the lower control arm.

14. Install a new cotter pin into the upper and lower ball joint studs.

NOTE: *When installing the cotter pin, never loosen the castle nut to expose the cotter pin hole.*

15. To complete the installation, reverse the removal procedures. Torque the tie rod end-to-steering knuckle nut to 40 ft. lbs., the splash shield-to-steering knuckle bolts to 10 ft. lbs. Check and/or adjust the wheel bearing and the front end alignment.

16. Remove the jackstands and lower the vehicle. Refill the brake master cylinder.

4WD Model

NOTE: *The following procedure requires the use of the Universal Steering Linkage Puller tool No. J-24319-01 or equivalent, the Axle Shaft Boot Seal Protector tool No. J-28712 or equivalent, the Ball Joint Separator tool No. J-34026 or equivalent, and the Steering Knuckle Seal Installation tool No. J-28574 or equivalent.*

1. Refer to the "Torsion Bar, Removal and Installation" procedures in this Chapter and relieve the torsion bar pressure.

2. Raise and support the front of the truck on jackstands; place the jackstands under the frame.

3. Remove the wheel and tire.

4. Using the Axle Shaft Boot Seal Protector tool No. J-28712 or equivalent, attach it to the tripot axle joint.

5. Remove the disc brake caliper-to-steering knuckle bolts, lift the brake caliper and support it (out of the way) on a wire.

6. Remove the brake disc from the wheel hub.

7. At the wheel hub, remove the cotter pin, the retainer, the castle nut, the thrust washer.

8. From the tie-rod-to-steering knuckle assembly, remove the cotter pin and the castle nut.

9. Using the Universal Steering Linkage Puller tool No. J-24319-01 or equivalent, tie-rod from the steering knuckle.

10. Remove the hub/bearing assembly-to-steering knuckle bolts and the hub/bearing assembly from the steering knuckle.

11. From the upper and lower ball joints, remove the cotter pin(s) and back off the castle nut(s).

12. Using the Ball Joint Separator tool No. J-34026 or equivalent, disconnect the ball joints from the steering knuckle. Remove the

ball joint nut(s) and separate the ball joint(s) from the steering knuckle.

NOTE: *When removing the steering knuckle from the wheel hub, be careful not to damage the splined surface of the half shaft.*

13. Remove the spacer and the seal from the steering knuckle.

14. Clean and inspect the parts for nicks, scores and/or damage, then replace them as necessary.

15. Using the Steering Knuckle Seal Installation tool No. J-28574 or equivalent, install a new seal into the steering knuckle.

16. Install the spacer, then the upper and lower ball joints to the steering knuckle. Torque the upper ball joint-to-steering knuckle nut to 61 ft. lbs. and the lower ball joint-to-

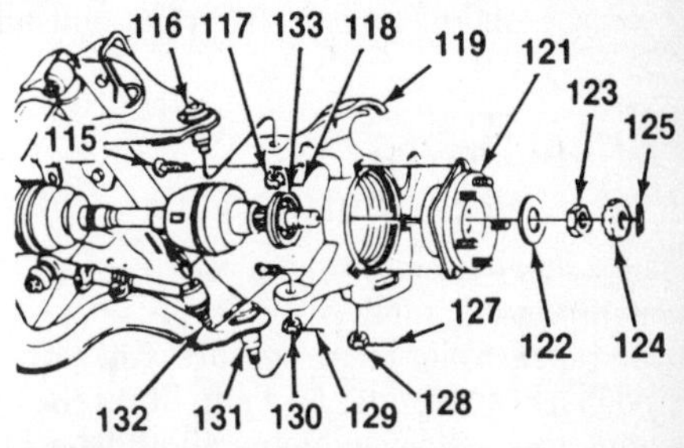

115. Bolt
116. Upper control arm ball joint
117. Nut
118. Pin
119. Knuckle
121. Hub and bearing assembly
122. Washer
123. Nut
124. Retainer
125. Pin
127. Pin
128. Nut
129. Pin
130. Nut
131. Lower control arm ball joint
132. Tie rod end
133. Seal

Steering knuckle and hub assembly on 4WD

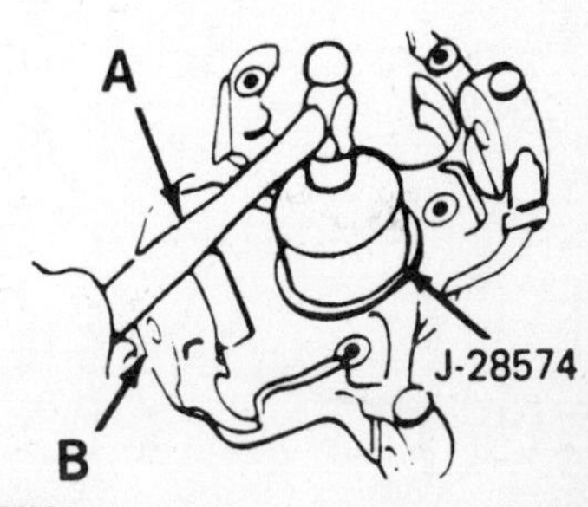

A. Hammer
B. Knuckle

Installing the new steering knuckle seal on 4WD

steering knuckle nut to 83 ft. lbs. DO NOT loosen the nut for the cotter pin installation, simply turn the nut a $\frac{1}{6}$ turn further; bend the pin ends against the nut flats.

17. Install the wheel hub/bearing assembly-to-steering knuckle, be careful to align the threads and splines carefully. Torque the hub/bearing assembly-to-steering knuckle bolts to 86 ft. lbs.

18. Install the tie-rod end-to-steering knuckle, then torque the tie-rod end nut to 35 ft. lbs. Install the cotter pin and bend the ends against the nut flats.

19. To complete the installation, reverse the removal procedures. Before torquing the wheel hub/bearing, put the vehicle on the ground. The torque is high enough to cause the truck to fall off the jack stands. Torque the wheel hub/bearing assembly-to-half shaft nut to 181 ft. lbs. Check and/or adjust the front end alignment.

2-Wheel Drive
Front Wheel Bearings

The proper functioning of the front suspension cannot be maintained unless the front wheel taper roller bearings are correctly adjusted. The cones must be a slip fit on the spindle and the inside diameter should be lubricated to insure that the cones will creep. The spindle nut must be a free-running fit on threads.

ADJUSTMENT

1. Raise and support the front of the vehicle on jackstands, then remove the grease cap from the hub.

2. Remove the cotter pin from axle spindle and spindle nut.

3. Tighten the spindle nut to 12 ft. lbs. while turning the wheel assembly forward by hand to fully seat the bearings. This will remove any grease or burrs which could cause excessive wheel bearing play later.

4. Back off the nut to the "just loose" position.

5. Hand tighten the spindle nut. Loosen the spindle nut until either hole in the spindle aligns with a slot in the nut; not more than $\frac{1}{2}$ flat.

6. Install a new cotter pin; bend the ends against nut flat, cut off extra length to ensure ends will not interfere with the grease cap.

7. Measure the looseness in the wheel hub assembly. There will be from 0.03–0.13mm (0.001–0.005 in.) end play when properly adjusted.

8. Install the grease cap onto the wheel hub.

REMOVAL AND INSTALLATION

NOTE: *The following procedure requires the use of the Wheel Bearing Removal tool No. J-29117 or equivalent, the Wheel Bearing Installation tools No. J-8092 and J-8850 or equivalent.*

1. Remove to the "Disc Brake Caliper, Removal and Installation" procedures in the Chapter 9 and remove the disc brake caliper.

CAUTION: *Brake shoes and pads contain asbestos, which has been determined to be a cancer causing agent. Never clean the brake surfaces with compressed air! Avoid inhaling any dust from any brake surface! When cleaning brake surfaces, use a commercially available brake cleaning fluid.*

2. Remove the grease cup from wheel hub.

3. Remove the cotter pin, the castle nut and the thrust washer from the spindle.

4. Carefully pull wheel hub assembly from the spindle.

5. Remove the outer wheel bearing from the wheel hub. The inner wheel bearing will remain in the hub and may be removed after prying out the inner wheel bearing grease seal; discard the seal.

6. Using the Wheel Bearing Removal tool No. J-29117 or equivalent, remove the inner

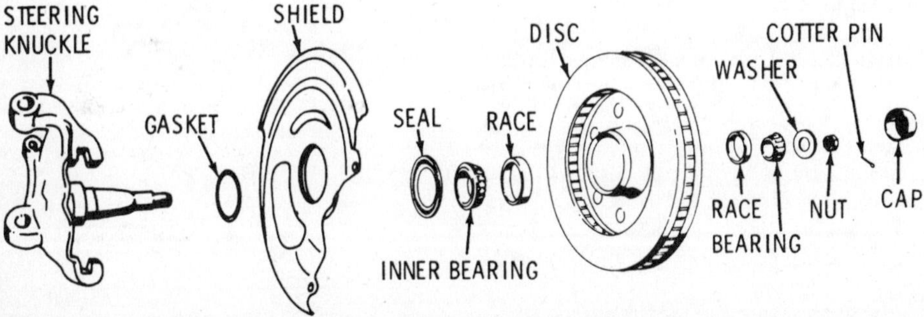

Front rotor and wheel bearings, 2WD

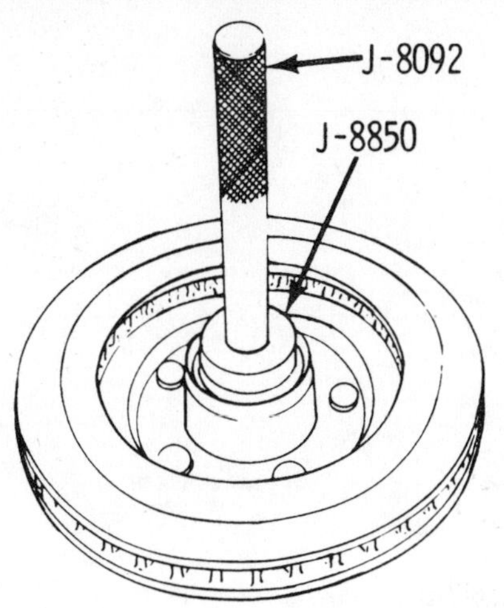

Installing inner bearing race

and outer wheel bearing races from the wheel hub.

7. Clean all of the parts in clean solvent and air dry.

8. Inspect the bearings for cracks, worn or pitted rollers.

9. Inspect the bearing races for cracks, scores or a brinelled condition.

10. If the the outer races were removed, use the Wheel Bearing Installation tools No. J-8092 and J-8850 or equivalent, drive or press the races into the hub.

11. Clean off any grease in the hub/spindle and thoroughly clean out any grease in the bearings. Use clean solvent and a small brush, with no loose bristles, to clean out all old grease. DO NOT spin the bearing with compressed air while drying it or the bearing may be damaged.

12. Use an approved high temperature front wheel bearing grease.

NOTE: *DO NOT mix greases as mixing may change the grease properties and result in poor performance.*

13. Apply a thin film of grease to the spindle at the outer bearing seat and at the inner bearing seat, the shoulder and the seal seat.

14. Put a small quantity of grease inboard of each bearing cup in the hub. This can be applied with your finger, forming a dam to provide extra grease availability to the bearing and to keep thinned grease from flowing out of the bearing.

15. Fill the bearing cone and roller assemblies full of grease.

NOTE: *A preferred method for doing this is with a cone type grease machine that forces grease into the bearing. If a cone greaser is*

not available, the bearings can be packed by hand. If hand packing is used, it is extremely important to work the grease thoroughly into the bearings between the rollers, cone and the cage. Failure to do this could result in premature bearing failure.

16. Place the inner bearing cone and roller assembly in the hub. Then using your finger, put an additional quantity of grease outboard of the bearing.

17. Install a new grease seal using a flat plate until the seal is flush with the hub. Lubricate the seal lip with a thin layer of grease.

18. Carefully install the hub and rotor assembly. Place the outer bearing cone and roller assembly in the outer bearing cup. Install the washer and nut and initially tighten the nut to 12 ft. lbs. while turning the wheel assembly forward by hand. Put an additional quantity of grease outboard the bearing. This provides extra grease availability to the bearing.

19. Check and/or adjust the wheel bearing.

4-Wheel Drive

Front Wheel Bearings

The wheel bearing is installed in the wheel hub assembly and is serviced by replacement only.

Refer to the "Steering Knuckle, Removal and Installation" procedures in this Chapter and replace the wheel hub assembly.

Front End Alignment

CASTER

Caster is the tilting of the front steering axis either forward or backward from the vertical. A backward tilt is said to be positive (+) and a forward tilt is said to be negative (–).

CAMBER

Camber is the inward or outward tilting of the front wheels from the vertical. When the wheels tilt outward at the top, the camber is said to be positive (+). When the wheels tilt inward at the top, the camber is said to be negative (–). The amount of tilt is measured in degrees from the vertical and this measurement is called the camber angle.

TOE-IN

Toe-in is the turning in of the front wheels. The actual amount of toe-in is normally only a fraction of a degree. The purpose of toe-in is to ensure parallel rolling of the front wheels. Excessive toe-in or toe-out will cause tire wear.

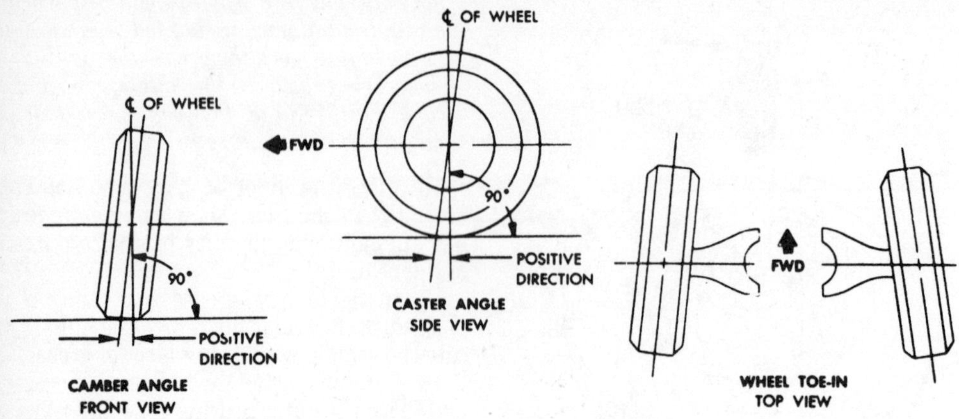

Camber, caster and toe are adjusted in degrees

REAR SUSPENSION

The rear suspension system consists of several major components: The double acting shock absorbers, variable rate multi-leaf springs and various attachment parts. The multi-leaf springs are connected to the frame by a hanger assembly with integral bushings in the front and a shackle assembly with integral bushings in the rear. The shackle assembly, in response to different road and payload conditions, allows the leaf spring to "change its length". The rear axle is connected to both the leaf springs and the shock absorbers by various attaching parts.

Leaf Springs

REMOVAL AND INSTALLATION

NOTE: *The following procedure requires the use of two sets of jackstands.*

1. Raise and safely support the rear frame of the vehicle on jackstands. support the rear axle with the second set of jackstands.

NOTE: *When supporting the rear of the vehicle, support the axle and the body separately to relieve the load on the rear spring.*

2. Remove the wheel and tire assembly.

3. At the rear of the spring, loosen (DO NOT remove) the shackle-to-frame bolt and the shackle-to-spring bolt.

4. Remove the shock absorber.

5. Remove the axle U-bolt-to-anchor plate nuts, the lower plate-to-anchor plate nuts, the U-bolts and the lower plate, then jack up the axle on that side only just enough to lift off of the spring.

6. At the front of the spring, remove the retainer-to-hanger assembly nuts, the washers and the retainer(s).

7. At the rear of the spring, remove the spring-to-shackle nut, washer and bolt. Remove the spring from the vehicle.

To install:

8. When installing a new spring, it is usually easier to put the rear end up first. Put the bolts through one of the shackle plates, hang the shackle on the frame, hang the spring on the shackle and put on the other shackle plate. Install the nuts finger tight.

9. It should be possible to move the spring enough on the shackle to line up the holes for the front mounting bolt. Install the washers and nut finger tight.

10. Lower the axle to rest on the spring and install the U-bolts and anchor plates. Torque the nuts in a cross pattern first to 18 ft. lbs., then to 85 ft. lbs. It is important that the U-bolts are tightened evenly.

11. Raise the axle so there is about 6.75 inches (171mm) between the axle housing and the frame of the truck. Measure from the housing between the U-bolts to the metal part of the rubber bump stop on the frame.

12. Torque the front spring mounting bolt

Wheel Alignment Specifications

Toe-in		Camber		Caster	
Range (in.)	Preferred (in.)	Range (deg.)	Preferred (deg.)	Range (deg.)	Preferred (deg.)
1/16–3/32P	1/16P	5/16–13/16P	13/16P	1 1/2–2 1/2P	2P

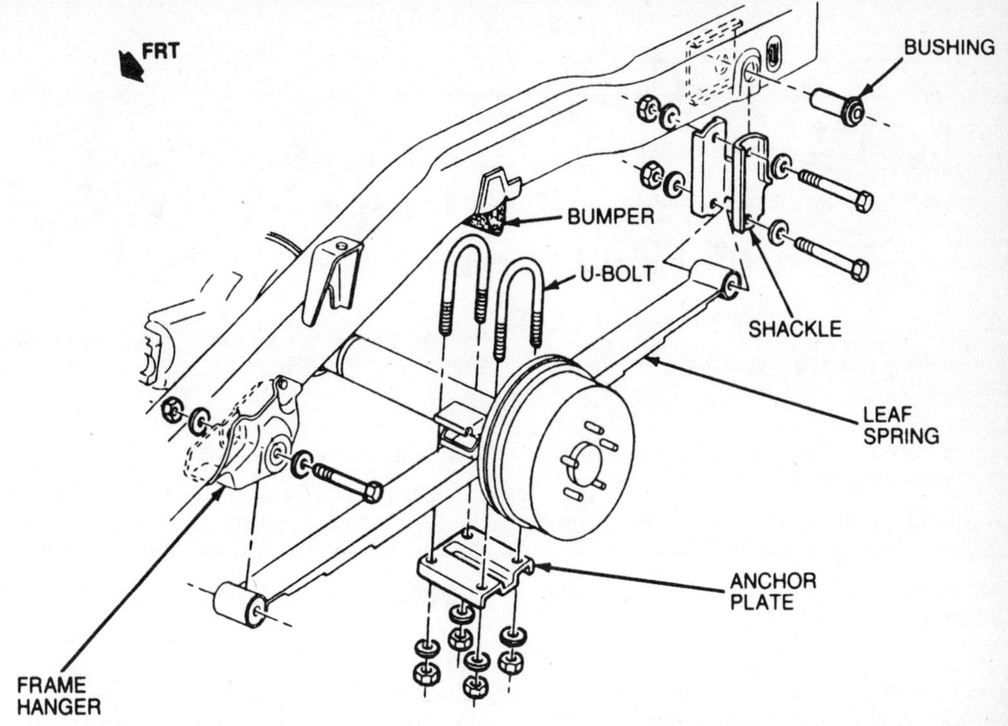

Rear leaf spring and axle attachment

and the rear shackle bolts to 92 ft. lbs. Install the shock absorber and wheel.

Shock Absorbers

REMOVAL AND INSTALLATION

1. Raise and support the rear of the truck on jackstands; support the rear axle.

2. At the upper mounting location, disconnect shock absorber bolts.

3. At the lower mounting location, remove the nut and washer.

4. Remove the shock absorber(s) from the vehicle.

5. To install the shock absorber, place it into position and reattach at upper mounting location.

6. Align the lower-end of the shock absorber with the anchor plate stud and install the washer and nut.

7. Torque the shock absorber-to-body bolts to 15 ft. lbs. and the shock absorber-to-axle nut to 50 ft. lbs.

8. Lower vehicle and remove from hoist.

TESTING

Visually inspect the shock absorber. If there is evidence of leakage and the shock absorber is covered with oil, the shock is defective and should be replaced.

If there is no sign of excessive leakage (a small amount of weeping is normal) bounce the truck at one corner by pressing down on the bumper and releasing it. When you have the truck bouncing as much as you can, release the bumper. The truck should stop bouncing after the first rebound. If the bouncing continues past the center point of the bounce more than once, the shock absorbers are worn and should be replaced.

STEERING

Steering Wheel

REMOVAL AND INSTALLATION

NOTE: *The following procedure requires the use of the GM Steering Wheel Puller tool No. J-1859-03 or equivalent.*

1. Disconnect the negative battery cable from the battery.

2. Position the steering wheel so that it is in the horizontal position and the front wheel are straight.

3. If equipped with a horn cap, pry the cap from the center of the steering wheel. If equipped with a steering wheel shroud, remove

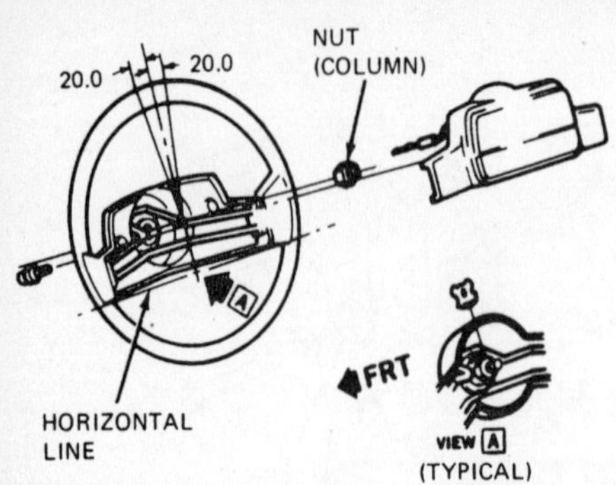

Make sure the wheel is properly aligned when installing it

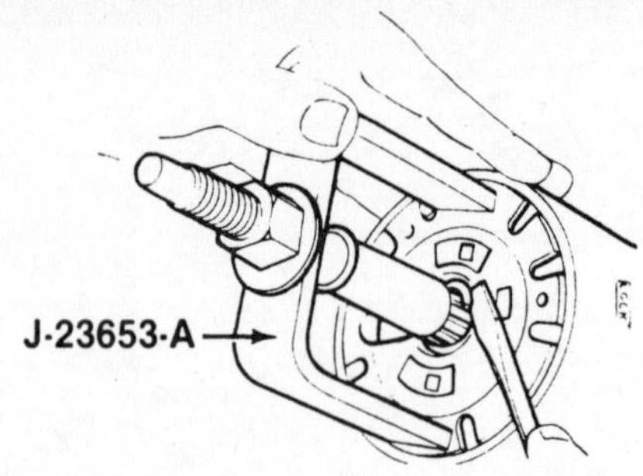

Removing the steering column lock plate with the compressor tool installed

the screw from the rear of the steering wheel and remove the shroud.

NOTE: *If the horn cap or shroud is equipped with an electrical connector, disconnect it.*

4. Remove the steering wheel-to-steering shaft retainer (snapring) and nut.

NOTE: *Since the steering column is designed to collapse upon impact, it is recommended NEVER to hammer on it.*

5. Matchmark the relationship of the steering wheel to the steering shaft.

6. Using the GM Steering Wheel Puller tool No. J-1859-03 or equivalent, press the steering wheel from the steering column.

NOTE: *Before installing the steering wheel, be sure that the turn signal switch is in the Neutral position. DO NOT misalign the steering wheel more than 1 in. (25mm) from the horizontal centerline.*

7. To install the steering wheel, align the matchmarks and push it onto the steering shaft splines, torque the steering wheel-to-steering shaft nut to 30 ft. lbs. Install the horn cap or pad.

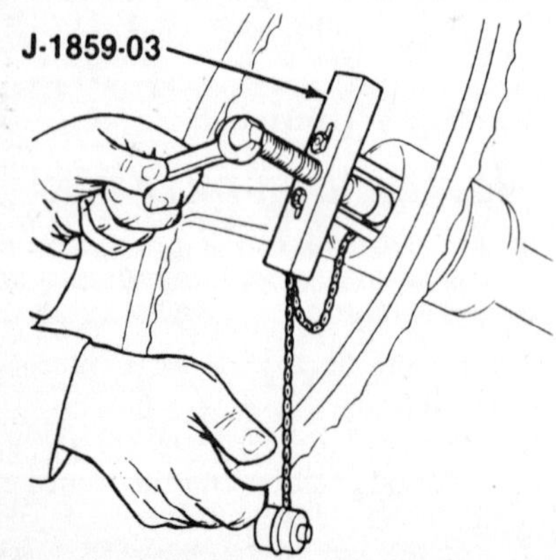

Using a steering wheel puller

Combination Switch

The combination switch is a combination of the turn signal, the windshield wiper/washer, the dimmer and the cruise control switches.

REMOVAL AND INSTALLATION

NOTE: *The following procedure requires the use of the GM Lock Plate Compressor tool No. J-23653 or equivalent.*

1. Disconnect the negative battery cable. Refer to the "Steering Wheel, Removal and Installation" procedures in this Chapter and remove the steering wheel.

2. If necessary, remove the steering column-to-lower instrument panel cover. Disconnect the electrical harness connector from the steering column jacket (under the dash).

3. Using a screwdriver, insert into the slots between the steering shaft lock plate cover and the steering column housing, then pry upward to remove the cover from the lock plate.

4. Using the GM Lock Plate Compressor tool No. J-23653-A or equivalent, screw the center shaft onto the steering shaft (as far as it will go), then screw the center post nut clockwise until the lock plate is compressed.

5. Pry the snapring from the steering shaft slot.

NOTE: *If the steering column is being disassembled on a bench, the steering shaft will slide out of the mast jacket when the snapring is removed.*

6. Remove the GM Lock Plate Compressor tool No. J-23653 or equivalent, and the lock plate.

7. Remove the multi-function lever-to-switch screw and the lever.

8. To remove the hazard warning switch, press the knob inward and unscrew it.

9. Remove the combination switch assembly-to-steering column screws.

10. Lift the combination switch assembly from the steering column, then slide the elec-

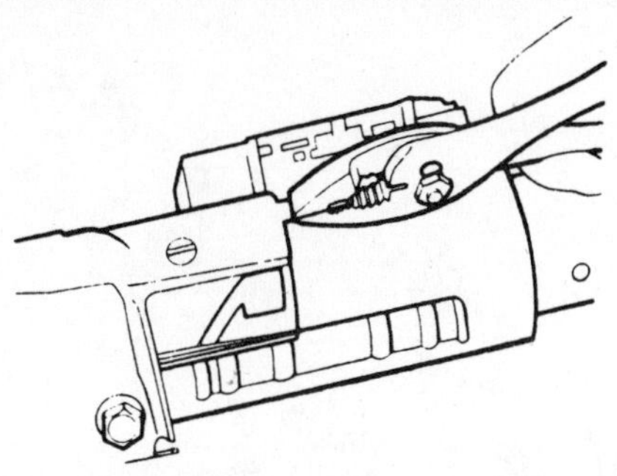

Removing the wire protector

trical connector through the column housing and the protector.

NOTE: *If the steering column is the tilting type, position the steering housing into the Low position.*

11. To remove the harness cover, pull it toward the lower end of the column; be careful not to damage the wires.

12. To remove the wire protector, grab the protector's tab with a pair of pliers, then pull the protector downward, out of the steering column.

NOTE: *When assembling the steering column, use only fasteners of the correct length; over length fasteners could prevent a portion of the assembly from compressing under impact.*

To install:

13. To install the combination switch electrical connector, perform the following procedures:

   a. On the non-tilt columns, be sure that the electrical connector is on the protector, then feed it and the cover down through the housing and under the mounting bracket.

   b. On the tilt columns, feed the electrical connector down through the housing and under the mounting bracket, then install the cover onto the housing.

14. Install the clip on the electrical connector to the clip on the jacket, the combination

switch-to-steering column mounting screws, the lower instrument trim panel, the turn signal lever/screws and the hazard warning knob.

NOTE: *With the multi-function lever installed, place it into the Neutral position. With the hazard warning knob installed, pull it Outward.*

15. Onto the upper end of the steering shaft, install the washer, the upper bearing preload spring, the canceling cam, the lock plate and a new retaining ring (snapring). Using the GM Lock Plate Compressor tool No. J-23653 or equivalent, compress the lock plate and slide the new retaining ring into the steering shaft groove.

16. To complete the installation, reverse the removal procedures. Torque the multi-function switch-to-steering column screws to 35 inch lbs. and the steering wheel nut to 30 ft. lbs.

Ignition Switch

The ignition switch, for anti-theft reasons, is located inside the channel section of the brake pedal support and is completely inaccessible without first lowering the steering column. The switch is actuated by a rod and rack assembly. A gear on the end of the lock cylinder engages the toothed upper end of the actuator rod.

REMOVAL AND INSTALLATION

1. Remove the lower instrument panel-to-steering column cover. Remove the steering column-to-dash bolts and lower the steering column; be sure to properly support it.

2. Place the ignition switch in the Locked position.

NOTE: *If the lock cylinder was removed, the actuating rod should be pulled up until it stops, then moved down one detent; the switch is now in the Lock position.*

3. Remove the two ignition switch-to-steering column screws and the switch assembly.

4. Before installing the ignition switch, place it in the Locked position, then make sure that the lock cylinder and actuating rod are in the Locked position (1st detent from the top).

5. Install the activating rod into the ignition switch and assemble the switch onto the steering column. Torque the ignition switch-to-steering column screws to 35 inch lbs.

NOTE: *When installing the ignition switch, use only the specified screws since over length screws could impair the collapsibility of the column.*

6. To complete the installation, install the steering column and the lower instrument panel cover. Torque the steering column-to-instrument bolts to 22 ft. lbs.

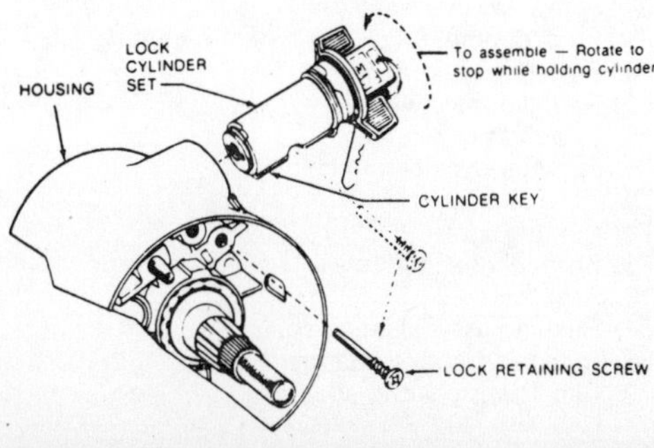

Ignition lock cylinder replacement

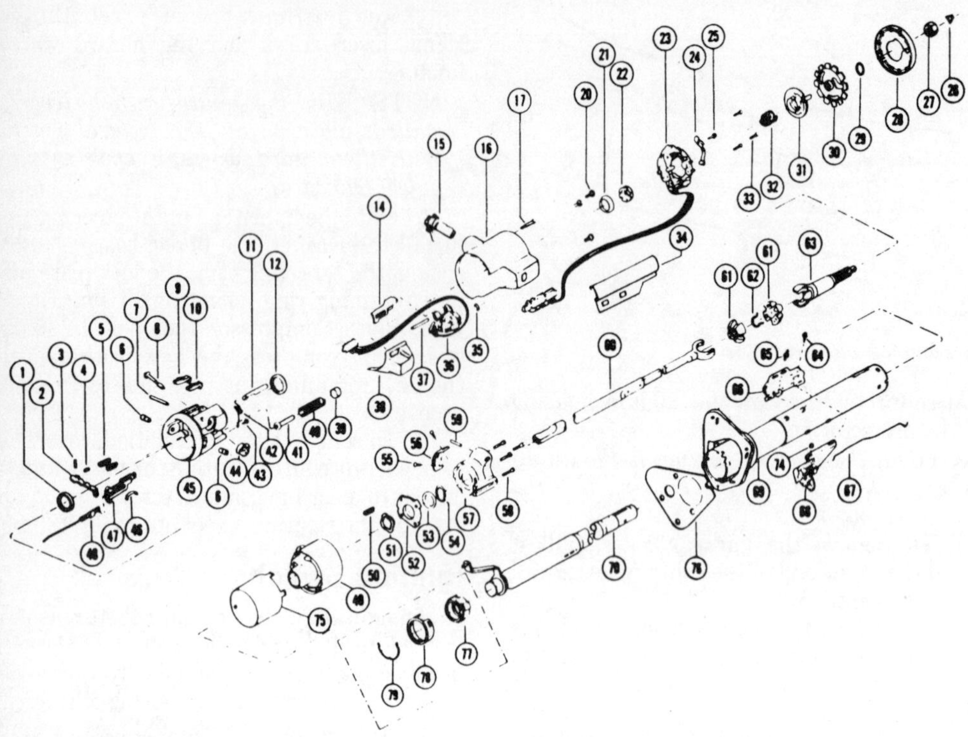

1. Bearing assy
2. Lever, shoe release
3. Pin, release lever
4. Spring, release lever
5. Spring, shoe
6. Pin, pivot
7. Pin, dowel
8. Shaft, drive
9. Shoe, steering wheel lock
10. Shoe, steering wheel lock
11. Bolt, lock
12. Bearing assy
14. Actuator, dimmer switch rod
15. Lock cylinder set, strg column
16. Cover, lock housing
17. Screw, lock retaining
20. Screw, pan head cross recess
21. Race, inner
22. Seat, upper bearing inner race
23. Switch assy, turn signal
24. Arm assy, signal switch
25. Screw, round washer head
26. Retainer
27. Nut, hex jam
28. Cover, shaft lock
29. Ring, retaining
30. Lock, shaft
31. Cam assy, turn signal cancelling
32. Spring, upper bearing
33. Screw, binding head cross recess
34. Protector, wiring
35. Spring, pin preload
36. Switch assy, pivot &
37. Pin, switch actuator pivot
38. Cap, column housing cover end
39. Retainer, spring
40. Spring, wheel tilt

41. Guide, spring
42. Spring, lock bolt
43. Screw, hex washer head
44. Sector, switch actuator
45. Housing, steering column
46. Spring, rack preload
47. Rack, switch actuator
48. Actuator assy, ignition switch
49. Bowl, gearshift lever
50. Spring, shift lever
51. Washer, wave
52. Plate, lock
53. Washer, thrust
54. Ring, shift tube retaining
55. Screw, oval head cross recess
56. Gate, shift lever
57. Support, strg column housing
58. Screw, support
59. Pin, dowel
60. Shaft assy, lower steering
61. Sphere, centering
62. Spring, joint preload
63. Shaft assy, race & upper
64. Screw, washer head
65. Stud, dimmer & ignition switch mounting
66. Switch assy, ignition
67. Rod, dimmer switch
68. Switch assy, dimmer
69. Jacket assy, steering column
70. Tube assy, shift
74. Nut, hexagon
75. Shroud, gearshift bowl
76. Seal, dash
77. Bushing assy, steering shaft
78. Retainer, bearing adapter
79. Clip, lower bearing adapter

Tilt steering column components

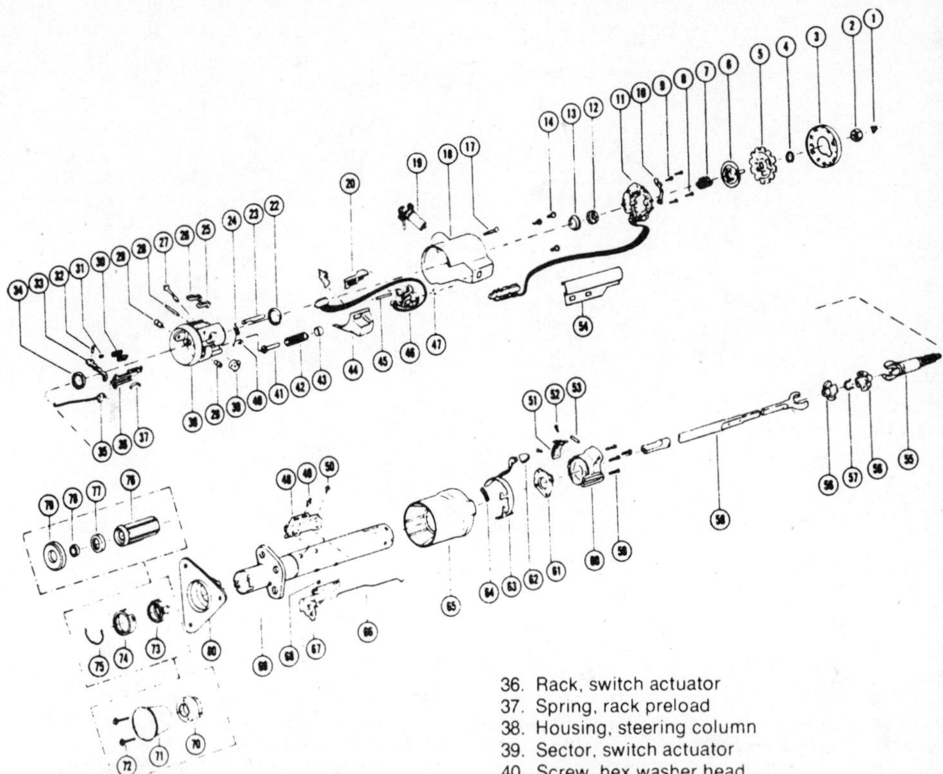

1. Retainer
2. Nut, hexagon jam
3. Cover, shaft lock
4. Ring, retaining
5. Lock, shaft
6. Cam assy, turn signal cancelling
7. Spring, upper bearing
8. Screw, binding head cross recess
9. Screw, round washer head
10. Arm assy, signal switch
11. Switch assy, turn signal
12. Seat, upper bearing inner race
13. Race, inner
14. Screw, pan head cross recess
17. Screw, lock retaining
18. Cover, lock housing
19. Lock cylinder set, steering column
20. Actuator, dimmer switch rod
22. Bearing assy
23. Bolt, lock
24. Spring, lock bolt
25. Shoe, steering wheel lock
26. Shoe, steering wheel lock
27. Shaft, drive
28. Pin, dowel
29. Pin, pivot
30. Spring, shoe
31. Spring, release lever
32. Pin, release lever
33. Lever, shoe release
34. Bearing assy
35. Actuator assy, ignition switch

36. Rack, switch actuator
37. Spring, rack preload
38. Housing, steering column
39. Sector, switch actuator
40. Screw, hex washer head
41. Guide, spring
42. Spring, wheel tilt
43. Retainer, spring
44. Cap, column housing cover end
45. Pin, switch actuator pivot
46. Switch assy, pivot &
47. Spring, pin preload
48. Switch assy, ignition
49. Stud, dimmer & ignition switch mounting
50. Screw, washer head
51. Plate, shroud retaining
52. Screw, oval head cross recess
53. Pin, dowel
54. Protector, wiring
55. Shaft assy, race & upper
56. Sphere, centering
57. Spring, joint preload
58. Shaft assy, lower steering
59. Screw, support
60. Support, steering column housing
61. Plate, lock
62. Finger pad, release lever
63. Lever, key release
64. Spring, key release
65. Shroud, steering column housing
66. Rod, dimmer switch
67. Switch assy, dimmer
68. Nut, hexagon
69. Jacket assy, steering column
73. Bushing assy, steering shaft
74. Retainer, bearing adapter
75. Clip, lower bearing adapter
80. Bracket assy, column dash

Tilt steering column with key release components

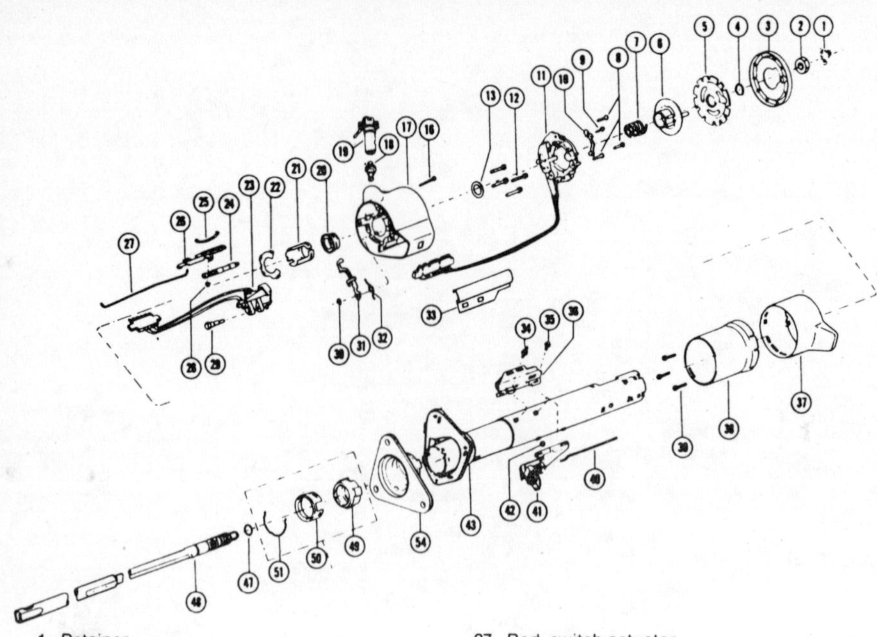

1. Retainer	27. Rod, switch actuator
2. Nut, hexagon jam	28. Washer, spring thrust
3. Cover, shaft lock	29. Pin, switch actuator pivot
4. Ring, retaining	30. Washer, wave
5. Lock, steering shaft	31. Lever, key release
6. Cam assy, turn signal cancelling	32. Spring, key release
7. Spring, upper bearing	33. Protector, wiring
8. Screw, binding head cross recess	34. Stud, dimmer and ignition switch mounting
9. Screw, round washer head	35. Screw, washer head
10. Arm assy, switch actuator	36. Switch assy, ignition
11. Switch assy, turn signal	37. Bowl, floor shift
12. Screw, hex washer head tapping	38. Shroud, shift bowl
13. Washer, thrust	39. Screw, binding head cross recess
16. Screw, lock retaining	40. Rod, dimmer switch actuator
17. Housing, steering column	41. Switch assy, dimmer
18. Sector assy, switch actuator	42. Nut, hexagon
19. Lock cylinder set, steering column	43. Jacket assy, steering column
20. Bearing assy	47. Ring, retaining
21. Bushing, bearing retaining	48. Shaft assy, steering
22. Retainer, upper bearing	49. Bushing assy. steering shaft
23. Switch assy, pivot &	50. Retainer, bearing adapter
24. Bolt assy, spring &	51. Clip, lower bearing adapter
25. Spring, rack preload	54. Bracket assy, column dash
26. Rack, switch actuator	

Key release standard steering column components

Ignition Lock Cylinder

REMOVAL AND INSTALLATION

1. Disconnect the negative battery cable. Refer to the "Combination Switch, Removal and Installation" procedures in this Chapter and remove the combination switch.

2. Place the lock cylinder in the **Run** position.

3. Remove the buzzer switch, the lock cylinder screw and the lock cylinder.

CAUTION: *If the screw is dropped upon removal, it could fall into the steering column, requiring complete disassembly to retrieve the screw.*

4. To install, rotate the lock cylinder clockwise to align the cylinder key with the keyway in the housing.

5. Push the lock cylinder all the way in.

6. Install the cylinder lock-to-housing screw. Tighten the screw to 14 inch lbs.

Steering Column

REMOVAL AND INSTALLATION

NOTE: *The following procedure requires the use of the Steering Column Holding Fixture tool No. J-23074 or equivalent.*

1. Disconnect the negative battery cable. Refer to the "Steering Wheel, Removal and In-

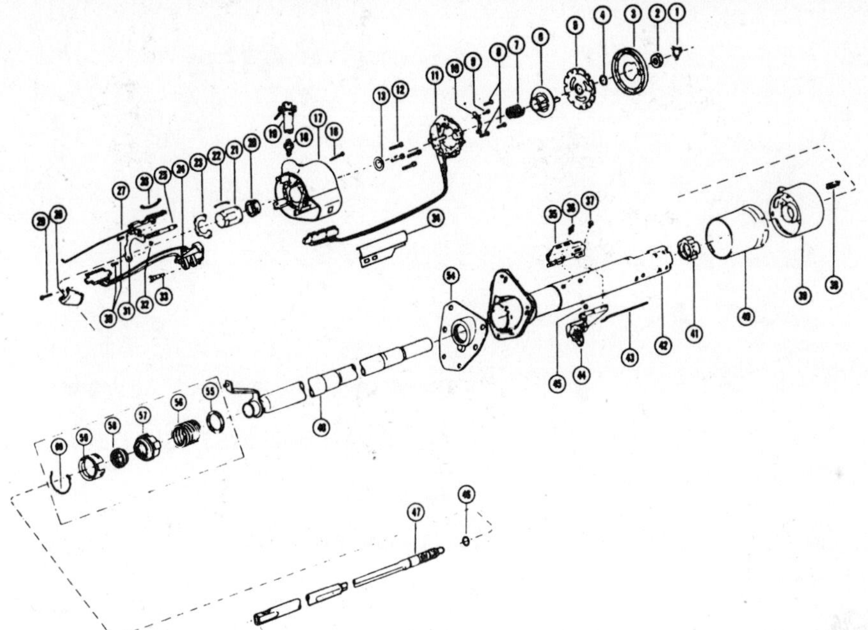

1. Retainer
2. Nut, hexagon
3. Cover, shaft lock
4. Ring, retaining
5. Lock, steering shaft
6. Cam assy, turn signal cancelling
7. Spring, upper bearing
8. Screw, binding head cross recess
9. Screw, round washer head
10. Arm assy, switch actuator
11. Switch assy, turn signal
12. Screw, hex washer head tapping
13. Washer, thrust
16. Screw, lock retaining
17. Housing, steering column
18. Sector assy, switch actuator
19. Lock cylinder set, steering column
20. Bearing assy

21. Bushing, bearing retaining
22. Contact, horn circuit
23. Retainer, upper bearing
24. Switch assy, pivot &
25. Bolt assy, spring &
26. Spring, rack preload
27. Rack assy, switch actuator rod &
28. Cover, housing
29. Screw, binding head cross recess
30. Screw, flat head cross recess
31. Gate, shift lever
32. Washer, spring thrust
33. Pin, switch actuator pivot
34. Protector, wiring
35. Switch assy, ignition
36. Stud, dimmer & ignition switch mounting
37. Screw, washer head
38. Spring, upper shift lever

39. Bowl, gearshift lever
40. Shroud, gearshift bowl
41. Bearing, bowl lower
42. Jacket assy, steering column
43. Rod, dimmer switch actuator
44. Switch assy, dimmer
45. Nut, hexagon
46. Ring, retaining
47. Shaft assy, steering
48. Tube assy, shift
54. Seal, dash
55. Washer spring thrust
56. Spring shift tube return
57. Adapter, lower bearing
58. Bearing assembly
59. Retainer bearing adapter
60. Clip, lower bearing adapter

Standard steering column components

stallation'' procedures in this Chapter and remove the steering wheel.

2. Disconnect the negative battery terminal from the battery.

3. If equipped with a column shift, disconnect the transmission control linkage from the column shift tube levers.

4. From inside the engine compartment, remove the intermediate shaft-to-steering column shaft (pot-joint) bolt.

NOTE: *Before separating the intermediate shaft from the steering column shaft, mark the relationship of the two shafts.*

5. Remove the lower instrument panel-to-steering column cover, the steering column bracket-to-dash nuts/bolts (support the steer-

ing column) and the steering column-to-firewall cover (if necessary).

6. From under the dash, disconnect the electrical harness connectors from the steering column.

NOTE: *Some models are equipped with a back-up light switch and a neutral/start switch, be sure to disconnect the electrical connectors from them.*

7. Remove the steering column from the vehicle.

NOTE: *If equipped with a column shifter, rotate the steering column so that the shift lever clears the dash opening.*

8. To install, align the matchmarks of the steering column shaft and the intermediate

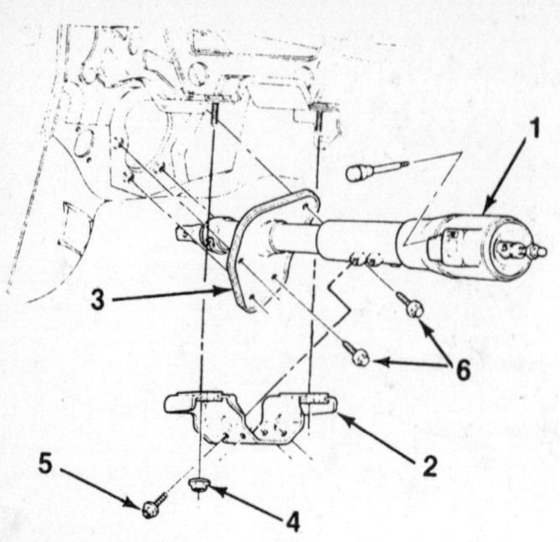

1. Steering column
2. Support bracket
3. Seal
4. Nut
5. Bolt
6. Screws

Steering column removal

shaft, tighten the fasteners finger tight and reverse the removal procedures.

9. Torque the intermediate shaft-to-steering column shaft (pot-joint) pinch bolt to 30 ft. lbs., the steering column bracket-to-dash nuts to 25 ft. lbs. and the steering column-to-firewall screws to 7 ft. lbs.

10. Reconnect the electrical harness-to-steering column connectors. Reinstall the steering wheel and the negative battery terminal.

NOTE: *If equipped with steering column shifter, reconnect the transmission-to-steering column linkage.*

Steering Linkage

The steering linkage consists of: a forward mounted linkage, crimp nuts at the inner pivots, castellated nuts at the steering knuckle arm, an idler arm, a steering gear pitman arm, a relay rod and a steering damper (manual steering). Grease fittings are equipped with each joint, for durability.

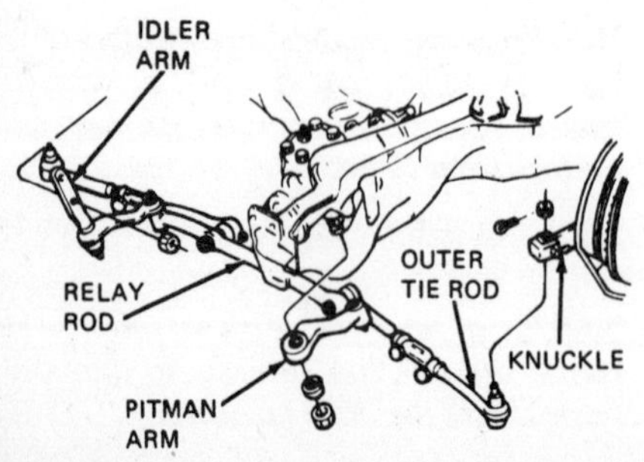

Steering linkage

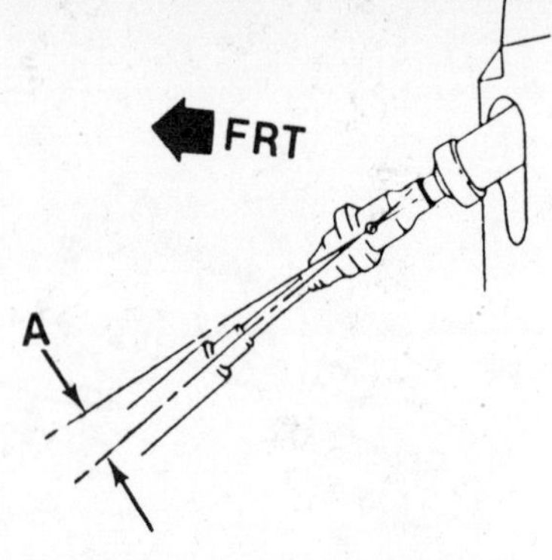

Pot joint angle not to exceed 12.5 degrees

REMOVAL AND INSTALLATION

Pitman Arm

NOTE: *The following procedure requires the use of the GM Steering Linkage Puller tool No. J-24319-01 or equivalent, the GM Pitman Arm Remover tool No. J-6632 or equivalent, and the GM Steering Linkage Installer tool No. J-29193 (12mm) or J-29194 (14mm) or equivalent.*

1. Raise and safely support the front frame of the vehicle on jackstands.

2. Disconnect the nut from the pitman arm ball joint stud.

3. Using the GM Steering Linkage Puller tool No. J-24319-01 or equivalent, separate the relay rod from the pitman arm. Pull down on the relay rod and separate it from the stud.

4. Remove the pitman arm-to-pitman shaft nut, mark the relationship the arm to the shaft. Using the GM Pitman Arm Remover tool No. J-6632 or equivalent, separate the pitman arm from the pitman shaft.

NOTE: *When separating the pitman arm from the shaft, DO NOT use a hammer or apply heat to the arm.*

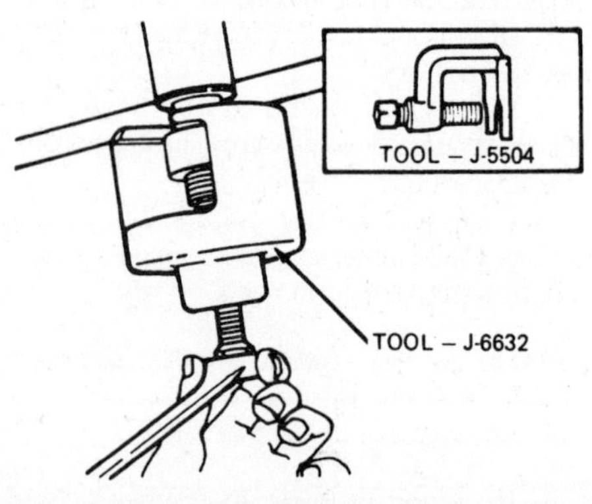

Pitman arm removal using the proper tool

5. To install, align the pitman arm-to-pitman shaft matchmark and the pitman shaft nut; torque the pitman arm-to-pitman shaft nut to 185 ft. lbs.

6. Connect the pitman arm to the relay rod ball stud (make sure that the seal is on the stud). Using the GM Steering Linkage Installer tool No. J-29193 (12mm) or J-29194 (14mm) or equivalent, install the correct one onto the ball stud and torque it to 40 ft. lbs. to seat the taper.

7. After seating, remove the tool, install the lock washer and nut and torque to 60 ft. lbs.

Idler Arm

NOTE: *The following procedure requires the use of the GM Steering Linkage Puller tool No. J-24319-01 or equivalent, the GM Steering Linkage Installer tool No. J-29193 (12mm) or J-29194 (14mm) or equivalent, and a spring scale.*

1. Raise and safely support the front frame of the vehicle on jackstands.

NOTE: *Jerking the right wheel assembly back and forth is not an acceptable testing procedure; there is no control on the amount of force being applied to the idler arm. Before suspecting idler arm shimmying complaints, check the wheels for imbalance, runout, force variation and/or road surface irregularities.*

2. To inspect for a defective idler arm, perform the following procedures:

   a. Position the wheels in the straight ahead position.

   b. Using a spring scale, position it near the relay rod end of the idler arm, then exert 25 lbs. of force upward and then downward.

   c. Measure the distance between the upward and downward directions that the idler arm moves. The allowable deflection is $1/8$ in. (3mm) for each direction; a total difference of $1/4$ in. (6mm); if the idler arm deflection is beyond the allowable limits, replace it.

3. Remove the idler arm-to-frame bolts and the idler arm-to-relay rod ball joint nut.

4. Using the GM Steering Linkage Puller tool No. J-24319-01 or equivalent, separate the relay rod from the ball joint stud.

5. Inspect and/or replace (if necessary) the idler arm.

6. Install the idler arm-to-frame bolts and torque them to 60 ft. lbs.

7. Connect the relay rod to the idler arm ball joint stud. Using the GM Steering Linkage Installer tool No. J-29193 (12mm) or J-29194 (14mm) or equivalent, seat (torque) the relay rod-to-idler arm ball joint stud to 40 ft. lbs., then remove the tool.

8. Install the idler arm-to-relay rod stud nut and torque it to 35 ft. lbs. (2WD) or 60 ft. lbs. (4WD).

9. Lower the vehicle. Check and/or adjust the toe-in.

Relay Rod

NOTE: *The following procedure requires the use of the GM Steering Linkage Puller tool No. J-24319-01 or equivalent, and the GM Steering Linkage Installer tool No. J-29193 (12mm) or J-29194 (14mm) or equivalent.*

1. Refer to the "Tie Rod, Removal and Installation" procedures in this Chapter and disconnect the inner tie rod ends from the relay rod.

2. Remove the idler arm stud-to-relay rod nut.

3. Using the GM Steering Linkage Puller tool No. J-24319-01 or equivalent, disconnect the relay rod from the idler arm, then remove the relay rod from the vehicle.

4. Clean and inspect the threads on the tie rod, the tie rod ends and the ball joints for damage, and replace them (if necessary). Inspect the ball joint seals for excessive wear, and replace them (if necessary).

5. To install, position the relay rod onto the idler arm (no mounting nut). Using the GM Steering Linkage Installer tool No. J-29193 (12mm) or J-29194 (14mm) or equivalent, install it onto the idler arm stud and torque the idler arm-to-relay rod stud nut to 35 ft. lbs. (to seat the taper). Remove the installer tool, then install the mounting nuts and torque the idler arm-to-relay arm stud nut to 35 ft. lbs. (2WD) or 60 ft. lbs. (4WD).

6. Position the inner tie rod ball joints onto the relay rod. Install the mounting nuts and torque the tie rod-to-relay rod stud nuts to 35 ft. lbs.

7. Lower the vehicle and check the steering linkage performance.

Tie Rod

NOTE: *The following procedure requires the use of the Steering Linkage Installer tool No. J-29193 (12mm) or J-29194 (14mm) or equivalent, and the GM Wheel Stud and Tie Rod Remover tool No. J-6627-A or equivalent.*

1. Raise and safely support the front frame of the vehicle on jackstands.

2. Remove the cotter pin from the tie rod-to-steering knuckle stud.

3. Remove the tie rod-to-relay rod stud nut and the tie rod-to-steering knuckle stud nut.

NOTE: *DO NOT attempt to separate the tie rod-to-steering knuckle joint using a wedge type tool for seal damage could result.*

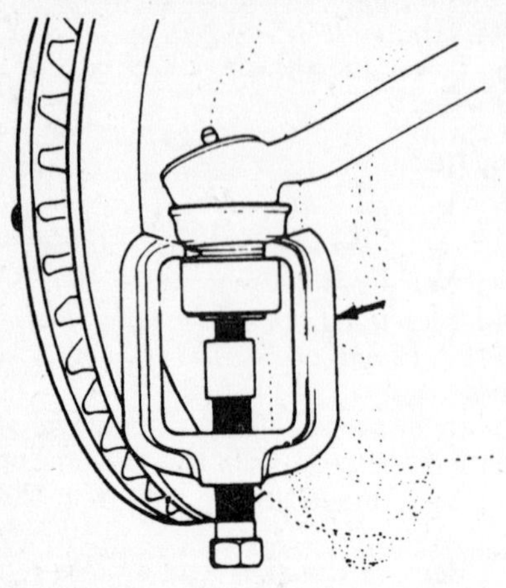

Disconnecting the tie rod end with the proper tool

4. Using the GM Wheel Stud Remover tool No. J-6627-A or equivalent, separate the outer tie rod stud from the steering knuckle and the inner tie rod stud from the relay rod. Remove the tie rod from the vehicle.

5. If removing ONLY the tie rod end, perform the following procedures:

a. Disconnect the defective ball joint end of the tie rod.

b. Loosen the adjuster tube clamp bolt.

c. Unscrew the tie rod end from the adjuster tube; count the number of turns necessary to remove the tie rod end.

d. Clean, inspect and lubricate the adjuster tube threads.

e. To install a new tie rod end, screw it into the adjuster tube using the same number of turns necessary to remove it.

f. Position the clamp bolts between the adjuster tube dimples (located at each end) and in the proper location (see illustration). Torque the adjuster tube clamp bolt 13 ft. lbs.

6. To install, position the tie rod onto the steering knuckle and the relay rod. Using the Steering Linkage Installer tool No. J-29193 (12mm) or J-29194 (14mm) or equivalent, install them onto the studs and torque them to 35 ft. lbs. (to seat the tapers). After seating the tapers, remove the tool.

7. At the tie rod-to-steering knuckle stud, tighten the nut until the castle nut slot aligns with the hole in the stud, then install a new cotter pin.

8. Lower the vehicle and check the steering linkage performance.

Damper Assembly

The damper assembly is used to the remove steering wheel vibration and vehicle wonder; not all vehicles are equipped with it.

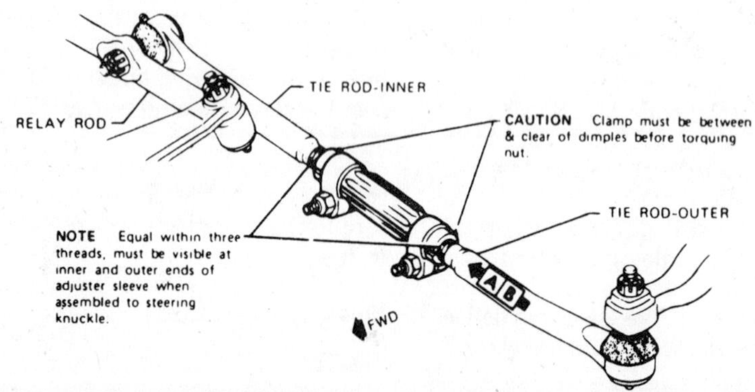

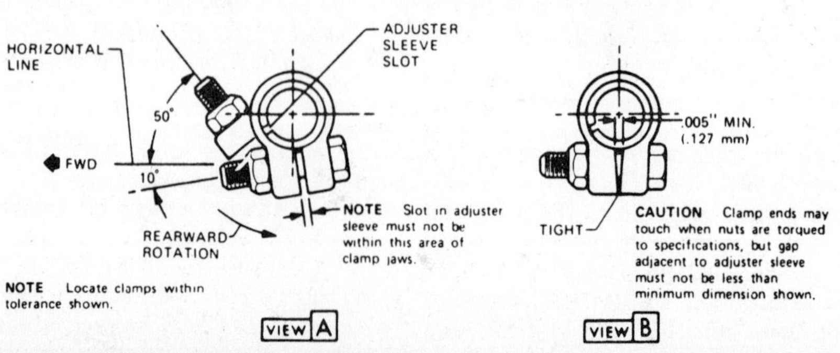

Tie rod clamp and sleeve positioning

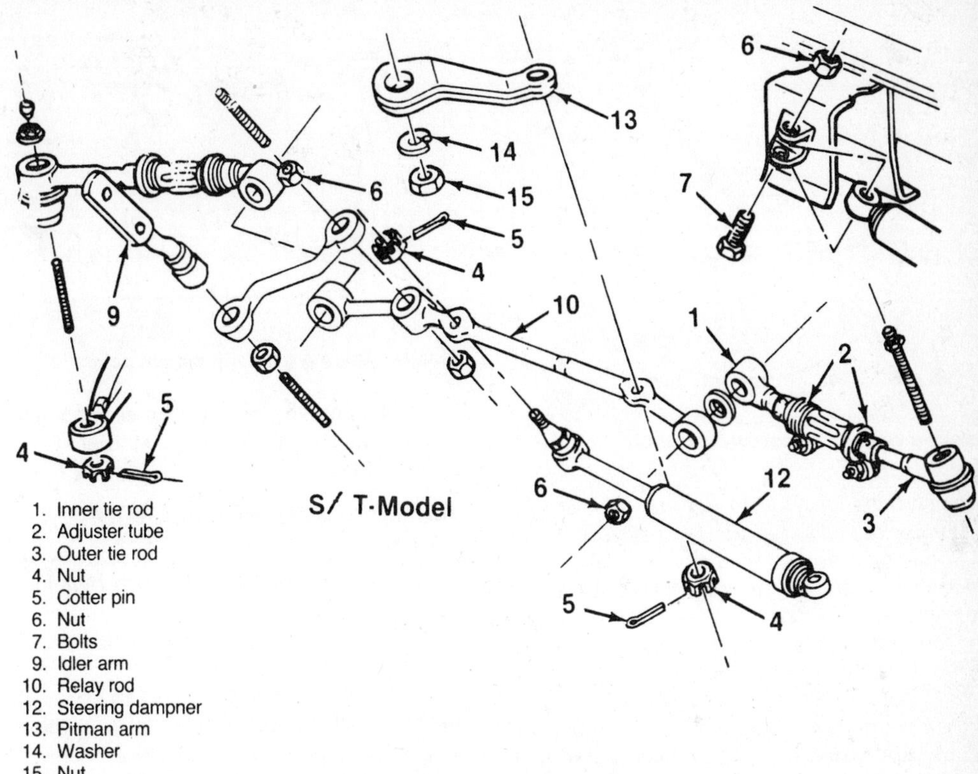

Steering linkage with damper

NOTE: *The following procedure requires the use of the Steering Linkage Puller tool No. J-24319-01 or equivalent.*

1. Raise and safely support the front frame of the vehicle on jackstands.

2. Remove the damper assembly-to-relay rod cotter pin and nut.

3. Using the Steering Linkage Puller tool No. J-24319-01 or equivalent, separate the damper assembly from the relay rod.

4. Remove the damper assembly-to-bracket nut/bolt and the damper assembly from the vehicle.

5. If necessary, use a new damper assembly and reverse the removal procedures. Torque the damper assembly-to-bracket nut/bolt to 26 ft. lbs. and the damper assembly-to-relay rod nut to 45 ft. lbs. Align the castle nut slot with the hole in the ball joint stud and install a new cotter pin.

Manual Steering Gear

The recirculating ball type manual steering gear is manufactured by Saginaw and is equipped with a mechanical ratio of 24:1.

ADJUSTMENTS

NOTE: *The following procedure requires the use the GM Steering Linkage Puller tool No. J-6632 or equivalent, and a 0–50 inch lbs. torque wrench.*

1. Disconnect the negative battery cable from the battery.

2. Raise and safely support the front frame of the vehicle on jackstands.

NOTE: *Before adjustments are made to the steering gear, be sure to check the front end alignment, the shock absorbers, the wheel balance and the tire pressure.*

3. Remove the pitman arm-to-pitman shaft nut and matchmark the pitman arm to the pitman shaft. Using the GM Steering Linkage Puller tool No. J-6632 or equivalent, remove the pitman arm from the pitman shaft.

4. Loosen the steering gear adjuster plug locknut and back-off the adjuster plug 1/4 turn.

5. From the steering wheel, remove the horn cap or cover.

6. Gently, turn the steering wheel (in one direction) to the stop; then, turn it back 1/2 turn.

NOTE: *When the steering linkage is disconnected from the steering gear, DO NOT turn*

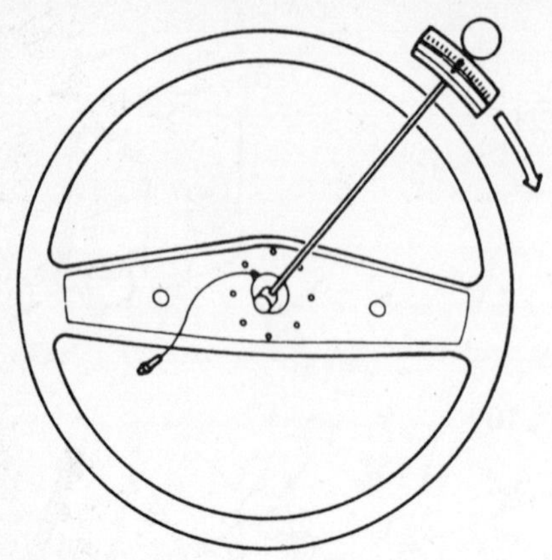

Measure steering wheel rotation effort

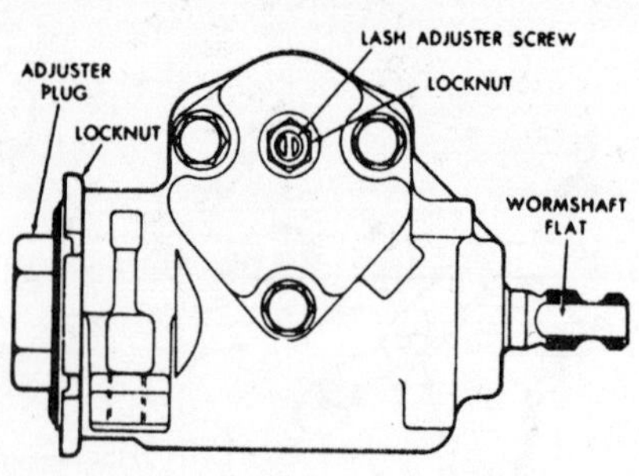

Manual steering gear adjustment points

the steering wheel hard against the stops for damage to the ball guides may result.

7. Using a torque wrench (0–50 inch lbs.), position it onto the steering wheel nut, then measure and record the bearing drag. To measure the bearing drag, use the torque wrench to rotate the steering wheel 90°.

8. Using a torque wrench (0–50 inch lbs.), tighten the adjuster plug (on the steering gear) to obtain a thrust bearing preload of 5–8 inch lbs. After the thrust bearing preload is obtained, torque the adjuster plug locknut to 25 ft. lbs.

NOTE: *If the steering gear feels lumpy (after adjustment), suspect damage to the bearings, probably due to the improper adjustment or severe impact.*

9. To adjust the overcenter preload, perform the following procedures:

a. Turn the steering wheel, from one stop all the way to the other stop, counting the number of turns. Turn the steering wheel back exactly $^1/_2$ way, to the center position.

b. Turn the overcenter adjusting screw clockwise, until the lash is removed between the ball nut and the pitman shaft sector teeth, then tighten the locknut.

c. Using a torque wrench (0–50 inch lbs.), check the highest force necessary to turn the steering wheel through the center position; the usable torque is 4–10 inch lbs.

d. If necessary, loosen the locknut and readjust the overcenter adjusting screw to obtain the proper torque. Retorque the locknut to 25 ft. lbs. and recheck the steering wheel torque through the center of travel.

NOTE: *If the maximum is too high, turn the overcenter adjuster screw counterclockwise, then torque the adjuster lock nut in the clockwise motion to achieve the proper torque.*

10. To install, realign the pitman arm-to-pitman shaft, torque the pitman shaft nut to 185 ft. lbs.

REMOVAL AND INSTALLATION

NOTE: *The following procedure requires the use of the GM Pitman Arm Remover tool No. J-6632 or equivalent.*

1. Disconnect the negative battery cable from the battery.

2. Raise and safely support the front frame of the vehicle on jackstands. Position the wheel in the straight ahead direction.

3. Remove the intermediate shaft-to-steering gear pinch bolt.

4. Remove the pitman arm-to-pitman shaft nut, mark the relationship the arm to the shaft. Using the GM Pitman Arm Remover tool No. J-6632 or equivalent, separate the pitman arm from the pitman shaft.

NOTE: *When separating the pitman arm from the shaft, DO NOT use a hammer or apply heat to the arm.*

5. Remove the steering gear-to-frame bolts and the gear from the vehicle.

NOTE: *When installing the steering gear, be sure that the intermediate shaft bottoms on the worm shaft, so that the pinch bolt passes through the undercut on the worm shaft.*

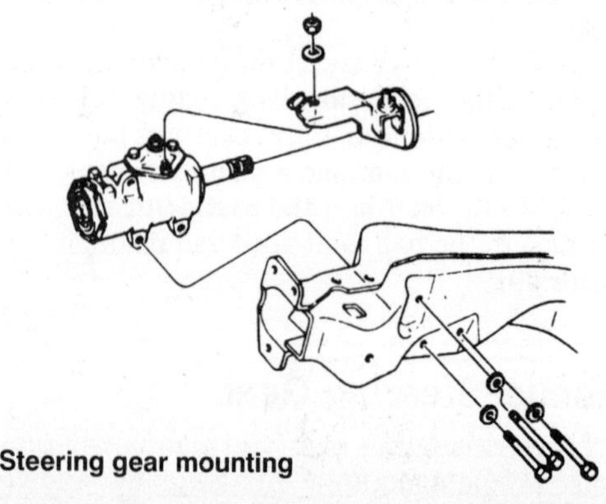

Steering gear mounting

Removing the adjuster plug lock nut from the power steering gear

Check and/or adjust the alignment of the pitman arm-to-pitman shaft.

6. To install, align the matchmarks and reverse the removal procedures. Torque the steering gear-to-frame bolts to 60 ft. lbs., the pitman arm-to-pitman shaft nut to 185 ft. lbs. and the intermediate steering shaft-to-steering gear bolt to 30 ft. lbs.

Power Steering Gear

The recirculating ball type power steering gear is basically the same as the manual steering gear, except that it uses a hydraulic assist on the rack piston.

The power steering gear control valve directs the power steering fluid to either side of the rack piston, which rides up and down the worm shaft. The steering rack converts the hydraulic pressure into mechanical force. Should the vehicle loose the hydraulic pressure, it can still be controlled mechanically.

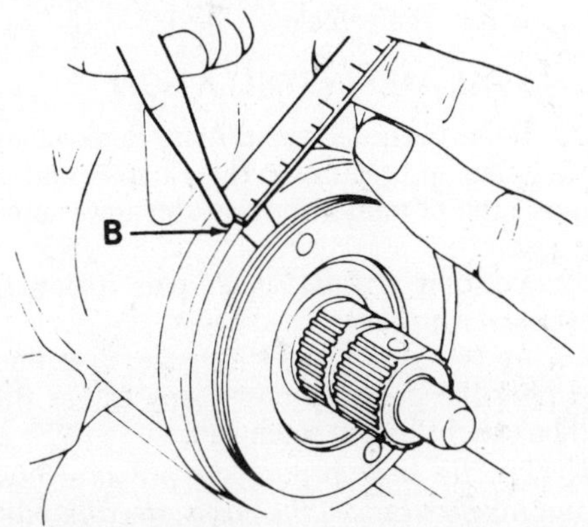

B. Second index mark

Make the second index mark

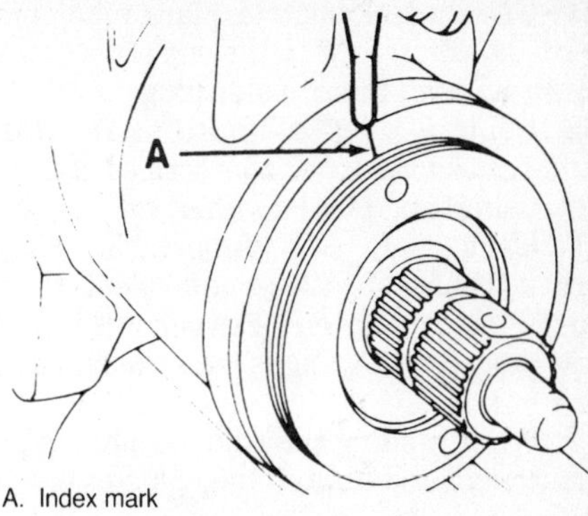

A. Index mark

Marking the housing with the adjuster plug hole

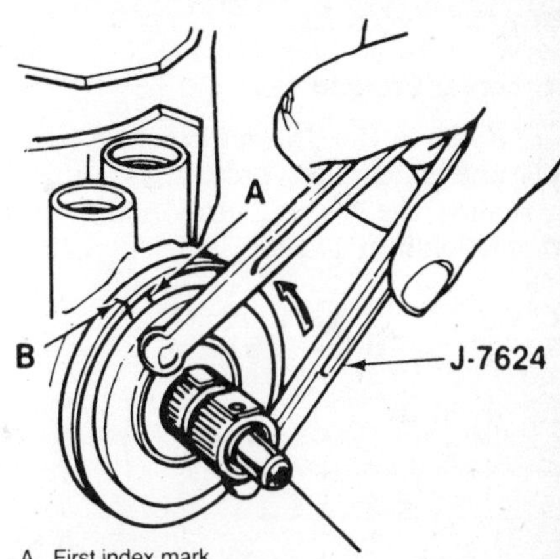

A. First index mark
B. Second index mark

Using the spanner to align the adjuster plug with the second mark

ADJUSTMENTS

NOTE: *To perform adjustments to the power steering gear, it is recommended to remove the power steering gear from the vehicle and place it in a vise. Before adjustments are performed to the system, be sure to check problems relating to hydraulic pressures and performance.*

Worm Bearing Preload

NOTE: *The following procedure requires the use of the GM Adjustable Spanner Wrench tool No. J-7624 or equivalent.*

1. Refer to the "Power Steering Gear, Removal and Installation" procedures in this Chapter, remove the steering gear from the vehicle and position it in a vise.

2. Using a hammer and a brass punch, drive the adjuster plug lock nut counterclockwise and remove it from the end of the steering gear.

3. Using the GM Adjustable Spanner Wrench tool No. J-7624 or equivalent, turn the adjuster plug inward, until it firmly bottoms in the housing with a torque of 20 ft. lbs.

4. Using a scribing tool, place a matchmark (on the housing) next to the one of the spanner wrench holes in the adjuster plug.

5. Using a ruler, measure $^1/_2$ in. (13mm) counterclockwise from the scribed mark (on the housing) and place another mark.

6. Using the GM Adjustable Spanner Wrench tool No. J-7624 or equivalent, turn the adjuster plug (counterclockwise) until the hole in the adjuster plug aligns with the 2nd scribed mark.

7. While holding the adjuster plug in alignment, install and tighten the adjuster plug lock nut.

8. Perform the overcenter preload adjustment.

Overcenter Preload

1. Refer to the "Power Steering Gear, Removal and Installation" procedures in this Chapter, remove the steering gear from the vehicle and position it in a vise.

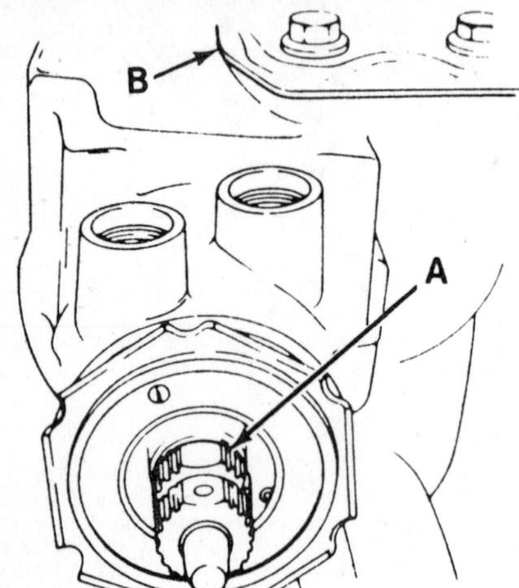

A. Stub shaft flat
B. Side cover

Alining the stub shaft with the side cover

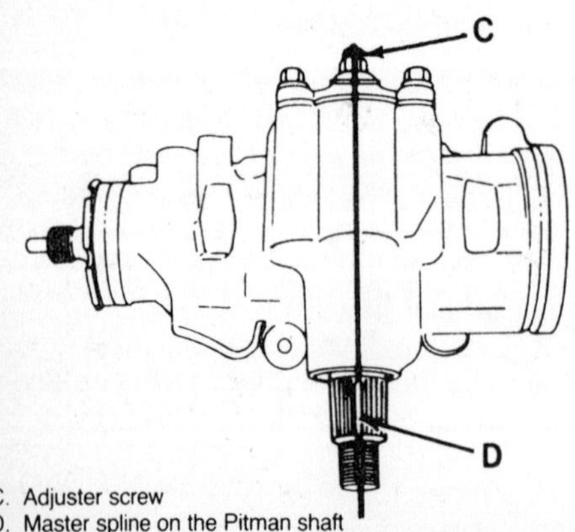

C. Adjuster screw
D. Master spline on the Pitman shaft

Align the pitman arm shaft master spline

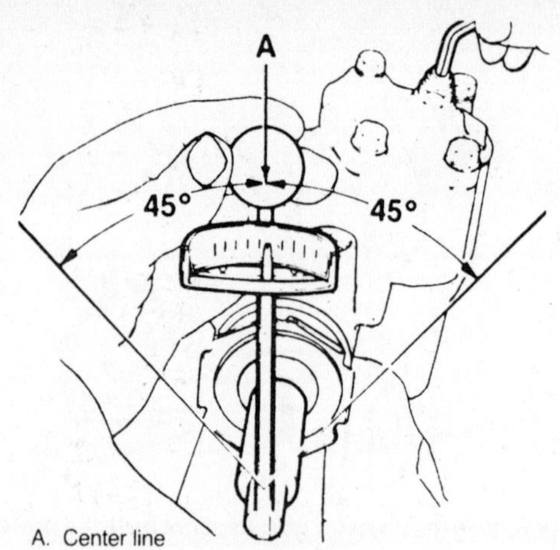

A. Center line

Reading over center rotation torque

2. Rotate the stud shaft from stop-to-stop and count the number of turns necessary.

3. Starting from one stop, turn the stub shaft back $^1/_2$ the number of turns (center of the gear).

NOTE: *With the stub gear centered, the flat on top of the shaft should face upward and be parallel with the side cover; the master spline on the pitman shaft should be in line with the adjuster screw.*

4. Loosen the pitman shaft adjuster screw locknut and turn the adjuster screw counterclockwise until it is fully extended, then turn it clockwise one full turn.

5. Using a torque wrench (0–50 inch lbs.), position it onto the stub shaft, rotate it 45° (to each side) and record the highest drag measured near or on the center.

6. Turn the adjuster screw inward until the torque on the stub shaft is 6–10 inch lbs. greater than the initial reading.

7. Install the adjuster screw jam nut and torque it to 20 ft. lbs. Reinstall the power steering gear into the vehicle.

REMOVAL AND INSTALLATION

1. Refer to the "Pitman Arm, Removal and Installation" procedures in this Chapter and disconnect the pitman arm from the power steering gear.

2. Position a fluid catch pan under the power steering gear.

3. At the power steering gear, disconnect and plug the pressure hoses; any excess fluid will be caught by the catch pan.

NOTE: *Be sure to plug the pressure hoses and the openings of the power steering pump to keep dirt out of the system.*

4. Remove the intermediate shaft-to-steering gear bolt. Matchmark the intermediate

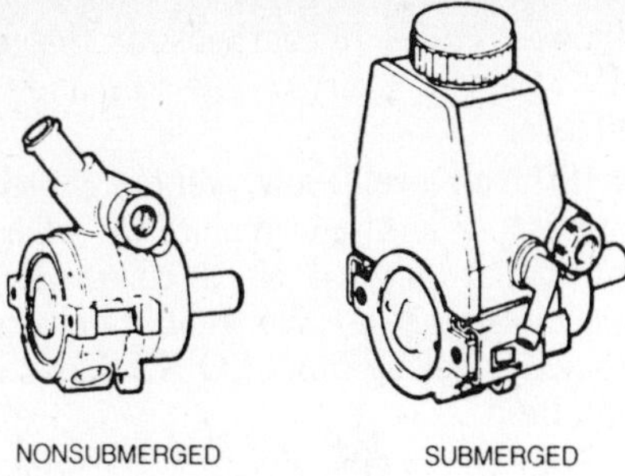

Two pumps are in production

shaft-to-power steering gear and separate the shaft from the gear.

5. Remove the power steering gear-to-frame bolts, washers and the steering gear from the vehicle.

6. To install, reverse the removal procedures. Torque the power steering gear-to-frame bolts to 55 ft. lbs., the intermediate shaft-to-power steering gear bolt to 30 ft. lbs. and the pitman arm-to-pitman shaft nut to 185 ft. lbs.

7. Connect the pressure hoses to the power steering gear, refill the power steering reservoir and bleed the power steering system.

8. Road test the vehicle.

Power Steering Pump

Two types of power steering pumps are offered, they are: The submerged and the non-submerged. The submerged pump has a housing and internal parts which are inside the reservoir and operate submerged in oil. The non-submerged pump functions the same as the submerged pump except the reservoir is separate from the housing and internal parts.

REMOVAL AND INSTALLATION

NOTE: *The following procedure requires the use of the GM Puller tool No. J-29785-A or equivalent, and the GM Pulley Installer tool No. J-25033-B or equivalent.*

1. Position a fluid catch pan under the power steering pump.

2. Remove the pressure hoses from the power steering pump and drain the excess fluid into the catch pan.

NOTE: *On models equipped with a remote fluid reservoir, disconnect and plug the hose(s).*

3. Loosen the power steering pump adjusting bolt, the washer and the pivot bolt, then remove the drive belt.

4. Using the GM Puller tool No. J-29785-A or equivalent, install it onto the power steering pump pulley. While holding the tool body, turn the pilot bolt counterclockwise to press the drive pulley from the pump.

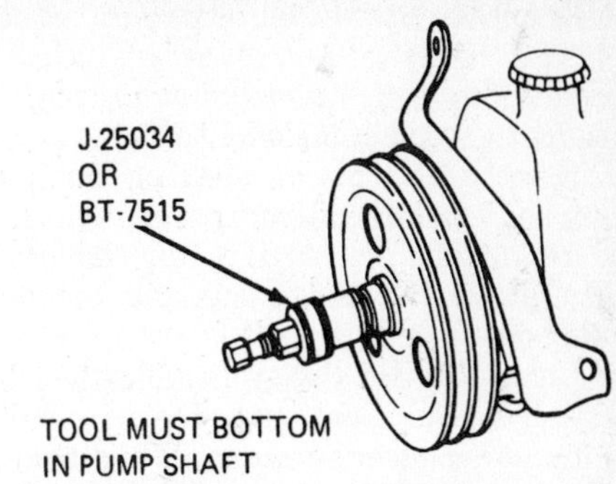

Installing pilot bolt

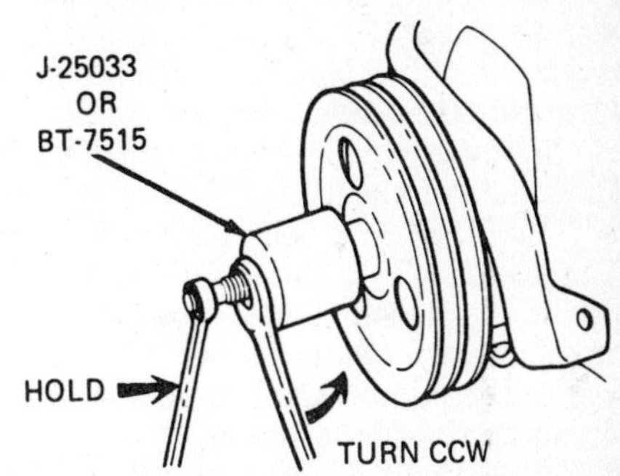

Removing the power steering pump pulley

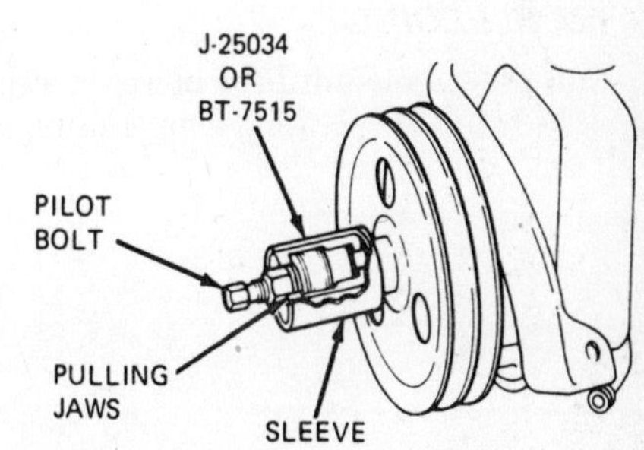

Installing the puller

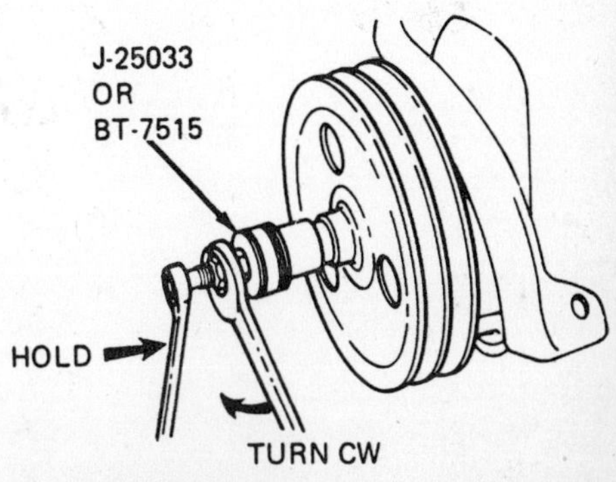

Installing the pulley

NOTE: *When installing the puller tool onto the power steering pump pulley, be sure that the pilot bolt bottoms in the pump shaft by turning the head of the pilot bolt.*

5. Remove the power steering pump-to-bracket bolts and the pump from the vehicle.

6. To install, reverse the removal procedures. Torque the power steering pump-to-bracket bolts to 18 ft. lbs.

7. Using the GM Pulley Installer tool No. J-25033-B or equivalent, press the drive pulley onto the power steering pump. While holding the tool body, turn the pilot bolt clockwise to press the drive pulley onto the pump.

NOTE: *When installing the installer tool onto the power steering pump pulley, be sure that the pilot bolt bottoms in the pump shaft by turning the head of the pilot bolt.*

8. Hand tighten the pivot bolt, the adjusting bolt and the washer.

9. Install the drive belt and adjust the drive belt tension. Torque the mounting bolts and nut to 36 ft. lbs. (submerged type) or 20 ft. lbs. (non-submerged type). Install the pressure hoses (to the pump), refill the power steering reservoir and bleed the system.

NOTE: *Be sure to secure any hoses which may get in the way or rub other components.*

10. Test drive the vehicle.

SYSTEM BLEEDING

1. Run the engine until the power steering fluid reaches normal operating temperature, approximately 170°F (76°C), then shut the engine Off. Remove the reservoir filler cap and check the oil level.

2. If the oil level is low, add power steering fluid to proper level and replace the filler cap. When adding or making a complete fluid change, always use GM No. 1050017 or equivalent, power steering fluid. DO NOT use transmission fluid.

3. Start the engine and turn the wheels in both directions (to the stops) several times. Stop the engine and add power steering fluid to the level indicated on the reservoir.

NOTE: *Maintain the fluid level just above the internal pump casting. Fluid with air in it will have a light tan or milky appearance. This air must be eliminated from the fluid before normal steering action can be obtained.*

4. Return the wheels to the center position and continue to run it for 2–3 minutes, then shut the engine Off.

5. Road test the vehicle to make sure the steering functions normally and is free from noise.

6. Allow the vehicle to stand for 2–3 hours, then recheck the power steering fluid.

BRAKE SYSTEM

The trucks are equipped with independent front and rear brake systems. The systems consist of a power booster, a master cylinder, a combination valve, front disc and rear drum assemblies.

The master cylinder, mounted on the left firewall or power booster, consists of two fluid reservoirs, a primary (rear) cylinder, a secondary (front) cylinder and springs. The reservoirs, being independent of one another, are contained within the same housing; fluid cannot pass from one to the other. The rear reservoir supplies fluid to the front brakes while the front reservoir supplies fluid to the rear brakes.

During operation, fluid drains from the reservoirs to the master cylinder. When the brake pedal is applied, fluid from the master cylinder is sent to the combination valve (mounted on a bracket, directly under the master cylinder), here it is monitored and proportionally distributed to the front or rear brake systems. Should a loss of pressure occur in one system, the other system will provide enough braking pressure to stop the vehicle. Also, should a loss of pressure in one system occur, the differential warning switch (located on the combination valve) will turn ON the brake warning light (located on the dash board).

As the fluid enters each brake caliper or wheel cylinder, the pistons are forced outward. The outward movement of the pistons force the brake pads against a round flat disc or the brake shoes against a round metal drum. The brake lining attached to the pads or shoes comes in contact with the revolving disc or drum, causing friction, which brings the wheel to a stop.

In time, the brake linings wear down. If not replaced, their metal support plates (bonded type) or rivet heads (riveted type) will come in contact with the disc or drum; damage to the disc or drum will occur. Never use brake pads or shoes with a lining thickness less than $\frac{1}{32}$ in. (0.8mm).

Most manufacturers provide a wear sensor, a piece of spring steel, attached to the rear edge of the inner brake pad. When the pad wears to the replacement thickness, the sensor will contact the disc and produce a high pitched squeal.

Adjustments

FRONT DISC BRAKES

Disc brakes are not adjustable. They are, in effect, self adjusting.

ADJUSTMENT OF REAR BRAKES

Normal adjustments of the rear drum brakes are automatic and are made during the reverse applications of the brakes. ONLY, if the lining has been renewed, should the following procedure be performed.

NOTE: *The following procedure requires the use of the GM Brake Adjustment tool No. J-4735 or equivalent.*

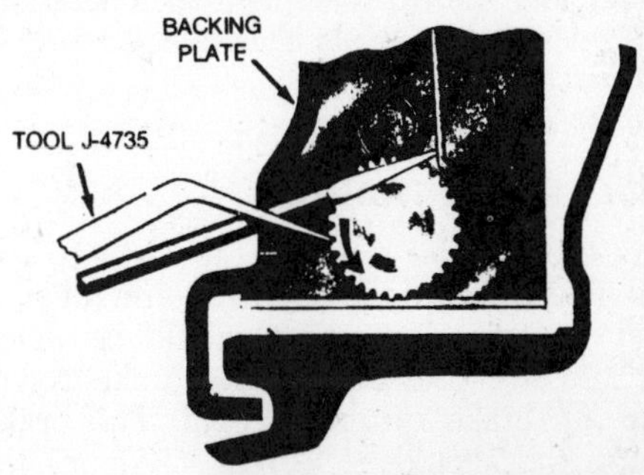

Adjusting the rear brake star wheel

1. Raise and safely support the rear of the vehicle on jackstands.

2. Using a punch and a hammer, at the rear of the backing plate, knock out the lanced metal area near the starwheel assembly.

NOTE: *When knocking out the lanced metal area from the backing plate, the wheels must be removed and all of the metal pieces discarded.*

3. Using the GM Brake Adjustment tool No. J-4735 or equivalent, insert it into the slot and engage the lowest possible tooth on the starwheel. Move the end of the brake tool downward to move the starwheel upward and expand the adjusting screw. Repeat this operation until the brakes just lock the wheel.

4. Insert a small screwdriver or piece of firm wire (coat hanger wire) into the adjusting slot and push the automatic adjuster lever out and free of the starwheel on the adjusting screw.

5. While holding the adjusting lever out of the way, engage the topmost tooth possible on the starwheel (with the brake tool). Move the end of the adjusting tool upward to move the adjusting screw starwheel downward and contact the adjusting screw. Back off the adjusting screw starwheel until the wheel spins freely with a minimum of drag. Keep track of the number of turns the starwheel is backed off.

6. Repeat this operation for the other side. When backing off the brakes on the other side, the adjusting lever must be backed off the same number of turns to prevent side-to-side brake pull.

NOTE: *Backing off the starwheel 12 notches (clicks) is usually enough to eliminate brake drag.*

7. Repeat this operation on the other side of the rear brake system.

8. After the brakes are adjusted, install a rubber hole cover into the backing plate slot. To complete the brake adjustment operation, make several stops while backing the truck to equalize the adjustment.

9. Road test the vehicle.

BRAKE PEDAL TRAVEL

The brake pedal travel is the distance the pedal moves toward the floor from the fully released position. Inspection should be made with 100 lbs. pressure on the brake pedal, when the brake system is Cold. The brake pedal travel should be $4^3/4$ in. (120mm) for manual, or $2^1/2$ in. (61mm) for power.

NOTE: *If equipped with power brakes, be sure to pump the brake pedal at least 3 times with the engine Off, before making the brake pedal check.*

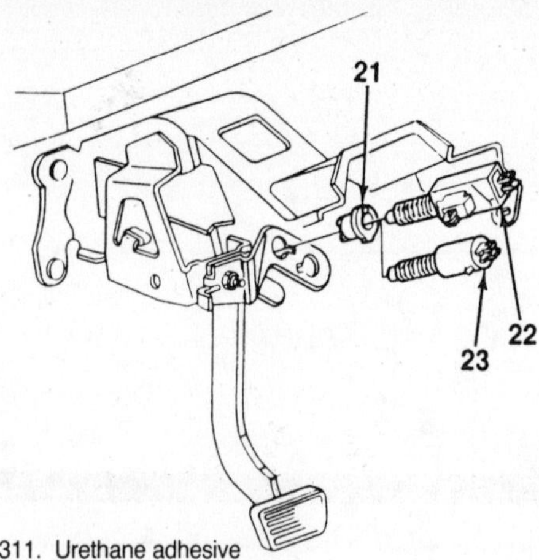

311. Urethane adhesive
333. Window frame pinchweld
334. Glass assembly
335. Clip

Adjusting the brake light switch

1. From under the dash, remove the pushrod-to-pedal clevis pin and separate the pushrod from the brake pedal.

2. Loosen the pushrod adjuster lock nut, then adjust the pushrod.

3. After the correct travel is established, reverse the removal procedure.

Brake Light Switch

REMOVAL AND INSTALLATION

1. Disconnect the negative battery cable from the battery.

2. Disconnect the electrical connector from the brake light switch.

3. Turn the brake light switch retainer (to align the key with the bracket slot), then remove the switch with the retainer.

4. To install, reverse the removal procedures. Adjust the brake light switch.

ADJUSTMENT

1. Depress the brake pedal and press the brake light switch inward until it seats firmly against the clip.

NOTE: *As the switch is being pushed into the clip, audible clicks can be heard.*

2. Release the brake pedal, then pull it back against the pedal stop until the audible click can no longer be heard.

3. The brake light switch will operate when the pedal is depressed 0.53 in. (13mm) from the fully released position.

Master Cylinder

REMOVAL AND INSTALLATION

1. Apply the parking brakes and block the wheels.

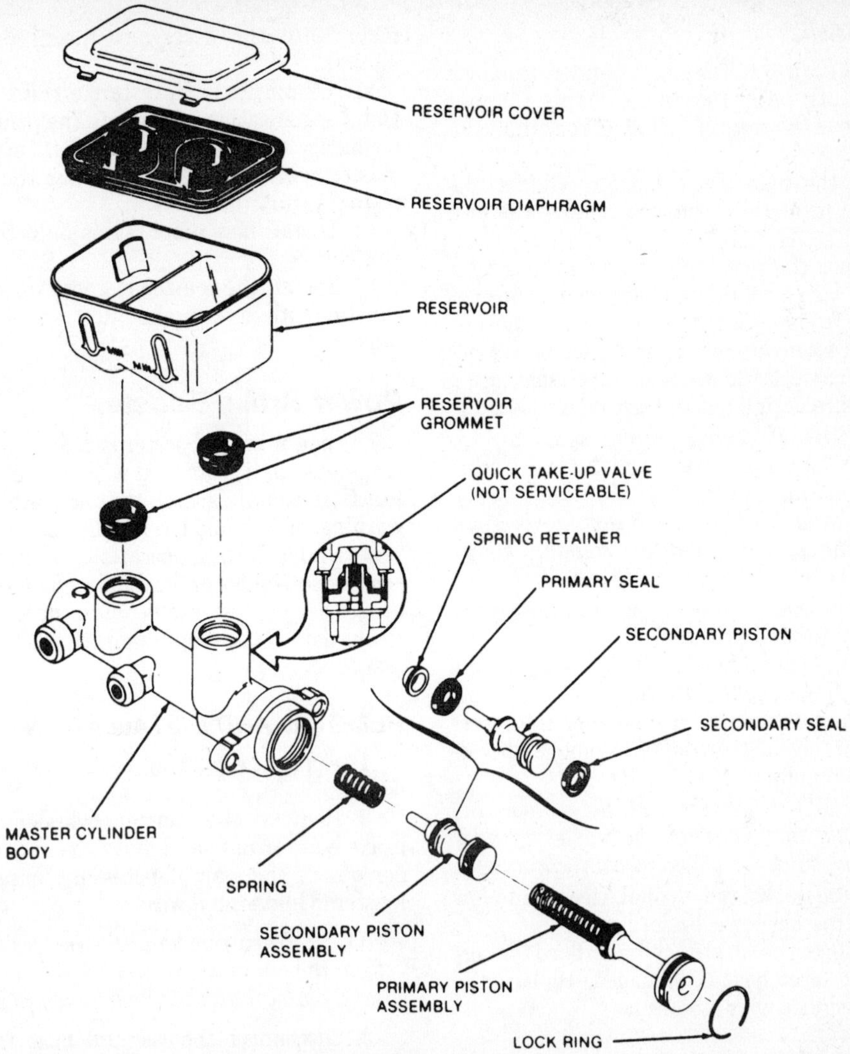

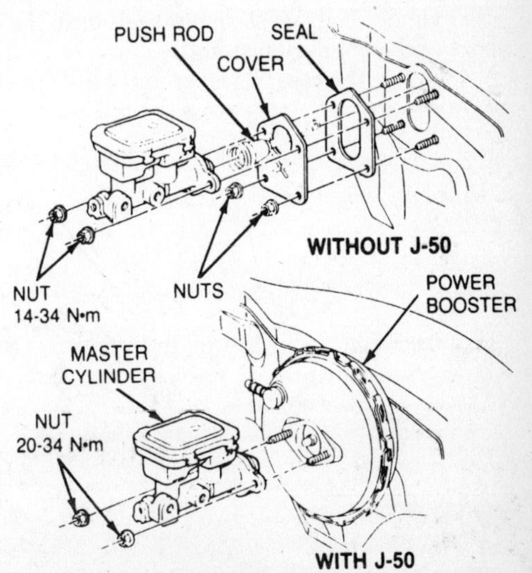

Master cylinder exploded view

2. Use a line wrench to disconnect and plug the hydraulic lines from the master cylinder.

3. If equipped with a manual brake system, disconnect the pushrod from the brake pedal.

4. Remove the master cylinder-to-bracket (manual) or vacuum booster (power) nuts, then separate the combination valve/bracket from the master cylinder.

5. Remove the master cylinder, the gasket and the rubber boot from the vehicle.

6. To install, bench bleed the master cylinder and reverse the removal procedures. Torque the master cylinder mounting nuts to 20 ft. lbs.

7. Refill the master cylinder with clean brake fluid, bleed the brake system and check the brake pedal travel.

NOTE: *If equipped with manual brakes, be sure to reconnect the pushrod to the brake pedal.*

Master cylinder attachment

OVERHAUL

1. Refer to the "Master Cylinder, Removal and Installation" procedures in this Chapter and remove the master cylinder from the vehicle.

2. At the rear of the master cylinder, depress the primary piston and remove the lock ring.

3. Block the rear outlet hole on the master cylinder. Using compressed air, gently direct it into the front outlet hole to remove the primary and secondary pistons from the master cylinder. If compressed air is not available, use a hooked wire to pull out the secondary piston.

CAUTION: *If using compressed air to remove the pistons from the master cylinder, DO NOT stand in front of the pistons, for too much air will cause the pistons to be fired from the master cylinder, causing bodily harm.*

4. From the secondary piston, remove the spring retainer and the seals.

5. Using the mounting flange (ear) on the master cylinder, clamp it into a vise.

6. Using a medium pry bar, pry the reservoirs from the master cylinder. Remove the reservoir grommets.

NOTE: *DO NOT attempt to remove the quick take-up valve from the master cylinder body; the valve is not serviceable separately.*

7. Using denatured alcohol, clean and blow dry all of the master cylinder parts.

8. Inspect the master cylinder bore for corrosion or scratches; if damaged, replace the master cylinder with a new one.

To install:

9. Use new reservoir grommets (lubricated with brake fluid) and press them into the master cylinder body. Install new seals onto the primary and secondary pistons.

10. Position the reservoirs on flat, hard surfaces (block of wood), then press the master cylinder onto the reservoirs, using a rocking motion.

11. Using heavy duty brake fluid, meeting Dot 3 specifications, lubricate the primary and secondary pistons, then install them into the master cylinder. While depressing the primary piston, install the lock ring.

12. Install new diaphragms onto the reservoir covers.

13. Install the master cylinder on the vehicle, fill with new brake fluid and bleed the brakes.

Power Brake Booster

The power brake booster is a tandem vacuum suspended unit, equipped with a single or dual function vacuum switch that activates a brake warning light should low booster vacuum be present. Under normal operation, vacuum is present on both sides of the diaphragms. When the brakes are applied, atmospheric air is admitted to one side of the diaphragms to provide power assistance.

REMOVAL AND INSTALLATION

1. Apply the parking brake and block the wheels.

2. Remove the master cylinder-to-power brake booster nuts and move the master cylinder out of the way; if necessary, support the master cylinder on a wire.

NOTE: *When removing the master cylinder from the power brake booster, it is not necessary to disconnect the hydraulic lines.*

3. Disconnect the vacuum hose from the power brake booster.

4. From under the dash, disconnect the pushrod from the brake pedal.

5. From under the dash, remove the power brake booster-to-cowl nuts.

6. From the engine compartment, remove

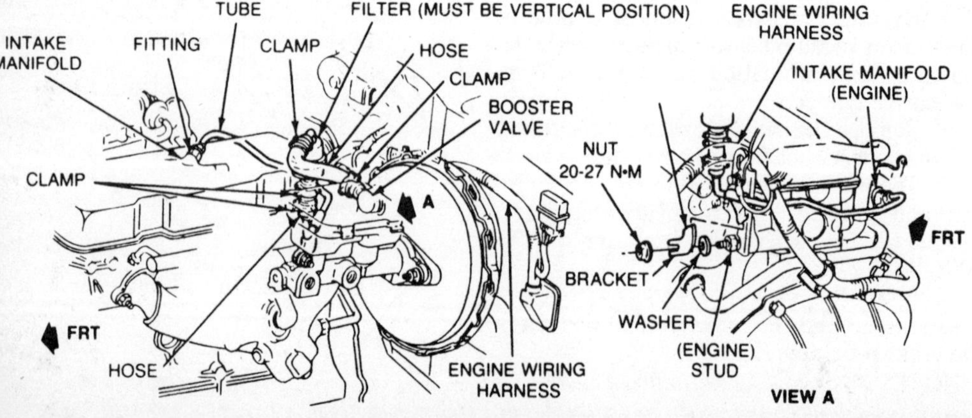

4-cylinder engine vacuum lines

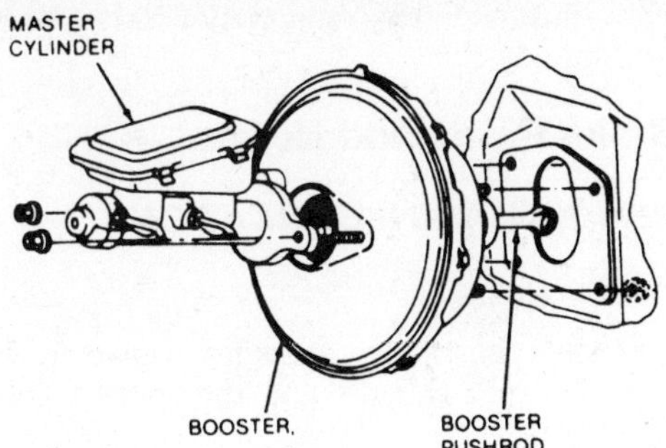

Power brake booster attachment

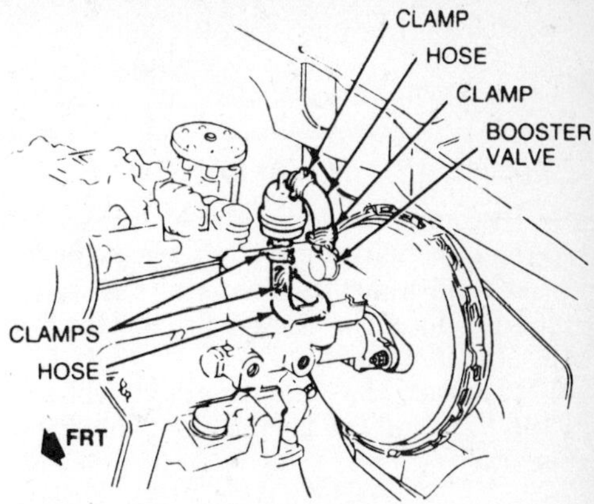

6-cylinder engine vacuum lines

the power brake booster and the gasket from the vehicle.

7. To install, use a new gaskets and reverse the removal procedures. Torque the power brake booster-to-cowl nuts to 15 ft. lbs. and the master cylinder-to-power brake booster nuts to 20 ft. lbs. Start the engine and check the brake system operation.

Combination Valve

The combination valve is located in the engine compartment, directly under the master cylinder. It consists of three sections: the metering valve, the warning switch and the proportioning valve.

The metering section limits the pressure to the front disc brakes until a predetermined front input pressure is reached, enough to overcome the rear shoe retractor springs. Under 3 psi, there is no restriction of the inlet pressures; the pressures are allowed to equalize during the no brake period.

The proportioning section controls the outlet pressure to the rear brakes after a predetermined rear input pressure has been reached; this feature is provided for vehicles with light loads, to help prevent rear wheel lock-up. The by-pass feature of this valve assures full system pressure to the rear brakes in the event of a front brake system malfunction. Also, full front pressure is retained if the rear system malfunctions.

The pressure differential warning switch is designed to constantly compare the front and the rear brake pressures; if one should malfunction, the warning light (on the dash) will turn On. The valve and switch are designed to lock On the warning position once the malfunction

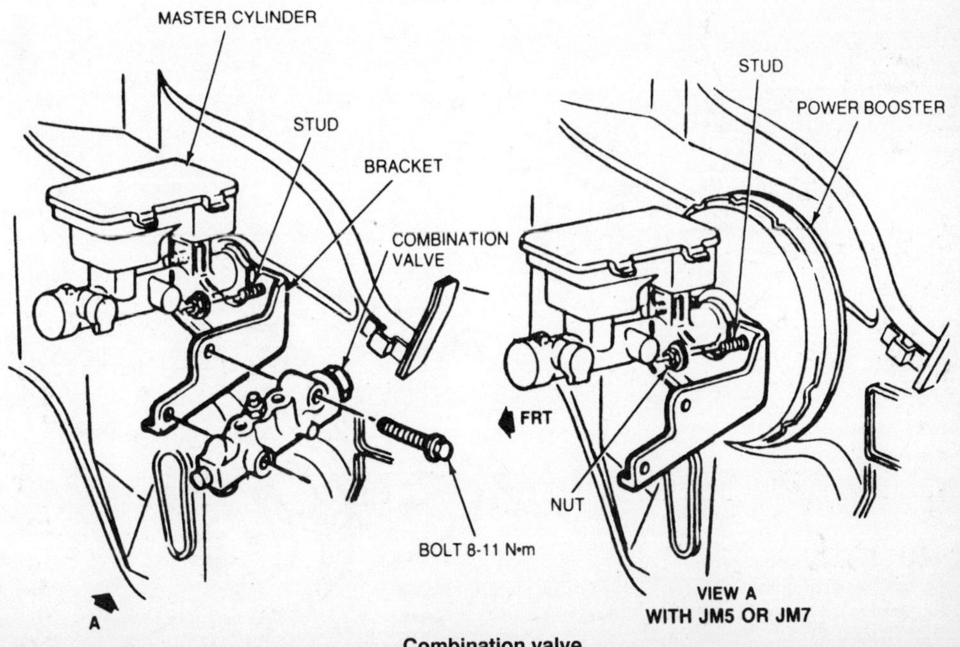

Combination valve

has occurred. The only way the light can be turned Off is to repair the malfunction and apply a brake line force of 450 psi.

REMOVAL AND INSTALLATION

1. Disconnect and plug the hydraulic lines from the combination valve to prevent the loss of brake fluid or dirt from entering the system.

2. Disconnect the electrical connector from the combination valve.

3. Remove the combination valve-to-bracket nuts and the combination valve from the vehicle.

NOTE: *The combination valve is not repairable and must be replaced as a complete assembly.*

4. To install, use a new combination valve (if defective) and reverse the removal procedures. Torque the combination valve-to-bracket nuts to 12 ft. lbs. Reconnect the electri-

cal connector to the combination valve. Bleed the brake system.

Brake Pipes and Hoses

REMOVAL AND INSTALLATION

Flexible Hoses

Flexible hoses are installed between the frame-to-front calipers and the frame-to-rear differential.

1. Using a wire brush, clean the dirt and/or grease from both ends of the hose fittings.

2. Disconnect the steel pipes from the flexible hose.

3. To remove the brake hose from the front brake caliper or the rear differential, perform the following procedures:

a. Remove the brake hose-to-frame bracket retaining clip.

b. Remove the brake hose-to-brake cali-

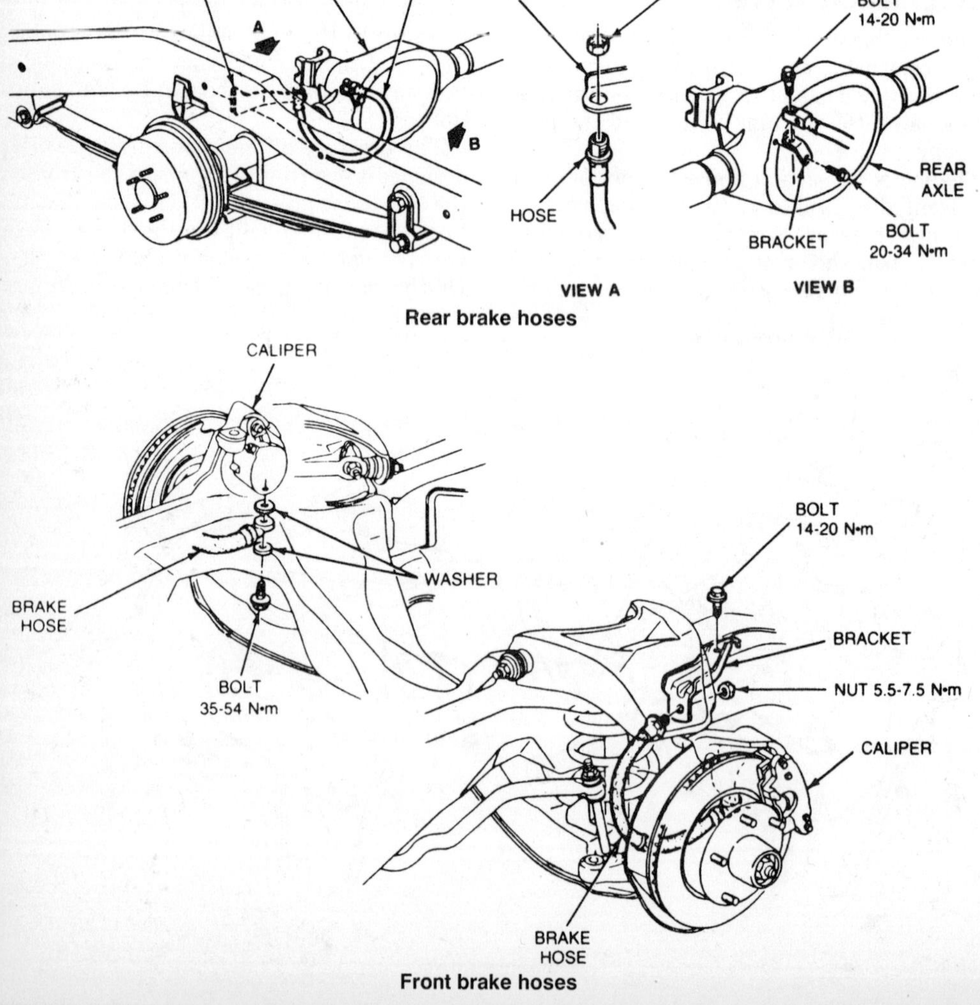

Rear brake hoses

Front brake hoses

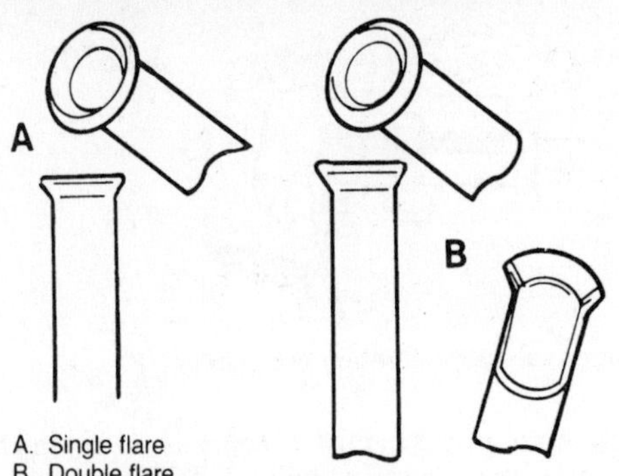

A. Single flare
B. Double flare

Single and double flare tube ends

per or differential junction block bolt.

c. Remove the brake hose and the gaskets from the vehicle.

NOTE: *After disconnecting the brake hose(s) from the fittings, be sure to plug the fittings to keep the fluid from discharging or dirt from entering the system.*

5. Clean and inspect the brake hose(s) for cracking, chafing or road damage; replace the hose(s) if any signs are observed.

6. Using new flexible hose-to-caliper gaskets, install the flexible hose(s) and reverse the removal procedures. Torque the flexible hose(s)-to-front caliper bolt(s) to 32 ft. lbs. and all other brake pipe fittings to 13 ft. lbs. Bleed the brake system.

NOTE: *Be sure that the hoses do not make contact with any of the suspension components.*

Steel Pipes

When replacing the steel brake pipes, always use steel piping which is designed to withstand high pressure, resist corrosion and is of the same size.

CAUTION: *Never use copper tubing, for it is subject to fatigue, cracking, and/or corrosion, which will result in brake line failure.*

NOTE: *The following procedure requires the use of the GM Tube Cutter tool No. J-23533 or equivalent, and the GM Flaring tool No. J-23530 or equivalent.*

1. Disconnect the steel brake pipe(s) from the flexible hose connections or the rear wheel cylinders; be sure to remove any retaining clips.

2. Remove the steel brake pipe from the vehicle.

3. Using new steel pipe (same size) and the GM Tube Cutter tool No. J-23533 or equivalent, cut the pipe to length; be sure to add $^1/_8$ in. (3mm) for each flare.

NOTE: *Be sure to install the correct pipe fittings onto the tube before forming any flares.*

4. Using the Flaring tool No. J-23530 or equivalent, follow the instructions equipped

with the tool to form double flares on the ends of the pipes.

5. Using the small pipe bending tool, bend the pipe to match the contour of the pipe which was removed.

6. To install, reverse the removal procedures. Bleed the hydraulic system.

Bleeding

WITHOUT ABS

The hydraulic brake system must be bled any time one of the lines is disconnected or any time air enters the system. If the brake pedal feels spongy upon application, and goes almost to the floor but regains height when pumped, air has entered the system. It must be bled out. Check for leaks that would have allowed the entry of air and repair them before bleeding the system. The correct bleeding sequence is; right rear, left rear, right front and left front.

CAUTION: *If the vehicle has rear wheel or 4 wheel anti–lock braking, do not use this procedure. Improper service procedures on anti-lock braking systems can cause serious personal injury. Refer to the ABS service procedures.*

MANUAL

This method of bleeding requires two people, one to depress the brake pedal and the other to open the bleeder screws.

NOTE: *The following procedure requires the use of a clear vinyl hose, a glass jar and clean brake fluid.*

1. Clean the top of the master cylinder, remove the cover and fill the reservoirs with clean fluid. To prevent squirting fluid, replace the cover.

NOTE: *On vehicles equipped with front disc brakes, it will be necessary to hold in the me-*

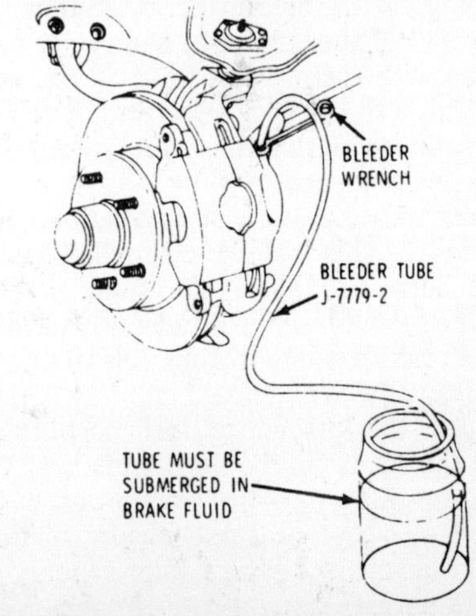

Brake bleeding

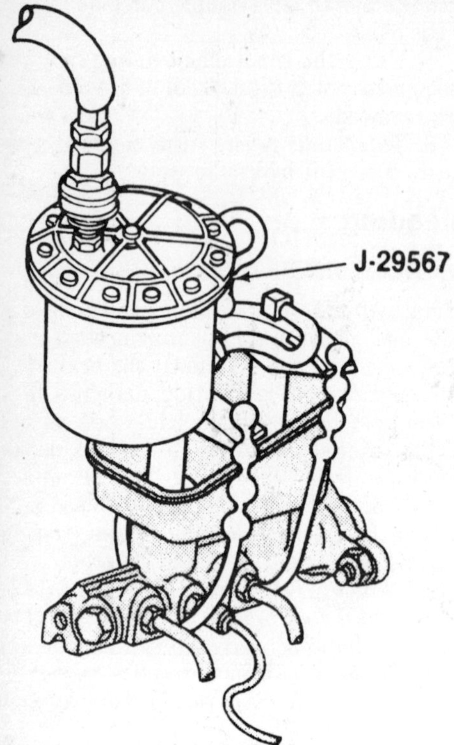

Pressure bleeding the brake system

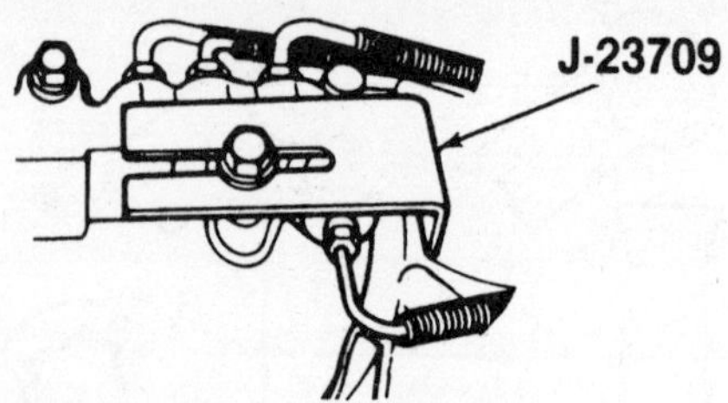

Depressing the combination valve

the brake pedal firmly. If there is no air in the system, the dash light will turn Off.

PRESSURE

NOTE: *The following procedure requires the use of the GM Brake Bleeder Adapter tool No. J-29567 or equivalent, and the GM Combination Valve Depressor tool No. J-23709 or equivalent.*

1. Using the GM Brake Bleeder Adapter tool No. J-29567 or equivalent, fill the pressure tank to at least $1/3$ full of brake fluid. Using compressed air, charge the pressure tank to 20–25 psi., then install it onto the master cylinder.

2. Using the GM Combination Valve Depressor tool No. J-35856 or equivalent, install it onto the combination valve to hold the valve open during the bleeding operation.

3. Bleed each wheel cylinder or caliper in the following sequence: right rear, left rear, right front and left front.

4. Connect a hose from the bleeder tank to the adapter at the master cylinder, then open the tank valve.

5. Attach a clear vinyl hose to the brake bleeder screw, then immerse the opposite end into a container partially filled with clean brake fluid.

6. Open the bleeder screw $3/4$ turn and allow the fluid to flow until no air bubbles are seen in the fluid, then close the bleeder screw.

7. Repeat the bleeding process to each wheel.

8. Inspect the brake pedal for sponginess and if necessary, repeat the entire bleeding procedure.

9. Remove the depressor tool from the combination valve and the bleeder adapter from the master cylinder.

10. Refill the master cylinder to the proper level with brake fluid.

tering valve pin during the bleeding procedure. The metering valve is located beneath the master cylinder and the pin is situated under the rubber boot on the end of the valve housing. This may be tapped in or held by an assistant.

2. Fill the master cylinder with clean brake fluid.

3. Install a box end wrench onto the bleeder screw on the right rear wheel.

4. Attach a length of small diameter, clear vinyl tubing to the bleeder screw. Submerge the other end of the tubing in a glass jar partially filled with clean brake fluid. Make sure the tube fits on the bleeder screw snugly or you may be squirted with brake fluid when the bleeder screw is opened.

5. Have your assistant slowly depress the brake pedal. As this is done, open the bleeder screw $1/2$ turn and allow the fluid to run through the tube. Close the bleeder screw, then return the brake pedal to its fully released position.

6. Repeat this procedure until no bubbles appear in the jar. Refill the master cylinder.

7. Repeat this procedure on the left rear, right front and the left front wheels, in that order. Periodically, refill the master cylinder so that it does not run dry.

8. If the brake warning light is On, depress

FRONT DISC BRAKES

CAUTION: *Brake shoes contain asbestos, which has been determined to be a cancer causing agent. Never clean the brake sur-*

faces with compressed air! Avoid inhaling any dust from any brake surface! When cleaning brake surfaces, use a commercially available brake cleaning fluid.

Brake Pads

INSPECTION

Brake pads should be inspected once a year or at 7,500 miles, which ever occurs first. Check both ends of the outboard shoe, looking in at each end of the caliper; then check the lining thickness on the inboard shoe, looking down through the inspection hole. The lining should be more than 0.032 in. (0.8mm) thick above the rivet (so that the lining is thicker than the metal backing). Keep in mind that any applicable state inspection standards that are more stringent, take precedence. All four pads must be replaced if one shows excessive wear.

NOTE: *All models have a wear indicator that makes a noise when the linings wear to a degree where replacement is necessary. The spring clip is an integral part of the inboard shoe and lining. When the brake pad reaches a certain degree of wear, the clip will contact the rotor and produce a warning noise.*

REMOVAL AND INSTALLATION

NOTE: *The following procedure requires the use of a C-clamp and adjustable pliers.*

1. If the fluid reservoir is full, siphon off about ²/₃ of the brake fluid from the master cylinder reservoirs.

CAUTION: *The insertion of thicker replacement pads will push the piston back into its bore and will cause a full master cylinder reservoir to overflow, possibly causing paint damage. In addition to siphoning off fluid, it would be wise to keep the reservoir cover on during pad replacement.*

2. Raise and safely support the front of the vehicle on jackstands. Remove the wheels.

NOTE: *When replacing the pads on just one wheel, uneven braking will result; always replace the pads on both wheels.*

3. Install a C-clamp on the caliper so that the frame side of the clamp rests against the back of the caliper and so the screw end rests

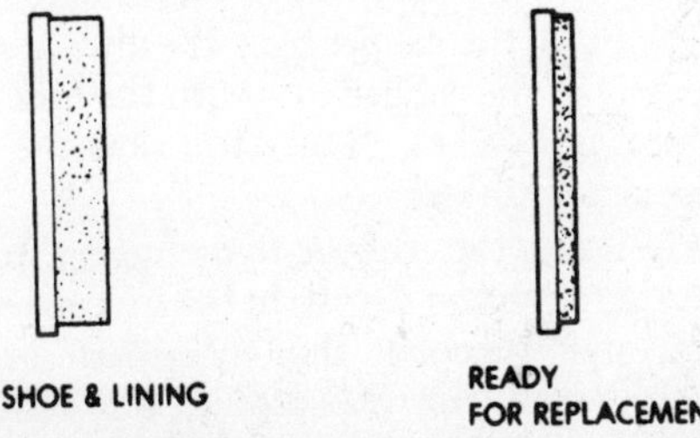

New and worn brake pads

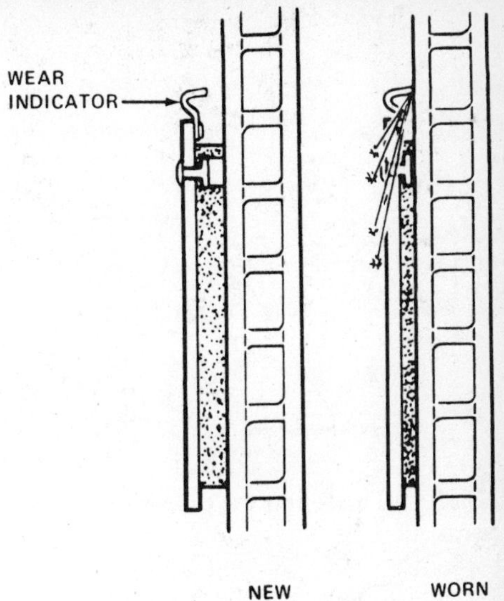

Disk brake pad wear indicator operation

against the metal part (shoe) of the outboard pad.

4. Tighten the clamp until the caliper moves enough to bottom the piston in its bore. Remove the clamp.

5. Remove the two Allen head caliper mounting bolts enough to allow the caliper to be pulled off the disc.

6. Remove the inboard pad and loosen the outboard pad. Place the caliper where it will not strain the brake hose; hang it from the suspension with wire.

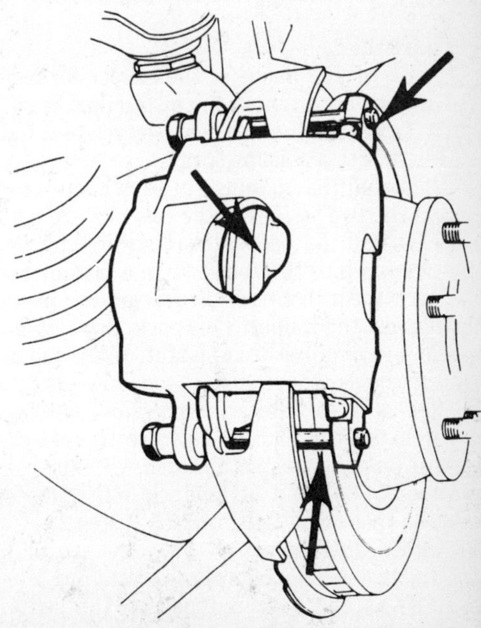

Inspecting the front brake pads

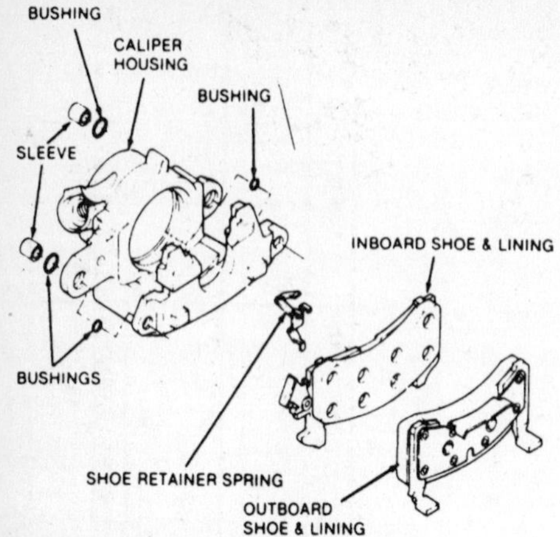

Removing the pads from the caliper

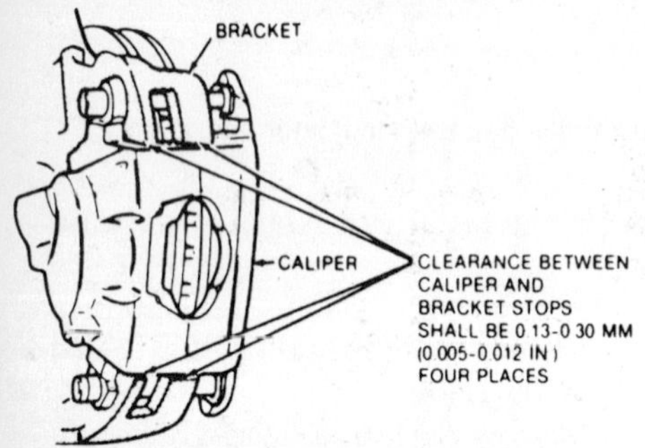

Checking caliper-to-bracket stop clearance

7. Remove the pad support spring clip from the piston.

8. Remove the two bolt ear sleeves and the four rubber bushings from the ears.

9. Brake pads should be replaced when they are worn to within $\frac{1}{32}$ in. (0.8mm) of the rivet heads.

To install:

10. Check the inside of the caliper for leakage and the condition of the piston dust boot.

11. Lubricate the two new sleeves and four bushings with a silicone spray.

12. Install the bushings in each caliper ear. Install the two sleeves in the two inboard ears.

13. Install the pad support spring clip and the old pad into the center of the piston. You will then push this pad down to get the piston flat against the caliper. This part of the job is a hassle and requires an assistant. While the assistant holds the caliper and loosens the bleeder valve to relieve the pressure, obtain a medium pry bar and try to force the old pad inward, making the piston flush with the caliper surface. When it is flush, close the bleeder valve so that no air gets into the system.

NOTE: *Make sure that the wear sensor is facing toward the rear of the caliper.*

14. Place the outboard pad in the caliper with its top ears over the caliper ears and the bottom tab engaged in the caliper cutout.

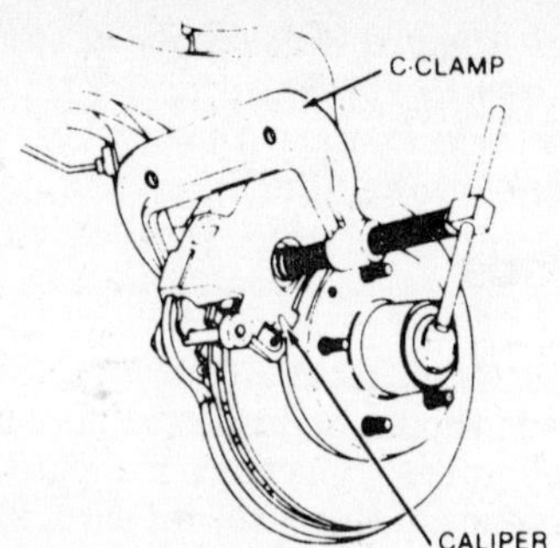

Using a C-clamp to bottom the brake caliper piston

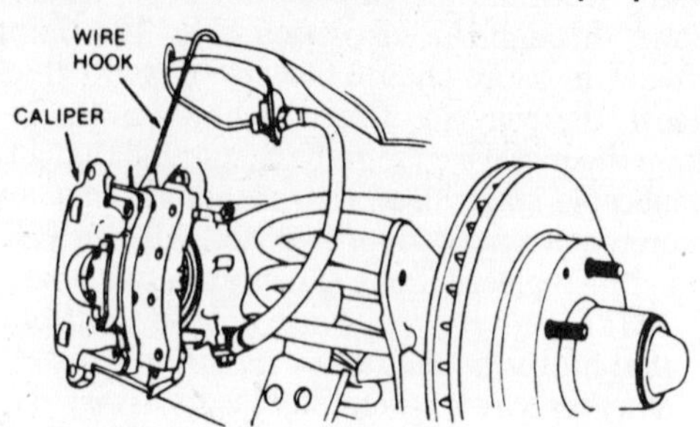

Suspending the caliper out of the way during brake servicing

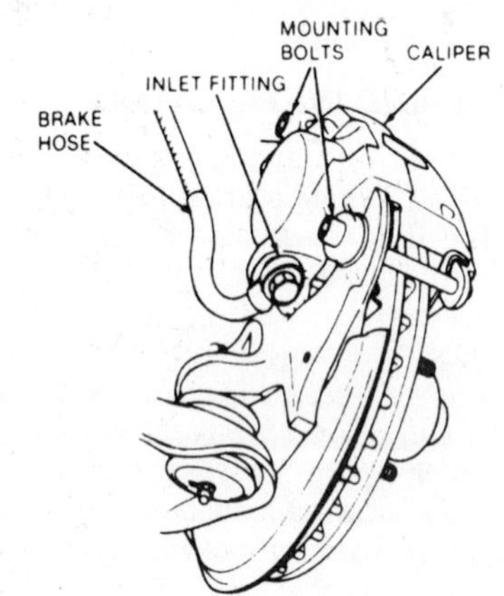

Caliper mounting

15. After both pads are installed, lift the caliper and place the bottom edge of the outboard pad on the outer edge of the disc to make sure that there is no clearance between the tab on the bottom of the shoes and the caliper abutment.

16. Place the caliper over the disc, lining up the hole in the caliper ears with the hole in the mounting bracket. Make sure that the brake hose is not kinked.

17. Start the caliper-to-mounting bracket bolts through the sleeves in the inboard caliper ears and through the mounting bracket, making sure that the ends of the bolts pass under the retaining ears of the inboard shoe.

18. Push the mounting bolts through to

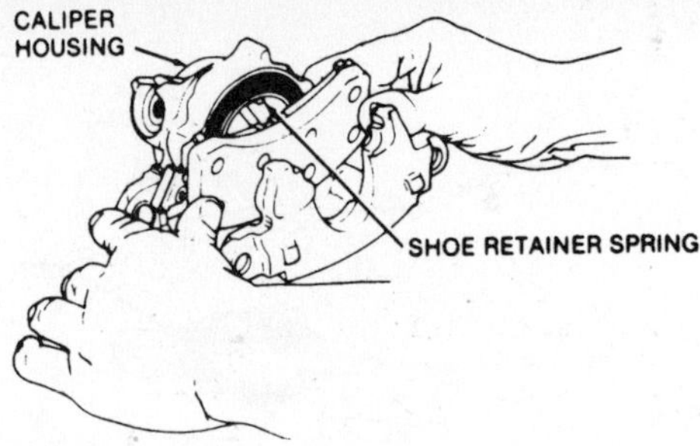

Installing the pads in the caliper

engage the holes in the outboard shoes and the outboard caliper ears and then thread them into the mounting bracket.

19. Torque the mounting bolts to 37 ft. lbs. Pump the brake pedal to seat the linings against the rotors.

20. Using a pair of channel lock pliers, place them on the notch on the caliper housing, bend the caliper upper ears until no clearance exists between the shoe and the caliper housing.

21. Install the wheels, lower the vehicle and refill the master cylinder reservoirs with brake fluid. Pump the brake pedal to make sure that it is firm. If it is not, bleed the brakes.

Brake Caliper

REMOVAL AND INSTALLATION

1. Refer to the "Brake Pads, Removal and Installation" procedures in this Chapter and remove the brake caliper from the steering knuckle.

2. Disconnect the flexible brake hose-to-caliper bolt, discard the pressure fitting washers, then remove the brake caliper from the vehicle and place it on a work bench.

3. To inspect the caliper assembly, perform the following procedures:

    a. Check the inside of the caliper assembly for signs of leakage; if necessary, replace or rebuild the caliper.

    b. Check the mounting bolts and sleeves

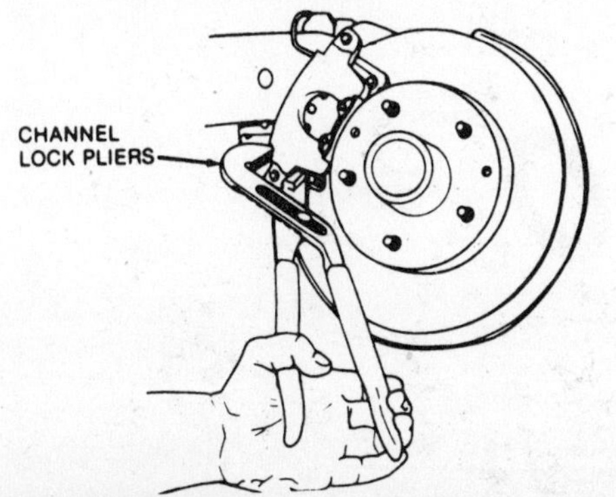

Seating the caliper

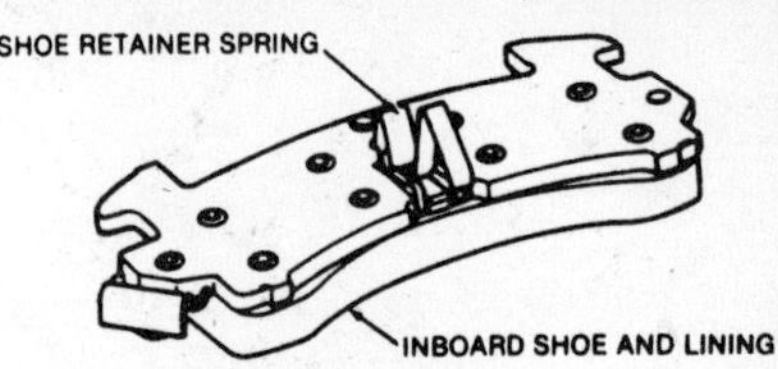

Installing the shoe retainer spring

for signs of corrosion; if necessary, replace the bolts.

NOTE: *If the mounting bolts have signs of corrosion, DO NOT attempt to polish away the corrosion.*

4. To install, use new caliper bushings and sleeves, use Delco® Silicone Lube or equivalent to lubricate the mounting bolts and new brake pads (if necessary).

5. After both pads are installed, lift the caliper and place the bottom edge of the outboard pad on the outer edge of the disc to make sure that there is no clearance between the tab on the bottom of the shoes and the caliper abutment.

6. Place the caliper over the disc, lining up the hole in the caliper ears with the hole in the mounting bracket.

7. Start the caliper-to-mounting bracket bolts through the sleeves in the inboard caliper ears and through the mounting bracket, making sure that the ends of the bolts pass under the retaining ears of the inboard shoe.

8. Push the mounting bolts through to engage the holes in the outboard shoes and the outboard caliper ears, then thread them into the mounting bracket.

9. To complete the installation, use new flexible brake hose-to-caliper washers and reverse the removal procedures. Torque the caliper-to-steering knuckle bolts to 37 ft. lbs. and the flexible brake hose-to-caliper bolt to 32 ft. lbs. Refill the master cylinder reservoirs and bleed the brake system. Pump the brake pedal to seat the linings against the rotors.

10. Using a pair of channel lock pliers, place them on the caliper housing notch, bend the caliper upper ears until no clearance exists between the shoe and the caliper housing.

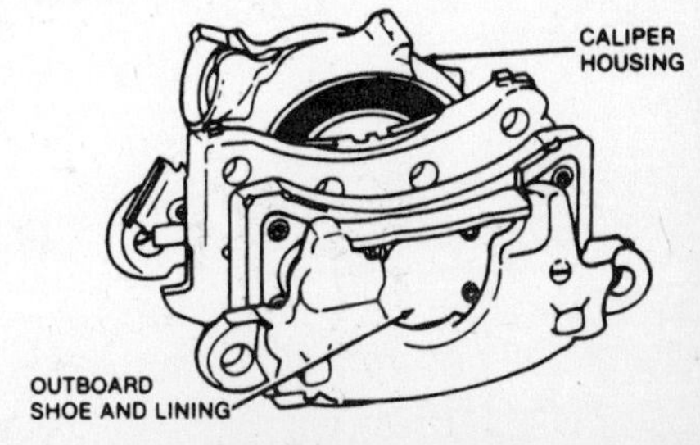

Positioning the shoe in the caliper

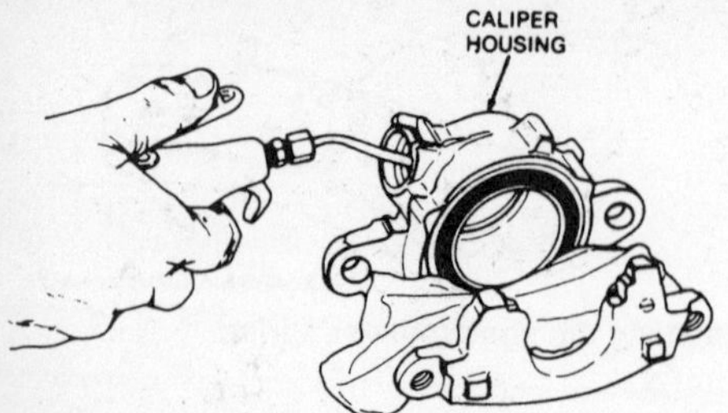

Place a clean rag as shown to catch the caliper piston when using compressed air to remove the piston from the bore

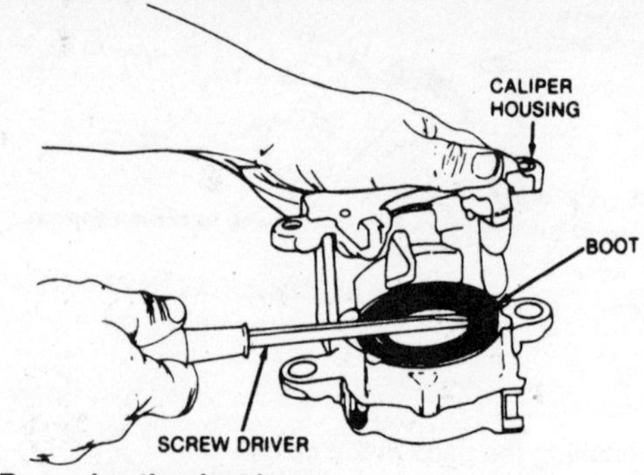

Removing the dust boot

11. Install the wheels, lower the vehicle. Pump the brake pedal to make sure that it is firm. Road test the vehicle.

OVERHAUL

1. Refer to the "Brake Caliper, Removal and Installation" procedures in this Chapter and remove the brake caliper from the vehicle.

2. Remove the inlet fitting from the brake caliper.

3. Position the caliper on a work bench and place clean shop cloths in the caliper opening. Using compressed air, force the piston from it's bore.

CAUTION: *DO NOT apply too much air pressure to the bore, for the piston may jump out, causing damage to the piston and/or the operator.*

4. Remove and discard the piston boot and seal. Be careful not to scratch the bore.

5. Clean all of the parts with non-mineral based solvent and blow dry with compressed air. Replace the rubber parts with those in the brake service kit.

6. Inspect the piston and the caliper bore for damage or corrosion. Replace the caliper and/or the piston (if necessary).

7. Remove the bleeder screw and it's rubber cap.

8. Inspect the guide pins for corrosion, replace them (if necessary). When installing the guide pins, coat them with silicone grease.

9. To install, perform the following procedures:

   a. Lubricate the piston, caliper and seal with clean brake fluid.

NOTE: *When positioning the piston seal on the piston, it goes in the groove nearest the piston's flat end with the lap facing the largest end. If placement is correct, the seal lips*

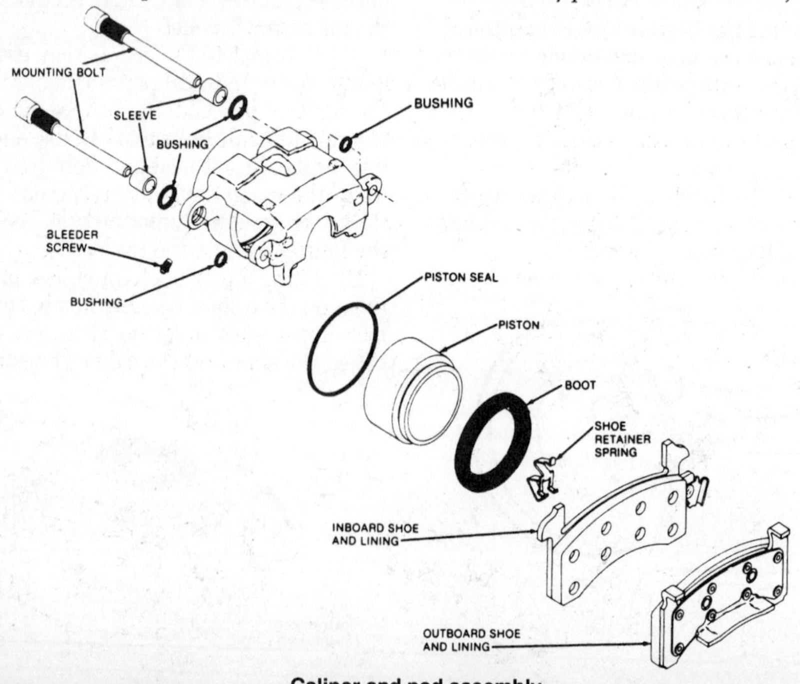

Caliper and pad assembly

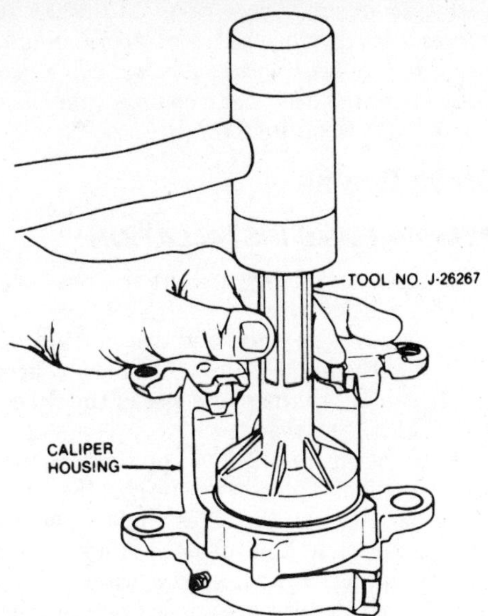

Installing the caliper seal

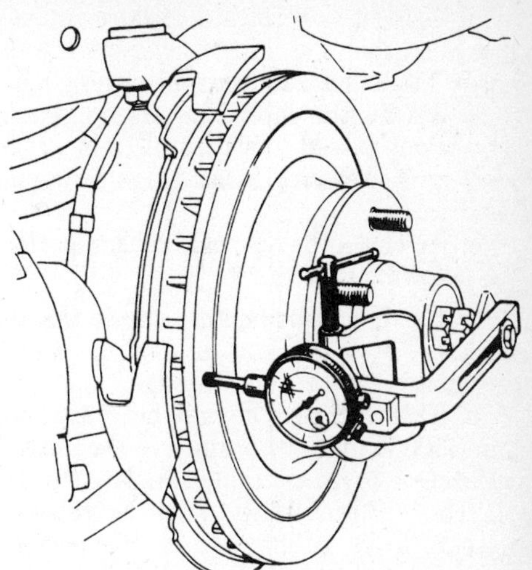

Use a dial indicator to determine the brake disc runout

will be in the groove and not extend over the groove's step.

b. Replace the caliper-to-steering knuckle bolts and torque the bolts to 37 ft. lbs.

10. To complete the installation, reverse the removal procedures. Bleed the brake system after installation.

Brake Disc (Rotor)

REMOVAL AND INSTALLATION

2WD Model

1. Siphon some brake fluid from the brake master cylinder.

2. Raise and safely support the front of the vehicle on jackstands. Remove the wheels.

3. Remove the brake caliper from the steering knuckle and hang it on a wire.

4. Remove the grease cup, the cotter pin, the castle nut and the hub assembly.

5. Inspect the brake discs for signs of wear or damage; if necessary, replace the brake disc.

6. To install the brake disc, reverse the removal procedures. Check and/or adjust the wheel bearing and the front end alignment.

7. Remove the jackstands and lower the vehicle. Refill the brake master cylinder.

4WD Model

1. Refer to the "Torsion Bar, Removal and Installation" procedures in Chapter 7 and relieve the torsion bar pressure.

2. Raise and safely support the front of the truck on jackstands; place the jackstands under the frame.

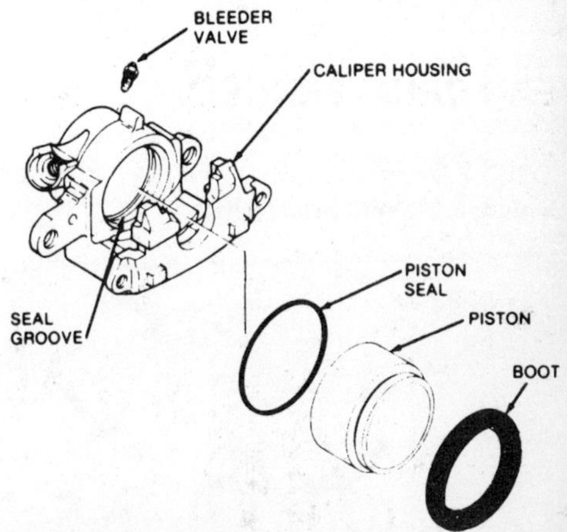

Caliper piston assembly

3. Remove the wheel and tire assembly.

4. Remove the disc brake caliper-to-steering knuckle bolts, lift the brake caliper and support it (out of the way) on a wire.

5. Remove the brake disc from the wheel hub.

NOTE: *When removing the steering knuckle from the wheel hub, be careful not to damage the splined surface of the half shaft.*

6. Inspect the disc for nicks, scores and/or damage, then replace it if necessary.

7. To install, reverse the removal procedures. Check and/or adjust the front end alignment.

INSPECTION

1. Raise and safely support the front of the vehicle on jackstands. Remove the wheels.

2. To check the disc runout, perform the following procedures:

a. Using a dial indicator, secure and position it so that the button contacts the disc about 1 in. (25.4mm) from the outer edge.

b. Rotate the disc. The lateral reading should not exceed 0.004 in. (0.1mm). If the reading is excessive, recondition or replace the disc.

3. To check the disc parallelism, perform the following procedures:

a. Using a micrometer, check the disc thickness at 4 locations around the disc, at the same distance from the edge.

b. The thickness should not vary more than 0.0005 in. (0.0127mm). If the readings are excessive, recondition or replace the disc.

4. The surface finish must be relatively smooth to avoid pulling and erratic performance, also, to extend the lining life. Light rotor surface scoring of up to 0.015 in. (0.38mm) in depth, can be tolerated. If the scoring depths are excessive, refinish or replace the rotor.

REAR DRUM BRAKES

CAUTION: *Brake shoes contain asbestos, which has been determined to be a cancer causing agent. Never clean the brake surfaces with compressed air! Avoid inhaling any dust from any brake surface! When cleaning brake surfaces, use a commercially available brake cleaning fluid.*

Brake Drums

REMOVAL AND INSTALLATION

1. Raise and safely support the rear of the vehicle on jackstands.

2. Remove the wheel and tire assemblies.

3. Pull the brake drum off. It may by necessary to gently tap the rear edges of the drum to start it off the studs.

4. If the drum will not come off past the shoes, it will be necessary to retract the adjusting screw. Remove the access hole cover from the backing plate and turn the adjuster to retract the linings away from the drum.

5. Install a replacement hole cover before reinstalling the drum.

6. Install the drums in the same position on the hub as removed.

NOTE: *The rear wheel bearings are not adjustable, they are serviced by replacement ONLY. If necessary to replace the rear wheel bearings, refer to the Axle Shaft, Bearing and*

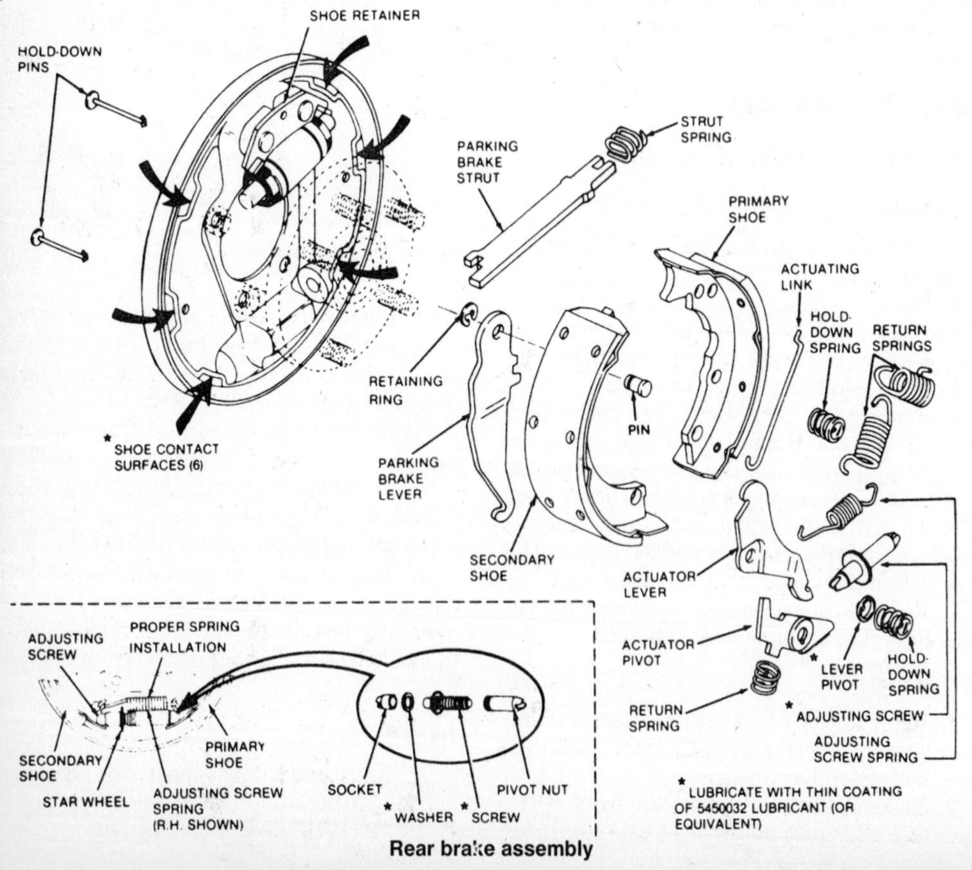

Rear brake assembly

Seal, Removal and Installation procedures and follow the replacement procedures.

INSPECTION

1. Check the drums for any cracks, scores, grooves or an out-of-round condition; if it is cracked, replace it. Slight scores can be removed with fine emery cloth while extensive scoring requires turning the drum on a lathe.

2. Never have a drum turned more than 0.060 in. (1.5mm) larger than the original inside diameter. The brake shoes will not make proper contact.

Brake Shoes

INSPECTION

Remove the drum and inspect the lining thickness of both brake shoes. The rear brake shoes should be replaced if the lining is less than $\frac{1}{16}$ in. (1.5mm) at the lowest point (bonded linings) or above the rivet heads (riveted linings) on the brake shoe. However, these lining thickness measurements may disagree with your state inspections laws.

NOTE: *Brake shoes should always be replaced in sets.*

REMOVAL AND INSTALLATION

NOTE: *The following procedure requires the use of the GM Brake Spring Pliers tool No. J-8057 or equivalent.*

1. Raise and safely support the rear of the vehicle on jackstands.

2. Slacken the parking brake cable.

3. Remove the rear wheels and the brake drum.

4. Using the GM Brake Spring Pliers tool No. J-8057 or equivalent, disconnect the brake shoe return springs, the actuator pullback spring, the holddown pins/springs and the actuator assembly.

NOTE: *Special brake spring tools are available from the auto supply stores, which will ease the replacement of the spring and anchor pin, but the job may still be performed with common hand tools.*

5. Disconnect the adjusting mechanism and spring, then remove the primary shoe. The primary shoe has a shorter lining than the secondary and is mounted at the front of the wheel.

6. Disconnect the parking brake lever from the secondary shoe and remove the shoe.

7. Clean and inspect all of the brake parts.

8. Check the wheel cylinders for seal condition and leaking.

9. Inspect the wheel bearing for leakage and replace, if necessary.

10. Inspect the replacement shoes for nicks or burrs, lightly lubricate the backing plate contact points, the brake cable, the levers and adjusting screws with brake grease, then reassemble them.

11. Make sure that the right and left hand adjusting screws are not mixed. You can prevent this by working on one side at a time. This will also provide you with a reference for reassembly. The star wheel should be nearest to the secondary shoe when correctly installed.

12. To complete the installation, reverse the removal procedures. When completed, make an initial adjustment as previously described.

Wheel Cylinders

REMOVAL AND INSTALLATION

1. Refer to the "Brake Shoe, Removal and Installation" procedures in this Chapter and remove the brake shoe assembly from the backing plate.

2. Clean away all of the dirt, crud and foreign material from around the wheel cylinder. It is important that dirt be kept away from the brake line when the cylinder is disconnected.

3. Disconnect and plug the hydraulic line at the wheel cylinder.

4. Remove the wheel cylinder-to-backing plate bolts and the wheel cylinder from the backing plate.

NOTE: *If the wheel cylinder is sticking, use a hammer and a punch to drive the wheel cylinder from the backing plate.*

5. To install, reverse the removal procedures. Torque the wheel cylinder-to-backing plate bolts to 160 inch lbs. Adjust and bleed the rear brake system.

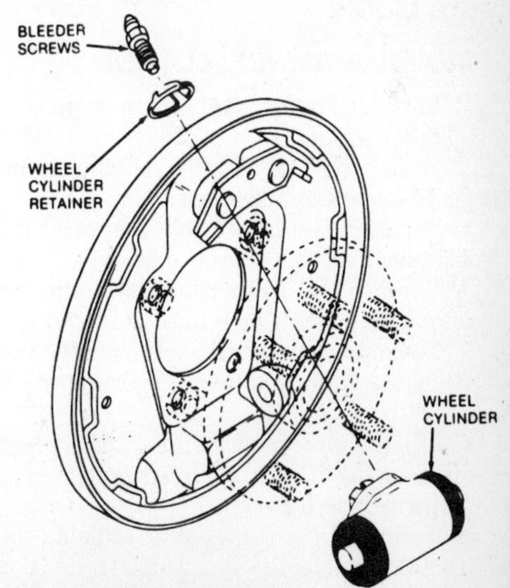

Wheel cylinder attachment

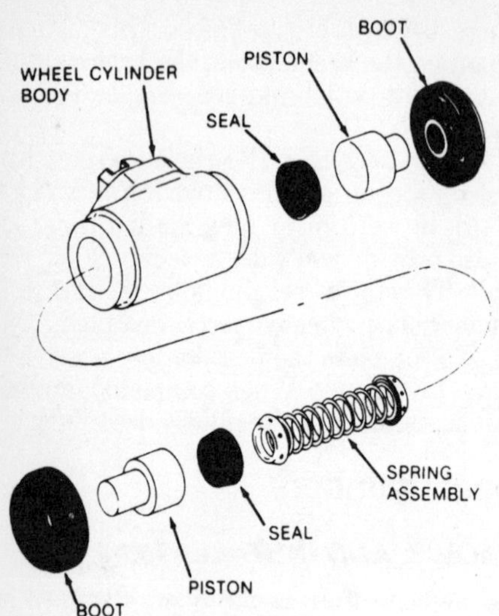

Wheel cylinder components

OVERHAUL

1. Remove the boots, pistons, seals and spring.

2. Dry the bore and pistons, then check for wear, scoring, pitting or corrosion. GM does not recommend honing of the bore. If light corrosion exists it may be removed with crocus cloth. If crocus cloth does not do the job, replace the cylinder.

3. To assemble, use new seals/boots, coat all of the parts with clean silicone brake fluid and reverse the removal procedures.

PARKING BRAKE

Front Cable

REMOVAL AND INSTALLATION

1. Raise and safely support the front of the vehicle on jackstands.

2. Under the left center of the vehicle, loosen the cable equalizer assembly.

3. Separate the front cable connector from the equalizer cable.

4. Remove the front cable retaining bolts and clips, then bend the retaining fingers.

5. Disconnect the front cable from the parking pedal assembly and the cable from the vehicle.

NOTE: *On some models, it may be necessary to remove the dash trim panels to gain access to the brake pedal.*

6. To install the front cable, attach a piece of wire to the cable, fish it through the cowl and reverse the removal procedures. Adjust the parking brake.

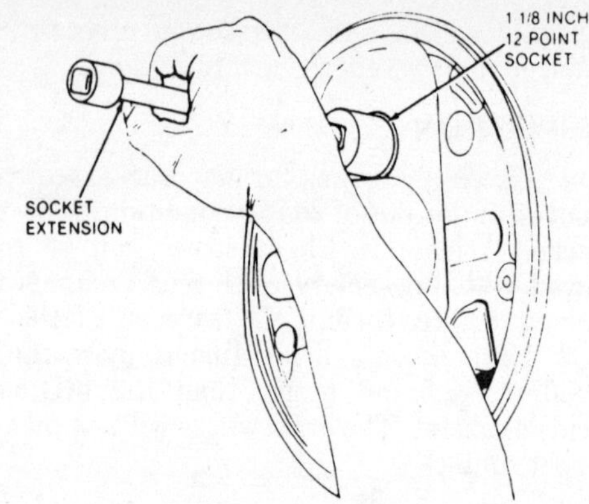

Installing the wheel cylinder retainer

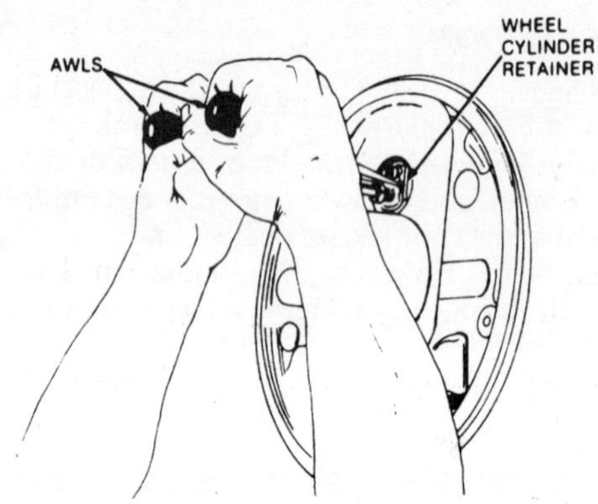

Removing the wheel cylinder retainer

7. Lower the vehicle and check the parking brake operation.

Rear Cable

REMOVAL AND INSTALLATION

Left and Right Rear Cables

1. Raise and safely support the rear of the vehicle on jackstands.

2. Under the left center of the vehicle, loosen the cable equalizer assembly.

3. Separate the front cable connector from the equalizer cable.

4. Refer to the "Brake Shoe, Removal and Installation" procedures in this Chapter and remove the brake shoes.

5. At the backing plate, bend the cable retaining fingers.

6. Disconnect the rear cable from the secondary brake shoe and the cable from the vehicle.

7. To install the rear cable, reverse the removal procedures. Adjust the parking brake.

NOTE: *When installing the rear parking brake cables, make sure that the retaining fin-*

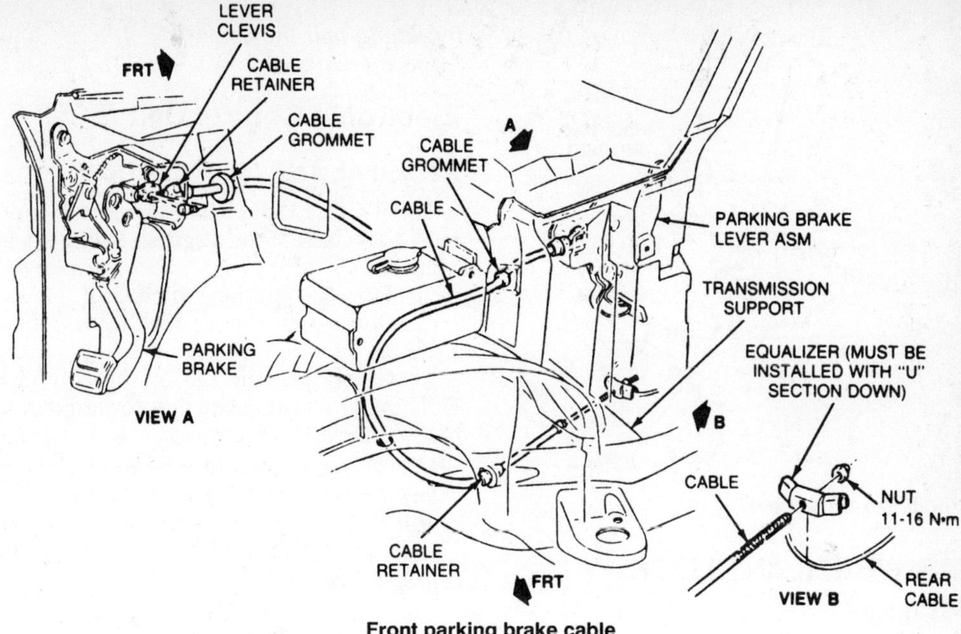

Front parking brake cable

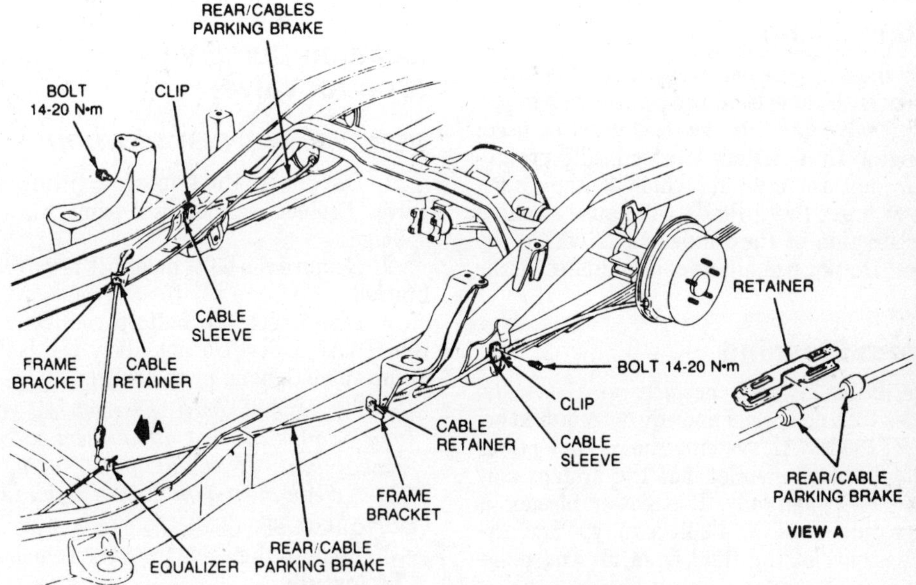

Intermediate rear parking brake cable

gers are completely through the backing plate.

8. Before lowering the vehicle, check the parking brake operation.

ADJUSTMENT

NOTE: *Before adjusting the parking brakes, check the condition of the service brakes; replace any necessary parts.*

1. Block the front wheels.

2. Raise and safely support the rear of the vehicle on jackstands.

3. Under the left center of the vehicle, loosen the equalizer.

4. On the 2WD model, position the parking brake pedal (ratchet) on the 8th click (1982–84) or 2nd click (1985–91); on the 4WD model, position the parking brake pedal on the 10th click (1983–84) or the 3rd click (1985–91).

5. Turn the cable equalizer until the rear wheel drags (when turned by hand).

6. Tighten the equalizer lock nut.

7. Release the parking brake pedal, then test it; the correct adjustment to specifications.

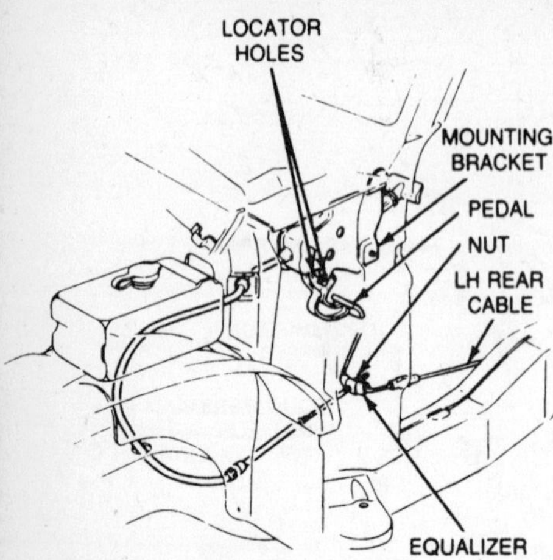

Parking brake adjustment

REAR WHEEL ANTILOCK (RWAL) SYSTEM

System Filling

The master cylinder is filled in the usual manner with no special procedures being necessary. Only DOT 3 brake fluid must be used; silicone or DOT 5 fluid is specifically prohibited. Do not use any fluid which contains a petroleum base; these fluids will cause swelling and distortion of the rubber parts within the system. Do not use old or contaminated brake fluid.

System Bleeding

The brake system is bled in the usual manner with no special procedures required because of the RWAL system. The use of a power bleeder is recommended but the system may also be bled manually. If a power bleeder is used, it must be of the diaphragm type and provide isolation of the fluid from air and moisture.

Do not pump the pedal rapidly when bleeding; this can make the circuits very difficult to bleed. Instead, press the brake pedal slowly 1 time and hold it down while bleeding takes place. Tighten the bleeder screw, release the pedal and wait 15 seconds before repeating the sequence. Because of the length of the brake lines and other factors, it may take 10 or more repetitions of the sequence to bleed each line properly. When necessary to bleed all 4 wheels, the correct order is right rear, left rear, right front and left front.

CAUTION: *Do not move the vehicle until a firm brake pedal is achieved. Failure to properly bleed the system may cause impaired*

braking and the possibility of injury and/or property damage

Electronic Control Unit (ECU)

REMOVAL AND INSTALLATION

The RWAL ECU is a non–serviceable unit. It must be replaced when diagnosis indicates a malfunction.

1. Turn the ignition switch **OFF**.
2. Disconnect the wiring harness to the ECU.
3. Gently pry the tab at the rear of the ECU; remove the control unit toward the front of the vehicle.

NOTE: *Do not touch the electrical connectors or pins; do not allow them to contact brake fluid. If contaminated with brake fluid, clean them with water followed by isopropyl alcohol.*

4. Install the RWAL ECU by sliding it into the bracket until the tab locks into the hole.
5. Connect the wiring harness to the ECU.

Isolation/Dump Valve (Control Valve)

REMOVAL AND INSTALLATION

1. Disconnect the brake line fittings at the valve. Protect surrounding paint work from spillage.
2. Remove the bolts holding the valve to the bracket.
3. Disconnect the bottom connector from the RWAL ECU. Do not allow the isolation/dump valve to hang by the wiring.

NOTE: *Do not touch the electrical connectors or pins; do not allow them to contact brake fluid. If contaminated with brake fluid, clean them with water followed by isopropyl alcohol.*

4. Remove the valve from the vehicle.
To install:
5. Place the valve in position and install the retaining bolts. Tighten the bolts to 21 ft. lbs. (29 Nm).
6. Connect the electrical connector to the RWAL ECU.
7. Install the brake lines; tighten the fittings to 18 ft. lbs. (24 Nm)
8. Bleed the brake system at all 4 wheels.

Speed Sensor

REMOVAL AND INSTALLATION

The speed sensor is not serviceable and must replaced if malfunctioning. The sensor is located in the left rear of the transmission case

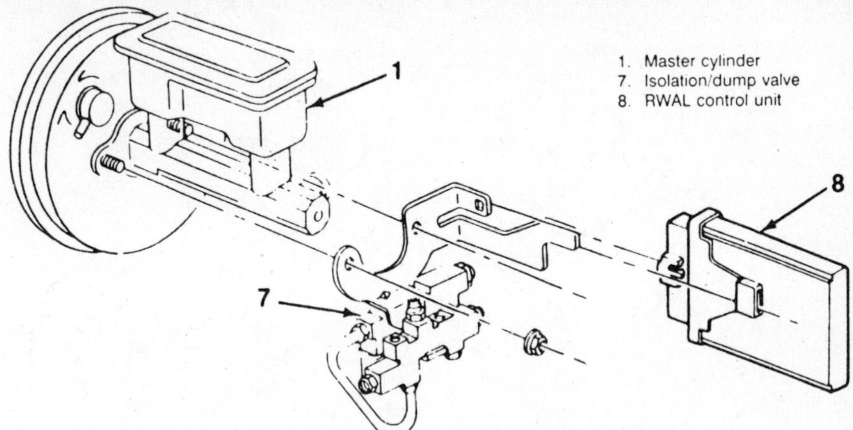

Rear wheel anti-lock ECU and isolation/dump valve

on 2wd vehicles and on the transfer case of 4wd vehicles.

The speed sensor may be tested with an ohmmeter; the correct resistance is 900–2000 ohms. To remove the speed sensor:

1. Disconnect the electrical connector from the speed sensor.

2. Remove the sensor retaining bolt if one is used.

3. Remove the speed sensor; have a container handy to catch transmission fluid when the sensor is removed.

4. Recover the O-ring used to seal the sensor; inspect it for damage or deterioration.

To install:

5. When installing, coat the new O-ring with a thin film of transmission fluid.

6. Install the O-ring and speed sensor.

7. If a retaining bolt is used, tighten the bolt to 8 ft. lbs. (11 Nm) in automatic transmissions or 9 ft. lbs. (12 Nm) for all other transmissions.

8. If the sensor is a screw-in unit, tighten it to 32 ft. lbs. (43 Nm).

9. Connect the wire harness to the sensor.

4-WHEEL ANTILOCK SYSTEM

System Filling

The master cylinder reservoirs must be kept properly filled to prevent air from entering the system. No special procedures are required because of the 4 wheel anti-lock brakes.

When adding fluid, use only DOT 3 fluid. The use of DOT 5 or silicone fluids is specifically prohibited. Use of improper or contaminated fluid may cause the fluid to boil or cause the rubber components in the system to deteriorate. Never use any fluid with a petroleum base or any fluid which has been exposed to water or moisture.

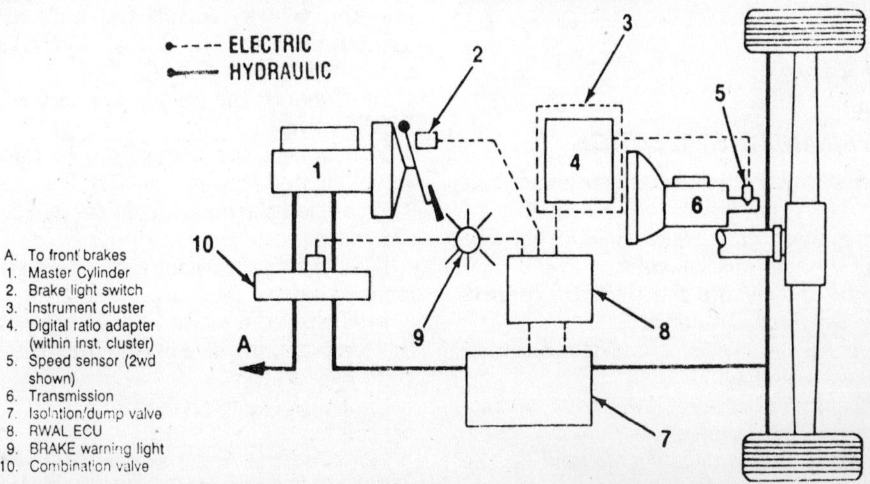

Rear wheel anti-lock system schematic

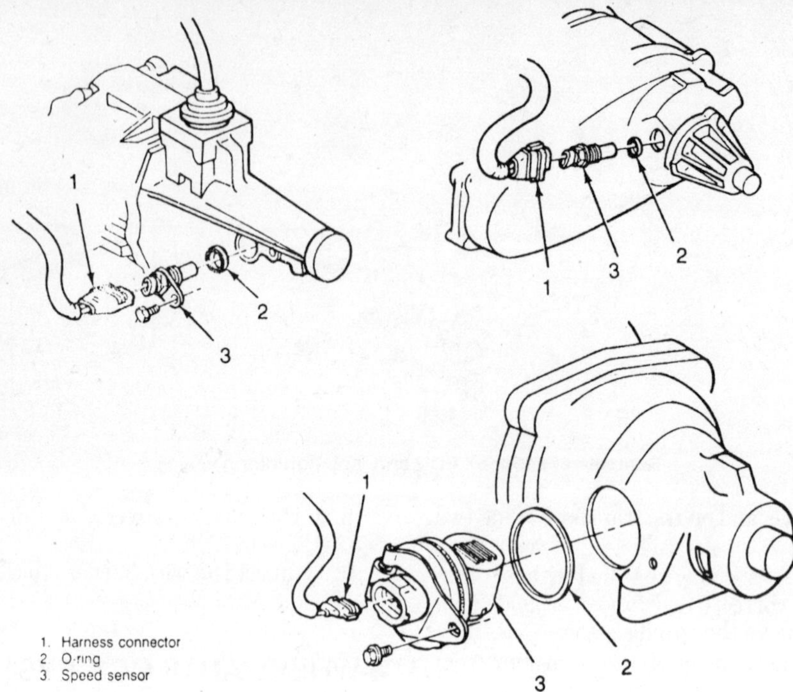

Speed sensor locations and installation

System Bleeding

Bleeding the system is also done in the usual fashion. The vacuum booster reserve should be released by pumping the pedal several times before beginning bleeding procedures. Bleeding may be done manually or with a pressure bleeder; if a pressure bleeder is used, it must contain a diaphragm to separate the air supply from the brake fluid.

When it is necessary to bleed all wheels, the correct order is right rear, left rear, right front and left front. The EHCU valve is not routinely bled; it only requires bleeding after replacement.

EHCU Valve

REMOVAL AND INSTALLATION

1. Remove the intermediate steering shaft from the steering column.
2. Disconnect the brake lines from the bottom of the combination valve.
3. Label and remove the electrical connectors from the combination valve.
4. Remove the master cylinder and combination valve assembly.
5. Label and disconnect the wiring connectors from the EHCU valve.
6. Remove the nuts and bolt holding the EHCU valve bracket to the firewall. Remove the valve and bracket assembly as a unit.

7. Separate the EHCU valve from the bracket on the workbench.

NOTE: *The EHCU valve is not serviceable. Do not attempt to disassemble or repair the unit.*

To Install:

8. Place the EHCU valve on the bracket and install the 6 screws. Tighten these screws only to 60 inch lbs. (7 Nm); over tightening may result in excessive noise transfer from the EHCU valve to the interior.
9. Install the valve and bracket assembly into the vehicle. Install the nuts and bolt. Tighten the bolt to 33 ft. lbs. (45 Nm) and the nuts to 20 ft. lbs. (27 Nm).
10. Connect the wiring connectors to the EHCU valve.
11. Connect the brake lines to the EHCU valve. Tighten the lines to 16 ft. lbs. (25 Nm).
12. Install the master cylinder and combination valve assembly.
13. Connect the wiring connector to the combination valve.
14. Install the brake lines to the bottom of the combination valve and tighten the lines to 15 ft. lbs. (20 Nm).
15. Install the intermediate shaft to the steering column.
16. Bleed the brake system at the calipers and wheel cylinders.
17. Bleed the EHCU valve.

EHCU Bleeding

The EHCU valve should be bled only after replacement. It should not be necessary to bleed the valve during normal brake bleeding operations. The valve should be bled after the calipers and wheel cylinders have been bled. Use the 2 bleed screws on the EHCU valve to bleed the unit.

NOTE: *There are also 2 bleeders on the front of the unit that look like normal brake bleeders. These are NOT the correct ports for bleeding the EHCU valve and should not be loosened.*

Bleeding the EHCU valve requires the use of a combination valve depressor such as tool J–35856 or its equivalent. To bleed the EHCU valve:

1. Make sure the ignition switch is ‹cf35›OFF‹cf33› or false trouble codes will be set. Install the combination valve depressor on the left high pressure accumulator bleed stem of the EHCU valve.
2. Slowly depress the brake pedal 1 time and hold in the depressed position.
3. Loosen the left bleeder screw $1/4$–$1/2$ turn to purge the air from the EHCU valve.
4. Tighten the bleeder screw to 60 inch lbs. (7 Nm) and slowly release the pedal.
5. Wait 15 seconds, then repeat the bleeding sequence including the 15 second wait until all air is purged from the unit. Correct final torque on the bleeder is 60 inch lbs. (7 Nm).
6. Install the combination valve depressor on the right high pressure accumulator bleed stem and repeat the bleeding sequence.
7. Remove the valve depressor tools.

Front Wheel Speed Sensor

REMOVAL AND INSTALLATION

1. Elevate and safely support the vehicle.
2. Remove the tire and wheel.
3. Remove the brake caliper.
4. Remove the hub and rotor assembly (2WD). On 4WD vehicles, remove the rotor first, then the hub and bearing assembly.
5. Disconnect the wheel speed sensor wire connector.
6. Release the sensor wire from the clip on the upper control arm.

7. On 2WD vehicles, remove the bolts holding the splash shield to the knuckle.
8. Remove the splash shield and sensor assembly from the knuckle.

To Install:

9. To install, position the splash shield and sensor assembly on the knuckle.
10. On 2WD vehicles, install the retaining bolts and tighten them to 11 ft. lbs. (15 Nm).
11. Place the sensor wire into the clip on the upper control arm.
12. Connect the sensor wire to the harness connector.
13. On 4WD vehicles, install the hub and bearing assembly followed by the brake rotor.
14. On 2WD vehicles, install the hub and rotor assembly.
15. Install the brake caliper.
16. Install the tire and wheel. Lower the vehicle to the ground.

Rear Wheel Speed Sensors

REMOVAL AND INSTALLATION

1. Elevate and safely support the vehicle.
2. Remove the wheel and tire.
3. Remove the brake drum.
4. Remove the primary brake shoe.
5. Disconnect the sensor wiring at the connector.
6. Remove the sensor wire from the rear axle clips.
7. Remove the 2 bolts holding the sensor.
8. Remove the speed sensor by tracking the wire through the hole in the backing plate.

To Install:

9. To install, route the wire through the hole in the backing plate and fit the sensor into position.
10. Install the 2 bolts and tighten them to 26 ft. lbs. (35 Nm).
11. Secure the sensor wire within the rear axle clips.
12. Connect the sensor wiring to the harness connector.
13. Install the primary brake shoe.
14. Install the brake drum.
15. Install the wheel and tire assembly.
16. Lower the vehicle to the ground.

BRAKE SPECIFICATIONS
(All specifications in inches)

| Years | Model | Master Cyl. Bore | Brake Disc | | | Bake Drum | | | Wheel Cyl. or Caliper Bore | |
			Original Thickness	Minimum Thickness	Maximum Run-out	Orig. Inside Dia.	Max. Wear Limit	Maximum Machine O/S	Front	Rear
1982–91	All	0.945	1.03	0.965①	0.004	9.50	9.59	9.56	—	0.874

① Do not reface if rotor thickness is less than 0.980.

Body 10

EXTERIOR

Doors

REMOVAL AND INSTALLATION

NOTE: *The following procedure requires the use of the GM Door Hinge Spring Compressor tool No. J-28625-A or equivalent.*

1. If equipped with power door components, perform the following procedures:

    a. Disconnect the negative battery cable from the battery.

    b. Refer to the "Door Trim Panel, Removal and Installation" procedures in this Chapter and remove the door panel.

    c. Disconnect the electrical harness connector from the power door lock motor and/or the power window regulator.

    d. Remove the electrical harness from the door.

CAUTION: *Before removing the hinge spring from the door, be sure to cover it (to keep it from flying); it could cause personal injury!*

2. Using the GM Door Hinge Spring Compressor tool No. J-28625-A or equivalent, compress the door hinge spring and remove it.

3. To remove the door hinge pin clips, spread the clips and move them above the recess on the pin; when the pin is removed, the clip will ride on the pin and fall free of it.

4. Using a soft-head hammer and a pair of locking pliers, remove the lower pin from the door hinge; then, install a bolt (in the lower pin hole) to hold the door in place until the upper hinge pin is removed.

5. Remove the upper door hinge pin and support the door, then remove the bolt from the lower hinge pin hole and the door from the truck.

6. To install the door, position it on the hinges and insert a bolt through the lower hinge pin hole.

7. Using a new hinge pin clip, install the upper hinge pin.

8. Remove the bolt from the lower hinge pin hole. Using a new hinge pin, install it into the lower hinge pin holes.

9. Using the GM Door Hinge Spring Compressor tool No. J-28625-A or equivalent, compress the door hinge spring and install it into the door hinge.

10. If equipped with power door components, reconnect the electrical harness connector(s), install the door panel and the reconnect the negative battery terminal.

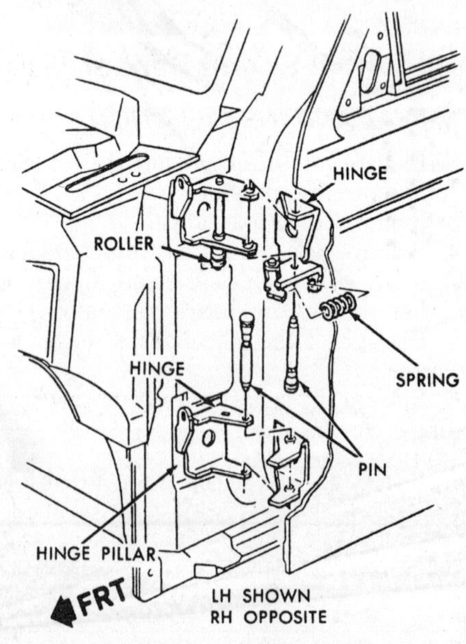

Door hinge pins — exploded view

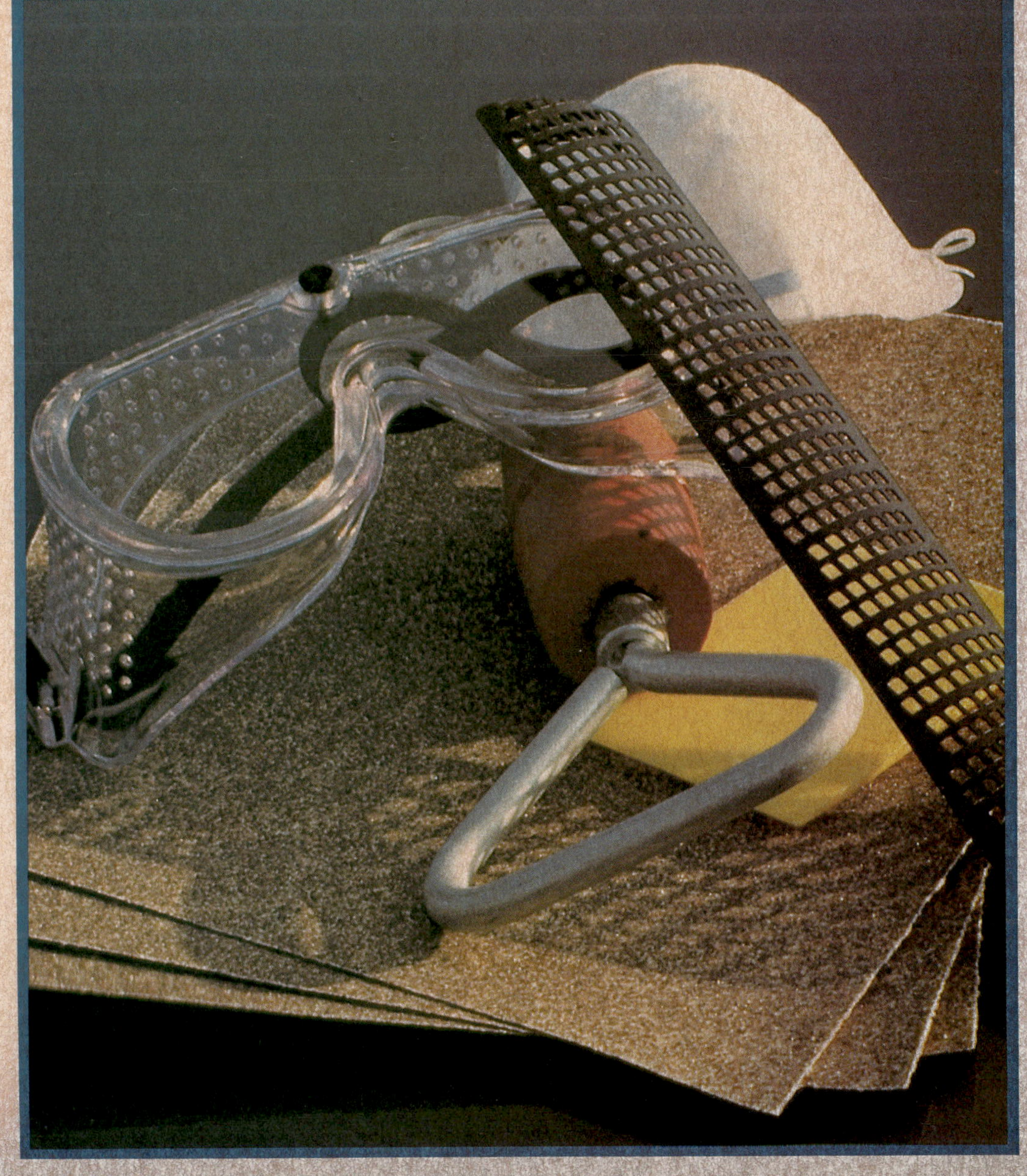

CHILTON'S
AUTO BODY REPAIR TIPS

Tools and Materials • Step-by-Step Illustrated Procedures
How To Repair Dents, Scratches and Rust Holes
Spray Painting and Refinishing Tips

With a little practice, basic body repair procedures can be mastered by any do-it-yourself mechanic. The step-by-step repairs shown here can be applied to almost any type of auto body repair.

TOOLS & MATERIALS

You may already have basic tools, such as hammers and electric drills. Other tools unique to body repair — body hammers, grinding attachments, sanding blocks, dent puller, half-round plastic file and plastic spreaders — are relatively inexpensive and can be obtained wherever auto parts or auto body repair parts are sold. Portable air compressors and paint spray guns can be purchased or rented.

Auto Body Repair Kits

The best and most often used products are available to the do-it-yourselfer in kit form, from major manufacturers of auto body repair products. The same manufacturers also merchandise the individual products for use by pros.

Kits are available to make a wide variety of repairs, including holes, dents and scratches and fiberglass, and offer the advantage of buying the materials you'll need for the job. There is little waste or chance of materials going bad from not being used. Many kits may also contain basic body-working tools such as body files, sanding blocks and spreaders. Check the contents of the kit before buying your tools.

BODY REPAIR TIPS

Safety

Many of the products associated with auto body repair and refinishing contain toxic chemicals. Read all labels before opening containers and store them in a safe place and manner.

• Wear eye protection (safety goggles) when using power tools or when performing any operation that involves the removal of any type of material.

• Wear lung protection (disposable mask or respirator) when grinding, sanding or painting.

Sanding

1 Sand off paint before using a dent puller. When using a non-adhesive sanding disc, cover the back of the disc with an overlapping layer or two of masking tape and trim the edges. The disc will last considerably longer.

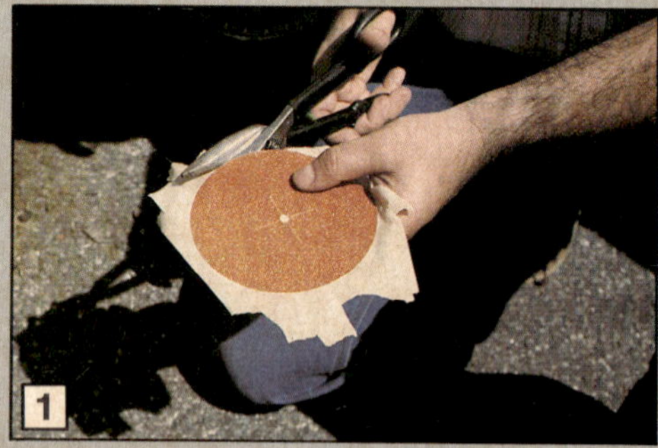

2 Use the circular motion of the sanding disc to grind *into* the edge of the repair. Grinding or sanding away from the jagged edge will only tear the sandpaper.

3 Use the palm of your hand flat on the panel to detect high and low spots. Do not use your fingertips. Slide your hand slowly back and forth.

WORKING WITH BODY FILLER

Mixing The Filler

Cleanliness and proper mixing and application are extremely important. Use a clean piece of plastic or glass or a disposable artist's palette to mix body filler.

1 Allow plenty of time and follow directions. No useful purpose will be served by adding more hardener to make it cure (set-up) faster. Less hardener means more curing time, but the mixture dries harder; more hardener means less curing time but a softer mixture.

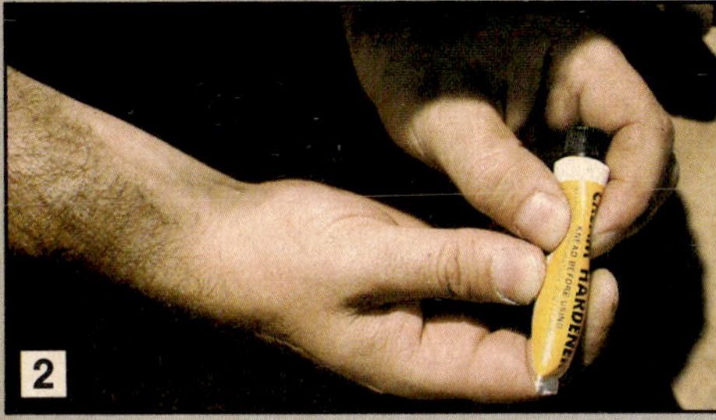

2 Both the hardener and the filler should be thoroughly kneaded or stirred before mixing. Hardener should be a solid paste and dispense like thin toothpaste. Body filler should be smooth, and free of lumps or thick spots.

Getting the proper amount of hardener in the filler is the trickiest part of preparing the filler. Use the same amount of hardener in cold or warm weather. For contour filler (thick coats), a bead of hardener twice the diameter of the filler is about right. There's about a 15% margin on either side, but, if in doubt use less hardener.

3 Mix the body filler and hardener by wiping across the mixing surface, picking the mixture up and wiping it again. Colder weather requires longer mixing times. Do not mix in a circular motion; this will trap air bubbles which will become holes in the cured filler.

Applying The Filler

1 For best results, filler should not be applied over 1/4" thick.

Apply the filler in several coats. Build it up to above the level of the repair surface so that it can be sanded or grated down.

The first coat of filler must be pressed on with a firm wiping motion.

Apply the filler in one direction only. Working the filler back and forth will either pull it off the metal or trap air bubbles.

REPAIRING DENTS

Before you start, take a few minutes to study the damaged area. Try to visualize the shape of the panel before it was damaged. If the damage is on the left fender, look at the right fender and use it as a guide. If there is access to the panel from behind, you can reshape it with a body hammer. If not, you'll have to use a dent puller. Go slowly and work the metal a little at a time. Get the panel as straight as possible before applying filler.

1 This dent is typical of one that can be pulled out or hammered out from behind. Remove the headlight cover, headlight assembly and turn signal housing.

2 Drill a series of holes ½ the size of the end of the dent puller along the stress line. Make some trial pulls and assess the results. If necessary, drill more holes and try again. Do not hurry.

3 If possible, use a body hammer and block to shape the metal back to its original contours. Get the metal back as close to its original shape as possible. Don't depend on body filler to fill dents.

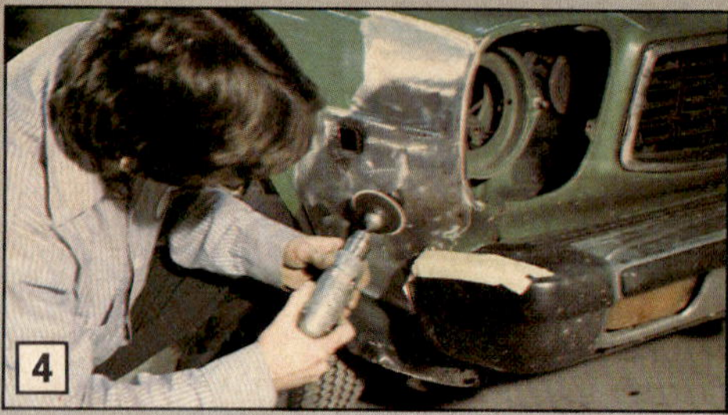

4 Using an 80-grit grinding disc on an electric drill, grind the paint from the surrounding area down to bare metal. Use a new grinding pad to prevent heat buildup that will warp metal.

5 The area should look like this when you're finished grinding. Knock the drill holes in and tape over small openings to keep plastic filler out.

6 Mix the body filler (see Body Repair Tips). Spread the body filler evenly over the entire area (see Body Repair Tips). Be sure to cover the area completely.

7 Let the body filler dry until the surface can just be scratched with your fingernail. Knock the high spots from the body filler with a body file ("Cheesegrater"). Check frequently with the palm of your hand for high and low spots.

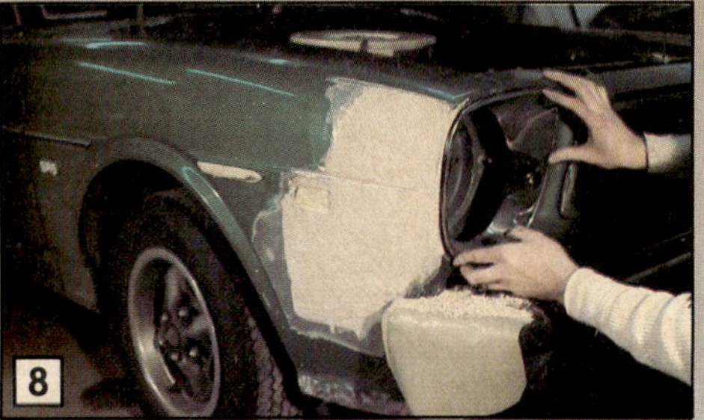

8 Check to be sure that trim pieces that will be installed later will fit exactly. Sand the area with 40-grit paper.

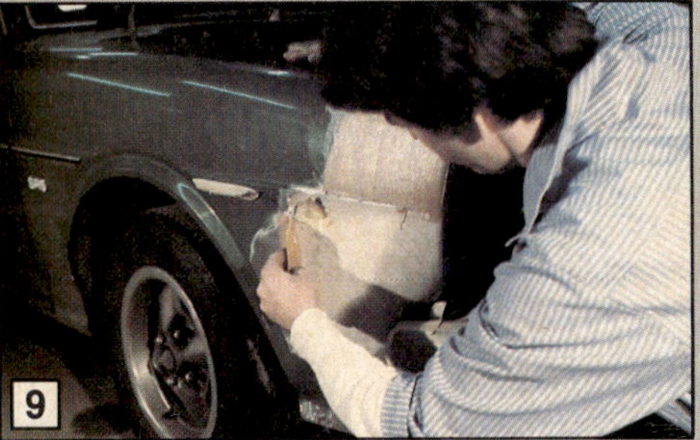

9 If you wind up with low spots, you may have to apply another layer of filler.

10 Knock the high spots off with 40-grit paper. When you are satisfied with the contours of the repair, apply a thin coat of filler to cover pin holes and scratches.

11 Block sand the area with 40-grit paper to a smooth finish. Pay particular attention to body lines and ridges that must be well-defined.

12 Sand the area with 400 paper and then finish with a scuff pad. The finished repair is ready for priming and painting (see Painting Tips).

Materials and photos courtesy of Ritt Jones Auto Body, Prospect Park, PA.

REPAIRING RUST HOLES

There are many ways to repair rust holes. The fiberglass cloth kit shown here is one of the most cost efficient for the owner because it provides a strong repair that resists cracking and moisture and is relatively easy to use. It can be used on large and small holes (with or without backing) and can be applied over contoured areas. Remember, however, that short of replacing an entire panel, no repair is a guarantee that the rust will not return.

1 Remove any trim that will be in the way. Clean away all loose debris. Cut away all the rusted metal. But be sure to leave enough metal to retain the contour or body shape.

2 Grind away all traces of rust with a 24-grit grinding disc. Be sure to grind back 3-4 inches from the edge of the hole down to bare metal and be sure all traces of paint, primer and rust are removed.

3 Block sand the area with 80 or 100 grit sandpaper to get a clear, shiny surface and feathered paint edge. Tap the edges of the hole inward with a ball peen hammer.

4 If you are going to use release film, cut a piece about 2-3″ larger than the area you have sanded. Place the film over the repair and mark the sanded area on the film. Avoid any unnecessary wrinkling of the film.

5 Cut 2 pieces of fiberglass matte to match the shape of the repair. One piece should be about 1″ smaller than the sanded area and the second piece should be 1″ smaller than the first. Mix enough filler and hardener to saturate the fiberglass material (see Body Repair Tips).

6 Lay the release sheet on a flat surface and spread an even layer of filler, large enough to cover the repair. Lay the smaller piece of fiberglass cloth in the center of the sheet and spread another layer of filler over the fiberglass cloth. Repeat the operation for the larger piece of cloth.

7 Place the repair material over the repair area, with the release film facing outward. Use a spreader and work from the center outward to smooth the material, following the body contours. Be sure to remove all air bubbles.

8 Wait until the repair has dried tack-free and peel off the release sheet. The ideal working temperature is 60°-90° F. Cooler or warmer temperatures or high humidity may require additional curing time. Wait longer, if in doubt.

9 Sand and feather-edge the entire area. The initial sanding can be done with a sanding disc on an electric drill if care is used. Finish the sanding with a block sander. Low spots can be filled with body filler; this may require several applications.

10 When the filler can just be scratched with a fingernail, knock the high spots down with a body file and smooth the entire area with 80-grit. Feather the filled areas into the surrounding areas.

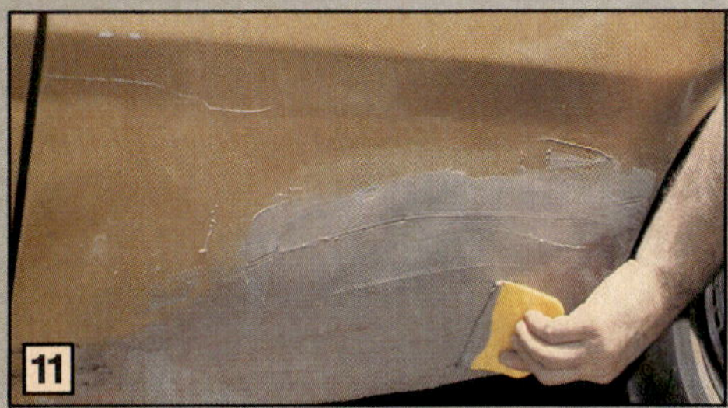

11 When the area is sanded smooth, mix some topcoat and hardener and apply it directly with a spreader. This will give a smooth finish and prevent the glass matte from showing through the paint.

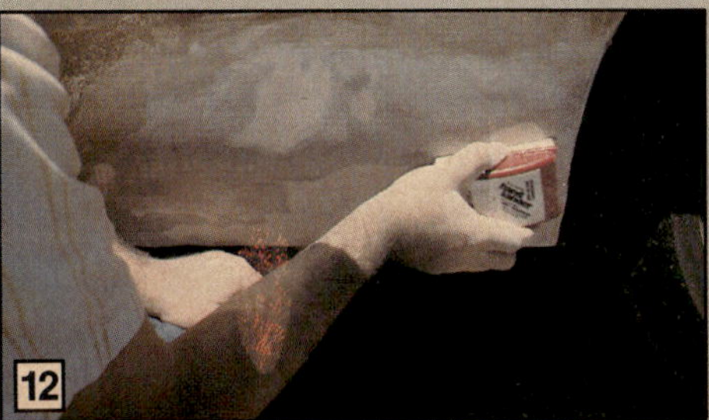

12 Block sand the topcoat smooth with finishing sandpaper (200 grit), and 400 grit. The repair is ready for masking, priming and painting (see Painting Tips).

Materials and photos courtesy Marson Corporation, Chelsea, Massachusetts

PAINTING TIPS

Preparation

1 SANDING — Use a 400 or 600 grit wet or dry sandpaper. Wet-sand the area with a 1/4 sheet of sandpaper soaked in clean water. Keep the paper wet while sanding. Sand the area until the repaired area tapers into the original finish.

2 CLEANING — Wash the area to be painted thoroughly with water and a clean rag. Rinse it thoroughly and wipe the surface dry until you're sure it's completely free of dirt, dust, fingerprints, wax, detergent or other foreign matter.

3 MASKING — Protect any areas you don't want to overspray by covering them with masking tape and newspaper. Be careful not get fingerprints on the area to be painted.

4 PRIMING — All exposed metal should be primed before painting. Primer protects the metal and provides an excellent surface for paint adhesion. When the primer is dry, wet-sand the area again with 600 grit wet-sandpaper. Clean the area again after sanding.

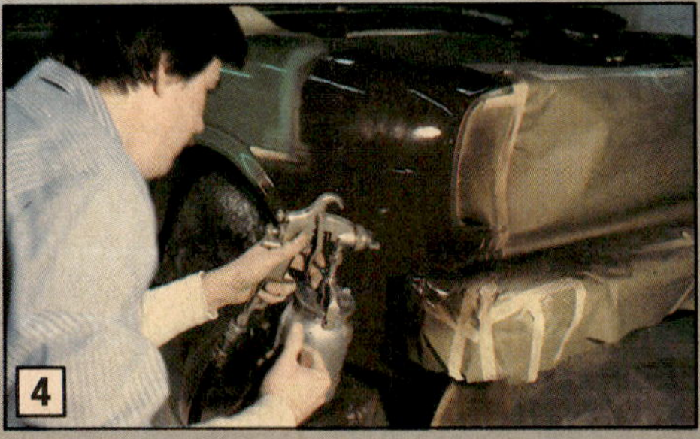

Painting Techniques

P aint applied from either a spray gun or a spray can (for small areas) will provide good results. Experiment on an old piece of metal to get the right combination before you begin painting.

SPRAYING VISCOSITY (SPRAY GUN ONLY) — Paint should be thinned to spraying viscosity according to the directions on the can. Use only the recommended thinner or reducer and the same amount of reduction regardless of temperature.

AIR PRESSURE (SPRAY GUN ONLY) — This is extremely important. Be sure you are using the proper recommended pressure.

TEMPERATURE — The surface to be painted should be approximately the same temperature as the surrounding air. Applying warm paint to a cold surface, or vice versa, will completely upset the paint characteristics.

THICKNESS — Spray with smooth strokes. In general, the thicker the coat of paint, the longer the drying time. Apply several thin coats about 30 seconds apart. The paint should remain wet long enough to flow out and no longer; heavier coats will only produce sags or wrinkles. Spray a light (fog) coat, followed by heavier color coats.

DISTANCE — The ideal spraying distance is 8"-12" from the gun or can to the surface. Shorter distances will produce ripples, while greater distances will result in orange peel, dry film and poor color match and loss of material due to overspray.

OVERLAPPING — The gun or can should be kept at right angles to the surface at all times. Work to a wet edge at an even speed, using a 50% overlap and direct the center of the spray at the lower or nearest edge of the previous stroke.

RUBBING OUT (BLENDING) FRESH PAINT — Let the paint dry thoroughly. Runs or imperfections can be sanded out, primed and repainted.

Don't be in too big a hurry to remove the masking. This only produces paint ridges. When the finish has dried for at least a week, apply a small amount of fine grade rubbing compound with a clean, wet cloth. Use lots of water and blend the new paint with the surrounding area.

WRONG

Thin coat. Stroke too fast, not enough overlap, gun too far away.

CORRECT

Medium coat. Proper distance, good stroke, proper overlap.

WRONG

Heavy coat. Stroke too slow, too much overlap, gun too close.

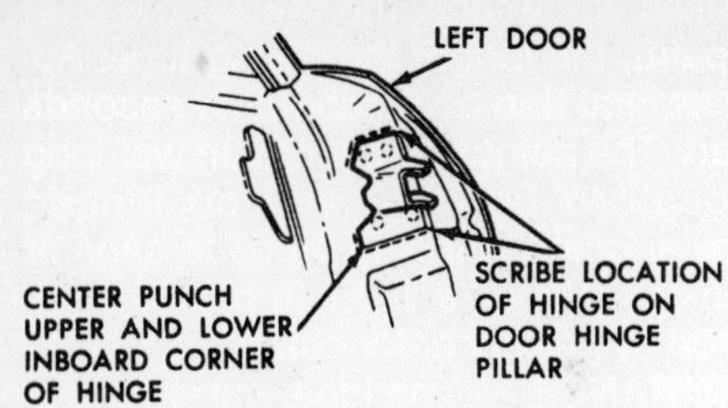

Marking the door hinges for replacement

ADJUSTMENTS

Factory installed hinges are welded in place, so no adjustment of the system is necessary or recommended.

Door Hinges

NOTE: *The following procedure requires the use of an $^1/_8$ in. (3mm) drill bit, $^1/_2$ in. (13mm) drill bit, a center punch, a cold chisel, a portable body grinder, a putty knife and a scribing tool.*

REMOVAL AND INSTALLATION

1. Refer to the "Door, Removal and Installation" procedures in this Chapter and remove the door(s), then place the door on a padded workbench.
2. Using a putty knife, remove the sealant from the around the edge of the hinge.
3. Using a scribing tool, outline the position of the hinge(s) on the door and the body pillar.
4. Using a center punch, mark the center position of the hinge-to-door and the hinge-to-body pillar welds.
5. Using a $^1/_8$ in. (3mm) drill bit, drill a pilot hole completely through each weld.

NOTE: *When drilling the holes through the hinge welds, DO NOT drill through the door or the body pillar.*

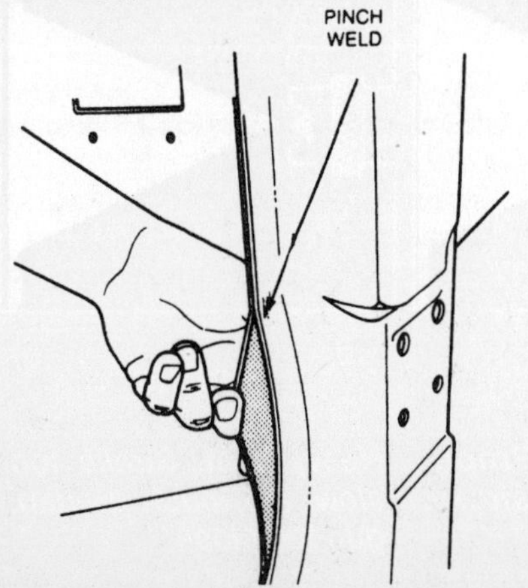

Opening the door pillar to insert the tapped anchor plate

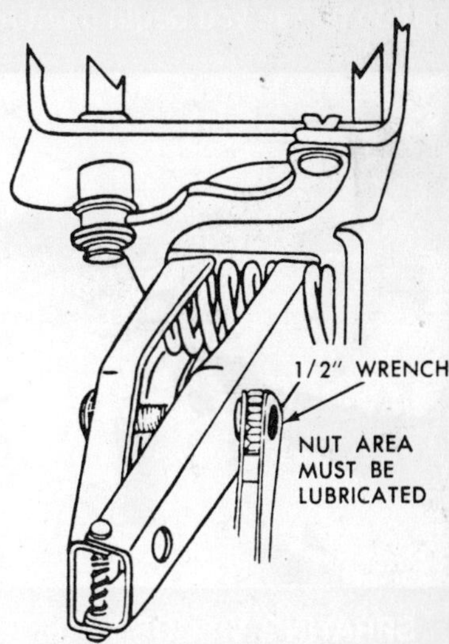

Using a spring compressor to replace the door hinge pins

6. Using a $^1/_2$ in. (13mm) drill bit, drill a hole through the hinge base, following the $^1/_8$ in. (3mm) pilot hole.
7. Using a cold chisel and a hammer, separate the hinge from the door and/or the body pillar. Using a portable grinder, clean off any welds remaining on the door or the body pillar.
8. To fasten the replacement hinge(s) to the door and/or body pillar, perform the following procedures:

   a. Align the replacement hinge, with the scribe lines, previously made.

   b. Using a center punch and the new hinge as a template, mark the location of each bolt hole.

   c. Using a $^1/_2$ in. (13mm) drill bit, drill holes (using the center marks) through the door and body pillar.

   d. If the upper body-side hinge is to be replaced, remove the instrument panel fasteners, pull the panel outwards and support it. Using a cold chisel, open the door pillar pinch weld to install the tapped anchor plate.

9. To install, use medium body sealant (apply it to the hinge-to-door or body pillar surface), the hinge-to-door/body pillar bolts and tapped anchor plate. Torque the hinge-to-door/body pillar bolts to 14–26 ft. lbs. Apply paint to the hinge and the surrounding area.

NOTE: *If the instrument panel was removed, replace it.*

ADJUSTMENT

NOTE: *The $^1/_2$ in. (13mm) drill hinge holes provide for some adjustment.*

1. Loosen, adjust, then tighten the hinge-to-door/body pillar bolts; close the door, then

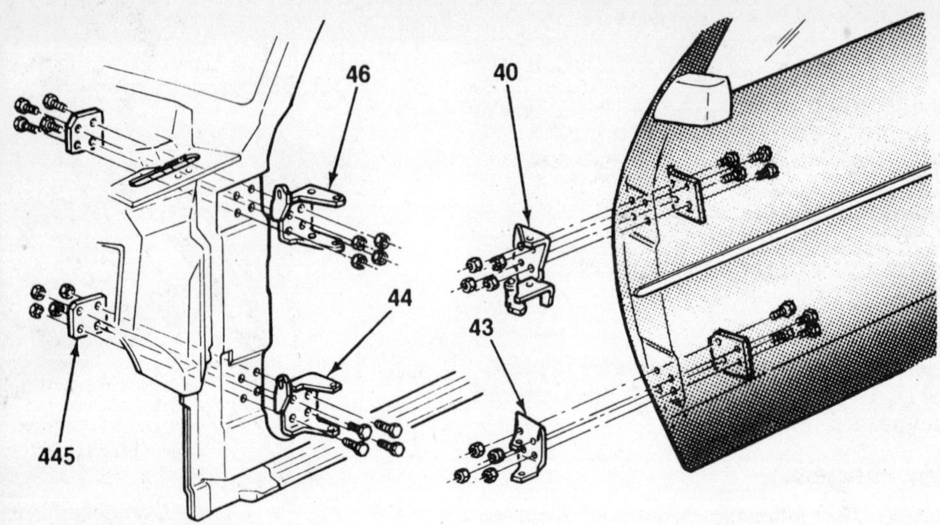

40. Upper door side hinge
43. Lower door side hinge
44. Lower body side hinge
46. Upper body side hinge
445. Backing plate

Exploded view of the door hinge

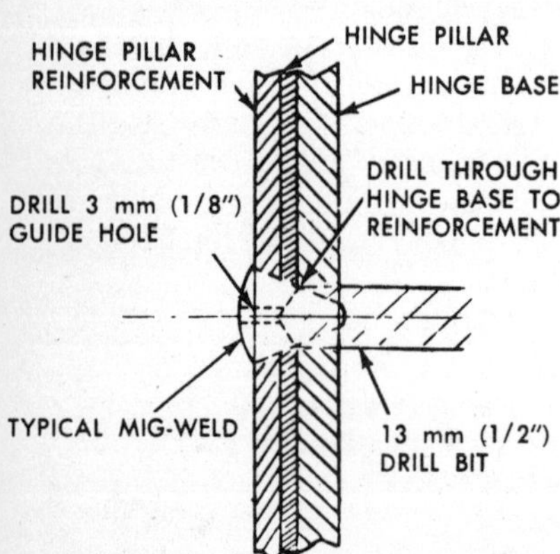

Using a drill to remove the door hinge welds

check the door gap, it should be 0.157–0.235 in. (4–6mm) between the door and the door frame.

2. With the door closed, it should be flush (± 0.039 in. [± 1.0mm]) with the body; if not, enlarge the striker hole.

3. Make sure that the striker properly engages the lock fork bolt.

Hood

REMOVAL AND INSTALLATION

1. This job requires fender covers on the fenders and an assistant.

2. Disconnect the electrical wiring connector from the underhood light.

3. Using a scribing tool, mark the area around the hinges to make the installation easier.

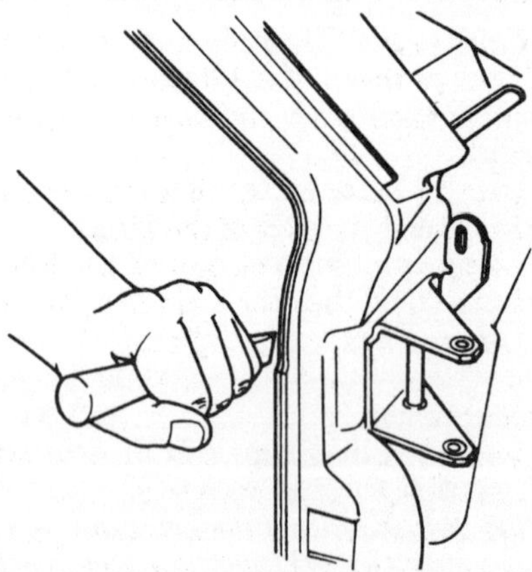

Using a cold chisel to open the door pillar pinch weld

4. Support the hood with one person at each side and remove the hinge-to-hood bolts to remove the hood.

5. To install, reverse the removal procedures and align the hood.

ALIGNMENT

If there are no alignment marks from removal, center the hood in the opening between the fenders, the cowl and the radiator grille. Be careful not to locate the hood too close to the cowl, or it will contact the cowl when closing and damage the paint. If it is difficult to center the hood or if the hood appears to be out of square, the front end sheet metal may need to be adjusted.

Tailgate

REMOVAL AND INSTALLATION

1. Remove the torque rod retainers and the torque rod. This may be easier to do from below the bumper with the gate closed.

2. Lower and support the tailgate on a table or saw horses.

3. If equipped, disconnect the rear window release wire inside the trim panel.

4. Remove the cable supports.

5. Spread the hinge pin clips and remove the pins to remove the tailgate.

6. When installing the tailgate, position the gate and insert the hinge pins.

7. Attach the cable support and operate the tailgate to make sure it is properly aligned and the latch works.

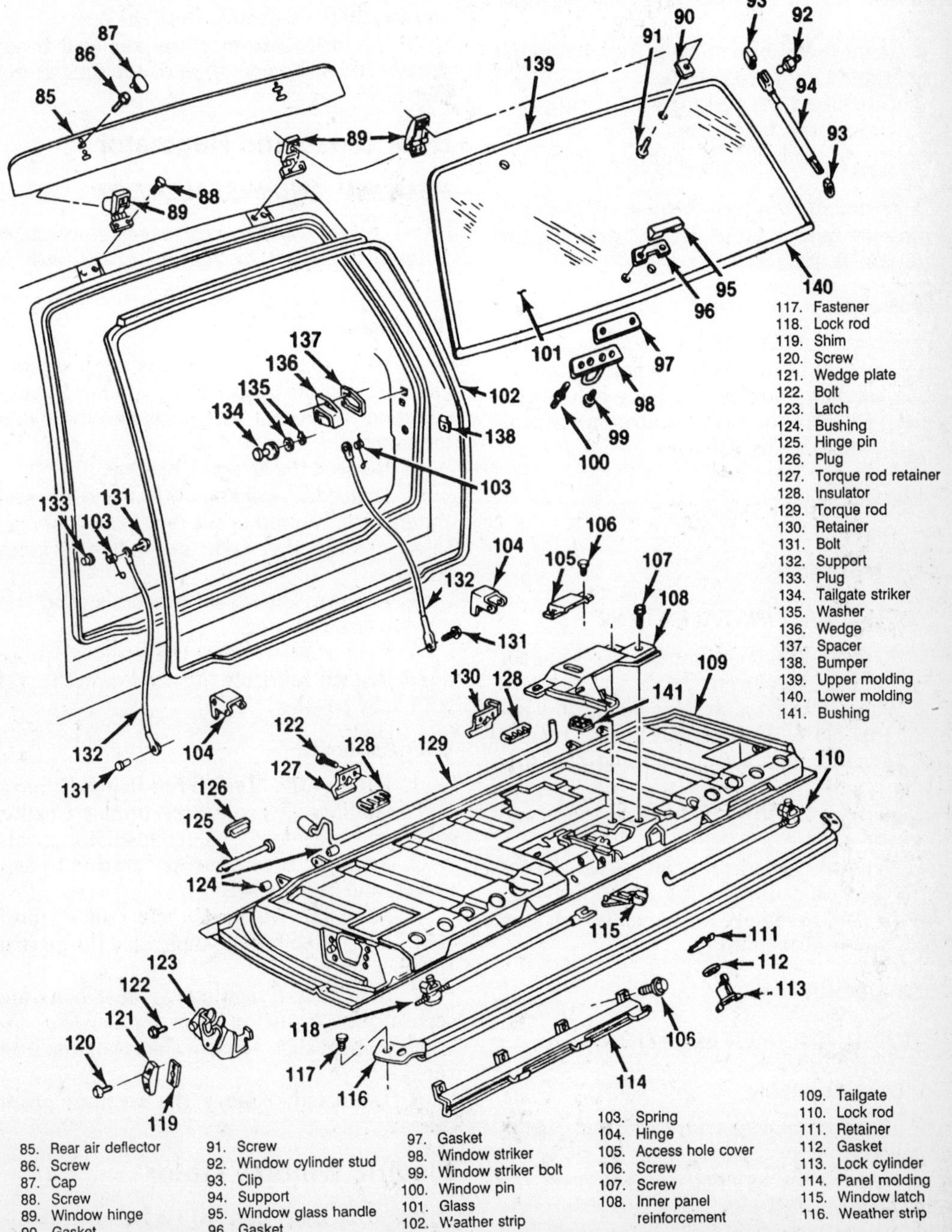

Tailgate components

8. Connect any wiring that was removed and install the interior panel.

9. Install the torque rod.

Bumpers

REMOVAL AND INSTALLATION

Front Bumper

1. On vehicles equipped with a front air dam with fog lights, disconnect the fog light wiring.

2. Remove the air dam bolts from below the bumper and remove the air dam.

3. Disconnect the parking light wiring.

4. Unbolt the brace from the ends of the bumper and unbolt the bumper from the frame.

5. Installation is the reverse of removal. Torque the nuts to 20 ft. lbs. (27 Nm) and the bolts to 37 ft. lbs. (50 Nm).

Rear Bumper

The rear bumper simply attaches to the frame with nuts and bolts. When installing, torque the large bumper-to-frame bolts to 77 ft. lbs. (105 Nm) and the smaller brace nuts and bolts to 20 ft. lbs. (27 Nm).

INTERIOR

Door Panels

REMOVAL AND INSTALLATION

1. Remove the door handle bezel-to-door screws and the bezel from the door.

2. Using the Window Handle Spring Removal tool No. J-9886 or equivalent, remove the window handle spring clip and the door handle.

3. Remove the armrest-to-door screws and the armrest.

4. Remove the door trim panel-to-door screws and carefully pry the panel fasteners from the door to remove the panel. Installation is the reverse of removal.

Door Locks

REMOVAL AND INSTALLATION

Door Lock Assembly

1. Remove the door trim panel and insulator panel.

2. Remove the lock rod and the lever rod from the inner door handle housing.

3. Disconnect the outside handle and lock cylinder rods from the lock assembly.

4. Remove the lock assembly-to-door

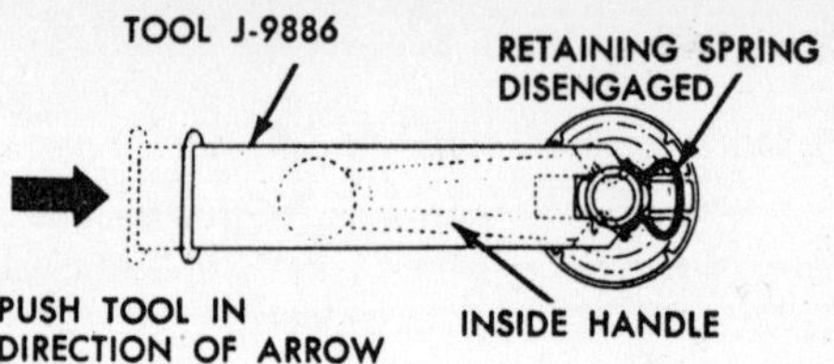

Removing the window regulator handle retaining spring

screws and the assembly from the door.

5. To install, reverse the removal procedures. Check the operation of the lock assembly.

Door Glass and Regulator

REMOVAL AND INSTALLATION

CAUTION: *Always wear heavy gloves when handling glass to minimize the risk of injury!*

Door Glass

1. Refer to the "Door Trim Panel, Removal and Installation" procedures in this Chapter and remove the door trim panel and the insulator panel.

2. Remove the arm rest bracket.

3. Lower the window until it and the sash channel can be seen in the door panel opening, then remove the sash assembly-to-window bolts.

4. Remove the sash assembly and the window from the door.

5. To install, reverse the removal procedures. Lightly lubricate the window in the sash with baby powder.

Door Regulator

1. Refer to the "Door Trim Panel, Removal and Installation" procedures in this Chapter and remove the door trim and insulator panels.

2. Remove the armrest bracket-to-door screws and the bracket.

3. Raise the window to the Full Up position. Using cloth backed tape, tape the glass to the door frame.

4. Remove the regulator-to-door bolts and separate the regulator lift arm roller from the window sash, then remove the regulator from the door.

5. To install, reverse the removal procedures.

Electric Window Motor

REMOVAL AND INSTALLATION

NOTE: *The following procedure requires the use of the Trim Pad Removal tool No. J-*

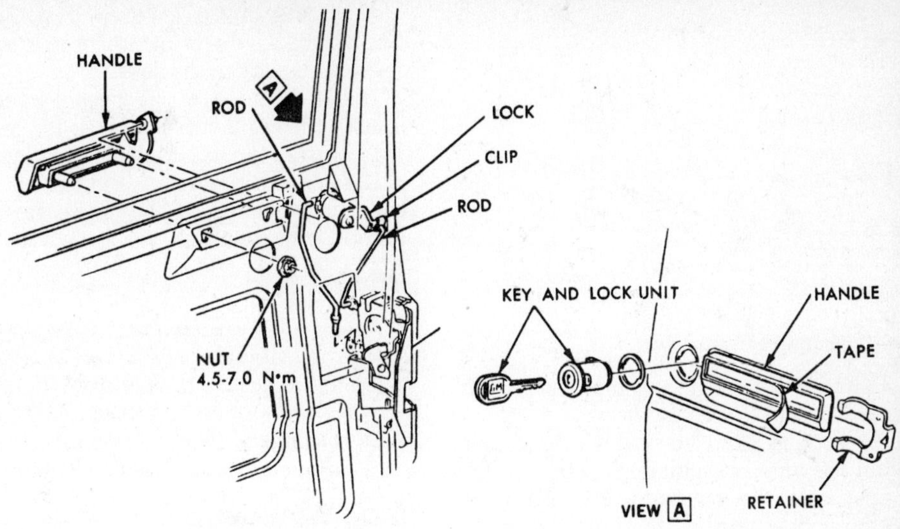

Outside door handle and cylinder lock assembly — exploded view

24595 or equivalent, the Water Deflector Removal tool No. J-21104 or equivalent, the Rivet Installation tool No. J-29022 or equivalent, the Window Regulator Clip Removal tool No. J-9886-01 or equivalent, and $^3/_{16}$ in. rivets.

1. Refer to the "Door Trim Panel, Removal and Installation" procedures in this Chapter and remove the door trim panel.

2. Disconnect the negative battery terminal from the battery.

3. Remove the armrest bracket-to-door screws and the bracket.

4. Using the Water Deflector Removal tool No. J-21104 or equivalent, remove the water deflector from the door.

5. Raise the window to the Full Up posi-

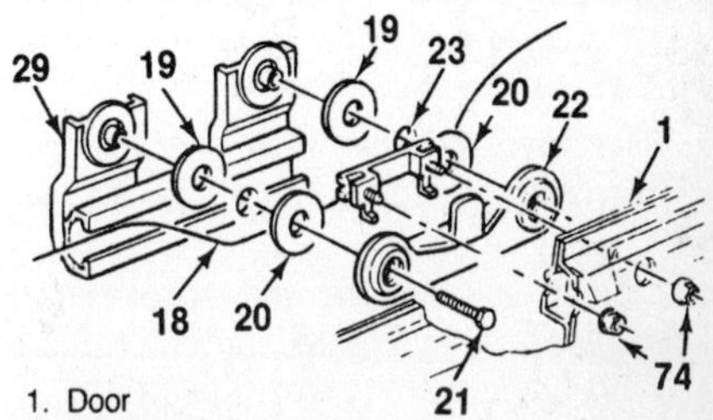

1. Door
18. Glass
19. Window glass mount washer
20. Window mount bushing
21. Bolt
22. Window mount sash
23. Side window retainer
29. Window mount sash
74. Nut

Window sash components

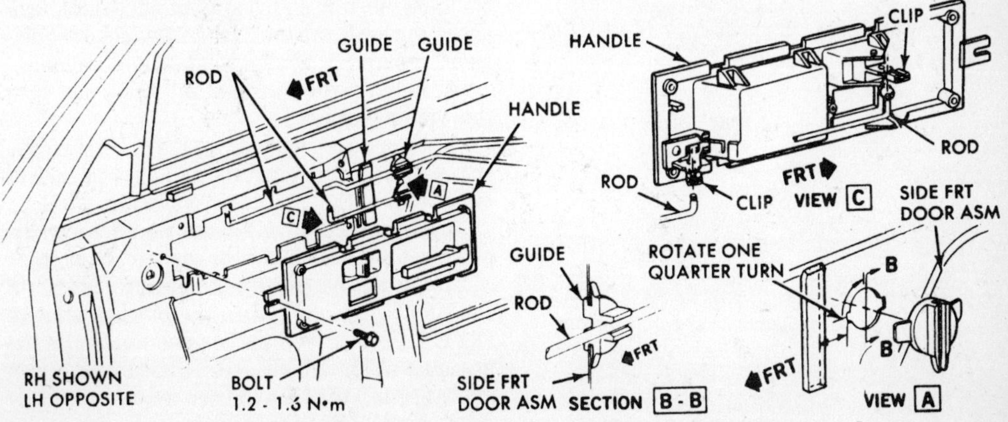

Inner door handle and lock assembly — exploded view

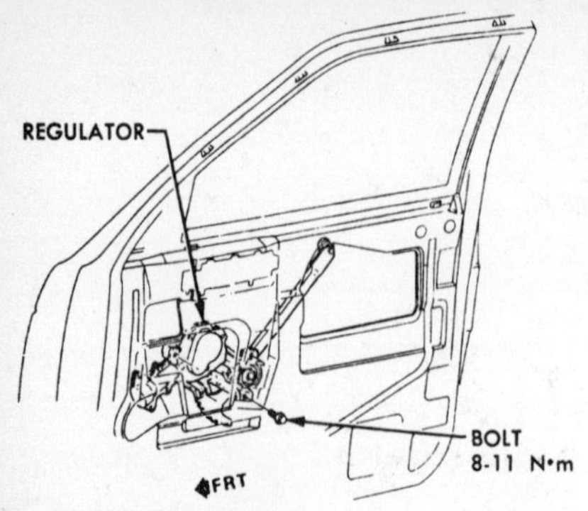

Electric window regulator

tion. Using cloth backed tape, tape the glass to the door frame.

6. Disconnect the electrical wiring connector from the window regulator motor.

7. Separate the regulator lift arm roller from the window sash.

CAUTION: *The sector gear must be locked into position. The lift arm is balanced by a spring that is now under tension and could cause injury if the sector gear is not properly secured!*

8. If removing the window regulator motor from the door, perform the following procedure:

    a. Drill a hole through the regulator sector gear and backplate, then install a bolt/nut to lock the sector gear in position.

    b. Using a $^{3}/_{16}$ in. (5mm) drill bit, drill out the motor-to-door rivets.

    c. Remove the motor from the door.

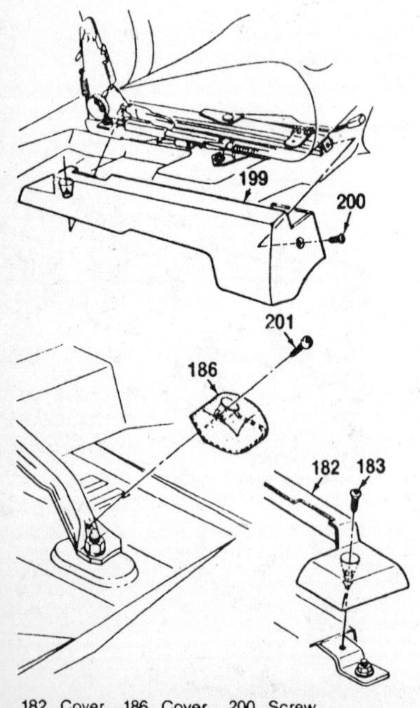

182. Cover 186. Cover 200. Screw
183. Screw 199. Cover 201. Screw

Front seat track comes out with the seat

9. To install, use the Rivet Installation tool No. J-29022 or equivalent, rivet the window regulator motor to the door.

10. After the motor is riveted to the door, remove the nut/bolt from the sector gear.

11. Install the lift arm to the window mount.

12. Connect the wiring and battery and test the window before installing the water deflector and trim panel.

Windshield

NOTE: *Bonded windshields require special tools and special removal procedures to be performed to ensure the windshield will be removed without being broken. For this reason we recommend that you refer all removal and installation to a qualified technician.*

Side Window

REMOVAL AND INSTALLATION

Stationary

NOTE: *The following procedure requires the use of the Urethane Glass Sealant Remover (hot knife) tool No. J-24709-1 or equivalent, and the Glass Sealant Remover Knife tool No. J-24402-A or equivalent.*

1. Remove the vinyl reveal molding.

2. Use a razor knife to cut the molding from around the window.

NOTE: *If the glass is cracked, it should be crisscrossed with masking tape to reduce the risk of damage to the vehicle. If a crack extends to the edge of the glass, mark the cab with a piece of chalk at the point where the crack meets the cab; this will aid the inspection later.*

3. Working inside the vehicle, use the Urethane Glass Sealant Remover (hot knife) tool No. J-24709-1 or equivalent, or the Glass Sealant Remover Knife tool No. J-24402-A or equivalent, separate the window glass and molding.

4. Remove the molding and the glass from the window frame.

5. Using a scraper or a chisel, remove the adhesive from the pinchweld flange; be sure to remove all of the mounds or loose adhesive.

6. Using alcohol and a clean cloth, clean the pinchweld flange. Allow the alcohol to air dry.

7. Using the pinchweld primer, found in the service kit, apply it to the pinchweld area. DO NOT let any of the primer touch the exposed paint for damage to the finish may occur; allow five minutes for the primer to dry.

8. Apply a smooth continuous bead of adhesive around the molding edge. Be sure that the adhesive contacts the entire edge of the molding and extends to fill the gap between the glass and the primed sheet metal.

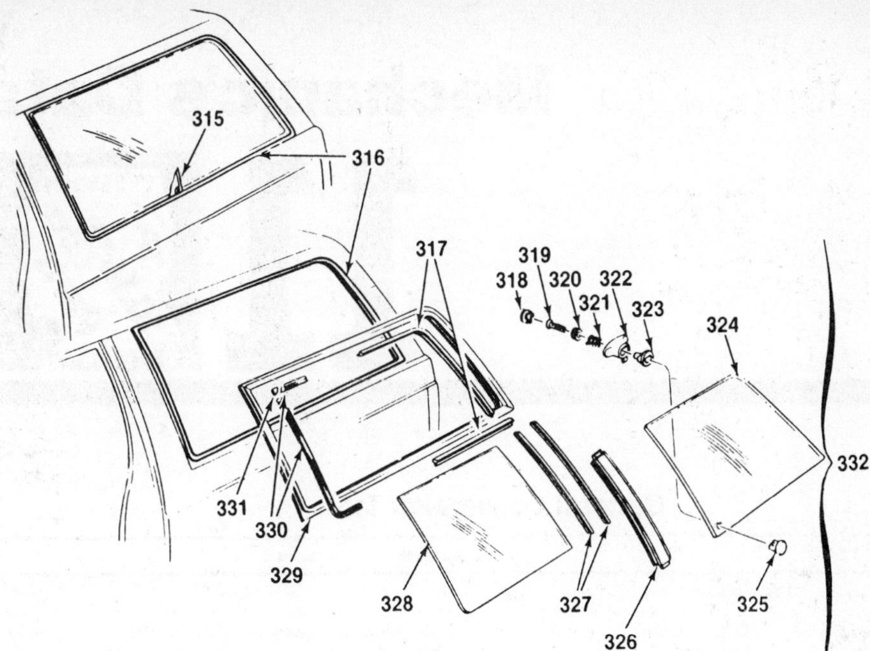

Procedure is the same for one or two piece side glass

9. Using hand pressure, press the glass/molding assembly onto the pinchweld flange. Using retaining clips, secure the glass/molding assembly to the pinchweld.

10. Spray a mist of warm or hot water onto the urethane. Water will assist in the curing process. Dry the area where the reveal molding will contact the body and glass.

Seats

REMOVAL AND INSTALLATION

Front

1. Remove the cover screws and covers from the seat tracks.

2. Remove the nuts and lift the seat and track from the vehicle.

3. When installing, torque the track retaining nuts to 24 ft. lbs. (32 Nm).

Rear

1. Remove the front support cover screws and covers.

2. Remove the front support bracket bolts and fold the seat forward.

3. Support the seat and remove the center support bracket nuts. Remove the seat.

4. When installing, torque the nuts to 28 ft. lbs. (38 Nm).

General Conversion Table

Multiply By	To Convert	To	
	LENGTH		
2.54	Inches	Centimeters	.3937
25.4	Inches	Millimeters	.03937
30.48	Feet	Centimeters	.0328
.304	Feet	Meters	3.28
.914	Yards	Meters	1.094
1.609	Miles	Kilometers	.621
	VOLUME		
.473	Pints	Liters	2.11
.946	Quarts	Liters	1.06
3.785	Gallons	Liters	.264
.164	Cubic inches	Liters	61.02
16.39	Cubic inches	Cubic cms.	.061
28.32	Cubic feet	Liters	.0353
	MASS (Weight)		
28.35	Ounces	Grams	.035
.4536	Pounds	Kilograms	2.20
—	To obtain	From	Multiply by

Multiply By	To Convert	To	
	AREA		
6.45	Square inches	Square cms.	.155
.836	Square yds.	Square meters	1.196
	FORCE		
4.448	Pounds	Newtons	.225
.138	Ft. lbs.	Kilogram/meters	7.23
1.356	Ft. lbs.	Newton-meters	.737
.113	In. lbs.	Newton-meters	8.844
	PRESSURE		
.068	Psi	Atmospheres	14.7
6.89	Psi	Kilopascals	.145
	OTHER		
1.104	Horsepower (DIN)	Horsepower (SAE)	.9861
.746	Horsepower (SAE)	Kilowatts (KW)	1.34
1.609	Mph	Km/h	.621
.425	Mpg	Km/L	2.35
—	To obtain	From	Multiply by

Tap Drill Sizes

National Coarse or U.S.S.

Screw & Tap Size	Threads Per Inch	Use Drill Number
No. 5	40	39
No. 6	32	36
No. 8	32	29
No. 10	24	25
No. 12	24	17
1/4	20	8
5/16	18	F
3/8	16	5/16
7/16	14	U
1/2	13	27/64
9/16	12	31/64
5/8	11	17/32
3/4	10	21/32
7/8	9	49/64

National Coarse or U.S.S.

Screw & Tap Size	Threads Per Inch	Use Drill Number
1	8	7/8
1 1/8	7	63/64
1 1/4	7	1 7/64
1 1/2	6	1 11/32

National Fine or S.A.E.

Screw & Tap Size	Threads Per Inch	Use Drill Number
No. 5	44	37
No. 6	40	33
No. 8	36	29
No. 10	32	21

National Fine or S.A.E.

Screw & Tap Size	Threads Per Inch	Use Drill Number
No. 12	28	15
1/4	28	3
6/16	24	1
3/8	28	Q
7/16	20	W
1/2	20	29/64
9/16	18	33/64
5/8	18	37/64
3/4	16	11/16
7/8	14	13/16
1 1/8	12	1 3/64
1 1/4	12	1 11/64
1 1/2	12	1 27/64

Drill Sizes In Decimal Equivalents

Inch	Decimal	Wire	mm
1/64	.0156		.39
	.0157		.4
	.0160	78	
	.0165		.42
	.0173		.44
	.0177		.45
	.0180	77	
	.0181		.46
	.0189		.48
	.0197		.5
	.0200	76	
	.0210	75	
	.0217		.55
	.0225	74	
	.0236		.6
	.0240	73	
	.0250	72	
	.0256		.65
	.0260	71	
	.0276		.7
	.0280	70	
	.0292	69	
	.0295		.75
	.0310	68	
1/32	.0312		.79
	.0315		.8
	.0320	67	
	.0330	66	
	.0335		.85
	.0350	65	
	.0354		.9
	.0360	64	
	.0370	63	
	.0374		.95
	.0380	62	
	.0390	61	
	.0394		1.0
	.0400	60	
	.0410	59	
	.0413		1.05
	.0420	58	
	.0430	57	
	.0433		1.1
	.0453		1.15
	.0465	56	
3/64	.0469		1.19
	.0472		1.2
	.0492		1.25
	.0512		1.3
	.0520	55	
	.0531		1.35
	.0550	54	
	.0551		1.4
	.0571		1.45
	.0591		1.5
	.0595	53	
	.0610		1.55
1/16	.0625		1.59
	.0630		1.6
	.0635	52	
	.0650		1.65
	.0669		1.7
	.0670	51	
	.0689		1.75
	.0700	50	
	.0709		1.8
	.0728		1.85

Inch	Decimal	Wire	mm
	.0730	49	
	.0748		1.9
	.0760	48	
	.0768		1.95
5/64	.0781		1.98
	.0785	47	
	.0787		2.0
	.0807		2.05
	.0810	46	
	.0820	45	
	.0827		2.1
	.0846		2.15
	.0860	44	
	.0866		2.2
	.0886		2.25
	.0890	43	
	.0906		2.3
	.0925		2.35
	.0935	42	
3/32	.0938		2.38
	.0945		2.4
	.0960	41	
	.0965		2.45
	.0980	40	
	.0981		2.5
	.0995	39	
	.1015	38	
	.1024		2.6
	.1040	37	
	.1063		2.7
	.1065	36	
	.1083		2.75
7/64	.1094		2.77
	.1100	35	
	.1102		2.8
	.1110	34	
	.1130	33	
	.1142		2.9
	.1160	32	
	.1181		3.0
	.1200	31	
	.1220		3.1
1/8	.1250		3.17
	.1260		3.2
	.1280		3.25
	.1285	30	
	.1299		3.3
	.1339		3.4
	.1360	29	
	.1378		3.5
	.1405	28	
9/64	.1406		3.57
	.1417		3.6
	.1440	27	
	.1457		3.7
	.1470	26	
	.1476		3.75
	.1495	25	
	.1496		3.8
	.1520	24	
	.1535		3.9
	.1540	23	
5/32	.1562		3.96
	.1570	22	
	.1575		4.0
	.1590	21	
	.1610	20	

Inch	Decimal	Wire & Letter	mm
	.1614		4.1
	.1654		4.2
	.1660	19	
	.1673		4.25
	.1693		4.3
	.1695	18	
11/64	.1719		4.36
	.1730	17	
	.1732		4.4
	.1770	16	
	.1772		4.5
	.1800	15	
	.1811		4.6
	.1820	14	
	.1850	13	
	.1850		4.7
	.1870		4.75
3/16	.1875		4.76
	.1890		4.8
	.1890	12	
	.1910	11	
	.1929		4.9
	.1935	10	
	.1960	9	
	.1969		5.0
	.1990	8	
	.2008		5.1
	.2010	7	
13/64	.2031		5.16
	.2040	6	
	.2047		5.2
	.2055	5	
	.2067		5.25
	.2087		5.3
	.2090	4	
	.2126		5.4
	.2130	3	
	.2165		5.5
7/32	2188		5.55
	.2205		5.6
	.2210	2	
	.2244		5.7
	.2264		5.75
	.2280	1	
	.2283		5.8
	.2323		5.9
	.2340	A	
15/64	.2344		5.95
	.2362		6.0
	.2380	B	
	.2402		6.1
	.2420	C	
	.2441		6.2
	.2460	D	
	.2461		6.25
	.2480		6.3
1/4	.2500	E	6.35
	.2520		6.
	.2559		6.5
	.2570	F	
	.2598		6.6
	.2610	G	
	.2638		6.7
17/64	.2656		6.74
	.2657		6.75
	.2660	H	
	.2677		6.8

Inch	Decimal	Letter	mm
	.2717		6.9
	.2720	I	
	.2756		7.0
	.2770	J	
	.2795		7.1
	.2810	K	
9/32	.2812		7.14
	.2835		7.2
	.2854		7.25
	.2874		7.3
	.2900	L	
	.2913		7.4
	.2950	M	
	.2953		7.5
19/64	.2969		7.54
	.2992		7.6
	.3020	N	
	.3031		7.7
	.3051		7.75
	.3071		7.8
	.3110		7.9
5/16	.3125		7.93
	.3150		8.0
	.3160	O	
	.3189		8.1
	.3228		8.2
	.3230	P	
	.3248		8.25
	.3268		8.3
21/64	.3281		8.33
	.3307		8.4
	.3320	Q	
	.3346		8.5
	.3386		8.6
	.3390	R	
	.3425		8.7
11/32	.3438		8.73
	.3445		8.75
	.3465		8.8
	.3480	S	
	.3504		8.9
	.3543		9.0
	.3580	T	
	.3583		9.1
23/64	.3594		9.12
	.3622		9.2
	.3642		9.25
	.3661		9.3
	.3680	U	
	.3701		9.4
	.3740		9.5
3/8	.3750		9.52
	.3770	V	
	.3780		9.6
	.3819		9.7
	.3839		9.75
	.3858		9.8
	.3860	W	
25/64	.3906		9.92
	.3937		10.0
	.3970	X	
	.4040	Y	
13/32	.4062		10.31
	.4130	Z	
	.4134		10.5
27/64	.4219		10.71

Inch	Decimal	mm
	.4331	11.0
7/16	.4375	11.11
	.4528	11.5
29/64	.4531	11.51
15/32	.4688	11.90
	.4724	12.0
31/64	.4844	12.30
	.4921	12.5
1/2	.5000	12.70
	.5118	13.0
33/64	.5156	13.09
17/32	.5312	13.49
	.5315	13.5
35/64	.5469	13.89
	.5512	14.0
9/16	.5625	14.28
	.5709	14.5
37/64	.5781	14.68
	.5906	15.0
19/32	.5938	15.08
39/64	.6094	15.47
	.6102	15.5
5/8	.6250	15.87
	.6299	16.0
41/64	.6406	16.27
	.6496	16.5
21/32	.6562	16.66
	.6693	17.0
43/64	.6719	17.06
11/16	.6875	17.46
	.6890	17.5
45/64	.7031	17.85
	.7087	18.0
23/32	.7188	18.25
	.7283	18.5
47/64	.7344	18.65
	.7480	19.0
3/4	.7500	19.05
49/64	.7656	19.44
	.7677	19.5
25/32	.7812	19.84
	.7874	20.0
51/64	.7969	20.24
	.8071	20.5
13/16	.8125	20.63
	.8268	21.0
53/64	.8281	21.03
27/32	.8438	21.43
	.8465	21.5
55/64	.8594	21.82
	.8661	22.0
7/8	.8750	22.22
	.8858	22.5
57/64	.8906	22.62
	.9055	23.0
29/32	.9062	23.01
59/64	.9219	23.41
	.9252	23.5
15/16	.9375	23.81
	.9449	24.0
61/64	.9531	24.2
	.9646	24.5
31/64	.9688	24.6
	.9843	25.0
63/64	.9844	25.0
1	1.0000	25.4

AIR/FUEL RATIO: The ratio of air to gasoline by weight in the fuel mixture drawn into the engine.

AIR INJECTION: One method of reducing harmful exhaust emissions by injecting air into each of the exhaust ports of an engine. The fresh air entering the hot exhaust manifold causes any remaining fuel to be burned before it can exit the tailpipe.

ALTERNATOR: A device used for converting mechanical energy into electrical energy.

AMMETER: An instrument, calibrated in amperes, used to measure the flow of an electrical current in a circuit. Ammeters are always connected in series with the circuit being tested.

AMPERE: The rate of flow of electrical current present when one volt of electrical pressure is applied against one ohm of electrical resistance.

ANALOG COMPUTER: Any microprocessor that uses similar (analogous) electrical signals to make its calculations.

ARMATURE: A laminated, soft iron core wrapped by a wire that converts electrical energy to mechanical energy as in a motor or relay. When rotated in a magnetic field, it changes mechanical energy into electrical energy as in a generator.

ATMOSPHERIC PRESSURE: The pressure on the Earth's surface caused by the weight of the air in the atmosphere. At sea level, this pressure is 14.7 psi at 32°F (101 kPa at 0°C).

ATOMIZATION: The breaking down of a liquid into a fine mist that can be suspended in air.

AXIAL PLAY: Movement parallel to a shaft or bearing bore.

BACKFIRE: The sudden combustion of gases in the intake or exhaust system that results in a loud explosion.

BACKLASH: The clearance or play between two parts, such as meshed gears.

BACKPRESSURE: Restrictions in the exhaust system that slow the exit of exhaust gases from the combustion chamber.

BAKELITE: A heat resistant, plastic insulator material commonly used in printed circuit boards and transistorized components.

BALL BEARING: A bearing made up of hardened inner and outer races between which hardened steel balls roll.

BALLAST RESISTOR: A resistor in the primary ignition circuit that lowers voltage after the engine is started to reduce wear on ignition components.

BEARING: A friction reducing, supportive device usually located between a stationary part and a moving part.

BIMETAL TEMPERATURE SENSOR: Any sensor or switch made of two dissimilar types of metal that bend when heated or cooled due to the different expansion rates of the alloys. These types of sensors usually function as an on/off switch.

BLOWBY: Combustion gases, composed of water vapor and unburned fuel, that leak past the piston rings into the crankcase during normal engine operation. These gases are removed by the PCV system to prevent the buildup of harmful acids in the crankcase.

BRAKE PAD: A brake shoe and lining assembly used with disc brakes.

BRAKE SHOE: The backing for the brake lining. The term is, however, usually applied to the assembly of the brake backing and lining.

BUSHING: A liner, usually removable, for a bearing; an anti-friction liner used in place of a bearing.

BYPASS: System used to bypass ballast resistor during engine cranking to increase voltage supplied to the coil.

CALIPER: A hydraulically activated device in a disc brake system, which is mounted straddling the brake rotor (disc). The caliper contains at least one piston and two brake pads. Hydraulic pressure on the piston(s) forces the pads against the rotor.

CAMSHAFT: A shaft in the engine on which are the lobes (cams) which operate the valves. The camshaft is driven by the crankshaft, via a belt, chain or gears, at one half the crankshaft speed.

CAPACITOR: A device which stores an electrical charge.

CARBON MONOXIDE (CO): A colorless, odorless gas given off as a normal byproduct of combustion. It is poisonous and extremely dangerous in confined areas, building up slowly to toxic levels without warning if adequate ventilation is not available.

CARBURETOR: A device, usually mounted on the intake manifold of an engine, which mixes the air and fuel in the proper proportion to allow even combustion.

CATALYTIC CONVERTER: A device installed in the exhaust system, like a muffler, that converts harmful byproducts of combustion into carbon dioxide and water vapor by means of a heat-producing chemical reaction.

CENTRIFUGAL ADVANCE: A mechanical method of advancing the spark timing by using fly weights in the distributor that react to centrifugal force generated by the distributor shaft rotation.

CHECK VALVE: Any one-way valve installed to permit the flow of air, fuel or vacuum in one direction only.

CHOKE: A device, usually a movable valve, placed in the intake path of a carburetor to restrict the flow of air.

CIRCUIT: Any unbroken path through which an electrical current can flow. Also used to describe fuel flow in some instances.

CIRCUIT BREAKER: A switch which protects an electrical circuit from overload by opening the circuit when the current flow exceeds a predetermined level. Some circuit breakers must be reset manually, while most reset automatically

COIL (IGNITION): A transformer in the ignition circuit which steps up the voltage provided to the spark plugs.

COMBINATION MANIFOLD: An assembly which includes both the intake and exhaust manifolds in one casting.

COMBINATION VALVE: A device used in some fuel systems that routes fuel vapors to a charcoal storage canister instead of venting them into the atmosphere. The valve relieves fuel tank pressure and allows fresh air into the tank as the fuel level drops to prevent a vapor lock situation.

COMPRESSION RATIO: The comparison of the total volume of the cylinder and combustion chamber with the piston at BDC and the piston at TDC.

CONDENSER: 1. An electrical device which acts to store an electrical charge, preventing voltage surges.
2. A radiator-like device in the air conditioning system in which refrigerant gas condenses into a liquid, giving off heat.

CONDUCTOR: Any material through which an electrical current can be transmitted easily.

CONTINUITY: Continuous or complete circuit. Can be checked with an ohmmeter.

COUNTERSHAFT: An intermediate shaft which is rotated by a mainshaft and transmits, in turn, that rotation to a working part.

CRANKCASE: The lower part of an engine in which the crankshaft and related parts operate.

CRANKSHAFT: The main driving shaft of an engine which receives reciprocating motion from the pistons and converts it to rotary motion.

CYLINDER: In an engine, the round hole in the engine block in which the piston(s) ride.

CYLINDER BLOCK: The main structural member of an engine in which is found the cylinders, crankshaft and other principal parts.

CYLINDER HEAD: The detachable portion of the engine, fastened, usually, to the top of the cylinder block, containing all or most of the combustion chambers. On overhead valve engines, it contains the valves and their operating parts. On overhead cam engines, it contains the camshaft as well.

DEAD CENTER: The extreme top or bottom of the piston stroke.

DETONATION: An unwanted explosion of the air/fuel mixture in the combustion chamber caused by excess heat and compression, advanced timing, or an overly lean mixture. Also referred to as ''ping''.

DIAPHRAGM: A thin, flexible wall separating two cavities, such as in a vacuum advance unit.

DIESELING: A condition in which hot spots in the combustion chamber cause the engine to run on after the key is turned off.

DIFFERENTIAL: A geared assembly which allows the transmission of motion between drive axles, giving one axle the ability to turn faster than the other.

DIODE: An electrical device that will allow current to flow in one direction only.

DISC BRAKE: A hydraulic braking assembly consisting of a brake disc, or rotor, mounted on an axle, and a caliper assembly containing, usually two brake pads which are activated by hydraulic pressure. The pads are forced against the sides of the disc, creating friction which slows the vehicle.

DISTRIBUTOR: A mechanically driven device on an engine which is responsible for electrically firing the spark plug at a predetermined point of the piston stroke.

DOWEL PIN: A pin, inserted in mating holes in two different parts allowing those parts to maintain a fixed relationship.

DRUM BRAKE: A braking system which consists of two brake shoes and one or two wheel cylinders, mounted on a fixed backing plate, and a brake drum, mounted on an axle, which revolves around the assembly. Hydraulic action applied to the wheel cylinders forces the shoes outward against the drum, creating friction, slowing the vehicle.

DWELL: The rate, measured in degrees of shaft rotation, at which an electrical circuit cycles on and off.

ELECTRONIC CONTROL UNIT (ECU): Ignition module, amplifier or igniter. See Module for definition.

ELECTRONIC IGNITION: A system in which the timing and firing of the spark plugs is controlled by an electronic control unit, usually called a module. These systems have no points or condenser.

ENDPLAY: The measured amount of axial movement in a shaft.

ENGINE: A device that converts heat into mechanical energy.

EXHAUST MANIFOLD: A set of cast passages or pipes which conduct exhaust gases from the engine.

FEELER GAUGE: A blade, usually metal, of precisely predetermined thickness, used to measure the clearance between two parts. These blades usually are available in sets of assorted thicknesses.

F-HEAD: An engine configuration in which the intake valves are in the cylinder head, while the camshaft and exhaust valves are located in the cylinder block. The camshaft operates the intake valves via lifters and pushrods, while it operates the exhaust valves directly.

FIRING ORDER: The order in which combustion occurs in the cylinders of an engine. Also the order in which spark is distributed to the plugs by the distributor.

FLATHEAD: An engine configuration in which the camshaft and all the valves are located in the cylinder block.

FLOODING: The presence of too much fuel in the intake manifold and combustion chamber which prevents the air/fuel mixture from firing, thereby causing a no-start situation.

FLYWHEEL: A disc shaped part bolted to the rear end of the crankshaft. Around the outer perimeter is affixed the ring gear. The starter drive engages the ring gear, turning the flywheel, which rotates the crankshaft, imparting the initial starting motion to the engine.

FOOT POUND (ft.lb. or sometimes, ft. lbs.): The amount of energy or work needed to raise an item weighing one pound, a distance of one foot.

FUSE: A protective device in a circuit which prevents circuit overload by breaking the circuit when a specific amperage is present. The device is constructed around a strip or wire of a lower amperage rating than the circuit it is designed to protect. When an amperage higher than that stamped on the fuse is present in the circuit, the strip or wire melts, opening the circuit.

GEAR RATIO: The ratio between the number of teeth on meshing gears.

GENERATOR: A device which converts mechanical energy into electrical energy.

HEAT RANGE: The measure of a spark plug's ability to dissipate heat from its firing end. The higher the heat range, the hotter the plug fires. **HUB:** The center part of a wheel or gear.

HYDROCARBON (HC): Any chemical compound made up of hydrogen and carbon. A major pollutant formed by the engine as a byproduct of combustion.

HYDROMETER: An instrument used to measure the specific gravity of a solution.

INCH POUND (in.lb. or sometimes, in. lbs.): One twelfth of a foot pound.

INDUCTION: A means of transferring electrical energy in the form of a magnetic field. Principle used in the ignition coil to increase voltage.

INJECTION PUMP: A device, usually mechanically operated, which meters and delivers fuel under pressure to the fuel injector.

INJECTOR: A device which receives metered fuel under relatively low pressure and is activated to inject the fuel into the engine under relatively high pressure at a predetermined time.

INPUT SHAFT: The shaft to which torque is applied, usually carrying the driving gear or gears.

INTAKE MANIFOLD: A casting of passages or pipes used to conduct air or a fuel/air mixture to the cylinders.

JOURNAL: The bearing surface within which a shaft operates.

KEY: A small block usually fitted in a notch between a shaft and a hub to prevent slippage of the two parts.

MANIFOLD: A casting of passages or set of pipes which connect the cylinders to an inlet or outlet source.

MANIFOLD VACUUM: Low pressure in an engine intake manifold formed just below the throttle plates. Manifold vacuum is highest at idle and drops under acceleration.

MASTER CYLINDER: The primary fluid pressurizing device in a hydraulic system. In automotive use, it is found in brake and hydraulic clutch systems and is pedal activated, either directly or, in a power brake system, through the power booster.

MODULE: Electronic control unit, amplifier or igniter of solid state or integrated design which controls the current flow in the ignition primary circuit based on input from the pick-up coil. When the module opens the primary circuit, the high secondary voltage is induced in the coil.

NEEDLE BEARING: A bearing which consists of a number (usually a large number) of long, thin rollers.

OHM:(Ω) The unit used to measure the resistance of conductor to electrical flow. One ohm is the amount of resistance that limits current flow to one ampere in a circuit with one volt of pressure.

OHMMETER: An instrument used for measuring the resistance, in ohms, in an electrical circuit.

OUTPUT SHAFT: The shaft which transmits torque from a device, such as a transmission.

OVERDRIVE: A gear assembly which produces more shaft revolutions than that transmitted to it.

OVERHEAD CAMSHAFT (OHC): An engine configuration in which the camshaft is mounted on top of the cylinder head and operates the valves either directly or by means of rocker arms.

OVERHEAD VALVE (OHV): An engine configuration in which all of the valves are located in the cylinder head and the camshaft is located in the cylinder block. The camshaft operates the valves via lifters and pushrods.

OXIDES OF NITROGEN (NOx): Chemical compounds of nitrogen produced as a byproduct of combustion. They combine with hydrocarbons to produce smog.

OXYGEN SENSOR: Used with the feedback system to sense the presence of oxygen in the exhaust gas and signal the computer which can reference the voltage signal to an air/fuel ratio.

PINION: The smaller of two meshing gears.

PISTON RING: An open ended ring which fits into a groove on the outer diameter of the piston. Its chief function is to form a seal between the piston and cylinder wall. Most automotive pistons have three rings: two for compression sealing; one for oil sealing.

PRELOAD: A predetermined load placed on a bearing during assembly or by adjustment.

PRIMARY CIRCUIT: Is the low voltage side of the ignition system which consists of the ignition switch, ballast resistor or resistance wire, bypass, coil, electronic control unit and pick-up coil as well as the connecting wires and harnesses.

PRESS FIT: The mating of two parts under pressure, due to the inner diameter of one being smaller than the outer diameter of the other, or vice versa; an interference fit.

RACE: The surface on the inner or outer ring of a bearing on which the balls, needles or rollers move.

REGULATOR: A device which maintains the amperage and/or voltage levels of a circuit at predetermined values.

RELAY: A switch which automatically opens and/or closes a circuit.

RESISTANCE: The opposition to the flow of current through a circuit or electrical device, and is measured in ohms. Resistance is equal to the voltage divided by the amperage.

RESISTOR: A device, usually made of wire, which offers a preset amount of resistance in an electrical circuit.

RING GEAR: The name given to a ring-shaped gear attached to a differential case,or affixed to a flywheel or as part a planetary gear set.

ROLLER BEARING: A bearing made up of hardened inner and outer races between which hardened steel rollers move.

ROTOR: 1. The disc-shaped part of a disc brake assembly, upon which the brake pads bear; also called, brake disc.
  2. The device mounted atop the distributor shaft, which passes current to the distributor cap tower contacts.

SECONDARY CIRCUIT: The high voltage side of the ignition system, usually above 20,000 volts. The secondary includes the ignition coil, coil wire, distributor cap and rotor, spark plug wires and spark plugs.

SENDING UNIT: A mechanical, electrical, hydraulic or electromagnetic device which transmits information to a gauge.

SENSOR: Any device designed to measure engine operating conditions or ambient pressures and temperatures. Usually electronic in nature and designed to send a voltage signal to an on-board computer, some sensors may operate as a simple on/off switch or they may provide a variable voltage signal (like a potentiometer) as conditions or measured parameters change.

SHIM: Spacers of precise, predetermined thickness used between parts to establish a proper working relationship.

SLAVE CYLINDER: In automotive use, a device in the hydraulic clutch system which is activated by hydraulic force, disengaging the clutch.

SOLENOID: A coil used to produce a magnetic field, the effect of which is to produce work.

SPARK PLUG: A device screwed into the combustion chamber of a spark ignition engine. The basic construction is a conductive core inside of a ceramic insulator, mounted in an outer conductive base. An electrical charge from the spark plug wire travels along the conductive core and jumps a preset air gap to a grounding point or points at the end of the conductive base. The resultant spark ignites the fuel/air mixture in the combustion chamber.

SPLINES: Ridges machined or cast onto the outer diameter of a shaft or inner diameter of a bore to enable parts to mate without rotation.

TACHOMETER: A device used to measure the rotary speed of an engine, shaft, gear, etc., usually in rotations per minute.

THERMOSTAT: A valve, located in the cooling system of an engine, which is closed when cold and opens gradually in response to engine heating, controlling the temperature of the coolant and rate of coolant flow.

TOP DEAD CENTER (TDC): The point at which the piston reaches the top of its travel on the compression stroke.

TORQUE: The twisting force applied to an object.

TORQUE CONVERTER: A turbine used to transmit power from a driving member to a driven member via hydraulic action, providing changes in drive ratio and torque. In automotive use, it links the driveplate at the rear of the engine to the automatic transmission.

TRANSDUCER: A device used to change a force into an electrical signal.

TRANSISTOR: A semi-conductor component which can be actuated by a small voltage to perform an electrical switching function.

TUNE-UP: A regular maintenance function, usually associated with the replacement and adjustment of parts and components in the electrical and fuel systems of a vehicle for the purpose of attaining optimum performance.

TURBOCHARGER: An exhaust driven pump which compresses intake air and forces it into the combustion chambers at higher than atmospheric pressures. The increased air pressure allows more fuel to be burned and results in increased horsepower being produced.

VACUUM ADVANCE: A device which advances the ignition timing in response to increased engine vacuum.

VACUUM GAUGE: An instrument used to measure the presence of vacuum in a chamber.

VALVE: A device which control the pressure, direction of flow or rate of flow of a liquid or gas.

VALVE CLEARANCE: The measured gap between the end of the valve stem and the rocker arm, cam lobe or follower that activates the valve.

VISCOSITY: The rating of a liquid's internal resistance to flow.

VOLTMETER: An instrument used for measuring electrical force in units called volts. Voltmeters are always connected parallel with the circuit being tested.

WHEEL CYLINDER: Found in the automotive drum brake assembly, it is a device, actuated by hydraulic pressure, which, through internal pistons, pushes the brake shoes outward against the drums.

A: Ampere

AC: Alternating current

A/C: Air conditioning

A–h: Amper hour

AT: Automatic transmission

ATDC: After top dead center

μA: Microampere

bbl: Barrel

BDC: Bottom dead center

bhp: Brake horsepower

BTDC: Before top dead center

BTU: British thermal unit

C: Celsius (Centigrade)

CCA: Cold cranking amps

cd: Candela

cm^2: Square centimeter

cm^3, cc: Cubic centimeter

CO: Carbon monoxide

CO_2: Carbon dioxide

cu.in., in^3: Cubic inch

CV: Constant velocity

Cyl.: Cylinder

DC: Direct current

ECM: Electronic control module

EFE: Early fuel evaporation

EFI: Electronic fuel injection

EGR: Exhaust gas recirculation

Exh.: Exhaust

F: Farenheit

F: Farad

pF: Picofarad

μF: Microfarad

FI: Fuel injection

ft.lb., ft. lb., ft. lbs.: foot pound(s)

gal: Gallon

g: Gram

HC: Hydrocarbon

HEI: High energy ignition

HO: High output

hp: Horsepower

Hyd: Hydraulic

Hz: Hertz

ID: Inside diameter

in.lb; in. lbs.; in. lbs.: inch pound(s)

Int: Intake

K: Kelvin

kg: Kilogram

kHz: Kilohertz

km: Kilometer

km/h: Kilometers per hour

kΩ: Kilohm

kPa: Kilopascal

kV: Kilovolt

kW: Kilowatt

l: Liter

l/s: Liters per second

m: Meter

mA: Milliampere

mg: Milligram

mHz: Megahertz

mm: Millimeter

mm^2: Square millimeter

m^3: Cubic meter

MΩ: Megohm

m/s: Meters per second

MT: Manual transmission

mV: Millivolt

μm: Micrometer

N: Newton

N–m: Newton meter

NOx: Nitrous oxide

OD: Outside diameter

OHC: Over head camshaft

OHV: Over head valve

Ω: Ohm

PCV: Positive crankcase ventilation

psi: Pounds per square inch

pts: Pints

qts: Quarts

rpm: Rotations per minute

rps: Rotations per second

R–12: refrigerant gas (Freon)

SAE: Society of Automotive Engineers

SO$_2$: Sulfur dioxide

T: Ton

t: Megagram

TBI: Throttle Body Injection

TPS: Throttle Position Sensor

V: 1. Volt; 2. Venturi

μV: Microvolt

W: Watt

∞: Infinity

‹: Less than

›: Greater than

CHILTON'S REPAIR MANUAL MODEL INDEX
Car and truck model names are listed in alphabetical and numerical order

Part No.	Model	Repair Manual Title
6980	Accord	Honda 1973-88
7747	Aerostar	Ford Aerostar 1986-90
7165	Alliance	Renault 1975-85
7199	AMX	AMC 1975-86
7163	Aries	Chrysler Front Wheel Drive 1981-88
7041	Arrow	Champ/Arrow/Sapporo 1978-83
7032	Arrow Pick-Ups	D-50/Arrow Pick-Up 1979-81
6637	Aspen	Aspen/Volare 1976-80
6935	Astre	GM Subcompact 1971-80
7750	Astro	Chevrolet Astro/GMC Safari 1985-90
6934	A100, 200, 300	Dodge/Plymouth Vans 1967-88
5807	Barracuda	Barracuda/Challenger 1965-72
6844	Bavaria	BMW 1970-88
5796	Beetle	Volkswagen 1949-71
6837	Beetle	Volkswagen 1970-81
7135	Bel Air	Chevrolet 1968-88
5821	Belvedere	Roadrunner/Satellite/Belvedere/GTX 1968-73
7849	Beretta	Chevrolet Corsica and Beretta 1988
7317	Berlinetta	Camaro 1982-88
7135	Biscayne	Chevrolet 1968-88
6931	Blazer	Blazer/Jimmy 1969-82
7383	Blazer	Chevy S-10 Blazer/GMC S-15 Jimmy 1982-87
7027	Bobcat	Pinto/Bobcat 1971-80
7308	Bonneville	Buick/Olds/Pontiac 1975-87
6982	BRAT	Subaru 1970-88
7042	Brava	Fiat 1969-81
7140	Bronco	Ford Bronco 1966-86
7829	Bronco	Ford Pick-Ups and Bronco 1987-88
7408	Bronco II	Ford Ranger/Bronco II 1983-88
7135	Brookwood	Chevrolet 1968-88
6326	Brougham 1975-75	Valiant/Duster 1968-76
6934	B100, 150, 200, 250, 300, 350	Dodge/Plymouth Vans 1967-88
7197	B210	Datsun 1200/210/Nissan Sentra 1973-88
7659	B1600, 1800, 2000, 2200, 2600	Mazda Trucks 1971-89
6840	Caballero	Chevrolet Mid-Size 1964-88
7657	Calais	Calais, Grand Am, Skylark, Somerset 1985-86
6735	Camaro	Camaro 1967-81
7317	Camaro	Camaro 1982-88
7740	Camry	Toyota Camry 1983-88
6695	Capri, Capri II	Capri 1970-77
6963	Capri	Mustang/Capri/Merkur 1979-88
7135	Caprice	Chevrolet 1968-88
7482	Caravan	Dodge Caravan/Plymouth Voyager 1984-89
7163	Caravelle	Chrysler Front Wheel Drive 1981-88
7036	Carina	Toyota Corolla/Carina/Tercel/Starlet 1970-87
7308	Catalina	Buick/Olds/Pontiac 1975-90
7059	Cavalier	Cavalier, Skyhawk, Cimarron, 2000 1982-88
7309	Celebrity	Celebrity, Century, Ciera, 6000 1982-88
7043	Celica	Toyota Celica/Supra 1971-87
8058	Celica	Toyota Celica/Supra 1986-90
7309	Century FWD	Celebrity, Century, Ciera, 6000 1982-88
7307	Century RWD	Century/Regal 1975-87
5807	Challenger 1965-72	Barracuda/Challenger 1965-72
7037	Challenger 1977-83	Colt/Challenger/Vista/Conquest 1971-88
7041	Champ	Champ/Arrow/Sapporo 1978-83
6486	Charger	Dodge Charger 1967-70
6845	Charger 2.2	Omni/Horizon/Rampage 1978-88

Part No.	Model	Repair Manual Title
6739	Cherokee 1974-83	Jeep Wagoneer, Commando, Cherokee, Truck 1957-86
7939	Cherokee 1984-89	Jeep Wagoneer, Comanche, Cherokee 1984-89
6840	Chevelle	Chevrolet Mid-Size 1964-88
6836	Chevette	Chevette/T-1000 1976-88
6841	Chevy II	Chevy II/Nova 1962-79
7309	Ciera	Celebrity, Century, Ciera, 6000 1982-88
7059	Cimarron	Cavalier, Skyhawk, Cimarron, 2000 1982-88
7049	Citation	GM X-Body 1980-85
6980	Civic	Honda 1973-88
6817	CJ-2A, 3A, 3B, 5, 6, 7	Jeep 1945-87
8034	CJ-5, 6, 7	Jeep 1971-90
6842	Colony Park	Ford/Mercury/Lincoln 1968-88
7037	Colt	Colt/Challenger/Vista/Conquest 1971-88
6634	Comet	Maverick/Comet 1971-77
7939	Comanche	Jeep Wagoneer, Comanche, Cherokee 1984-89
6739	Commando	Jeep Wagoneer, Commando, Cherokee, Truck 1957-86
6842	Commuter	Ford/Mercury/Lincoln 1968-88
7199	Concord	AMC 1975-86
7037	Conquest	Colt/Challenger/Vista/Conquest 1971-88
6696	Continental 1982-85	Ford/Mercury/Lincoln Mid-Size 1971-85
7814	Continental 1982-87	Thunderbird, Cougar, Continental 1980-87
7830	Continental 1988-89	Taurus/Sable/Continental 1986-89
7583	Cordia	Mitsubishi 1983-89
5795	Corolla 1968-70	Toyota 1966-70
7036	Corolla	Toyota Corolla/Carina/Tercel/Starlet 1970-87
5795	Corona	Toyota 1966-70
7004	Corona	Toyota Corona/Crown/Cressida/Mk.II/Van 1970-87
6962	Corrado	VW Front Wheel Drive 1974-90
7849	Corsica	Chevrolet Corsica and Beretta 1988
6576	Corvette	Corvette 1953-62
6843	Corvette	Corvette 1963-86
6542	Cougar	Mustang/Cougar 1965-73
6696	Cougar	Ford/Mercury/Lincoln Mid-Size 1971-85
7814	Cougar	Thunderbird, Cougar, Continental 1980-87
6842	Country Sedan	Ford/Mercury/Lincoln 1968-88
6842	Country Squire	Ford/Mercury/Lincoln 1968-88
6983	Courier	Ford Courier 1972-82
7004	Cressida	Toyota Corona/Crown/Cressida/Mk.II/Van 1970-87
5795	Crown	Toyota 1966-70
7004	Crown	Toyota Corona/Crown/Cressida/Mk.II/Van 1970-87
6842	Crown Victoria	Ford/Mercury/Lincoln 1968-88
6980	CRX	Honda 1973-88
6842	Custom	Ford/Mercury/Lincoln 1968-88
6326	Custom	Valiant/Duster 1968-76
6842	Custom 500	Ford/Mercury/Lincoln 1968-88
7950	Cutlass FWD	Lumina/Grand Prix/Cutlass/Regal 1988-90
6933	Cutlass RWD	Cutlass 1970-87
7309	Cutlass Ciera	Celebrity, Century, Ciera, 6000 1982-88
6936	C-10, 20, 30	Chevrolet/GMC Pick-Ups & Suburban 1970-87

Chilton's Repair Manuals are available at your local retailer or by mailing a check or money order for **$15.95** per book plus **$3.50** for 1st book and **$.50** for each additional book to cover postage and handling to:

Chilton Book Company
Dept. DM
Radnor, PA 19089

NOTE: When ordering be sure to include your name & address, book part No. & title.

CHILTON'S REPAIR MANUAL MODEL INDEX
Car and truck model names are listed in alphabetical and numerical order

Part No.	Model	Repair Manual Title
8055	C-15, 25, 35	Chevrolet/GMC Pick-Ups & Suburban 1988-90
6324	Dart	Dart/Demon 1968-76
6962	Dasher	VW Front Wheel Drive 1974-90
5790	Datsun Pickups	Datsun 1961-72
6816	Datsun Pickups	Datsun Pick-Ups and Pathfinder 1970-89
7163	Daytona	Chrysler Front Wheel Drive 1981-88
6486	Daytona Charger	Dodge Charger 1967-70
6324	Demon	Dart/Demon 1968-76
7462	deVille	Cadillac 1967-89
7587	deVille	GM C-Body 1985
6817	DJ-3B	Jeep 1945-87
7040	DL	Volvo 1970-88
6326	Duster	Valiant/Duster 1968-76
7032	D-50	D-50/Arrow Pick-Ups 1979-81
7459	D100, 150, 200, 250, 300, 350	Dodge/Plymouth Trucks 1967-88
7199	Eagle	AMC 1975-86
7163	E-Class	Chrysler Front Wheel Drive 1981-88
6840	El Camino	Chevrolet Mid-Size 1964-88
7462	Eldorado	Cadillac 1967-89
7308	Electra	Buick/Olds/Pontiac 1975-90
7587	Electra	GM C-Body 1985
6696	Elite	Ford/Mercury/Lincoln Mid-Size 1971-85
7165	Encore	Renault 1975-85
7055	Escort	Ford/Mercury Front Wheel Drive 1981-87
7059	Eurosport	Cavalier, Skyhawk, Cimarron, 2000 1982-88
7760	Excel	Hyundai 1986-90
7163	Executive Sedan	Chrysler Front Wheel Drive 1981-88
7055	EXP	Ford/Mercury Front Wheel Drive 1981-87
6849	E-100, 150, 200, 250, 300, 350	Ford Vans 1961-88
6320	Fairlane	Fairlane/Torino 1962-75
6965	Fairmont	Fairmont/Zephyr 1978-83
5796	Fastback	Volkswagen 1949-71
6837	Fastback	Volkswagen 1970-81
6739	FC-150, 170	Jeep Wagoneer, Commando, Cherokee, Truck 1957-86
6982	FF-1	Subaru 1970-88
7571	Fiero	Pontiac Fiero 1984-88
6846	Fiesta	Fiesta 1978-80
5996	Firebird	Firebird 1967-81
7345	Firebird	Firebird 1982-90
7059	Firenza	Cavalier, Skyhawk, Cimarron, 2000 1982-88
7462	Fleetwood	Cadillac 1967-89
7587	Fleetwood	GM C-Body 1985
7829	F-Super Duty	Ford Pick-Ups and Bronco 1987-88
7165	Fuego	Renault 1975-85
6552	Fury	Plymouth 1968-76
7196	F-10	Datsun/Nissan F-10, 310, Stanza, Pulsar 1976-88
6933	F-85	Cutlass 1970-87
6913	F-100, 150, 200, 250, 300, 350	Ford Pick-Ups 1965-86
7829	F-150, 250, 350	Ford Pick-Ups and Bronco 1987-88
7583	Galant	Mitsubishi 1983-89
6842	Galaxie	Ford/Mercury/Lincoln 1968-88
7040	GL	Volvo 1970-88
6739	Gladiator	Jeep Wagoneer, Commando, Cherokee, Truck 1962-86
6981	GLC	Mazda 1978-89
7040	GLE	Volvo 1970-88
7040	GLT	Volvo 1970-88

Part No.	Model	Repair Manual Title
7593	Golf	VW Front Wheel Drive 1974-90
7165	Gordini	Renault 1975-85
6937	Granada	Granada/Monarch 1975-82
6552	Gran Coupe	Plymouth 1968-76
6552	Gran Fury	Plymouth 1968-76
6842	Gran Marquis	Ford/Mercury/Lincoln 1968-88
6552	Gran Sedan	Plymouth 1968-76
6696	Gran Torino 1972-76	Ford/Mercury/Lincoln Mid-Size 1971-85
7346	Grand Am	Pontiac Mid-Size 1974-83
7657	Grand Am	Calais, Grand Am, Skylark, Somerset 1985-86
7346	Grand LeMans	Pontiac Mid-Size 1974-83
7346	Grand Prix	Pontiac Mid-Size 1974-83
7950	Grand Prix FWD	Lumina/Grand Prix/Cutlass/Regal 1988-90
7308	Grand Safari	Buick/Olds/Pontiac 1975-87
7308	Grand Ville	Buick/Olds/Pontiac 1975-87
6739	Grand Wagoneer	Jeep Wagoneer, Commando, Cherokee, Truck 1957-86
7199	Gremlin	AMC 1975-86
6575	GT	Opel 1971-75
7593	GTI	VW Front Wheel Drive 1974-90
5905	GTO 1968-73	Tempest/GTO/LeMans 1968-73
7346	GTO 1974	Pontiac Mid-Size 1974-83
5821	GTX	Roadrunner/Satellite/Belvedere/GTX 1968-73
5910	GT6	Triumph 1969-73
6542	G.T.350, 500	Mustang/Cougar 1965-73
6930	G-10, 20, 30	Chevy/GMC Vans 1967-86
6930	G-1500, 2500, 3500	Chevy/GMC Vans 1967-86
8040	G-10, 20, 30	Chevy/GMC Vans 1987-90
8040	G-1500, 2500, 3500	Chevy/GMC Vans 1987-90
5795	Hi-Lux	Toyota 1966-70
6845	Horizon	Omni/Horizon/Rampage 1978-88
7199	Hornet	AMC 1975-86
7135	Impala	Chevrolet 1968-88
7317	IROC-Z	Camaro 1982-88
6739	Jeepster	Jeep Wagoneer, Commando, Cherokee, Truck 1957-86
7593	Jetta	VW Front Wheel Drive 1974-90
6931	Jimmy	Blazer/Jimmy 1969-82
7383	Jimmy	Chevy S-10 Blazer/GMC S-15 Jimmy 1982-87
6739	J-10, 20	Jeep Wagoneer, Commando, Cherokee, Truck 1957-86
6739	J-100, 200, 300	Jeep Wagoneer, Commando, Cherokee, Truck 1957-86
6575	Kadett	Opel 1971-75
7199	Kammback	AMC 1975-86
5796	Karmann Ghia	Volkswagen 1949-71
6837	Karmann Ghia	Volkswagen 1970-81
7135	Kingswood	Chevrolet 1968-88
6931	K-5	Blazer/Jimmy 1969-82
6936	K-10, 20, 30	Chevy/GMC Pick-Ups & Suburban 1970-87
6936	K-1500, 2500, 3500	Chevy/GMC Pick-Ups & Suburban 1970-87
8055	K-10, 20, 30	Chevy/GMC Pick-Ups & Suburban 1988-90
8055	K-1500, 2500, 3500	Chevy/GMC Pick-Ups & Suburban 1988-90
6840	Laguna	Chevrolet Mid-Size 1964-88
7041	Lancer	Champ/Arrow/Sapporo 1977-83
5795	Land Cruiser	Toyota 1966-70
7035	Land Cruiser	Toyota Trucks 1970-88
7163	Laser	Chrysler Front Wheel Drive 1981-88
7163	LeBaron	Chrysler Front Wheel Drive 1981-88
7165	LeCar	Renault 1975-85

Chilton's Repair Manuals are available at your local retailer or by mailing a check or money order for **$15.95** per book plus **$3.50** for 1st book and **$.50** for each additional book to cover postage and handling to:

Chilton Book Company
Dept. DM
Radnor, PA 19089

NOTE: When ordering be sure to include your name & address, book part No. & title.

CHILTON'S REPAIR MANUAL MODEL INDEX
Car and truck model names are listed in alphabetical and numerical order

Part No.	Model	Repair Manual Title
5905	LeMans	Tempest/GTO/LeMans 1968-73
7346	LeMans	Pontiac Mid-Size 1974-83
7308	LeSabre	Buick/Olds/Pontiac 1975-87
6842	Lincoln	Ford/Mercury/Lincoln 1968-88
7055	LN-7	Ford/Mercury Front Wheel Drive 1981-87
6842	LTD	Ford/Mercury/Lincoln 1968-88
6696	LTD II	Ford/Mercury/Lincoln Mid-Size 1971-85
7950	Lumina	Lumina/Grand Prix/Cutlass/Regal 1988-90
6815	LUV	Chevrolet LUV 1972-81
6575	Luxus	Opel 1971-75
7055	Lynx	Ford/Mercury Front Wheel Drive 1981-87
6844	L6	BMW 1970-88
6844	L7	BMW 1970-88
6542	Mach I	Mustang/Cougar 1965-73
6812	Mach I Ghia	Mustang II 1974-78
6840	Malibu	Chevrolet Mid-Size 1964-88
6575	Manta	Opel 1971-75
6696	Mark IV, V, VI, VII	Ford/Mercury/Lincoln Mid-Size 1971-85
7814	Mark VII	Thunderbird, Cougar, Continental 1980-87
6842	Marquis	Ford/Mercury/Lincoln 1968-88
6696	Marquis	Ford/Mercury/Lincoln Mid-Size 1971-85
7199	Matador	AMC 1975-86
6634	Maverick	Maverick/Comet 1970-77
6817	Maverick	Jeep 1945-87
7170	Maxima	Nissan 200SX, 240SX, 510, 610, 710, 810, Maxima 1973-88
6842	Mercury	Ford/Mercury/Lincoln 1968-88
6963	Merkur	Mustang/Capri/Merkur 1979-88
6780	MGB, MGB-GT, MGC-GT	MG 1961-81
6780	Midget	MG 1961-81
7583	Mighty Max	Mitsubishi 1983-89
7583	Mirage	Mitsubishi 1983-89
5795	Mk.II 1969-70	Toyota 1966-70
7004	Mk.II 1970-76	Toyota Corona/Crown/Cressida/Mk.II/Van 1970-87
6554	Monaco	Dodge 1968-77
6937	Monarch	Granada/Monarch 1975-82
6840	Monte Carlo	Chevrolet Mid-Size 1964-88
6696	Montego	Ford/Mercury/Lincoln Mid-Size 1971-85
6842	Monterey	Ford/Mercury/Lincoln 1968-88
7583	Montero	Mitsubishi 1983-89
6935	Monza 1975-80	GM Subcompact 1971-80
6981	MPV	Mazda 1978-89
6542	Mustang	Mustang/Cougar 1965-73
6963	Mustang	Mustang/Capri/Merkur 1979-88
6812	Mustang II	Mustang II 1974-78
6981	MX6	Mazda 1978-89
6844	M3, M6	BMW 1970-88
7163	New Yorker	Chrysler Front Wheel Drive 1981-88
6841	Nova	Chevy II/Nova 1962-79
7658	Nova	Chevrolet Nova/GEO Prizm 1985-89
7049	Omega	GM X-Body 1980-85
6845	Omni	Omni/Horizon/Rampage 1978-88
6575	Opel	Opel 1971-75
7199	Pacer	AMC 1975-86
7587	Park Avenue	GM C-Body 1985
6842	Park Lane	Ford/Mercury/Lincoln 1968-88
6962	Passat	VW Front Wheel Drive 1974-90
6816	Pathfinder	Datsun/Nissan Pick-Ups and Pathfinder 1970-89

Part No.	Model	Repair Manual Title
5790	Patrol	Datsun 1961-72
6934	PB100, 150, 200, 250, 300, 350	Dodge/Plymouth Vans 1967-88
5982	Peugeot	Peugeot 1970-74
7049	Phoenix	GM X-Body 1980-85
7027	Pinto	Pinto/Bobcat 1971-80
6554	Polara	Dodge 1968-77
7583	Precis	Mitsubishi 1983-89
6980	Prelude	Honda 1973-88
7658	Prizm	Chevrolet Nova/GEO Prizm 1985-89
8012	Probe	Ford Probe 1989
7660	Pulsar	Datsun/Nissan F-10, 310, Stanza, Pulsar 1976-88
6529	PV-444	Volvo 1956-69
6529	PV-544	Volvo 1956-69
6529	P-1800	Volvo 1956-69
7593	Quantum	VW Front Wheel Drive 1974-87
7593	Rabbit	VW Front Wheel Drive 1974-87
7593	Rabbit Pickup	VW Front Wheel Drive 1974-87
6575	Rallye	Opel 1971-75
7459	Ramcharger	Dodge/Plymouth Trucks 1967-88
6845	Rampage	Omni/Horizon/Rampage 1978-88
6320	Ranchero	Fairlane/Torino 1962-70
6696	Ranchero	Ford/Mercury/Lincoln Mid-Size 1971-85
6842	Ranch Wagon	Ford/Mercury/Lincoln 1968-88
7338	Ranger Pickup	Ford Ranger/Bronco II 1983-88
7307	Regal RWD	Century/Regal 1975-87
7950	Regal FWD 1988-90	Lumina/Grand Prix/Cutlass/Regal 1988-90
7163	Reliant	Chrysler Front Wheel Drive 1981-88
5821	Roadrunner	Roadrunner/Satellite/Belvedere/GTX 1968-73
7659	Rotary Pick-Up	Mazda Trucks 1971-89
6981	RX-7	Mazda 1978-89
7165	R-12, 15, 17, 18, 18i	Renault 1975-85
7830	Sable	Taurus/Sable/Continental 1986-89
7750	Safari	Chevrolet Astro/GMC Safari 1985-90
7041	Sapporo	Champ/Arrow/Sapporo 1978-83
5821	Satellite	Roadrunner/Satellite/Belvedere/GTX 1968-73
6326	Scamp	Valiant/Duster 1968-76
6845	Scamp	Omni/Horizon/Rampage 1978-88
6962	Scirocco	VW Front Wheel Drive 1974-90
6936	Scottsdale	Chevrolet/GMC Pick-Ups & Suburban 1970-87
8055	Scottsdale	Chevrolet/GMC Pick-Ups & Suburban 1988-90
5912	Scout	International Scout 1967-73
8034	Scrambler	Jeep 1971-90
7197	Sentra	Datsun 1200, 210, Nissan Sentra 1973-88
7462	Seville	Cadillac 1967-89
7163	Shadow	Chrysler Front Wheel Drive 1981-88
6936	Siera	Chevrolet/GMC Pick-Ups & Suburban 1970-87
8055	Siera	Chevrolet/GMC Pick-Ups & Suburban 1988-90
7583	Sigma	Mitsubishi 1983-89
6326	Signet	Valiant/Duster 1968-76
6936	Silverado	Chevrolet/GMC Pick-Ups & Suburban 1970-87
8055	Silverado	Chevrolet/GMC Pick-Ups & Suburban 1988-90
6935	Skyhawk	GM Subcompact 1971-80
7059	Skyhawk	Cavalier, Skyhawk, Cimarron, 2000 1982-88
7049	Skylark	GM X-Body 1980-85

Chilton's Repair Manuals are available at your local retailer or by mailing a check or money order for **$15.95** per book plus **$3.50** for 1st book and **$.50** for each additional book to cover postage and handling to:

Chilton Book Company
Dept. DM
Radnor, PA 19089

NOTE: When ordering be sure to include your name & address, book part No. & title.

CHILTON'S REPAIR MANUAL MODEL INDEX
Car and truck model names are listed in alphabetical and numerical order

Part No.	Model	Repair Manual Title
7675	Skylark	Calais, Grand Am, Skylark, Somerset 1985-86
7657	Somerset	Calais, Grand Am, Skylark, Somerset 1985-86
7042	Spider 2000	Fiat 1969-81
7199	Spirit	AMC 1975-86
6552	Sport Fury	Plymouth 1968–76
7165	Sport Wagon	Renault 1975-85
5796	Squareback	Volkswagen 1949-71
6837	Squareback	Volkswagen 1970-81
7196	Stanza	Datsun/Nissan F-10, 310, Stanza, Pulsar 1976-88
6935	Starfire	GM Subcompact 1971-80
7583	Starion	Mitsubishi 1983-89
7036	Starlet	Toyota Corolla/Carina/Tercel/Starlet 1970-87
7059	STE	Cavalier, Skyhawk, Cimarron, 2000 1982-88
5795	Stout	Toyota 1966-70
7042	Strada	Fiat 1969-81
6552	Suburban	Plymouth 1968-76
6936	Suburban	Chevy/GMC Pick-Ups & Suburban 1970-87
8055	Suburban	Chevy/GMC Pick-Ups & Suburban 1988-90
6935	Sunbird	GM Subcompact 1971-80
7059	Sunbird	Cavalier, Skyhawk, Cimarron, 2000 1982-88
7163	Sundance	Chrysler Front Wheel Drive 1981-88
7043	Supra	Toyota Celica/Supra 1971-87
8058	Supra	Toyota Celica/Supra 1986-90
6837	Super Beetle	Volkswagen 1970-81
7199	SX-4	AMC 1975-86
7383	S-10 Blazer	Chevy S-10 Blazer/GMC S-15 Jimmy 1982-87
7310	S-10 Pick-Up	Chevy S-10/GMC S-15 Pick-Ups 1982-87
7383	S-15 Jimmy	Chevy S-10 Blazer/GMC S-15 Jimmy 1982-87
7310	S-15 Pick-Up	Chevy S-10/GMC S-15 Pick-Ups 1982-87
7830	Taurus	Taurus/Sable/Continental 1986-89
6845	TC-3	Omni/Horizon/Rampage 1978-88
5905	Tempest	Tempest/GTO/LeMans 1968-73
7055	Tempo	Ford/Mercury Front Wheel Drive 1981-87
7036	Tercel	Toyota Corolla/Carina/Tercel/Starlet 1970-87
7081	Thing	Volkswagen 1970-81
6696	Thunderbird	Ford/Mercury/Lincoln Mid-Size 1971-85
7814	Thunderbird	Thunderbird, Cougar, Continental 1980-87
7055	Topaz	Ford/Mercury Front Wheel Drive 1981-87
6320	Torino	Fairlane/Torino 1962-75
6696	Torino	Ford/Mercury/Lincoln Mid-Size 1971-85
7163	Town & Country	Chrysler Front Wheel Drive 1981-88
6842	Town Car	Ford/Mercury/Lincoln 1968-88
7135	Townsman	Chevrolet 1968-88
5795	Toyota Pickups	Toyota 1966-70
7035	Toyota Pickups	Toyota Trucks 1970-88
7004	Toyota Van	Toyota Corona/Crown/Cressida/Mk.II/Van 1970-87
7459	Trail Duster	Dodge/Plymouth Trucks 1967-88
7046	Trans Am	Firebird 1967-81
7345	Trans Am	Firebird 1982-90
7583	Tredia	Mitsubishi 1983-89

Part No.	Model	Repair Manual Title
7040	Turbo	Volvo 1970-88
5796	Type 1 Sedan 1949-71	Volkswagen 1949-71
6837	Type 1 Sedan 1970-80	Volkswagen 1970-81
5796	Type 1 Karmann Ghia 1960-71	Volkswagen 1949-71
6837	Type 1 Karmann Ghia 1970-74	Volkswagen 1970-81
5796	Type 1 Convertible 1964-71	Volkswagen 1949-71
6837	Type 1 Convertible 1970-80	Volkswagen 1970-81
5796	Type 1 Super Beetle 1971	Volkswagen 1949-71
6837	Type 1 Super Beetle 1971-75	Volkswagen 1970-81
5796	Type 2 Bus 1953-71	Volkswagen 1949-71
6837	Type 2 Bus 1970-80	Volkswagen 1970-81
5796	Type 2 Kombi 1954-71	Volkswagen 1949-71
6837	Type 2 Kombi 1970-73	Volkswagen 1970-81
6837	Type 2 Vanagon 1981	Volkswagen 1970-81
5796	Type 3 Fastback & Squareback 1961-71	Volkswagen 1949-71
7081	Type 3 Fastback & Squareback 1970-73	Volkswagen 1970-70
5796	Type 4 411 1971	Volkswagen 1949-71
6837	Type 4 411 1971-72	Volkswagen 1970-81
5796	Type 4 412 1971	Volkswagen 1949-71
6845	Turismo	Omni/Horizon/Rampage 1978-88
5905	T-37	Tempest/GTO/LeMans 1968-73
6836	T-1000	Chevette/T-1000 1976-88
6935	Vega	GM Subcompact 1971-80
7346	Ventura	Pontiac Mid-Size 1974-83
6696	Versailles	Ford/Mercury/Lincoln Mid-Size 1971-85
6552	VIP	Plymouth 1968-76
7037	Vista	Colt/Challenger/Vista/Conquest 1971-88
6933	Vista Cruiser	Cutlass 1970-87
6637	Volare	Aspen/Volare 1976-80
7482	Voyager	Dodge Caravan/Plymouth Voyager 1984-88
6326	V-100	Valiant/Duster 1968-76
6739	Wagoneer 1962-83	Jeep Wagoneer, Commando, Cherokee, Truck 1957-86
7939	Wagoneer 1984-89	Jeep Wagoneer, Comanche, Cherokee 1984-89
8034	Wrangler	Jeep 1971-90
7459	W100, 150, 200, 250, 300, 350	Dodge/Plymouth Trucks 1967-88
7459	WM300	Dodge/Plymouth Trucks 1967-88
6842	XL	Ford/Mercury/Lincoln 1968-88
6963	XR4Ti	Mustang/Capri/Merkur 1979-88
6696	XR-7	Ford/Mercury/Lincoln Mid-Size 1971-85
6982	XT Coupe	Subaru 1970-88
7042	X1/9	Fiat 1969-81
6965	Zephyr	Fairmont/Zephyr 1978-83
7059	Z-24	Cavalier, Skyhawk, Cimarron, 2000 1982-88
6735	Z-28	Camaro 1967-81
7318	Z-28	Camaro 1982-88
6845	024	Omni/Horizon/Rampage 1978-88
6844	3.0S, 3.0Si, 3.0CS	BMW 1970-88
6817	4-63	Jeep 1981-87

Chilton's Repair Manuals are available at your local retailer or by mailing a check or money order for **$15.95** per book plus **$3.50** for 1st book and **$.50** for each additional book to cover postage and handling to:

Chilton Book Company
Dept. DM
Radnor, PA 19089

NOTE: When ordering be sure to include your name & address, book part No. & title.

CHILTON'S REPAIR MANUAL MODEL INDEX
Car and truck model names are listed in alphabetical and numerical order

Part No.	Model	Repair Manual Title
6817	4 × 4-63	Jeep 1981-87
6817	4-73	Jeep 1981-87
6817	4 × 4-73	Jeep 1981-87
6817	4-75	Jeep 1981-87
7035	4Runner	Toyota Trucks 1970-88
6982	4wd Wagon	Subaru 1970-88
6982	4wd Coupe	Subaru 1970-88
6933	4-4-2 1970-80	Cutlass 1970-87
6817	6-63	Jeep 1981-87
6809	6.9	Mercedes-Benz 1974-84
7308	88	Buick/Olds/Pontiac 1975-90
7308	98	Buick/Olds/Pontiac 1975-90
7587	98 Regency	GM C-Body 1985
5902	100LS, 100GL	Audi 1970-73
6529	122, 122S	Volvo 1956-69
7042	124	Fiat 1969-81
7042	128	Fiat 1969-81
7042	131	Fiat 1969-81
6529	142	Volvo 1956-69
7040	142	Volvo 1970-88
6529	144	Volvo 1956-69
7040	144	Volvo 1970-88
6529	145	Volvo 1956-69
7040	145	Volvo 1970-88
6529	164	Volvo 1956-69
7040	164	Volvo 1970-88
6065	190C	Mercedes-Benz 1959-70
6809	190D	Mercedes-Benz 1974-84
6065	190DC	Mercedes-Benz 1959-70
6809	190E	Mercedes-Benz 1974-84
6065	200, 200D	Mercedes-Benz 1959-70
7170	200SX	Nissan 200SX, 240SX, 510, 610, 710, 810, Maxima 1973-88
7197	210	Datsun 1200, 210, Nissan Sentra 1971-88
6065	220B, 220D, 220Sb, 220SEb	Mercedes-Benz 1959-70
5907	220/8 1968-73	Mercedes-Benz 1968-73
6809	230 1974-78	Mercedes-Benz 1974-84
6065	230S, 230SL	Mercedes-Benz 1959-70
5907	230/8	Mercedes-Benz 1968-73
6809	240D	Mercedes-Benz 1974-84
7170	240SX	Nissan 200SX, 240SX, 510, 610, 710, 810, Maxima 1973-88
6932	240Z	Datsun Z & ZX 1970-87
7040	242, 244, 245	Volvo 1970-88
5907	250C	Mercedes-Benz 1968-73
6065	250S, 250SE, 250SL	Mercedes-Benz 1959-70
5907	250/8	Mercedes-Benz 1968-73
6932	260Z	Datsun Z & ZX 1970-87
7040	262, 264, 265	Volvo 1970-88
5907	280	Mercedes-Benz 1968-73
6809	280	Mercedes-Benz 1974-84
5907	280C	Mercedes-Benz 1968-73
6809	280C, 280CE, 280E	Mercedes-Benz 1974-84
6065	280S, 280SE	Mercedes-Benz 1959-70
5907	280SE, 280S/8, 280SE/8	Mercedes-Benz 1968-73
6809	280SEL, 280SEL/8, 280SL	Mercedes-Benz 1974-84
6932	280Z, 280ZX	Datsun Z & ZX 1970-87
6065	300CD, 300D, 300SD, 300SE	Mercedes-Benz 1959-70
5907	300SEL 3.5, 300SEL 4.5	Mercedes-Benz 1968-73
5907	300SEL 6.3, 300SEL/8	Mercedes-Benz 1968-73
6809	300TD	Mercedes-Benz 1974-84
6932	300ZX	Datsun Z & ZX 1970-87
5982	304	Peugeot 1970-74
5790	310	Datsun 1961-72
7196	310	Datsun/Nissan F-10, 310, Stanza, Pulsar 1977-88
5790	311	Datsun 1961-72
6844	318i, 320i	BMW 1970-88
6981	323	Mazda 1978-89
6844	325E, 325ES, 325i, 325iS, 325iX	BMW 1970-88
6809	380SEC, 380SEL, 380SL, 380SLC	Mercedes-Benz 1974-84
5907	350SL	Mercedes-Benz 1968-73
7163	400	Chrysler Front Wheel Drive 1981-88
5790	410	Datsun 1961-72
5790	411	Datsun 1961-72
7081	411, 412	Volkswagen 1970-81
6809	450SE, 450SEL, 450 SEL 6.9	Mercedes-Benz 1974-84
6809	450SL, 450SLC	Mercedes-Benz 1974-84
5907	450SLC	Mercedes-Benz 1968-73
6809	500SEC, 500SEL	Mercedes-Benz 1974-84
5982	504	Peugeot 1970-74
5790	510	Datsun 1961-72
7170	510	Nissan 200SX, 240SX, 510, 610, 710, 810, Maxima 1973-88
6816	520	Datsun/Nissan Pick-Ups and Pathfinder 1970-89
6844	524TD	BMW 1970-88
6844	525i	BMW 1970-88
6844	528e	BMW 1970-88
6844	528i	BMW 1970-88
6844	530i	BMW 1970-88
6844	533i	BMW 1970-88
6844	535i, 535iS	BMW 1970-88
6980	600	Honda 1973-88
7163	600	Chrysler Front Wheel Drive 1981-88
7170	610	Nissan 200SX, 240SX, 510, 610, 710, 810, Maxima 1973-88
6816	620	Datsun/Nissan Pick-Ups and Pathfinder 1970-89
6981	626	Mazda 1978-89
6844	630 CSi	BMW 1970-88
6844	633 CSi	BMW 1970-88
6844	635CSi	BMW 1970-88
7170	710	Nissan 200SX, 240SX, 510, 610, 710, 810, Maxima 1973-88
6816	720	Datsun/Nissan Pick-Ups and Pathfinder 1970-89
6844	733i	BMW 1970-88
6844	735i	BMW 1970-88
7040	760, 760GLE	Volvo 1970-88
7040	780	Volvo 1970-88
6981	808	Mazda 1978-89
7170	810	Nissan 200SX, 240SX, 510, 610, 710, 810, Maxima 1973-88
7042	850	Fiat 1969-81
7572	900, 900 Turbo	SAAB 900 1976-85
7048	924	Porsche 924/928 1976-81
7048	928	Porsche 924/928 1976-81
6981	929	Mazda 1978-89
6836	1000	Chevette/1000 1976-88
6780	1100	MG 1961-81
5790	1200	Datsun 1961-72
7197	1200	Datsun 1200, 210, Nissan Sentra 1973-88
6982	1400GL, 1400DL, 1400GF	Subaru 1970-88
5790	1500	Datsun 1961-72

Chilton's Repair Manuals are available at your local retailer or by mailing a check or money order for **$15.95** per book plus **$3.50** for 1st book and **$.50** for each additional book to cover postage and handling to:

Chilton Book Company
Dept. DM
Radnor, PA 19089

NOTE: When ordering be sure to include your name & address, book part No. & title.

CHILTON'S REPAIR MANUAL MODEL INDEX
Car and truck model names are listed in alphabetical and numerical order

Part No.	Model	Repair Manual Title	Part No.	Model	Repair Manual Title
6844	1500	DMW 1970-88	6844	2000	BMW 1970-88
6936	1500	Chevy/GMC Pick-Ups & Suburban 1970-87	6844	2002, 2002Ti, 2002Tii	BMW 1970-88
8055	1500	Chevy/GMC Pick-Ups & Suburban 1988-90	6936	2500	Chevy/GMC Pick-Ups & Suburban 1970-87
6844	1600	BMW 1970-88	8055	2500	Chevy/GMC Pick-Ups & Suburban 1988-90
5790	1600	Datsun 1961-72	6844	2500	BMW 1970-88
6982	1600DL, 1600GL, 1600GLF	Subaru 1970-88	6844	2800	BMW 1970-88
6844	1600-2	BMW 1970-88	6936	3500	Chevy/GMC Pick-Ups & Suburban 1970-87
6844	1800	BMW 1970-88	8055	3500	Chevy/GMC Pick-Ups & Suburban 1988-90
6982	1800DL, 1800GL, 1800GLF	Subaru 1970-88	7028	4000	Audi 4000/5000 1978-81
6529	1800, 1800S	Volvo 1956-69	7028	5000	Audi 4000/5000 1978-81
7040	1800E, 1800ES	Volvo 1970-88	7309	6000	Celebrity, Century, Ciera, 6000 1982-88
5790	2000	Datsun 1961-72			
7059	2000	Cavalier, Skyhawk, Cimarron, 2000 1982-88			

Chilton's Repair Manuals are available at your local retailer or by mailing a check or money order for **$15.95** per book plus **$3.50** for 1st book and **$.50** for each additional book to cover postage and handling to:

Chilton Book Company
Dept. DM
Radnor, PA 19089

NOTE: When ordering be sure to include your name & address, book part No. & title.